THE
DIY
MANUAL

THE
DIY
MANUAL

THE
DIY
MANUAL

Colour Library Direct

First published in 1992 by
HarperCollinsPublishers
London

20262
This edition published 1997 by
Colour Library Direct
Godalming, Surrey
Printed and bound in Italy
ISBN 1-85833-636-8

Design, art direction
and project management
Simon Jennings

Text
Albert Jackson
David Day

Text
and editorial direction
Albert Jackson

Illustrations editor
David Day

Designer
Alan Marshall

Illustrators
David Day
Robin Harris

Additional illustrations
Brian Craker
Michael Parr
Brian Sayers

HarperCollinsPublishers

Publishing Director
Robin Wood

Executive editor
Polly Powell

The text and illustrations in this book
were previously published in
Collins Complete Do-it-Yourself Manual

Copyright © 1986, 1989, 1992, 1994
HarperCollins**Publishers** Ltd

ISBN 1-85833-636-8

Printed and bound in Italy
by Rotolito Lombarda

Cross-references

There are few DIY projects that do not require a combination of skills. Decorating a single room, for instance, might also involve modifying the plumbing or electrical wiring, installing ventilation, repairing the structure of the building and so on. As a result, you might have to refer to more than one section of this book. To help you locate the relevant sections, a symbol (▷) in the text refers you to a list of cross-references in the page margin. Those references printed in bold type are directly related to the task in hand. Other references which will broaden your understanding of the subject are printed in lightweight type.

1 DECORATING

Colour selection	**8**
Tone	10
Texture	12
Pattern	13
Manipulating space	14
Interior schemes	**16**
Access	20
Preparation & priming	**23**
Primers/sealers	23
Masonry	24
Plaster	30
Wallcoverings	32
Woodwork	33
Metalwork	36
Tiling	38
Applying finishes	**39**
Paints	39
Exterior masonry	40
Walls & ceilings	43
Woodwork	46
Finishes	47
Doors	49
Window frames	50
Graining	51
Staining	52
Varnishing	54
French polishing	55
Cold cure lacquer	56
Metalwork	57
Textured coatings	59
Wallcoverings	60
Tiling	69
Wall tiles	72
Floor tiles	75
Ceiling tiles	80

2 HOUSEHOLD REPAIRS

Plasterwork	**82**
Types of plaster	83
Techniques of plasterwork	84
Repairing plasterwork	88
Doors	**90**
Windows	**92**
Glass	92
Repairing glass	94
Re-cording windows	95
Spiral balances	96
Securing doors	97
Securing windows	98
Stairs	**99**
Repairs	99
Roofs	**102**
Maintenance	102
Sheet roofing	103
Flat roofs	104
Flashings	106

3 INSULATING & VENTILATION

Insulation	**108**
Insulating plumbing	109
Draughtproofing	110
Roof and loft insulation	113
Double glazing	116
Ventilation	**119**
Cooker hoods	120
Extractor fans	121

CONTENTS

CONTENTS

4 ELECTRICITY

Economics	124
Basics	126
Safety	**127**
Bathroom safety	128
Electric shock	129
Replacements & repairs	**130**
Flex	131
Plugs and lampholders	133
Main switch equipment	**134**
Fuse boards	134
Consumer units	136
Fuses	137
Circuits	139
Cables	**140**
Cable types	140
Installing cables	141
Checklists	144
Power circuits	**146**
Mounting sockets	146
Replacing socket outlets	148
Adapting circuits	149
Fixed appliances	**152**
Fused connection units	152
Heaters	153
Small appliances	154
Larger appliances	**155**
Cookers	155
Immersion heaters	156
Doorbells, buzzers & chimes	158
Showers	159
Lighting	**159**
Circuits	159
Fittings	161
Switches	163
Installing	165
Complete rewiring	166

5 PLUMBING

Plumbing systems	168
Repairs & maintenance	**171**
Emergency repairs	171
Tap repairs	172
Cisterns maintenance	174
Drainage	**177**
Maintenance	177
Blockages	178
Pipework	**181**
Metal pipework	181
Plastic plumbing	186
Plumbing installations	**190**
WC	190
Wash basins	193
Baths	197
Showers	199
Bidets	203
Sinks	204
Waste disposal units	205
Washing machines	206
Storage cisterns	208

6 WORKING OUTDOORS

Fences	**210**
Supporting	210
Erecting	212
Walls	**215**
Brickwork	216
Blockwork	223
Paths/Drives/Patios	**224**
Concrete	224
Paving slabs	232
Crazy paving	234
Brick paving	235

INDEX	**237**

1

COLOUR SELECTION	**8**
ACCESS	**20**
PREPARATION AND PRIMING	**23**
PREPARING MASONRY	24
PREPARING PLASTER	30
PREPARING WALLCOVERINGS	32
PREPARING WOODWORK	33
PREPARING METALWORK	36
PREPARING TILES	38
APPLYING FINISHES	**39**
MASONRY	40
WALLS/CEILINGS	43
WOODWORK	46
METALWORK	57
TEXTURED COATINGS	59
WALLCOVERINGS	60
TILING	69

DECORATING

A BASIS FOR SELECTING COLOUR

SEE ALSO

◁ Details for:
Tone	10-11
Texture	12
Pattern	13
Manipulating space	14-15

Developing a sense of the 'right' colour is not the same as learning to paint a door or hang wallpaper. There are no 'rules' as such but there are simple guidelines which will help. In magazine articles on interior design or colour selection you will come across terms such as harmony and contrast. Colours are described as being cool or warm, or as tints or shades. These specialized terms form a basis for developing a colour scheme. By considering colours as the spokes of a wheel, you will see how one colour relates to another and how such relationships create a particular mood or effect.

Primary colours
All colours are derived from three basic 'pure' colours – red, blue and yellow. They are known as the primary colours.

Secondary colours
When you mix two primary colours in equal proportions, a secondary colour is produced. Red plus blue makes violet, blue with yellow makes green and red plus yellow makes orange. When a secondary colour is placed between its constituents on the wheel, it sits opposite its complementary colour – the one primary not used in its make-up. Complementary colours are the most contrasting colours in the spectrum and are used in colour schemes for dramatic effects.

Tertiary colours
When a primary is mixed equally with one of its neighbouring secondaries, it produces a tertiary colour. The complete wheel illustrates a simplified version of all colour groupings. Colours on opposite sides of the wheel are used in combination to produce vibrant, contrasting colour schemes, while those colours grouped together on one side of the wheel form the basis of a harmonious scheme.

Warm and cool colours
The wheel also groups colours with similar characteristics. On one side are the warm red and yellow combinations, colours we associate with fire and sunlight. A room decorated with warm colours feels cosy or exciting depending on the intensity of the colours used. Cool colours are grouped on the opposite side of the wheel. Blues and greens suggest vegetation, water and sky, and create a relaxed airy feeling when used together.

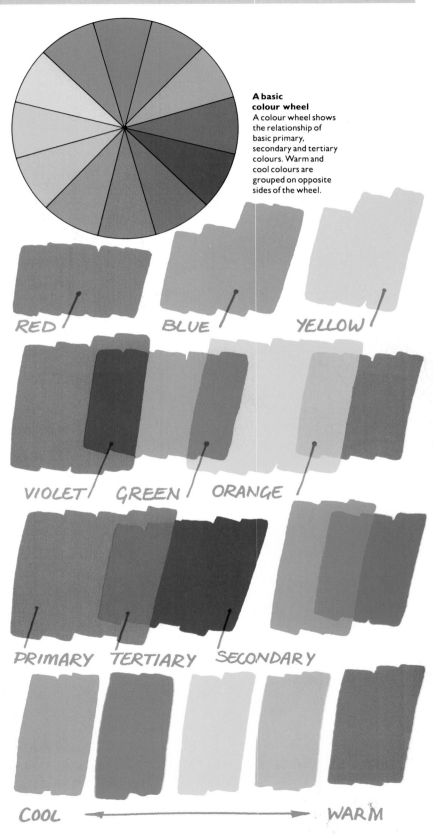

A basic colour wheel
A colour wheel shows the relationship of basic primary, secondary and tertiary colours. Warm and cool colours are grouped on opposite sides of the wheel.

RED BLUE YELLOW

VIOLET GREEN ORANGE

PRIMARY TERTIARY SECONDARY

COOL ←——————→ WARM

SELECTING COLOUR

1△

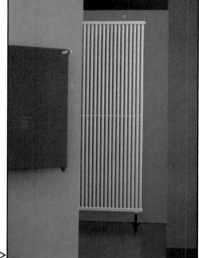

3▷

4▷

5▷

2▽

SEE ALSO	
Details for: ▷	
Tone	10-11
Texture	12
Pattern	13
Manipulating space	14-15

1 Bold treatment for a living room
A bold red treatment always creates a warm atmosphere. In this interior, obvious brush strokes add the extra element of texture.

2 A child's playroom
Primary colours make a lively, invigorating playroom. The grey floor and expanse of white accentuate the bright colours.

3 Coloured equipment
Basic appliances such as baths, sinks or storage heaters were invariably produced in neutral colours so that they blended into any interior. Now it is possible to order equipment like these wall-mounted radiators which become important elements of a colour scheme.

4 Adding colour with window blinds
Coloured or patterned curtains are fairly commonplace but fewer people choose from the available range of brightly coloured venetian blinds. Strong sunlight contributes to the colourful effect.

5 Using colour outside
Most buildings do not lend themselves to being painted in bright colours. In areas of the country where colour is traditionally acceptable, a bold treatment can be very exciting.

USING TONE FOR SUBTLETY

Pure colours are used to great effect for exterior colour schemes and interior decor but a more subtle combination of colours is called for in the majority of situations. Subtle colours are made by mixing different percentages of pure colour, or simply by changing the tone of a colour by adding a neutral.

SEE ALSO

◁ Details for:
Colour theory	8-9
Texture	12
Pattern	13
Manipulating space	14-15

Neutrals

The purest form of neutral is the complete absence of 'colour' – black or white. By mixing the two together, the range of neutrals is extended almost indefinitely as varying tones of grey. Neutrals are used extensively by decorators because they do not clash with any other colour, but in their simplest forms neutrals can be either stark or rather bland. Consequently, a touch of colour is normally added to a grey to give it a warm or cool bias so that it can pick up the character of another colour in harmony, or provide an almost imperceptible contrast within a range of colours.

Tints

Changing the tone of pure colours by adding white creates pastel colours or tints. Used in combination, tints are safe colours. It is difficult to produce anything but a harmonious scheme whatever colours you use together. The effect can be very different, however, if a pale tint is contrasted with dark tones to produce a dramatic result.

Shades

The shades of a colour are produced by adding black to it. Shades are rich dramatic colours which are used for bold yet sophisticated schemes. It is within this range of colours that browns appear – the interior designer's stock in trade. Brown blends so harmoniously into almost any colour scheme that it is tantamount to a neutral.

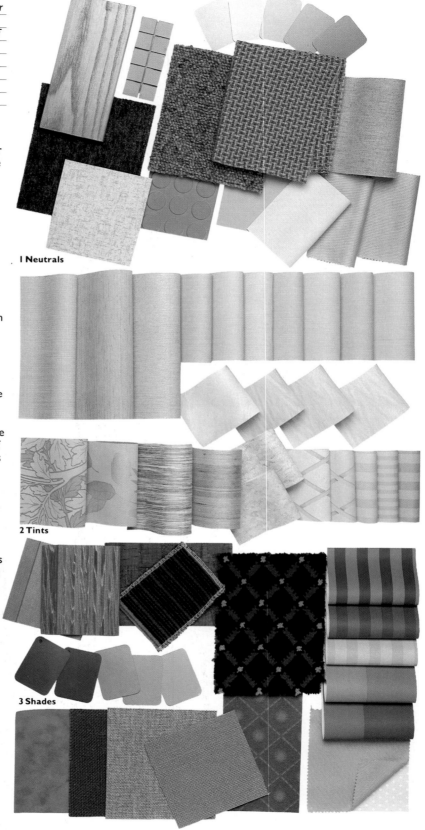

1 Neutrals

2 Tints

3 Shades

1 Neutrals
A range of neutral tones introduces all manner of subtle colours.

2 Tints
A composition of pale tints is always harmonious and attractive.

3 Shades
Use darker tones, or shades, for rich dramatic effects.

USING TONE

1△

3▷

<2

SEE ALSO

Details for: ▷	
Colour theory	8-9
Texture	12
Pattern	13
Manipulating space	14-15

1 White makes a room spacious
White paint, fabric and carpet take full advantage of available natural light to create a fresh airy interior. In this bedroom, the crisp black frames accentuate the beautifully proportioned windows.

2 Using tints creatively
Pale colours are often used when a safe harmonious scheme is required but you can create vibrant effects by juxtaposing cool and warm tints.

3 Dark dramatic tones
The very dark tone used for walls, ceiling and floors in this room is relieved by a carefully painted frieze and white accessories. Gloss paint will reflect some light even when such a dark colour is used.

TAKING TEXTURE INTO ACCOUNT

Colour is an abstraction, merely the way we perceive different wavelengths of light, and yet we are far more aware of the colour of a surface than its more tangible texture which we almost take for granted. Texture is a vital ingredient of any decorative scheme and merits careful thought.

SEE ALSO

◁ Details for:
Colour theory	8-9
Tone	10-11
Manipulating space	14-15

Natural and man-made textures
(Far right)
Many people are not conscious of the actual texture of materials. This selection ranges from the warmth of wood and coarsely woven materials to the smooth coolness of marble, ceramics, plastic and metal.

Textural variety
(Below)
It's relatively simple to achieve interesting textural variety with almost any group of objects. Here, a few stylish kitchen artefacts contrast beautifully with a patterned tile splashback and warm oak cupboards.

The visual effect of texture is also created by light. A smooth surface reflects more light than one that is rough. Coarse textures absorb light, even creating shadows if the light falls at a shallow angle. Consequently, when you paint a coarse texture, the colour will look entirely different from the same colour applied to a smooth one.

Even without applied colour, texture adds interest to a scheme. You can contrast bare brickwork with smooth paintwork, for instance, or use the reflective qualities of glass, metal or glazed ceramics to produce some stunning decorative effects.

Just as colour is used to create an atmosphere, texture will produce an almost instinctive impression – it's as if we could feel texture with our eyes. Cork, wood, coarsely woven fabrics or rugs add warmth, even a sense of luxury, to an interior, while smooth hard materials such as polished stone, stainless steel, vinyl, or even a black lacquered surface, give a clean, almost clinical feeling to a room.

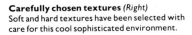

Carefully chosen textures *(Right)*
Soft and hard textures have been selected with care for this cool sophisticated environment.

USING PATTERN FOR EFFECT

Recent, purist approaches to design have made us afraid to use pattern boldly, and yet our less-inhibited forefathers felt free to cover their homes with pattern and applied decoration with spectacular results, creating a sense of gaiety, excitement – 'punch', if you like – which is difficult to evoke in any other way.

A well-designed patterned wallpaper, fabric or rug can provide the basis for the entire colour scheme and a professional designer will have chosen the colours to form a pleasing combination. There is no reason why the same colours shouldn't look equally attractive when applied to the other surfaces of a room but perhaps the safest way to incorporate a pattern is to use it on one surface only to contrast with plain colours elsewhere.

Combining different patterns can be tricky, but a small regular pattern normally works well with large, bold decoration. Also, different patterns with a similar dominating colour can coordinate well even if you experiment with contrasting tones. Another approach is to use the same pattern in different colourways, one for the walls perhaps and the other for curtains. You should also select patterns according to the atmosphere you want to create. Simple geometric shapes are likely to be more restful than bold swirling motifs.

SEE ALSO

Details for: ▷	
Colour theory	8-9
Tone	10-11
Manipulating space	14-15

Be bold with pattern
There is no reason to be afraid of using pattern when you consider that manufacturers have done most of the thinking for you. Well-designed materials are available to clad just about any surface in your home.

1 Coordinated pattern
The colours used for the striped curtain and furniture fabrics are the basis of this coordinated colour scheme.

2 A profusion of pattern
This bedroom combines a wealth of pattern with the rich colour of natural mahogany furniture. It shows what can be achieved if one has the courage to opt for the bold approach.

MANIPULATING SPACE

SEE ALSO

◁ Details for:
Colour theory	8-9
Tone	10-11
Texture	12
Pattern	13

There are nearly always areas of a house that feel uncomfortably small or, conversely, so spacious that one feels isolated, almost vulnerable. Perhaps the first reaction is to consider structural alterations like knocking down a wall or installing a false ceiling. In some cases, such measures will prove to be the most effective solution, but there is no doubt that they will be more expensive and disruptive than the alternative measures of manipulating space – using colour, tone and pattern.

Our eyes perceive colours and tones in such a way that it is possible to create optical illusions that apparently change the dimensions of a room. Warm colours appear to advance, so that a room painted overall with brown or red, for instance, will feel smaller than the same room decorated in cool colours such as blue or green which have a tendency to recede.

Tone can be used to modify or reinforce the desired illusion. Dark tones, even when you are using cool colours, will advance, while pale tones will open up a space visually.

The same qualities of colour and tone will change the proportion of a space. Adjusting the height of a ceiling is an obvious example. If you paint a ceiling a darker tone than the walls it will appear lower. If you treated the floor in a similar way, you could almost squeeze the room between the two. A long narrow passageway will feel less claustrophobic if you push out the walls by decorating them with pale, cool colours which will, incidentally, reflect more light as well.

Using linear pattern is another way to alter our perception of space. A vertically striped wallpaper or woodstrip panelling on the walls counteracts the effect of a low ceiling. Venetian blinds make windows seem wider, and stripped wooden floors are stretched in the direction of the boards. Any large-scale pattern draws attention to itself and will advance like warm, dark colours, but small patterns appear as an overall texture from a distance so have less effect.

Practical experiments *(Right)*
A model will help to determine whether an optical illusion will have the desired effect.

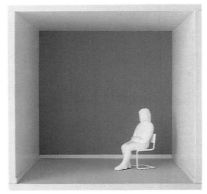

Warm colours appear to advance

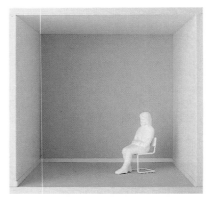

A cool colour or pale tone will recede

A dark ceiling will appear lower

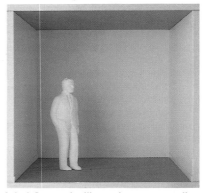

A dark floor and ceiling make a room smaller

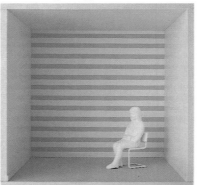

Horizontal stripes make a wall seem wider

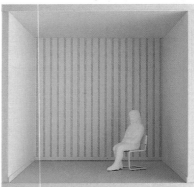

Vertical stripes increase the height

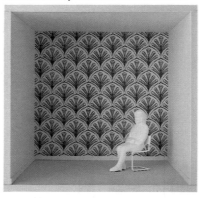

Large-scale patterns advance

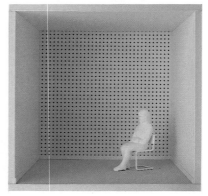

A small regular pattern recedes

1 Using mirrors
Floor to ceiling mirrors appear to double the size of a room.

2 Lowering a ceiling
A dark-tone carpet and deep-blue ceiling reduce the height of a room.

3 Incorporating an alcove
Disguise a small kitchen alcove by using colours or pattern which make it feel like part of the living room.

4 Creating space with pattern
A three-dimensional pattern can make a small space seem larger.

1△

2△

◁3

4▷

VERIFYING YOUR SCHEME

Before you spend money on paint, carpet or wallcoverings, collect samples of the materials you propose to use in order to gauge the effect of one colour or texture on another.

Collecting samples
Make your first selection from the limited choice of furniture fabrics or carpets. Collect offcuts of the other materials you are considering or borrow sample books or display samples from the suppliers to compare them at home. As paint charts are printed you can never be absolutely confident they will match the actual paint. Consequently, some manufacturers produce small sample pots of paint to try on the wall or woodwork.

Making a sample board
Professional designers make sample boards to check the relative proportions of materials as they will appear in the room. Usually a patch of floor- or wallcovering will be the largest dominating area of colour, painted woodwork will be proportionally smaller and accessories might be represented by small spots of colour. Make your own board by gluing your assembly of materials to stiff card, butting one piece against another to avoid leaving a white border around each sample which would change the combined effect.

Incorporating existing features
Most schemes will have to incorporate existing features such as a bathroom suite or kitchen units. Use these items as starting points, building the colour scheme around them. Cut a hole in your sample board to use as a window for viewing existing materials or borrowed examples against those on the card.

SEE ALSO

Details for: ▷	
Colour theory	8-9
Tone	10-11
Texture	12
Pattern	13

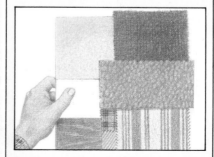

Checking your colour selection
View your completed sample board in natural and artificial light to check your colour selection.

SCHEMES FOR LIVING ROOMS

In most homes the living room is the largest area in the house. It's where you spend most of your leisure time and entertain your friends. It's the room upon which most money is spent on furnishings, curtains and carpets, not to mention expensive hi-fi units, the television set and so on. For all these reasons, you will want to make sure that the living room decor has lasting appeal. After all, you are unlikely to replace costly furniture and materials frequently.

Unless you are lucky enough to have more than one reception or living room, it is an area that must feel comfortable during the day, relaxing in the evening and lively enough for the occasional party. Unless the room receives an unusual amount of sunlight, a warm colour scheme is often the best, to create a cosy atmosphere. Dark cool tones will produce a similar result under artificial light, but very deep tones can have the opposite effect by creating dark shadowy areas. Predominantly neutral schemes or a range of browns and beiges lend themselves to change in the future by simply swapping the

accessories without having to spend a lot of money on replacing the essentials. Natural textures are equally versatile.

Patterned carpets or rugs are less likely to be ruined by the inevitable spillages than plain colours, but very dark tones are almost as difficult to keep clean as pale colours.

Curtains or blinds provide the perfect solution to a change of mood. During the day, they are pulled aside or withdrawn and therefore contribute very little to the general appearance of the room, but in the evening they can become a wall of colour or pattern which can transform the scheme.

SEE ALSO

◁ Details for:	
Colour theory	8-9
Neutrals	10
Tone	10-11
Texture	12
Pattern	13
Manipulating space	14-15
Interior wall paints	43
Wood finishes	46-47
Metal finishes	58
Wallcoverings	60-61
Tiles	69-71

An adaptable scheme
(Right)
A safe yet comfortable scheme lends itself to change by swapping the accessories.

Typically traditional
(Far right)
Pink-washed walls and floral pattens suit a typical country cottage.

Sympathetic style
(Below)
A surviving period living room deserves appropriate styling.

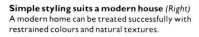
Simple styling suits a modern house *(Right)*
A modern home can be treated successfully with restrained colours and natural textures.

SCHEMES FOR BEDROOMS

A bedroom is first and foremost a personal room. Its decor should reflect the character of its occupant and the functions to which the room is put. At night, a bedroom should be relaxing, even romantic. Much depends on the lighting, but pattern and colour can create a luxurious and seductive mood.

Strangely, very few people ever use pattern on a ceiling, and yet a bedroom provides the ideal opportunity, especially as you are unlikely to spend much of your waking life there so can afford to be adventurous with the decor. Bedroom carpet is invariably of inferior quality because it need not be hardwearing but you could give the colour scheme a real lift by investing in an expensive rug or deep-pile carpet knowing that it will come to no harm.

If a bedroom faces south, early sunlight will provide the necessary stimulus to wake you up, but a north-facing room will benefit from bright invigorating colours.

Some bedrooms may serve a dual function. A teenager's bedroom may have to double as a study or a private sitting room so needs to be stimulating rather than restful. A child's room will almost certainly function as a playroom. The obvious choice would be for strong, even primary colours, but as most children accumulate brightly coloured toys, books and pictures you might select a neutral background to the colourful accessories. The smallest bedrooms are usually reserved for guests, but they can be made to appear larger and more inviting by the judicious manipulation of the proportions with colour or tone.

SEE ALSO

Details for: ▷	
Colour theory	8-9
Tone	10-11
Texture	12
Pattern	13
Manipulating space	14-15
Interior wall paints	43
Wood finishes	46-47
Metal finishes	58
Wallcoverings	60-61
Tiles	69-71

◁1

2▷

◁3

4▷

1 An elegant master bedroom
The peaceful character of this elegant bedroom is a result of a basically neutral scheme which is warmed very slightly by a hint of cream and pale yellow.

2 Bright and refreshing
The combination of bright yellow and white makes for a cheerful start to the day.

3 Dual-purpose room
When a bedroom doubles as a sitting room it needs to be stimulating during the day and cosy at night.

4 A guest room
A guest room should make a visitor feel at home immediately. The warmth of stripped pine makes this room very inviting.

DECOR FOR COOKING AND EATING

Kitchens need to be functional areas capable of taking a great deal of wear and tear, so the materials you choose will be dictated largely by practicalities. But that doesn't mean you have to restrict your use of colour in any way. Kitchen sinks and appliances are made in bright colours as well as the standard stainless steel and white enamel. Tiled worktops and splashbacks, vinyl floorcoverings and melamine surfaces offer further opportunity to introduce a range of colours.

Textures are an important consideration with a range of possibilities. Natural timber is still a popular material for kitchen cupboards, and wherever wood is employed, it will provide a warm element which you can choose to contrast with cool colours and textures, or pick up the warm theme with paint, paper or floor-covering. Some people prefer to rely entirely on metallic, ceramic and plastic surfaces which impose a clean, purposeful and practical character.

If the kitchen incorporates a dining area, you may decide to create within the same room a separate space that is more conducive to relaxation and conversation. Softer textures such as carpet tiles, cork flooring and fabric upholstery absorb some of the sound generated by appliances and the clatter of kitchen utensils. You could also decorate the walls in a different way to change the mood, perhaps using darker tones or a patterned wallcovering to define the dining area.

SEE ALSO

◁ Details for:

Colour theory	8-9
Tone	10-11
Texture	12
Pattern	13
Manipulating space	14-15
Interior wall paints	43
Wood finishes	46-47
Metal finishes	58
Wallcoverings	60-61
Tiles	69-71

1 A functional kitchen
This simple kitchen, laid out to form a perfect work triangle, looks extremely functional without feeling clinical.

2 A family kitchen
Some people like the kitchen to be part of an informal sitting and dining area where the family can relax.

3 A breakfast room
A sunny alcove linked to the kitchen makes an ideal breakfast room.

4 A kitchen extension
Colourful fabric blinds shade this kitchen extension from direct sunlight.

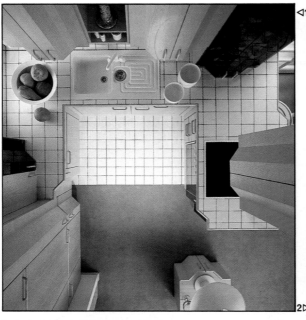

◁1

2▷

◁3

4▷

BATHROOMS

Bathrooms like kitchens must fulfil quite definite functions efficiently but they should never look clinical. Even when a bathroom is centrally heated, a cold uninviting colour scheme would not be a wise choice as enamelled and tiled surfaces are inevitable. Coloured bathroom appliances are commonplace but choose carefully as they are likely to remain the dominating influence on any future colour schemes.

A bathroom is another area where you can afford to be inventive with your use of colour or pattern. A bold treatment which might become tiresome with overexposure can be highly successful in a room used at intervals only. Try to introduce some sound-absorbing materials like ceiling tiles, carpet or cork flooring to avoid the hollow acoustics associated with old-fashioned tiled bathrooms. If you want to use delicate materials that might be affected by steam, make sure the bathroom is

properly ventilated. Bathrooms are usually small rooms with relatively high ceilings, but painting a ceiling a dark tone which might improve the proportion of a larger room can make a bathroom feel like a box. A more successful way to counter the effect of a high ceiling is to divide the walls with a dado rail, using a different colour or material above and below the line.

If you live in a hard-water area, avoid dark-coloured bathroom suites which will emphasize lime-scale deposits.

SEE ALSO

Details for: ▷	
Colour theory	8-9
Tone	10-11
Texture	12
Pattern	13
Manipulating space	14-15
Interior wall paints	43
Wood finishes	46-47
Metal finishes	58
Wallcoverings	60-61
Tiles	69-71
Extractor fans	121-122

1 Warm and luxurious
There is no reason why a bathroom cannot be warm and inviting when there is such a choice of luxurious wallcoverings and ceramic tiles.

2 Changing the proportion
Improve the proportion of a bathroom with a high ceiling by a change of colour at dado height.

3 Fashionable styling
A clever combination of colour and shape changes a simple bathroom into a room with distinctive character.

4 A period bathroom
Reproduction fittings and marbled paintwork re-create a period bathroom.

SEE ALSO

◁ Details for:
Work platforms   22

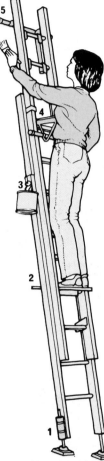

Ladder accessories
Kit out your ladder with a range of helpful devices to make working easier and safer. This ladder features adjustable feet (1) for uneven ground, a foot rest for comfort (2), a clamp for a paint can (3), a tool tray (4), and a stay (5), to hold the top away from eaves or gutters.

BEFORE YOU BEGIN

Timing, weather and the condition of the site are important factors to consider before you decorate outside. Indoors, you have the problem of what to do with a room full of furniture and furnishings while you work.

OUTSIDE THE HOUSE

Plan your work so that you can begin the actual decoration of the house exterior in late summer and autumn so that the previous warm weather will have dried out the fabric of the building sufficiently.

The best weather for decorating is a warm but overcast day. Avoid painting on rainy days or in direct sunlight, as both can ruin new paintwork. You should follow the sun around the house, however, so that its warmth dries out the night's dew before you get there.

Don't work on windy days either, or dust will be deposited on the fresh paint. Sprinkle water around doorways or spray with a houseplant spray before you paint as this settles dust, which you would churn up with your feet.

Clear away any rubbish from around the house, which will slow down your progress or even cause accidents. Cut back overhanging foliage from trees or shrubs. Protect plants and paving with dust sheets in the work area.

INSIDE THE HOUSE

Before you decorate a room inside, carry out all repairs necessary and have the chimney swept if you use an open fire: a soot fall would ruin your decorations. Clear as much furniture from the room as possible, and group what is left under dust sheets.

Lift any rugs or carpets then spray water on the floor and sweep it to collect loose dust before you begin to paint. Protect finished wood or tiled floors with dust sheets.

Remove all furnishings such as pictures and lampshades and unscrew door handles and fingerplates. Keep the knob handy in the room with you, in case you get shut in accidentally.

WHAT TO WEAR

Naturally, you will wear old clothes when decorating, but avoid woollen garments, which tend to leave hairs sticking to paintwork. Dungarees with loops and large pockets for tools are ideal for decorating and other work.

MEANS OF ACCESS

Whether you are decorating inside or outside, you must provide adequate means of reaching the area you are working on. Using inefficient equipment and makeshift structures is dangerous; but even if you don't want to buy your own ladders, you can hire them quite cheaply. Safety and comfort while working are other important considerations, and there's a range of devices and accessories to make the job that much easier.

Types of ladders and access equipment

Stepladders are essential for interior decoration. Traditional wooden stepladders are still available, but they have been largely superseded by lightweight aluminium alloy types. You should have at least one pair which stand about 2m (6ft 6in) high to reach a ceiling, without having to stand on the top step. Another, shorter ladder might be more convenient for other jobs and you can use them both, with scaffold boards, to build a platform.

Outdoors you'll need ladders to reach up to eaves height. Double and triple wooden extension ladders are very heavy, so consider a metal one.

Some doubles and most triples are operated by a rope and pulley so that they can be extended single-handed.

To estimate the length of ladder you need, add together the ceiling heights of your house. Add at least one metre (about 3ft) to the length to allow for the angle and access to a platform.

There are many versions of dual- or even multi-purpose ladders, which convert from stepladder to straight ladder. A well-designed, versatile ladder is a good compromise.

Sectional scaffold frames can be built up to form towers at any convenient height for decorating inside and outside. Wide feet prevent the tower sinking into the ground, and adjustable versions allow you to level it. Some models have locking castors, which enable you to move the tower.

Towers are ideal for painting a large expanse of wall outdoors. Indoors, smaller platforms made from the same scaffold components bring high ceilings within easy reach.

Accessories for ladders

• **Ladder stay** A stay holds the ladder away from the wall. It is an essential piece of equipment when painting overhanging eaves and gutters: you would otherwise be forced to lean back and possibly overbalance.
• **Clip-on platform** A wide flat board, which clamps to the rungs, provides a comfortable platform to stand on while working for long periods.
• **Adjustable legs** Bolt-on accessories, which enable you to level the foot of a ladder on uneven ground.

• **Paint can holder** You should always support yourself with one hand on a ladder, so use a metal S-hook to hang the paint can from a rung. A special clamp, which can be fixed to the stile, enables you to position the can at one side of the ladder.
• **Tool tray** A clip-on tray is ideal for holding a small selection of tools.

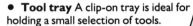

Alloy stepladder   **Dual-purpose ladder**   **Scaffold tower**   **Extending ladder**

WORKING WITH LADDERS

When you buy or hire a ladder, wooden or metal, bear in mind that:
● Wooden ladders should be made from straight-grained, knot-free timber.
● Good-quality wooden ladders have hardwood rungs tenoned through the upright stiles and secured with wedges.
● Wooden rungs with reinforcing metal rods stretched under them are safer than ones without.
● End caps or foot pads are an advantage to prevent the ladder from slipping on hard ground.
● Adjustability is a prime consideration. Choose a ladder that enables you to gain access to various parts of the building and which converts to a compact unit for storage.
● The rungs of overlapping sections of an extension ladder should align or the gap between the rungs might be too small to secure a good foothold.
● Choose an extension ladder with a rope, pulley and an automatic latch, which locks the extension to its rung.
● Check that you can buy or hire a range of accessories (see opposite) to fit your make of ladder.
● Choose a stepladder with a platform at the top to take cans and trays.
● Treads should be comfortable to stand on. Stepladders with wide, flat treads are the best choice.
● Stepladders with extended stiles give you a handhold at the top of the steps.
● Wooden stepladders often have a rope to stop the two halves sliding apart. A better solution used on most metal stepladders is a folding stay, which locks in the open position.

Is the ladder safe to use?

Check ladders regularly and before you use them after a winter's break. Inspect a hired ladder before use.

Look for splits opening along the stiles, check that there are no missing or broken rungs and that the joints are tight. Sight along the stiles to make sure they are aligned, or the ladder could rock when leant against a wall.

Inspect wooden ladders for signs of woodworm or rot. Even a few holes or sponginess could signify serious damage below the surface. Test that the wood is sound before using the ladder and treat it with a woodworm fluid or preservative. If in doubt, scrap the ladder for safety's sake.

Check that fixings for hinges and pulleys are secure and lubricate them. Inspect the pulley rope for fraying and renew if necessary.

Oil or varnish wooden ladders regularly to stop them drying out. Apply extra coats to the rungs (which take most wear). Don't paint a ladder as this may hide serious defects.

How to handle a ladder

Ladders are heavy and unwieldy; handle them properly so you don't damage property or injure yourself.

Carry a ladder upright, not slung across your shoulder. Hold the ladder vertically, bend your knees slightly then rock the ladder back against your shoulder. Grip one rung lower down while you support the ladder at head height with your other hand, then straighten your knees.

To erect a ladder, lay it on the ground with its feet against the wall. Gradually raise it to vertical as you walk towards the wall. Pull the feet out from the wall so that the ladder is resting at an angle of about 70 degrees – if the ladder extends to 8m (26ft) for example, its feet should be 2m (6ft 6in), or one quarter of its height, from the wall.

Raise an extending ladder to the required height while holding it upright. If it is a heavy ladder, get someone to hold it while you operate the pulley.

Handling a ladder
Carry the ladder upright, leaning back against your shoulder; grip one rung low down, another at head height. When erected, the base of the ladder should be one quarter of its height away from the wall so that it is correctly balanced.

HOW TO USE A LADDER SAFELY

More accidents are caused by using ladders unwisely than as a result of faulty equipment. Erect the ladder safely before you ascend and move it when the work is out of reach – never lean out to the side or you'll overbalance. Follow these simple, common-sense rules:

Securing the ladder
If the ground is soft, spread the load of the ladder by placing a wide board under the feet; screw a batten across the board to wedge the ladder in place.

On hard ground, make sure the ladder has anti-slip end caps and lay a sandbag (or a tough polythene bag filled with earth) at the base.

Secure the stiles near the base with rope tied to timber stakes driven into the ground at each side and just behind the ladder (**1**). When extending a ladder, the sections should overlap by at least one quarter of their length – but don't lean the top against the gutters, soil pipes and drainpipes, and especially glass, as they may give way.

Anchor the ladder near the top by tying it to a stout timber rail, held across the inside of the window frame. Make sure the rail extends about 300mm (1ft) on each side of the window and pad the ends to protect the wall (**2**).

It's a good idea to fix ring bolts at regular intervals into the masonry just below the fascia board: this is an excellent way to secure the top of a ladder as you have equally good anchor points wherever you position it. Alternatively, fix screw eyes to the masonry or a sound fascia board and attach the ladder to them.

Safety aloft
Never climb higher than four rungs from the top of the ladder or you will not be able to balance properly, and handholds will be out of reach. Don't lean sideways from a ladder either. Keep both feet on a rung and your hips centred between the stiles.

Avoid a slippery foothold by placing a sack or old doormat at the foot of the ladder to dry your boots and wipe off any mud before you ascend.

Unless the manufacturer states otherwise, do not use a ladder to form a horizontal walkway, even with a scaffold board lying on it.

Stepladders are prone to topple sideways. Clamp a strut to the ladder on uneven floors (**3**).

SEE ALSO

Details for: ▷	
Work platforms	22
Varnishing	54
Oiling wood	56

1 Staking a ladder
Secure the base of the ladder by lashing it to stakes in the ground.

2 Securing the top
Anchor the ladder to a batten held inside the window frame.

3 Supporting a stepladder
Clamp a strut to the stile to prop up a pair of stepladders.

ERECTING WORK PLATFORMS INDOORS

SEE ALSO

◁ Details for:
Ladders   20
Scaffold tower   20

A lot of work can be carried out by moving a ladder little by little as the work progresses, but it can become tedious, perhaps leading to an accident as you try to reach just a bit further before having to move along, and then overbalance.

It's more convenient to build a work platform which allows you to tackle a large area without moving the structure. You can hire decorators' trestles and bridge a pair with a scaffold board, or make a similar structure with two pairs of stepladders (1).

Clamp or tie the board to the rungs and use two boards, one on top of the other, if two people need to use the platform at once.

An even better arrangement is to use scaffold tower components to make a mobile platform (2). Choose one with locking castors for the ideal solution for painting or papering ceilings.

2 Mobile platform
An efficient structure made from scaffold tower frames.

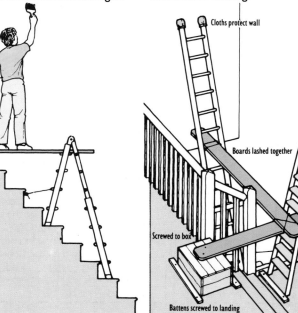

1 Improvised platform
A simple yet safe platform made from stepladders and a scaffold board.

Gaining access to a stairwell

Stairwells present particular problems when building work platforms. The simplest method is to use a dual-purpose staircase ladder, which can be adjusted to stand evenly on a flight (3). Anchor the steps with rope through a couple of screw eyes fixed to the stair treads; the holes will be concealed by carpet later. Rest a scaffold board between the ladder and the landing to form a bridge. Screw the board to the landing and tie the other end.

Alternatively, construct a tailor-made platform from ladders and boards to suit your staircase (4). Make sure the boards and ladders are clamped or lashed together, and that ladders can't slip on the treads. If necessary, screw wooden battens to the stairs to prevent the foot of the ladder moving.

Stair scaffold
Erect a platform to compensate for the slope of a staircase with scaffold frames.

3 Dual-purpose ladder
Use a stair ladder to straddle the flight with a scaffold board to give a level work platform.

Cloths protect wall

Boards lashed together

Screwed to box

Battens screwed to landing

4 Tailor-made platform
Build a network of scaffold boards, stepladders, ladders and boxes to suit your stairwell layout.

ERECTING PLATFORMS OUTSIDE

Scaffolding is by far the best method of building a work platform to decorate the outside of a house. Towers made from slot-together frames are available for hire. Heights up to about 9m (30ft) are possible; the tallest ones require supporting 'outriggers'.

Build the lower section of the frame first and level it with adjustable feet before erecting a tower on top. As you build, climb and stand on the inside of the tower.

Erect a proper platform at the top with toe boards all round to prevent tools and materials being knocked off the tower, and extend the framework to provide hand rails all round.

Secure the tower to the house by tying it to ring bolts fixed into the masonry, as with ladders.

Some towers incorporate a staircase inside the scaffold frame; floors with a trapdoor enable you to ascend to the top of the tower. If you cannot find such a tower, the safest access is via a ladder. Make sure it extends at least 1m (about 3ft) above the staging so that you can step on and off safely.

It is difficult to reach windows and walls above an extension with just a ladder. With a scaffold tower, however, you can construct a cantilevered section fixed to the main tower, which rests on the roof of the extension.

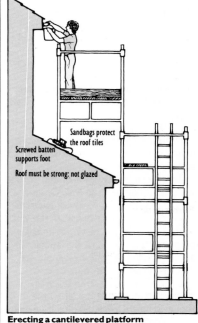

Cloths protect wall

Sandbags protect the roof tiles

Screwed batten supports foot

Roof must be strong: not glazed

Erecting a cantilevered platform
The cantilever section rests on a board to spread load.

PREPARATION AND PRIMING

Thorough preparation of all surfaces is the vital first step in redecorating. If you neglect this stage, subsequent finishes will be rejected. Preparation means removing dirt, grease and loose or flaky previous finishes, as well as repairing serious deterioration such as cracks, holes, corrosion and decay. It's not just old surfaces that need attention: new masonry, timber and metalwork must be sealed against attack and priming is called for to ensure a surface is in a suitable condition to accept its finish. Consult the charts on this page for details of primers and sealers for all the materials you're likely to encounter in and around the home, then read the following sections, which examine each material in detail.

TYPES OF PRIMERS AND SEALERS

There are numerous primers and sealers to suit a variety of materials.

Stabilizing primer
Used to bind powdery or flaky materials. A clear or white liquid.

Wood primer
Standard pink or white primer prevents other coats of paint soaking in.

Aluminium wood primer
Used to seal oily hardwoods, it will also cover creosote.

General-purpose primer
Seals porous building materials and covers patchy walls and ceilings.

Metal primers
Essential to prevent corrosion in metals and to provide a key for paint.

PVA bonding agent
A general-purpose liquid adhesive for many building materials. An excellent primer and sealer when diluted, even for bituminous paints.

Water repellent
A liquid which dries colourless to seal masonry against water penetration.

Alkali-resistant primer
Used to prevent the alkali content of some materials attacking oil paints.

Aluminium spirit-based sealer
Formulated to obliterate materials likely to 'bleed' through subsequent coatings. Effective over bituminous paints, creosote, metallic paints and nicotine.

SEE ALSO

Details for: ▷	
Priming brickwork	26
Waterproofing masonry	26
Priming flaky paint	28
Priming plaster	30
Priming wood	33
Priming metal	36

PRIMERS AND SEALERS SUITABILITY: DRYING TIME: COVERAGE

●Black dot denotes that primer and surface are compatible.

●Red dot denotes metal primers.

	Stabilizing primer	Wood primer	Aluminium wood primer	General-purpose primer	Zinc phosphate	Red oxide	Calcium plumbate	Red lead	Chromate primer	PVA bonding agent	Water repellent	Alkali-resistant primer	Aluminium sealer spirit-based
SUITABLE FOR													
Brick	●			●						●	●	●	
Stone	●			●						●	●	●	
Cement rendering	●			●						●	●	●	
Concrete	●			●						●	●	●	
Plaster	●			●						●		●	
Plasterboard	●			●								●	
Distemper	●												
Limewash	●												
Cement paint	●												
Bituminous paints										●			●
Asbestos cement	●			●						●		●	
Softwood		●	●	●					●				
Hardwood			●				●		●				
Chipboard		●	●	●					●				
Hardboard		●	●	●					●				
Plywood		●	●	●					●				
Creosoted timber			●										●
Absorbent fibre boards	●											●	
Ferrous metals (inside)					●	●							
Ferrous metals (outside)					●		●	●					
Galvanized metal							●						
Aluminium					●				●				
DRYING TIME: HOURS													
Touch dry	3	6	6	4	4	4	8	10	10	3	1	4	¼
Recoatable	16	16	16	16	10	16	24	24	24	16	12	16	1
COVERAGE (Sq. metre per litre)													
Smooth surface	9	13	15	12	13	13	13	13	13	9	3-4	10	4
Rough/Absorbent surface	7	10	11	9	10	10	10	10	10	7	2-3	7	3

● **Lead content in paint**
Lead, which is a poison, was widely used in the past as a drier in solvent-based paints including primers. (Emulsions, which are water-based, have never contained lead). Many solvent-based paints are now made without lead. If possible, choose one labelled 'no lead added' or similar. Don't let children chew old painted surfaces, which may have a high lead content.

CLEANING BRICK AND STONE

SEE ALSO

◁ Details for:
**Spirit-thinned
masonry paint**   41
Painting masonry   40-42

Before you decorate the outside of your house, check the condition of the brick and stonework, and carry out any necessary repairs. There's no reason why you can't paint brick or stone walls – indeed, in some areas it is traditional to do so – but if you consider masonry most attractive in its natural state, you could be faced with a problem: once masonry is painted, it is not possible to restore it to its original condition. There will always be particles of paint left in the texture of brickwork, and even smooth stone, which can be stripped successfully, may be stained by the paint.

Stained brickwork

Organic growth

Efflorescence

Treating new masonry

New brickwork or stonework should be left for about three months until it is completely dry before any further treatment is considered. White powdery deposits called efflorescence may come to the surface over this period, but you can simply brush it off with a stiff-bristled brush or a piece of dry sacking (◁). After that, bricks and mortar should be weatherproof and therefore require no further protection or treatment.

Cleaning organic growth from masonry

There are innumerable species of mould growth or lichens which appear as tiny coloured specks or patches on masonry. They gradually merge until the surface is covered with colours ranging from bright orange to yellow or green, grey and black.

Moulds and lichen will only flourish in damp conditions, so try to cure the source of the problem before treating the growth. If one side of the house always faces away from the sun, it will have little chance to dry out. Relieve the situation by cutting back overhanging trees or shrubs to increase ventilation to the wall.

Make sure the damp-proof course (DPC) is working adequately and is not being bridged by piled earth or debris.

Cracked or corroded rainwater pipes leaking onto the wall are another common cause of organic growth. Feel behind the pipe with your fingers or use a hand mirror to locate the leak.

Removing the growth
Brush the wall vigorously with a stiff-bristled brush. This can be an unpleasant, dusty job, so wear a gauze facemask. Brush away from you to avoid debris being flicked into your eyes.

Microscopic spores will remain even after brushing. Kill these with a solution of bleach or, if the wall suffers persistently from fungal growth, use a proprietary fungicide, available from most DIY stores.

Using a bleach solution
Mix one part household bleach with four parts water. Paint the solution onto the wall using an old paintbrush, then 48 hours later wash the surface with clean water, using a scrubbing brush. Brush on a second application of bleach solution if the original fungal growth was severe.

Using a fungicidal solution
Dilute the fungicide with water according to the manufacturer's instructions and apply it liberally to the wall with an old paintbrush. Leave it for 24 hours then rinse the wall with clean water. In extreme cases, give the wall two washes of fungicide, allowing 24 hours between applications and a further 24 hours before washing it down with water.

Removing efflorescence from masonry

Soluble salts within building materials such as cement, brick, stone and plaster gradually migrate to the surface along with the water as a wall dries out. The result is a white crystalline deposit called efflorescence.

The same condition can occur on old masonry if it is subjected to more than average moisture. Efflorescence itself is not harmful but the source of the damp causing it must be identified and cured before decoration proceeds.

Regularly brush the deposit from the wall with a dry stiff-bristled brush or coarse sacking until the crystals cease to form – don't attempt to wash off the crystals; they'll merely dissolve in the water and soak back into the wall. Above all, don't attempt to decorate a wall which is still efflorescing, and therefore damp.

When the wall is completely dry, paint the surface with an alkali-resistant primer to neutralize the effect of the crystals before you paint with oil paint; water-thinned paints or clear sealants let the wall breathe, so are not affected by the alkali content of the masonry. Some specially formulated masonry paint can be used without primer (◁).

CLEANING OLD MASONRY

Whatever type of finish you intend to apply to a wall, all loose debris and dirt must be brushed off with a stiff-bristled brush. Don't use a wire brush unless the masonry is badly soiled as it may leave scratch marks.

Brush along the mortar joints to dislodge loose pointing. Defective mortar can be repaired easily at this stage (see right), but if you fail to disturb it now by being too cautious, it will fall out as you paint, creating far more work in the long run.

Removing unsightly stains

Improve the appearance of stone or brick left in its natural state by washing it with clean water. Play a hose gently onto the masonry while you scrub it with a stiff-bristled brush (**1**). Scrub heavy deposits with half a cup of ammonia added to a bucketful of water, then rinse again.

Abrade small cement stains or other marks from brickwork with a piece of similar-coloured brick, or scrub the area with a household kitchen cleanser.

Remove spilled oil paint from masonry with a proprietary paint stripper (▷). Put on gloves and protective goggles, then paint on the stripper, stippling it into the rough texture (**2**). After about ten minutes, remove it with a scraper and a soft wire brush. If paint remains in crevices, dip the brush in stripper and gently scrub it with small circular strokes. When the wall is clean, rinse with water.

1 Remove dirt and dust by washing

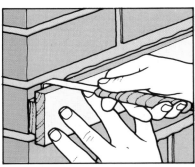

2 Stipple paint stripper onto spilled oil paint

REPOINTING MASONRY

The mortar joints between bricks and stone can become porous with age, allowing rainwater to penetrate to the inside, causing damp patches to appear, ruining decorations. Replacing the mortar pointing, which deflects the water, is quite straightforward but time consuming. Tackle only a small, manageable area at a time, using a ready-mixed mortar or your own mix.

Applying the pointing mortar

Rake out the old mortar pointing with a thin wooden lath to a depth of about 12mm (½in). Use a cold chisel or a special plugging chisel and a club hammer to dislodge firmly embedded sections, then brush out the joints with a stiff-bristled brush.

Flick water into the joints using an old paintbrush, making sure the bricks or stones are soaked so they will not absorb too much water from the fresh mortar. Mix up some mortar in a bucket and transfer it to a hawk. If you're mixing your own mortar, use the proportions 1 part cement: 1 part lime: 6 parts builders' sand.

Pick up a little sausage of mortar on the back of a small pointing trowel and push it firmly into the upright joints. This can be difficult to do without the mortar dropping off, so hold the hawk under each joint to catch it.

Try not to smear the face of the bricks with mortar, or it will stain. Repeat the process for the horizontal joints. The actual shape of the pointing is not vital at this stage.

Once the mortar is firm enough to retain a thumb print, it is ready for shaping. Match the style of pointing used on the rest of the house (see below). When the pointing has almost hardened, brush the wall to remove traces of surplus mortar.

Shaping the mortar joints

The joints shown here are commonly used for brickwork but they are also suitable for stonework. Additionally, stone may have raised mortar joints.

Flush joints

The easiest profile to produce, a flush joint is used where the wall is sheltered or painted. Rub each joint with sacking; start with the verticals.

Rubbed (rounded) joints

Bricklayers make a rubbed or rounded joint with a tool shaped like a sled runner with a handle: the semi-circular blade is run along the joints.

Improvise by bending a short length of metal tube or rod. Use the curved section only or you'll gouge the mortar. Alternatively, use a length of 9mm (⅜in) diameter plastic tube.

Raked joints

A raked joint is used to emphasize the type of bonding pattern of a brick wall. It's not suitable for soft bricks or for a wall that takes a lot of weathering. Scrape out a little of the mortar then tidy up the joints by running a 9mm (⅜in) lath along them.

Weatherstruck joints

The sloping profile is intended to shed rainwater from the wall. Shape the mortar with the edge of a pointing trowel. Start with the vertical joints, and slope them in either direction but be consistent. During the process, mortar will tend to spill from the bottom of a joint, as surplus is cut off. Bricklayers use a tool called a 'frenchman' to neaten the work: it has a narrow blade with the tip bent at right-angles. Make your own by bending a thin metal strip then bind insulating tape round the other end to form a handle, or bend the tip of an old kitchen knife after heating it in the flame of a blowtorch or cooker burner.

You will find it easiest to use a wooden batten to guide the blade of the frenchman along the joints, but nail scraps of plywood at each end of the batten to hold it off the wall.

Align the batten with the bottom of the horizontal joints, then draw the tool along it, cutting off the excess mortar, which drops to the ground.

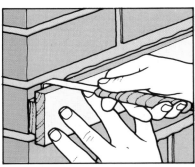

Use a frenchman to trim weatherstruck joints

SEE ALSO

Details for: ▷	
Paint stripper	35
Mixing mortar	215

● **Mortar dyes**
Liquid or powder additives are available for changing the colour of mortar to match existing pointing. Colour matching is difficult and smears can stain the bricks permanently.

Flush joint

Rubbed joint

Raked joint

Weatherstruck joint

REPAIRING MASONRY

Cracks in external walls can be the source of penetrating damp which ruins your decorations inside. They may be the result of a much more serious problem: subsidence in the foundations. Whatever the cause, it's obvious that you shouldn't just ignore the danger signs, but effect immediate cures.

SEE ALSO

◁ Details for:
Work platform	22
Efflorescence	24
Organic growth	24
Reinforced emulsion	41
Primers	23

Filling cracked masonry

If substantial cracks are apparent in a brick or stone wall, consult a builder or your local Building Control Officer to ascertain the cause.

If the crack seems to be stable, it can be filled. Where the crack follows the line of the mortar joints, rake out those affected and repoint in the normal way, as previously described. A crack that splits one or more bricks or stones cannot be repaired, and the damaged area should be removed and replaced, unless you are painting the wall.

Use a ready-mixed mortar with a little PVA bonding agent added to help it to stick. Soak the cracked masonry with a hose to encourage the mortar to flow deeply into the crack.

Crack may follow pointing only

Cracked bricks could signify serious faults

Priming brickwork

Brickwork will only need to be primed in certain circumstances. An alkali-resistant primer will guard against efflorescence (◁) and a stabilizing solution will bind crumbling masonry and help to seal it at the same time.

If you are planning to paint the wall for the first time with an exterior emulsion, you may find that the first coat is difficult to apply due to the suction of the dry, porous brick. Thin the first coat slightly with water.

To economize when using a reinforced emulsion (◁) prime the wall with a cement paint with a little fine sand mixed in thoroughly.

Waterproofing masonry

1 Replacing a spalled brick
Having mortared top and one end, slip the new brick into the hole you have cut.

Colourless water-repellent fluids are intended to make masonry impervious to water without colouring it or stopping it from breathing (important to allow moisture within the walls to dry out).

Prepare the surface thoroughly before applying the fluid: make good any cracks in bricks or pointing and remove organic growth (◁) and allow the wall to dry out thoroughly.

Apply the fluid generously with a large paintbrush and stipple it into the joints. Apply a second coat as soon as the first has been absorbed to ensure that there are no bare patches where water could seep in. To be sure that you're covering the wall properly, use a sealant containing a fugitive dye, which disappears gradually after a few weeks.

Carefully paint up to surrounding woodwork; if you accidentally splash sealant onto it, wash it down immediately with a cloth dampened with white spirit.

If the area you need to treat is large, consider spraying on the fluid, using a hired spray gun. You'll need to rig up a substantial work platform (◁) and mask off all timber and metalwork that adjoins the wall. The fumes from the fluid can be dangerous if inhaled, so be sure to wear a proper respirator, which you can also hire.

REPAIRING SPALLED MASONRY

Moisture penetrating soft masonry will expand in icy weather, flaking off the outer face of brickwork and stonework. The process, known as spalling, not only looks unattractive but also allows water to seep into the surface. Repairs to spalled bricks or stones can be made, although the treatment depends on the severity of the problem.

If spalling is localized, it is possible to cut out individual bricks or stones and replace them with matching ones. The sequence below describes how it's tackled with brickwork, but the process is similar for a stone wall.

Spalling bricks caused by frost damage

Where the spalling is extensive, it's likely that the whole wall is porous and your best remedy is to paint on a stabilizing solution to bind the loose material together, then apply a textured wall finish, as used to patch pebbledash, which will disguise the faults and waterproof the wall at the same time.

Replacing a spalled brick

Use a cold chisel and club hammer to rake out the pointing surrounding the brick then chop out the brick itself. If the brick is difficult to prise out, drill into it many times with a large-diameter masonry bit, then attack the brick with a cold chisel and hammer: it should crumble, enabling you to remove the pieces easily.

To fit the replacement brick, first dampen the opening and spread mortar on the base and one side. Butter the dampened replacement brick on the top and one end and slot it into the hole **(1)**.

Shape the pointing to match the surrounding brickwork then, once it is dry, apply a clear water repellent.

REPAIRING RENDER

Brickwork may be clad with a smooth or roughcast cement-based render for improved weatherproofing and to give a decorative finish; often the render is susceptible to the effects of damp and frost, which can cause cracking, bulging and staining. Before you redecorate a rendered wall, make good any damage, clean off surface dirt, mould growth and flaky material to achieve a long-lasting finish.

Cracked render allows moisture to penetrate

Blown pebbledash parts from the masonry

Rust staining due to leaky guttering

Repairing defective render

Before you repair cracked render, correct any structural faults which may have contributed to it. Brush to remove loose particles. Apply a stabilizing solution if the wall is dusty.

Ignore fine hair cracks if you paint the wall with reinforced emulsion, which covers minor faults. Rake out larger cracks using a cold chisel, dampen with water and fill flush with the surface with exterior filler. Fill major cracks with a mortar mix comprising 1 part cement: 4 parts builders' sand, with a little PVA bonding agent added to help it stick to the masonry.

Bulges in render can indicate that the cladding has parted from the masonry. Tap gently with a hammer to find the extent of these hollow areas; hack off the material to sound edges. Undercut the perimeter of the hole to give a grip for the filler material.

Brush out debris then apply a coat of PVA bonding agent. When PVA is tacky, trowel on a mortar mix as for filling cracks then smooth with a wet trowel.

Reinforcing a crack in render

To prevent a crack in render opening up again, reinforce the repair with a fine scrim embedded in a bitumen base coat. Rake out the crack to remove any loose material, then wet it. Fill the crack just proud of the surface with a mortar mix of 1 part cement: 4 parts builders' sand. When this has stiffened scrape it flush with the render.

When the mortar has hardened, brush on a generous coat of bitumen base coat, making sure it extends at least 75mm (3in) on both sides of the crack. Embed strips of open weave scrim (sold with the base coat) into the bitumen, using a stippling and brushing action **(1)**. While it is still wet, feather the edges of the bitumen with a foam roller **(2)**, bedding the scrim into it. After 24 hours, the bitumen will be hard, black and shiny. Apply a second coat, feather with a roller and, when it has dried, apply two full coats of a compatible reinforced emulsion (▷).

1 Embed the scrim

2 Feather with roller

Patching pebbledash

Pebbledash comprises small stones stuck to a thin coat of render over a thicker base coat. If damp gets behind pebbledashing, one or both layers may separate. Hack off any loose render to a sound base and seal it with stabilizer. If necessary, repair the first 'scratchcoat' of render. Restore the texture of the top 'buttercoat' with a thick paste made from PVA bonding agent. Mix one part of cement paint powder with three parts clean, sharp (plastering) sand. Stir in one measure of bonding agent diluted with three parts water to form a thick, creamy paste. Load a banister brush and scrub the paste onto the bare surface.

Apply a second generous coat of paste, stippling it to form a coarse texture **(1)**. Leave for about 15 minutes to firm up then, with a loaded brush, stipple it to match the texture of the pebbles. Let the paste harden fully before painting.

To leave the pebbledash unpainted, make a patch using replacement pebbles. The result will not be a perfect match but could save you painting the entire wall. Cut back the blown area and apply a scratchcoat followed by a buttercoat. While this is still wet, fling pebbles onto the surface from a dustpan; they should stick to the soft render but you'll have to repeat until the coverage is even.

1 Stipple the texture

Removing rust stains

Faulty plumbing will often leave rusty streaks on a rendered wall. Before decorating, prime the stains with an aluminium spirit-based sealer or they will bleed through. Rust marks may also appear on a pebbledashed wall, well away from any metalwork: these are caused by iron pyrites in the aggregate. Chip out the pyrites with a cold chisel, then seal the stain.

SEE ALSO

Details for: ▷
Reinforced emulsion 41
Masonry paints 41

27

PAINTED MASONRY

SEE ALSO

◁ Details for:
Spalled brick   26
Primers   23
Bitumen basecoat   27

Painted masonry inside the house is usually in fairly good order, and apart from a good wash down to remove dust and grease, and a light sanding to give a key for the new finish, there's little else you need to do. Outside, however, it's a different matter: subjected to extremes of heat, cold and rain, the surface is likely to be detrimentally affected by stains, flaking and chalkiness.

Chalky surface needs stabilizing

Strip flaky paintwork to a sound surface

Chimney stained by tar deposits from the flue

Curing a chalky surface

Rub the palm of your hand lightly over the surface of the wall to see if it is chalky. If the paint rubs off as a powdery deposit, treat the wall before you redecorate. Brush the surface with a stiff-bristled brush then liberally paint the whole wall with a stabilizing primer, which binds the chalky surface so that paint will adhere to it. Use a white stabilizing primer, which can act as an undercoat. Clean splashes of the fluid from surrounding woodwork with white spirit. If the wall is very dusty, apply a second coat of stabilizer after about 12 hours. Wait a further 12 hours before painting over.

Dealing with flaky paintwork

Flaking is commonly due to poor surface preparation or because the paint and preparatory treatments were incompatible. Damp walls will cause flaking, so remedy this and let the wall dry out before further treatment. Another cause could be too many previous coats of paint, which makes the top layers flake off.

Subsequent coats of paint will not bind to a flaky surface, so this must be removed. Use a paint scraper and stiff-bristled brush to remove all loose material. Coarse glasspaper should finish the job or at least feather the edges of any stubborn patches. Stabilize the surface as for chalky walls before repainting.

If the flaking is as a result of spalling brickwork (◁), stabilize the affected bricks with a bitumen base coat. Feather the edges with a foam roller, leave the bitumen to harden for 24 hours then paint the wall with two coats of reinforced emulsion.

Treating a stained chimney

A painted brick chimney stack with the outline of courses showing clearly through the paint as brown staining is caused by a breakdown of the internal rendering or 'pargeting' of the chimney; this allows tar deposits to migrate through the mortar to the outer paintwork. To solve the problem, fit a proprietary flue liner in the chimney, then treat the stains with an aluminium spirit-based sealer before applying a new coat of paint.

ASBESTOS CEMENT

Asbestos cement is used to make various items in and around the home, typically wallboards, corrugated lightweight roof cladding, gutters and downpipes. Nowadays, asbestos is regarded as an unnecessary danger – the dust is a real health hazard if inhaled – and it's consequently not recommended where an alternative is available. But if your home already contains the material, there's a safe way to treat it and keep it looking good.

Whenever you are working with any material containing asbestos, take the precaution of wearing a gauze facemask and of damping the surface with water whenever rubbing down. If asbestos sheets or boards are in a friable (crumbly) condition, seek professional advice.

Dealing with new asbestos
Asbestos cement boards or sheets vary in their alkali content but oil paints are likely to be attacked if the boards become damp, unless they are primed with an alkali-resistant primer. Where possible, prime both sides and edges of asbestos sheets, particularly where condensation might occur.

Before you fill fixing nails or screws, treat them with a metal primer to prevent rust stains.

Normally no primer is needed for emulsion paint, except perhaps a coat of stabilizing solution. Apply a thinned coat of paint or seal with cement paint then reinforced emulsion.

If you want to decorate over asbestos sheets with wallcovering, prime and fill all fixings and treat with one coat of white spirit-thinned stabilizing primer. Follow with one coat of size and allow it to dry before you hang the paper.

Previously painted asbestos
Wash down paintwork that's in good condition with a sugar soap or detergent solution, then rinse with clean water. Lightly key gloss paint with wet and dry abrasive paper dipped in water. Avoid rubbing through to the surface of the asbestos.

Use a stiff-bristled brush to remove flaky paint then wash down as previously described. Let the surface dry then bind it with a stabilizing primer, before painting. Build up low patches with undercoat, rubbing down with wet and dry abrasive paper.

REPAIRING CONCRETE

Concrete is used in and around the house as a surface for solid floors, drives, paths and walls. In common with other building materials, it suffers from the effects of damp – spalling and efflorescence – and related defects such as cracking and crumbling. Repairs can usually be made in much the same way as for brickwork and render, although there are some special considerations you should be aware of. If the damage is widespread, however, it's quite straightforward to resurface it prior to decorating.

Sealing concrete

New concrete has a high alkali content and efflorescence can develop on the surface as it dries out. Do not use any finish other than a water-thinned paint until the concrete is completely dry. Treat efflorescence on concrete as for brickwork (▷).

A porous concrete wall should be water-proofed with a clear sealant on the exterior. Some reinforced emulsions will cover bitumen satisfactorily but it will bleed through most paints unless you prime it with a PVA bonding agent diluted 50 per cent with water. Alternatively, use an aluminium spirit-based sealer.

Cleaning dirty concrete

Clean dirty concrete as you would brickwork. Where a concrete drive or garage floor, for instance, is stained with patches of oil or grease, soak up fresh spillages immediately to prevent them becoming permanent stains. Sprinkle dry sand onto patches of oil to absorb any liquid deposits, collect it up and wash the area with white spirit or degreasing solution.

Binding dusty concrete

Concrete is trowelled when it is laid to give a flat finish; if this is overdone, cement is brought to the surface and when the concrete dries out, this thin layer begins to break up within a short time, producing a loose, dusty surface. You must not apply a decorative finish to concrete in this condition.

Treat a concrete wall with stabilizing primer but paint a dusty floor with one or two coats of PVA bonding agent mixed with five parts of water. Use the same solution to prime a particularly porous surface.

Making good cracks and holes

Rake out and brush away loose debris from cracks or holes in concrete. If the crack is less than about 6mm (¼in) wide, open it up a little with a cold chisel so that it will accept a filling. Undercut the edges to form a lip so the filler will grip.

To fill a hole in concrete, add a fine aggregate such as gravel to the sand and cement mix. Make sure the fresh concrete sticks in shallow depressions by priming the damaged surface with 3 parts bonding agent: 1 part water. When the primed surface becomes tacky, trowel in the concrete and smooth it.

Treating spalled concrete

When concrete breaks up or spalls due to the action of frost, the process is accelerated when steel reinforcement is exposed and begins to corrode. Fill the concrete as described above but prepare and prime the metalwork first (▷). If spalling recurs, particularly in exposed conditions, protect the wall with a bitumen base coat and a compatible reinforced emulsion paint.

Spalling concrete ▷
Rusting metalwork causes concrete to spall

REPAIRING A CONCRETE FLOOR

An uneven or pitted concrete floor must be made flat and level before you apply any form of floorcovering. You can do this fairly easily using a proprietary self-levelling screed. But first of all you must ensure the surface is free from dampness.

Testing for dampness
Do not lay any tiles or sheet floorcoverings (or apply a levelling screed) to a floor that's damp. A new floor should incorporate a damp-proof membrane (DPM) but must be left to dry out for six weeks before any covering is added.

If you suspect an existing floor is damp, make a simple test by laying a small piece of polythene on the concrete then seal it all round with adhesive tape. After one or two days, look to see if there are any traces of moisture on the underside.

For a more accurate assessment, hire a moisture meter. This device has contact pins or deep wall probes, which, when stuck into the suspect surface, gives a moisture saturation percentage: if the moisture reading does not exceed 6 per cent proceed with covering or levelling the floor.

If either test indicates treatment is necessary, paint the floor with a waterproofing compound. Prime the surface first with a slightly diluted coat, then brush on two full-strength coats, allowing each to dry between applications. If necessary you can then lay a self-levelling screed over the waterproofing compound.

Applying a self-levelling compound
Fill holes and cracks deeper than about 3mm (⅛in) by first raking out and undercutting the edges (1), then spreading self-levelling compound over the entire floor surface. This material is supplied as a powder, which you mix with water.

Make sure the floor is clean and free from damp, then pour some of the compound in a corner furthest from the door. Spread the compound with a trowel (2) until it is about 3mm (⅛in) thick, then leave it to seek its own level.

Continue across the floor, joining the area of compound until the entire surface is covered. You can walk on the floor after about one hour, but leave the compound to harden for a few days before laying permanent floorcovering.

SEE ALSO

Details for: ▷	
Efflorescence	24
Priming metal	36
Primers	23
Repairing brickwork	26
Repairing render	27
Masonry paints	41
Mixing concrete	225

1 Rake out cracks

2 Apply compound
Spread levelling compound with a trowel.

29

PLASTERWORK: MAKING GOOD

SEE ALSO

◁ Details for:
Lining paper	64
Plasterboard joints	148
Primers	23

Plaster is used to finish the inner surfaces of the walls and ceilings in most houses. Ceilings are traditionally clad with slim wood laths which are then plastered over: the plaster grips between the laths. Walls are usually covered directly with a backing (floating) coat of plaster and a smooth finish coat – various grades of plaster are used to suit the condition and quality of the masonry.

In very old houses, the walls might be lath-and-plaster covered. In modern houses, plasterboard is used instead for convenience. A plastered or boarded surface can be decorated with paint, paper or cladding such as tiles; the preparation is similar for each. Whatever you intend to use as a decorative finish, the plastered wall or ceiling must be made good by filling cracks or holes.

Cracks in solid plaster

Rake loose material from a crack with the blade of a scraper or filling knife **(1)**. Undercut the edges of larger cracks to provide a key for the filling. Mix up interior-grade cellulose filler to a stiff consistency or use a pre-mixed filler.

Dampen the crack with a paintbrush, then press the filler in with a filling knife. Drag the blade across the crack to force the filler in then draw it along the crack **(2)** to smooth the filler. Leave the filler standing slightly proud of the surface ready for rubbing down smooth and flush with abrasive paper.

Fill shallow cracks with one application, but for deep ones, build up the filler in stages, letting each set before adding more.

Cracks sometimes appear in the corner between walls or a wall and ceiling; fill these by running your finger dipped in filler along the crack. When the filler has hardened, rub it down with medium-grade abrasive paper.

Fill and rub down small holes and dents in solid plasterwork in the same way as for filling cracks.

PREPARING TO DECORATE

NEW PLASTER

New plaster must dry out thoroughly before it can be decorated with paint or paper. Allow efflorescence to form on the surface then wipe off with coarse sacking; repeat periodically until the crystals cease to appear.

Use an alkali-resistant primer if you are applying oil paint. Priming isn't necessary for emulsion, but apply a thinned coat on absorbent plaster.

Size new, absorbent plaster before wallpapering, or the water will be sucked too quickly from the paste, resulting in poor adhesion. Use a proprietary size or heavy-duty wallpaper paste. If you are hanging vinyl wallcovering, make sure the size contains fungicide as the covering can't breathe like a plain paper can.

For tiling, no further preparation is needed, once the plaster is dry.

Smooth finish
Smooth the surface of small repairs with a wet brush or knife to reduce the amount of sanding required later.

OLD PLASTER

Apart from filling minor defects and dusting down, old dry plaster needs no further preparation. If the wall is patchy, apply a general purpose primer. If the surface is friable apply a stabilizing solution before you decorate.

Don't decorate damp plaster; cure, then let the plaster dry out first.

PLASTERBOARD

Fill all joints between newly fixed plasterboard then, whether you're painting or papering the board, daub all nail heads with zinc phosphate primer.

Before you paint plasterboard with oil paint, prime it with one coat of general-purpose primer. One coat of thinned emulsion may be needed on an absorbent board before the normal full-strength coats are applied.

Prior to hanging wallcovering on plasterboard, seal the surface with a general-purpose primer thinned with white spirit. After 48 hours, apply a coat of size. This allows wet-stripping without disturbing the board's paper facing.

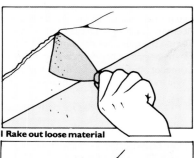

1 Rake out loose material

PAINTED PLASTER

Wash any paintwork in good condition with sugar soap or detergent solution to remove dirt and grease. Use water and medium-grade wet and dry abrasive paper to key the surface of gloss paint, particularly if covering with emulsion. Prime and allow to dry.

If the ceiling is severely stained by smoke and nicotine, prime it with an alkali-resistant primer or an aluminium spirit-based sealer.

If you want to hang wallcovering on oil paint, key then size the wall. Add dry plaster or cellulose filler to the size to provide an additional key. Cross-line the wall with lining paper (◁) before hanging a heavy embossed paper on oil paint.

Remove flaky materials with a scraper or stiff-bristled brush. Feather off the edges of the paintwork with wet and dry abrasive paper. Treat bare plaster patches with a general-purpose-primer. Should the edges of old paintwork continue to show, prime those areas again, rubbing down afterwards. Apply stabilizing primer if the paint is friable.

Apply tiles over sound paintwork after you have removed any loose material.

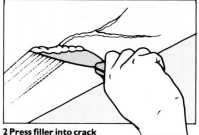

2 Press filler into crack

PATCHING HOLES IN PLASTER

A lath-and-plaster wall

If the laths are intact, plaster up the holes as for solid plasterwork. A hole under 75mm (3in) wide can simply be packed out with a ball of wet newspaper dipped in plaster. Fill flush to the surface with cellulose filler.

If some laths are broken, reinforce the repair with a piece of fine expanded metal mesh. Rake out loose plaster and undercut the edge of the hole with a bolster chisel. Use tinsnips to cut the metal to the shape of the hole but a little larger (1).

The mesh is flexible so you can bend it in order to tuck the edge behind the sound plaster all round (2). Flatten it against the laths with light taps from a hammer and if possible staple the mesh to a wall stud to hold it (3).

Gently apply one thin coat of backing plaster (4) and let it dry for about one hour before you continue patching.

1 Cut with tinsnips

2 Tuck mesh into hole

3 Staple mesh to stud

4 Trowel on plaster

A plasterboard wall or ceiling

A large hole punched through a plasterboard wall or ceiling cannot be patched with wet plaster only. Cut back the damaged board to the nearest studs or joists at each side using a sharp trimming knife against a straightedge. Keep the cut-out slim to avoid having to fit braces at the long sides (1).

Cut a new panel of plasterboard to fit snugly within the hole and nail it to the joists or studs using galvanized plasterboard nails. Use a steel trowel to spread finish plaster over the panel, forcing it well into the edges (2). Allow the plaster to stiffen then smooth over it with a dry trowel. You may have to add another layer to bring the patch to the level of the wall or ceiling.

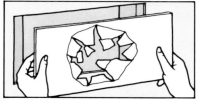

1 Cut damaged panel to nearest supports

2 Nail on the new panel and coat with plaster

A small hole in plasterboard

For very small holes in plasterboard use cellulose filler instead of plaster. Use a glass-fibre patching tape for holes up to about 90mm (3½in) across. Stick on the self-adhesive strips in a star shape over the hole then apply filler (1).

Alternatively, use an offcut of plasterboard just larger than the hole yet narrow enough to slot through. Bore a hole in the middle and thread a length of string through. Tie a galvanized nail to one end of the string (2). Butter the ends of the offcut with filler then feed it into the hole (3). Pull on the string to force it against the back of the cladding then press more filler into the hole so it's not quite flush with the surface. When the filler is hard, cut off the string then apply a thin coat of filler for a flush finish.

1 Fill and feather the patch

2 Fix string to offcut

3 Pull on string

DEALING WITH DISTEMPER

Distemper was once a popular finish, so you may have to deal with it if your house is old. Distemper is basically powdered chalk or whiting, mixed with glue size and water. It makes a poor base for decorating: when wet it redissolves and comes away from the surface along with the new decorations.

To remove it, brush away all loose material and wash off what you can. A little wallpaper stripper in the water will help. Apply a stabilizing primer to bind any traces left on the surface.

Many delicate plaster mouldings have been obliterated over the years with successive coats of distemper. Being water-soluble, you can remove it with a lot of care and patience. Work on a small area at a time, wetting it through with water. Remove the distemper with an old toothbrush until the detail of the moulding becomes clear, then scrape out the softened paint with pointed sticks such as wooden skewers. Wash over the moulding finally and apply a stabilizing primer.

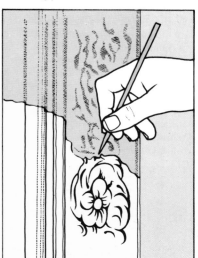

How to remove distemper
Scrub with a toothbrush, then scrape out the softened paint with a pointed stick.

Limewash and cement paints

Other water-thinned paints such as limewash and cement paints are less likely to cause problems when they're overpainted, unless they are in poor condition. Scrape and brush down with a stiff-bristled brush, then wipe the surface with white spirit to remove grease (it is best not to use water on these paints). Ensure the surface is sound by applying a stabilizing primer.

SEE ALSO

Details for: ▷
Finish plaster	83
Primers	23

External corners
Dampen the chipped corner then use a filling knife to scrape the filler onto the damaged edge, working from both sides of the angle (1). Let the filler stiffen then shape it with a wet finger to closely resemble the original profile (2).

1 Use filler knife

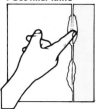

2 Shape with finger

● **Lath-and-plaster ceiling**
If the laths are sound, plaster over as for solid plasterwork. If the laths are broken, cut back to the nearest joist and secure with galvanized nails. Fit a panel of plasterboard and spread on a coat of bonding plaster followed by a coat of finish plaster (▷).

SEE ALSO

◁ Details for:
Painted plaster	30
Repairing plaster	30-31
Blown vinyl	60
Consumer unit	134
Primers	23
Wallcoverings	60-68

2 Steam stripper
To remove painted and washable wallpapers, use a steam stripper – little more than a water boiler which exudes steam from a sole plate. To use the machine, hold the plate against the wall until the steam penetrates, soaks and softens the paper, then remove it with a scraper. Wash the wall to remove traces of paste.

Mould growth ▷
Mould, typified by black specks, will grow on damp plaster or paper.

32

ERADICATING MOULD GROWTH

When provided with damp conditions, mould can develop, usually in the form of black specks. The cause of the damp should be remedied before you treat the walls or ceiling.

Sterilize the mould growth before you carry out any other preparatory work to avoid distributing spores into the atmosphere. Apply a liberal wash of a solution made from 1 part household bleach: 16 parts water. Don't make the solution any stronger as it may damage the wall decoration. Leave the solution for at least four hours then carefully scrape off the mould, wipe it onto newspaper and burn it outside.

Wash the wall again with the solution but leave it for three days to sterilize the wall completely. When the wall is dry, paint it with a stabilizing primer thinned with white spirit. If you plan to hang wallpaper, size the wall using a size containing a fungicide solution.

Where mould growth is affecting wallpaper, soak the area in a warm water and bleach solution, then scrape off the contaminated paper and burn it. Wash the wall with a fresh bleach solution to remove paste residue.

Apply a liberal wash of similar solution to sterilize the wall and leave it for at least three days, but preferably one week, to make sure no further growth occurs. When the wall is completely dry, apply a stabilizing primer thinned with white spirit, followed by a coat of size if you plan to re-paper the wall.

PREPARING WALLCOVERINGS

Faced with a previously papered surface the best solution is to strip it completely before hanging new wallcoverings. However, if the paper is perfectly sound, you can paint it with emulsion or oil paints (but be warned: it will be difficult to remove in the future). Don't paint vinyl wallcovering except blown vinyl (◁). If the paper has strong reds, greens or blues, the colours may show through the finished paint; metallic inks have a similar tendency. You can mask strong colours by applying knotting thinned by 25 per cent with methylated spirit, but over a large area, use an aluminium spirit-based sealer. If you opt for stripping off the old covering, the method you use depends on the material and how it's been treated.

Stripping wallpaper

Soak the paper with warm water with a little washing-up liquid or proprietary stripping powder or liquid added to soften the adhesive. Apply the liquid with a sponge or houseplant sprayer. Repeat and leave the water to penetrate for 15 to 20 minutes.

Use a wide metal-bladed scraper to lift the softened paper, starting at the seams. Take care not to dig the points of the blade into the plaster. Re-soak stubborn areas of paper and return to strip them later.

Electricity and water are a lethal combination: where possible, dry-strip around switches and sockets. If the paper cannot be stripped dry, switch off the power at the consumer unit (◁) when you come to strip around electrical fittings. Unscrew the faceplates so that you can get at the paper trapped behind. Don't use the sprayer near electrical accessories.

Collect all the stripped paper in plastic sacks, then wash the wall with warm water containing a little detergent. From then on, treat the wall as for plaster (◁).

Scoring washable wallpaper

Washable wallpaper has an impervious plastic surface film, which you must break through to allow the water to penetrate to the adhesive.

Use a wire brush, coarse abrasive paper or a serrated scraper to score the surface, then soak it with warm water and stripper. It may take several applications of the liquid before the paper begins to lift.

Peeling off vinyl wallcovering

Vinyl wallcovering consists of a thin vinyl layer, which is fused with the pattern, on a paper backing. It is possible to peel off the film, leaving the backing paper on the wall; this can then be painted or used as a lining for a new wallcovering.

To remove the top layer, lift both bottom corners, then pull firmly but steadily away from the wall. Either soak and scrape off the backing paper or, if you want to leave it as a lining paper, smooth the seams with medium-grade abrasive paper, but use very light pressure or you'll wear a hole.

Stripping painted wallcoverings

Wallcoverings which have been painted previously can be difficult to remove, especially if a heavy embossed paper was used. If the paper is sound, prepare in the same way as painted plaster (◁) and decorate over it.

Use a wire brush or home-made scraper (**1**) to score the surface then soak with warm water plus a little paper stripper. Painted papers (and washables) can easily be stripped using a hired steam stripper. Hold the stripper plate against the paper until the steam penetrates, then remove the soaked paper with a wide-bladed scraper (**2**).

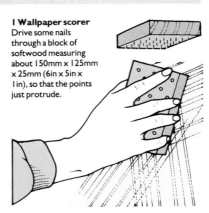

1 Wallpaper scorer
Drive some nails through a block of softwood measuring about 150mm x 125mm x 25mm (6in x 5in x 1in), so that the points just protrude.

PREPARING WOODWORK

The wooden joinery in our homes needs redecorating long before any other part of the house, particularly on the exterior of windows and doors, bargeboards and fascias. The cause is the nature of the wood itself, which swells when it becomes moist, then shrinks again when the sun or central heating dries it out. Paint will not adhere for long under these conditions, nor will any other finish. Wood is also vulnerable to woodworm and various forms of rot caused primarily by damp, so it is not surprising that careful preparation is essential to preserve most types of timber.

SEE ALSO	
Details for: ▷	
Primers	23
Finishing woodwork	46-56
Wood stains	52
Timber preservatives	47

Treating new timber

A lot of new joinery is primed at the factory but check that the primer is in good condition before it is installed: there may have been a long delay before it was delivered. Don't leave it uncovered outside, either, as primer itself is not sufficient protection against prolonged exposure to the weather. If the primer seems to be satisfactory, rub it down lightly with fine-grade abrasive paper, dust it off, then apply a second coat of wood primer to the areas that will be inaccessible after installation.

To prepare bare timber, first make sure it is dry, then sand the surface in the direction of the grain only, using a fine-grade glasspaper (wrap it round a wood block for flat surfaces; roll it round a pencil or piece of dowel for moulded sections).

Once you have removed all raised grain and lightly rounded sharp edges, dust the wood down. Rub it over finally with a tack rag – an impregnated cloth to which dust will stick; they're sold in many DIY stores.

Seal resinous knots with shellac knotting

Knots and other resinous areas of the wood must be treated to prevent them staining subsequent paint layers. Pick off any hardened resin, then seal the knots by painting them with two coats of shellac knotting. This is the best material to use when you plan to paint with pale finishing colours; for darker paints, seal the knots and prime the timber in one operation using aluminium primer.

Alternatively, paint bare timber with a standard resin-based primer or use a quick-drying water-thinned acrylic primer. Apply either liberally, taking care to work it well into the joints and particularly the end grain (which will require at least two coats to give it adequate protection).

Wash oily hardwoods with white spirit immediately prior to priming with an aluminium primer. For other hardwoods, use oil- or water-thinned wood primers, thinned slightly to encourage penetration into the grain.

When the primer is dry, fill open-grained timber with a fine surface filler. Use a piece of coarse cloth to rub it well into the wood. Use circular strokes followed by parallel strokes in the direction of the grain. When the filler is dry, rub it down with a fine abrasive paper to a smooth finish.

Fill larger holes, open joints, cracks and similar imperfections with interior or exterior wood filler. Press it into holes with a filling knife, leaving it slightly proud of the surface so that it can be sanded flush with fine-grade abrasive paper once it has set. Dust down ready for painting. If you find a hole you have missed just before you start applying the undercoat, fill it with putty; unlike other fillers, you can paint straight over putty without having to wait for it to dry, although you should wait until it forms a skin.

Filling the grain

If you plan to clear-finish an open-grained timber, apply a proprietary grain filler after sanding. Use a natural filler for pale timbers: for darker wood, buy a filler that matches the timber. Rub the filler across the grain with a coarse rag, leave to harden for several hours, then rub off the excess along the grain with a clean coarse rag.

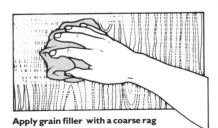
Apply grain filler with a coarse rag

Preparing for a clear finish

There's no need to apply knotting when you intend to finish the timber with a clear varnish or lacquer. Sand the wood in the direction of the grain using progressively finer grades of abrasive paper, then seal it with a slightly thinned coat of the intended finish.

If the wood is in contact with the ground or in proximity to previous outbreaks of dry rot, treat it first with a liberal wash of clear timber preservative. Check with the maker's recommendations that the liquid is compatible with the finish. This treatment is equally well suited to a painted finish.

Cellulose filler would show through a clear finish, so use a proprietary stopper to fill imperfections: these are thick pastes made in a range of colours to suit the type of timber. You can adjust the colour further by mixing it with wood stains. As stoppers can be oil- or water-based, make sure you use a similarly-based stain. Where possible, use an oil-based stopper outside. Fill the blemishes as before and rub down when the stopper hardens.

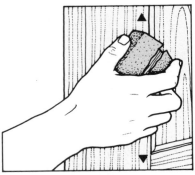
Sand along the grain with abrasive paper

PAINTED AND VARNISHED WOODWORK

SEE ALSO

◁ Details for:
Painting	46-50
Gas torch	183
Primers	23

Most of the joinery in and around your house will have been painted or varnished at some time and so long as it is in good condition, it will form a sound base for new paintwork. But when too many coats of paint have been applied, mouldings around door and window frames begin to look poorly defined and the paintwork has an unattractive, lumpy appearance; it's best to strip off all the old paint to bare wood and start again. Stripping off is also essential where the paintwork has deteriorated and is blistering, crazing or flaking.

Preparing paintwork in good condition

Wash the paintwork from the bottom upwards with a solution of warm water and sugar soap or detergent. Pay particular attention to the areas around door handles and window catches, where dirt and grease will be heaviest. Rinse with fresh water from top to bottom to prevent runs of dirty liquid on a newly cleaned surface.

Use fine grade wet and dry abrasive paper dipped in water to rub down gloss paintwork, providing a key for the new finish coat, and remove any blemishes. Prime bare patches of wood. Build up these low spots gradually with undercoat, rubbing down between each application.

Fill any open joints or holes with filler and rub down when set. Renew old and crumbling window putty and seal around window and door frames with mastic. Proceed with your chosen undercoat and top coat, following the basic paint system (◁).

Preparing unsound paintwork or varnish

Unsound paintwork or varnish such as the examples pictured left must be stripped to bare wood. There are several methods you can use but always scrape off loose material first.

In some cases, where the paint is particularly dry and flaky, dry-scraping may be all that is required, using a proprietary hook scraper, plus a light rub down with abrasive paper. Where most of the paint is stuck firmly to the woodwork, remove it using one of the methods described below and on the facing page.

Stripping paint and varnish with a blowtorch

The traditional method for stripping old paint is to burn it off with a flame. The paraffin-fuelled blowlamp has now been largely superseded by the more convenient, safer blowtorch, which is fuelled by liquid gas in a replaceable pressurized canister.

More sophisticated tools are designed so that the torch itself is connected by a hose to a metal gas bottle, the type used for camping or in caravans. This type of gas torch is finely adjustable, so is useful for other jobs such as brazing and soldering (◁).

To reduce the risk of fire, take down curtains and pelmets and, outside, rake out old bird's nests from behind your roof fascia board and soffit.

It's only necessary to soften the paint with a flame, but it is all too easy to heat the paint so that it is actually burning when you scrape it off. Deposit these scrapings in a paint kettle or metal bucket as you remove them.

Start by stripping mouldings from the bottom upwards. Never direct the flame at one spot but keep it moving all the time, so that you do not scorch the wood. As soon as the paint has softened, use a shavehook to scrape it off easily. If it is sticky or hard, heat it a little more then try scraping again.

Having dealt with the mouldings, strip flat areas of woodwork, using a wide-bladed stripping knife. When you have finished stripping, sand the wood with medium-grade abrasive paper to remove hardened specks of paint and any accidental light scorching.

Liquid sander
You can chemically prepare paintwork in good condition using a liquid sander: wipe it onto the surface with a cloth or sponge and leave it to slightly soften the top layer of paint, leaving a matt finish. It is an ideal surface for applying the new top coat of paint. The chemical cleans and degreases the paintwork, too.

Dry, flaky paintwork

Heavily overpainted woodwork

Badly weathered varnish

Shavehook, used for mouldings

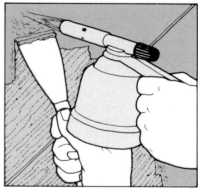
Scraper, used for flat surfaces

SELECTING AND USING CHEMICAL STRIPPERS

An old finish can be removed using a stripper which reacts chemically with paint or varnish. There are basically two types: those with a liquid or gel consistency based on methylene chloride; and strippers in the form of a thick paste, which are caustic based.

All chemical strippers can be dangerous if splashed on your skin or eyes, so take proper precautions:
●Wear vinyl work gloves and safety spectacles. If you have a respiratory problem, wear a face mask, too.
●Work in a well-ventilated area and never smoke near the chemicals: some give off fumes which are toxic when inhaled through a cigarette.
●If you get stripper on your skin, wash it off immediately with copious amounts of cold water. If it gets in your eyes, wash it out under running water and seek medical advice.
●Keep pets and small children out of the way when using chemical strippers.

GEL OR LIQUID STRIPPERS

Liquid strippers are only suitable when you can lay an object horizontal. For stripping household joinery, use a gel stripper, which is stiff enough to cling to vertical surfaces.

Lay polythene sheet or plenty of newspaper on the floor, then apply a liberal coat of stripper to the paint, working well into the mouldings.

Leave it for about 10 minutes then try scraping a patch to see if the paint has softened through to the wood. If not, don't waste time removing the top layers only, but apply more stripper and stipple the softened paint back down with a brush. Leave for five minutes.

Once the chemicals have completed their work, use a stripping knife to scrape the paint from flat surfaces and a shavehook to remove it from mouldings.

Wipe the paint from deep carvings with fine wire wool; use small pieces of coarse sacking when stripping oak as particles of metal can stain the wood.

When you have removed the bulk of the paint, clean off residual patches with a wad of wire wool dipped in fresh stripper. Rub with the grain, turning the wad inside out to present a clean face as it becomes clogged with paint.

Neutralize the stripper by washing the wood with white spirit or water (depending on the manufacturer's advice). It is cheaper to use water when washing large areas but it will raise the grain and can cause joints to swell. Let the wood dry out thoroughly then treat as new timber ($\triangleright$).

PASTE STRIPPERS

Spread a paste stripper onto wood in a thick layer, working it well into crevices and mouldings and making sure all air bubbles are expelled.

The paste must be kept moist long enough for the chemicals to work – it may dry out too quickly in direct sunlight or a heated room – so cover it with a thin polythene sheet. Some manufacturers supply a blanket which seals the moisture in. Leave the stripper in place for several hours, then lift the leathery substance at the edge with a scraper and peel it off, complete with paint, in one layer. If it has become too hard to peel, soften it by soaking.

Discard the paste wrapped in newspaper, then wash the wood with water and a scrubbing brush. Leave it to dry before priming and finishing.

INDUSTRIAL STRIPPING

Any portable woodwork can be taken to a professional stripper, who will immerse the whole thing in a tank of stripping solution. Many companies use a solution of hot caustic soda, which must be washed out of the wood by hosing down with water. It is an efficient process (which incidentally kills woodworm at the same time) but there is a risk of splitting the panels, warping the wood and of opening up joints. At best, you can expect a reasonable amount of raised grain, which you will have to sand before refinishing.

Some companies use a cold chemical dip, which does little harm to solid timber and raises the grain less. This process is likely to be more expensive than the caustic soda method.

Most stripping companies will collect, many will rehang a door for you, and some offer a finishing service, too.

Never submit veneered items to either treatment: it may peel off.

Using a hot air stripper

Although stripping paint with a flame is fast and efficient, there is always the risk that you will burn the wood. Scorching can be covered by paint, but if you want to varnish the stripped wood, scorch marks will mar the finish.

Electrically-heated guns – like powerful hair dryers – work almost as quickly as a torch with less risk of scorching or fire. They do operate at an extremely high temperature: under no circumstances test the stripper by holding your hand over the nozzle.

Some guns come with variable heat settings and a selection of nozzles for various uses (see below). Hold the gun about 50mm (2in) from the surface of the paintwork and move it slowly backwards and forwards until the paint blisters and bubbles. Immediately remove the paint with a shavehook or scraper. Aim to heat the paint just ahead of the scraper so you develop a continuous work action.

Fit a shaped nozzle onto the gun when stripping glazing bars to concentrate the jet of hot air and reduce the risk of cracking the glass.

Old primer can sometimes be difficult to remove with a hot air stripper. If you are repainting the timber this is no problem; just rub the surface down with abrasive paper. For a clear finish remove residues of paint from the grain with wads of wire wool dipped in chemical stripper (see left).

SEE ALSO

Details for: $\triangleright$	
Preparing timber	33
Primers	23
Finishing wood	46-56

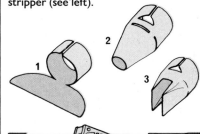

Nozzles for hot air guns
Hot air strippers come with a standard wide mouth for general usage but most offer optional extras, typically a push-on nozzle for stripping thin glazing bars (**1**) and a conical nozzle to concentrate the heat on a small area (**2**). Some offer nozzles for a wide spread of heat (**3**).

With a hot air gun there's less risk of scorching

METALWORK: IRON AND STEEL

Metal is a strong, hardwearing material that's used extensively throughout the home – for window frames, railings, gutters, pipework and radiators, to name but a few. Oddly, they're areas that are in close proximity to water, and consequently particularly prone to attack by metal's worst enemy: rust. Paint alone won't guard against this corrosive menace, so special treatments are necessary to ensure the long life of metal.

SEE ALSO

◁ Details for:

Industrial stripping	35
Primers	23
Finishing metal	57-58

Cast iron railings deeply pitted with rust

Flaking casement window as a result of rust

Severely corroded cast iron drainpipe

What is rust?

Rust is a form of corrosion that affects only the ferrous metals – notably iron and steel – due to the combination of water, oxygen and carbon dioxide. Although paint slows down the rate at which moisture penetrates, it doesn't stop it altogether; inhibitors and primers are needed to complete the protection, and the type you use depends on the condition of the metal and how you plan to decorate it. Prepare thoroughly or the job will be ruined.

Treating bare metal

Remove light deposits of rust by rubbing with wire wool or wet and dry abrasive paper dipped in white spirit. If the rust is heavy and the surface of the metal pitted, use a wire brush or, for extensive corrosion, a wire wheel or cup brush in a power drill. Wear goggles while wire brushing to protect your eyes from flying particles.

Paint a proprietary rust inhibitor onto the cleaned metal, following the manufacturer's instructions: some inhibitors remain on the surface to protect the metal, others must be washed off after a few minutes. Some car accessory shops carry a range of suitable inhibitors.

Wash off deposits of grease with white spirit and wire wool. As soon as the metal is clean and dry, apply a primer. For general inside use, choose a zinc phosphate or red oxide primer. For exterior paintwork, use calcium plumbate, red lead or zinc phosphate primers. Work the primer into crevices and fixings, and make sure sharp edges and corners where corrosion often begins are coated generously.

Preparing previously painted metal

If the paint is perfectly sound, wash it with sugar soap or a detergent solution, rinse and dry. Key gloss paint with fine wet and dry abrasive.

If the paint film is blistered or flaking where water has penetrated and corrosion has set in, remove all loose paint and rust with a wire brush or rotary attachment to an electric drill. Apply rust inhibitor to bare patches, working it well into joints, bolt heads and other fixings. Prime bare metal immediately: rust can reform rapidly.

When you're preparing cast iron guttering, brush out dead leaves and other debris and wash it clean. Paint the inside with a bitumen paint. If you want to paint over old bitumen paint, use an aluminium primer first to prevent it bleeding to the surface.

Stripping painted metal

Delicately moulded sections – on fire surrounds, garden furniture and other cast or wrought ironwork – can't easily be rubbed down with a wire brush, and will often benefit from stripping off old paint and rust which is masking fine detail. A hot air stripper cannot be used here as the metal dissipates the heat before the paint softens. A gas blowtorch can be used to strip wrought ironwork, but cast iron might crack if it becomes distorted by localized heating.

Chemical stripping is the safest method but before you begin, check that what appears to be a metal fire surround is not in fact made from plaster mouldings on a wooden background: the stripping process can play havoc with soft plasterwork. Tap the surround to see if it is metallic, or scrape an inconspicuous section.

Apply a proprietary rust-killing jelly or liquid, chemicals which will remove and neutralize rust: usually based on phosphoric acid, they combine with the rust to leave it quite inert in the form of iron phosphate. Some rust killers will deal with minute particles invisible to the naked eye, and are self-priming, so no additional primer is required.

Alternatively, if the metalwork is portable, you can take it to a sandblaster or an industrial stripper (◁). None of the disadvantages of industrial stripping apply to metal.

Clean the stripped metal with a wire brush then wash with white spirit before finishing it.

TREATING OTHER METALS

Corrosion in aluminium

Aluminium does not corrode to the same extent as ferrous metals. Indeed, modern aluminium alloy window and door frames, for example, are designed to withstand weathering without a coat of protective paint. Nevertheless, in adverse conditions, aluminium may corrode to a dull grey and even produce white crystals on the surface.

To remove the corrosion, rub the aluminium with fine wet and dry abrasive paper using white spirit as a lubricant until you get back to bright, but not gleaming, metal. Wipe the metal with a cloth dampened with white spirit to remove particles and traces of grease. When dry, prime the surface with a chromate primer. Never use a primer containing lead on aluminium, as there is likely to be an adverse chemical reaction between the metals in the presence of moisture.

Painting galvanized metal

Galvanized iron and steel has a coating of zinc applied by hot dipping; when new, it provides a poor key for most paints. Leaving the galvanizing to weather for six months will remedy this, but in many cases the manufacturer of galvanized metalwork will prepare it chemically for instant priming. If possible, check when you purchase it.

Treating chipped galvanizing
Any small rust spots caused by accidental chipping of the zinc coating should be removed by gentle abrasion with wire wool but take care not to damage the surrounding coating. Wash the area with white spirit then allow the surface to dry. Prime with calcium plumbate primer.

Protecting corrugated iron
For long-term protection of corrugated iron, first remove rust deposits then prime with a bitumen basecoat before finishing with a compatible reinforced emulsion paint.

Maintaining brass and copper

Ornamental brassware – typically door knobs, fingerplates and other door furniture – should not be painted, especially as there are clear lacquers which protect it from the elements. Strip painted brass with a chemical stripper; deal with corroded brass as described right.

Copper – mainly plumbing pipework and fittings – doesn't require painting for protection but visible pipe runs are usually painted so they blend in with the room decor (it is possible to make a feature of them by polishing, but it's a chore to keep them looking pristine).

Don't just paint onto the bare pipes: degrease and key the surface with fine wire wool lubricated with white spirit. Wipe away metal particles with a cloth dampened with white spirit. Apply undercoat and top coats direct: no primer is needed.

Painting over lead

In order to decorate old lead pipework, scour the surface with wire wool dipped in white spirit; no further preparation is required before you apply paint.

Advanced lead corrosion
The cames (grooved retaining strips) of stained glass windows can become corroded, producing white stains.

Mix some mild white vinegar in a little water and rub the cames thoroughly with the solution until the corrosion disappears. Next, apply a solution of washing soda and water to neutralize the acid content of the vinegar, then rinse several times with clean water and cloths.

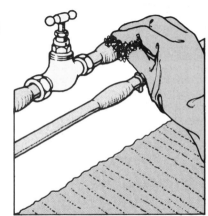

Key lead pipes for painting with wire wool

REMOVING CORROSION FROM BRASS FITTINGS

Brass corrodes to a dull brown colour but corrosion is normally easy to remove with a standard metal polish. However, if exterior brass door fittings have been left unprotected, deposits build up until they are difficult to polish off.

Mix one level tablespoonful of salt plus the same amount of vinegar in 275 ml (½ pint) of hot water. Soften the corrosion by applying liberal washes of the solution to the brass using very fine wire wool.

Wash the metal in hot water containing a little detergent, then rinse and dry it before polishing.

Clean brass with salt and vinegar solution

Removing verdigris
Badly weathered brass can develop green deposits called verdigris. This heavy corrosion may leave the metal pitted, so clean it as soon as possible.

Line a plastic bowl with ordinary aluminium cooking foil. Attach a piece of string to each item of brassware then place in the bowl on top of the foil. Dissolve a cup of washing soda in four pints of hot water and pour it into the bowl to cover the metalware.

Leave the solution to fizz and bubble for a couple of minutes, then lift out the brass items with the string. Replace any that are still corroded. If necessary, the process can be repeated using fresh solution and new foil.

Rinse the brass with hot water, dry it with a soft cloth, then polish.

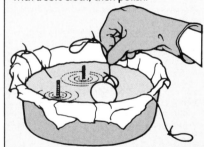

Remove verdigris with a washing soda dip

SEE ALSO

Details for: ▷	
Primers	23
Finishing metal	57-58

TILED SURFACES

Tiles are used to clad walls, floors and ceilings, and are made in a vast range of materials – ceramic, cork, vinyl and polystyrene are popular – and in a host of different surface textures and finishes. If they're looking shabby it's possible to either revive their existing finish or decorate them with paint or wallcoverings – with some it's even possible to stick new tiles on top for a completely new look.

SEE ALSO

◁ Details for:
Levelling compound	29
Glass-fibre wallcovering	61, 67
Lining paper	64
Tiling	69-80

CLEANING AN OLD QUARRY TILED FLOOR

Old quarry tiles are absorbent and dirt and grease become ingrained in the surface. If normal washing with detergent fails to revitalize their colour and finish, clean the tiles with a diluted hydrochloric acid (available from a chemist as spirits of salts).

Add a drop or two of acid to some warm water in a plastic bucket. Stir it gently with a wooden stick and try it on a small patch of floor. Don't make the solution any stronger than is necessary: the solution attacks the grouting, so work quickly in small sections. Wash the floor with the solution, rinsing off the diluted acid with clean, warm water.

Removing ingrained dirt
Wash tiles with hydrochloric acid solution

WHEN USING ACID

● **Wear PVC gloves, old clothes and goggles.**
● **Add acid to water, never the other way around.**
● **Keep acid out of reach of children and animals.**

Removing ceramic or quarry tiles
To remove old tiles, first chop out at least one of them with a cold chisel, then prise the others off the surface by driving a bolster chisel behind them. Chop away any remaining tile adhesive or mortar with the bolster.

Ceramic wall and floor tiles

Ceramic tiles are stuck to the wall or floor with a special adhesive or, in the case of quarry tiles, mortar. Removing them in their entirety in order to redecorate the wall is messy and time-consuming, but is often the most satisfactory longterm solution.

So long as a ceramic tiled wall is sound, you can paint it with oil-based paint. Wash the surface thoroughly with sugar soap or detergent solution. The problem with this treatment is that glazed tiles do not provide a good key for paintwork and you'd find that the new surface would chip easily. You can lay new tiles directly over old ones but make sure the surface is perfectly flat – check by holding a long spirit level or straight-edged batten across the surface. Tap the tiles to locate any loose ones and either glue them firmly in place or chop them out with a cold chisel and club hammer and fill the space with mortar. Wash the wall to remove grease and dirt.

It's also possible to tile over old quarry or ceramic floor tiles in the same way. Treat an uneven floor with a self-levelling compound (◁).

It is not practicable to paper over old ceramic wall tiles, as the adhesive would not be able to grip on the shiny surface. Instead, you could hang a woven glass-fibre wallcovering, which is designed to be painted afterwards (◁). The tiles must be perfectly sound and free from dirt and grease, or this rather coarse material might peel off.

Polystyrene ceiling tiles

Polystyrene tiles are stuck directly onto the surface with a water- or solvent-based adhesive that can be difficult to remove. The adhesive was commonly applied in five small dabs: this method is now unapproved due to the risk of fire. Manufacturers recommend a complete bed of adhesive, which makes removal even worse.

Remove tiles by prising them off with a wide-bladed scraper then prise off the adhesive dabs. On stubborn patches, try to soften the adhesive with warm water, wallpaper stripper or even paint stripper (but wear goggles and PVC gloves: it's difficult to avoid splashes). For larger areas of adhesive try a solution of ammonia (see below). One way to give the tiles a facelift is to paint them. These tiles should never be painted with an oil paint, which increases the risk of fire spreading across the tiles. Brush the tiles to remove dust, then apply emulsion paint.

Vinyl floor tiles

Vinyl floor tiles are not a good foundation so resurface them or remove them completely. Soften the tiles and their adhesive with a domestic iron, then use a scraper to prise them up. Remove the old adhesive by applying a solution of half a cupful of household ammonia and a drop of liquid detergent in a bucketful of cold water. When the floor is clean, rinse it with water.

If vinyl tiles are firmly glued to the floor, you can clean them then resurface them with a latex self-levelling screed (◁). Before you apply this method, however, check the recommendations of your floorcovering manufacturer: it may not be suitable for laying after this treatment.

Cork floor and wall tiles

It's possible to decorate over cork tiles, although absorbent types will need priming first. The advice given for vinyl floor tiles applies for cork tiles also. Hard, sound wall tiles can be painted so long as they are clean. Prime absorbent cork first with a general-purpose primer before painting over it.

Unless the tiles are textured or pierced, they can be papered over but size the surface with commercial size or heavy-duty wallpaper paste, then line them horizontally (◁) to prevent joins showing through.

Fibre ceiling tiles

Acoustic fibre tiles can be painted with water-based paints. Wash them with a mild detergent but do not soak the tiles as they're quite absorbent.

APPLYING FINISHES

A finish in decorating terms means a liquid or semi-liquid substance which sets, dries or cures to protect and sometimes colour materials such as wood or masonry. Apart from paint, other finishes for wood include stains, varnishes, oil, wax and French polish, all of which are used specifically where you want to display the grain of the timber for its natural beauty.

The make-up of paint

Paint is basically made from solid particles of pigment suspended in a liquid binder or medium. The pigment provides the colour and body of the paint, the medium allows the material to be brushed, rolled or sprayed and, once applied, forms a solid film binding the pigment together and adhering to the surface. Binder and pigment vary from paint to paint, but the commonest two families are solvent- (sometimes known as oil) and water-based.

COMMON PAINT FINISHES AND ADDITIVES

The type of paint you choose depends on the finish you want and the material you're decorating. Various additives adapt the paint's qualities.

SOLVENT-BASED (OIL) PAINT

The medium for solvent-based paints (commonly called oil paints) is a mixture of oils and resin. A paint made from a natural resin is slow-drying, but modern paints contain synthetic resins such as alkyd, urea, epoxy, acrylic and vinyl, which all make for fast-drying paints. A white pigment, titanium dioxide, is added, plus other pigments to alter the colour.

WATER-BASED PAINT

Emulsion is the commonest water-based paint. It has a binder made from synthetic resins similar to those used for oil paints, but it is dispersed in a solution of water. Titanium is the white pigment used for good-quality paints. It is also used with additional pigments for a wide range of colours.

ADDITIVES IN PAINT

No paint is made from simply binder and pigment. Certain additives are included during manufacture to give the paint qualities such as faster drying, high gloss, easy flow, longer pot life, or to make the paint non-drip.

● **Thixotropic** paints are the typical non-drip types; they are thick, almost jelly-like in the can, enabling you to pick up a brush load without dripping.

● **Extenders** are added as fillers to strengthen the paint film. Cheap paint contains too much filler, reducing its covering power.

PAINT THINNERS

If a paint is too thick it cannot be applied properly and must be thinned before it is used. Some finishes require special thinners provided by the manufacturer, but most oil paints can be thinned with white spirit, and emulsions with water.

Turpentine will thin oil paint but has no advantages over white spirit for household paints and it is much more expensive.

GLOSS OR MATT FINISH?

The proportion of pigment to resin affects the way the paint sets. A gloss (shiny) paint contains approximately equal amounts of resin and pigment, whereas a higher proportion of pigment produces a matt (dull) paint. By adjusting the proportions, it is possible to make satin or eggshell paints. Matt paints tend to cover best due to their high pigment content, but the greater proportion of resin in gloss paints is responsible for their strength.

Applying a paint system

No paint will provide protection for long if you apply one coat only. It is necessary to apply successive layers to build up a paint system.

● Paint for walls requires a simple system comprising two or three coats of the same paint.

● Paint intended for woodwork and metalwork needs a more complex system using paints with different qualities. A typical paint system for woodwork is illustrated below.

SEE ALSO

Details for: ▷	
Choosing colours	8-9
Primers	23
Lead content	23
Preparing paint	40

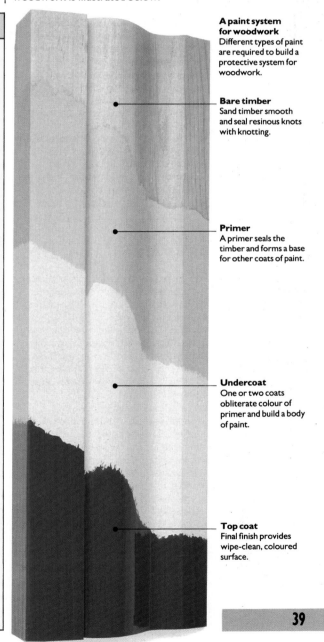

A paint system for woodwork
Different types of paint are required to build a protective system for woodwork.

Bare timber
Sand timber smooth and seal resinous knots with knotting.

Primer
A primer seals the timber and forms a base for other coats of paint.

Undercoat
One or two coats obliterate colour of primer and build a body of paint.

Top coat
Final finish provides wipe-clean, coloured surface.

SEE ALSO

◁ Details for:
Ladders and towers 20-22
Preparing masonry 24-29

SAFETY WHEN PAINTING

Decorating isn't dangerous so long as you take sensible precautions to protect your health.

● **Ensure good ventilation indoors while applying a finish and when it is drying. Wear a facemask if you have respiratory problems.**
● **Do not smoke while painting or in the vicinity of drying paint.**
● **Contain paint spillages outside with sand or earth and don't allow it to enter a drain.**
● **If you splash paint in your eyes, flush them with copious amounts of water with your lids held open; if symptoms persist, visit a doctor.**
● **Wear barrier cream or gloves on sensitive hands. Use a proprietary skin cleanser to remove paint from the skin or wash it off with warm soapy water. Do not use paint thinners to clean your skin.**
● **Keep any finish and thinners out of reach of children. If a child swallows a substance, do not attempt to make it vomit but seek medical treatment.**

Strain old paint
If you're using leftover paint, filter it through a piece of muslin or old tights stretched over the rim of a container.

Resealing the lid
Wipe the rim of the can clean before you replace the lid, then tap it down all round with a hammer over a softwood block.

PREPARING THE PAINT

Whether you're using newly purchased paint or leftovers from previous jobs, there are some basic rules to observe before you apply it.

● Wipe dust from the paint can, then prise off the lid with the side of a knife blade. Don't use a screwdriver: it only buckles the edge of the lid, preventing an airtight seal and making subsequent removal difficult.
● Gently stir liquid paints with a wooden stick to blend the pigment and medium. There's no need to stir thixotropic paints unless the medium has separated; if you have to stir it, leave it to gel again before using.
● If a skin has formed on paint, cut round the edge with a knife and lift out in one piece with a stick. It's a good idea to store the can on its lid, so that a skin cannot form on top of the paint.
● Whether the paint is old or new, transfer a small amount into a paint kettle or plastic bucket. Old paint should be filtered at the same time, tying a piece of muslin or old nylon tights across the rim of the kettle.

PAINTING EXTERIOR MASONRY

The outside walls of your house need painting for two major reasons: to give a clean, bright appearance and to protect the surface from the rigours of the climate. What you use as a finish and how you apply it depends on what the walls are made of, their condition and the degree of protection they need. Bricks are traditionally left bare, but may require a coat of paint if they're in bad condition or previous attempts to decorate have resulted in a poor finish. Rendered walls are normally painted to brighten the naturally dull grey colour of the cement; pebbledashed surfaces may need a colourful coat to disguise previous conspicuous patches. On the other hand, you may just want to change the present colour of your walls for a fresh appearance.

Working to a plan

Before you start painting the outside walls of your house, plan your time carefully. Depending on the preparation even a small house will take a few weeks to complete.

It's not necessary to tackle the whole job at once, although it is preferable – the weather may change to the detriment of your timetable. You can split the work into separate stages with days (even weeks) in between, so long as you divide the walls into manageable sections. Use window and door frames, bays, downpipes and corners of walls to form break lines that will disguise joins.

Start at the top of the house, working right to left if you are right-handed (vice versa if you are left-handed).

FINISHES FOR MASONRY

Black dot denotes compatibility. All surfaces must be clean, sound, dry and free from organic growth.

	Cement paint	Exterior emulsion paint	Reinforced emulsion paint	Spirit-thinned masonry paint	Textured coating	Floor paint
SUITABLE TO COVER						
Brick	●	●	●	●	●	●
Stone	●	●	●	●	●	●
Concrete	●	●	●	●	●	●
Cement rendering	●	●	●	●	●	●
Pebbledash	●	●	●	●	●	
Asbestos cement	●	●	●	●	●	
Emulsion paint		●	●	●	●	
Oil-based paint		●		●	●	
Cement paint	●					
DRYING TIME: HOURS						
Touch dry	1-2	1-2	2-3	1-2	6	2-3
Re-coatable	24	4	24	24	24-48	12-24
THINNERS: SOLVENTS						
Water-thinned	●	●	●		●	
White spirit-thinned				●		●
NUMBER OF COATS						
Normal conditions	2	2	1-2	2	1	1-2
COVERAGE: DEPENDING ON WALL TEXTURE						
Sq.metres per litre		4-10	3-6.5	3-6		5-15
Sq.metres per kg	1.5-3.5				1-2	
METHOD OF APPLICATION						
Brush	●	●	●	●	●	●
Roller	●	●	●	●	●	●
Spray gun	●	●	●	●		●

SUITABLE PAINTS FOR EXTERIOR MASONRY

There are various grades of paint suitable for decorating and protecting exterior masonry, which take into account economy, standard of finish, durability and coverage. Use the chart opposite for quick reference.

CEMENT PAINT

Cement paint is supplied as a dry powder, to which water is added. It is based on white cement but pigments are added to produce a range of colours. Cement paint is the cheapest of the paints suitable for exterior use, although it is not as weatherproof as some others. Spray new or porous surfaces with water before you apply two coats.

Mixing cement paint
Shake or roll the container to loosen the powder, then add two volumes of powder to one of water in a clean bucket. Stir it to a smooth paste then add a little more water until you achieve a full-bodied, creamy consistency. Mix up no more than you can use in one hour, or it will start to dry.

Adding an aggregate
When you're painting a dense wall or one treated with a stabilizing solution so that its porosity is substantially reduced, it is advisable to add clean sand to the mix. It also provides added protection for an exposed wall and helps to cover dark colours. If the sand changes the colour of the paint, add it to the first coat only. Use one volume of sand to four of powder, but stir it in when the paint is still in its paste-like consistency.

EXTERIOR-GRADE EMULSION

Exterior-grade emulsion resembles the interior type; it is water-thinnable and dries to a similar smooth, matt finish. However, it is formulated to make it weatherproof and includes an additive to prevent mould growth; so apart from reinforced emulsions, it is the only emulsion paint recommended for use on outside walls.

The paint is ready for use but thin the first coat on porous walls with 20 per cent water. Follow up with one or two full-strength coats (depending on the colour of the paint).

REINFORCED EMULSION

Reinforced emulsion is a water-thinnable, resin-based paint to which has been added powdered mica or a similar fine aggregate. It dries with a textured finish that is extremely weatherproof, even in coastal districts or industrial areas where darker colours are especially suitable.

Although cracks and holes must be filled prior to painting, reinforced emulsion will cover hair cracks and crazing. Apply two coats of paint in normal conditions but you can economize by using sanded cement paint for the first coat.

SPIRIT-THINNED MASONRY PAINT

A few masonry paints suitable for exterior walls are thinned with white spirit but they are based on special resins so that, unlike most oil-based paints, they can be used on new walls without priming first with an alkali-resistant primer (▷). Check with manufacturer's recommendations. However, it is advisable to thin the first coat with 15 per cent white spirit.

TEXTURED COATING

A thick textured coating can be applied to exterior walls. It is a thoroughly weatherproof, self-coloured coating, but it can be overpainted to match other colours. The usual preparation is necessary and brickwork should be pointed flush. Large cracks should be filled, but a textured coating will cover fine cracks. The paste is brushed or rolled onto the wall, then left to harden, forming an even texture. On the other hand, you can produce a texture of your choice using a variety of simple tools (▷). It's an easy process, but practise on a small section first.

EXTERIOR MASONRY

Concrete floor paints

Floor paints are specially prepared to withstand hard wear. They are especially suitable for concrete garage or workshop floors, but they are also used for stone paving, steps and other concrete structures. They can be used inside for playroom floors.

The floor must be clean and dry and free from oil or grease. If the concrete is freshly laid, allow it to mature for at least three months before painting. Thin the first coat of paint with 10 per cent white spirit.

Don't use floor paint over a surface sealed with a proprietary concrete sealer, but you can cover other paints so long as they are keyed first.

The best way to paint a large area is to use a paintbrush around the edges, then fit an extension to a paint roller for the bulk of the floor.

SEE ALSO

Details for: ▷	
Primers	23
Textured coating	59
Preparing masonry	24-29

Apply paint with a roller on an extension

Paint in manageable sections
You can't hope to paint an entire house in one session, so divide each elevation into manageable sections to disguise the joins. The horizontal moulding divides the wall neatly into two sections, and the raised door and window surrounds are convenient break lines.

TECHNIQUES FOR PAINTING MASONRY

SEE ALSO

◁ Details for:
| Work platforms | 20-22 |
| Preparing masonry | 24-29 |

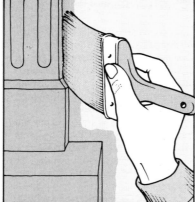
I Cut in with a gentle scrubbing motion

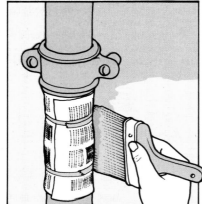
2 Protect downpipes with newspaper

3 Use a banister brush
Tackle deeply textured wall surfaces with a banister brush, using a scrubbing action.

4 Use a roller
For speed in application, use a paint roller with a deep pile for heavy textures, a medium pile for light textures and smooth wall surfaces.

5 Spray onto the apex of external corners

6 Spray internal corners as separate surfaces

Using paintbrushes

Choose a 100 to 150mm (4 to 6in) wide paintbrush for walls; larger ones are heavy and tiring to use. A good-quality brush with coarse bristles will last longer on rough walls. For a good coverage, apply the paint with vertical strokes, criss-crossed with horizontal ones. You will find it necessary to stipple paint into textured surfaces.

Cutting in

Painting up to a feature such as a door or window frame is known as cutting in. On a smooth surface, you should be able to paint a reasonably straight edge following the line of the feature, but it's difficult to apply the paint to a heavily textured wall with a normal brush stroke. Don't just apply more paint to overcome the problem; instead, touch the tip of the brush only to the wall, using a gentle scrubbing action (1), then brush excess paint away from the feature once the texture is filled.

Wipe splashed paint from window and door frames with a cloth dampened with the appropriate thinner.

Painting behind pipes

To protect rainwater downpipes, tape a roll of newspaper around them. Stipple behind the pipe with a brush then slide the paper tube down the pipe to mask the next section (2).

Painting with a banister brush

Use a banister brush (3) to paint deep textures such as pebbledash. Pour some paint into a roller tray and dab the brush in to load it. Scrub the paint onto the wall using circular strokes to work it well into the uneven surface.

Using a paint roller

A roller (4) will apply paint three times faster than a brush. Use a deep-pile roller for heavy textures or a medium-pile for lightly textured or smooth walls. Rollers wear quickly on rough walls, so have a spare sleeve handy. Vary the angle of the stroke when using a roller to ensure an even coverage and use a brush to cut into angles and obstructions.

A paint tray is difficult to use at the top of a ladder, unless you fit a tool support, or better still erect a flat platform to work from (◁).

Using a spray gun

Spraying is the quickest and most efficient way to apply paint to a large expanse of wall. But you will have to mask all the parts you do not want to paint, using newspaper and masking tape. The paint must be thinned by about 10 per cent for spraying: set the spray gun according to the manufacturer's instructions to suit the particular paint. It is advisable to wear a respirator when spraying.

Hold the gun about 225mm (9in) away from the wall and keep it moving with even, parallel passes. Slightly overlap each pass and try to keep the gun pointing directly at the surface — tricky while standing on a ladder. Trigger the gun just before each pass and release it at the end of the stroke.

When spraying a large, blank wall, paint it into vertical bands overlapping each band by 100mm (4in).

Spray external corners by aiming the gun directly at the apex so that paint falls evenly on both surfaces (5). When two walls meet at an internal angle, treat each surface separately (6).

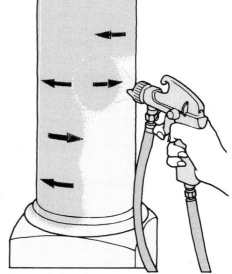
Spray-painting columns
Columns, part of a front door portico, for instance, should be painted in a series of overlapping vertical bands. Apply the bands by running the spray gun from side to side as you work down the column.

PAINTING INTERIOR WALLS AND CEILINGS

Most interior walls and ceilings will be plastered and most probably papered or painted, unless the house has been recently built. Apart from their preparation, the methods for painting them are identical and they can be considered smooth surfaces in terms of paint coverage. Although a flat, matt finish is usually preferred indoors for walls and ceilings, there's no reason why you shouldn't use a gloss or even a textured paint in your scheme.

Finishes for bare masonry

Some interior walls are left unplastered – and some may even have been stripped on purpose – either for their decorative appearance or because it was considered unnecessary to clad the walls of certain rooms such as the basement, workshop or garage. A stripped brick or stone chimney breast makes an attractive focal point in a room, and an entire wall of bare masonry can create a dramatic effect or suggest a country cottage style.

If you want to finish brick, concrete or stone walls, follow the methods described for exterior walls. However, because they will not have to withstand weathering, you can use paint designed for interior use. Newly stripped masonry will require sealing to bind the surface (▷).

SEE ALSO

Details for: ▷	
Primers and sealers	23
Cement paint	41
Preparation	24-31
Stripping wallcoverings	32

SELECTING PAINTS FOR INTERIOR SURFACES

Although you really only have a choice of two finishes for interior walls and ceilings – emulsion or oil paint – there are various qualities which offer depth of sheen, texture, one-coat coverage and good obliteration.

EMULSION PAINT

The most popular and practical finish for walls and ceilings, emulsions are available in liquid or thixotropic consistencies with matt or satin (semi-gloss) finishes.

A satin finish emulsion is less likely to show fingerprints or scuffs. A non-drip, thixotropic paint has obvious advantages when painting ceilings, and covers in one coat. But apply a thinned coat on new, porous plaster, followed by a full-strength coat to achieve the required finish.

Emulsion is also available in a solid form, which comes in its own roller tray. It paints out well with minimal spatter and no drips.

REINFORCED EMULSION

Emulsion paints, reinforced with fine aggregate, are primarily for use on exterior walls but their fine textured finish is just as attractive inside and will cover minor imperfections, which would show through standard emulsions.

OIL PAINT

Oil paints dry to a hard, durable finish. Although these paints are mainly intended for woodwork, they can be used on walls that require an extra degree of protection: they were once popular in bathrooms and kitchens, where you might expect condensation, but this is unnecessary with the development of modern water-thinned emulsions, which resist moisture.

High-gloss paints accentuate uneven wall surfaces, so most people prefer a satin finish. Both types are available in liquid or thixotropic form. Most gloss paints should be preceded by one or two undercoats, but satin finishes, which have a very fine texture, form their own undercoats.

UNDERCOAT

Undercoat is a relatively cheap paint used to build up the full system of protective paintwork. It will obliterate underlying colours and fill minor irregularities. If speed is essential, choose a quick-drying primer/undercoat – a three-coat system of two undercoats and a top coat can be built up in one day.

CEMENT PAINT

Cement paint is an inexpensive exterior finish which is ideal for a utilitarian area indoors, such as a cellar, workshop or garage. Sold in dry powder form, it must be made up with water and dries to a matt finish (▷).

Paints for walls and ceilings
Emulsion paint, in its many forms, is the most practical finish for interior walls and ceilings, but use oil paints on wall-fixed joinery like skirtings and picture rails. The example above illustrates the advantage of contrasting textures: matt emulsion for the cornice up to the ceiling; gloss oil paint for the picture rail; satin emulsion for the woodchip covered walls.

USING BRUSHES, PADS AND ROLLERS

SEE ALSO

◁ Details for:
Work platforms	22
Radiator roller	57
Spraying	42

Applying paint by brush

Choose a good-quality brush for painting walls and ceilings. Cheap brushes tend to shed bristles – infuriating and less economical in the long run. Buy a brush about 200mm (8in) wide for quickest coverage: if you're not used to handling a brush your wrist will soon tire and you may find a 150mm (6in) brush, plus a 50mm (2in) brush for the edges and corners, more comfortable to use, although take into account that the job will take longer.

Loading the brush

Don't overload a brush with paint; it leads to messy work and ruins the bristles if it is allowed to dry in the roots. Dip no more than the first third of the brush into the paint, wiping off excess on the side of the container to prevent drips (1). When using thixotropic paint, load the brush and apply paint without removing excess.

Using a brush

You can hold the brush whichever way feels comfortable to you, but the 'pen' grip is the most versatile, enabling your wrist to move the brush freely in any direction. Hold the brush handle between your thumb and forefinger, with your fingers on the ferrule (metal band) and your thumb supporting it from the other side (2).

Apply the paint in vertical strokes then spread it at right angles to even out the coverage. Emulsion paint will not show brush marks when it dries but finish oil paints with light upward vertical strokes for the best results.

1 Dip only the first third of bristles in paint

2 Place fingers on ferrule, thumb behind

Applying paint by roller

A paint roller with interchangeable sleeves is an excellent tool for applying paint to large areas. Choose a roller about 300mm (1ft) long for painting walls and ceilings.

There are a number of different sleeves to suit the type of paint and texture of the surface. Long-haired sheepskin and woven wool sleeves are excellent on texture surfaces, especially with emulsion paint. Choose a short-pile for smooth surfaces, and with oil paints.

Disposable plastic foam rollers can be used to apply any paint to a smooth surface but they soon lose their resilience and have a greater tendency to skid across the wall.

Special rollers

Rollers with long extension handles are designed for painting ceilings without having to erect a work platform (◁).

Some have a built-in paint reservoir for automatic reloading.

Narrow rollers are available for painting behind radiators, if you are unable to remove them (◁).

Loading a roller

You will need a special paint tray to load a standard roller. Having dipped the sleeve lightly into the paint reservoir, roll it gently onto the ribbed part of the tray to coat the roller evenly (1).

Using a roller

Use zig-zag strokes with a roller (2), covering the surface in all directions. Keep it on the surface at all times. If you let it spin at the end of a stroke it will spray paint onto the floor or adjacent surface. When applying oil paint, finish in one direction, preferably towards prevailing light.

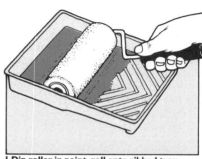

1 Dip roller in paint, roll onto ribbed tray

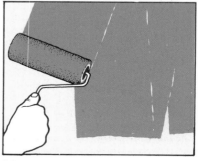

2 Apply in zig-zags, finish in one direction

Applying paint by pad

Paint pads for large surfaces have flat rectangular faces covered with a short mohair pile. A plastic foam backing gives the pad flexibility so that the pile will always be in contact with the wall, even on a rough surface.

The exact size of the pad will be determined by the brand you choose but one about 200mm (8in) long is best for applying paint evenly and smoothly to walls and ceilings. You will also need a small pad or paintbrush for cutting in at corners and ceilings.

Loading a pad

Load a pad from its own special tray, drawing the pad across the captive roller so that you pick up an even amount of paint (1).

Using a pad

To apply the paint consistently, keep the pad flat on the wall and sweep it gently and evenly in any direction (2). Use criss-cross strokes for emulsion, but finish with vertical strokes with oil paints to prevent streaking.

1 Loading a paint pad
Load the pad evenly by drawing it across the integral roller on the tray without squeezing.

• **Spraying**
It is possible to spray paint onto interior walls and ceilings, but it is only practical for large rooms: you'll have to mask everything you don't want to paint; and the sprayed paint would be forced through even the narrowest gaps between doors and frames. Adequate ventilation is vital when spraying indoors.

2 Sweep pad gently in any direction

APPLYING PAINT TO WALLS AND CEILINGS

Even the most experienced painter can't help dripping a little paint, so always paint a ceiling before the wall, especially if they are to be different colours. Erect a work platform so that you can cover as much of the surface as possible without having to change position: you will achieve a better finish and will be able to work in safety. When you start to paint, follow a strict working routine to ensure a faultless finish. Choose your tools wisely so you can work efficiently. Refer to the chart below for professional results.

Painting the ceiling

Start in a corner near the window and carefully paint along the edges with a small paintbrush.

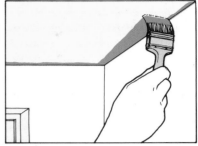

Paint edges first

Working from the wet edges, paint in 600mm (2ft) wide bands, working away from the light. Whether you use a brush, a pad or a roller, apply each fresh load of paint just clear of the previous application, blending in the junctions for even coverage.

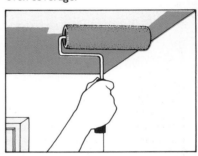

Work from wet edges

SEE ALSO

Details for: ▷	
Consumer unit	134
Work platforms	22
Primers	23
Preparing masonry	24-26
Preparing paint surfaces	28, 30
Preparing concrete	29
Preparing plaster	30-31
Stripping wallpaper	32

● Black dot denotes compatibility. All surfaces must be clean, sound, dry and free from organic growth.

FINISHES FOR INTERIOR WALLS & CEILINGS

	Emulsion paint	Reinforced emulsion paint	Oil-based paints	Undercoat	Primer/ undercoat	Cement paint	Textured coating
SUITABLE TO COVER							
Plaster	●	●	●	●	●	●	●
Wallpaper	●		●	●	●		
Brick	●	●	●	●		●	●
Stone	●	●	●	●		●	●
Concrete	●	●	●	●	●	●	●
Previously painted surface	●	●	●	●	●		
DRYING TIME: HOURS							
Touch dry	1-2	2-3	4	4	½	1-2	6
Re-coatable	4	24	16	16	2	24	24-48
THINNERS: SOLVENTS							
Water	●	●				●	●
White spirit			●	●	●		
NUMBER OF COATS							
Normal conditions	2	1-2	1-2	1-2	1-2	2	1
COVERAGE: APPROXIMATE							
Sq. metres per litre	9-15	3-6.5	12-17	15-18	15		
Sq. metres per kg						1.5-3.5	1-2
METHOD OF APPLICATION							
Brush	●	●	●	●	●	●	●
Roller	●	●	●	●	●	●	●
Paint pad	●		●	●	●	●	
Spray	●	●	●	●	●	●	

Electrical fittings

Unscrew a ceiling rose cover so that you can paint right up to the backplate with a small brush. Loosen the faceplate or mounting box of sockets and switches to paint behind them.

Remember: switch off at the mains before exposing electrical connections (▷).

Paint reservoir
Use a special roller with a pressurized paint reservoir to avoid having to constantly reload a roller; it's an excellent boon for painting ceilings and high walls, when frequent returns to the tray would be tiresome.

Painting the walls

Use a small brush to paint the edges starting at a top corner of the room. If you are right-handed, work right to left. Paint an area of about 600mm (2ft) square at a time. If you are left-handed, paint the wall in the opposite direction. When using emulsion, paint in horizontal bands **(1)**, but, with oil paints, use vertical strips **(2)** as the junctions are more likely to show unless you blend in the wet edges quickly. Always finish a complete wall before you take a break or a change of tone will show between separate painted sections.

1 Paint emulsion in horizontal bands

2 Apply oil paints in vertical strips

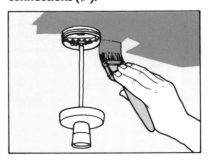

Unscrew rose cover to keep it clean

FINISHING WOODWORK

Paint is the usual finish for woodwork in and around the house — it gives a protective, decorative coating and there's a vast choice of colours and surface finishes. But stains, varnishes or polishes can also be used not just for furniture but as an attractive, durable finish for joinery. They enable

you to add colour to woodwork without obliterating the natural beauty of its grain; transparent finishes are also a good alternative where you don't want to alter the natural wood colour. Bear in mind the location of the woodwork and the amount of wear it is likely to get when choosing a finish.

Left to right
1 Wax polish
2 Coloured preserver
3 Satin oil paint
4 Cold cure lacquer
5 Gloss oil paint
6 Oil finish

7 Unsealed wood stain
8 Opaque microporous wood stain
9 Clear microporous wood stain
10 Polyurethane varnish

SEE ALSO

◁ Details for:

Colour and texture	8-12
Painting wood	48-51
Staining wood	52-53
Varnishing wood	54, 56
Polishing wood	55, 56
Oiling wood	56

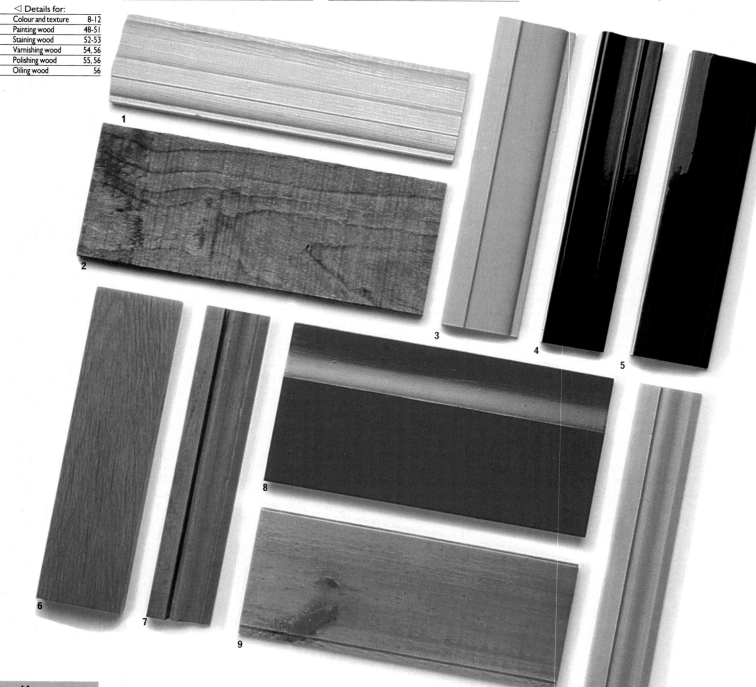

THE CHOICE OF FINISHES FOR WOOD

The list below comprises a comprehensive range of finishes available for decorating and protecting woodwork in and around the house. Each finish has qualities particular to its intended usage, although many can be used simply for their attractive appearance rather than for any practical considerations – this, however, depends on the location of timberwork, as some finishes are much more durable than others.

OIL PAINT

Oil (solvent-based) paints are still the most popular finish, primarily for the range of colours offered by all paint manufacturers, secondarily because they last for many years with only the occasional wash down to remove finger marks. Outside, their durability is reduced considerably due to the combined action of sun and rain: consider redecoration every two or three years. They are available as a gloss or satin finish with both liquid and thixotropic consistencies.

One or two undercoats are essential, especially for outside.

GLOSS EMULSION PAINT

Emulsion-based gloss paint was introduced by several manufacturers but is still quite rare. Beneficially, it dries much faster than oil paint and without the strong smell associated with such paint. It is suitable for both interior and exterior use. It allows moisture to escape from the wood while protecting it from rainwater – which oil paint does not – so reduces the risk of flaking and blistering. Gloss emulsion requires its own compatible primer/undercoat. The usual system of two undercoats and one top coat can be applied in one day.

WOOD STAIN

Unlike paint, which after the initial priming coat rests on the surface of timber, stain penetrates the wood. Its main advantage is to enhance the natural colour of the woodwork or to unify the slight variation in colour found in even the same species.

Water- or oil-based stains are available ready for use but powdered pigments are available for mixing with methylated spirit. None of these stains will actually protect the timber and you will have to seal them with a clear varnish or polish.

There are protective wood stains (often sold as *microporous paints* or *breathing paints*) specially made for use on exterior joinery. The microporous nature of the coating allows water to escape from the wood, yet provides a weather-resistant satin finish. Being a stain, it does not crack, peel or flake. Choose a semi-transparent stain when you want the grain to show, or an opaque one for less attractive timbers.

COLOURED PRESERVERS

Sawn timber fencing, wall cladding and outbuildings look particularly unattractive when painted, yet they need protection. Use a wood preserver, which penetrates deeply into the timber to prevent rot and insect attack. There are clear preservers, plus a range of browns and greens, and usually one for red cedar.

Traditional preservers such as creosote have a strong, unpleasant smell and are harmful to plants, but there are several organic solvent preservers, which are perfectly safe – even for greenhouses and propagators.

VARNISH

Varnish is a clear protective coating for timber. Most modern varnishes are made with polyurethane resins to provide a waterproof scratch- and heat-resistant finish. The majority are ready to apply, although some are supplied with a catalyst, which must be added before the varnish is used. These two-component varnishes are even tougher than standard polyurethanes and are especially suitable for treating wooden floors: you can choose from high gloss, satin or matt.

An exterior grade of varnish is more weather-resistant. Yacht varnish, which is formulated to withstand even salt water, would be an ideal finish for exterior woodwork in a coastal climate.

Coloured varnishes are designed to provide a stain and clear finish at the same time. They are available in the normal wood shades and some strong primary colours. Unlike a true stain, a coloured varnish does not sink into the timber, so there is a possibility of a local loss of colour in areas of heavy wear or abrasion unless you apply additional coats of clear varnish.

COLD CURE LACQUER

Cold cure lacquer is a plastic coating, which is mixed with a hardener just before it is used. It is extremely durable, even on floors, and is heat- and alcohol-resistant. The standard type dries to a high gloss, which can be burnished to a lacquer-like finish if required. There is also a matt finish grade but a smoother matt surface can be obtained by rubbing down the gloss coating with fine steel wool and wax. It is available in clear, black or white.

OIL

Oil is a subtle finish which soaks into the wood, leaving a mellow sheen on the surface. Traditional linseed oils remain sticky for hours but a modern oil will dry in about one hour and provides a tougher, more durable finish. Oil can be used on softwood as well as open-grained oily hardwoods, such as teak or afrormosia. It's suitable for interior and exterior woodwork.

WAX POLISH

Wax can be used as a dressing to preserve and maintain another finish, or it can be used as a finish itself. A good wax should be a blend of beeswax and a hard polishing wax such as carnauba. Some contain silicones to make it easier to achieve a high gloss.

Polishes are white or tinted to various shades of brown to darken the wood. Although it is attractive, wax polish is not a durable finish and should be used indoors only.

FRENCH POLISH

French polish is made by dissolving shellac in alcohol and if properly applied, can be burnished to a mirror-like finish. It is easily scratched and alcohol, or even water, will etch the surface, leaving white stains. Consequently, it can be used only on furniture unlikely to receive normal wear and tear.

There are several varieties of shellac polish. Button polish is the best quality standard polish and is reddish brown in colour. It is bleached to make white polish for light coloured woods and if the natural wax is removed from the shellac, a clear, transparent polish is produced. For mahogany, choose a darker red garnet polish.

SEE ALSO

Details for: ▷
Primers   23

PAINTING WOODWORK

When you're painting wood, take into account that it's a fibrous material, which has a definite grain pattern, different rates of absorbency, knots *that may ooze resin – all qualities that influence the type of paint you use and the techniques and tools you'll need to apply it.*

SEE ALSO

◁ Details for:

Primers	23
Preparing wood	33
Preparing paintwork	34-35
Paint system	39

Basic application

Prepare and prime all new woodwork thoroughly (◁) before applying the final finish. If you are using gloss paint, apply one or two undercoats, depending on the covering power of the paint. As each coat hardens, rub down with fine wet and dry paper to remove blemishes and wipe the surface with a cloth dampened with white spirit.

Best quality paintbrushes are the most efficient tools for painting woodwork. You will need 25mm (1in) and 50mm (2in) brushes for general work and a 12mm (½in) paintbrush for painting narrow glazing bars. Apply the paint with vertical strokes then spread sideways to even out the coverage. Finish with light strokes – called laying off – in the direction of the grain. Blend the edges of the next application while the paint is still wet, or a hard edge will show. Don't go back over a painted surface that has started to dry, or it will leave a blemish in the surface.

It is not necessary to spread thixotropic paint in the same way. Simply lay on the paint in almost parallel strokes leaving the brush strokes to settle out naturally.

THE ORDER OF WORK

Follow the sequences recommended below for painting interior and exterior woodwork successfully:

INSIDE

Start painting windows early in the day, so you can close them at night without the new film sticking. Paint doors, then picture rails; finish with skirting boards so that any specks of dust picked up on the brush won't be transferred to other areas.

OUTSIDE

Choose the order of painting according to the position of the sun. Avoid painting in direct sunlight as this will cause glare with light colours and results in runs or blistering. Never paint on wet or windy days: rain specks will pit the finish and airborne dust will ruin the surface. Paint windows and exterior doors early, so that they are touch-dry by the evening.

● **Removing a blemish**
If you find specks of fluff or a brush bristle embedded in fresh paintwork, don't attempt to remove them once a skin has begun to form on the paint. Let it harden then rub down with wet and dry paper. The same applies if you discover runs.

Painting a panel
When painting up to the edge of a panel, brush from the centre out: if you flex the bristles against the edge, the paint will run.

Similarly, moulding flexes the bristles unevenly and too much paint flows: spread it well, taking care at corners of moulded panels.

Making a straight edge
To finish an area with a straight edge, use one of the smaller brushes and place it a few millimetres from the edge. As you flex the bristles, they'll spread to the required width, laying on an even coat of paint.

● Black dot denotes compatibility. All surfaces must be clean, sound, dry and free from organic growth.

FINISHES FOR WOODWORK	Oil paint	Gloss emulsion	Wood stain	Protective wood stain	Coloured preserver	Varnish	Coloured varnish	Cold cure lacquer	Oil	Wax polish	French polish
SUITABLE FOR											
Softwoods	●	●	●	●	●	●	●	●	●	●	
Hardwoods	●	●	●	●	●	●	●	●	●		●
Oily hardwoods	●	●	●			●	●	●	●		●
Planed wood	●	●	●	●	●	●	●	●	●		●
Sawn wood				●	●						
Interior use	●	●	●	●		●	●	●	●	●	●
Exterior use	●		●	●	●	●	●		●		
DRYING TIME: HOURS											
Touch-dry	4	1	½	4	1-2	4	4	1	1		½
Re-coatable	14	3	6	6-8	2-4	14	14	2	6	1	24
THINNERS: SOLVENTS											
Water		●	●		●						
White spirit	●		●	●	●	●	●		●		
Methylated spirit											●
Special thinner								●			
NUMBER OF COATS											
Interior use	1-2	1-2	2-3	2		2-3	2-3	2-3	3	2	10-15
Exterior use	2-3	1-2		2	2	3-4	3-4		3		
COVERAGE											
Sq metres per litre	12-16	10-15	16-30	10-25	4-12	15-16	15-16	16-17	10-15	VARIABLE	VARIABLE
METHOD OF APPLICATION											
Brush	●	●	●	●	●	●	●	●	●	●	●
Paint pad	●	●	●	●		●	●		●		
Cloth pad (rubber)			●			●	●		●	●	●
Spray gun	●	◎	●		●	●	●	●	●		

PAINTING DOORS

Doors have a variety of faces and conflicting grain patterns that need to be painted separately – yet the end result must look even in colour without ugly brush marks or heavily painted edges. There's a strict system for painting panel, flush or glazed doors.

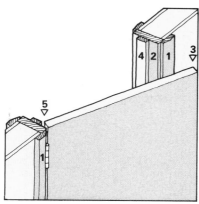

Painting each side a different colour
Make sure all the surfaces that face you when the door is open are painted the same colour.

Opening side: paint the architrave (1) and door frame up to and including the edge of the door stop (2) one colour. Paint the face of the door and its opening edge (3) the same colour.

Opposite side: paint the architrave and frame up to and over the door stop (4) the second colour. Paint the opposite face of the door and its hinged edge (5) with the second colour.

Preparation and technique

Remove the door handles and wedge the door open so that it cannot be closed accidentally, locking you in the room. Keep the handle in the room with you, just in case.

Aim to paint the door and its frame separately so that there is less chance of touching wet paintwork when passing through a freshly painted doorway. Paint the door first and when it is dry finish the framework.

If you want to use a different colour for each side of the door, paint the hinged edge the colour of the closing face (the one that comes to rest against the frame). Paint the outer edge of the door the same colour as the opening face. This means that there won't be any difference in colour when viewed from either side.

Each side of the frame should match the corresponding face of the door. When painting in the room into which the door swings, paint that side of the frame, including the edge of the stop bead against which the door closes, to match the opening face. Paint the rest of the frame the colour of the closing face.

System for a flush door

To paint a flush door, start at the top and work down in sections, blending each one into the other. Lay on the paint, then finish each section with light vertical brush strokes. Finally, paint the edges. Brush from edges, never onto them, or the paint will build up, run and a ridge will form.

System for a panel door

The different parts of a panelled door must be painted in logical order. Finish each part with parallel strokes in the direction of the grain.

Whatever the style of panelled door you are painting, start with the mouldings (1) followed by the panels (2). Paint the centre verticals – muntins (3) next, then the cross rails (4).

Finish the face by painting the outer verticals – stiles (5). Paint the edge of the door (6).

To achieve a superior finish, paint the muntins, rails and stiles together, picking up the wet edges of paint before they begin to dry, show brush strokes and pull out bristles. To get the best results you must work quickly.

SEE ALSO

Details for: ▷	
Glazing bars	50
Primers	23
Preparing wood	33
Preparing paintwork	34
Staining a door	53

Glazed doors
To paint a glazed door, begin with the glazing bars (▷) then follow the sequence as described for panel doors.

Flush door
Apply square sections of paint, working down from the top, and pick up the wet edges for a good blend. Lay off with light vertical brush strokes.

Panel door: basic painting method
Follow the numbered sequence for painting the various parts of the door, each finished with strokes along the grain to prevent streaking.

Panel door: advanced painting method
Working rapidly, follow the alternative sequence to produce a finish free from joins between sections.

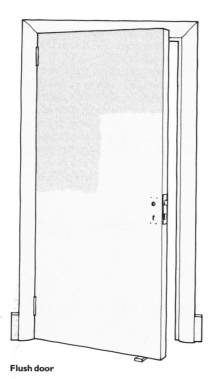

Flush door

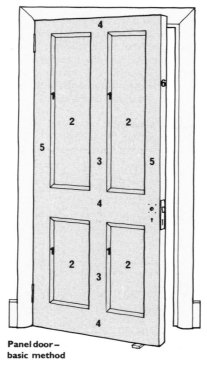

Panel door – basic method

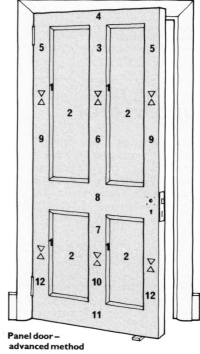

Panel door – advanced method

SEE ALSO

◁ Details for:

Primers 23
Preparing wood 33
Preparing paintwork 34

● **Clean windows first**
Clean the glass in your windows before decorating to avoid picking up particles of dust in the paint.

Cutting-in brush
Paint glazing bars with a cutting-in brush, which has its bristles cut at an angle to enable you to work right up to the glass with a thin line of paint.

● **Painting French windows**
Although French windows are really glazed doors, treat them like large casement windows.

PROTECTING THE GLASS

When painting the edge of glazing bars, overlap the glass by about 2mm (¹⁄₁₆in) to prevent rain or condensation seeping between the glass and woodwork.

If you find it difficult to achieve a satisfactory straight edge, use a proprietary plastic or metal paint shield held against the edge of the frame to protect the glass.

Alternatively, run masking tape around the edges of the window pane, leaving a slight gap so that the paint will seal the join between glass and frame. When the paint is touch-dry, carefully peel off the tape. Don't wait until the paint is completely dry or the film may peel off with the tape.

Scrape off any paint accidentally dripped onto the glass using a razor blade, once it has set. Plastic handles to hold blades are sold by many DIY stores for this purpose.

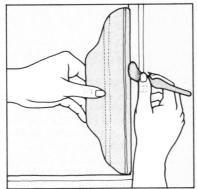

Using a paint shield
A plastic or metal paint shield enables you to paint a straight edge up to glass.

KEEPING THE WINDOW OPEN

With the catch and stay removed there's nothing to stop the frame closing. Make a stay with a length of stiff wire, hook the other end and slot it into one of the screw holes in the frame.

Temporary stay
Wind wire around a nail driven in the underside of the frame and use as a stay.

PAINTING WINDOW FRAMES

Window frames need to be painted in strict order, like doors, so that the various components will be evenly treated and so that you can close them at night. You *also need to take care not to splash panes with paint or apply a crooked line around the glazing bars – the mark of poor workmanship.*

Painting a casement window

A casement window hinges like a door, so if you plan to paint each side a different colour, follow a similar procedure to that described for painting doors and frames.

Remove the stay and catch before you paint the window. So that you can still operate the window during decorating without touching wet paint, drive a nail into the underside of the bottom rail as a makeshift handle.

Painting sequence
First paint the glazing bars (1), cutting into the glass on both sides. Carry on with the top and bottom horizontal rails (2) followed by the vertical stiles (3). Finish the casement by painting the edges (4) then paint the frame (5).

Painting sequence for casement window ▷

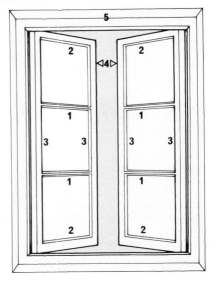

Painting a sash window

Sash windows are the most difficult type to paint, as the two panes slide vertically, overlapping each other.

The following sequence describes the painting of a sash window from the inside. To paint the outside face, use a similar procedure but start with the lower sash. When using different colours for each side, the demarcation lines are fairly obvious. When the window is closed, all the visible surfaces from one side should be the same.

Painting sequence
Raise the bottom sash and pull down the top one. Paint the bottom meeting rail of the top sash (1) and the accessible parts of the vertical members (2). Reverse the position of the sashes, leaving a gap top and bottom and complete the painting of the top sash (3). Paint the bottom sash (4) then the frame (5) except for the runners in which the sashes slide.

Leave the paint to dry then paint the inner runners (6) plus a short section of the outer runners (7). When painting the runners, pull the cords aside to avoid splashing paint on them, as this will make them brittle, shortening their working life. Make sure the window slides before the paint dries.

Raise bottom sash and pull down top **Reverse the position of the sashes** **Lower both sashes for access to runners**

PAINTING FIXED JOINERY

Staircase
Paint banisters first, making sure that you do not precipitate runs by stroking the brush against the edges or mouldings. Start at the top of the stairs, painting the treads, risers and strings (▷) together to keep the edges of the paintwork fresh.

If there is any chance that the paint will not dry before the staircase is used again, paint all risers but alternate treads only. The next day, paint the remainder.

Skirting boards
The only problem with painting a skirting board is to protect the floor from paint and at the same time avoid picking up dust on the wet paintbrush.

Slide strips of thin card under the skirting as a paint shield (don't use newspaper; it will tear and remain stuck to the skirting).

PAINTING EXTERIOR WEATHERBOARDING

Start at the top of the wall and apply paint to one or two boards at a time. Paint the under-edge first, then the face of the boards; finish parallel with the edge. Make sure you coat exposed end grain well, as it is more absorbent and requires extra protection.

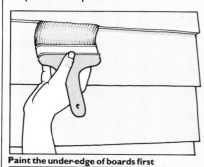
Paint the under-edge of boards first

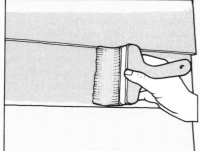
Paint the face of boards next

GRAINING TIMBER

Graining is a technique for simulating natural wood with paint. It was used extensively on cheap softwood joinery to imitate expensive hardwoods. Doors and panels can look attractive treated in this way. The basic method is simple to describe but practice on a flat board is essential before you can achieve convincing results. A skilled grainer can simulate actual species of timber, but just try to suggest ordinary wood grain rather than attempt to produce a perfect copy.

Equipment and preparation for graining

The simplest graining effects can be achieved by removing dark paint to reveal a paler basecoat below. The traditional way to carry out this effect is to use a special hog's- or squirrel's-hair brush called a mottler or grainer. To compromise, try any soft-bristled paintbrush or even a dusting brush. You can also buy steel, rubber or leather combs from decorator's suppliers to achieve similar effects.

Applying a basecoat (ground)
Prepare the basecoat as normal paintwork, finishing with a satin oil paint. It should represent the lightest colour of the timber you want to reproduce and is normally beige or olive green. The basecoat will look more convincing if it is slightly dull rather than being too bright.

Choosing the graining colour
Translucent, flat-drying paints are produced especially for graining in a range of appropriate colours. These paints must be thinned with a mixture comprising 2 parts white spirit: 1 part raw linseed oil to make a graining glaze. The quantity of thinners controls the colour of the graining, so add it to the paint sparingly until you achieve the required result. Try the method on a practice panel first.

Producing the effect

Paint an even coat of glaze onto the ground with a 50mm (2 in) paintbrush. After only two or three minutes, lightly drag the tip of the mottler or comb along the line of the rail or panel, leaving faint streaks in the glaze.

When two rails meet at right-angles, mask the joint with a piece of card to prevent the simulated grain being disturbed on one rail while you paint a rail next to it.

The grain does not have to be exactly parallel with the rail. You can vary the pattern by allowing the comb or mottler to streak out the glaze at a slight angle and over the edge of some of the rails.

Leave the graining to dry overnight then apply one or two coats of clear varnish to protect and seal the effects.

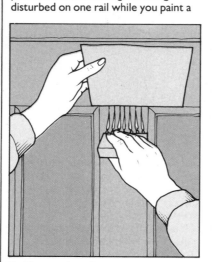
Masking meeting rails
Hold a piece of card over the joint between two meeting rails – on a panel door, for instance, where muntins meet cross rails – to prevent spoiling the graining effect on one while you treat the other.

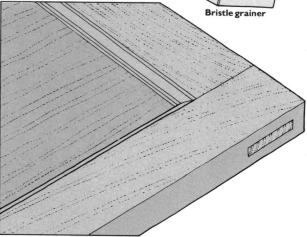
Applying graining patterns
Produce graining patterns that are as authentic as possible. Don't just run the streaks in one direction, or parallel to the timber: simulate actual wood grain by running the pattern at an angle.

SEE ALSO

Details for: ▷	
Staircases	99-101
Preparing wood	33
Painting wood	48
Varnishing wood	54

Steel graining comb

Rubber or leather comb

Bristle grainer

STAINING WOODWORK

SEE ALSO

◁ Details for:
Making a rubber	55
Preparing wood	33
Filling grain	33
Stripping wood	34-35
Stains	46-47

Testing the stain
Make a test strip (far right) to assess the depth of colour of various stains before embarking on the final job. Apply a band of varnish along the bottom half of the strip to see how the colours are affected.

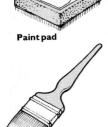

Paint pad

Paintbrush

Rubber

Unless the wood is perfectly clean and free from grease, the stain will be rejected, producing an uneven, patchy appearance. Strip any previous finish and sand the wood with progressively finer abrasive papers, always in the direction of the grain. Scratches made across the grain will tend to be emphasized by the stain.

Making a test strip

The final colour is affected by the nature of the timber, the number of coats and the overlying clear finish. You can also mix compatible stains to alter the colour or dilute them with the appropriate thinner.

Make a test strip so that you will have an accurate guide from which you can choose the depth of stain to suit your purpose. Use a piece of timber from the same batch you are staining, or one that resembles it closely.

Paint the whole strip with one coat of stain. Allow the stain to be absorbed then apply a second coat, leaving a strip of the first application showing. It is rarely necessary to apply more than two coats of stain, but for the experiment add a third and even a fourth coat, always leaving a strip of the previous application for comparison.

When the stain has dried completely, paint a band of clear varnish along the strip: some polyurethane varnishes react unfavourably with oil-based stains, so it is advisable to use products made by the same manufacturer.

USING A RUBBER

Wear gloves to protect your skin and pour some stain into a shallow dish. Saturate the rubber with stain then squeeze some out so that it is not dripping but still wet enough to apply a liberal coat of stain to the surface.

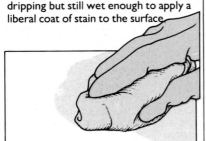

Apply stain by rubber

If you wet a piece of timber, water is absorbed by the wood, raising a mass of tiny fibres across the surface. A water-based stain will produce the same result and the final finish will be ruined. Solve the problem by sanding the wood until it is perfectly smooth, then dampen the whole surface with a wet rag. Leave it to dry out then sand the raised grain with very fine abrasive paper before you apply the stain. If you are using an

oil-based stain, this preliminary process is unnecessary.

If you want to fill the grain, first apply a seal coat of clear finish over the stain. Choose a grain filler that matches the stain closely, adjusting the colour by adding a little stain to it, but make sure that the stain and filler are compatible. An oil-based stain will not mix with a water-based filler and vice versa, so check before you buy either.

How to apply wood stain

Use a 100mm (4in) paintbrush to apply stains over a wide, flat surface. Do not brush out a stain like paint, but apply it liberally and evenly, always in the direction of the grain.

It is essential to blend wet edges of stain, so work fairly quickly and don't take a break until you have completed the job. If you have brushed a water-based stain onto the wood it is sometimes advantageous to wipe over the wet surface with a soft cloth and remove excess stain.

A paint pad is one of the best applicators for achieving an even coverage of wood stain over a flat surface. However, you may find that you will still need a paintbrush to get the stain into awkward corners and for tackling mouldings.

Because stains are so fluid, it's often easier to apply them with a wad of soft, lint-free rag called a rubber (◁). You'll be able to control runs on a vertical panel and it's the best way to stain turned wood and rails.

STAINING PANELS, FLOORS AND DOORS

Staining a flat panel

Whenever possible, set up a panel horizontally for staining, either on trestles or raised on softwood blocks. Shake the container before use and pour the stain into a flat dish so that you can load your applicator properly.

Apply the stain, working swiftly and evenly along the grain. Stain the edges at the same time as the top surface. The first application may have a slightly patchy appearance as it dries because some parts of the wood will absorb more stain than others. The second coat normally evens out the colour without difficulty. If powdery deposits are left on the surface of the dry stain, wipe them off with a coarse, dry cloth, before applying the second coat in the same way as the first.

Leave the stain to dry overnight then proceed with the clear finish of your choice to seal the colourant.

Staining floors

Because a wooden floor is such a large area it is more difficult to blend the wet edges of the stain. Work along two or three boards at a time, using a paintbrush, so that you can finish at the edge of a board each time.

Wood block floors are even trickier, so try to complete one panel at a time, and use a soft cloth to blend in any overlapping areas.

Staining a door

Stain a new or stripped door before it is hung so that it can be layed horizontally. A flush door is stained just like any other panel but use a rubber to carefully colour the edges so that stain does not run under to spoil the other side.

When staining a panelled door, it is essential to follow a sequence which will allow you to pick up the edges of stain before they dry. Use a combination of brush and rubber to apply the stain.

Follow the numbered sequence below and note that, unlike painting a panel door, the mouldings are stained last – this is to prevent any overlapping showing on the finished door. Stain the mouldings carefully with a narrow brush and blend in the colour with a rubber.

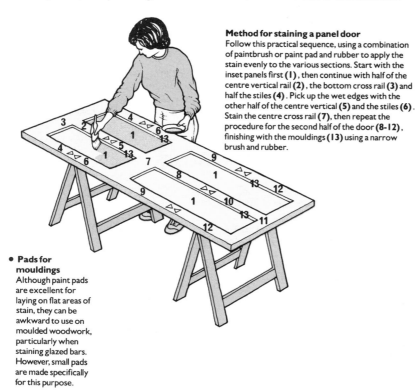

Method for staining a panel door
Follow this practical sequence, using a combination of paintbrush or paint pad and rubber to apply the stain evenly to the various sections. Start with the inset panels first (**1**), then continue with half of the centre vertical rail (**2**), the bottom cross rail (**3**) and half the stiles (**4**). Pick up the wet edges with the other half of the centre vertical (**5**) and the stiles (**6**). Stain the centre cross rail (**7**), then repeat the procedure for the second half of the door (**8-12**), finishing with the mouldings (**13**) using a narrow brush and rubber.

● **Pads for mouldings**
Although paint pads are excellent for laying on flat areas of stain, they can be awkward to use on moulded woodwork, particularly when staining glazed bars. However, small pads are made specifically for this purpose.

USING WOOD STAINS OUTSIDE

Standard wood stains are not suitable for exterior use. They have no protective properties of their own and they have a tendency to fade in direct sunlight. For planed joinery and weatherboarding, use a microporous protective wood stain (▷). For sawn timber use a coloured wood preserver. Both materials are much thinner than paint, so take care to avoid splashing.

Protective wood stain
Make sure the surface is clean, dry and sanded. All previous paint or varnish must be stripped. For blemished timber, use an opaque wood stain so that you can fill cracks and holes. For extra protection treat the timber with a clear wood preserver before staining.

Apply two coats with a paintbrush, making sure that the coating is even, and avoid any overlaps.

Stain wall cladding one board at a time (treating the under-edge first).

Wood preserver
Before you apply wood preserver, remove surface dirt with a stiff-bristled brush. Paint or varnish must be stripped completely, but previously preserved or creosoted timber can be treated, so long as it has weathered.

For additional protection against insect and fungal attack, treat the timber first with a clear wood preserver, either by immersion or by full brush coats (▷).

Paint a full coat of coloured preserver onto the wood followed by a second coat as soon as the first has soaked in. Brush out sufficiently to achieve an even colour and avoid overlaps by following immediately with the edges of boards, rails and posts.

Replacing putty
Stain will not colour putty. In any case, microporous stains allow the wood to breathe, so there's likely to be some movement, which puts greater strain on the glass. For both reasons, remove the old putty (▷) and stain the frame. Seal the rebate with mastic (**1**).

Set lengths of stained wooden beading into the mastic and secure them with panel pins (**2**). You'll find it easiest to fix the beading if you tap in the pins beforehand, so they just protrude through the other side. Remove excess mastic squeezed from beneath the beading with a putty knife (**3**).

SEE ALSO

Details for: ▷	
Protective stains	47
Wood preservers	47
Removing putty	94
Preparing wood	33
Stripping wood	34-35
Painting a door	49

I Apply mastic

2 Fix beading

3 Trim mastic

VARNISHING WOODWORK

Varnish serves two main purposes: to protect the wood from knocks, stains and other marks, and to give it a sheen that accentuates the beautiful grain pattern. In some cases, it can even be used to change the colour of the wood to that of another species – or to give it a fresh, new look with a choice of bright primary colours.

SEE ALSO

◁ Details for:

Linseed oil	47
Using a rubber	52
Test strip	52
Preparing wood	33
Stripping wood	34-35
Varnishes	47
Wax polish	47

The effect of varnish
The example below demonstrates how different varnishes affect the same species of wood. From top to bottom: untreated birch plywood; matt clear varnish; gloss clear varnish; wood shade coloured varnish; pure coloured varnish.

How to apply varnish

Use paintbrushes to apply varnish in the same way as paint. You will need a range of sizes for general work: 12mm (½in), 25mm (1in) and 50mm (2in) are useful widths. For varnishing floors use a 100mm (4in) brush for quick coverage. With any brush, make sure it's spotlessly clean; any previous traces of paint may mar the finish.

Load a brush with varnish by dipping the first third of the bristles into the liquid, then touch off the excess on the side of the container. Don't scrape the brush across the rim of the container as it causes bubbles in the varnish, which can spoil the finish if transferred to the woodwork.

A soft cloth pad, or rubber (◁) can be used to apply the first thinned coat of varnish into the grain. It is not essential to use a rubber – even for the sealing coat – but it is a convenient method, especially for coating shaped or turned pieces of wood.

Applying the varnish

Thin the first coat of varnish with 10 per cent white spirit and rub it well into the wood with a cloth pad in the direction of the grain. Brush on the sealer coat where the rubber is difficult to use.

Apply the second coat of varnish not less than six hours later. If more than 24 hours have elapsed, key the surface of gloss varnish lightly with fine abrasive paper. Wipe it over with a cloth dampened with white spirit to remove dust and grease, then brush on a full coat of varnish as for paint.

Apply a third coat if the surface is likely to take hard wear.

Using coloured varnish

A wood stain can only be used on bare timber, but you can use a coloured varnish to darken or alter the colour of woodwork that has been varnished previously without having to strip the finish. Clean the surface with wire wool and white spirit mixed with a little linseed oil (◁). Dry the surface with a clean cloth then apply the varnish.

Apply tinted varnish in the same way as the clear type. It might be worth making a test strip to see how many coats you will need to achieve the depth of colour you want (◁).

Varnishing floors

Varnishing a floor is no different to finishing any other woodwork but the greater area can produce an unpleasant concentration of fumes in a confined space. Open all windows for ventilation and wear a gauze facemask.

Start in the corner furthest from the door and work back towards it. Brush the varnish out well to make sure it does not collect in pools.

DEALING WITH DUST PARTICLES

Minor imperfections and particles of dust stuck to the varnished surface can be rubbed down with fine abrasive paper between coats. If your top coat is to be a high-gloss finish, take even more care to ensure that your brush is perfectly clean.

If you are not satisfied with your final finish, dip very fine wire wool in wax polish and rub the varnish with parallel strokes in the direction of the grain. Buff the surface with a soft duster. This will remove the high gloss but it leaves a pleasant sheen on the surface with no obvious imperfections.

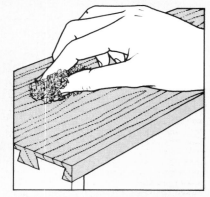

Produce a soft sheen with wire wool and wax

FRENCH POLISHING

The art of French polishing has always been considered the province of the expert, which a wise amateur would leave well alone. It is true that an expert will make a better job of the polishing and can work much faster than an amateur, but there's no reason why anyone cannot produce a satisfactory finish with a little practice.

Basic French polishing

Try out French polishing using one of the prepared proprietary kits available from DIY stores. A kit typically contains a bottle of thin shellac for building up the body of polish and a separate clear burnishing liquid.

Brush coating

Pour some shellac into a shallow dish so that you can use a brush to paint the polish onto the wood. Keep the coating even and work quickly to pick up the moist edges. Don't go over an area more than once.

Half an hour later, brush coat the work again then leave it for another hour. Next, lightly sand the polish with a silicon carbide paper (grey with a dry lubricant embedded in its surface) to remove any blemishes.

Building up the polish

With the workpiece set up at a comfortable working height and in good light, distribute the polish along the surface of the wood with continuous, circular strokes of the rubber.

There's no need to press too hard at first as a fully charged rubber flows easily. As the rubber gradually dries out, increase the pressure.

Never bring the pad to rest on the surface of the polish. As you reach the edge of the workpiece, sweep the rubber off the surface and sweep it back on again for the next pass. If you pull the

rubber off the workpiece it will leave a blemish in the polish.

Cover the surface, perhaps ten or twelve times. As you feel the rubber drying out, open it up and pour a little more shellac onto the back of the cotton wool filling. Occasionally change the rag for a spare one, leaving the used one to soak in a jar of methylated spirit to wash out the polish ready for the next exchange.

Seal the rubber in an empty glass jar and leave the surface to harden for about one hour, then if necessary, lightly flatten the polish with silicon carbide paper using fingertip pressure.

Build up another layer of polish with the rubber. Vary the size and shape of your strokes so that every part of the surface is covered (see below). In between each coat, make straight parallel strokes along the grain.

Repeat the process for a third time, more if you want a deeper colour. Make your final coat with slightly less polish; allow it to harden overnight.

Burnishing the polished surface

Take a handful of clean cotton wool and dampen the sole with burnishing liquid. Use it to burnish a small section at a time, rubbing forcefully along the grain. As the sole of the pad becomes dirty, pull it off to reveal a clean surface. Buff each section with a soft duster before burnishing the next.

Woodwork must be prepared immaculately before polishing, as every blemish will be mirrored in the finish. The grain should be filled, either with a proprietary filler (▷) or by layers of polish, which are rubbed down and repeated until the pores of the wood are filled flush with polish.

Work in a warm, dust-free room:

dust's effect is obvious, but a low temperature will make the polish go cloudy (bloom).

Work in a good light so that you can glance across the surface to gauge the quality of the finish you are applying.

TRADITIONAL FRENCH POLISHING

With traditional polishing, the shellac is thicker therefore do not soak the rag with meths. Charge the rubber and dab linseed oil on the sole.

Apply all the shellac with a rubber, using a combination of strokes (see below). Recharge the rubber and add a touch of oil to the sole when it starts to drag or catch. Leave to dry for twenty minutes. Repeat four or five times.

Leave to harden overnight then build up more layers – ten may be enough but continue until you're happy with the depth of colour. To remove surface marks, rub down the hard polish with silicon carbide paper. The top layer may be streaked due to the linseed oil: add meths to the rubber's cotton wool. Burnish with straight strokes parallel with the grain, sweeping the rubber on and off at each end. As the rubber drags, recharge. Leave for a few minutes to see if the streaking disappears. If not, repeat with more meths. Polish with a duster and leave to harden.

SEE ALSO

Details for: ▷	
Grain filler	33
Preparing wood	33
Stripping wood	34-35
French polish	47

Apply French polish with a rubber

Using the rubber
Apply the polish with a combination of circular and figure-of-eight strokes so that every part of the surface is covered. When you finish each coat, run the rubber in long straight strokes, parallel to the wood grain. Keep the pad moving constantly and smoothly: if you lift it from the surface a scar will form.

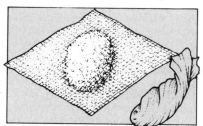

Making a rubber for basic polishing
Saturate a 300mm (1ft) square of white cotton rag with meths, wring out until damp, dip a handful of cotton wool into the shellac and squeeze out excess. Wrap in rag, twist excess into a handgrip; smooth sole of rubbber.

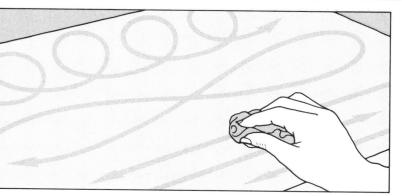

COLD CURE LACQUER

Due to its chemical composition, careful preparation is essential or plastic coating will take days to cure instead of only two hours. It must be applied to a clean, grease-free surface, which has been sanded smooth. Strip the old finish but do not use a caustic stripper, as this will react against the coating.

Clean old wax polish from the wood. You must remove every trace, even from the pores of the timber. Wash it with white spirit, using a ball of fine wire wool in the direction of the grain. When the wood is dry, scrub it with water and detergent, then rinse the surface with clean water with a little white vinegar added.

If you use wood stain, make sure it is made by the manufacturer of the lacquer, otherwise it might change colour. Use the same manufacturer's stopping to fill cracks and holes and never use plaster or plastic fillers.

SEE ALSO

◁ Details for:	
Using a rubber	52
Preparing wood	33
Stripping wood	34-35
Cold cure lacquer	47
Oil	47
Wax polish	47

Mixing cold cure lacquer

In most cases, it's best to use a paintbrush to apply plastic coating, although you can use a plastic foam roller instead, especially for large areas of woodwork.

When you are ready to apply the lacquer, mix the coating and hardener in a glass, polythene or enamel container.

Use the proportions recommended by the manufacturer. Mix just enough for your immediate needs, as it will set in two to three days in an open dish. Don't be tempted to economize by pouring mixed lacquer back into its original container: the hardener will ruin any remaining substance.

Applying the lacquer

Plastic coating must be applied in a warm atmosphere. Use a well-loaded applicator and spread the lacquer onto the wood. There is no need to over-brush the liquid as it will flow unaided and even a thick coat will cure thoroughly and smoothly. Plastic coating dries quickly and will begin to show brush marks if disturbed after 10 to 15 minutes, so you should work swiftly to pick up the wet edges.

After two hours, apply the second coat. If necessary, rub down the hardened lacquer with fine abrasive paper to remove blemishes, then add a third coat. You will achieve better adhesion between the layers if you can apply all the coats in one day, so long as each has time to dry.

Burnishing lacquer
If you want a mirror finish, wait for 24 hours then use a proprietary burnishing cream. Rub down the lacquer with very fine abrasive paper or wire wool, then rub the cream onto the surface with a soft cloth. Burnish it vigorously with a clean soft duster to achieve the required depth of sheen.

Matting lacquer
To produce a subtle satin coat, rub the hardened lacquer along the grain with fine wire wool dipped in wax polish. The grade of the wire wool will effect the degree of matting. Use very fine 000 grade for a satin finish and a coarse 0 grade for a fully-matted surface. Polish with a clean, soft duster.

● **Spontaneous combustion**
It is essential to dispose of oily rags immediately you have finished with them as they have been known to burst into flames.

SAFETY WHEN USING LACQUER

Although cold cure lacquer is safe to use, you should take care when applying it to a large surface such as a floor, due to the concentration of fumes.

Open all windows and doors if possible for ventilation – but remember the necessity for a warm atmosphere, too – and take the extra precaution of wearing a simple gauze facemask to prevent you breathing in the fumes. You can buy cheap masks and spare lint filters, which you should renew frequently, from chemists and DIY stores.

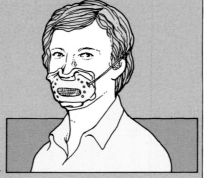

OILING AND WAXING WOODWORK

Applying the oil
Clean and prepare the wood for oiling. Remove previous finishes carefully so that oil can penetrate the grain.

The most efficient way to apply a finishing oil is to rub it into the wood with a soft, lint-free rag in the form of a rubber (◁). Don't store oily rags: keep them in a sealed tin while the job is in progress then unfold them and leave them outside to dry before throwing them away.

A brush is a convenient way to spread oil liberally over large surfaces and into carvings or deep mouldings.

Rub or brush a generous coating of oil into the wood grain. Leave it to soak in for a few minutes, then rub off excess oil with a clean cloth. After about six hours, coat the wood with oil once more. The next day, apply a third and final coat; raise a faint sheen by burnishing with a soft duster.

Wax polishing timber
If you want to wax-polish new timber, seal the wood first with one coat of clear varnish (or French polish on fine furniture). This will stop the wax being absorbed too deeply into the wood and provides a slightly more durable finish. Before waxing an old clear finish, clean it first to remove deposits of dirt and possibly an old wax dressing.

To remove dirty wax, mix up white spirit with 25 per cent linseed oil. Use the liquid to clean the surface quite hard with a coarse cloth. If there is no obvious improvement, try dipping very fine wire wool into the cleaner and rub in the direction of the grain. Don't press too hard as you want to remove wax and dirt only without damaging the finish below. Wash the cleaned surface with a cloth dipped in white spirit and leave to dry before refinishing.

You can use a soft cloth to apply wax polish but use a paintbrush to spread liquid wax over a wide area. Pour liquid wax polish onto a cloth pad and rub it into the sealed wood with a circular motion followed by strokes parallel with the grain. Make this first coat a generous one.

Buff up the wax after one hour then apply a second, thinner coat in the direction of the grain only. Burnish this coat lightly and leave it for several hours to harden. Bring the surface to a high gloss by burnishing vigorously with a soft duster.

FINISHING METALWORK

Ferrous metals that are rusty will shed any paint film rapidly, so the most important aspect of finishing metalwork is thorough preparation and priming to prevent this corrosion from returning; then applying the finish is virtually the same as painting woodwork.

When you are choosing a finish for metalwork in and around the house (see chart below and table overleaf for suitable types) make sure it fulfils your requirements. Many of the finishes listed are easy to apply to metal, but the ability of some to withstand heavy wear is likely to be poor (▷)

Methods of application

Most of the finishes suggested for use on metalwork can be applied with a paintbrush. The exception is black lead (▷). In the main, use the standard techniques for painting woodwork (▷), but bitumen-based paints should be laid on only and not brushed out like conventional coatings.

Remove metal door and window fittings for painting, suspending them on wire hooks to dry. Make sure that sharp or hard edges are coated properly, as the finish can wear thin quickly.

Some paints can be sprayed but there are few situations where it is advantageous, except perhaps for intricately moulded ironwork such as garden furniture, which you can paint outside – otherwise ventilation is a necessity indoors.

A roller is suitable on large flat surfaces and pipework requires its own special V-section roller, which is designed to coat curved surfaces.

SEE ALSO

Details for: ▷	
Preparing metal	36-37
Painting wood	48
Metal finishes	58
Primers	23

● Black dot denotes compatibility. Thorough preparation is essential before applying any finish to metals (▷).

FINISHES FOR METALWORK

	Oil paint	Emulsion paint	Metallic paint	Bituminous based paint	Security paint	Radiator enamel	Black lead	Varnish	Bath paint	Non-slip paint
DRYING TIME: HOURS										
Touch-dry										
Re-coatable										
THINNERS: SOLVENTS										
Water		●		●						
White spirit	●		●	●	●		●	●	●	●
Special						●				
Cellulose thinners							●			
NUMBER OF COATS										
Normal conditions						VARIABLE				
COVERAGE										
Sq metres per litre						VARIABLE				
METHOD OF APPLICATION										
Brush	●	●	●	●	●	●	●	●	●	●
Roller	●	●		●						
Spray gun	●	●		●				●		
Cloth pad (Rubber)							●			

1 Corner roller
You cannot paint into a corner with a standard roller, so unless there are to be different adjacent colours, paint the corner first with a shaped corner roller.
2 Pipe roller
A pipe roller has two narrow sleeves, mounted side by side, which locate over the cylindrical pipework to paint it.
3 Radiator roller
This is a thin roller on a long wire handle for painting behind radiators and pipes.

PAINTING RADIATORS AND PIPES

Leave radiators and hot water pipes to cool before you paint them. The only problem with decorating a radiator is how to paint the back: the best solution is to remove it completely or, if possible, swing it away from the wall, paint the back, reposition the radiator then paint the front.

If this is inconvenient, use a special radiator brush with a long metal handle (see right). Use the same tool to paint in between the leaves of a double radiator. It is difficult to achieve a perfect finish even with the brush, so aim at covering areas you are likely to see when the radiator is fixed in position rather than a complete application.

Don't paint over radiator valves or fittings or you will not be able to operate them afterwards.

Paint pipework lengthwise rather than across, or runs are likely to form. The first coat on metal piping will be streaky, so be prepared to apply two or three coats. Unless you are using radiator enamel, allow the paint to harden thoroughly before turning on the heat, or it may blister.

Using a radiator brush
A long, slim-handled radiator brush enables you to paint the back of the radiator without having to remove it from the wall. You can also use this brush to paint between the leaves of a double radiator.

METALWORK

Gutters and downpipes

It is best to coat the inside of gutters with a bituminous paint for thorough protection against moisture, but you can finish the outer surfaces with oil paint or security paint.

To protect the wall behind a downpipe, slip a scrap of card between while painting the back of the pipe (1).

Metal casement windows

Paint metal casement windows using the sequence described for wooden casements (◁), which allows you to close the frame at night without spoiling a freshly-painted surface.

Varnishing metalwork

Polish the metal to a high gloss then use a nail brush to scrub it with warm water containing some liquid detergent. Rinse the metal in clean water then dry it thoroughly with an absorbent cloth.

Use a large, soft artist's brush to paint on acrylic lacquer (2), working swiftly from the top. Let the lacquer flow naturally, working all round the object to keep the wet edge moving.

If you do leave a brush stroke in partially-set varnish, do not try to overpaint it but finish the job then warm the metal (by standing it on a radiator if possible). As soon as the blemish disappears, remove the object from the heat and allow it to cool gradually in a dust-free atmosphere.

Blacking cast iron

Black lead produces an attractive finish for cast iron. It is not a permanent or durable finish and will have to be renewed periodically. It may transfer if rubbed hard.

The material is supplied in a toothpaste-like tube. Squeeze some of the black cream onto a soft cloth and spread it onto the metal. Use an old toothbrush (3) to scrub it into decorative ironwork for best coverage.

When you have covered the surface, buff the black lead to a satin sheen with a clean, dry cloth. Build up a patina with several applications of black lead for a moisture-proof finish.

SEE ALSO

◁ Details for:	
Painting casements	50
Primers	23
Preparing metal	36-37
Painting radiators	57

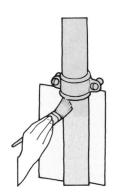

1 Protect wall
Use card behind a downpipe when painting behind it.

2 Apply lacquer
Use a large, soft artist's paintbrush.

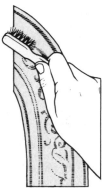

3 Apply black lead
Scrub cream into intricate surfaces using an old toothbrush.

SUITABLE FINISHES FOR METALWORK

OIL PAINT

Standard oil paints are perfectly suitable for metal. Having primed the surface, interior metalwork will need at least one undercoat plus a top coat. Add an extra undercoat for greater protection of exterior metalwork.

EMULSION PAINT

Strictly, emulsion paint is not suitable for finishing metal. Being water-based, it may promote corrosion on ferrous metals if applied directly; it can be used to paint radiators to match the wall colour if the metal has been factory-painted.

METALLIC PAINT

For a metallic-like finish, choose a paint containing aluminium, copper, gold or bronze powders: these paints are water-resistant and are able to withstand very high temperatures – up to about 100°C (212° F).

BITUMINOUS PAINT

Bitumen-based paints give economical protection for exterior storage tanks and piping. Standard bituminous paint is black but there is also a limited range of colours, plus 'modified' bituminous paint, which contains aluminium.

Before coating the inside of drinking water tanks, make sure the paint is non-contaminating. Don't apply over other types of paint.

SECURITY PAINT

Non-setting security paint, primarily for rainwater and waste downpipes, remains slippery to prevent intruders from scaling the wall via the pipe. Restrict it to pipework over about 1.8m (6ft) above the ground, out of reach.

RADIATOR ENAMEL

A heat-stoving acrylic paint which is applied in two thin coats. It can be used over emulsion or oil paints so long as these have not been recently applied (don't rub them down first).

Apply a compatible metal primer over new paint or factory priming to prevent strong solvents in the enamel reacting with the previous coating. A special thinner is required for brush cleaning. A choice of satin and gloss finishes is available.

Finish the radiator in position then turn the heating on (boiler set to maximum) for a minimum of two hours to bake the enamel onto the metal. Apply a second coat six to eight hours later.

Also use to repaint central heating boiler cabinets, refrigerators, cookers and washing machines.

BLACK LEAD

A cream used to colour cast ironwork, it is a mixture of graphite and waxes. After several coats it is moisture-proof, but it is not suitable for exterior use.

VARNISHES

Virtually any clear lacquer can be used on polished metalwork without spoiling its appearance, but many polyurethanes yellow with age. An acrylic lacquer is clear and will protect chrome-plating, brass and copper – even outside.

NON-SLIP PAINT

Designed to provide good foot-holding on a wide range of surfaces, including metal, non-slip paint is ideal for painting metal spiral staircase treads and exterior fire escapes. The surface must be primed before application.

APPLYING TEXTURED COATING

You can apply the coating with either a roller or a broad wall brush: finer textures are possible using the latter. Buy a special roller if recommended by the coating manufacturer.

With a well-loaded roller, apply a generous coat in a 600mm (2ft) wide band across the ceiling or down a wall. Do not press too hard and vary the angle of the stroke.

If you decide to brush on the coating, do not spread it out like paint. Lay it on with one stroke and spread it back again with one or two strokes only.

Clean up any splashes then apply a second band and texture it, blending both bands together. Continue in this way until the wall or ceiling is complete. Keep the room ventilated until the coating has hardened.

Painting around fittings
Use a small paintbrush to fill in around electrical fittings and along edges, trying to copy the texture used on the surrounding wall or ceiling. Some people prefer to form a distinct margin around fittings by drawing a small paintbrush along the perimeter to give a smooth finish.

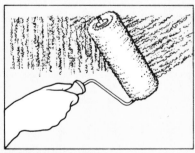

Creating a texture
You can experiment with a variety of tools to make any number of textures. You can use a standard roller, or use ones made with special surfaces to produce diagonal or diamond patterns, or you can apply a swirling, ripple or stipple finish with improvized equipment, as shown right.

TEXTURED COATINGS

Textured coatings can be obtained as a dry powder for mixing with warm water, or in a ready-mixed form for direct application from the tub. Most manufacturers supply a fine or a thick mix; if you want a heavy texture, choose the thicker mix. Where you're likely to rub against the wall – in a narrow hall, small bathroom or children's room, a fine texture is preferable: the coating dries very hard and could graze your skin.

Textured coatings are suitable for exterior walls as well as indoors. They are also available in a range of colours – you can cover the texture with emulsion paint if a standard colour does not fit your decorative scheme.

Preparing for textured coatings

New surfaces will need virtually no preparation, but joints between plasterboard must be reinforced with tape (▷). Strip any wallcoverings and key gloss paint with glasspaper. Old walls and ceilings must be clean, dry, sound and free from organic growth. Treat friable surfaces with stabilizing solution (▷).

Although large cracks and holes must be filled, a textured coating will conceal minor defects in walls and ceilings by filling small cracks and bridging shallow bumps and hollows.

Masking joinery and fittings
Use 50mm (2in) wide masking tape to cover door and window frames, electrical socket outlets, switches and ceiling roses, plumbing pipework, picture rails and skirting boards. Lay dust sheets over the floor.

1 Diamond pattern

3 Swirl design

5 Tree bark simulation

2 Stipple effect

4 Combed arcs

6 Stucco finish

SEE ALSO

Details for: ▷	
Friable surfaces	28
Plasterboard tapes	50
Using texture	12
Preparing plaster	30-31
Stripping wallpaper	32

1 Geometric patterns
Use a roller with diamond or diagonal grooves: load the roller and draw lightly across the textured surface.

2 Stippled finish
Pat the coating with a damp sponge to create a pitted profile. Rinse out frequently. Alter your wrist angle and overlap sections.

3 Random swirls
Twist a damp sponge on the textured surface, then pull away to make a swirling design. Overlap swirls for a layered effect.

4 Combed arcs
A toothed spatula sold with the finish is used to create combed patterns: arcs, criss-cross patterns or wavy scrolls.

5 Imitation tree bark
Produce a bark texture by applying parallel strokes with a roller then lightly drawing the straight edge of a spatula over it.

6 Stucco finish
Apply parallel roller strokes, then run the rounded corner of a spatula over it in short straight strokes.

WALLCOVERINGS

Although wallcoverings are often called 'wallpaper', only a proportion of the wide range available is made solely from wood pulp. There is a huge range of paper-backed fabrics from exotic silks to coarse hessians; other types include natural textures such as cork or woven grass on a paper backing. Plastics have widened the choice of wallcoverings still further: there are paper- or cotton-backed vinyls, and plain or patterned foamed plastics. Before wallpaper became popular, fabric wall hangings were used to decorate interiors and this is still possible today, using unbacked fabrics glued or stretched across walls.

SEE ALSO

◁ Details for:	
Sizing wall	30
Choosing colour/pattern	8-9, 13
Preparing plaster	30-31
Mould growth	32
Stripping wallpaper	32

Top right
1 Expanded polystyrene
2 Lining paper
3 Woodchip

Bottom left
4 Hand-printed
5 Machine-printed

Bottom right
6 Anaglypta
7 Supaglypta
8 Lincrustas
9 Vinaglypta

Ensuring a suitable surface

Although many wallcoverings will cover minor blemishes, walls and ceilings should be clean, sound and smooth. Eradicate damp and organic growth before hanging any wallcovering. Consider whether you should size the walls to reduce paste absorption (◁).

COVERINGS THAT CAMOUFLAGE

Although a poor surface should be repaired, some coverings hide minor blemishes as well as providing a foundation for other finishes.

Expanded polystyrene sheet
Thin polystyrene sheet is used for lining a wall before papering. It reduces condensation but will also bridge hairline cracks and small holes. Polystyrene dents easily, so don't use where it will take a lot of punishment. A patterned ceiling version is made.

Lining paper
A cheap, buff coloured wallpaper for lining uneven or impervious walls prior to hanging a heavy or expensive wallcovering. Can also provide an even surface for emulsion paint.

Woodchip paper
Woodchip or ingrain paper is a relief covering made by sandwiching particles of wood between two layers of paper. It's inexpensive, easy to hang (but a problem to cut), and must be painted.

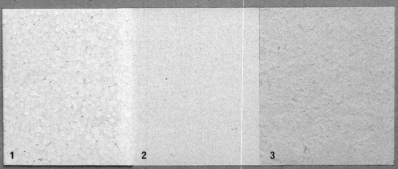

1   2   3

Relief papers ▷
'Whites', or relief papers, with a deeply embossed pattern, are for hiding minor imperfections and for over-painting.

Anaglypta is made by bonding two sheets of paper together, which then pass between embossing rollers. A stronger version, *Supaglypta,* is made using cotton fibres instead of wood pulp, and withstands deeper embossing.

The raised pattern on *Lincrusta* is a solid film of linseed oil and fillers fused onto a backing paper before the pattern is applied by an engraved steel roller. Deep relief wallcoverings are made from vinyl – notably *Vinaglypta* – either as solid plastic, or it is heated in an oven, which 'blows' or expands the vinyl, embossing it. Relief vinyls are intended to be painted over.

◁ Printed wallpapers
One advantage of ordinary wallpaper is the superb range of printed colours and patterns, which is much wider than for any other covering. Most papers – the cheapest – are machine-printed.

Hand-printed papers are more costly. Inks have a tendency to run if you smear paste on the surface, are prone to tearing when wet, and are not really suitable for walls exposed to wear or condensation. Pattern matching can be awkward, because hand-printing isn't as accurate as machine printing.

4

5

6

7

8

9

WALLCOVERINGS

Washable papers

Ordinary printed papers with a thin, impervious glaze of PVA to make a spongeable surface, washables are suitable for bathrooms and kitchens. The surface must not be scrubbed or the plastic coating will be worn away.

Vinyl wallcoverings

A base paper, or sometimes a cotton backing, is coated with a layer of vinyl upon which the design is printed. Heat is used to fuse the colours and vinyl. The result is a durable, washable wallcovering ideally suited to bathrooms and kitchens. Many vinyls are sold ready-pasted for easy application.

Foamed polyethylene coverings

A lightweight wallcovering, called *Novamura,* made solely of foamed plastic with no backing paper. It is printed with a wide range of patterns, colours and designs. You paste the wall instead of the covering. It is best used on walls that are not exposed to wear.

Flock wallcoverings

Flock papers have the major pattern elements picked out with a fine pile produced by gluing synthetic or natural fibres (such as silk or wool) to the backing paper, so that it stands out in relief, with a velvet-like texture.

Standard flocks are difficult to hang as paste will ruin the pile. Vinyl flocks are less delicate, can be hung anywhere, and may even be ready-pasted.

You can sponge flock paper to remove stains, but brush to remove dust from the pile. Vinyl flocks can be washed without risk of damage.

Foil wallcoverings

Paper-backed foils are coated with a metallized plastic film to give a shiny finish. They are expensive but come in a range of beautiful contrasting textures (over-printed designs allow the foil to show through). Foils should not be used on uneven walls, as the shine will highlight imperfections.

Glass fibre wallcovering

Woven glass fibre fabric is a durable fire-resistant wallcovering that will bridge minor irregularities. After 24 hours, the fabric can be painted.

Grass cloth

Natural grasses are woven into a mat, which is glued to a paper backing. These wallcoverings are very attractive but fragile and difficult to hang.

Cork-faced paper

A wallpaper surfaced with thin sheets of coloured or natural cork, which is not as easily spoiled as other special papers.

Paper-backed fabrics

Finely woven cotton, linen or silk on a paper backing must be applied to a flat surface. They are expensive, not easy to hang, and you must avoid smearing the fabric with adhesive. Most fabrics are delicate but some are plastic-coated to make them scuff-resistant.

Unbacked fabrics

Upholstery width fabric — typically hessian — can be wrapped around panels, glued to the wall.

SEE ALSO	
Details for: ▷	
Sizing wall	30
Choosing colour/pattern	8-9, 13
Preparing plaster	30-31
Mould growth	32
Stripping wallpaper	32
Preparing tiles	38

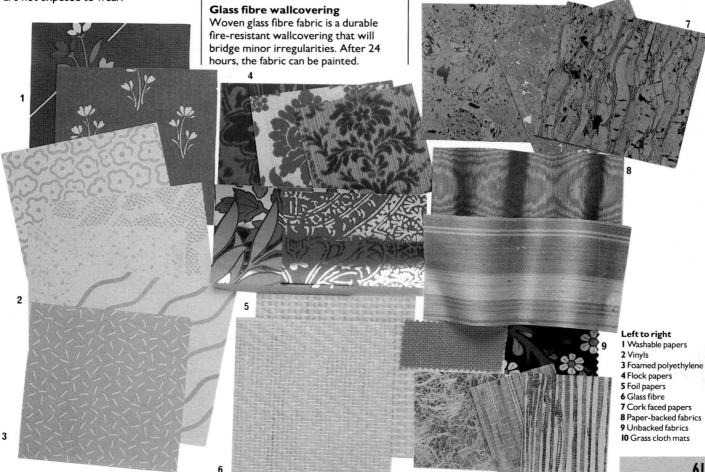

Left to right
1 Washable papers
2 Vinyls
3 Foamed polyethylene
4 Flock papers
5 Foil papers
6 Glass fibre
7 Cork faced papers
8 Paper-backed fabrics
9 Unbacked fabrics
10 Grass cloth mats

WALLCOVERINGS: ESTIMATING QUANTITIES

Calculating the number of rolls of wallcovering you will need to cover your walls and ceiling depends on the size of the roll – both length and width – the pattern repeat and the obstructions you have to avoid. Because of variations in colour between batches, you must take into account all these points – and allow for wastage, too. A standard roll of wallcovering measures 530mm (1ft 9in) wide and 10.05 metres (33ft) long. Use the two charts on this page to estimate how many rolls you will need for walls and ceilings.

SEE ALSO

◁ Details for:

Wallcoverings 60-61
Papering walls 64-67
Papering ceilings 68

Estimating non-standard rolls

If the wallcovering is not cut to a standard size, calculate the amount you need in this way:

Walls

Measure the height of the walls from skirting to ceiling. Divide the length of the roll by this figure to find the number of wall lengths you can cut from a roll.

Measure around the room, excluding windows and doors, to work out how many widths fit into the total length of the walls. Divide this number by the number of wall lengths you can get from one roll to find how many rolls you need.

Make an allowance for short lengths above doors and under windows.

Ceilings

Measure the length of the room to determine one strip of paper. Work out how many roll widths fit across the room. Multiply the two figures. Divide the answer by the length of a roll to find out how many rolls you need. Check for waste and allow for it.

Checking for shading

If rolls of wallcovering are printed in one batch, there should be no problem with colour matching one roll to another. When you buy, look for the batch number printed on the wrapping.

Make a visual check before hanging the covering, especially for hand-printed papers or fabrics. Unroll a short length of each roll and lay them side by side. You may get a better colour match by changing the rolls around, but if colour difference is obvious, ask for a replacement roll.

Some wallcoverings are marked 'reverse alternate lengths' in order to even out any colour variations. Take this into account when checking.

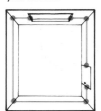

Measuring walls for standard rolls
You can include windows and doors in your estimate.

Measuring walls for non-standard rolls
Do not include doors and windows when estimating for expensive materials. Allow for short lengths afterwards.

Walls:
Standard rolls
Measure your room, then look down height column and across wall column to assess number of standard rolls required.

WALLS	HEIGHT OF ROOM IN METRES FROM SKIRTING							
	2.0-2.25m	2.25-2.50m	2.50-2.75m	2.75-3.0m	3.0-3.25m	3.25-3.50m	3.50-3.75m	3.75-4.0m
	NUMBER OF ROLLS REQUIRED FOR WALLS							
10.0m	5	5	6	6	7	7	8	8
10.5m	5	6	6	7	7	8	8	9
11.0m	5	6	7	7	8	8	9	9
11.5m	6	6	7	7	8	8	9	9
12.0m	6	6	7	8	8	9	9	10
12.5m	6	7	7	8	9	9	10	10
13.0m	6	7	8	8	9	10	10	10
13.5m	7	7	8	9	9	10	10	11
14.0m	7	7	8	9	10	10	11	11
14.5m	7	8	8	9	10	10	11	12
15.0m	7	8	9	9	10	11	12	12
15.5m	7	8	9	9	10	11	12	13
16.0m	8	8	9	10	11	11	12	13
16.5m	8	9	9	10	11	12	13	13
17.0m	8	9	10	10	11	12	13	14
17.5m	8	9	10	11	12	13	14	14
18.0m	9	9	10	11	12	13	14	15
18.5m	9	10	11	12	12	13	14	15
19.0m	9	10	11	12	13	14	15	16
19.5m	9	10	11	12	13	14	15	16
20.0m	9	10	11	12	13	14	15	16
20.5m	10	11	12	13	14	15	16	17
21.0m	10	11	12	13	14	15	16	17
21.5m	10	11	12	13	14	15	17	18
22.0m	10	11	13	14	15	16	17	18
22.5m	11	12	13	14	15	16	17	18
23.0m	11	12	13	14	15	17	18	19
23.5m	11	12	13	15	16	17	18	19
24.0m	11	12	14	15	16	17	18	20
24.5m	11	13	14	15	16	18	19	20
25.0m	12	13	14	15	17	18	19	20
25.5m	12	13	14	16	17	18	20	21
26.0m	12	13	15	16	17	19	20	21
26.5m	12	14	15	16	18	19	20	22
27.0m	13	14	15	17	18	19	21	22
27.5m	13	14	16	17	18	20	21	23
28.0m	13	14	16	17	19	20	21	23
28.5m	13	15	16	18	19	20	22	23
29.0m	13	15	16	18	19	21	22	24
29.5m	14	15	17	18	20	21	23	24
30.0m	14	15	17	18	20	21	23	24

MEASUREMENT IN METRES AROUND WALLS INCLUDING DOORS AND WINDOWS

Ceilings:
Standard rolls
Number of standard rolls required are shown next to overall room dimensions.

Dimensions
All dimensions are shown in metres.
(1m = 39in)

CEILINGS: NUMBER OF ROLLS REQUIRED							
Measurement around room (m)	Number of rolls	Measurement around room (m)	Number of rolls	Measurement around room (m)	Number of rolls	Measurement around room (m)	Number of rolls
11.0	2	16.0	4	21.0	6	26.0	9
12.0	2	17.0	4	22.0	7	27.0	10
13.0	3	18.0	5	23.0	7	28.0	10
14.0	3	19.0	5	24.0	8	29.0	11
15.0	4	20.0	5	25.0	8	30.0	11

TRIMMING AND CUTTING TECHNIQUES

Most wallcoverings are already machine-trimmed to width so that you can butt-join adjacent lengths accurately. Some hand-printed papers and speciality coverings are left untrimmed. These are usually expensive, so don't attempt to trim them yourself: ask the supplier to do this for you – it's worth the slight additional cost.

Cutting plain wallcoverings
To cut a plain paper to length, measure the height of the wall at the point where you will hang the first 'drop'. Add an extra 100mm (4in) for trimming top and bottom. Cut several pieces from your first roll to the same length and mark the top of each one.

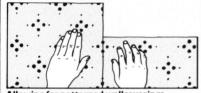

Allowing for patterned wallcoverings
You may have to allow extra on alternate lengths of patterned wallcoverings to match patterns. Check before you cut your second length.

CHOOSING PASTE

Most wallpaper pastes are supplied as powder or flakes for mixing with water. There are several specific types:

All-purpose paste
Standard wallpaper paste is suitable for most light- to medium-weight papers. By adding less water, it can be used to hang heavyweight papers.

Heavy-duty paste
Specially prepared to hang embossed papers, paper-backed fabrics and other heavyweight wallcoverings.

Fungicidal paste
Most pastes contain a fungicide to prevent mould growth under certain impervious wallcoverings, which slow down the drying rate of the paste. It is essential to use a fungicidal paste when hanging vinyls, washable papers, foils and foamed plastic coverings.

Ready-mixed paste
Tubs of ready-mixed, thixotropic paste are specially made to give the high adhesion required for heavyweight luxury wallcoverings such as fabric.

PASTING WALLCOVERINGS

You can use any wipe-clean table for pasting, but a narrow fold-up pasting table is a good investment if you are doing a lot of decorating. Lay several cut lengths of paper on top of each other face down on the table to keep it clean. Tuck the ends under a length of string tied loosely round the table legs to stop the paper rolling up while you paste it.

Applying the paste

Use a large, soft wall brush or pasting brush to apply the paste. Mix the paste in a plastic bucket and tie string across the rim to support the brush, keeping its handle clean while you paperhang.

Align the covering with the far edge of the table (so you don't get paste on the table, then transfer it to the face of the wall covering). Apply the paste by brushing away from the centre. Paste the edges and remove any lumps.

If you prefer, apply the paste with a short-piled paint roller; pour the paste into a roller tray. Roll in one direction only towards the end of the paper.

Pull the covering to the front edge of the table and paste the other half. Fold the pasted end over – don't press it down – and slide the length along the table to expose an unpasted part.

Paste the other end then fold it over to almost meet the first cut end: the second fold is invariably deeper than the first, a good way to denote the bottom of patterned wallcoverings. Fold long drops concertina-fashion.

Leave the pasted covering to soak, draped over a broom handle spanning two chair backs. Some heavy or embossed coverings may need to soak for 15 minutes: let one length soak while you hang another. Vinyls and lightweight papers can be hung immediately.

Pasting the wall

Hang exotic wallcoverings by pasting the wall, to reduce the risk of marking their delicate faces. Apply a band of paste just wider than the length of covering, so that you will not have to paste right up to its edge for the next length. Use a brush or roller.

Ready-pasted wallcoverings

Many wallcoverings come pre-coated with adhesive, activated by soaking a cut length in a trough of cold water ($\triangleright$). Mix ordinary paste to recoat dry edges.

SEE ALSO

Details for: $\triangleright$
| Ready-pasted paper | 66 |
| Wallcoverings | 60-61 |

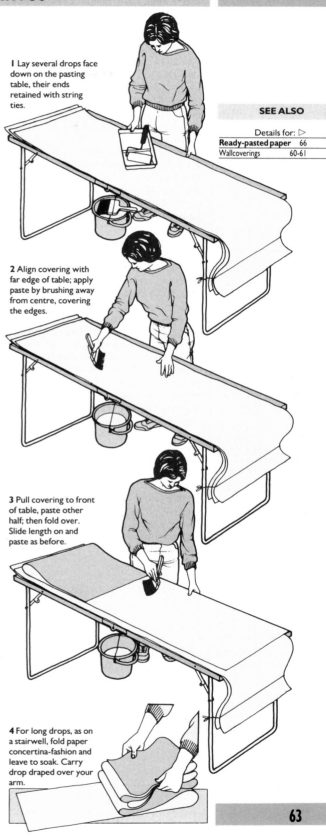

1 Lay several drops face down on the pasting table, their ends retained with string ties.

2 Align covering with far edge of table; apply paste by brushing away from centre, covering the edges.

3 Pull covering to front of table, paste other half; then fold over. Slide length on and paste as before.

4 For long drops, as on a stairwell, fold paper concertina-fashion and leave to soak. Carry drop draped over your arm.

SEE ALSO

◁ Details for:	
Painting ceiling	**45**
Painting wood	**48-50**
Varnishing	**54**
Papering ceiling	**68**
Preparing plaster	30-31
Wallcoverings	60-61

● **Hide a join in a corner**
When you are using a wallcovering with a large pattern, try to finish in a corner where you will not notice if the pattern does not match.

Sticking down the edges
Ensure that the edges of the paper adhere firmly by running a seam roller along the butt join.

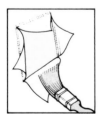

Losing air bubbles
Slight blistering usually flattens out as wet paper dries and shrinks slightly. If you find that a blister remains, either inject a little paste through it and roll it flat, or cut across it in two directions, peel back the triangular flaps and paste them down.

LINING A WALL

Lining a wall prior to decorating is only necessary if you are hanging embossed or luxury wallcoverings, or if the wall is uneven and imperfections might show through a thin paper. Lining paper is hung horizontally so that the joins cannot align with those in the top layer. Work from right to left if you are right-handed, vice versa if you are left-handed.

Mark a horizontal line near the top of the wall, one roll width from the ceiling. Holding the concertina-folded length in one hand, start at the top right-hand corner of the wall, aligning the bottom edge with the marked line. Smooth the paper onto the wall with a paperhanger's brush, working from the centre towards the edges.

Work along the wall gradually, unfolding the length as you do so. Take care not to stretch or tear the wet paper. Use the brush to gently stipple the edge into the corner at each end.

Use the point of a pair of scissors to lightly mark the corner, peel back the paper and trim to the line. Brush the paper back in place. You may have to perform a similar operation along the ceiling if the paper overlaps slightly. Work down the wall butting each strip against the last, or leave a tiny gap between the lengths.

Trim the bottom length to the skirting. Leave the lining paper to dry out for 24 hours before covering.

Lining prior to painting

If you line a wall for emulsion painting, hang the paper vertically as for other wallcoverings as the joins will be minimally visible.

Hanging lining paper horizontally
Hold the concertina-folded paper in one hand and smooth onto the wall from top right, butting strips.

PAPERING A WALL

Where to start

Don't apply wallcovering until all the woodwork has been painted or varnished (◁) and start by painting or papering the ceiling (◁).

The traditional method for papering a room is to hang the first length next to a window close to a corner, then work in both directions away from the light, but you may find it easier to paper the longest uninterrupted wall to get used to the basic techniques before tackling corners or obstructions.

If your wallcovering has a large regular motif, centre the first length over the fireplace for symmetry. You could centre this first length between two windows, unless you will be left with narrow strips each side, in which case it's best to butt two lengths on the centre line.

Centre a large motif over fireplace

Or butt two lengths between windows

Hanging on a straight wall

The walls of an average room are rarely truly square, so use a plumb line to mark a vertical guide against which to set the first length of wallcovering. Start at one end of the wall and mark the vertical line one roll width away from the corner, minus 12mm (½in) so the first length will overlap the adjacent wall.

Allowing enough wallcovering for trimming at the ceiling, unfold the top section of the pasted length and hold it against the plumbed line. Using a paperhanger's brush, work gently out from the centre in all directions to squeeze out any trapped air.

When you are sure the paper is positioned accurately, mark the ceiling line with outer edge of your scissors blade, peel back the top edge and cut along the crease. Smooth the paper back and stipple it down carefully with the brush. Unpeel the lower fold of the paper, smooth it onto the wall with the brush then stipple it firmly into the corner. Trim the bottom edge against the skirting, peel away, trim and brush back against the wall.

Hang the next length in the same way. Slide it with your fingertips to align the pattern and produce a perfect butt joint. Wipe any paste from the surface with a damp cloth. Continue to the other side of the wall, allowing the last drop to overlap the adjoining wall by 12mm (½in).

I Mark first length
Use a roll of paper to mark the wall one width away from the corner – less 12mm (½in) for an overlap onto the return wall – then draw a line from ceiling to skirting using a plumb line.

2 Hang first drop
Cut the first drop of paper, allowing about 50mm (2in) at each end for trimming, paste and allow to soak. Hang the top fold against the plumbed line and brush out from the centre, working down.

3 Trim at ceiling
When the paper is smoothly brushed on, run the outer edge of your scissors along the ceiling angle, peel away the paper, cut off the excess then brush back onto the wall.

4 Trim at skirting
Hang the lower fold of paper. At the skirting, tap your brush gently into the top edge, peel away the paper and cut along the folded line with scissors, then brush back.

PAPERING PROBLEM AREAS

Papering around doors and windows

Hang the length next to a door frame, brushing down the butt joint to align the pattern, but allow the other edge to loosely overlap the door.

Make a diagonal cut in the excess towards the top corner of the frame (**1**). Crease the waste along the frame with scissors, peel it back, trim it off then brush it back. Leave a 12mm (½in) strip for turning onto the top of the frame. Fill in over the door.

Butt the next full length over the door and cut the excess diagonally into the frame so that you can paste the rest of the strip down the side of the door. Mark and cut off the waste.

When papering up to flush window frames, treat them like a door. Where a window is set into a reveal, hang the length of wallcovering next to the window and allow it to overhang the opening. Make a horizontal cut just above the edge of the window reveal. Make a similar cut near the bottom then fold the paper around to cover the side of the reveal. Crease and trim along the window frame and sill.

Cut a strip of paper to match the width and pattern of the overhang above the window reveal. Paste it, slip it under the overhang and fold it around the top of the reveal (**2**). Cut through the overlap with a smooth, wavy stroke, remove the excess paper and roll down the join (**3**).

To continue, hang short lengths on the wall below and above the window, wrapping top lengths into the reveal.

Papering around a fireplace

Paper around a fireplace as for a door. Make a diagonal cut in the waste overlapping the fireplace, up to the edge of the mantel shelf, so that you can tuck the paper in all round for creasing and trimming to the surround.

To cut to an ornate surround, paper the wall above the surround; cut strips to fit under the mantel at each side, turning them around the corners of the chimney breast. Gently press the wallcovering into the moulding, peel it away and cut round the impression using nail scissors. Brush the paper back.

Papering internal and external corners

Turn an internal corner by marking another plumbed line so that the next length of paper covers the overlap from the first wall. If the piece you trimmed off at the corner is wide enough, use it as your first length on the new wall.

To turn an external corner, trim the last length so that it wraps around it, lapping the next wall by about 25mm (1in). Plumb and hang the remaining strip with its edge about 12mm (½in) from the corner.

Papering behind radiators

If you can't remove a radiator, turn off the heating and allow it to cool. Use a steel tape to measure the positions of the brackets holding the radiator to the wall. Transfer these measurements to a length of wallcovering, slit it from the bottom up to the top of the bracket. Feed the pasted paper behind the radiator, down both sides of the brackets. Use a radiator roller to press it to the wall (▷). Crease and trim to the skirting board.

Papering around switches and sockets

Turn off the electricity at the mains (▷). Hang the wallcovering over the switch or socket. Make diagonal cuts from the centre of the fitting to each corner. Trim off the waste leaving 6mm (¼in) all round. Loosen the faceplate, tuck the margin behind and retighten it. Don't switch the power back on until the paste is dry. Don't use for foils: the metallic surface can conduct electricity.

SEE ALSO

Details for: ▷	
Radiator roller	57
Turning off power	134
Preparing plaster	30-31
Wallcoverings	60-61

1 Cut the overlap diagonally into the frame

2 Fold onto reveal top   **3 Cut with wavy line**

Internal corner

External corner

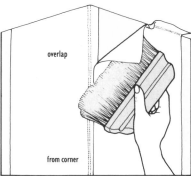

Slit to top of bracket behind radiator

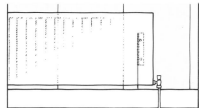

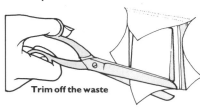

Trim off the waste

- **Papering archways**
  Arrange strips to leave even gaps between arch sides and the next full-length strips. Hang strips over face of arch, cut curve leaving 25mm (1in) margin. Fold it onto underside snipping into margin to prevent creasing. Fit a strip on the underside to reach from floor to top of arch. Repeat on opposite side of arch.

- **Trimming foils around electrical fittings**
  Make diagonal cuts (See left), but crease the waste against the fitting and trim off with a sharp knife when the paste has dried.

STAIRWELLS

The only real problem with papering a stairwell is the extra long drops on the side walls. You will need to build a safe work platform over the stairs (◁). Plumb and hang the longest drop first, lapping the head wall above the stairs by 12mm (½in).

Carrying the long drops of wallcovering – sometimes as much as 4.5m (15ft) long – is awkward: paste the covering liberally so it's not likely to dry out while you hang it, then fold it concertina-fashion. Drape it over your arm while you climb the platform. You'll need a helper to support the weight of the pasted length while you apply it. Unfold the flaps as you work down.

SEE ALSO

◁ Details for:
Work platforms	22
Preparing plaster	30-31
Wallcoverings	60-61

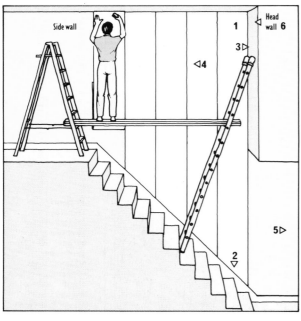

Papering sequence
Follow this sequence for papering a stairwell.
1 Hang the longest drop
2 Crease it into the angled skirting and cut
3 Lap the paper onto the head wall
4, 5 Work away from the first drop in both directions
6 Paper the head wall

Crease and cut the bottom of the paper against the angled skirting. Don't forget – when first you cut the length – to allow for this angle; work to the longest edge measurement. Work away from this first length in both directions, then hang the head wall.

Where the banister rail is let into the stairwell wall, try to arrange the rolls so that the rail falls between the two butted drops. Hang the drops to the rail and cut horizontally into the edge of the last strip at the centre of the rail, then make radial cuts so the paper can be moulded around the rail. Crease the flaps, peel away the wallcovering and cut them off. Smooth the covering back.

Hang the next drop at the other side of the rail, butting it to the previous piece and make similar radial cuts.

SPECIAL TECHNIQUES FOR WALLPAPERING

Whatever you are using as a wallcovering, follow the standard wallpapering techniques as explained previously. However, there are some additional considerations and special techniques involved in using certain types of wallcovering, as explained below and opposite.

RELIEF WALLCOVERINGS

When hanging *Anaglypta*, line the wall first and use a heavy-duty paste. Apply the paste liberally and evenly but try not to leave too much paste in the depressions. Allow it to soak for 10 minutes. *Supaglypta* will need 15 minutes soaking time.

Don't use a seam roller on the joins: tap the paper gently with a paperhanger's brush to avoid flattening the embossing.

Don't turn a relief wallcovering around corners. Measure the distance from the last drop to the corner and cut your next length to fit. Trim and hang the offcut to meet at the corner. Fill external corners with cellulose filler once the paper has dried thoroughly.

To use *Lincrusta*, sponge the back with hot water until it is thoroughly soaked. Apply the paste and hang the length, rubbing it down with a felt or rubber roller.

Use a sharp knife and straightedge to trim *Lincrusta*. Treat the corners with filler as for *Anaglypta*.

VINYL WALLCOVERINGS

Paste paper-backed vinyls in the normal way, but cotton-backed vinyl hangs better if you paste the wall and leave it to become tacky before applying the wallcovering. Use fungicidal paste.

Hang and butt join lengths of vinyl using a sponge to smooth them onto the wall rather than a brush. Crease a length top and bottom, then trim it to size with a sharp knife.

Vinyl will not stick to itself, so when you turn a corner, use a knife to cut through both pieces of paper where they overlap. Peel away the excess and rub down the vinyl to produce a perfect butt join.

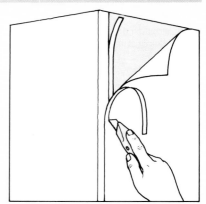

Cut through overlap and remove excess

READY-PASTED WALLCOVERINGS

Place the trough of cold water next to the skirting at the position of the first drop. Roll a cut length loosely from the bottom with the pattern on the outside. Immerse the roll in the trough for the prescribed time, according to the manufacturer's instructions.

Take hold of the cut end and lift the paper, allowing it to unroll naturally, draining the surface water back into the trough at the same time.

Hang and butt join the coverings in the usual way — use a sponge to apply vinyls but use a paperhanger's brush for other coverings.

Hanging a long wet length can be difficult if you follow the standard procedure. Instead, roll the length from the top with the pattern outermost. Place it in the trough and immediately re-roll it through the water. Take it from the trough in roll form and drain excess water. Hang it by feeding from the roll as you proceed.

Pull paper from trough and hang on the wall

SPECIAL TECHNIQUES FOR WALLPAPERING

METALLIC FOILS

The acid content of old paste may discolour metallic foil papers, so coat either the paper or the wall with fresh fungicidal paste.

FLOCK PAPER

Protect the flocking with a piece of lining paper and remove air bubbles with a paperhanger's brush. Cut through both thicknesses of overlapped joins and remove the surplus; press back the edges to make a neat butt join.

FOAMED POLYETHYLENE

Novamura (foamed polyethylene) can be hung straight from the roll onto a pasted wall. Sponge in place and trim it top and bottom with scissors.

FABRICS AND SPECIAL COVERINGS

Try to keep paste off the face of paper-backed fabrics and any other special wallcoverings. There are so many different coverings, so check with the supplier which paste to use.

So you don't damage a delicate surface, use a felt or rubber roller to press in place or stipple with a brush.

Most fabric coverings will be machine-trimmed but if the edges are frayed, overlap the joints and cut through both thicknesses then peel off the waste to make a butt join. Make a similar join at a corner.

Many fabrics are sold in wide rolls: even one cut length will be heavy and awkward to handle. Paste the wall, then support the rolled length on a batten between two stepladders. Work from the bottom upwards.

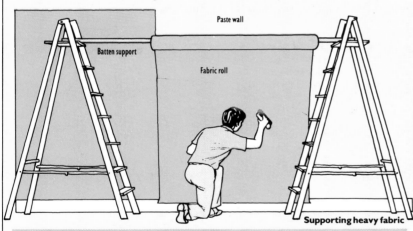

Paste wall

Batten support

Fabric roll

Supporting heavy fabric

GLASS FIBRE WALLCOVERINGS

Hang glass fibre coverings by applying the special adhesive to the wall with a roller. Hang and butt the lengths, then use a spatula to smooth the covering from the centre outwards (or use a felt or rubber roller).

Crease and trim glass fibre as for ordinary wallcoverings, or use a knife and straightedge. Leave the glue to set for 24 hours, then paint. When the first coat has dried, lightly rub down to remove raised fibres, then recoat.

EXPANDED POLYSTYRENE

Paint or roll special adhesive onto the wall. Hang the covering straight from the roll, smooth gently with the flat of your hand, then roll over it lightly with a dry paint roller.

If the edge is square, butt adjacent drops. If it is crushed or crumbled, overlap the join and cut through both thicknesses with a sharp trimming knife, peel away the offcuts and rub the edges down. Unless the edges are generously glued, they will curl apart. Trim top and bottom with a knife and straightedge. Allow the adhesive to dry for 72 hours then hang the wallcovering using a thick fungicidal paste.

UNBACKED FABRICS

If you want to apply a plain coloured medium-weight fabric, you can glue it directly to the wall. However, it is easy to stretch an unbacked fabric so that aligning a pattern is difficult.

For more control, stretch the fabric onto 12mm (½in) thick panels of lightweight insulation board (you'll then have the added advantage of insulation and a pin-board). Stick the boards directly onto the wall.

SEE ALSO

Details for: ▷	
Preparing plaster	30-31
Preparing tiles	38
Wallcoverings	60-61

Using paste
Test an offcut of the fabric first to make sure that the adhesive will not stain it. Use a ready-mixed paste and roll it onto the wall.

Wrap a cut length of fabric around a cardboard tube (from a carpet supplier) and gradually unroll it on the surface, smoothing it down with a dry paint roller. Take care not to distort the weave. Overlap the joins but do not cut through them until the paste has dried, in case the fabric shrinks. Re-paste and close the seam.

Press the fabric into the ceiling line and skirting and trim away the excess with a sharp trimming knife when the paste has set.

Making wall panels
Cut the insulation board to suit the width of the fabric and the height of the wall. Stretch the fabric across the panel, wrap it around the edges, then use latex adhesive to stick it to the back. Hold it temporarily with drawing pins, while the adhesive dries.

Either use wallboard adhesive to glue the panels to the wall or pin them, tapping the nail heads through the weave of the fabric to conceal them.

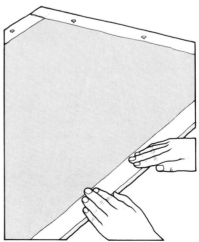

Stretch unbacked fabric over insulation board

67

PAPERING A CEILING

Papering a ceiling isn't as difficult as you may think: the techniques are basically the same as for papering a wall, except that the drops are usually longer and more unwieldy to hold while you brush the paper into place. Set up a sensible work platform - it's virtually impossible to work by moving a single stepladder along - and enlist a helper to support the pasted, folded paper while you position one end, and progress backwards across the room. If you've marked out the ceiling first, the result should be faultless.

SEE ALSO

◁ Details for:
Work platforms	22
Pasting paper	63
Preparing plaster	30-31
Wallcoverings	60-61

Setting out the ceiling

Arrange your work platform (◁) before you begin to plan out the papering sequence for the ceiling. The best type of platform to use is a purpose-made decorator's trestle, but you can manage with a scaffold board spanning between two pairs of stepladders.

Now mark the ceiling to give a visual guide to positioning the strips of paper. Aim to work parallel with the window wall and away from the light, so you can see what you are doing and so that the light will not highlight the joins between strips. If the distance is shorter the other way, hang the strips in that direction for ease.

Mark a guide line along the ceiling, one roll-width minus 12mm (½in) from the side wall, so that the first strip of paper will lap onto the wall.

Putting up the paper

Paste and fold the paper as for wallcovering, concertina fashion (◁), drape it over a spare roll and carry it to the work platform. You'll certainly find it easier to get a helper to hold the folded paper, giving you both hands free for brushing into place.

Hold the strip against the guideline, using a brush to stroke it onto the ceiling. Tap it into the wall angle then gradually work backwards along the scaffold board, brushing on the paper as your helper unfolds it.

If the ceiling has a cornice, crease and trim the paper at the ends. Otherwise, leave it to lap the walls by 12mm (½in) so that it will be covered by the wallcovering. Work across the ceiling in the same way, butting the lengths of paper together. Cut the final strip to roughly the width, and trim into the wall angle.

Working from a ladder
If you have to work from a stepladder, an assistant can support the paper on a cardboard tube taped to a broom.

Papering a ceiling
The job is so much easier if two people work together.
1 Mark guide line on ceiling
2 Support folded paper on tube
3 Brush on paper, from centre outwards
4 Overlap covered by wallpaper
5 Use two boards to support two people

LIGHTING FITTINGS AND CENTREPIECES

There are usually few obstructions on a ceiling to make papering difficult – unlike walls, which have doors, windows and radiators to contend with. The only problem areas occur where there's a pendant light fitting or a decorative plaster centrepiece.

Cutting around a pendant light
Where the paper passes over a ceiling rose, cut several triangular flaps so that you can pass the light fitting through the hole. Tap the paper all round the rose with a paperhanging brush and continue to the end of the strip. Return to the rose and cut off the flaps with a knife.

Papering around a centrepiece
If you have a decorative plaster centrepiece, work out the position of the strips so that a joint will pass through the middle. Cut long flaps from the side of each piece of paper so that you can tuck it in all round the plaster moulding.

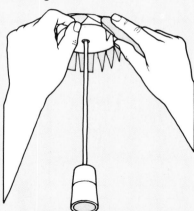

Cut off triangular flaps when paste is dry

Cut long strips to fit around moulding

CHOOSING TILES

Tiling is a universally popular method of decorating a surface, with an almost inexhaustible range of colours, textures and patterns to choose from depending on the degree of durability required. Tiling provides the facility of finishing a surface with small, regular units which can be cut and fitted into an awkward shape far easier than sheet materials.

Glazed ceramic tiles

Hard ceramic tiles, usually glazed and fired, are made for walls and floors. Unglazed tiles are available but only to provide a surer grip for flooring. A textured surface reduces the risk of accidents where a floor might become wet. All ceramic tiles are durable and waterproof, but be sure to use special heat- and frost-resistant tiles where appropriate. Do not use wall tiles on the floor as they cannot take the weight of traffic or furniture.

The majority of tiles are square but dimensions vary according to use and the manufacturer's preference. Rectangular and more irregular shaped tiles are available. Typical shapes include hexagons, octagons, diamonds and interlocking units with curved elaborate edges. Other units include slim rectangles with pointed (pic) or slanted (cane) ends. Use them in combination to produce patterned floors and walls.

Mosaic tiles

Mosaic tiles are small versions of the standard ceramic tiles. To lay them individually would be time consuming and lead to inaccuracy, so they are usually joined by a paper covering, or a mesh background, into larger panels. Square tiles are common but rectangular, hexagonal and round mosaics are also available. Because they are small, mosaics can be used on curved surfaces, and will fit irregular shapes better than large ceramic tiles.

Quarry tiles

Quarry tiles are thick, unglazed ceramic tiles used for floors which need a hardwearing, waterproof surface. Colours are limited to browns, reds, black and white. Machine-made tiles are regular in size and even in colour but hand-made tiles are variable, producing a beautiful mottled effect. Quarry tiles are difficult to cut so do not use them where you will have to fit them against a complicated shape. Rounded-edge quarry tiles can be used as treads for steps, and a floor can be finished with skirting tiles.

Stone and slate flooring

A floor laid with real stone or slate tiles will be exquisite but expensive. Sizes and thicknesses will vary according to the manufacturer – some will even cut to measure. A few materials are so costly that you should consider hiring a professional to lay them, otherwise treat cheaper ones like quarry tiles.

SEE ALSO

Details for: ▷	
Choosing colour/pattern	8-9, 13
Levelling concrete	29
Preparing plaster	30-31
Wall tiling	72-74
Floor tiling	78-79

Standard tile sections
A range of sections is produced for specific functions:

Field tile for general tiling with spacing lugs moulded onto them.

Rounded-edge (RE) tile for edging the field.

REX tile with two adjacent rounded edges.

Universal tile with two glazed, square edges for use in any position.

Tile selection
The examples shown left are a typical cross-section of commercially available ceramic tiles.
1 Glazed ceramic
2 Shape and size variation
3 Mosaic tiles
4 Quarry tiles
5 Slate and stone

69

CHOOSING TILES

SEE ALSO

◁ Details for:	
Choosing colour/pattern	8-9, 13
Levelling concrete	29
Preparing plaster	30-31
Floor tiling	75-77

Stone and brick tiles

Thin masonry facing tiles can be used to simulate a stone or brick wall as a feature area for a chimney breast, for example, or to clad a whole wall. Stone tiles are typically made from reconstituted stone in moulds, and most look unconvincing as an imitation of the real thing. Colour choice is intended to reflect local stone types, and is typically white, grey or buff. Some 'weathered' versions are also made.

Brick tiles look much more authentic. The best ones are actually brick 'slips' – slivers cut from kiln-produced bricks. A very wide range of traditional brick colours is available.

Left to right
1 Brick tiles
2 Vinyl floor tiles

Vinyl tiles

Vinyl tiles are among the cheapest and easiest floorcoverings to use. Vinyl can be cut easily, and so long as the tiles are firmly glued, with good joints, the floor will be waterproof. However, it will still be susceptible to scorching. A standard coated tile has a printed pattern between a vinyl backing and a harder, clear vinyl surface. Solid vinyl tiles are made entirely of the hardwearing plastic. Some vinyl tiles have a high proportion of mineral filler. As a result they are stiff and must be laid on a perfectly flat base. Unlike standard vinyl tiles, they will resist some rising damp in a concrete sub-floor. Most tiles are square or rectangular but there are interlocking shapes and hexagons. There are many patterns and colours to choose from, including embossed vinyl which represents ceramic, brick or stone tiling.

CARPET TILES

Carpet tiles have advantages over wall-to-wall carpeting. There is less to fear when cutting a single tile to fit, and, being loose-laid, a worn, burnt or stained tile can be replaced instantly. However, you can't substitute a brand new tile several years later, as the colour will not match. Buy several spares initially and swap them around regularly to even out the wear and colour change. Most types of carpet are available as tiles, including cord, loop and twist piles in wool as well as a range of man-made fibres. Tiles are normally plain in colour but some are patterned to give a striking grid effect. Some tiles have an integral rubber underlay.

A selection of carpet tiles
Tiles are used extensively for contract carpeting but they are equally suitable as a hard-wearing floor covering in the home.

1

CHOOSING TILES

Polystyrene tiles

Although expanded polystyrene tiles will not reduce heat loss from a room by any significant amount, they will deter condensation as well as mask a ceiling in poor condition. Polystyrene cuts easily so long as the trimming knife is very sharp. For safety in case of fire, choose a self-extinguishing type and do not overpaint with an oil paint. Wall tiles are made but they will crush easily and aren't suitable for use in a vulnerable area. There are flat or decoratively-embossed tiles.

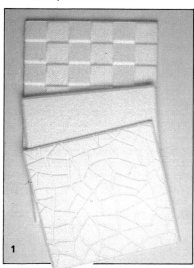

Mirror tiles

Square and rectangular mirror tiles can be attached to walls with self-adhesive pads in each corner. There is a choice of silver, bronze or smoke grey finish. Don't expect tiles to produce a perfect reflection unless they are mounted on a really flat surface.

Mineral fibre tiles

Ceiling tiles made from compressed mineral fibre are dense enough to be sound and heat insulating. They often have tongued-and-grooved edges so that, once stapled to the ceiling, the next interlocking tile covers the fixings. Fibre tiles can also be glued directly to a flat ceiling. A range of textured surfaces is available.

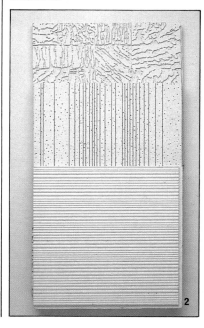

Metal tiles

Lightweight pressed metal tiles are fixed in the same way as mirror tiles. Choose from aluminium, bronze and gold coloured tiles with satin or bright finishes. These tiles are not grouted so do not use them where food particles can gather in the crevices.

Rubber tiles

Soft rubber tiles were originally made for use in shops and offices, but they are equally suitable for the home, being hardwearing yet soft and quiet to walk on. The surface is usually studded or textured to improve the grip. Choice is limited to a few plain colours.

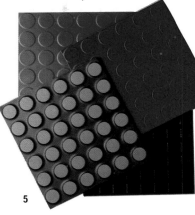

SEE ALSO

Details for: ▷	
Choosing colour/pattern	8-9, 13
Levelling concrete	29
Preparing plaster	30-31
Floor tiling	75-77
Tiling a ceiling	80

Cork tiles

Cork is a popular covering for walls and floors. It is easy to lay with contact adhesive and can be cut to size and shape with a knife. There's a wide range of textures and warm colours to choose from. Pre-sanded but unfinished cork will darken in tone when you varnish it. Alternatively, you can buy ready-finished tiles with various plastic and wax coatings. Soft, granular insulating cork is suitable as a decorative finish for walls only. It crumbles easily, so should not be used where it will be exposed on external corners.

Left to right
1 Polystyrene tiles
2 Mineral fibre tiles
3 Mirror tiles
4 Metal wall tiles
5 Rubber tiles
6 Cork floor tiles

SETTING OUT FOR WALL TILES

Setting out
The setting out procedure described on this page is applicable to the following tiles: cork, mosaics, ceramic, mirror, metal.

SEE ALSO

◁ Details for:
Flaky paint	28
Preparing plaster	30-31
Stripping wallpaper	32
Tiles	69-71

Whatever tiles you plan to use, the walls must be clean, sound and dry. You cannot tile over wallpaper, and flaking or powdery paint must be treated first to give a suitably stable base for the tiles. It's important that you make the surface as flat as possible so the tiles will stick firmly. Setting out the prepared surface accurately is a vital aid to hanging the tiles properly.

MAKING A GAUGE STICK

First make a gauge stick (a tool for plotting the position of tiles on the wall) from a length of 50 x 12mm (2 x ½in) softwood. Lay several tiles along it, butting together those with lugs, or add spacers for square-edged tiles, unless they're intended to be close-butted. Mark the position of each tile on the softwood batten.

Mark tile increments along a gauge stick

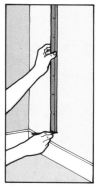

Using a gauge stick
Hold a home-made gauge stick firmly against the wall and mark the positions of the tiles on the surface.

Setting out a plain wall

On a plain uninterrupted wall, use the gauge stick to plan horizontal rows starting at skirting level. If you are left with a narrow strip at the top, move the rows up half a tile-width to create a wider margin. Mark the bottom of the lowest row of whole tiles. Temporarily nail a thin guide batten to the wall aligned with the mark (**1**). Make sure it is horizontal by placing a level on top.

Mark the centre of the wall (**2**), then use the gauge stick to set out the vertical rows at each side of it. If the border tiles are less than half a width, reposition the rows sideways by half a tile. Use a spirit level to position a guide batten against the last vertical line and nail it (**3**).

Plotting a half-tiled wall

If you are tiling part of a wall only, up to a dado rail for instance, set out the tiles with a row of whole tiles at the top (**4**).

This is even more important if you are using RE or REX tiles which are used for the top row of a half-tiled wall.

Arranging tiles around a window

Setting out for tiling
Plan out the tiling arrangement on the walls as shown right, but first plot the symmetry of the tile field with a gauge stick to ensure a wide margin all round.
1 Temporarily fix a horizontal batten at the base of the field
2 Mark the centre of the wall
3 Gauge from the mark then fix a vertical batten to indicate the side of the field
4 Start under a dado rail with whole tiles
5 Use a row of whole tiles at sill level
6 Place cut tiles at back of a reveal
7 Support tiles over window while they set

Use a window as your starting point so that the tiles surrounding it are equal and not too narrow. If possible, begin a row of whole tiles at sill level (**5**), and position cut tiles at the back of a window reveal (**6**). Fix a guide batten over a window to support the rows of tiles temporarily (**7**).

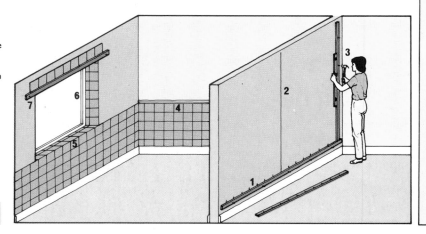

RENOVATING TILES

A properly tiled surface should last for many years but the appearance is often spoiled by one or two damaged tiles, by discoloured grouting on ceramic tiles, lifting or curling of cork, vinyl or polystyrene tiles. There is usually no need to redecorate – most problems can be solved fairly easily.

Renewing the grouting
It's not necessary to rake out old, drab grouting: use a renovation kit to brighten up the existing grout.

Brush on the liquid colourant (supplied in red, white, blue, green, beige or brown), following the lines of the grout which must be clean and dry. After about an hour, wet the area with a sponge, leave it for three minutes, then wipe excess colourant from the tiles. The liquid forms a strong bond with the grout and provides a water-resistant finish which can be polished with a dry cloth if required.

Replacing a cracked ceramic tile
Scrape the grout from around the damaged tiles then use a fine cold chisel to carefully chip out the tile, working from the centre. Take care not to dislodge its neighbours.

Scrape out the remains of the adhesive and vacuum the recess. Butter the back of the replacement tile with adhesive then press it firmly in place. Wipe off excess adhesive, allow it to set, then renew the grouting.

Lifting a cork or vinyl floor tile
Try to remove a single tile by chopping it out from the centre with a wood chisel. If the adhesive is firm, try warming the tile with a domestic iron.

Scrape the floor clean of old adhesive and try the new tile for fit. Trim the edges if necessary. Spread adhesive on the floor, then place one corner of the tile in position. Gradually lower it into the recess. Spread the tile with your finger tips to squeeze out any air bubbles, place a heavy weight on it and leave overnight.

Removing a ceiling tile
Loosen a polystyrene tile by picking it out from the centre with a sharp knife and paint scraper. Don't lever it out or you will crush the adjoining tile. Stick the replacement tile back on a complete bed of special adhesive. Remove a stapled ceiling tile by cutting through the tongues all round.

TILING A WALL: CERAMIC TILES

Choosing the correct adhesive

Most ceramic tile adhesives are sold ready-mixed, although a few need to be mixed with water. Tubs or packets will state the coverage.

A standard adhesive is suitable for most applications but use a waterproof type in areas likely to be subjected to running water or splashing. If the tiles are to be laid on a wallboard, use a flexible adhesive and make sure it is heat resistant for worktops or around a fireplace. Some adhesives can also be used for grouting the finished wall.

A notched plastic spreader is usually supplied with each tub, or you can use a serrated trowel.

Hanging the tiles

Spread enough adhesive on the wall to cover about one metre square (about 3ft square). Press the teeth of the spreader against the surface and drag it through the adhesive so that it forms horizontal ridges (1).

Press the first tile into the angle formed by the setting-out battens (2) until it is firmly fixed, then butt up tiles on each side. Build up three or four rows at a time. If the tiles do not have lugs, place matchsticks, thick card or proprietary plastic spacers between them to form the grout lines. Wipe away adhesive from the surface with a damp sponge.

Spread more adhesive and tile along the batten until the first rows of whole tiles are complete. From time to time, check that your tiling is accurate by holding a batten and spirit level across the faces and along the top and edge. When you have completed the entire field, scrape adhesive from the border and allow it to set before removing the setting-out battens.

Grouting tiles and sealing joins

Use a ready-mixed paste called grout to fill the gaps between the tiles. Standard grout is white, grey or brown, but there is also a range of coloured grouts to match or contrast with the tiles. Alternatively, mix pigments with dry, powdered grout before adding water to match any colour.

Waterproof grout is essential for showers and bath surrounds, and you should use an epoxy-based grout for worktops to keep them germ-free.

Leave the adhesive to harden for 24 hours, then use a rubber-bladed squeegee or plastic scraper to press the grout into the joins (3). Spread it in all directions to make sure all joins are well filled.

Wipe grout from the surface of the tiles with a sponge before it sets and smooth the joins with a blunt-ended stick – a dowel will do.

When the grout has dried, polish the tiles with a dry cloth. Do not use a tiled shower for about seven days to let the grout harden thoroughly.

Sealing around bathroom fittings

Don't use grout or ordinary filler to seal the gap between a tiled wall and shower tray, bath or basin: the fittings can flex enough to crack a rigid seal, and frequent soakings will allow water to seep in, create stains and damage the floor and wall. Use a silicone rubber caulking compound to fill the gaps; it remains flexible enough to accommodate any movement.

Sealants are sold in a choice of colours to match popular tile and sanitaryware colourways. They come in tubes or cartridges and can cope with gaps up to 3mm (1/8in) wide: over that, pack out with soft rope or twists of soaked newspaper.

If you're using a tube, trim the end off the plastic nozzle and press the tip into the joint at an angle of 45 degrees. Push forward at a steady rate while squeezing the tube to apply a bead of sealant. Smooth any ripples with the back of a wetted teaspoon.

If you're using a cartridge, again, snip the end off the angled nozzle – the amount you cut off dictates the thickness of the bead – and use the container's finger-action dispenser to squirt out the sealant (4).

Alternatively, use ceramic coving or quadrant tiles to edge a bath or shower unit, or glue on a plastic coving strip which you cut to length.

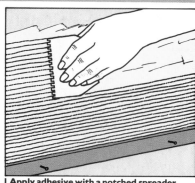

1 Apply adhesive with a notched spreader

SEE ALSO

Details for: ▷	
Preparing plaster	30-31
Ceramic tiles	69

2 Stick first tile in angle of 'setting-out' battens

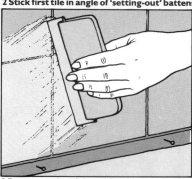

3 Press grout into joins with rubber squeegee

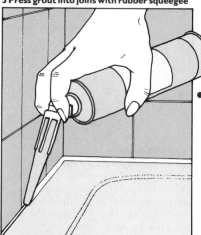

4 Seal between tiles and fittings with sealant

Ceramic coving tiles

Quadrant
Used to fill the joint between bath and wall

Mitred tile
Use at the end if you want to turn a corner

Bullnose tile
Use this tile to finish the end of a straight run

● **Tiling around pipes and fittings**
Check with the gauge stick how the tiles will fit round socket outlets and switches, pipes and other obstructions. Make slight adjustments to the position of the main field to avoid difficult shaping around these features.

73

CUTTING CERAMIC TILES

SEE ALSO

◁ Details for:
Preparing plaster	30-31
Ceramic tiles	69

Having finished the main field of tiles you will have to cut the ceramic tiles to fill the border and to fit around obstructions such as window frames, *electrical fittings, pipes and the basin. Making straight cuts is easy using a purpose-made cutter but shaping tiles to fit curves takes practice.*

Cutting thin strips
A cutting jig is the most accurate way to cut a thin strip cleanly from the edge of a tile. If you do not want to use the strip itself, nibble away the waste a little at a time with pincers or special tile nibblers.

Tile cutting jig
A worthwhile investment if you're cutting a lot of tiles, a proprietary jig incorporates a device for measuring and scoring tiles. The cutter is drawn down the channel of the adjustable guide. The tile is snapped with a special pincer-action tool.

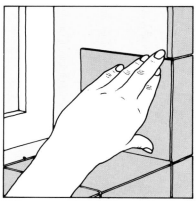

Tiling around a window
Tile up to the edges of a window, then stick RE tiles to the reveal so that they lap the edges of surrounding tiles. Fill in behind the edging tiles with cut tiles.

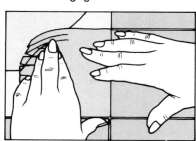

Cutting a curve
To fit a tile against a curved shape, cut a template from thin card to the exact size of a tile. Cut 'fingers' along one edge; press them against the curve to reproduce the shape. Transfer the curve onto the face of the tile and score the line freehand. Nibble away the waste a little at a time using pincers or a tile nibbler and smooth the edge with a slipstone.

Mark two edges   **Cut and fit tile**

Fitting around a pipe
Mark the centre of the pipe on the top and side edges of a tile and draw lines across the tile from these points. Where they cross, draw round a coin or something slightly larger than the diameter of the pipe.

Make one straight cut through the centre of the circle and either nibble out the waste, having scored the curve, or clamp it in a vice, protected with softening, and cut it out with a saw file – a thin rod coated with hard, abrasive particles which will cut in any direction. Stick one half of the tile on each side of the pipe.

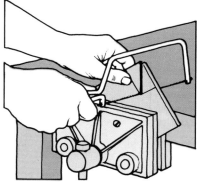

Fitting around a socket or switch
In order to fit around a socket or switch you may have to cut the corner out of a tile. Mark it from the socket then clamp the tile in a vice, protected with softening. Score both lines then use a saw file to make one diagonal cut from the corner of the tile to where the lines meet. Snap out both triangles.

If you have to cut a notch out of a large tile, cut down both sides with a hacksaw then score between them and snap the piece out of the middle.

CUTTING BORDER TILES

It's necessary to cut border tiles one at a time to fit the gap between the field tiles and the adjacent wall: walls are rarely truly square and the margin is bound to be uneven.

Making straight cuts
Mark a border tile by placing it face down over its neighbour with one edge against the adjacent wall **(1)**. Make an allowance for normal spacing between the tiles. Transfer the marks to the edge of the tiles using a felt-tip pen.

Use a proprietary tile cutter held against a straightedge to score across the face with one firm stroke to cut through the glaze **(2)**. You may have to score the edge of thick tiles.

Stretch a length of thin wire across a panel of chipboard, place the scored line directly over the wire and press down on both sides to snap the tile **(3)**.

Alternatively use a tile cutter, which has a wheel to score the tile and jaws to snap it along the line. If you're doing a lot of tiling, invest in a purpose-made jig. The jig will hold the tile square with a cutting edge; pressing down on the guide snaps the tile cleanly. Some jigs include a device for measuring border tiles, too.

Smooth the cut edges of the tile with a tile sander or small slipstone.

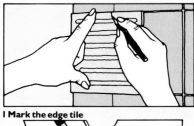

1 Mark the edge tile

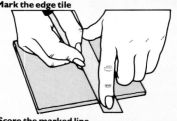

2 Score the marked line

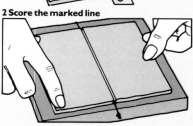

3 Snap the tile over a wire

SETTING OUT FOR DIAGONAL TILING

Arranging the tiles diagonally can create an unusual decorative effect, especially if your choice of tiles enables you to mix colours. Setting out and laying the tiles off centre isn't complicated – it's virtually the same as fixing them at right-angles, except that you'll be working into a corner instead of a wall. Mark a centre line, and bisect it at right-angles using an improvised compass (right). Draw a line from opposite diagonal corners of the room through the centre point. Dry lay a row of tiles to plot the margins (See below). Mark a right-angle to the diagonal. Fix a batten along one diagonal as a guide to laying the first row of tiles.

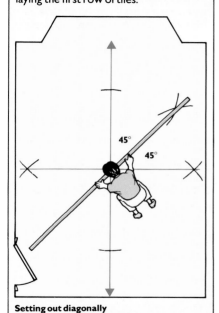

Setting out diagonally
Bisect the quartered room at 45 degrees

SETTING OUT FOR SOFT FLOOR TILES

Vinyl, rubber, cork and carpet tiles are relatively large, so you can complete the floor fairly quickly. Some vinyl tiles are self-adhesive, and carpet tiles are loose-laid, both of which speed up the process still further. Soft tiles such as these can be cut easily with a sharp trimming knife or even scissors, so fitting to irregular shapes is easier.

Marking out the floor

You can lay tiles onto a solid concrete or suspended wooden floor, so long as the surface is level, clean and dry. Most soft tiles can be set out in a similar way: find the centre of two opposite walls, snap a chalked string between them to mark a line across the floor (**1**). Lay loose tiles at right-angles to the line up to one wall (see below left). If there is a gap of less than half a tile-width, move the line sideways by half a tile to give a wider margin.

To draw a line at right-angles to the first, use string and a pencil as an improvised compass to scribe arcs on the marked line, at equal distances each side of the centre (**2**).

From each point, scribe arcs on both sides of the line (**3**), which bisect each other. Join the points to form a line across the room (**4**). As before, lay tiles at right-angles to the new line to make sure border tiles are at least half width. Nail a guide batten against one line to align the first row of tiles.

If the room is noticeably irregular in shape, centre the first line on the fireplace or the door opening (see below right).

Details for: ▷	
Levelling concrete	29
Floor tiles	70-71

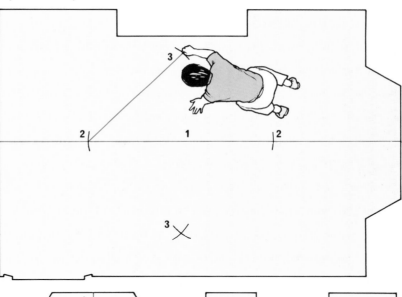

Setting out
When marked out, the quartered room ensures that the tiles can be laid symmetrically. This method is suitable for the following tiles: vinyl, rubber, cork, carpet.

4 Right angle complete

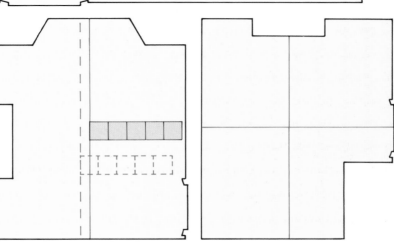

Plotting margin width *(near right)*
Lay loose tiles to make sure there is a reasonable gap at the margins. If not, move the line half a tile-width to the left.

Plotting an odd-shaped room *(far right)*
When a room is not a single rectangle, set out the lines using the fireplace and door as focal points.

LAYING VINYL FLOOR TILES

SEE ALSO

◁ Details for:
Levelling concrete	29
Vinyl tiles	70

Tiles pre-coated with adhesive can be laid quickly and simply, plus there is no risk of squeezing glue onto the surface. If you're not using *self-adhesive tiles, however, follow the tile manufacturer's instructions concerning the type of adhesive to use.*

Fixing self-adhesive tiles

Stack the tiles in the room for 24 hours before you lay them so they become properly acclimatized.

If the tiles have a directional pattern – some have arrows printed on the back to indicate this – make sure you lay them the correct way.

Remove the protective paper backing from the first tile prior to laying (**1**), then press the edge against the guide batten. Align one corner with the centre line (**2**). Gradually lower the tile onto the floor and press it down.

Lay the next tile on the other side of the line, butting against the first one (**3**). Form a square with two more tiles. Lay tiles around the square to form a pyramid (**4**). Continue in this way to fill one half of the room, remove the batten and tile the other half.

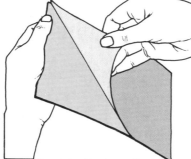

1 Peel off paper backing from adhesive tiles

GLUING VINYL TILES

Spread adhesive thinly but evenly across the floor, using a notched spreader, to stick about two or three tiles only. Lay the tiles carefully and wipe off surplus adhesive that's squeezed out with a rag.

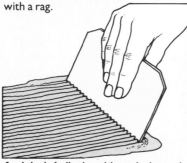

Apply bed of adhesive with notched spreader

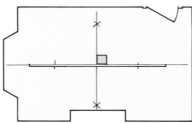

2 Place first tile in angle of intersecting lines

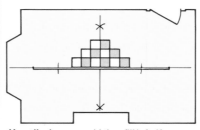

3 Butt up next tile on other side of line

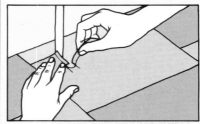

4 Lay tiles in a pyramid then fill in half room

Finishing off the floor

As soon as you have laid all the floor tiles, wash over the surface with a damp cloth to remove any finger marks. It is not often necessary to polish vinyl tiles, but you can apply an emulsion floor polish if you wish.

Fit a straight metal strip (available from carpet suppliers) over the edge of the tiles when you finish at a doorway. When the tiles butt up to an area of carpet, fit a single threshold bar onto the edge of the carpeting.

CUTTING TILES TO FIT

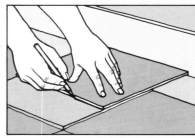

Trimming border tiles
Edges are rarely square, so cut border tiles to the skirting profile. To make a border tile, lay a loose one exactly on top of the last full tile. Place another tile on top but with its edge touching the wall. Draw along the edge of this tile with a pencil to mark the tile below. Remove the marked tile and cut along the line, then fit the cut off portion of the tile into the border.

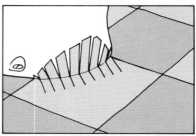

Cutting irregular shapes
To fit curves and mouldings, make a template for each tile out of thin card. Cut fingers which can be pressed against the object to reproduce its shape. Transfer the template to a tile and cut it out. You can also use a profile gauge to mark tiles for cutting complex curves.

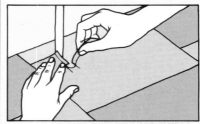

Fitting around pipes
Mark the position of the pipe on the tile using a compass. Draw parallel lines to the edge of the tile, taken from the perimeter of the circle. Measure halfway between the lines and cut a straight slit to the edge of the tile. Fold back the slit and slide the tile in place.

LAYING OTHER TYPES OF SOFT FLOOR TILES

Carpet tiles

Carpet tiles are laid as for vinyl tiles, except that they are not usually glued down. Set out centre lines on the floor (▷) but don't fit a guide batten: simply aligning the row of tiles with the marked lines is sufficient.

Carpet tiles have a pile which must be laid in the correct direction, sometimes indicated by arrows on the back face. One problem with loose-laid carpet tiles is preventing them from slipping – particularly noticeable in a large room.

Some tiles have ridges of rubber on the back which mean they will slip easily in one direction but not in another. The non-slip direction is typically denoted by an arrow on the back of the tile. It's usual to lay the tiles in pairs so that one prevents the other from moving.

Stick down every third row of tiles using double-sided carpet tape to make sure the tiles don't slide.

Cut and fit carpet tiles as described for vinyl tiles.

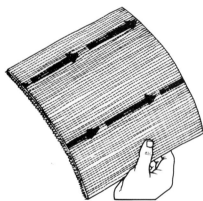

Checking direction of pile
Some carpet tiles have arrows on their back to indicate laying direction.

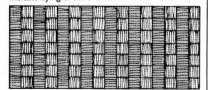

Using pile for decoration
Two typical arrangements of tiles using the pile to make decorative textures.

Cork tiles

Use the methods described for laying vinyl tiles to cut and fit cork tiles, but use a contact adhesive: thixotropic types allow a degree of movement as you position the tiles.

Make sure the tiles are level by tapping down the edges with a block of wood. Unfinished tiles can be sanded lightly to remove minor irregularities.

Vacuum then seal unfinished tiles with three or four coats of clear polyurethane varnish.

Bedding cork tiles
Bed the edges of cork tiles with a wood block.

Rubber tiles

Use the same methods for laying rubber tiles as for vinyl types. Use a latex flooring adhesive.

Laying rubber tiles
Lay large rubber tiles by placing one edge and corner against neighbouring tiles before lowering it onto a bed of adhesive.

NEAT DETAILING FOR SOFT FLOOR TILES

Covering a plinth

Create the impression of a floating bath panel or kitchen base units by running floor tiles up the face of the plinth. Hold carpet tiles into a tight bend with gripper strip (**1**) or glue other tiles in place for a similar detail. Glue a plastic moulding, normally used to seal around the edge of a bath, behind the floor covering to produce a curved detail which makes cleaning the floor a lot easier (**2**).

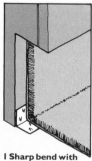
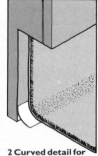

1 Sharp bend with gripper strip

2 Curved detail for easy cleaning

Cutting holes for pipes

With most soft floor tiles you can cut neat holes for central heating pipes using a home-made punch: cut a 150mm (6in) length of the same diameter pipe and sharpen the rim on the inside at one end with a metalworking file. Plot the position for the hole on the tile then place the punching tool on top. Hit the other end of the punch with a hammer to cut through the tile cleanly. With some carpet tiles you may have to cut round the backing to release the cut-out and prevent fraying with tape.

Punch holes for pipes with sharpened offcut

SEE ALSO

Details for: ▷	
Setting out	75
Levelling concrete	29
Carpet tiles	70
Cork tiles	71
Rubber tiles	71

● **Access to plumbing**
If you are covering completely a bath panel with tiles, remember to make a lift-off section in the panel to gain access to pipes and taps around the bath.

LAYING CERAMIC FLOOR TILES

Ceramic floor tiles make a durable, hard surface that can also be extremely decorative. Laying the tiles on a floor is similar to hanging them on a wall, *although being somewhat thicker than wall tiles, you have to be especially careful when cutting them to fit for neat and accurate results.*

SEE ALSO

◁ Details for:	
Levelling concrete	29
Border wall tiles	74
Sawing tiles	74
Marking out	75
Ceramic tiles	69
Grouting tiles	73

● **Battens on concrete**
Use masonry nails to hold battens onto a concrete floor.

Spacing the tiles
Use offcuts of thick card to set ceramic floor tiles apart consistently to allow for grouting.

● **Grouting the joins**
Grout the tiles as for walls, but fill the joins flush rather than indenting them, so that dirt will not clog them. A dark grout is less likely to show up dirt.

Setting out for tiling
Mark out the floor as for soft floor tiles then set out the field with battens.
1 Fix temporary guide battens at the edge of the field on two adjacent walls farthest from the door
2 Ensure that the battens are at true right-angles by measuring the diagonal
3 Dry-lay a square of 16 tiles in the angle as a final check

Setting out

You cannot lay ceramic tiles on a suspended wooden floor without constructing a solid, level surface that will not flex. A flat, dry concrete floor is an ideal base (◁).

Mark out the floor as for soft floor tiles (◁) and work out the spacing to achieve even, fairly wide border tiles. Nail two softwood guide battens to the floor, aligned with the last row of whole tiles on two adjacent walls farthest from the door. Set the battens at a right-angle – even a small error will become obvious by the time you reach the other end of the room. Check the angle by measuring three units from one corner along one batten and four units along the other. Measure the diagonal between the marks: it should measure five units if the battens form an angle of 90 degrees. Make a final check by dry-laying a square of tiles in the angle.

Laying the tiles

Use a proprietary floor tile adhesive that is waterproof and slightly flexible when set. Spread it on using a plain or notched trowel, according to the manufacturer's recommendations. The normal procedure is to apply adhesive to the floor for the main area of tiling but to butter the back of individual cut tiles as well.

Spread enough adhesive on the floor for about sixteen tiles. Press the tiles into the adhesive, starting in the corner. Work along both battens then fill in between, to form the square. Few floor tiles have spacing lugs, so use plastic spacers or card.

Check the alignment of the tiles with a straightedge and make sure they're lying flat by spanning them with a spirit level. Work along one batten laying squares of sixteen tiles each time. Tile the rest of the floor in the same way, working back towards the door. Leave the floor for 24 hours before you walk on it to remove the guide battens and fit the border tiles.

Cutting ceramic floor tiles
Measure and cut the tiles to fit the border as described for wall tiles (◁). Because they are thicker, floor tiles will not snap quite so easily, so if you have a large area to fill, buy or hire a tile cutting jig.

Alternatively, make your own device by nailing two scraps of 12mm (½in) thick plywood to 50 × 25mm (2 × 1in) softwood battens, leaving a parallel gap between them which is just wide enough to take a tile. Hold the device on edge, insert a scored tile into the gap, up to the scored line – which should be uppermost – and press down on the free end (see below right). Snap thin strips from the edge in this way. Saw or nibble curved shapes (◁).

LAYING MOSAIC FLOOR TILES

Set out mosaic tiles on a floor as for ceramic floor tiles. Spread on the adhesive then lay the tiles, paper facing uppermost, with spacers that match the gaps between individual pieces. Press the sheets into the adhesive, using a block of wood to tamp them level. Remove the spacers and soak then peel off the facing with warm water 24 hours later. Grout as normal.

If you have to fit a sheet of mosaic tiles around an obstruction remove individual mosaic pieces as close to the profile as possible. Fit the sheet (**1**) then cut and replace the pieces to fit around the shapes.

If you're using mosaics in areas of heavy traffic – a step on the patio, for example – protect vulnerable edges with a nosing of ordinary ceramic floor tiles to match or contrast (**2**).

1 Remove mosaic pieces to fit around pipe

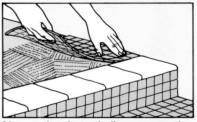

2 Lay a nosing of ceramic tiles on step treads

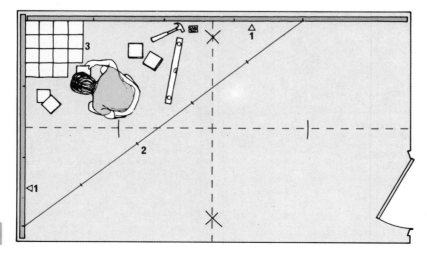

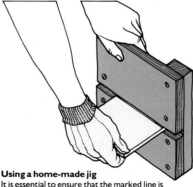

Using a home-made jig
It is essential to ensure that the marked line is positioned parallel to the edge of the plywood or the tile will not snap accurately.

LAYING QUARRY TILES

Quarry tiles are the best choice for a tough, hardwearing flooring that will receive a lot of heavy foot traffic. But beware: they're fairly thick and making even a straight cut is not easy. Reserve them for areas that don't require a lot of complex shaping.

Don't lay quarry tiles on a suspended wooden floor: replace the floorboards with 18 or 22 mm (¾ or 1 in) *exterior-grade plywood to provide a sufficiently flat and rigid base. A concrete floor will present few problems, providing it is free from damp. So long as the floor is reasonably flat, the mortar bed on which the quarry tiles are laid will take care of any fine levelling problems.*

Setting out for tiling

Set out two guide battens in a corner of the room at right-angles to each other, as described for ceramic floor tiles, opposite. The depth of the battens should measure about twice the thickness of the tiles to allow for the mortar bed. Fix them temporarily to a concrete floor with long masonry nails. The level of the battens is essential, so check with a spirit level; pack out under the battens with scraps of hardboard or card where necessary. Mark tile widths along each batten, leaving 3mm (⅛in) gaps between for grouting, as a guide to positioning.

Dry-lay a square of sixteen tiles in the angle, then nail a third batten to the floor, butting the tiles and parallel with one of the other battens. Level and mark it as before.

Bedding down the tiles

Quarry tiles are laid on a bed of mortar mixed from 1 part cement: 3 parts builder's sand. When water is added, the mortar should be stiff enough to hold an impression when squeezed in your hand.

Soak quarry tiles in water prior to laying to prevent them sucking water from the mortar too rapidly, when a poor bond could result. Cut a stout board to span the parallel battens: this will be used to level the mortar bed and tiles. Cut a notch in each end to fit between the battens, and the thickness of a tile less 3mm (⅛in).

Spread the mortar to a depth of about 12mm (½in) to cover the area of sixteen tiles. Level it by dragging the notched side of the board across.

Dust dry cement on the mortar to provide a good key for the tiles, then lay the tiles along three sides of the square against the battens. Fill in the square, spacing the tiles equally by adjusting them with a trowel.

Tamp down the tiles gently with the un-notched side of the board until they are level with the battens. If the mortar is too stiff, brush water into the joins. Wipe mortar from the faces of the tiles before it hardens, or it will stain.

Fill in between the battens then move one batten back to form another bay of the same dimension. Level it with the first section of tiles. Tile section-by-section until the main floor is complete. When the floor is hard enough to walk on, lift the battens and fill in the border tiles.

CUTTING QUARRY TILES

Because quarry tiles are difficult to cut you may think it worthwhile having them cut by a specialist tile supplier. Measure border tiles as described for wall tiles then, having scored the line, number each one on the bottom and mark the waste with a felt-tip pen.

If you want to cut the tiles yourself, scribe them with a tile cutter, then make a shallow cut down each edge with a saw file (▷). With the face side of the tile held in a gloved hand, strike behind the scored line with the cross pein of a hammer.

Score tile face: tap the back with a hammer

SEE ALSO

Details for: ▷	
Levelling concrete	29
Damp floors	29
Mixing mortar	216

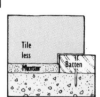

Notching the levelling board
Cut the same notch at each end of the board for levelling the mortar.

Levelling the mortar
With a notch located over each guide batten, drag the levelling board towards you.

Levelling border tiles
Use a notched piece of plywood to level the mortar in the margin and tamp down the tiles with a block.

● **Finishing off the quarry tiling**
Grout quarry tiles as for ceramic floor tiles, using cement or proprietary waterproof grout. Clean it off the surface by sprinkling sawdust onto it and wiping off with a cloth. Wash the finished floor with a soapless detergent.

The set-up for a quarry tiled floor
The arrangement for quarry tiles is similar to glazed tiles.
1 Fix two guide battens – about twice the tile thickness – at right-angles to each other
2 Fix a third batten, parallel with one of the others
3 Dry-lay sixteen tiles between the battens so check their accuracy then proceed with tiling

FITTING CEILING TILES

There are basically two types of tiles which you can use on a ceiling: the most popular, polystyrene tiles, are easy to cut and – because they're so lightweight – they can be stuck to the ceiling without any difficulty. For a more *luxurious finish, consider using mineral fibre ceiling tiles. They, too, can be glued directly to a ceiling, although some have tongued-and-grooved edges which are best stapled to a timber framework nailed to the ceiling.*

SEE ALSO

◁ Details for:
Preparing plaster	30-31
Marking out	75
Gluing tiles	76
Border tiles	76
Using template	76
Turning off power	134
Connecting a rose	160

I Make a spacing gauge
Set out the furring strips at the correct spacing using a gauge made from two battens nailed together.

2 Securing the tiles
Fix the tiles groove outwards and staple through the grooved edge. Slot the tongues of butting tiles into them.

Installing stapled tiles

Mineral fibre tiles are stapled to a batten framework nailed to the ceiling joists. The first job is to locate the joists and arrange the battens to suit the tile size.

Locating the joists
Start by marking out two bisecting lines across the ceiling (◁), so that you can work out the spacing of the tiles with even borders. Mark the edges of the last whole tile on the ceiling.

Check the direction of the joists by examining the floor above if you're in a downstairs room, or by looking in the loft if you're upstairs.

To locate the joists on the ceiling, poke a bradawl through the plaster at each side of a few joists (if you can gain access via the loft). Don't go to the trouble of lifting floorboards in a room above: floorboards run at right-angles to joists, so to locate them, try tapping the ceiling with your knuckles. Listen for the dull thud when you're over a joist. Use the bradawl – or a small-diameter drill bit – to locate the approximate centre of the joists.

Measure from these points to the next joists – they'll be anything from 300 to 450mm (1 to 1ft 8in) apart – and mark their centres. Nail parallel strips of 50 × 25mm (2 × 1in) sawn timber to

the joists, at right-angles to them. Space them so the distance between the centre of each strip is a tile width. Fitting the strips is easier with a spacer – two softwood battens nailed together (1) to set the spacing. Finish by nailing the last strip against the far wall. Transfer the line marking the edge of the border tiles to the battens along both sides of the ceiling.

Fitting stapled tiles
Unlike any other form of tiling, you must start by fixing stapled tiles at the borders. Mark and cut off the tongued edges of two adjacent rows of border tiles, starting with the one in the corner. Staple them through the grooved edge to the furring strips but secure the cut edges with panel pins driven through their faces.

Proceed diagonally across the ceiling by fixing whole tiles into the angle formed by the border tiles. Slide the tongues of the loose tile into the groove of its neighbours, then staple it through its own grooved edge (2).

To fit the remaining border tiles, cut off the tongues and nail them through their face.

FIXING POLYSTYRENE CEILING TILES

Where to use the tiles
Polystyrene tiles can be used in virtually any room in the house except the kitchen, where they would be directly over a source of heat – the cooker or a gas-fired water heater.

Setting out the ceiling
Remove any friable material and make sure the ceiling is clean and free from grease (◁). Snap two chalked lines which cross each other at right-angles in the centre of the ceiling (◁). Hang the tiles to the chalked lines, checking their alignment frequently (◁).

Sticking up the tiles
Use a proprietary polystyrene adhesive or a heavy-duty wallpaper paste. Spread the adhesive across the back of the tile to cover all but the very edge.

Press the first tile into one of the angles formed by the marked lines. Use the flat of your hand: fingertip pressure can crush polystyrene. Proceed with subsequent tiles to complete one half of the ceiling, then the other.

Cutting the tiles
Mark the border tiles (◁) then use a sharp trimming knife with a blade long enough to cut through a tile with one stroke. Cut the tiles on a flat piece of scrap board. Clean up the edges but don't rub too hard or the polystyrene granules will crumble.

Mark out curves with a card template (◁), then follow the marked line freehand with a trimming knife.

How stapled ceiling tiles are fixed
Mineral fibre tiles require a set-up of battens attached to the ceiling surface.
1 Nail battens to the joists at right-angles, a tile-width apart. Arrange substantial borders by altering the starting point
2 Fix the border tiles first on two adjacent rows, starting with the corner tile
3 Staple the remaining tiles to the battens through their grooves, working diagonally across the ceiling

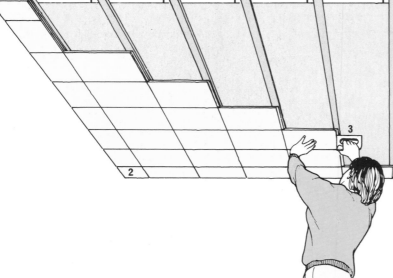

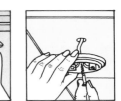

1 Fix battens to joists   **2 Replace ceiling rose**

Dealing with electrical fittings
Turn off the power at the mains (◁) unscrew the ceiling rose cover, and release the flex conductors.

Nail battens to the ceiling joists to correspond with the screw fixings of the rose (1). Cut a hole through the covering tile for the cable, replace the rose (2), screwing it through the tile to the battens. Reconnect the conductors (◁), replace the rose cover then restore the power.

2

PLASTERWORK	82
DOORS	90
WINDOWS	92
STAIRS	99
ROOFS	102

HOUSEHOLD REPAIRS

PLASTERWORK

Plasterwork is used to provide internal walls and ceilings with a smooth, flat surface suitable for decorating with paint or paper. The plaster also provides sound and thermal insulation as well as protection from fire. Decorative mouldings – a feature of walls and ceilings in many older houses – are also made of plaster; they're still available for renovations. There are basically two methods for providing a plaster finish: the traditional way is wet plastering; the modern one uses plasterboard, and is known as 'dry lining'.

Traditional plastering techniques

Traditional plastering uses a mix of plastering materials and water, which is spread over the rough background in one, two or even three layers. Each layer is applied with a trowel and levelled accordingly; when set, the plaster forms an integral part of the wall or ceiling. The background may be solid masonry for walls, or timber-framed walls and ceilings finished with lath-and-plaster. Laths are thin strips of wood nailed to the timber framework to support plaster, which, forced between the laths, spreads to form nibs that grip on the other side. With traditional plastering, it takes practice to achieve a smooth, flat surface over a large area. With care, an amateur can produce satisfactory results, provided the right tools and plaster are employed and the work is divided into manageable sections. All-purpose one-coat plasters are now available to make traditional plastering easier for amateurs.

Dry lining with plasterboard

Manufactured boards of paper-covered plaster are widely used to dry-line the walls and ceilings in modern homes and during renovations. Its use overcomes the drying out period required for wet plasters and requires less skill to apply.

The large flat boards are nailed or bonded to walls and ceilings to provide a separate finishing layer. The surface may be decorated directly once the boards are sealed, or covered with a thin coat of finish plaster.

BUYING AND STORING PLASTER

Plaster powder is normally sold in 50kg (1cwt) paper sacks. Smaller sizes, including 2.5kg (5½lb) bags are available from DIY stores for repair work. It's generally more economical to buy the larger sacks, but this depends on the scale of the work. Try to buy only as much plaster as you need. It's better to overestimate, however, to allow for wastage and prevent running short (◁).

Store plaster in dry conditions: if it is to be kept in an outbuilding for some time, cover it with plastic sheeting to protect it from moisture. Keep the paper bags off a concrete floor by placing them on boards or plastic sheeting. Open bags are more likely to absorb moisture, which can shorten the setting time and weaken the plaster. Keep an opened bag in a sealed plastic sack. Use self-adhesive tape to seal it. Discard plaster which contains lumps.

Ready-to-use plaster is also available in plastic tubs. It can be more expensive to buy it this way but it is easier for amateurs to use and it will keep for a long time, provided the airtight lid is well sealed.

SEE ALSO

◁ Details for:
Plaster coverage	85
Patching plasterboard	31

Storing plaster
Keep an open bag of plaster in a plastic sack sealed with adhesive tape.

Traditional Plastering
(Right)
The construction of a lath-and-plaster ceiling and plastered masonry wall.
1 Brick background
2 Ceiling joists
3 Lath background
4 Rendering coat
5 Floating coat
6 Finishing coat
7 Cornice moulding

Dry lining
(Far right)
The construction of a modern dry-lined wall and ceiling.
1 Block background
2 Batten fixing
3 Ceiling joists
4 Noggings
5 Plasterboard
6 Coving
7 Tape
8 Filler

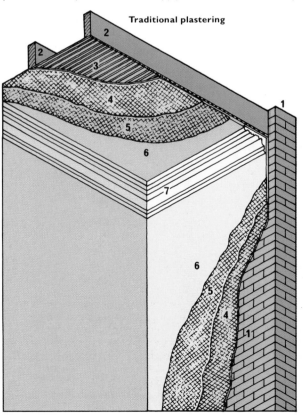

Traditional plastering

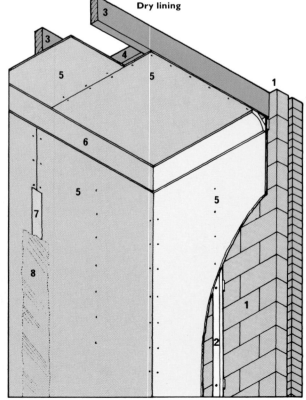

Dry lining

TYPES OF PLASTER

Plastering is carried out using modern gypsum plasters or mixes based on cement, lime and sand. By varying the process and introducing additives, a range of plasters can be produced within a given type to suit different background materials.

Plasters are basically produced in two grades – one as a base or 'floating' coat, the other for finishing coats. Base coat gypsum plasters are pre-mixed types, which contain lightweight aggregates. Base coat sanded plasters which are based on cement or cement/lime have to be mixed on site with a suitable grade of clean, sharp sand (although finish plasters are ready to use with the addition of water).

The following information deals only with those materials suitable for domestic work.

SEE ALSO

Details for: ▷
Applications   85

CHOOSING PLASTERS FOR DOMESTIC WORK

GYPSUM PLASTERS

Most plasters in common use are produced from ground gypsum rock by a process which removes most of the moisture from the rock to produce a powder that sets hard when mixed with water. Setting times are controlled by the use of retarding additives which give each of the several types of plaster a setting time suitable to its use.

Gypsum plasters are intended for interior work only, they should not be used on permanently damp walls. They must not be remixed with water once they start to set.

PLASTER OF PARIS

This quick-setting non-retarded gypsum plaster gives off heat as it sets. It is white or pinkish, and is mixed to a creamy consistency with clean water. It is unsuitable for general plastering but good for casting, and can be used for repairs to decorative mouldings.

CARLITE PLASTER

Carlite refers to a range of retarded gypsum plasters which are premixed with a lightweight aggregate and need only water to prepare them for use. The undercoat bonds well to most backgrounds, and this, coupled with their light weight – about half that of plasters mixed with sand – makes Carlite plasters fairly easy to use. The lightweight aggregate also gives improved thermal insulation. Setting time for Carlite plasters is about 1 to 2 hours.

Three types of Carlite undercoat plasters – 'browning', 'bonding' and 'metal lathing' – are available, each formulated to suit a background of a particular surface texture and suction. Browning is generally used for backgrounds with average suction, such as brickwork. For low-suction surfaces like dense brick and concrete blocks the bonding undercoat is preferred. The metal lathing is less commonly used and is primarily for metal lath backgrounds.

When more than one undercoat layer is needed to build up a thickness the same plaster should be used for all layers to ensure compatibility.

There is only one Carlite finishing plaster and it can be used over all the undercoats, being applied as soon as the undercoat has set.

THISTLE PLASTERS

Thistle is the brand name of a range of building plasters used for a variety of conditions and backgrounds.

Two types of finishing plaster are made, both mixed with water only: the finish plaster, for use over sanded undercoats, and the board finish plaster, used for finishing plasterboard surfaces.

Two special 'renovating' plasters are for use on walls with residual dampness. The undercoat is a pre-mixed gypsum plaster with special additives and the finish, formulated specially for use with the undercoat, contains a fungicide. The plaster is for use on damp walls which are slow to dry out, as in new, exposed building work or in old houses with new damp-proof courses installed. The plaster is not itself a damp-proofing material, but it allows the background material to breathe and dry out without letting the moisture show on the surface.

The cause of the problem must be dealt with before the plaster is applied.

SIRAPITE B

Sirapite B is a finish coat gypsum plaster for use over undercoats which contain sand, including cement rendering. It is not suitable for application to plasterboard. Only water is needed to prepare it. It contains additives which improve its workability, it has a gradual, progressive set and it can be brought to a high standard of finish.

Sirapite B is widely used by skilled professional plasterers.

SANDED PLASTERS

Before the advent of modern gypsums, lime and sand for undercoats and neat lime for finishes were used in traditional wet plastering, often with animal hair added to the undercoat mix as a binder. Lime plasters are generally less strong than gypsum and cement-based plasters.

Lime is still used, but mainly as an additive to improve the workability of a sand-and-cement plaster or rendering. Cement-based sanded plaster undercoats may be required by some authorities for kitchen and bathroom walls constructed on timber and expanded-metal lathing. These undercoats can also be used on old brickwork or where a strong impact-resistant covering is required.

SINGLE-COAT PLASTERS

A universal one-coat plaster can, as its name implies, be used in a single application on a variety of backgrounds and trowelled to a normal finish.

The plaster is available in 40kg (88lb) bags and only water is added to prepare it for use. It will stay workable for up to an hour and can be built up to a thickness of 50mm (2in) in one coat.

One-coat plaster is also available in small packs contained in mixing tubs, and these are ideal for such small repair jobs as making good where a fireplace has been removed. For larger areas than this it is more economical to buy bigger bags and mix on a board in the usual way.

FILLERS

Fillers are fine plaster powders used for repairs. Some, reinforced with cellulose resin, are sold in small packs and need only mixing with clean water for use. They are non-shrinking, adhere well and are ideal for filling cracks and holes in plaster and wood. Extra-fine fillers are also available ready-mixed in small tubs for levelling dents in woodwork.

● **Avoiding old plaster**
Plaster may deteriorate if stored for more than two months so suppliers try to ensure it is sold in rotation. The paper sacks in which plaster is supplied are usually date-stamped by the manufacturer. If you are buying from a self-service supplier, choose a sack with the latest date.

TYPES OF SURFACE

SEE ALSO

◁ Details for:
Efflorescence   24

● **Providing a 'key'**
Rake out mortar
joints to help plaster
and cement
renderings grip.

A well-prepared background is the first step to successful plastering. New surfaces of block or brickwork may need only dampening or priming with a bonding agent, depending on their absorbency. *Old plastered surfaces needing repair should be thoroughly checked. If the plaster has 'blown', hack it off back to sound material, then treat the surface and replaster the area.*

Background preparation and absorbency

Brush down the surface of a masonry background to remove loose particles, dust and efflorescent salts (◁). Test the absorption of the background by splashing on water; if it stays wet, consider the surface 'normal' – this means that it will only require light dampening with clean water prior to applying the plaster.

A dry background which absorbs the water immediately takes too much water from the plaster, making it difficult to work, prevents it from setting properly and can result in cracking. Soak the masonry with clean water applied with a brush.

High-absorbency surfaces

For very absorbent surfaces, such as aerated concrete blocks, prime the background with 1 part PVA bonding agent: 3 to 5 parts clean water. When dry, apply a bonding coat of 3 parts bonding agent: 1 part water. Apply the plaster when the bonding coat is tacky.

Low-absorbency surfaces

Prime low-absorption smooth brickwork or concrete with a solution of 1 part bonding agent: 3 to 5 parts water. Allow to dry. Apply a second coat of 3 to 5 parts bonding agent: 1 part water, and apply the plaster when tacky or allow it to dry for no more than 24 hours before plastering.

Non-absorbent surfaces

Glazed tiles and painted walls are considered non-absorbent and will require a coating of neat bonding agent to enable the plaster to stick. The plaster is applied while the agent is still wet. An alternative for glazed tiles is to apply a slurry of 2 parts sharp sand: 1 part cement mixed with a solution of 1 part bonding agent: 1 part water. Apply the slurry with a stiff-bristled brush to form a stippled coating. Allow to dry for 24 hours then apply the plaster.

Another option is to chip off the old tiles. Always remove loose tiles.

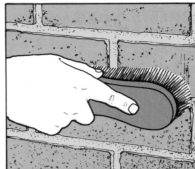
Remove loose particles with a stiff brush

Prime porous surfaces to control the suction

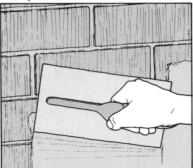
A bonding agent improves adhesion

Smooth tiles can be 'keyed' with a slurry

MAKING FILLER AND MORTAR BOARDS

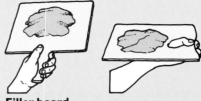

Filler board

You can make a useful board for mixing and working with filler from 6mm (¼in) marine plywood. Cut out a 300mm (1ft) square with a projecting handle on one side, or make a thumb hole like an artist's palette. Seal the surface with a polyurethane varnish or apply a plastic laminate for a smooth finish.

Mortar board

Cut a piece of 12mm (½in) or 18mm (¾in) marine plywood approximately 900mm (3ft) square. Round off the corners and chamfer the edges all round. Screw three lengths of 50 x 25mm (2 x 1in) softwood across the underside, spread equally apart. A smaller board, known as a 'spotboard', 600mm (2ft) square, can be made in a similar way.

Using a stand ▶
You will find it easier to handle plaster with the mix at table height.

Using a stand

A stand is used to support the mortar board at table height, about 700mm (2ft 4in) from the ground. This enables the plaster to be picked up on a hawk by placing it under the edge of the board and drawing the plaster onto it (◁).

Make a folding stand using 50 x 38mm (2 x 1½in) softwood for the legs and 75 x 25mm (3 x 1in) softwood for the rails. Make one leg frame fit inside the other and bolt them securely together at the centre.

A portable Workmate bench can be used to support the board instead of making a stand: grip the centre batten in the vice jaws.

MIXING PLASTER

With the background prepared, the next step for the amateur plasterer is to make a good mix. It is best to mix your plaster close to the working place, as it can be messy. Also cover the floor with old newspapers and remember to wipe your feet when leaving the room.

A plaster that is well mixed to the right consistency will be easier to apply. Use a plastic bucket to acccurately measure the cement, lime and sand, or plaster. For large quantities of plaster, multiply the number of bucket measures. For small quantities, just use half-bucket measures or less.

Old hard plaster stuck to your equipment can shorten the setting time and reduce the strength of the newly mixed plaster. Do not try to re-work plaster that has begun to set by adding more water: discard it and make a fresh batch. Mix only as much plaster as you will need. For larger areas, mix as much as you can apply in about twenty minutes – judge this by practice.

BONDING AGENTS

Bonding agents modify the suction of the background or improve the adhesion of the plastering. When used, the base coat plaster should not exceed 10mm (3/8in) in thickness. If you need to build up the thickness, scratch the surface to provide an extra key, and allow at least 24 hours between coats.

Bonding agents can be mixed with plaster or sand and cement to fill cracks. First brush away any loose particles and then apply a solution of 1 part agent: 3 to 5 parts water with a brush.

Mix the plaster or sand and cement with 1 part bonding agent: 3 parts water to a stiff mix. Apply the filler with a trowel pressing it well into the crack.

Wash tools and brushes thoroughly in clean water when you are finished. It may be necessary to rinse out the brushes as the work progresses on a large job.

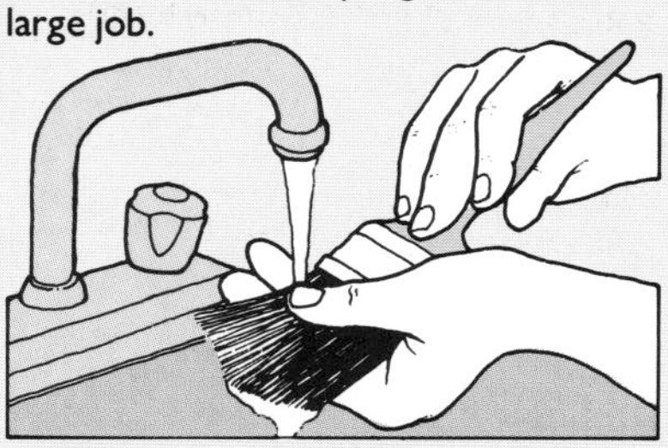

Wash agent from brushes before it sets

Base coat plasters

Mix base coat plasters on a mortar board (see opposite). For sanded plasters, measure out each of the materials and thoroughly dry-mix them with a shovel or trowel for small quantities (▷). Make a well in the heaped plaster and pour in some clean water. Turn in the plaster, adding water to produce a thick, creamy consistency.

Just add water to pre-mixed gypsum plaster (which already contains an aggregate). Mix them on the board in the same way. Always wash down the board after use.

You can mix small quantities of pre-mixed plaster in a bucket. Pour the plaster into the water and stir to a creamy consistency; 1kg (2lb 4oz) of plaster will need about 0.75 of a litre (1 1/3 pints) of water.

SEE ALSO

Details for: ▷
Trowel 218
Preparing plaster 30-31

Finish plaster

Mix finish plaster in a clean plastic bucket. Add the powder to the water. Pour not more than 2 litres (4 pints) of water into the bucket. Sprinkle the plaster into the water and stir it with a stout length of wood to a thick, creamy consistency. Tip the plaster out onto a clean, damp mortar board ready for use. Wash the bucket out with clean water before the plaster sets in it.

PLASTER TYPES, APPLICATION AND COVERAGE.

Type	Background	Type of coat	Coat thickness	Average coverage ●
CARLITE				
Browning *Normal suction*	Brick walls	Undercoat	10mm (3/8in)	6.5-7.5 sq.m. (7¾-9 sq yd)
	Block walls	Undercoat	10mm (3/8in)	6.5-7.5 sq.m. (7¾-9 sq yd)
	Concrete bricks	Undercoat	10mm (3/8in)	6.5-7.5 sq.m. (7¾-9 sq yd)
	Coarse concrete	Undercoat	10mm (3/8in)	6.5-7.5 sq.m. (7¾-9 sq yd)
Bonding *Low suction*	Brick walls	Undercoat	10mm (3/8in)	5.0-8.25 sq.m. (6-9¾ sq yd)
	Block walls	Undercoat	10mm (3/8in)	5.0-8.25 sq.m. (6-9¾ sq yd)
	Concrete bricks	Undercoat	10mm (3/8in)	5.0-8.25 sq.m. (6-9¾ sq yd)
	Smooth pre-cast concrete	Undercoat	8mm (5/16in)	5.0-8.25 sq.m. (6-9¾ sq yd)
	Plasterboards (Greyface)	Undercoat	8mm (5/16in)	5.0-8.25 sq.m. (6-9¾ sq yd)
	Polystyrene	Undercoat	10mm (3/8in)	5.0-8.25 sq.m. (6-9¾ sq yd)
Metal lathing	Expanded metal	Undercoat	10mm (3/8in)	3.0-3.5 sq.m. (3½-4 sq yd)
Finish	Carlite plaster Undercoats	Finish top coat	2mm (1/16in)	20.5-25.0 sq.m. (24½-30 sq yd)
THISTLE				
Finish	Sanded undercoats	Finish top coat	2mm (1/16in)	17.5-22.5 sq.m. (21-27 sq yd)
Board Finish	Plasterboards (Greyface)	Finish top coat	5mm (3/16in)	8.0-8.5 sq.m. (9½-10 sq yd)
Renovating *Normal suction*	Brick walls	Undercoat	10mm (3/8in)	6.0 sq.m. (7 sq yd)
	Block walls	Undercoat	10mm (3/8in)	6.0 sq.m. (7 sq yd)
	Concrete bricks	Undercoat	10mm (3/8in)	6.0 sq.m. (7 sq yd)
Renovating finish	Renovating plaster	Finish top coat	2mm (1/16in)	19.0-21.0 sq.m. (22¾-25 sq yd)
SIRAPITE				
	Sanded undercoats	Finish top coat	3mm (1/8in)	12.5-13.5 sq.m. (15-16 sq yd)
ONE COAT				
	All types	Undercoat/finish	12mm (1/2in)	4.5 sq.m. (5½ sq yd)

● m^2 per 50kg (sq yd per 50kg)

Plaster fillers

Pour out a small heap of the powder on to a small board, make a hollow in its centre and pour in water. Stir the mix to a creamy thickness; if it seems too runny add more powder. Use a rather drier mix for filling deeper holes.

APPLYING PLASTER

To the beginner plastering can seem a daunting business, yet it has only two basic requirements: that the plaster should stick well to its background and that it should be brought to a smooth, flat finish. Good preparation, the careful choice of plaster and working with the right tools should ensure good adhesion of the material, but the ability to achieve the smooth, flat surface will come only after some practice. Most of the plasterer's tools are rather specialized and unlikely to be found in the ordinary jobbing toolkit, but their cost may prove economical in the long term if you are planning several jobs.

SEE ALSO

◁ Details for:
Wallcoverings   60-68

● **Plasterer's rule**
Use a straight piece of wood to level a patch of plaster. A length of wooden architrave is ideal for the job.

Problems to avoid

Uneven surfaces
Many amateurs tackle plastering jobs, large or small, planning to rub the surface down level when it has set. This approach is very dust-creating and laborious, and invariably produces a poor result. If a power sander is used the dust is unpleasant to work in and permeates other parts of the house, making more work. Far better to try for a good surface as you put the plaster on, using wide-bladed tools to spread the material evenly. Ridges left by the corners of trowel or knife can be carefully shaved down afterwards with the knife – not with abrasive paper.

When covering a large area with finishing plaster it is not always easy to see if the surface is flat as well as smooth. Look obliquely across the wall or shine a light across it from one side to detect any irregularities.

Crazing
Fine cracks in finished plaster may be due to a sand-and-cement undercoat still drying out, and therefore shrinking. Such an undercoat must be fully dry before the plaster goes on, though if the plaster surface is sound the fine cracks can be wallpapered over.

Top coat and undercoat plaster can also crack if made to dry out too fast. Never heat plaster to dry it out.

Loss of strength
Gypsum and cement set chemically when mixed with water. If they dry out before the chemical set takes place they do not develop their full strength, and become friable. Should this happen it may be necessary to strip the wall and replaster it.

PLASTERING TECHNIQUES

Picking up

Hold the edge of the hawk below the mortar board and scrape a manageable amount of plaster onto the hawk, using the trowel (**1**). Take no more than a trowelful to start with.

Tip the hawk towards you and in one movement cut away about half of the plaster with the trowel, scraping and lifting it off the hawk and onto the face of the trowel (**2**).

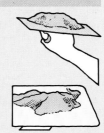

1 Load the hawk   **2 Lift off the plaster**

Application

Hold the loaded trowel horizontally but tilted at an angle to the face of the wall (**1**). Apply the plaster with a vertical upward stroke, pressing firmly so that plaster is fed to the wall. Flatten the angle of the trowel as you go (**2**) but never let its whole face come into contact with the plaster as suction can pull it off the wall again.

1 Tilt the trowel   **2 Apply the plaster**

Levelling up

Build a slight extra thickness of plaster with the trowel, applying it as evenly as possible. Use the rule to level the surface, starting at the bottom of the wall, the rule held against original plaster or wooden screeds nailed on at either side. Work the rule upwards while moving it from side to side, then lift it carefully away and the surplus plaster with it. Fill in any hollows with more plaster from the trowel, then level again. Let the plaster stiffen before a final smoothing with the trowel.

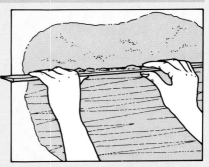

Work the rule up the wall to level the surface

Finishing

You can apply the finishing coat to a gypsum plaster undercoat as soon as it is set. A cement-based sanded plaster must dry thoroughly, but dampen its surface to adjust suction before finish-plastering. The grey face of plasterboard is finished immediately and is not wetted.

Apply the finish with a plasterer's trowel as described above, spreading it evenly, no more than 2 to 3mm (1/16 to 1/8in) judging this by eye, as screeds are not used. To plasterboard apply two coats to build a 5mm (3/16in) thickness.

As the plaster stiffens, brush or lightly spray it with water, then trowel the surface to consolidate it and produce a smooth matt finish. Avoid pressing hard and overworking the surface. Lastly remove surplus water with a sponge.

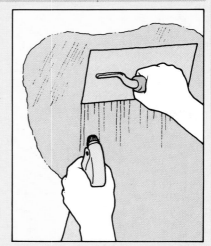

Spray plaster occasionally as you smooth it

REINFORCING A CORNER

When damage to a corner extends along most of the edge you can reinforce the repair plasterwork with a metal corner beading (1). As well as strengthening and protecting the new corner it will considerably speed up the repair work because it cuts out the need to use a board as a guide. You can obtain the beading from a good builders' merchant or DIY store.

Cut the beading to the required length with snips and a hacksaw. It has a galvanized protective coating, and the cut ends must be sealed with a metal primer or bituminous paint.

Cut back the old plaster from the damaged edge, wet the brickwork and apply patches of undercoat plaster at each side of the corner. Press the expanded metal wings of the beading into the plaster patches (2), using your straightedge to align its outer nose with both original plaster surfaces or checking the beading for plumb with a builder's level. Allow the plaster to set.

Build up the undercoat as before (3), but this time scrape it back to 2mm (1/16in) below the old finished level.

Apply the finishing coat, using the beading as a level to achieve flush surfaces. Take care not to damage the beading's galvanized coating with your trowel; rust can come through later and stain wallcoverings. To be on the safe side you can brush metal primer over the new corner before decorating.

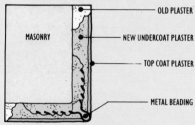

- OLD PLASTER
- MASONRY
- NEW UNDERCOAT PLASTER
- TOP COAT PLASTER
- METAL BEADING

1 Section through a repaired corner

2 Set in plaster　　**3 Trim undercoat back**

REPAIRING PLASTERWORK

Every decorator will at some time have to fill small holes and cracks with plaster or filler as part of normal preparations (▷), and these should present few problems. But once you start tackling more ambitious jobs, like removing fireplaces and taking down walls, you will need to develop some of the professional plasterer's skills in order to handle larger areas.

Plastering over a fireplace

A bricked-in fireplace provides an area large enough to give the amateur good practice without the work becoming unmanageable. Jobs of this kind can be done with a one-coat plaster, or you can apply an undercoat plaster followed by a top coat of finishing plaster.

Using a one-coat plaster

Prepare the background by cutting away any loose plaster above and around the brickwork. Remove dust and loose particles with a stiff brush.

Mix the plaster in a tub according to the maker's instructions.

Dampen the background with clean water and place a strip of hardboard below the work area to help you to pick up dropped plaster cleanly.

Tip the mixed plaster onto a dampened mortar board, then scoop some onto a hawk, and with a trowel (or the spreader provided) apply the plaster to the brickwork.

Work in the sequence shown (1), starting at the bottom of each section and spreading the plaster vertically. Work each area in turn, blending the edge of one into the next to build up a slight extra thickness, then level with a rule (▷). Fill any hollows and level again.

Leave the plaster to stiffen for about 45 minutes, when firm finger pressure should leave no impression, and lightly dampen the surface with a close-textured plastic sponge.

Wet the trowel or spreader and give the plaster a smooth finish, using firm pressure vertically and horizontally and keeping the tool wet.

Let the plaster dry thoroughly, for about six weeks, before decorating.

Two-coat plastering

Apply undercoat and finishing coat plasters as described above, scraping the undercoat back to allow for the thickness of the finishing coat.

Repairing a chipped corner

When part of the external corner of a plastered wall has broken away to show the brickwork behind, you can rebuild it with either one- or two-coat plaster. Use a 100mm (4in) wide board as a guide to get the corner straight.

With a bolster (▷), cut the plaster back from the damaged edge and reveal about 100mm (4in) of the brickwork.

For two-coat plaster, place the guide board against the old plaster work, set back about 3mm (1/8in) from the surface of the plaster on the other side of the corner (1). Fix the board to the brickwork temporarily with masonry nails through the mortar joints, placing them well away from the corner.

Mix up the undercoat plaster, wet the brickwork and edge of the old plaster, then fill the one side of the corner flush with the edge of the board but not the wall (2). Scratch-key the new plaster with the trowel.

When the plaster is stiff remove the board, pulling it straight from the wall to prevent the new plaster breaking away. The exposed edge represents the finished surface, so scrape it back about 3mm (1/8in) with the trowel and straight edge (3) to allow for the top coat.

For such a job a professional would simply hold the board over the new repair and fill the second side of the corner immediately. But this leaves only one hand to lift and apply the plaster, a difficult trick for the amateur. An easier, though slower, method is to let the new plaster harden, then nail the board through it before applying and keying fresh plaster as before (4). Or, if the new plaster is set hard, you can use the scraped edge as a guide.

Let the undercoat set, then nail the board to the wall as before, but this time set it flush with the corner and level off with finishing plaster. Dampen the undercoat if necessary, to help the top coat to stick.

When both sides are firm, polish the new plaster with a wet trowel, rounding over the sharp edge slightly, then leave it to dry out.

If you choose to carry out the repair with a one-coat plaster you must set the board flush with the corner before applying the material.

SEE ALSO

Details for: ▷
Preparing plaster 30-31
Preparing the background 84

1 Plastering sequence
Divide the area into manageable portions and apply the plaster in the sequence shown.

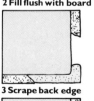

1 Set board back

2 Fill flush with board

3 Scrape back edge

4 Fill second side

SEE ALSO

◁ Details for:
Preparing plaster	30-31
Taping joints	82
Types of plaster	83
Switching off	134

2 Cut an opening

3 Nail in noggings

4 Nail in battens

PATCHING A PLASTERBOARD CEILING

A misplaced foot in the attic, a roof leak not attended to, a leaking water pipe – any of these can cause damage to a ceiling. Fortunately the damage is usually of a localized kind that can be simply patch-repaired.

Before starting work turn off the electricity supply at the mains (◁). The next job is to check the direction in which the ceiling joists run and whether there is any electrical wiring close by the damaged area. If the damaged ceiling is below a floor such an inspection can usually be carried out from above, by raising a floorboard. Alternatively knock an inspection hole through the centre of the damage with a hammer. You will find that it is possible to look along the void with the help of a torch and a mirror (1).

I Use a mirror and torch to inspect a void

Close round the damaged area, mark out a square or rectangle on the ceiling. Cut away an area of the plasterboard slightly larger than the damage, working up to the sides of the nearest joists (2). Use a padsaw or, if there is wiring nearby, a craft knife which will just penetrate the thickness of the plasterboard.

Cut and skew-nail 50mm (2in) noggings between the joists at the ends of the cut-out, with half of their thickness projecting beyond the cut edges of the plasterboard (3).

Nail 50 x 25mm (2 x 1in) softwood battens to the sides of the joists flush with their bottom edges (4).

Cut your plasterboard patch to fit the opening with a 3mm (⅛in) gap all round, and nail it to the noggings and battens. Fill and tape over the joints to give a flush surface (◁).

Minor damage

Repair minor damage to plasterboard as when preparing to decorate (◁).

REPAIRING LATH AND PLASTER

When the plaster of a lath and plaster wall deteriorates with age it can lose its grip on the laths because its key has gone. This may show itself as a swelling, perhaps with some cracking. It will give a hollow sound if tapped and will yield when it is pressed. The loose plaster should be replaced.

Repairing a wall

Cut out the plaster with a bolster and hammer (1). If the laths are sound you can replaster over them. Dampen the wooden laths and plaster edges (2) round the hole and apply a one-coat plaster with a plasterer's trowel, pressing it firmly between the laths as you coat them (3). Build up the coating flush with the surrounding plaster and level it with a rule. Let the plaster stiffen and smooth it with a damp sponge and a trowel. Alternatively, apply it in two coats. Scratch-key the first coat and let it set (4), then apply the second and finish as before.

For large repairs use two coats of pre-mixed lightweight bonding undercoat or metal-lathing plaster followed by a finishing plaster. For a small patch repair use a cellulose filler, pressing it on and between the laths (◁).

If laths are damaged cut them out and replace them, or cover the studs with plasterboard and finish with plaster. When using plasterboard nail it in the opening with the grey side towards you.

I Cut away loose or damaged plaster

2 Dampen edges of old sound plaster

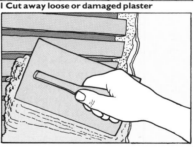

3 Apply plaster pressing it well between laths

4 Scratch key the undercoat

Repairing a ceiling

A water leak above a lath and plaster ceiling will cause localized damage to the plaster. Repair the ceiling with metal-lathing plaster, finishing with a top-coat gypsum plaster (◁).

Carefully cut back the plaster to sound material. Dampen the background and apply the undercoat (1). Don't build up a full thickness. Key the surface and let it set. Give the ceiling a second coat, scrape it back 3mm (⅛in) below the surface and lightly key it. When set, finish-coat the ceiling using a plasterer's trowel (2).

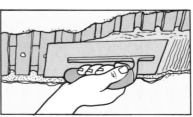

I Apply a thin first coat with firm pressure

2 Level top coat over keyed undercoat

CEILING CENTRE PIECES

Most Victorian and Edwardian houses of any quality had moulded cornices and centre pieces in at least some of their rooms. Though many of these disappeared in the modernism of recent decades, appreciation of them has now revived, and where they cannot be restored they are often replaced with reproductions.

Restoring originals

A ceiling centre piece, or 'rose', is a decorative plaster moulding placed at the centre of a ceiling and usually has a pendant light fitting hung from it. Old mouldings of this kind are often caked in accretions of ancient distemper that mask their fine detail. Restore them whenever possible by cleaning away the old paint build-up ($\triangleright$) and repairing any cracks and chipped details with filler.

Fitting a reproduction moulding

To replace original ceiling mouldings that are past repair or have been removed, there are some excellent reproduction mouldings made from fibrous plaster and available in a range of styles and sizes.

Prepare to fit such a reproduction by first carefully chipping away the old moulding, if present, with a hammer and chisel back to the ceiling plaster. Make good the surface with plaster.

If there is already a light fitting in place on the ceiling, turn off the power supply at the mains ($\triangleright$) and remove the whole fitting. If the ceiling is bare, find its centre by means of strings stretched across between diagonally opposite corners. The point where the strings cross is the centre. Mark the point and drill a hole there for the lighting cable.

If the new moulding itself lacks a hole for the lighting cable, drill one through its centre.

Apply a commercial plaster adhesive to the back of the moulding and press it firmly into place after first passing the cable through both holes. On a flat ceiling the suction of the adhesive should be enough, but if you are in any doubt use hired screw props.

The larger types of moulding should have the additional support of brass screws driven into the joists, the screw heads then being covered with filler.

Wipe away surplus adhesive from round the edges of the moulding with a damp brush or sponge.

When the adhesive is set, attach the light fitting. Longer screws will now be needed to secure it.

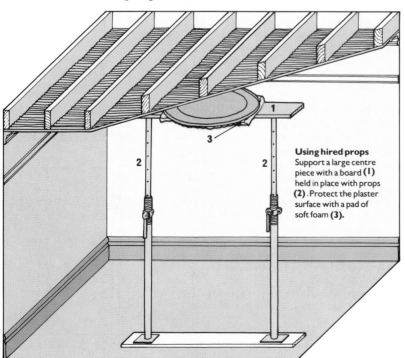

Using hired props
Support a large centre piece with a board (1) held in place with props (2). Protect the plaster surface with a pad of soft foam (3).

REPAIRING MOULDED CEILINGS

Sagging plaster on a traditional moulded ceiling can, if it is left unchecked, develop into an expensive repair job requiring the services of a professional. But if part of the plaster has broken away from its lath background, yet is otherwise intact, it can be re-fixed and prevented from collapsing.

Screw repair

Lift and support the sagging portion of the ceiling with wide boards propped in place with lengths of timber or hired screw props.

Drive countersunk plated screws fitted with galvanized or plated washers through the plaster and into the ceiling joists. The washers should be about 25mm (1in) in diameter and the fixings should be spaced about 300mm (12in) apart. They will bed themselves down into the plaster and can then be concealed with filler.

Plaster repair

A laborious but more substantial repair to a sagging ceiling can be made by using plaster of Paris to bond the plaster back to the laths.

Prop up the ceiling as for the screw repair, then lift the floorboards in the room above – this is not usually necessary in an attic – so that you can get at the back of the ceiling.

Thoroughly brush and vacuum-clean all loose material, dust and dirt away. If the groundwork is not clean the plaster of Paris will not hold.

Liberally soak the back of the ceiling with clean water, then mix the plaster of Paris to a creamy consistency and spread it quickly over the whole of the damaged area, covering both the laths and the plaster (1).

Plaster of Paris dries very quickly, but leave the props in place until it has set quite hard.

1 Spread plaster over laths and old plaster

SEE ALSO

Details for: $\triangleright$
Cleaning moulding	31
Switching off	134
Lighting	160-161

DOORS: FITTING AND HANGING

SEE ALSO

◁ Details for:	
Fitting locks	97
Draught excluders	110-111

Whatever the style of door you wish to fit, the procedure is the same, though minor differences between some external doors may show themselves. Two good-quality 100mm (4in) butt hinges are enough to support a standard door, but if you are hanging a heavy hardwood one you should add a third, central hinge.

All doors are fairly heavy, and as it is necessary to try a door in its frame several times to get the fit right you will find that the job goes much more quickly and easily if you have a helper working with you.

Fitting a door

Before attaching the hinges to a new door make sure that it fits nicely into its frame. It should have a clearance of 2mm (1/16in) at the top and sides and should clear the floor by at least 6mm (1/4in). As much as 12mm (1/2in) may be required for a carpeted floor.

Measure the height and width of the door opening and the depth of the rebate in the door frame into which the door must fit. Choose a door of the right thickness and, if you cannot get one that will fit the opening exactly, one which is large enough to be cut down.

Cutting to size

Some doors are supplied with 'horns', extensions to their stiles which protect the corners while the doors are in storage. Cut these off with a saw **(1)** before starting to trim the door to size.

Transfer the measurements from the frame to the door, making necessary allowance for the clearances all round. To reduce the width of the door stand it on edge with its latch stile upwards while it is steadied in a portable vice. Plane the stile down to the marked line, working only on the one side if a small amount is to be taken off. If a lot is to be removed, take some off each side. This is especially important with panel doors to preserve the symmetry.

If you need to take off more than 6mm (1/4in) to reduce the height of the door, remove it with a saw and finish off with a plane. Otherwise plane the waste off **(2)** . The plane must be sharp to deal with the end grain of the stiles. Work from each corner towards the centre to avoid 'chipping out' the corners.

Try the door in the frame, supporting it on shallow wedges **(3)** . If it still doesn't fit take it down and remove more wood where appropriate.

1 Saw off horns

2 Plane to size

3 Wedge the door

Fitting hinges

The upper hinge is set about 175mm (7in) from the door's top edge and the lower one about 250mm (10in) from the bottom. They are cut equally into the stile and door frame. Wedge the door in its opening and, with the wedges tapped in to raise it to the right floor clearance, mark the positions of the hinges on both the door and frame.

Stand the door on edge, the hinge stile uppermost, open a hinge and, with its knuckle projecting from the edge of the door, align it with the marks and draw round the flap with a pencil **(1)**. Set a marking gauge to match the thickness of the flap and mark the depth of the housing. With a chisel make a series of shallow cuts across the grain **(2)** and pare out the waste to the scored line. Repeat the procedure with the second hinge, then, using the flaps as guides, drill pilot holes for the screws and fix both hinges into their housings.

Wedge the door in the open position, aligning the free hinge flaps with the marks on the door frame. Make sure that the knuckles of the hinges are parallel with the frame, then trace the housings on the frame **(3)** and cut them out as you did the others.

Adjusting and aligning

Hang the door with one screw holding each hinge and see if it closes smoothly. If the latch stile rubs on the frame you may have to make one or both housings slightly deeper. If the door strains against the hinges it is what is called 'hinge bound'. In this case insert thin cardboard beneath the hinge flaps to pack them out. When the door finally opens and closes properly drive in the rest of the screws.

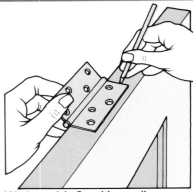

1 Mark round the flap with a pencil

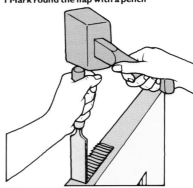

2 Cut across the grain with a chisel

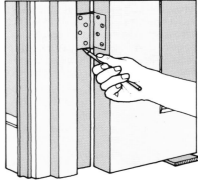

3 Mark the size of the flap on the frame

MEASUREMENTS

A door that fits well will open and close freely and look symmetrical in the frame. Use the figures given as a guide for trimming the door and setting out the position of the hinges.

3mm (1/8in) clearance at top and sides
Upper hinge 175mm (7in) from the top

Lower hinge 250mm (10in) from the bottom
6 to 12mm (1/4 to 1/2in) gap at the bottom

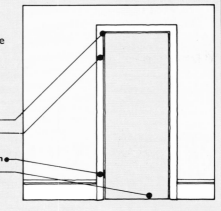

Rising butt hinges

Rising butt hinges lift a door as it is opened and are fitted to prevent it dragging on thick pile carpet.

They are made in two parts: a flap, with a fixed pin, which is screwed to the door frame, and another, with a single knuckle, which is fixed to the door, the knuckle sliding over the pin.

Rising butt hinges can be fixed only one way up, and are therefore made specifically for left- or right-hand opening. The countersunk screwholes in the fixed pin flap indicate the side to which it is made to be fitted.

Fitting

Trim the door and mark the hinge positions (See opposite), but before fitting the hinges plane a shallow bevel at the top outer corner of the hinge stile so that it will clear the frame as it opens. As the stile runs through to the top of the door, plane from the outer corner towards the centre to avoid splitting the wood. The top strip of the door stop will mask the bevel when the door is closed.

Fit the hinges to the door and the frame, then lower the door on to the hinge pins, taking care not to damage the architrave above the opening.

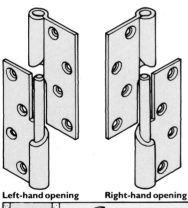

Left-hand opening   **Right-hand opening**

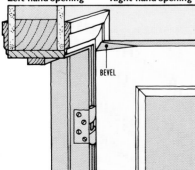

Plane a shallow bevel to clear the door frame

Weatherproofing a door

Fitting a weatherboard

A weatherboard is a special moulding fitted to the bottom of an outer door to shed rainwater away from the threshold. To fit one measure the width of the opening between the door stops and cut the moulding to fit, cutting one end at a slight angle where it meets the door frame on the latch side. This will allow it to clear the frame as the door swings open.

Make a weatherproof seal between the moulding and the door. On an unfinished door use screws and a waterproof adhesive to attach the moulding. On a pre-painted one apply a thick coat of primer to the back surface of the moulding and screw it into place while the primer is still wet. Fill or plug all screwholes and thoroughly prime and finish the surfaces.

Allowing for a weather bar

Though a rebate cut into the head and side posts of an outer door frame provides a seal round an inward opening door, a rebate cut into the sill at the foot of the door would merely encourage water to flow into the house.

Unless protected by a porch, a door in an exposed position needs to be fitted with a weather bar to prevent rainwater running underneath.

This is a metal or plastic strip which is set into the step or sill. If you are putting in a new door and wish to fit a weather bar, use a router or power saw to cut a rebate across the bottom of the door in order to clear the bar.

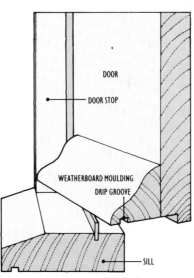

DOOR
DOOR STOP
WEATHERBOARD MOULDING
DRIP GROOVE
SILL

Door fitted with a weather board

ADJUSTING BUTT HINGES

Perhaps you have a door catching on a bump in the floor as it opens. You can, of course, fit rising butt hinges, but the problem can be overcome by resetting the lower hinge so that its knuckle projects slightly more than the top one. The door will still hang vertically when closed, but as it opens the out-of-line pins will throw it upwards so that the bottom edge will clear the bump.

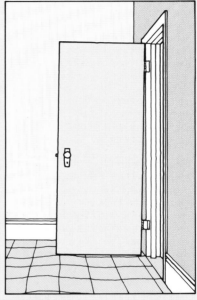

Resetting the hinge
You may have to reset both hinges to the new angle to prevent binding.

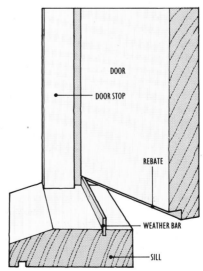

DOOR
DOOR STOP
REBATE
WEATHER BAR
SILL

Sill fitted with weather bar

BUYING GLASS

You can buy most types of glass from your local stockists. They will advise you on thickness, will cut the glass to your measurements and will also deliver larger sizes and amounts.

The thickness of glass, once expressed by weight, is now measured in millimetres. If you are replacing old glass, measure its thickness to the nearest millimetre, and, if it is slightly less than any available size, buy the next one up for the sake of safety.

Though there are no regulations about the thickness of glass, for safety reasons you should comply with the recommendations set out in the British Standard Code of Practice. The required thickness of glass depends on the area of the pane, its exposure to wind pressure and the vulnerability of its situation – e.g., in a window overlooking a play area. Tell your supplier what the glass is needed for – a door, a window, a shower screen etc. – to ensure that you get the right type.

Measuring up

Measure the height and width of the opening to the inside of the frame rebate, taking the measurement from two points for each dimension. Also check that the diagonals are the same length. If they differ markedly and show that the frame is out of square, or if it is otherwise awkwardly shaped, make a cardboard template of it. In any case deduct 3mm (1/8in) from the height and width to allow a fitting tolerance. When making a template allow for the thickness of the glass cutter.

When you order patterned glass, specify the height before the width. This will ensure that the glass is cut with the pattern running in the right direction. (Alternatively take a piece of the old glass with you, which you may need to do in any case to match the pattern.)

For an asymmetrically shaped pane of patterned glass supply a template, and mark the surface that represents the outside face of the pane. This ensures that the glass will be cut with its smooth surface outside and will be easier to keep clean.

WINDOWS: WORKING WITH GLASS

You should always carry glass on its edge. You can hold it with pads of folded rag or paper when gripping the top and bottom edge, though it is always better to wear stout work gloves.

Protect your hands with gloves and your eyes with goggles when removing broken glass from a frame. Wrap up the broken pieces in thick layers of newspaper if you have to dispose of it in your dustbin, but before doing so check with your local glazier, who may be willing to take the pieces from you and add them to his off-cuts, which are usually sent back to the manufacturers for recycling.

Basic glass-cutting

It is usually unnecessary to cut one's own glass as glass merchants are willing to do it, but you may have some surplus glass and wish to cut it yourself. Diamond-tipped cutters are available, but the type with a steel wheel is cheaper and quite adequate for normal use.

Cutting glass successfully is largely a matter of practice and confidence. If you have not done it before, you should make a few practice cuts on waste pieces of glass and get used to the 'feel' before doing a real job.

Lay the glass on a flat surface covered with a blanket. Patterned glass is placed patterned side downwards and cut on its smooth side. Clean the surface with methylated spirit.

Set a T-square the required distance from one edge, using a steel measuring tape **(1)**. If you are working on a small piece of glass or do not have a T-square, mark the glass on opposing edges with a felt-tipped pen or wax pencil and use a straight edge to join up the marks and guide the cutter.

Lubricate the steel wheel of the glass cutter by dipping it in thin oil or paraffin. Hold the cutter between middle finger and forefinger **(2)** and draw it along the guide in one continuous stroke. Use even pressure throughout and run the cut off the end. Slide the glass forward over the edge of the table **(3)** and tap the underside of the scored line with the back of the cutter to initiate the cut. Grip the glass on each side of the score line with gloved hands **(4)**, lift the glass and snap it in two. Alternatively, place a pencil under each end of the scored line and apply even pressure on both sides until the glass snaps.

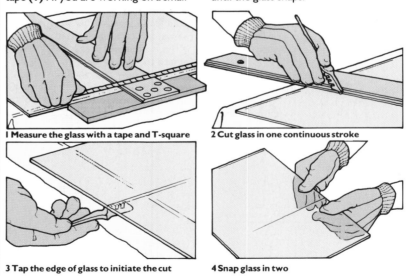

1 Measure the glass with a tape and T-square

2 Cut glass in one continuous stroke

3 Tap the edge of glass to initiate the cut

4 Snap glass in two

Cutting a thin strip of glass

A pane of glass may be slightly oversize due to inaccurate measuring or cutting or if the frame is distorted.

Remove a very thin strip of glass with the aid of a pair of pliers. Nibble away the edge by gripping the waste with the tip of the jaws close to the scored line.

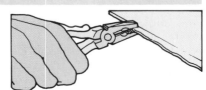

Nibble away a thin strip with pliers

CUTTING CIRCLES AND DRILLING HOLES

Fitting items such as an extractor fan may involve cutting a circular hole in a pane of glass. This can be done with a beam compass glass cutter.

Cutting a circle in glass

Locate the suction pad of the central pivot on the glass, set the cutting head at the required distance from it and score the circle round the pivot with even pressure (**1**). Now score another smaller circle inside the first one. Remove the cutter and score across the inner circle with straight cuts, then make radial cuts about 25mm (1in) apart in the outer rim. Tap the centre of the scored area from underneath to open up the cuts (**2**) and remove the inner area. Next tap the outer rim and nibble away the waste with pliers if necessary.

To cut a disc of glass, scribe a circle with the beam compass cutter, then score tangential lines from the circle to the edges of the glass (**3**). Tap the underside of each cut, starting close to the edge of the glass.

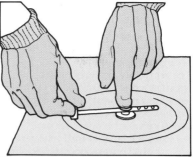

1 Score the circle with even pressure

SEE ALSO

Details for: ▷

Removing glass 94

Smoothing the edges of cut glass

You can grind down the cut edges of glass to a smooth finish using wet-and-dry paper wrapped round a wooden block. It is fairly slow work, though just how slow will depend on the degree of finish you require.

Start off with medium-grit paper wrapped tightly round the wood block. Dip the block complete with paper in water and begin by removing the 'arris' or sharp angle of the edge with the block held at 45 degrees to the edge. Keep the abrasive paper wet.

Follow this by rubbing down the vertical edge to remove any nibs and go on to smooth it to a uniform finish. Repeat the process with progressively finer grit papers. A final polish can be given with a wet wooden block coated with pumice powder.

2 Tap the centre of the scored area

3 Cutting a disc
Scribe the circle then make tangential cuts from it to the edge of the glass.

Using a glass cutting template

Semi-circular windows and glazed openings in Georgian-style doors are formed with segments of glass set between radiating glazing-bars.

Windows with semi-circular openings and modern reproductions of period doors can be glazed with ready-shaped panes available from joinery suppliers, but for an old glazed door you will probably have to cut your own. The pieces are segments of a large circle, beyond the scope of the beam compass glass cutter (See above), so you will have to make a card template.

Remove the broken glass, clean up the rebate, then tape a sheet of paper over the opening and, using a wax crayon, take a rubbing of the shape (**1**). Remove the paper pattern and tape it to a sheet of thick cardboard. Following the lines on the paper pattern, cut the card to shape with a sharp knife, but make the template about 2mm (1/16in) smaller all round, also allowing for the thickness of the glass cutter. The straight cuts can be aided by a straightedge, but you will have to make curved ones freehand. A slightly wavy line will be hidden by the frame's rebate.

Fix the template to the glass with double-sided tape, score round it with the glass cutter (**2**), running all cuts to the edge, and snap the glass in the normal way.

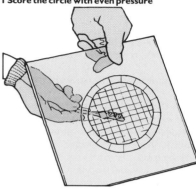

1 Take a rubbing of the shape with a crayon

● **Plastic glazing**
As an alternative to glass for awkward shapes you can use acrylic plastic, cutting it with a fret saw.

2 Cut round the template with even pressure

Drilling a hole in glass

There are special spear-point drilling bits available for drilling holes in glass. As glass should not be drilled at high speed, use a hand-held wheel brace.

Mark the position for the hole, no closer than 25mm (1in) to the edge of the glass, using a felt-tipped pen or a wax pencil. On mirror glass work from the back, or coated surface.

Place the tip of the bit on the marked centre and, with light pressure, twist it back and forth so that it grinds a small pit and no longer slides off the centre. Form a small ring with putty round the pit and fill the inner well with a lubricant such as white spirit, paraffin or water.

Work the drill at a steady speed and with even pressure. Too much pressure can chip the glass.

When the tip of the drill just breaks through, turn the glass over and drill from the other side. If you try to drill straight through from one side you risk breaking out the surface round the hole.

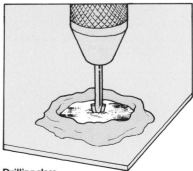

Drilling glass
Always run the drill in a lubricant to reduce friction.

REPAIRING A BROKEN WINDOW

A cracked window pane, even when no glass is missing from it, is a safety hazard and a security risk. If the window is actually lacking some of its glass, it is no longer weatherproof and should be repaired promptly.

SEE ALSO

◁ Details for:
Scaffold tower	20
Buying glass	92
Painting windows	50

Temporary repairs

For temporary protection from the weather a sheet of polythene can be taped or pinned with battens over the outside of the window frame, and a merely cracked window can be temporarily repaired with a special clear self-adhesive waterproof tape. Applied to the outside, the tape gives an almost invisible repair.

Safety with glass

The method you use to remove the glass from a broken window will to some extent depend on conditions. If the window is not at ground level, it may be safest to take out the complete sash to do the job. But a fixed window will have to be repaired on the spot, wherever it is.

Large pieces of glass should be handled by two people and the work done from a tower rather than ladders (◁). Avoid working in windy weather and always wear protective gloves for this work.

Weathered putty fixing

Wooden bead fixing
Unscrew beading and scrape out mastic. Bed new glass in fresh mastic and replace beading.

Repairing glass in wooden frames

In wooden window frames the glass is set into a rebate cut in the frame's moulding and bedded in linseed oil putty. Small wedge-shaped nails known as sprigs are also used to hold the glass in place. In some wooden-framed windows a screwed-on beading is used to hold the pane instead of the 'weathered' (outer) putty; this type of frame may have its rebate cut on the inside instead of the outside.

Removing the glass

If the glass in a window pane has shattered, leaving jagged pieces set in the putty, grip each piece separately (wearing gloves) and try to work it loose (1). It is safest always to start working from the top of the frame.

Old dry putty will usually give way, but if it is strong it will have to be cut away with a glazier's hacking knife and a hammer (2). Alternatively, the job can be done with a blunt wood chisel. Work along the rebate to remove the putty and glass. Pull out the sprigs with pincers (3).

If the glass is cracked but not holed, run a glass cutter round the perimeter of the pane about 25mm (1in) from the frame, scoring the glass (4). Fasten strips of self-adhesive tape across the cracks and the scored lines (5) and tap each piece of glass so that it breaks free and is held only by the tape. Carefully peel the inner pieces away, then remove the pieces round the edges and the putty as described above.

Clean out the rebate and seal it with a wood primer. Measure the height and width of the opening to the inside of the rebates and have your new glass cut 3mm (1/8in) smaller on each dimension (◁) to give a fitting tolerance.

Fitting new glass

Purchase new sprigs and enough putty for the frame. Your glass supplier should be able to advise you on this but, as a guide, 500g (1lb) of putty will fill an average-sized rebate of about 4m (13ft) in length.

Knead a palm-sized ball of putty to an even consistency. Very sticky putty is difficult to work with so wrap it briefly in newspaper to absorb some of the oil. You can soften putty that is too stiff by adding linseed oil to it.

Press a fairly thin, continuous band of putty into the rebate all round with your thumb. This is the bedding putty. Lower the edge of the new pane on to the bottom rebate, then press it into the putty. Press close to the edges only, squeezing the putty to leave a bed about 2mm (1/16in) behind the glass, then secure the glass with sprigs about 200mm (8in) apart. Tap them into the frame with the edge of a firmer chisel so that they lie flat with the surface of the glass (1). Trim the surplus putty from the back of the glass with a putty knife.

Apply more putty to the rebate all round, outside the glass. With a putty knife (2), work the putty to a smooth finish at an angle of 45 degrees. Wet the knife with water to prevent it dragging and make neat mitres in the putty at the corners. Let the putty set and stiffen for about three weeks, then apply an oil-based undercoat paint. Before painting, clean any putty smears from the glass with methylated spirit. Let the paint lap the glass slightly to form a weather seal.

A self-adhesive plastic foam can be used instead of the bedding putty. Run it round the back of the rebate in a continuous strip, starting from a top corner, press the glass into place on the foam and secure it with sprigs. Then apply the weathered putty in the same way described above.

Alternatively, apply a strip of foam round the outside of the glass and cover it with a wooden beading, then paint.

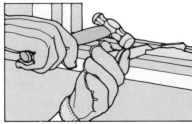

1 Work loose the broken glass

2 Cut away the old putty

3 Pull out the old sprigs

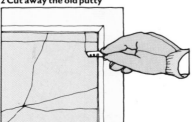

4 Score glass before removing a cracked pane

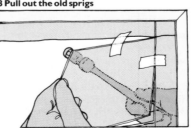

5 Tap the glass to break it free

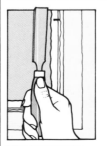

1 Tap in new sprigs

2 Shape the putty

RE-CORDING A SASH WINDOW

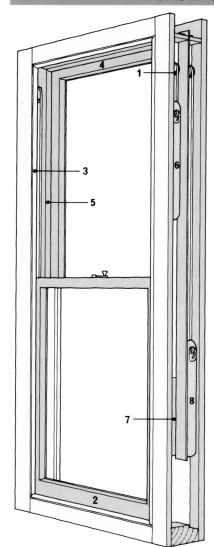

The workings of a double-hung sash window

1 Pulleys
2 Bottom sash
3 Staff bead
4 Top sash
5 Parting bead
6 Bottom sash weight
7 Pocket
8 Top sash weight

The sash cording from which the sashes are suspended will wear and in time will break. You should replace both cords even when only one has broken.

Waxed sash cording is normally sold in standard hanks, though some suppliers sell it by the metre. Each sash will require two lengths about three quarters the height of the window. Do not cut it to length beforehand.

Removing the sashes

Lower the sashes and cut through the cords with a knife to release the weights. Hold on to the cords and lower the weights as far as possible before letting them drop. Prise off the side staff beads from inside the frame, starting in the middle and bowing them to make their mitred ends spring out and avoid breakage.

Lean the inner sash forward and mark the ends of the cord grooves on the face of the sash stiles. Reposition the sash and carry the marks on to the pulley stiles **(1)**. The sash can now be pulled clear of the frame.

Carefully prise out the two parting beads from their grooves in the stiles. The top sash can then be removed, after marking the ends of the grooves as before. Place sashes safely aside.

To gain access to the weights take out the pocket pieces which were trapped by the parting bead and lift the weights out through the openings. Hanging pieces of thin wood known as parting strips may be fitted inside the box stiles to keep the pairs of weights apart. Push these aside to reach the outer weights.

Remove the old cording from the weights and sashes and clean them up ready for the new sash cords.

Fitting the sashes

The top sash is fitted first, but not before all of the sash cords and weights are in place. Clean away any build-up of paint from the pulleys. Tie a length of fine string to one end of the sash cord. Weight the other end of the string with small nuts or a piece of chain. Thread the weight – known as a mouse – over a pulley **(2)** and pull the string through the pocket opening until the cord is pulled through. Attach the end of the cord to a weight with a special knot (See below left).

Use the sash marks to measure the length of cord required. Pull on the cord to hoist the weight up to the pulley. Then let it drop back about 100mm (4in). Hold it temporarily in this position with a nail driven into the stile just below the pulley. Cut the cord level with the mark on the pulley stile **(3)**.

Repeat this procedure for the cord on the other side, and then for the bottom sash.

Replace the top sash on the sill, removing the temporary nails in turn. Lean the sash forward, locate the cords into the grooves in the stiles and nail them in place using three or four 25mm (1in) round wire nails. Nail only the bottom 150mm (6in), not all the way up **(4)**. Lift the sash to check that the weights do not touch bottom.

Replace the pocket pieces and pin the parting beads in their grooves. Fit the bottom sash in the same way. Finally replace the staff beads; take care to position them accurately.

HOW TO TIE A SASH WEIGHT KNOT

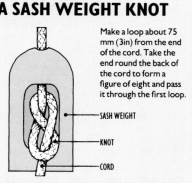

Make a loop about 75 mm (3in) from the end of the cord. Take the end round the back of the cord to form a figure of eight and pass it through the first loop.

SASH WEIGHT

KNOT

CORD

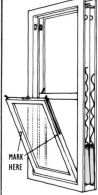

1 Mark cord grooves

MARK HERE

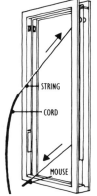

2 Pull cord through

STRING

CORD

MOUSE

3 Cut cords at mark

CUT HERE

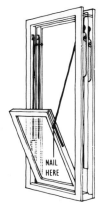

4 Nail cord to sash

NAIL HERE

SPIRAL BALANCES

SEE ALSO

◁ Details for:

Parting bead	95
Removing sashes	95

Instead of cords and counterweights, modern sash windows use spiral balances which are mounted on the faces of the frame stiles, eliminating the need for traditional box sections. The balances are made to order to match the size and weight of individual glazed sashes and can be ordered through builders' merchants or by post from the makers using an order form.

Spiral balance components

Each balance consists of a torsion spring and a spiral rod housed in a tube. The top end is fixed to the stile and the inner spiral to the bottom of the sash. The complete unit can be housed in a groove in the sash stile or in the jamb of the frame.

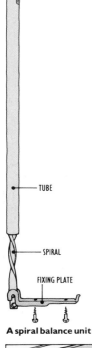

TUBE

SPIRAL

FIXING PLATE

A spiral balance unit

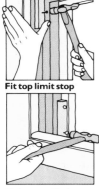

Fit top limit stop

Fit bottom limit stop

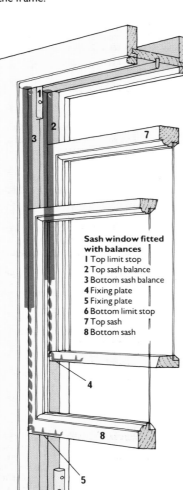

Sash window fitted with balances
1 Top limit stop
2 Top sash balance
3 Bottom sash balance
4 Fixing plate
5 Fixing plate
6 Bottom limit stop
7 Top sash
8 Bottom sash

Fitting the balances

You can fit spiral sash balances to replace the weights in a traditionally constructed sash window.

Remove the sashes and weigh them on your bathroom scales. Place your order, giving the weight of each sash and its height and width, also the height of the frame. Refit the sashes temporarily until the balances arrive, then take them out again and remove the pulleys.

Plug the holes and paint the stiles. Cut grooves, as specified by the manufacturers, in the stiles of each sash, to take the balances (**1**). Also cut a housing at each end of their bottom edges to receive the spiral rod fixing plates. Fit the plates with screws (**2**).

Sit the top sash in place, resting it on the sill, and fit the parting bead. Take the top pair of balances, which are shorter than those for the bottom sash, and locate each in its groove (**3**). Fix the top ends of the balance tubes to the frame stiles with the screw nails provided (**4**) and set the ends tight against the head.

Lift the sash to its full height and prop it with a length of wood. Hook the wire 'key', provided by the makers, into the hole in the end of each spiral rod and pull each one down about 150mm (6in). Keeping the tension on the spring, add three to five turns anti-clockwise (**5**). Locate the ends of the rods in the fixing plate and test the balance of the sash. If it drops add another turn on the springs until it is just held in position. Take care not to overwind the balances.

Fit the bottom sash in the same way, refitting the staff bead to hold it in place. Fit the stops that limit the full travel of the sashes in their respective tracks (See left).

RENOVATING SPIRAL BALANCES

In time the springs of spiral balances may weaken. Re-tension them by unhooking the spiral rods from the fixing plates, then turning the rods anti-clockwise once or twice.

The mechanisms can be serviced by releasing the tension and unwinding the rods from the tubes. Wipe them clean and apply a little thin oil, then rewind the rods back into the tubes and tension them as described above.

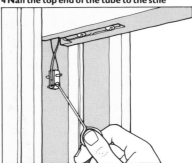

1 Cut a groove in the sash stiles

2 Fix the plates in their housings with screws

3 Fit the sash and locate the tube in its groove

4 Nail the top end of the tube to the stile

5 Tension the springs with the key provided

Fitting a mortise lock

Scribe a line centrally on the edge of the door with a marking gauge and use the lock body as a template to mark the top and bottom of the mortise (**1**). Choose a drill bit that matches the lock body thickness and drill out the majority of the waste.

Square up the edges of the mortise with a bevel-edged chisel (**2**) until the lock fits snugly in the slot. Mark around the edge of the faceplate with a knife (**3**), then chop a series of shallow cuts across the waste. Pare out the recess

until the faceplate is flush with the edge of the door.

Hold the lock against the face of the door and mark the centre of the keyhole with a bradawl (**4**). Clamp a block of scrap timber to the other side of the door over the keyhole position and drill right through on the centre mark: the block prevents the drill bit splintering the face of the door as it bursts through on the other side. Cut out the keyhole slot on both sides with a padsaw.

1 Mark the mortise   2 Chop out the waste   3 Mark the faceplate   4 Mark the keyhole

Screw the lock into its recess, check its operation; screw on the coverplate and then the escutcheons over each side of the hole (**5**). With the door closed, operate the bolt; it may incorporate a marking device to gauge the position of the striking plate on the

door frame. If it doesn't have a marking device, shoot the bolt fully open, push the door to, and draw round the bolt on the face of the frame (**6**).

Mark out and cut the mortise and recess for the striking plate as described for the lock (**7**).

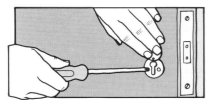  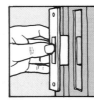

5 Screw on escutcheon to cover the keyhole   6 Mark bolt on frame   7 Fit striking plate

Fitting a cylinder rim lock

Tape the template provided with the lock to the door and mark then drill holes to accept the cylinder (**1**). They vary in size between models. Pass the cylinder into the hole from the outside and connect it to the mounting plate on the inside with machine screws (**2**).

Drill and insert the woodscrews to hold the plate to the door. Check the required length of the connecting bar, which projects through the plate and, if

necessary, cut it to the correct size with a hacksaw (**3**).

Mark and cut the recess in the door edge for the lock, and attach it to the door and mounting plate with screws (**4**). Mark the position of the lock on the frame and use the template to drill for staple fixing screws or stud. Hold the staple against the frame to mark its recess. Chop and pare out the recess then screw on the staple.

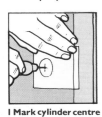 

1 Mark cylinder centre   2 Fit mounting plate   3 Cut connecting bar   4 Screw lock to door

FITTING RACK BOLTS

There are many strong bolts for securing a door from the inside, but the rack bolt can be fitted into the door edge: secure and unobtrusive. Fit them to front, back and side doors in addition to mortise and rim locks.

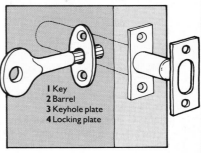

1 Key
2 Barrel
3 Keyhole plate
4 Locking plate

The components of a standard rack bolt

Drill a hole – usually 16mm (⅝in) in diameter – for the barrel of the bolt in the edge of the door. Use a try square to transfer the centre of the hole to the inside face of the door. Measure the keyhole and drill it with a 10mm (⅜in) bit. Insert the bolt (**1**).

With the key in position, mark the recess for the faceplate (**2**) then cut it out with a chisel. Screw the bolt and keyhole plate to the door. Operate the bolt to mark the frame, then drill a 16mm (⅝in) diameter hole to a depth that matches the length of the bolt. Fit the locking plate over the hole.

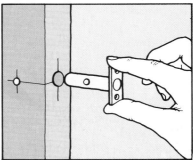

1 Drill holes for barrel and key then fit bolt

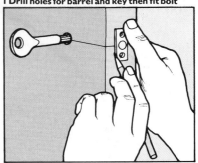

2 With the key holding bolt, mark faceplate

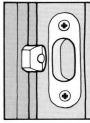

Fitting hinge bolts
Fit two bolts per door near the hinges. Drill hole in door edge for bolt and another in door frame. Recess the locking plate in frame.

Attaching a security chain
No special skills are needed to fit a chain, simply screw the fixing plates to the door and frame. Fit the chain just below the lock.

SECURING WINDOWS

SEE ALSO

◁ Details for:
Rack bolts 97

Windows are a common means of entry for burglars, so take particular care to ensure they're secured, especially those in vulnerable locations. There are special locks for both timber and metal windows: the best type for wooden frames are set in mortises, whereas locks for metal frames are more limited due to the necessity to cut threads in the material for the screw fixings.

How windows are locked

The way you lock a window depends on how it opens: sliding sashes, for instance, should be secured by locking the two frames together; casements, which open like doors, should be fastened to the outer frame or locked by rendering the catches and stays immovable. But whichever type of lock you choose, it makes sense to buy the best you can afford for the most vulnerable windows and to spend less on those which are difficult to reach.

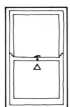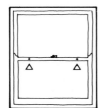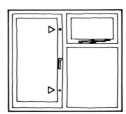

The best positions for window locks
The black dots in the illustrations above indicate where you should place bolts or locks.

Locks must be strong enough to resist forcing and they must be situated correctly for optimum security. For small windows, fit one lock as close to the centre as possible, but fit two locks spaced apart on large windows so that a thief cannot lever the opening edge and split the frame.

A window lock should be released by a removable key only. Some keys will open all locks of the same design (an advantage to some extent as you'll need to handle fewer keys – although a determined burglar may carry a range of standard keys). Other locks have several key variations.

Only fairly large windows can accommodate mortise-type locks, so many are surface-mounted. They're perfectly adequate, so long as the mechanism covers the screws, or where plugs are provided to seal them off once the lock is fixed. If neither is the case, drill out the centre of the screws once fitted so that they cannot be withdrawn.

Fitting sash window locks

Installing dual screws
Cheap but effective, dual screws comprise a bolt which passes through both meeting rails so that the sashes are immobilized. There is little to see when the window is closed and they are simple to operate with a special key.

With the window closed and the standard catch engaged, drill through the inner meeting rail into the outer one. Tape the drill bit to gauge the depth. Slide the sashes apart and tap the two bolt-receiving devices into their respective holes. Close the window and insert the threaded bolt with the key until it is flush with the window frame. If necessary, saw the bolt to length.

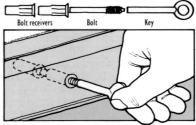

Bolt receivers   Bolt   Key

Turn a dual screw until it is flush with the frame

Using sash stops
When the bolt is withdrawn with a key, a sash stop fitted to each side of a window allows it to be opened slightly for ventilation. Apart from deterring a burglar, they will also prevent children from opening the window any further.

To fit the stop, drill a hole in the upper sash for the bolt and screw the faceplate over it. On close-fitting sashes, you will have to recess the faceplate. Screw the protective plate to the top edge of the lower sash.

Extract sash stop with key to secure window

Fitting a key-operated sash lock
A key-operated cylinder sash lock can be screwed to the outer frame at top and bottom, and drives a small bolt into a reinforced bolt hole. It's more obtrusive than other sash locks.

Locking casement windows

Fitting rack bolts
On a large casement window, fit a rack bolt as described for doors (◁).

Fitting a casement lock
A locking bolt can be attached to wooden window frames: the bolt is engaged by a simple catch but can only be released by a key.

With the lock body screwed to the opening part of the window, mark and cut a small mortise in the frame for the bolt. Screw on the coverplate.

For metal windows a similar device is a clamp which, fixed to the opening part of the casement, shoots a bolt that hooks onto the fixed frame.

Another metal casement lock fits within the metal section of the casement and a key-operated device expands the lock to secure the casement and frame together.

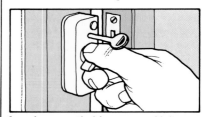

A good casement lock has a removable key

Locking the cockspur handle
The cockspur handle, which secures the opening edge of the casement to the fixed frame, can be locked using a device that you screw to the frame below the handle: when a key is turned, a bolt is extended to prevent the cockspur from moving. Lockable handles can be substituted for the standard handle; a key locks the handle, which can be fixed so the window is ajar for ventilation.

The extended bolt stops handle turning

Securing pivot windows

If a pivot window is not supplied with an integral lock, use the rack bolts or locks recommended for casement windows. Alternatively, fit the screw-mounted lock suggested for a fanlight window.

Creaking in stairs begins when joints become loose and start rubbing. The slight gaps that allow this movement are often the result of the timber having shrunk, though general wear and tear will also contribute to the problem.

The method you choose for dealing with it will depend on whether you have access to the backs of the treads. A better repair can be carried out from underneath, but if that means cutting into the plaster of a soffit it will be more convenient to work from above.

Working from underneath

If it is possible to get to the underside of the stairs, have someone walk slowly up the steps, counting them out loud, and from your position under the stair follow the counting, noting any loose steps and marking them with chalk. Have your assistant work the loose treads while you inspect them to discover the source of the creaking.

Loose housing joint
If the tread or the riser is loose in its housing in the string it may be because the original wedge has become loose. Remove the wedge (1), clean it up, apply PVA woodworking adhesive and re-wedge the joint (2). If the wedge has got damaged while being removed make a new one out of hardwood.

Loose blocks
Check the triangular blocks that fit in the angle between the tread and the riser. If the adhesive has failed on one face remove the blocks, clean off the old adhesive and reglue them in place. Before replacing the blocks slightly prise open the shoulder of the tongue-and-groove joint with a chisel and apply new adhesive to it (3), then pull the joint up tight using 38mm (1½in) countersunk screws set below the surface.

Rub-joint the blocks into the angle (4). You can use panel pins to hold them while the adhesive sets.

Try to avoid treading on the repaired steps before the adhesive has set.

If some of the blocks are missing you can make new ones from lengths of 50 x 50mm (2 x 2in) softwood. Set the wood upright in a vice and, sawing across the diagonal of the end, cut down the grain for about 175mm (7in). Remove the wood from the vice and holding it on a bench hook, or by repositioning it if you are using a Workmate bench, saw off 75mm (3in) long triangular blocks.

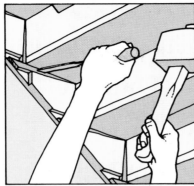
1 Prise out the old wedge with a chisel

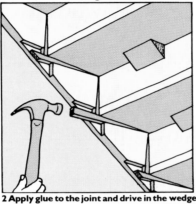
2 Apply glue to the joint and drive in the wedge

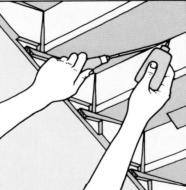
3 Prise open the joint and inject adhesive

4 Rub-joint the glued blocks into the angle

Working from the top

To identify the problem areas walk slowly up the stairs – which should first be stripped of any covering – and stop at the creaking step, then shift your weight to and fro on the offending tread to discover which part is moving. It is best to do this late at night or early in the morning, when the house is quiet and small noises will not be missed.

Nosing – loose joint
To cure looseness in a tongue-and-groove joint between the riser and the nosing of a tread drill clearance holes for 38mm (1½in) countersunk screws in the tread, centring on the thickness of the riser (1). Inject fresh PVA woodworking adhesive into the holes and work the joint a little so as to encourage the adhesive to spread into it, then pull the joint up tight with the screws. If the screws are not to be concealed by stair carpet you should counterbore the screw heads and plug the holes with matching wood.

Riser – loose joint
A loose joint at the back of the tread cannot be easily repaired from above. You can try working water-thinned PVA woodworking adhesive into the joint but you cannot use screws.

One form of reinforcement which may be of help is made by gluing a section of 12 x 12mm (½ x ½in) triangular moulding into the angle between the tread and the riser (2), but this is possible only if it does not leave the remaining width of the tread below the Building Regulation specification for treads of 220mm (8¾in). Cut the moulding slightly shorter than the width of the stair carpet, unless the carpet is of full stair width or a similar moulding is fitted on all of the steps.

1 Screw joint tight

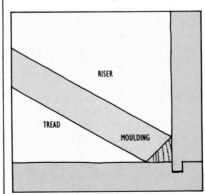

RISER

TREAD

MOULDING

2 Glue a triangular moulding into the angle

REPAIRING WORN STAIRS

Old softwood stairs which have not had the protection of a floor covering will eventually become very worn. Worn treads and nosings are dangerous, and should be repaired promptly. If all the treads are badly worn you should have the stair replaced by a builder.

Treads fitted between closed strings can be replaced only from below. If the soffit of the stair is enclosed with lath and plaster, or with plasterboard, you will have to cut an opening to reach the worn-out tread. Where a central bearer has been used in the construction of the stair the work involved in the repair can be extensive, and in such a case you should seek the advice of a professional builder.

Renewing a nosing

Wear on the nosing of a tread is usually concentrated round the centre, and you can repair it without having to renew the whole tread.

Mark three cutting lines just outside the worn area, one set parallel with the edge of the nosing and the other two at right angles to it **(1)**.

Adjust the blade depth of a portable powered circular saw to the thickness of the tread. Pin a batten the required distance from, and parallel to, the long cutting line to guide the edge of the saw's baseplate.

Cutting out
Position the saw, switch it on, then make the cut by lowering the blade into the wood **(2)**. Try not to overrun the short end lines. The cut made, remove the guide batten. Hand saw the end lines, making cuts at 45 degrees to the face of the tread and taking care not to go beyond the first saw cut. Make these cuts with a tenon saw **(3)**.

You will be left with uncut waste in the corners. Remove most of the cut waste with a chisel, working with the grain and taking care to avoid damaging the riser tongue and triangular reinforcing blocks. Pare away the waste from the uncut corners **(4)**.

Replacement
In the underside of a new section of nosing plane a groove to receive the tongue of the riser and cut its ends to 45 degrees. Check its fit in the opening, then apply PVA wood adhesive to all of the meeting surfaces and fix it in place. Cramp it down with a batten screwed at each end to the tread **(5)**. Place a packing strip of hardboard under the batten to concentrate the pressure, and a piece of polythene to prevent the hardboard sticking. Drill and insert 6mm (¼in) dowels into the edge of the nosing to reinforce the butt joint and, when the adhesive is set, plane and sand the repair flush. Refix any blocks that may have fallen off.

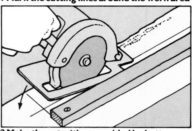
1 Mark the cutting lines around the worn area

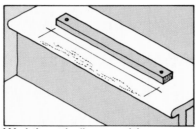
2 Make the cut with saw guided by batten

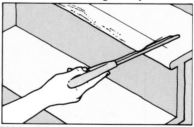
3 Make 45 degree cuts at each end

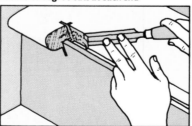
4 Pare away the waste from the corners

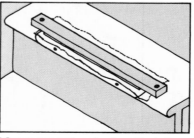
5 Cramp new section of nosing with a batten

REPLACING TREADS

Most stairs have tongue-and-groove joints between their risers and treads, though in some cases the tops of the risers are housed into the undersides of the treads and in other stairs simple butt joints are employed and secured with nails or screws.

You can determine which type of joint you are faced with by trying to pass a thin knife blade between the shoulders of the joint. It will help if you first remove any nails or screws. A butt joint will let the blade pass through, while a housed or a tongued and grooved one will not do so.

As the joints effectively lock the treads and risers together, those in contact with the damaged tread must be freed before the tread can be removed. A butt joint is relatively easy to take apart, whereas a housed or a tongue-and-groove joint will have to be cut.

Dismantling a butt joint
To take a butt joint apart first take out the nails or screws and, if adhesive has been used, give the tread a sharp tap to break the hardened adhesive, or prise it up with a chisel. In the same way remove the triangular glued blocks.

Cutting a tongue
Where the tongue of a riser is jointed into the underside of a tread you cut it working from the front of the stair, and where the riser's tongue is jointed into the top of the tread it must be cut from the rear **(1)**. If there is a scotia moulding fitted under the nosing try to prise it away first with a chisel.

Before cutting a tongue remove any screws, nails and glued reinforcement blocks, then drill a line of 3mm (⅛in) holes on the shoulders of the joint in which you can insert the blade of a padsaw **(2)**. Make a saw cut; when it is long enough, continue with a panel saw.

The method you will now use to remove the tread will depend on whether it is fitted between closed strings or has an open string at one end (See opposite).

1 Cut the tongue from the front or rear

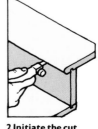
2 Initiate the cut with a padsaw

Closed string stair

Working from the underside of the stair, chisel out the tread-retaining wedges from the string housings at the ends of the tread (1), then free the joints by giving the tread a sharp tap from above with a hammer and block.

Next drive the tread backwards and out of its two housings, alternately tapping one end and then the other (2).

Make a tread to fit, shaping its front edge to match the nosings of the other steps, and cut a new pair of wedges. Slide the new tread and wedges into place from underneath, measure the gaps left by the sawcuts at its front and back (3) and cut wooden packing strips or pieces of veneer to fill them.

Remove the tread, apply PVA wood adhesive and replace it, with the wedges and packing pieces. Secure the tread with 38mm (1½in) countersunk wood screws into the risers.

1 Remove the wedges 2 Drive out the tread

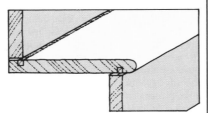
3 Pack out the saw cuts at front and back

Open string stairs

Prise off the moulding that covers the end grain of the tread, taking care not to split it (1), and carefully knock out the two balusters.

Chisel the wedge out of the wall string housing to free the inner end of the tread and drive the tread out from the rear of the stair, using a hammer and a wood block on the outer end of its back edge (2). In this way the end of the tread fitted to the outer string is released while the inner end is still partly engaged in its housing.

You will have to cut through or extract any nails that fix the tread to the outer string before it can be pulled completely clear.

Use the original tread as a template and mark its shape out on a new board, then cut the board accurately to size. Take care to preserve the shape of the nosing which must follow that of the return moulding.

Mark out and cut the housings for the balusters (3) and make a new wedge for the inner tread housing.

Fit the tread from the front, packing out and gluing and screwing it following the method described for a closed string tread (See above).

Apply adhesive to the balusters and replace them. Finally pin and glue the return moulding to the end of the tread and replace any scotia moulding.

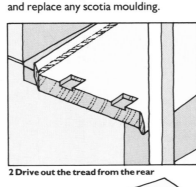
2 Drive out the tread from the rear

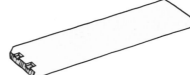
3 Cut the baluster housings in the new tread

1 Prise off the return cover moulding

REPAIRING A RISER

Risers take much less wear and tear than treads and will not ordinarily have to be replaced. Should a riser become weak through woodworm infestation it can be reinforced from behind by having a piece of new board screwed and glued to it, but the old and the new wood should both be thoroughly treated to eradicate the insects (▷). A riser which is seriously affected by woodworm should be replaced.

Closed string stair

In the case of a closed string stair remove the tread below the damaged riser using the method described (See left) but also saw through the tongue at the top of the riser. Knock the wedges out of the riser housings, then knock or prise out the riser (1).

Measure the distance between the strings and between the underside of one tread to the top of the other, then cut a new riser to fit. Though you could make tongue-and-groove joints on the new riser it is easier simply to butt-joint its top and bottom edges with the treads (2).

Glue and wedge the new riser into the housings and to its top edge glue and screw the upper tread (3).

If yours is a 'show-wood' staircase – one whose steps are not to be covered – counterbore the screw holes and use wood plugs to conceal the screws. Another way to secure a glued butt joint is by screwing and gluing blocks to both parts underneath.

Refit the tread as previously described (See left), but note that you need pack out only the front saw cut as the new riser has been made to fit.

Open string stair

First remove any scotia moulding that is fitted under the nosing, then saw through the tongues at the top and bottom of the infected riser and remove the wedge from its wall string housing.

Knock apart the mitred joint between the end of the riser and the outer string by hammering it from behind. Once the mitred joint is free, pull the inner end of the riser out of its housing, working from the front.

Make a new riser to fit between the treads, mitring its outer end to match the joint in the string. Apply adhesive and fit the riser from the front. Re-wedge the inner housing joint, screw the treads to the riser, nail the mitred end and replace the scotia moulding.

SEE ALSO

Details for: ▷
| Preservatives | 47 |
| Screw joints | 99 |

1 Prise out the riser

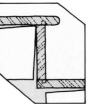
2 Cut riser to fit

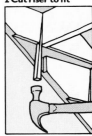
3 Wedge the riser

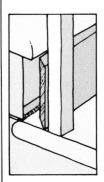
Free mitred joint

ROOFS: MAINTENANCE

SEE ALSO

◁ Details for:
Flashings   106

The roof and upper parts of a building, such as chimneys and parapet walls, must be kept in sound condition if they are to remain weatherproof. Failure of the roof covering can cause an expensive deterioration of the underlying timber structure, the interior plaster fabric and the decorative finishes.

All roof coverings have a limited life, *the length depending on the quality of materials used, the workmanship and the exposure of the house. An average roof covering might be expected to give good service for 40 to 60 years, and some materials can last for a hundred years or more, though some deterioration of the fixings and the flashings may take place. Reuse the old materials if you can.*

Patch repairs may prove to be of only temporary value and can look unsightly. If they become a recurrent chore it is time for the roof to be re-covered. This will mean stripping off the original old material and possibly reusing it, or perhaps replacing it with a new covering similar to the old.

Major roof work is not something you should tackle yourself. A contractor will do it more quickly and will guarantee the work.

Reroofing work may qualify for a discretionary improvement grant from your local authority, depending on the age and rateable value of the house. You will not require planning approval unless you live in a listed building or a conservation area.

Inspecting the roof
The roofs of older houses are likely to show their age and should be checked at least once a year.

Start by taking a general look at the whole roof from ground level. Slipped or disjointed tiles or slates should be easily spotted against the regular lines of the undisturbed covering. The colour of any newly exposed and unweathered slate will also pinpoint a fault. Look at the ridge against the sky to check for misalignment and gaps in the mortar jointing. Follow this with a closer inspection through binoculars, checking the state of the flashings at abutments and around the chimney brickwork (◁).

From inside an unlined roof you can easily spot chinks of daylight that indicate breaks in the covering, and with a light you can inspect the roof timbers for water stains, which may show as dark or white streaks. Trace the stain to find the source.

I Pull out nails

2 Nail strip to batten

3 Fold strip over edge

Removing and replacing a slate

A slate may slip out of place because of its nails becoming corroded or because of a breakdown of the material of the slate itself. Whatever the cause, slipped or broken slates must be replaced as soon as possible.

Use a slater's ripper to remove the trapped part of a broken slate. Slip the tool under the slate and locate its hooked end over one of the fixing nails **(I)**, then pull down hard on the tool to extract or cut through the nail. Remove the second nail in the same way. Even where an aged slate has already slipped out completely you may have to remove the nails in the same way to allow the replacement slate to be slipped in.

You will not be able to nail the new slate in place. Instead cut a 25mm (1 in) wide strip of lead or zinc to the length of the slate lap plus 25mm (1 in) and nail the strip to the batten, nailing between the slates of the lower course **(2)**. Then slide the new slate into position and turn back the end of the lead strip to secure it **(3)**.

Cutting slate

Cut from each edge

With a sharp point mark out the right size on the back of the slate, either by measuring it out or scribing round another slate of that size. Place the slate, bevelled side down, on a bench, the cutting line level with the bench's edge, then chop the slate with the edge of a bricklayer's trowel. Work from both edges towards the middle, using the edge of the bench as a guide. Mark the nail holes and punch them out with a nail or drill them with a bit the size of the nails. Support the slate well while making the holes.

Asbestos cement slates
These can be cut by scribing the lines, then breaking the slates over a straight edge or sawing with a general-purpose saw. If you saw them wear a mask, keep dust damped down well and sweep it into a plastic bag for disposal.

REPLACING A TILE

Individual tiles can be difficult to remove for two reasons: the retaining nibs on their back edges and their interlocking shape which holds them together.

You can remove a broken plain tile by simply lifting it so that the nibs clear the batten on which they rest, then drawing it out. This is made easier if the overlapping tiles are first lifted with wooden wedges inserted at both sides of the tile to be removed **(I)**.

If the tile is also nailed try rocking it loose. If this fails you will have to break it out carefully. You may then have to use a slater's ripper to extract or cut any remaining nails.

Use a similar technique for single-lap interlocking tiles, but in this case you will also have to wedge up the tile to the left of the one being removed **(2)**. If the tile is of a deep profile you will have to ease up a number of the surrounding tiles to get the required clearance.

If you are taking out a tile to put in a roof ventilator unit you can afford to smash it with a hammer. But take care not to damage any of the adjacent tiles. The remaining tiles should be easier to remove once the first is out.

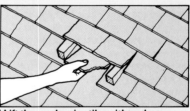
I Lift the overlapping tiles with wedges

2 Lift interlocking tiles above and to the left

CUTTING TILES

To cut tiles use an abrasive cutting disc in a power saw or hire an angle grinder for the purpose. Always wear protective goggles and a mask when cutting with a power tool.

For small work use a tungsten grit blade in a hacksaw frame or, if trimming only, pincers but score the cutting line first with a tile cutter.

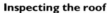

REBEDDING RIDGE TILES

Ridge tiles on old roofs often become loose because of a breakdown of the old lime mortar.

To rebed ridge tiles first lift them off and clear all the old crumbling mortar from the roof, and from the undersides of the tiles.

Give the tiles a good soaking in water before starting to fix them. Mix a new bedding mortar of I part cement to 3 parts sand. It should be a stiff mix and not at all runny. Load about half a bucketful and carry it on to the roof.

Dampen the top courses of the roof tiles and throw the mortar from the trowel to form a continuous edge bedding about 50mm (2in) wide and 75mm (3in) high, following the line left behind by the old mortar.

Where the ridge tiles butt together, or come against a wall, place a solid bedding of mortar, inserting pieces of slate in it to reduce shrinkage. Place the mortar for all the tiles in turn, setting each tile into place and pressing it firmly into the mortar. Strike off any squeezed-out mortar cleanly with the trowel, without smearing the tile. Ridge tiles should not be pointed.

Apply bands of bedding mortar on each side

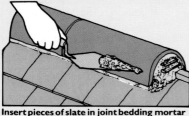

Insert pieces of slate in joint bedding mortar

HALF-ROUND   HOG-BACK   ANGLE

Typical ridge tile shapes

SHEET ROOFING

The commonest sheeting materials for roofing are corrugated asbestos cement and rigid PVC plastic. Aluminium and steel corrugated sheeting are made for roofing but are not generally used for domestic work.

Sheet roofings are used mainly for outbuildings such as garages and garden sheds, and the plastic types may be used for lean-to extensions.

Consult your local Building Control Officer when considering a plastic roofing to ensure that it complies with the fire regulations.

Corrugated sheet roofing

Corrugated sheeting is produced in standard profiles of 32mm (1¼in) for plastic, and 75mm (3in) and 150mm (6in) for plastic and asbestos cement. When calculating the number of sheets you need you must make an allowance for the side overlap. Small-profile sheeting should overlap at least two corrugations **(1)**, while larger ones can be used with only one **(2)**. The end overlap should be at least 150mm (6in) in sheltered locations for roofs with pitches of about 22 degrees or more. For pitches of less than this a 300mm (1ft) overlap should be allowed.

Corrugated sheeting is carried by purlins. They are of wood in most domestic buildings, though some system-built garages embody steel sections. Wood screws or drive screws fix the roofing to wooden purlins **(3)** and hooked bolts are used with metal ones **(4)**. There are special plastic washers and caps for sealing the heads of the screws or bolts.

Cutting corrugated plastic
On thin plastic sheet mark the cutting lines with a felt-tipped pen, then cut it with a fine-toothed tenon saw. Support the sheeting between two boards on trestles and use the top board as a guide for your saw.

When cutting to length saw across the peaks of the corrugations with the saw held at a very shallow angle. Cut halfway through, then turn the sheet over and cut from the other side.

When cutting to width make the cut along the peak of a corrugation, again working with the saw at a shallow angle. For a cut near the middle of the sheet support the sheet on both sides of the cutting line from below.

Cutting corrugated asbestos
Lay the sheet on boards supported by trestles. As the material is fairly thick you will not need a top supporting board and you can saw the sheet without turning it over. Use a sheet saw or general-purpose saw, damping down the dust and sweeping it into a plastic bag, to be sealed with adhesive tape and put in a dustbin. Damp newspaper under the trestles will help contain the dust.

Laying corrugated sheet

You can work from stepladders inside the structure or from above on boards, depending on the pitch of the roof.

Start at the eaves and work from left to right or vice versa.

Asbestos cement sheet is laid smooth side up.

Plastic sheet
Position the first sheet and drill oversized clearance holes for the fixing screws on the centre lines of the wooden purlins. Drill the holes in the crowns of the corrugations and space them at about every third or fourth corrugation. Never place fixings in the troughs of the sheeting.

Don't make holes where the next sheet will overlap the first. Instead lay the second sheet with two corrugations overlapping and drill through both sheets. Lay and fix the rest of the row of sheets in the same way.

Start the next row on the same side as the first one **(1)**, overlapping the ends by at least 150mm (6in), and drill and fix through both layers.

Finally fit the protective plastic caps over the fixing washers.

Laying asbestos sheet
Corrugated asbestos sheet is fairly thick material, and to deal with the bulk of four thickness at the end laps you should cut some of the corners away to form mitres **(2)**. The angle of the mitre is drawn between two points representing the length of the end lap and the width of the side lap.

Fix the sheets as for plastic sheet (See above). For the large profile sheeting use only two fixings to each purlin, placed adjacent to the side laps. The end laps are fixed through both layers.

SEE ALSO

Details for: ▷

Ladders	20-21
Sealing roofs	106

1 Small-profile lap

2 Large-profile lap

3 Wood purlin fixing

4 Metal purlin fixing

1 Overlap the ends

2 Mitre the corners

RENEWING A FELT ROOF

SEE ALSO

◁ Details for:
Flashings   106

Covering flat roofs, or stripping and re-covering them, should usually be left to professionals. A built-up felt system using hot bitumen or torching — using a gas-powered torch to soften bitumen coated felt — is beyond the amateur.

Yet a competent person can confidently replace perished felt on a garage roof, using a cold bitumen adhesive. The following example assumes a detached garage with a solid timber decking covered with three layers of felt.

Replacing perished felt

Wait for dry weather, then strip the old felt. Pull out any clout nails and check the deck for distorted or rotten boards. Lift and replace unsound ones with new ones, using galvanized wire nails and punching them below the surface.

Cutting to stagger joints

For a three-layer build-up start at one edge with a strip about one third of the roll width. The second layer starts with two-thirds width, the top layer with a full width. A two-layer roof starts with half a roll width, then with a full one. You can modify this to suit your roof and avoid a too-narrow strip at the other edge. If, for economy or ease of handling, you use short lengths the end should overlap at least 100mm (4in), the lower piece always lapped by the higher one as you work up the slope.

First layer

Cut the strips for the first felt layer slightly longer than the slope of the roof, and allow for an overlap of at least 50mm (2in) at the long edges. Cut one narrow side length so that successive lapped joints will be staggered.

Nail the felt down with 18mm (¾in) clout nails 50mm (2in) apart down the centres of the laps and 150mm (6in) apart overall (**1**). Tuck and trim the felt into the corners of the verge upstand to get mitred butt joints. Trim the felt

flush at eaves and verges and form and fit the drip at the eaves (See right).

Second layer

Cut lengths for the second layer, put the side piece in place, then roll it back halfway from the eaves end. Brush or trowel cold bitumen adhesive on the felt below but not on the verge upstand. Re-lay the felt, press it down, then roll up the other half and repeat, ensuring that the adhesive is continuous (**2**).

Fold and tuck the felt into the corner of the verge upstand and trim it to a mitred butt joint. Turn it back from the verge, apply adhesive and press it into place against the upstand. Trim the end to butt against the edge of felt for the eaves drip (See below) and trim the other edges flush with the verge. Place the next length, overlapping the first by at least 50mm (2in), and again roll back each half in turn, applying the adhesive. Repeat this across the roof, and cut and tuck the felt at the other verge corner.

Third layer

Cut and lay the mineral felt top layer or 'capsheet' in the same way as the second layer but lap the eaves drip and not the verge upstands (**3**).

Cut strips of the felt to form verge drips (See right) and nail and bond them into place around the side and near edges.

Built-up felt system
Lap the edges of the felt strips and stagger the joints in alternate layers.

1 Nail first layer

2 Bond second layer

3 Lap eaves drip

MAINTAINING A FLAT ROOF

Whatever the material used for covering your flat roof it is sensible to carry out a routine inspection of its current condition at least once a year.

Climb on to the roof to inspect it, wearing soft-soled shoes, and make the check in two parts: once on a dry day and again shortly after there has been rain, when standing water can be seen.

Remove any old leaves, twigs or other matter that may have found its way there and brush off any silt deposits that may have built up. Note the positions of puddles because, although

they may not present an immediate problem, leaks occurring later in the life of the roof will be more easily traced. In an asphalt or felted roof you should also note any blisters or ripples.

On a felted roof test the overlapping joints to see that they are still well bonded. Also make a close inspection of the vulnerable edges of the roof. Check the soundness of the coving at the verges and eaves and the flashings at abutments. You should also inspect the condition of the gutterings and outlets and remove any blockages.

MAKING DRIPS

Eaves

Cut 1m (3ft 3in) long strips from the length of a roll of felt. Calculate the width of the strips by measuring the depth of the drip batten and adding 25mm (1in), then doubling this figure and adding at least 100mm (4in). Cut away 50mm (2in) from one corner to enable the ends to be overlapped and make folds in the strips, using a straight edge. Nail the drip sections to the drip batten with galvanized clout nails and fold each strip back on itself and bond it over the first layer of felt (**1**).

Cutting the corners

Where the drip meets the verge, cut the corners to cover the end of the upstand (**2**). If necessary, make a paper pattern before cutting the felt. You may need an extra wide strip to allow for a tall upstand. Fold the tabs and bond into place, except the end one, which is left free to be tucked into the verge drip.

Verge drips

Cut and fix the verge drips in place after the top layer of roofing. Cut the strips 1m (3ft 3in) long and calculate their width as with the eaves drip, but allow extra for the top edge and slope of the upstand. Working from the eaves, notch the ends of the strips where they overlap, as described for eaves.

Cut and fold the end of the first strip where it meets the eaves (**3**), nail the strip to the batten and bond the remainder into place (**4**).

At the rear corners cut and fold the end strip covering the side verge (**5**). Cover the rear verge last, cutting and folding the corners to lap the side pieces and finishing with neat mitres (**6**).

1 Eaves drip strips

2 Corner detail

3 Verge drip at eaves

4 Verge after folding

5 Verge corner

6 Rear verge drip

FAULT-FINDING

Damp patches
Damp patches on a ceiling are a clear sign that the roof needs attention, but the source of the problem is not always obvious. If they are near an internal wall you should suspect a breakdown of the flashing details.

Locating the leak
A leak anywhere else in the roof may be hard to find, as the water can run downhill from its entry point before dripping on to the ceiling. Measure the distance between the patch and the edges of the ceiling, then locate the point on the roof surface and work from it up the slope seeking the source.

Splits and blisters
Splits and blisters on the smooth surface of an asphalt or bitumen felt covering may be obvious, but chippings on a covering can be troublesome and must be cleared away. This is not easy, and the attempt can obliterate the cause of the leak. Use a blowtorch or hot-air paint stripper to soften the bitumen and scrape the chippings away. The surface must be made smooth if it is to be patch-repaired.

Splits in the covering caused by some movement of the substrate can be recognised by the lines they follow. Blisters formed by trapped moisture or air should be pressed to locate any weaknesses in the covering, which will show as moisture is expelled. These must be sealed with patches. Their cause may be moisture permeating the substrate from below and, heated by the sun, expanding under the covering. If this is undamaged the blister can be left, but its cause must be dealt with.

Damp and condensation
Damp near a wall may be caused by porous brickwork above the flat roof, lack of pointing or DPC, slipped or inadequate coping on parapet walls and/or a breakdown of flashings, which should be made good as required. Condensation may also cause dampness, and is potentially a more serious problem. If warm moist air permeates the ceiling the vapour can condense under the cold roof and start rot in the structural timbers. In such a case upgrade the ceiling with a moisture check and fit some type of ventilation. If the problem is not solved so easily, have the roof recovered and also include better insulation.

FLAT ROOF REPAIRS

Just how a flat roof is to be repaired will depend on its general condition and age, and the extent of the damage. If inspection shows that the surface of the covering has decayed, as may happen to some traditional bitumen felts, it may be better to call in a contractor and have the roof re-covered.

Patch repairs

Such localised damage as splits and blisters can be patch-repaired with the aid of proprietary repair kits, but, as their effectiveness is only as good as their adhesion to the background, take care when cleaning the surface. Kill any lichen or moss spores with a good fungicide or bleach before starting the repair work.

A patched roof, if visible from above, can be rather an eyesore. This can be corrected with a finishing coat of bitumen and chippings or reflective paint to unify the surface area. Work on a warm day, preferably after a spell of dry weather.

Dealing with splits

You can use most self-adhesive repair tapes to patch-repair splits in all types of roof coverings.

First remove any chippings (See left), then clean the split and its surrounding surface thoroughly. Fill a wide split with a mastic compound before taping. Apply the primer supplied over the area to be covered and leave it for an hour.

Where a short split has occurred along a joint in the board substrate prepare the whole line of the joint for covering with tape.

Peel back the protective backing of the tape and apply it to the primed surface(1). If you are working on short splits cut the tape to length first. Otherwise work from the roll, unrolling the tape as you work along the repair.

Press it down firmly and, holding it in place with your foot, roll it out and tread it into place as you go, then cut it off at the end of the run. Go back and ensure that the edges are sealed (2).

1 Apply the tape

2 Press tape firmly

Dealing with blisters

Any blisters in asphalt or felted roofs should be left alone unless they have caused the covering to leak or they contain water.

To repair a blister in an asphalt roof first heat the area with a blow torch or hot-air stripper and, when the asphalt is soft, try to press the blister flat with a block of wood. If water is present cut into the asphalt to open the blister up and let the moisture dry out. This can be encouraged by careful use of the heat before pressing the asphalt back into place. Work mastic into the opening before closing it, then cover the repair with a patch of repair tape.

In a blister on a felted roof, make two crossed cuts and peel back the covering. Heating the felt will make this easier. Dry and clean out the opening, apply bitumen adhesive, and when it is tacky nail the covering back into place with galvanized clout nails (3) .

Cover the repair with a patch of roofing felt, bonded on with the bitumen adhesive. Cut the patch so as to lap at least 75mm (3in) all round. Alternatively you can use repair tape.

3 Nail cut edges
Use bitumen adhesive to glue a felt patch over the repair.

Treating the whole surface

A roof which has already been patch-repaired and is showing general signs of wear and tear can be given an extra lease of life by means of a liquid waterproofing treatment.

The treatment consists of a thick layer of cold-applied bitumen and latex rubber waterproofer which can also be reinforced with an open-weave glass fibre membrane.

First sweep the roof free of all dirt and loose material and treat the surface with a fungicide to kill off any traces of lichen and moss.

Following the maker's instructions, apply the first coat of waterproofer with a brush or broom (4) , then lay the glass fibre fabric into the wet material and stipple it with a loaded brush. Overlap the edges of the fabric strips by at least 50mm (2in) and bed them down well with the waterproofer. Clean the brush with soapy water.

Let the first coat dry thoroughly before laying the second and allow that one to dry before applying the third and last coat. When the last coat becomes tacky cover it with fine chippings or clean sharp sand to provide it with a protective layer.

4 Brush on first coat

SEE ALSO

Details for: ▷
Organic growth 24
Flashings 106

FLASHING REPAIRS

SEALING GLAZED ROOFS

Many problems come about with flashings because of corrosion of the flashing material or failure of the joints between different materials due to erosion or thermal movement.

A perished flashing should be stripped out and replaced. If this will require craft skills the work should be done by a specialist contractor, but in many cases leaks may be caused by shrinkage cracks, and you can repair these with self-adhesive flashing materials.

SEE ALSO

◁ Details for:
Primers	23
Glazing	92-94
Pointing	220

Using caulking compound

Cement fillets often shrink away from wall abutments. If the fillets are otherwise sound – free of cracks for example – fill the gap with a gun-applied flexible caulking compound, having chosen a colour to match the fillet. Brush the surfaces to remove any loose material before injecting the compound.

Flashing tape

Prepare the surfaces by removing all loose and organic material. A broken or crumbling cement fillet should be made good with mortar.

Ensure that the surfaces are dry and if necessary apply a primer – it is supplied with some tapes – about one hour before using the tape (1).

Cut the tape to length and peel away the protective backing as you press the tape into place. Work over the surface with a cloth pad, applying firm pressure to exclude any air trapped underneath the tape (2).

1 Apply a primer with a 50mm (2in) paintbrush

2 Press tape with a pad to exclude air bubbles

Repointing flashing

Metal flashings which are tucked into brickwork may have worked loose where the old mortar is badly weathered. If the flashing is otherwise sound rake out the mortar joint, tuck the lead or zinc into it and wedge it there with rolled strips of lead spaced about 500mm (20in) apart. Then repoint the joint. While you have the roof ladders and scaffolding in place, rake out and repoint all of the mortar joints if in poor condition.

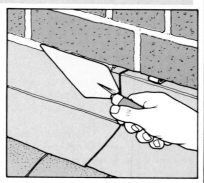

Rake out joint and repoint with fresh mortar

Patching lead

Lead will not readily corrode but splits can occur in it where it has buckled through expansion and contraction over the years.

Flashing tape can be used but it is possible to patch lead by soldering or, for a more substantial repair, cutting away a weak or damaged portion and joining on a new piece by lead 'burning' or welding. This is not a job you can easily do yourself and it should be handed over to a professional. It should be done only when it is more economical to have the old lead repaired than to have a new flashing made and fitted.

Traditional timber-framed conservatories, glazed porches and greenhouses can suffer from leaks caused by a breakdown of the seal between the glass and the glazing bars. Minor leaks should be dealt with promptly because the trapped moisture could lead to timber decay and expensive repair work.

Using aluminium tape

You can waterproof glazing bars with self-adhesive aluminium tape simply cut to length and pressed in place.

Clean all old material from the glazing bars and the edges of glass on both sides of them, let the wood dry out if necessary and apply wood primer. When the primer is dry fill the rebates with putty or mastic. The width of tape must cover the upstand of the bars and lap the glass each side by 18mm (¾in).

Start at the eaves and work up the roof, peeling off its backing as you unroll the tape. Mould it to the glazing bars' contour, excluding air bubbles.

At a step in the glass cut the tape for a 50mm (2in) overlap and mould the end over the stepped edge, then start a new length lapping the stuck-down end by 50mm (2in) and so on, to the ridge.

At the ridge you may cut the tape to butt against the framework or lap on to it. A horizontal tape should cover the turned ends. Where a lean-to roof has an apron flashing tuck the tape under it.

Self-adhesive aluminium tape can be painted or left its natural colour.

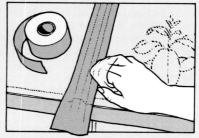

Clean the surfaces before applying the tape.

Clear tape

You can make a temporary repair to cracked glass with clear self-adhesive waterproofing tape.

Clean the glass and apply the tape over the crack on the weather side. It will make an almost invisible repair, especially if done promptly.

You can also use this tape for sealing the overlaps on translucent corrugated plastic roofing.

3

INSULATION	**108**
INSULATING PLUMBING	109
DRAUGHTPROOFING	110
ROOF AND LOFT INSULATION	113
DOUBLE GLAZING	116
VENTILATION	**119**
COOKER HOODS	120
EXTRACTOR FANS	121

INSULATION

No matter what fuel you use, the cost of heating a home has, over recent years, risen dramatically – and there's no reason to suppose it won't continue to rise, perhaps at an even faster rate. What makes matters worse for many householders is the heat escaping from their draughty, uninsulated homes. Even if the expense of heating wasn't an important factor, the improved comfort and health of the occupants would more than justify the effort of installing adequate insulation.

Local authority grants

The Government believe that home insulation is important to the economy of the country, so much so that they have made grants available through local authorities to encourage people to insulate their lofts, storage tanks and pipework. Everyone with less than 30mm (1¼in) of insulation is eligible for a grant of some sort. You must get local authority approval before you carry out the work or even purchase the insulation to qualify for the grant.

Specifications for insulation

When comparing thermal insulating materials, you will encounter certain technical specifications.

U-values
Elements of a house structure or the insulation itself are often given a U-value, which is a measurement of thermal transmittance. This represents the rate at which heat travels from one side to the other.

The U-value is an expression of watts of energy per square metre per °C difference ($W/m^2 °C$). If a solid brick wall is specified as having a U-value of 2.0, it means that 2 watts of heat is conducted from every square metre of the wall for every °C difference in the temperature on each side of the wall. If the temperature outside is 10 degrees lower than inside, each square metre of wall will conduct 20 watts of heat. For comparison, the lower the U-value the better the insulation.

R-values
In other cases, a material may be given an R-value, an indication of resistance to heat flow of a specified thickness. Materials with superior insulating qualities have the highest R-values.

SEE ALSO
◁ Details for:
Lagging pipes/cylinders	109
Radiator foil	109
Draughtproofing	110-112
Insulating roofs	113-115

Sound insulation
It is difficult to effectively insulate an existing building against sound, but attend to noisy plumbing (◁) and triple glaze your windows against airborne sound from outside (◁).

CHOOSING INSULATION PRIORITIES

To many people, the initial outlay for total house insulation is prohibitive, even though they will concede that it is cost-effective in the long term. Nevertheless, it's important to instigate a programme for insulation as soon as possible – every measure contributes some saving.

Most authorities suggest that 35 per cent of lost heat escapes through the walls of an average house, 25 per cent through its roof, 25 per cent through draughty doors and windows and 15 per cent through the floor. At best, this can be taken as a rough guide only as it is difficult to define an 'average' home and therefore to deduce the rate of heat loss. A terraced house, for instance, will lose less than a detached house of the same size, yet both may have a roof of the same area and a similar condition. Large, ill-fitting sash windows will permit far more draughts than small, well-fitting casements, and so on.

The figures identify the major routes for heat loss, but don't necessarily indicate where you should begin your programme in order to achieve the quickest return on your investment or, for that matter, the most immediate improvement in comfort. Start with the relatively inexpensive measures.

1 HOT WATER CYLINDER AND PIPES

Begin by lagging your hot water storage cylinder and any exposed pipework running through unheated areas of the house. This treatment will constitute a considerable saving in a matter of a few months only.

2 RADIATORS

Apply metallic foil behind any radiators on an outside wall: it will reflect heat back into the room; before the wall absorbs it.

3 DRAUGHTPROOFING

Seal off the major draughts around windows and doors. For a modest outlay, draughtproofing provides a substantial return both economically and in terms of your comfort. It is also easy to accomplish.

4 ROOF

Tackle the insulation of the roof next as, in addition to the eventual reduction in fuel bills, you may be eligible for a local authority grant towards the cost of its insulation (see left). It is a very economical proposition.

5 WALLS

Depending on the construction of your house, insulating the walls may be a sound investment. However, it's likely to be relatively expensive, so it will take several years to recoup your initial expenditure.

6 FLOORS

Most of us insulate our floors to some extent by laying carpets or tiles. Taking extra measures will depend on the degree of comfort you wish to achieve and whether you can install more efficient insulation while carrying out some other improvement to the floor, such as laying new boards.

7 DOUBLE GLAZING

Contrary to typical advertisements, double glazing will produce only a slow return on your investment, especially if you choose one of the more expensive systems. However, it may help to increase the value of your property – and a double-glazed room is definitely cosier and you will be less troubled by noise from outside especially if you choose to install triple glazing.

LAGGING PIPES, CYLINDER AND RADIATORS

Insulating a hot water cylinder

Many people think that an uninsulated cylinder is providing a useful source of heat in an airing cupboard, but in fact it squanders a surprising amount of energy. Even a lagged cylinder should provide ample background heat in an enclosed cupboard – but if not, an uninsulated pipe will.

Proprietary cylinder jackets are made from segments of 80 to 100mm (3¼ to 4in) thick mineral-fibre insulation material wrapped in plastic. Measure the approximate height and circumference of the cylinder to choose the right size. If necessary, buy a larger jacket rather than one that is too small. Make sure you buy a good-quality jacket by checking that it is marked with the British Standard kite mark (BS 5615).

If you should ever have to replace the cylinder, consider buying a pre-insulated version, of which there are various types on the market.

Thread the tapered ends of the jacket segments onto a length of string and tie it round the pipe at the top of the cylinder. Distribute the segments evenly around the cylinder and wrap the straps or string provided around it to hold the insulation in place.

Spread out the segments to make sure the edges are butted together and tuck the insulation around the pipes and the cylinder thermostat.

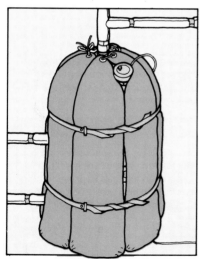

Lagging a hot water cylinder
Fit a jacket snugly around the cylinder and wrap insulating foam tubes (See above right) around the pipework, especially the vent pipe directly above the cylinder.

Lagging pipe runs

You should insulate hot water pipes where their radiant heat is not contributing to the warmth of your home, and also cold water pipe runs in unheated areas of the house, where they could freeze. You can wrap pipework in one of several lagging bandages, some of which are self-adhesive, but it is more convenient to use foamed plastic tubes designed for the purpose, especially along pipes running close and clipped to a wall, which would be awkward to wrap.

Plastic tubes are made to fit pipes of different diameters and the tube walls vary in thickness from 10mm to 20mm (½in to ¾in). More expensive tubing incorporates a metallic foil backing to reflect some of the heat back into hot water pipes.

Most tubes are pre-slit along their length so that they can be sprung over the pipe (1). Butt successive lengths of tube end-to-end and seal the joints with PVC adhesive tape.

At a bend, cut small segments out of the split edge so it bends without crimping. Fit it around the pipe (2) and seal the closed joints with tape. If pipe is joined with an elbow fitting (▷), mitre the ends of the two lengths of tube, butt them together (3) and seal with tape.

Cut lengths of tube to fit completely around a tee-joint, linking them with a wedge-shaped butt joint (4) and seal with tape as before.

 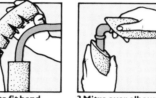

1 Spring onto pipe   2 Cut to fit bend   3 Mitre over elbows   4 Butt at tee-joint

SEE ALSO

Details for: ▷	
Plumbing joints	182
Radiator roller	57
Wallpaper paste	63

Reflecting heat from a radiator

Up to 25 per cent of the radiant heat from a radiator on an outside wall is lost to the wall behind. Reclaim perhaps half this wasted heat by installing a foil-faced, expanded polystyrene lining behind the radiator to reflect it back into the room.

The material is available as rolls, sheets or tiles to fit any size and shape of radiator. It is easier to stick the foil on the wall when the radiator is removed for decorating but it is not an essential requirement.

Turn off the radiator and measure it, including the position of the brackets. Use a sharp trimming knife or scissors to cut the foil to size so that it is slightly smaller than the radiator all round. Cut narrow slots to fit over the fixing brackets (1).

Apply heavy-duty fungicidal wallpaper paste to the back of the sheet and slide it behind the radiator (2). Rub it down with a radiator roller (▷) or smooth it against the wall with a wooden batten. Allow enough time for the adhesive to dry before turning the radiator on again.

 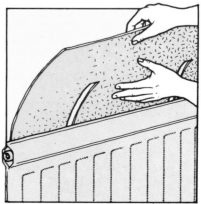

1 Cut slots to align with wall brackets   2 Slide lining behind radiator and press to wall

DRAUGHTPROOFING DOORS

SEE ALSO

◁ Details for:
**Proofing doors
and windows** 111-112

A certain amount of ventilation is desirable for a healthy environment and to keep water vapour at an acceptable level; it's also essential to enable certain heating appliances to operate properly and safely. But using uncontrolled draughts to ventilate a house is not the most efficient way of dealing with the problem. Draughts account for a large proportion of the heat lost from the home and are also responsible for a good deal of discomfort. Draughtproofing is easy to fit, requires no special tools, and there's a wide choice of excluders available to suit all locations.

Locating and curing draughts

Proof exterior doors– and windows– (◁) first, and seal only those interior doors which are the worst offenders to provide 'trickle' ventilation from room to room. Check out other possible sources of draughts, such as floorboards and skirtings, fireplaces, loft hatches, and overflow pipes from sanitaryware.

Locate draughts by running the flat of your hand along the likely gaps. Dampening your skin will enhance its sensitivity to cold, or wait for a very windy day to conduct your search.

There are so many manufacturers and variations of draught excluders, it's quite impossible to describe them all, but the following examples illustrate the principles commonly employed to seal out draughts. Choose the best you can afford, but perhaps more importantly, try to decide which type of draught excluder will suit your particular requirements best.

Flexible strip

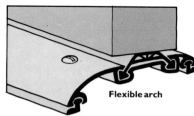
Brush seal

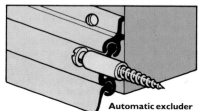
Automatic excluder

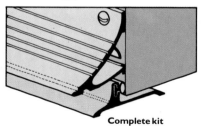
Flexible arch

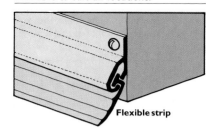
Complete kit

THRESHOLD DRAUGHT EXCLUDERS

The gap between the door and floor can be very large and will admit fierce draughts. Use a threshold excluder to seal this gap. If it is to be used on an exterior door, make sure it is suitable for this purpose. Buy a device that fits the opening exactly, or cut it to fit from a larger size.

FLEXIBLE STRIP EXCLUDERS

The simplest form of threshold excluder is a flexible strip of plastic or rubber, which sweeps against the floorcovering to form a seal. The basic versions are self-adhesive strips that are simply pressed along the bottom of the door but others have a rigid plastic or aluminium extrusion screwed to the door to hold the strip in contact with the floor. This type of excluder is rarely suitable for exterior doors and quickly wears out. However, it is inexpensive and easy to fit. Most types work best over smooth flooring.

BRUSH SEALS

A nylon bristle brush set into a metal or plastic extrusion acts as a draught excluder. It is suitable for slightly uneven or textured floorcoverings; the same excluder works on both hinged and sliding doors.

AUTOMATIC EXCLUDER

A plastic strip and its extruded clip are sprung-loaded to lift from the floor as the door is opened. On closing the door, the excluder is pressed against the floor by a stop screwed to the door frame. This is a good-quality interior and exterior excluder that reduces wear on the floorcovering.

FLEXIBLE ARCH

An aluminium extrusion with a vinyl arched insert, which presses against the bottom edge of the door. The extruder has to be nailed or screwed to the floor, so it would be difficult to use on a solid concrete floor. If you fit one for an external door, make sure it is fitted with additional under-seals to prevent the rain from seeping beneath it. You may have to plane the bottom of the door.

DOOR KITS

The best solution for an outside door is a kit combining an aluminium weather trim, which sheds the rainwater, and a weather bar with a built-in tubular rubber or plastic draught excluder screwed to the threshold.

WEATHERSTRIPPING THE DOOR EDGES

Any well-fitting door requires a gap of 2mm (1/16in) at top and sides so that it can be operated smoothly. However, the combined area of a gap this large loses a great deal of heat. There are several ways to seal it, some of which are described here. The cheaper varieties have to be renewed regularly.

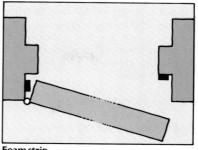

FOAM STRIPS

The most straightforward excluder is a self-adhesive foam plastic strip, which you stick around the rebate: it's compressed by the door, forming a seal. The cheapest polyurethane foam will be good for one or two seasons (but it's useless if painted) and is suitable for interior use only. Better-quality vinyl-coated polyurethane, rubber or PVC foams are more durable and do not perish on exposure to sunlight, as their cheaper counterparts do. Don't stretch foam excluders when applying them, as it reduces their efficiency. The door may be difficult to close at first but the excluder soon adjusts.

Foam strip

FLEXIBLE TUBE EXCLUDERS

A small vinyl tube held in a plastic or metal extrusion is compressed to fill the gap around the door. The cheapest versions have an integrally moulded flange, which can be stapled to the door frame, but they are not as neat.

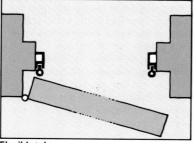

SPRING STRIP

Thin metal or plastic strips with a sprung leaf are pinned or glued to the door frame. The top and closing edges of the door brush past the leaf, which seals the gap, while the hinged edge compresses it. It can't cope with uneven surfaces unless it incorporates a foam strip on the flexible leaf.

Flexible tube

V-STRIP

A variation on the spring strip, the leaf is bent right back to form a V-shape. The strip can be mounted to fill the gap around the door or attached to the door stop so that the door closes against it. Most are cheap and unobtrusive.

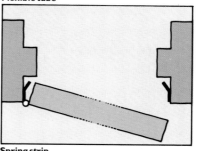

DRAUGHTPROOFING SEALANT

With this excluder, a bead of flexible sealant is squeezed onto the door stop: a low-tack tape applied to the surface of the door acts as a release agent. When the door is closed, it flattens the bead, which fills the gap perfectly. When it is set, the parting layer of tape is peeled from the door, leaving the sealant firmly attached to the door frame. If the door warps, the seal is not so good.

Spring strip

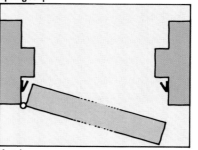

SEALING KEYHOLES AND LETTERBOXES

Make sure the outer keyhole for a mortise lock is fitted with a pivoting coverplate to seal out the draughts in the winter.

Special hinged flaps are made for screwing over the inside of a letterbox. Some types contain a brush seal behind the flap, forming an even better seal.

V-strip

Keyhole coverplate
The coverplate is part of the escutcheon.

Letterbox flap
A hinged flap neatens and draughtproofs a letterbox.

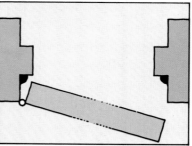

Sealant

GENERAL DRAUGHTPROOFING

*Hinged casement windows can be sealed
with any of the draught excluders
suggested for fitting around the edge
of a door, but draughtproofing a
sliding sash window presents a more
difficult problem.*

SEE ALSO

◁ Details for:
Sealant	111
Flue ventilation	119

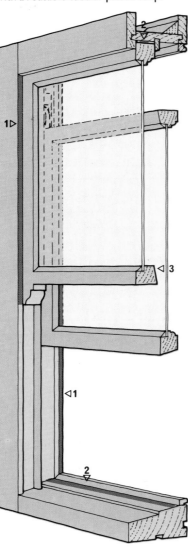

1 Brush seal

2 Spring or V-strip

3 Tubular strip

Sealing a sash window

The top and bottom closing rails of a
sash window can be sealed with any
form of compressible excluder; the
sliding edges admit fewer draughts but
they can be sealed with a brush seal
fixed to the frame, inside for the lower
sash, outside for the top one.

A spring or V-strip could be used to
seal the gap between the central
meeting rails but you may not be able to
reverse the sashes once it is fitted.
Perhaps the simplest solution is to seal it
with a reusable tubular plastic strip.

Clear liquid sealer

If you plan never to open a window
during the winter, you could seal all gaps
with a clear liquid draught seal, applied
from a tube. It is virtually invisible when
dry and can be peeled off, without
damaging the paintwork, when you
want to open the window again after
the winter.

Liquid sealer is supplied in a special injector

Sealing a pivot window

As you close a pivot window, the
moving frame comes to rest against
fixed stops, but the stops for the top
half of the window are on the outside of
the house. These exterior stops, at
least, must be sealed with draught
excluders that are weatherproof so use
spring or V-strip compressible
draughtproofing, or a good-quality
flexible tube strip. Alternatively, use a
draughtproofing sealant (◁).

DRAUGHTY FIREPLACES

A chimney can be an annoying source of
draughts. If the fireplace is unused, you
can seal it off completely, but be sure to
fit a 'hit-and-miss' ventilator to provide
ventilation for the flue (◁).

If you want to retain the appearance
of an open fireplace, cut a sheet of thick
polystyrene to seal the throat but leave
a hole about 50mm (2in) across to
provide some ventilation. Should you
ever want to use the fireplace again,
don't forget to remove the polystyrene,
which is flammable.

DRAUGHTPROOFING FLOORS AND SKIRTINGS

The ventilated void below a suspended
wooden floor is a prime source of
draughts through large gaps in the
floorboards and under the skirting. Fill
between floorboards or cover them
with hardboard panels (◁).

Seal the gap between the skirting
board and the floor with mastic applied
with an applicator gun or in the form of
caulking strips. For a neat finish, pin a
quadrant moulding to the skirting to
cover the sealed gap.

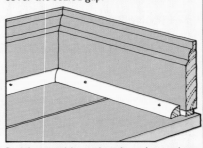

Seal the gap with mastic and wooden quadrant

DRAUGHTS FROM OVERFLOW PIPES

Overflow pipes leading directly from
bath tubs, sinks and basins can be the
passage for serious draughts when
there's a strong wind. The problem is
how to seal the pipes without
interfering with their function.

Covering the opening
The simplest solution is to cut the neck
off a balloon and stretch it over the end
of the pipe. It hangs down to cover the
opening but gushing water will pass
through safely.

Fitting a coverflap
Alternatively, cut a coverflap from a
lightweight metal such as zinc or
aluminium, which will not rust. Make a
simple pivot from the same metal and
attach the flap to the end of the tube
with a pipe clip. Inspect it regularly to
ensure that it is working smoothly.

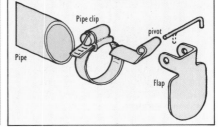

Pipe clip

pivot

Pipe

Flap

INSULATING ROOFS

About a quarter of the heat lost from an average house goes through the roof, so preventing this should be one of your priorities when it comes to insulating your home. Providing you're able to gain access to your loft floor, reducing substantial heat loss is just a matter of laying the insulation material between the joists: it's cheap, quick and effective. If you want to use the attic, insulating the sloping surface of the roof is a quite straightforward alternative.

Treating a flat roof

A flat roof – on an extension for instance – may also need insulating, but the only really practical solution for most householders is to apply a layer of insulation to the ceiling surface. It is not a particularly difficult task, providing the area is not too large, but you will have to re-locate lighting and take into consideration features such as cupboards or windows that extend to the ceiling. Fixing ceiling tiles is an alternative (▷) but their insulation value is minimal.

Preparing the loft

On inspection, you may find that the roof space has existing but inadequate insulation. At one time even 25mm (1in) of insulation was considered to be acceptable. It is worth installing extra insulation to bring it up to the recommended thickness of 100mm (4in). Check roof timbers for woodworm or signs of rot so that they can be treated first (▷). Make sure that the electrical wiring is sound; lift it clear so that you can lay insulation beneath it.

Plaster or plasterboard ceiling surfaces will not support your weight, so lay a plank or two, or a panel of chipboard, across the joists so that you can move about safely: don't allow it to overlap the joists; if you step on the edge it will tip over.

If there is no permanent lighting in the loft, rig up an inspection lamp on an extension lead, so you can move it wherever it is needed, or hang it high up for best overall light.

Most attics are very dusty, so wear old clothes and a gauze facemask. You may wish to wear protective gloves, particularly if you are handling glass-fibre batts or blanket insulation, which can irritate sensitive skin.

TYPES OF INSULATION

There's a wide range of different insulation materials available. Check out the recommended types with your local authority before you apply for a grant.

BLANKET INSULATION

Blanket insulation, which is made from glass fibre, mineral fibre or rock fibre, is widely available in the form of rolls that fit snugly between the joists. The same material, cut to shorter lengths, is also sold as 'batts'. A minimum thickness of 150mm (6in) is recommended for loft insulation. It may be unbacked, paper-backed to improve its tear-resistance, or it may have a foil backing that serves as a vapour barrier (see below).

The unbacked type is normally used for laying on the loft floor. The blankets are usually either 100mm (4in) or 150mm (6in) thick. Some 100mm blankets can be split into two for topping up existing insulation. The rolls are typically 6 to 8m (20 to 25ft) long and 400mm (1ft 4in) wide in order to be suitable for standard joist spacing. For wider-than-usual joist spacing, choose a roll 600mm (2ft) wide.

If you want to fit blanket insulation to the sloping part of a roof, buy it with a lip of backing along each side to staple to the rafters. Both mineral fibre and glass fibre are non-flammable, and are proofed against damp, rot and vermin.

LOOSE-FILL INSULATION

Loose-fill insulation in pellet or granular form is poured between the joists, up to the recommended depth of 150mm. This will inevitably bury some joists, but you can nail strips of wood to the tops of the joists that support walkway boarding.

Exfoliated vermiculite, made from the mineral mica, is the most common form of loose-fill insulation – but other types, such as mineral wool, cork granules or cellulose fibre (made from recycled paper), may be available. Loose-fill is supplied in 10 or 20kg (22 or 44lb) bags. A 10kg (22lb) bag covers about 1.6sq m (17sq ft) to a depth of 150mm (6in).

It's not advisable to use loose-fill in a draughty, exposed loft, as high winds can cause it to blow about. On the other hand, it is convenient to use if the joists are irregularly spaced.

BLOWN-FIBRE INSULATION

Fibrous inter-joist insulation is blown through a large hose by a professional contractor. It may not be suitable for a house in a windy location, but seek a contractor's advice. An even depth of at least 150mm (6in) is required.

RIGID AND SEMI-RIGID SHEET INSULATION

Sheet insulation, such as semi-rigid batts of glass fibre or mineral fibre, can be fixed between the rafters. They tend to perform better than lightweight rolls, so relatively thin sheets can be used, especially if covered with plasterboard. However, it pays to install the thickest insulation possible, allowing sufficient ventilation between it and the roof tiles or slates to avoid condensation.

VAPOUR BARRIERS

Installing insulation has the effect of making the areas of the house outside that layer of insulation colder than before, so increasing the risk of condensation (▷) either on or within the structure itself. In time this could result in decreased value of the insulation and may promote a serious outbreak of dry rot in household timbers (▷).

To prevent this happening, it's necessary to provide adequate ventilation for those areas outside the insulation or to install a vapour barrier on the inner, or warm, side of the insulation to prevent moisture-laden air passing through. This is usually a plastic sheet or layer of metal foil, which is sometimes supplied along with the insulation. It is essential that a vapour barrier is continuous and undamaged or its effect is greatly reduced.

SEE ALSO

Details for: ▷	
Preservatives	47
Ceiling tiles	80
Condensation	119
Extension lead	132
Checking electrics	144-145

ESTIMATING FOR BLANKET INSULATION
400mm wide rolls

Approx. loft area		
Square metres	Square feet	No. of rolls
29	314	13
31.5	339	14
34	363	15
36	387	16
38	411	17
40.5	435	18
43	460	19
45	487	20
56	605	25
67.5	726	30
79	847	35
90	968	40

Allows for average joist widths of 50mm (2in)

● **Ventilating the loft**
Laying insulation between the joists increases the risk of condensation in an unheated roof space above, but, provided there are gaps at the eaves, there will be enough air circulating to keep the loft dry.

INSULATING THE LOFT

Laying blanket insulation

Seal gaps around pipes, vents or wiring entering the loft with flexible mastic. Remove the blanket wrapping in the loft (it's compressed for storage and transportation but swells to its true thickness when released) and begin by placing one end of a roll into the eaves. Make sure you don't cover the ventilation gap – trim the end of the blanket to a wedge-shape so it does not obstruct the airflow, or fit eaves vents.

Unroll the blanket between the joists, pressing it down to form a snug fit, but don't compress it. If the roll is slightly wider than the joist spacing, allow it to curl up against the timbers on each side.

Continue at the opposite side of the loft with another roll: cut it to butt up against the end of the first one, using a large kitchen knife or long-bladed pair of scissors. Continue across the loft until all the spaces are filled. Cut the insulation to fit odd spaces.

Do not cover the casing of any light fittings which protrude into the loft space. Avoid covering electrical cables, as there's a risk it may cause overheating. Instead, lay the cables on top of the blanket, or clip them to the sides of the joists above it.

Do not insulate the area directly below a cold water tank, so that heat rising from the room below will help to prevent freezing. Cut a piece of insulation to fit the hatch cover and attach it with PVA adhesive or hold it down with cloth tapes and drawing pins. Fit foam draught excluder around the edge of the hatch.

Laying loose-fill insulation

Take similar precautions against condensation to those described for blanket insulation. To prevent blocking the eaves, wedge strips of plywood or thick cardboard between the joists. Pour insulation between the joists and distribute it roughly with a broom. Level it with a spreader cut from hardboard to fit between the joists: notch it to fit over the joists so the central piece levels the granules accurately.

To insulate the entrance hatch, screw battens around the outer edge of the cover, fill with granules and pin on a hardboard lid to contain them.

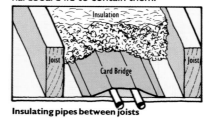

Insulating pipes between joists

SEE ALSO

◁ Details for:
Lagging pipes	109
Expansion (vent) pipe	208
Draught excluders	111
Insulant	113
Electrical wiring	142

INSULATING CISTERNS AND PIPES

Insulating cisterns

To comply with current bylaws, your cold-water-storage cistern must be insulated. It's simplest to buy a Bylaw 30 kit, which includes a cylinder jacket and all the other equipment that is required. Insulate your central-heating expansion tank at the same time.

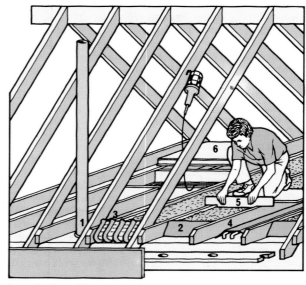

Buy a ready-made jacket for a cistern

Insulating pipes

If there are cold-water pipes running between the joists, lay the blanket insulation over them to prevent them from freezing. If that is not practical, insulate each pipe run separately.

Before pouring loose-fill insulation, lay a bridge made from thin card over cold-water pipes running between the joists, so they will benefit from warmth rising from the room below. If the joists are shallow, cover the pipes with foam sleeves before pouring the insulation.

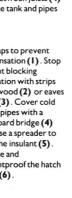

Left
Seal gaps around pipes and vents (**1**). Place end of roll against eaves and trim ends (**2**) or fit eaves vents (**3**). Press rolls between joists (**4**) Insulate tank and pipes (**5**).

Right
Seal gaps to prevent condensation (**1**). Stop insulant blocking ventilation with strips of plywood (**2**) or eaves vents (**3**). Cover cold water pipes with a cardboard bridge (**4**) then use a spreader to level the insulant (**5**). Insulate and draughtproof the hatch cover (**6**).

Laying blanket insulation in the loft

Spreading loose-fill insulant in the loft

INSULATING A SLOPING ROOF

Insulating between the rafters

If the attic is in use, you will need to insulate the sloping part of the roof in order to heat the living space. Repair tiles or slates first, as not only will leaks soak the insulation but also it will be difficult to spot them after insulating.

Condensation is a serious problem when you install insulation between the rafters, as the undersides of the tiles will become very cold. You must provide a 50mm (2in) gap between the tiles and the insulation to promote sufficient ventilation to keep the space dry, which in turn determines the maximum thickness of insulation you can install. The ridge and eaves must be ventilated ($\triangleright$) and you should include a vapour barrier on the warm side of the insulation, either by fitting foil-backed blanket or by stapling sheets of polythene to the lower edges of the rafters to cover unbacked insulation.

Whatever insulation you decide on, you can cover the rafters with sheets of plasterboard as a final decorative layer. The sizes of the panels will be dictated by the largest boards you can pass through the hatchway. Use plasterboard nails or screws to hold the panels against the rafters, staggering the joints ($\triangleright$). Alternatively, provide insulation and surface finish together by fitting insulated (thermal) plasterboard to the underside of the rafters ($\triangleright$).

Fixing blanket insulant

Unfold the side flanges from a roll of foil-backed blanket and staple them to the underside of the rafters. When fitting adjacent rolls, overlap the edges of the vapour barrier to provide a continuous layer.

Attaching sheet insulant

The simplest method is to cut the sheet insulation accurately so that it will be a wedge-fit between the rafters. If necessary, screw battens to the sides of the rafters to which you can fix the insulating sheets. Treat the battens beforehand with preservative. Staple a polythene sheet vapour barrier over the rafters. Double-fold the joints over a rafter and staple in place.

INSULATING AN ATTIC ROOM

If an attic room was built as part of the original dwelling, it will be virtually impossible to insulate the pitch of the roof unless you are prepared to hack off the old plaster and proceed as left. It may be simpler to insulate from the inside as for a flat roof ($\triangleright$) but your headroom may be seriously hampered.

Insulate the short vertical wall of the attic from inside the crawlspace, making sure the vapour barrier faces the inner, warm side of the partition. Insulate between the joists of the crawlspace at the same time.

Fit blankets with vapour barrier facing the room

Insulating a room in the attic
Surround the room itself with insulation but leave the floor uninsulated so that the room benefits from rising heat generated by the space below.

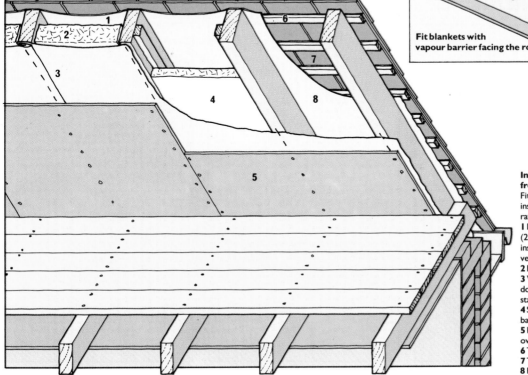

Insulating an attic from the inside
Fit blanket or sheet insulant between the rafters.
1 Minimum of 50mm (2in) between insulation and tiles for ventilation
2 Blanket or batts
3 Vapour barrier with double-folded joints stapled to rafters
4 Sheet insulant fixed to battens
5 Plasterboard nailed over vapour barrier
6 Tile battens
7 Tiles or slates
8 Roof felt

SECONDARY DOUBLE GLAZING

SEE ALSO

◁ Details for:
Draughtproofing   112

Secondary double glazing comprises a separate pane of glass or plastic sheet which is normally fitted to the inside of existing single-glazed windows. It *is a popular method for double glazing windows, being relatively easy for home installation – and usually at a fraction of the cost of other systems.*

How the glazing is fixed

Glazing can be fastened to the sash frames (**1**), the window frames (**2**), or across the window reveal (**3**). The choice depends on the ease of fixing, the type of glazing and personal requirements for ventilation.

Glazing fixed to the sash will cut down heat loss through the glass and provide accessible ventilation, but it will not stop draughts. That fixed to the window frame will reduce heat loss and stop draughts at the same time. Glazing fixed across the reveal will also offer improved sound insulation as the air gap can be wider. Any system should be readily demountable or preferably openable to provide a change of air in a room without some other form of ventilation.

Rigid glazing of plastic or glass can be fitted to the exterior of the window opening if secondary glazing would spoil the appearance of the interior. In this case, windows which are set in a deep reveal, such as the vertically sliding sash type, are the most suitable (**4**).

GLAZING POSITIONS

Secondary double glazing is particularly suitable for DIY installation, partly because it is so versatile. It is possible to fit a system to almost any style or shape of window.

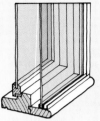

1 Sash fixed
Glazing fixed to the opening window frame

2 Frame fixed
Glazing fixed to the structural frame

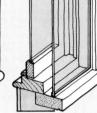

3 Reveal fixed
Glazing fixed to the reveal and interior window sill

4 Exterior fitted
Glazing fixed to the reveal and exterior window sill

Glazing with renewable film

Effective double glazing can be achieved using double-sided adhesive tape to stretch a thin, flexible sheet of plastic across the window frame. It can be removed at the end of the cold season without harming the paintwork.

Clean the window frame (**1**) then cut the plastic sheet roughly to size, allowing an overlap all round. Apply double-sided tape to the frame edges (**2**) and peel off its backing paper.

Attach the film to the top rail (**3**), then tension it onto the tape on the sides and bottom of the frame (**4**). Apply light pressure only until the film is positioned then rub it down onto the tape all round.

Use a hair dryer set to a high temperature to remove all creases and wrinkles in the film (**5**). Starting at an upper corner, move the dryer slowly across the film, holding it about 6mm (¼in) from the surface. When the film is tensioned, cut off the excess plastic (**6**).

1 Wipe woodwork to remove dust and grease

2 Apply double-sided tape to the fixed frame

3 Stretch the film across the top of the frame

4 Pull the film tight and fix to sides and bottom

5 Use a hair dryer to shrink the film

6 Trim the waste with a sharp knife

PLASTIC GLAZING

Demountable systems

A simple method for interior secondary glazing uses clear plastic film or sheet. These lightweight materials are secured by self-adhesive strips or rigid moulded sections, which form a seal. Most strip fastenings use magnetism or some form of retentive tape, which allows the secondary glazing to be removed for cleaning or ventilation. The strips and tapes usually have a flexible foam backing, which takes up slight irregularities in the woodwork. They are intended to remain in place throughout the winter and be removed for storage during the summer months.

Fitting a demountable system

Clean the windows and the surfaces of the window frame. Cut the plastic sheet to size. Place the glazing on the window frame and mark around it (**1**). Working with the plastic on a flat table, peel back the protective paper from one end of the self-adhesive strip. Tack it to the surface of the plastic, flush with one edge. Cut it to length and repeat on the other edges. Cut the mating parts of the strips and apply them to the window frame following the guidelines. Press the glazing into place (**2**).

When dealing with rigid moulded sections, cut the pieces to length with mitred corners. Fit the sections around the glazing, peel off the protective backing and press the complete unit against the frame (**3**).

I Mark round glazing **2 Position glazed unit**

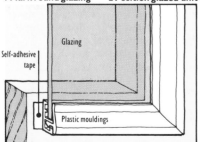

Glazing

Self-adhesive tape

Plastic mouldings

3 Rigid plastic mouldings support the glazing

PLASTIC MATERIALS FOR DOUBLE GLAZING

For economy and safety, plastic sheet materials can be used in place of glass to provide lightweight double glazing. They are available in clear thin flexible films or clear, textured and coloured rigid sheets.

Unlike glass, plastic glazing has a high impact-resistance and will not splinter when broken. Depending on thickness, plastic can be cut with scissors, drilled, sawn, planed and filed.

The clarity of new plastics is as good as glass but they will scratch. They are also liable to degrade with age and are prone to static. Plastic sheet should be washed with a liquid soap solution. Slight abrasions can be rubbed out with metal polish.

Film and semi-rigid plastics are sold by the metre or in rolls. Rigid sheets are available in a range of standard sizes or can be cut to order. Rigid plastic is covered with a protective film of paper or thin plastic on both faces which is peeled off only after cutting and shaping to keep the surface scratch-free.

POLYESTER FILM

A plastic film for inexpensive double glazing. It can be trimmed with scissors or a knife and fixed with self-adhesive tape or strip fasteners.

It is a tough, virtually tearproof film, which is very clear – ideal, in fact, for glazing living rooms. It is sold in 5, 10 and 25 metre (32, 64 and 160ft) rolls, 1143mm (3ft 9in) and 1300mm (4ft 3in) wide.

POLYSTYRENE

A relatively inexpensive clear or textured rigid plastic. Clear polystyrene does not have the clarity of glass and will degrade in strong sunlight. It should not be used for south-facing windows or where a distortion-free view is required. Depending on climatic conditions, the life of polystyrene is reckoned to be between three and five years. Its working life can be extended if the glazing is removed for storage in summer. It is available in thicknesses of 1.5mm ($\frac{1}{16}$in), 2.5mm ($\frac{3}{32}$in) and 4mm ($\frac{5}{32}$in) and sheet sizes up to 1220mm × 2440mm (4ft × 8ft).

ACRYLIC

A good-quality rigid plastic with the clarity of glass. It costs about the same as glass and about half as much again as polystyrene. Its working life is considered to be at least 10 years. Acrylic is also available in a wide range of translucent and opaque colours. The common thicknesses available for clear glazing are 1.5mm ($\frac{1}{16}$in), 2.5mm ($\frac{3}{32}$in) and 4mm ($\frac{5}{32}$in) and it is available in sheet sizes up to 1220mm×2440mm (4ft ×8ft).

POLYCARBONATE

A relatively new plastic glazing material, which is virtually unbreakable. It provides a lightweight vandal-proof glazing with a high level of clarity. The standard grade costs about twice the price of acrylic. It is made in clear, tinted, opal and opaque grades, some with textured surfaces. Thicknesses suitable for domestic glazing are 2mm ($\frac{1}{16}$in), 3mm ($\frac{1}{8}$in) and 4mm ($\frac{5}{32}$in), although greater thicknesses are made, some in grades which are even bullet-proof. Sheet size can be up to 2050mm × 3000mm (7ft × 10ft).

PVC GLAZING

PVC is available as a flexible film or as a semi-rigid sheet. The film provides inexpensive glazing where a high degree of clarity is not required such as in a bedroom. PVC is ultraviolet-stabilized so is suitable for outside or inside use. Consequently, it is very suitable for glazing conservatories (and carport roofs). Rigid PVC is 3mm ($\frac{1}{8}$in) thick in sheet sizes up to 1220mm × 2440mm (4ft × 8ft).

OPENABLE SECONDARY GLAZING SYSTEMS

SEE ALSO

◁ Details for:
Cutting glass   92-93

Hinged or sliding secondary glazing systems are available in kit form for home assembly. Sliding systems are also made and installed by glazing companies — and both sliding and hinged types are intended to be permanent fixtures.

Types of glass used

Normally, 4mm ($^5/_{32}$in) glass is used on openable secondary glazing systems. For sliding windows no pane of glass should exceed 1.85 sq m (20 sq ft), and no more than 1.1 sq m (12 sq ft) should be used for side-hung, hinged sections.

When top-hung, each pane can be 1.65 sq m (18 sq ft). The height of each pane should not exceed 1.5m (5ft) or be greater than twice its width. Use toughened glass for low windows or those at risk from impact.

Hinged system

A hinged system incorporates an aluminium extrusion to form a frame for the glass or rigid plastic sheet. The glazing is seated in a flexible gasket. Corner joints fix the four sides together. Pivot hinges are fitted into the extrusion to make side-hung or top-hung units. A meeting rail section is also made for one frame to close against another where the window is too large to cover in one.

The hinged frames are fitted to the face of a wooden window frame and secured by turn buttons. A flexible draughtproofing strip is fixed to the back of the aluminium.

Hinged system
1 Glazing
2 Flexible gasket
3 Corner joints
4 Hinges
5 Aluminium extrusion
6 Turn button
7 Draughtproofing strip

Sliding systems

A sliding system can operate horizontally or vertically. The horizontal version is normally used for casement windows and the vertical type for tall windows, such as double-hung sashes. You can get systems made of rigid plastic or aluminium.

Each pane of glass is framed by a lightweight extrusion which is jointed at the corners. The glass is sealed into its frame with a gasket. Two or more horizontally sliding panes can be used to suit the width of the window. They are held in a tracked frame, which is screwed to the window frame or the reveal. Fibre seals are fitted to the frame members to prevent draughts between the moving parts. The glazing is opened by a catch and each pane can be lifted out for cleaning.

A vertically sliding system uses a similar form of construction but incorporates catches to hold the panes open at any height.

Fixing a horizontally sliding system

Measure the width and height of your window opening. Buy the appropriate kit of parts to the nearest larger size. Cut the vertical and horizontal track members to size using a junior hacksaw (**1**) and fit the fibre seals in their grooves. Plug and screw them to the window reveal or the inside face of the window frame (**2**).

Following the manufacturer's instructions regarding tolerances, measure the opening for the glass and have it cut to size. Cut and fit the section of glazing frame, including the gasket. Join them together — usually with screw-fixed corner joints (**3**) but sometimes slot-together types — having inserted sliders and handles. Lift the glazing into the sliding tracks to complete the installation (**4**).

Sliding system
1 Glazing extrusion
2 Glazing
3 Corner joints
4 Gasket
5 Top track
6 Bottom/side track
7 Fibre draught seal
8 Catches
9 Rollers

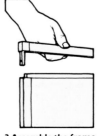

1 Cut track to length   2 Screw to the frame   3 Assemble the frame   4 Fit into the tracks

VENTILATION

Ventilation is essential for a fresh, comfortable atmosphere but it has a more important function with regard to the structure of our homes. It wasn't a problem when houses were heated with open fires, drawing fresh air through all the natural openings in the structure. With the introduction of central heating, insulation and draughtproofing, well-designed ventilation is vital. Without a constant change of air, centrally heated rooms quickly become stuffy and before long the moisture content of the air becomes so high that water is deposited as condensation (▷) – often with serious consequences. There are various ways to provide ventilation, some extremely simple, others much more sophisticated for total control.

Initial considerations

Whenever you undertake an improvement which involves insulation in one form or another, take into account how it is likely to affect the existing ventilation. It may change conditions sufficiently to create a problem in those areas outside the habitable rooms so that damp and its side-effects develop unnoticed under floorboards or in the loft. If there is a chance that damp conditions might occur, provide additional ventilation.

Fitting a fixed window vent

Provide continuous 'trickle' ventilation by installing a simple fixed vent in a window. A well-designed vent allows a free flow of air without draughts, normally by incorporating a wind shield on the outside. It is totally reliable as there are no moving parts to break down or produce those irritating squeaks which are a feature of wind-driven fans.

Have a glazier cut the recommended size of hole in the glass (▷), then place one louvred grille on each side, clamping them together with the central fixing bolt. Bolt the clear plastic windshield to the outer grille.

Ventilating a fireplace

An open fire needs oxygen to burn brightly. If the supply is reduced by thorough draughtproofing or double glazing, the fire smoulders and the slightest downdraught blows smoke into the room. There may be other reasons why a fire burns poorly, such as a blocked chimney for example, but if it picks up within minutes of partially opening the door to the room, you can be sure that inadequate ventilation is the problem.

The most efficient and attractive solution is to cut holes in the floorboards on each side of the fire and cover them with a ventilator grille. Cheap plastic grilles work just as well, but you may prefer brass or aluminium for a living room. Choose a 'hit-and-miss' ventilator, which you can open and close to seal off unwelcome draughts when the fire is not in use. Cut a hole in a fully fitted carpet and screw the grille on top.

If the floor is solid, your only alternative is to fit a grille over the door to the room. An aperture at that height will not create a draught because cold air will disperse across the room and warm as it falls slowly.

Ventilating an unused fireplace
An unused fireplace that has been blocked by brickwork, blockwork or plasterboard should be ventilated to allow air to flow up the chimney to dry out penetrating damp or condensation. Some people believe a vent from a warm interior aggravates the problem by introducing moist air to condense on the cold surface of the brick flue. However, so long as the chimney is uncapped, the updraught should draw moisture-laden air to the outside. An airbrick cut into the flue from outside is a safer solution but it is more difficult to accomplish and quite impossible if you live in a terraced house. Furthermore, the airbrick would have to be blocked should you want to re-open the fireplace at a later date.

To ventilate from inside the room, leave out a single brick, form an aperture with blocks, or cut a hole in the plasterboard used to block off the fireplace. Screw a face-mounted ventilator over the hole or use one that is designed for plastering in. The thin flange for screw-fixing the ventilator to the wall is covered as you plaster up to the slightly protruding grille.

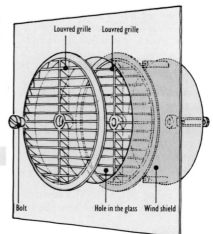

The components of a fixed window vent

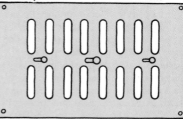

Hit-and-miss ventilator grille

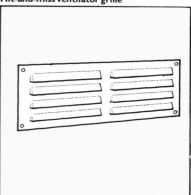

Face-mounted grille for ventilating a fireplace

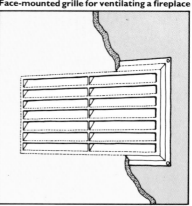

Hide the fixings of a grille with plaster

SEE ALSO

Details for: ▷
Cutting glass	93
Insulation	108-118

● **Condensation**
As air becomes warmer it can absorb more moisture in the form of water vapour. When water-laden air comes into contact with a surface that is colder than itself it condenses, depositing moisture in liquid form.

INSTALLING A COOKER HOOD

Window- and wall-mounted fans are designed for overall room extraction, but the ideal way to tackle steam and *greasy cooking smells from a cooker is to mount a specially designed extracting hood directly over it.*

SEE ALSO

◁ Details for:
Wiring cooker hood   154
Installing ducting   122

Where to mount the cooker hood

Mount a cooker hood between 600mm (2ft) and 900mm (3ft) above the hob or about 400 to 600mm (1ft 4in to 2ft) above an eye-level grill. Unless the manufacturer provides specific dimensions, mount a hood as low as possible within the recommended tolerances.

Depending on the model, a cooker hood may be cantilevered from the wall or, alternatively, screwed between or beneath kitchen cupboards. Some kitchen manufacturers produce a cooker hood housing unit, which matches the style of the cupboards. Opening the unit operates the fan automatically. Most cooker hoods have two or three speed settings and an inbuilt light fitting to illuminate the hob or cooker below.

Installing trunking

When a cooker hood is mounted on an outside wall, air is extracted through the back of the unit into a straight duct passing through the masonry. If the cooker is situated against another wall, it is possible to connect the hood with the outside by means of fire-resistant plastic trunking. Straight and curved components plug into each other to form a continuous shaft running along the top of the wall cupboards.

Plug the female end of the first trunking component over the outlet spigot fitted to the top of the cooker hood. Cutting them to fit with a hacksaw or a tenon saw, run the rest of the trunking, making the same female-to-male connections along the shaft. Some trunking is printed with airflow arrows to make sure each component is orientated correctly: if you were to reverse a component somewhere along the shaft, air turbulence might be created around the joint, reducing the effectiveness of the extractor. At the outside wall, cut a hole through the masonry for a straight piece of ducting and fit an external grille .

Fitting a cooker hood

Recycling and extracting hoods are hung from wall brackets supplied with the machines. Screw fixing points are provided for attaching them to wall cupboards. Cut a ducting hole through a wall as for a wall-mounted fan. Wire a cooker hood following the maker's instructions.

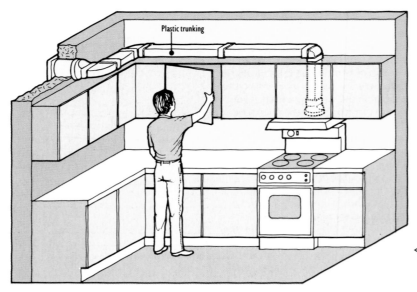

Plastic trunking

RECIRCULATION OR EXTRACTION?

The only real difference between one cooker hood and another is the way it deals with the stale air it captures. Some hoods filter out the moisture and grease before returning the freshened air to the room. Other machines dump stale air outside through a duct in the wall, just like a conventional wall-mounted extractor fan.

Because the air is actually changed, extraction is the more efficient method but it is necessary to cut a hole through the wall and, of course, the heated air is lost – excellent in hot weather but rather a waste in winter. Cooker hoods which recycle the air are much simpler to install but never filter out all the grease and odours, even when new. It is essential to clean and change the filters regularly to keep the hood working at peak efficiency.

Recirculation hood returns filtered air to room

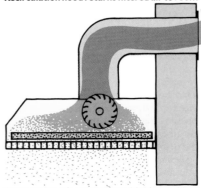

Extraction hoods suck air outside via trunking

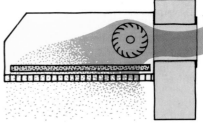

Alternatively, air is extracted through ducting

◁ **Running trunking outside**
When a cooker is placed against an inside wall, run plastic trunking from the extractor hood along the top of wall-hung cupboards.

FITTING AN EXTRACTOR FAN

Kitchens and bathrooms are particularly susceptible to problems of condensation so it is especially important to have a means of efficiently expelling moisture-laden air along with unpleasant odours. An electrically driven extractor fan will freshen a room faster than relying on natural ventilation and without creating uncomfortable draughts.

Positioning an extractor fan

The best place to site a fan is either in a window or on an outside wall but its exact position is more critical than that. Stale air extracted from the room must be replaced by fresh air, normally through the door leading to other areas of the house. If the fan is sited close to the source of replacement air it will promote local circulation but will have little effect on the rest of the room.

The ideal position would be directly opposite the source as high as practicable to extract the rising hot air (**1**). In a kitchen, try to locate the fan adjacent to the cooker but not directly over it. In that way, steam and cooking smells will not be drawn across the room before being expelled (**2**). If the room contains a flued, fuel-burning appliance, you must ensure there is an adequate supply of fresh air at all times or the extractor fan will draw fumes down the flue. The only exception is an appliance with a balanced flue, which takes its air directly from outside.

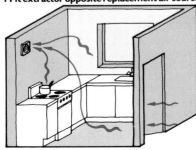
1 Fit extractor opposite replacement air source

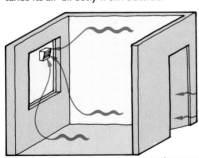
2 Place extractor near a cooker in a kitchen

Types of extractor fan

Many fans have integral switches but, if not, a switched connection unit can be wired into the circuit (▷) when you install the fan. Some models incorporate built-in controllers to regulate the speed of extraction and timers to switch off the fan automatically after a certain time. Fans can be installed in a window and some, with the addition of a duct, will extract air through a solid or cavity wall (see illustrations below). Choose a fan with external shutters that close when the fan is not in use, to prevent backdraughts.

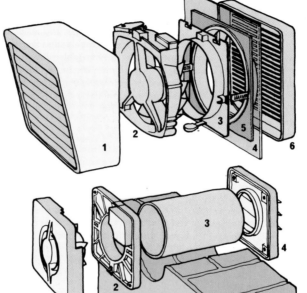

Window-mounted fan
1 Inner casing
2 Motor assembly
3 Interior clamping plate
4 Glass
5 Grille clamping plate
6 Exterior grille

Wall-mounted fan
1 Motor assembly
2 Interior backplate
3 Duct
4 Exterior grille

SEE ALSO

Details for: ▷

Switched connection unit	152
Cooker hoods	120

Choosing the size of a fan

The size of a fan, or to be accurate, its capacity, is determined by the type of room in which it is installed and the volume of air it must move.

A fan installed in a kitchen must be capable of changing the air completely ten to fifteen times per hour. A bathroom requires fifteen to twenty air changes per hour and a WC, ten to fifteen. A living room normally requires four to six changes per hour, but fit a fan with a slightly larger capacity in a smoky environment.

To calculate the capacity of the fan you require, find the volume of the room (length x width x height) then multiply that figure by the recommended number of air changes per hour. Choose a fan which is capable of the same or slightly higher capacity.

CALCULATING THE CAPACITY OF FAN FOR A KITCHEN

SIZE			
Length	**Width**	**Height**	**Volume**
3.35m (11ft)	3.05m (10ft)	2.44m (8ft)	$24.93m^3$ ($880ft^3$)

AIR CHANGES		
Per hour	**Volume**	**Fan capacity**
15	$24.93m^3$ ($880ft^3$)	$374m^3$ per hour ($13,200ft^3$)

SEE ALSO

◁ Details for:
Cutting glass	92-93
Fitting glass	94
Sash stop	98
Consumer unit	134

Metal detector
Detect buried pipes or cables by placing a hired electronic sensor against the plaster

I Hold panel with plank

2 Seal plate spigot

3 Insert duct in hole

4 Screw-fix grille

FITTING A WALL-MOUNTED UNIT

Satisfy yourself that there is no plumbing or wiring buried in the wall by looking in the loft or under the floorboards (see left). Make sure there are no drain pipes or other obstructions.

Cutting the hole

Wall-mounted fans are supplied with a length of plastic ducting for inserting in a hole which you must cut through the wall to the outside. Plot the centre of the hole and draw its diameter on the inside of the wall. Use a long-reach masonry drill to bore a central hole right through. To prevent the drill breaking out brickwork or rendering on the outside, hold a stout plywood panel against the wall and wedge it with a scaffold board supported by stakes driven into the ground **(I)** .

Before cutting the brick, drill holes close together around the inner edge of the hole. With a cold chisel, cut away the plaster using the holes as a guide, then continue to cut away the brickwork (try to avoid debris falling inside a cavity wall). When you reach the centre of the wall, remove the panel then use the same technique to finish the hole from the outside face.

Fitting the fan

Most wall fans are fitted in a similar manner, but check specific instructions beforehand. Separate the components of the fan, then attach a self-adhesive foam sealing strip to the spigot on the backplate to receive the duct **(2)** .

Insert the duct in the hole so that the backplate fits against the wall **(3)** . Mark the length of the duct on the outside, allowing sufficient to fit the similar spigot on the outer grille. Cut the duct to length with a hacksaw. Reposition the backplate and duct to mark the fixing holes on the wall. Drill and plug the holes then feed the electrical supply cable into the backplate before screwing it to the wall. Stick a foam sealing strip inside the spigot on the grille. Position it on the duct then mark, drill and plug the wall fixing holes. Use a screwdriver to stuff scraps of loft insulation between the duct and the cut edge of the hole, then screw on the exterior grille **(4)** .

If the grille does not fit flush with the wall, seal the gap with mastic. Wire the fan according to the manufacturer's recommendations. Attach the motor assembly to the backplate.

FITTING AN EXTRACTOR FAN

Installing a fan in a window

An extractor fan can only be installed in a fixed window. If you wish to fit one in a sash window, it's necessary to secure the top sash in which the fan is installed and fit a sash stop on each side of the window to prevent the lower sash damaging the casing of the fan should it be raised too far.

To install an extractor fan in an hermetically sealed double glazing system, ask the manufacturer to supply a special unit with a hole cut and sealed around its edges to receive the fan. Some manufacturers supply a kit which adapts a fan for installing in a window with secondary double glazing. It allows the inner window to be opened without dismantling the fan.

Cutting the glass

Every window-mounted fan requires a round hole to be cut in the glass. The size is specified by the manufacturer. It is possible to cut a hole in an existing window but stresses in the glass will sometimes cause it to crack, and while the glass is removed for cutting there is always a security risk, especially if you decide to take it to a glazier. All things considered, it is advisable to fit a new pane: it's easier to cut and can be installed immediately the old one has been removed.

Cutting a hole in glass is not easy (◁) and it may be more economical in the long run to order it from a glazier. You'll need to supply exact dimensions, including the size and position of the hole. Use 3mm glass for a pane that does not exceed 0.2 sq m (2 sq ft) in area. Cut a larger pane from 4mm glass.

Installing the fan

The exact assembly may vary but the following sequence is a typical example of how a fan is installed in a window. Take out the existing window pane and clean up the frame, removing traces of old putty and retaining sprigs. Fit the new pane, with its hole pre-cut, as for fitting window glass (◁).

From outside, fit the exterior grille by locating its circular flange in the hole **(I)** . Attach the plate on the inside, which clamps the grille to the glass. Tighten the fixing screws in rotation to achieve a good seal and an even clamping force on the glass **(2)** . Screw the motor assembly to the clamping plate **(3)** . Wire up the fan following the maker's instructions. Fit the inner casing over the motor assembly **(4)** .

WARNING

Never make electrical connections until the power is switched off at the consumer unit (◁).

I Place grille in the hole from outside

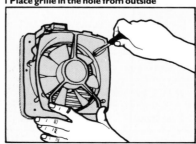

3 Screw the motor assembly to the plate

2 Clamp the inner and outer plate together

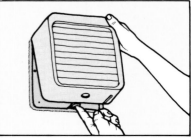

4 Attach the inner casing to cover the assembly

4

ECONOMICS	124
BASICS	126
SAFETY	127
BASIC REPAIRS	130
FUSE BOARDS	134
CIRCUITS	139
CABLES	140
CHECKLISTS	144
POWER CIRCUITS	146
FIXED APPLIANCES	152
LARGER APPLIANCES	155
LIGHTING	159
COMPLETE REWIRING	166

ELECTRICITY

REDUCING THE COST OF ELECTRICITY

Pressures from all sides urge us to conserve energy – electricity as well as fossil fuels like coal, oil and gas – but even without such encouragement the totals on our quarterly electricity bills should be stimulus enough to make us find ways of using less power. No-one wants to live in a poorly heated, dismally lit house without the comforts of hot baths, TV, record players and other conveniences, but you may be able to identify where energy is wasted, then find ways to reduce waste without compromising your comfort or pleasure.

SEE ALSO

◁ Details for:
Insulation	109
Immersion heaters	156-157

Avoid false economy

Whether you do your own wiring or employ a professional, don't try to economize by installing fewer sockets than you really need. When you rewire a room fit as many as you may possibly use. The inconvenience, later on, of running extra cable and disturbing decoration will far outweigh the cost of an extra socket or two.

Similarly, don't restrict your use of lighting unnecessarily. It uses relatively little power, so there is no point in risking, say, accidents on badly lit stairs. Nor need you strain your eyes in the glare from a single light hanging from the ceiling when extra lights can give comfortable and attractive background illumination where needed.

Fitting controls to save money

It will be clear from the chart (See opposite) that heating of one sort or another is the main consumer of power. One way to economize is to fit devices that are designed to regulate its use to suit your life style and keep your heating at comfortable but economic temperatures.

people are more comfortable at about 21°C (70°F).

An immersion heater thermostat both saves money and prevents water becoming dangerously hot. Set it at 60°C (140°F). (For Economy 7 setting see right.)

Thermostats
Most modern heating has some form of thermostatic control – a device that will switch power off when surroundings reach a certain temperature. Many thermostats are marked out simply to increase or decrease the temperature. In this case you have to experiment with various settings to find the one that suits you. If you can set it accurately try 18°C (65°F) for everyday use, though elderly

Time switches
Even thermostatically controlled heating is expensive if run continuously but an automatic time switch can turn it on and off at pre-set times so that you get up in the morning or home in the evening to a warm house. Set it to turn off the heating a half-hour before you leave home or go to bed, as the house will take time to cool down.

A similar device will ensure water at its hottest when it is needed.

● **Insulation**
Measures taken to save energy are of little use unless you insulate the house as well as the hot water cylinder and pipework (◁). You can do most of the work yourself with very little effort or cost.

Recording consumption

Keep an accurate record of your energy saving by taking weekly readings. Note the dates of measures taken to cut consumption and compare the corresponding drop in meter readings.

Digital meters
Modern meters simply display a row of figures or digits that represent the total number of units consumed since the meter was installed. To deduce the number of units used since your last electricity bill subtract the 'present reading' shown on the bill from the number of units now shown on the meter. Make sure that the bill shows an actual reading and not an estimate, indicated by an E before the reading.

ECONOMICAL OFF-PEAK RATES

Electricity is normally sold at a general-purpose rate, every unit used costing the same; but if you warm your home with storage heaters and heat your water electrically, then you can take advantage of the economical off-peak tariff. This system, called Economy 7, allows you to charge storage heaters and heat water at less than half the general-purpose rate for seven hours, starting between midnight and 1 a.m. Other appliances used during that time get cheap power too, so more savings can be made by running the dishwasher or washing machine after you've gone to bed. Each appliance must, of course, be fitted with a timer. The Economy 7 daytime rate is higher than the general-purpose one, but the cost of running 24-hour appliances such as freezers and refrigerators is balanced since they also use cheap power for seven hours.

For full benefit from off-peak water heating use a 182 to 227 litre (40 to 50 gallon) cylinder, to store as much cheap hot water as possible. You will need a twin-element heater or two separate units. One heater, near the base of the cylinder, heats the whole tank on cheap power; another, about half way up, tops up the hot water during the day. Set the night-time heater at 75°C (167°F), the daytime one at 60°C (140°F).

The Electricity Board provides Economy 7 customers with a special meter to record daytime and night-time consumption separately, plus a timer that automatically switches the supply from one rate to the other.

HOW TO READ DIAL METERS

The principle of a dial meter is simple. Ignore the dial marked 1/10, which is only for testing. Start with the dial indicating single units (kWh) and, working from right to left, record the readings from 10, 100, 1000 and finally 10,000 units. Note the digits the pointers have passed. If a pointer is, say,

between 5 and 6 record 5. If a pointer is right on a number, say 8, check the next dial on the right. If that point is between 9 and 0 record 7; if it is past 0 record 8.

Remember that adjacent dials revolve in opposite directions, alternating along the row.

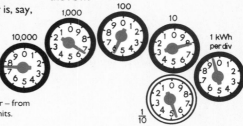

Reading a dial meter
Write down your reading in reverse order – from right to left. This meter records 76,579 units.

RUNNING COSTS OF YOUR APPLIANCES

Apart from the standing charge or hire-purchase payments, your electricity bill is calculated from the number of units of electricity you have used in a given period. Each unit represents the amount used in one hour by a 1kW appliance. An appliance rated at 3kW uses the same amount of energy in 20 minutes.

TYPICAL RUNNING COSTS

	Appliance	Typical usage	No. of units		Appliance	Typical usage	No. of units
	Cooker	Cooks one day's meals for four people	2½		Iron	In use for 2 hours	1
	Microwave	Cooks two joints of meat	1		Vacuum cleaner	Works for 1½-2 hours	1
	Slow cooker	Cooks for 8 hours	1		Cooker hood	Runs for 24 hours continuously	2
	Storage heater (2 kW)	Provides one day's heating	8½		Extractor fan	Runs for 24 hours continuously	1
	Bar fire or fan heater (3 kW)	Gives heat for one hour	3		Hair dryer	Runs for 2 hours	1
	Immersion heater	Supplies one day's hot water for family of four	9		Shaver	Provides 1800 shaves	1
	Instant water heater	Heats 2 to 3 bowls of washing up water	1		Single overblanket	Warms the bed for one week	2
	Instant shower	Delivers 1 to 2 showers	1		Single underblanket	Warms the bed for one week	1
	Dishwasher	Washes one full load	2		Power drill	Works for 4 hours	1
	Automatic washing machine	Deals with one full load with pre-wash	2½		Hedge trimmer	Trims for 2½ hours	1
	Tumble dryer	Dries same load	2½		Cylinder lawn mower	Cuts grass for 3 hours	1
	4 cu ft refrigerator	Keeps food fresh for one week	7		Hover mower	Cuts grass for 1 hour	1
	6 cu ft freezer	Maintains required temperature for one week	9		Stereo system	Plays for 8 hours	1
	Heated towel rail	Warms continuously for 6 hours	1½		Colour TV	Provides 6 hours viewing	1
	Electric kettle	Boils 40 cups of tea	1		VCR	Records for 10 hours	1
	Coffee percolator	Makes 75 cups of coffee	1		100W bulb	Gives 10 hours illumination	1
	Toaster	Toasts 70 slices of bread	1		40W fluorescent strip	Gives 20 hours illumination	1

SEE ALSO

Details for: ▷

Electric fires	153
Heated towel rail	153
Instant water heater	154
Wiring kitchen appliances	154
Wiring cooker hood	154
Wiring extractor fan	154
Wiring a cooker	155-156
Immersion heaters	156-157
Lighting	159-165

● **Typical running costs**
The table shows you how much electricity is used, on average, by common household appliances with different kW ratings. For example, a 100W light bulb can give you 10 hours of illumination before it uses up one 1 kilowatt unit, whereas a 3 kilowatt bar fire will give off heat for only 20 minutes for the same 1 kilowatt.

UNDERSTANDING THE BASICS

SEE ALSO

◁ Details for:
Earth bonding	128, 135
Flex	130
Fuses	133, 137
Circuits	139
Cable	140
Running cable	141-143

Though many people imagine working on the electrical circuits of their homes to be a complicated business it is, in fact, based on very simple principles.

For any electrical appliance to work, the power must have a complete circuit, flowing along a wire from its source – a battery, for instance – to the appliance – say a light bulb – then flowing back to the source along another wire. That is a circuit, and if it is broken at any point the appliance stops working – the bulb goes out.

Breaking the circuit – and restoring it as required – is what a switch is for. With the switch on, the circuit is complete and the bulb or other appliance operates. Switching off makes a gap in the circuit so that the electricity stops flowing.

Though a break in either wire will stop the power flow, in practice a

switch should be wired so that it interrupts the live wire, the one taking power to the appliance. In this way the appliance is completely dead when the switch is off. If the switch is wired so as to interrupt the neutral wire, which takes the electricity back to its source, the appliance will stop working but elements in it will still be 'live', which can be dangerous.

Though mains electricity is much more powerful than that produced by a battery it operates in exactly the same way, flowing through a live or 'phase' wire which is linked to every socket outlet, light and fixed electrical appliance in your home.

For purposes of identification when wiring is done the covering of the live wire is coloured red or brown. The covering on the neutral wire, which takes the current back out of the house after its work, is black or blue.

Identifying conductors ▶
The insulation covering the conductors in cable and flex are colour-coded to indicate live, neutral and earth.

LIVE	NEUTRAL	EARTH
Flex	Flex	Flex
Cable	Cable	Cable

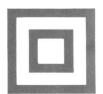

A basic circuit
Electricity runs from the source (battery) to the appliance (bulb) and returns to the source. A switch breaks the circuit to interrupt the flow of electricity.

Double insulation
A square within a square printed or moulded on an appliance means that it is double-insulated and its flex needs no earth wire.

Earthing

Any material through which electricity can flow is known as a conductor. Most metals conduct electricity well – which is why metal (usually copper, the most efficient conductor) is used for electrical wiring.

However, the earth itself, the ground on which we stand, is also an extremely good conductor. In fact, it is an even better conductor than the wiring that's used for electrical circuits – which is why electricity will always flow into the earth, if it has an opportunity to do so, by the shortest available route. This means that if you were to touch a live conductor, the current would divert and take the short route through your body to the earth – perhaps with fatal results.

A similar thing can occur if a live wire comes accidentally into contact with any exposed metal component of an appliance, including its casing. To prevent this, a third wire is included in the wiring system and connected to the earth, usually via the outer casing of the Electricity Board's main service

cable. This third wire – called the earth wire – is attached to the metal casing of some appliances and to special earth terminals in others, providing a direct route to the ground if a fault occurs. This sudden change of route by the electricity – known as an earth fault – causes a fuse to blow or circuit breaker to cut off the current.

Double-insulated appliances – which usually have a non-conductive plastic casing to insulate the user from metal parts that could become live – must not be be earthed with a third wire.

The earth wire either has a green-and-yellow covering or is a bare copper wire sandwiched between the insulated live and neutral wires in an electrical cable. If a bare earth wire is exposed for linking to socket outlets or lighting fittings, it should be covered with a green-and-yellow sleeve.

Metal pipes must also be connected to the earthing system by a separate cable to ensure they do not precipitate an accident during the time it would take for a fault to blow a fuse.

DIY WIRING

Many householders have a certain reluctance to undertake any but the simplest jobs involving electricity, no matter how competent they may be in other areas of home improvement.

To some extent the attitude is quite justifiable. It is sensible to have a healthy respect for anything as potentially dangerous as electricity, and it would be very foolhardy of anyone to jump in at the deep end and undertake a major installation before gaining some experience on less ambitious jobs.

In the end, though, many of us are driven to doing our own house wiring by the prohibitive cost of hiring the professionals. No-one minds paying for expert knowledge, but the truth is that much of the expert's time is taken up lifting floorboards, chopping out and repairing plaster and drilling holes in walls and timbers to run the cable – all jobs that most people would be happy to do themselves.

The electrician's 'Bible'

What unnerves the householder is the possibility of making mistakes with the connections or with the choice of equipment. Fortunately we are guided in this country by a set of detailed rules laid down by the Institition of Electrical Engineers in a document known as the IEE Wiring Regulations. This is the professional electrician's 'Bible', and it covers every aspect of electrical installation. If you follow its recommendations you can feel confident that your work will satisfy the Electricity Board. Indeed the Board will refuse to connect up an installation that doesn't comply with the Regulations.

You can buy a copy of the Wiring Regulations from the IEE itself or you can borrow one from your public library. Unfortunately the guide is notoriously difficult to understand, and it has even proved necessary to publish a 'guide to the guide', so that electricians can find their way through this exacting reference book.

The methods suggested in these pages comply with the Regulations, so you should have no need to refer to the originals unless you plan to undertake a job beyond the scope of this book.

Nevertheless, take the trouble to read all of the relevant information in the chapter so that you fully understand what you are doing. If at any time you become unsure of your competence don't hesitate to ask a professional electrician for help or advice.

FUSES AND CIRCUIT BREAKERS

A conductor will heat up if an unusually high current flows through it. This can damage electrical equipment and cause a serious risk of fire if it is allowed to continue in any part of a domestic wiring system. As a safeguard weak links are included in the wiring to break the circuit before the current can reach a dangerously high level.

The most common form of protection is a fuse, a thin wire designed to break the circuit by melting at a certain temperature depending on the part of the system it is protecting – an individual appliance, a single power or lighting circuit or a whole domestic wiring system.

Alternatively, a special automatic switch called a circuit breaker will trip and cut off the current as soon as it detects an overload on the wiring.

A fuse will 'blow' in the following circumstances:

- When too many appliances are operated on a circuit the excessive demand for current will blow the fuse in that circuit.
- When current reroutes to earth because of a faulty appliance the flow of current increases in the circuit and blows the fuse.

WARNING: The original fault must be dealt with before the fuse is replaced.

Measuring Electricity

Watts measure the amount of power used by an appliance when working. The wattage of an electrical appliance should be marked on its casing. One thousand watts (1000W) equals one kilowatt (1kW).

Amps measure the flow of electric power necessary to produce the required wattage for an appliance.

Volts measure the 'pressure' provided by the generators of the Electricity Board that drives the current along the conductors to the various outlets. In Britain 240 volts is standard.

If you know two of these factors you can determine the other:

Watts = Amps Volts	Amps x Volts = Watts
A method to determine a safe fuse or flex.	Indicates how much power is needed to operate an appliance.

WITH SAFETY IN MIND

Throughout this chapter you will find many references to safety while actually working on any part of your electrical system, but it cannot be stressed too strongly that you must take every step to safeguard yourself and others who will later be using the system. Faulty wiring and appliances are dangerous. When you deal with electricity the rule is 'safety first'.

- Never inspect or work on any part of an electrical installation without first switching off the power at the consumer unit and removing the circuit fuse (▷).
- Disconnect any portable appliance or light fitting that is plugged into a socket before you work on it.
- Double-check all your work, especially connections, before you turn the power on again.

- Always use the correct tools for any electrical job, and use good-quality equipment and materials.
- Fuses are important safety devices. Never fit one that is rated too highly for the circuit it is to protect (▷). No other type of wire or metal strip should be used in place of proper fuses or fusewire.
- Wear rubber-soled shoes when working on an electrical installation.

SEE ALSO

Details for: ▷	
Switching off	134, 136
Fuse ratings	137
Electric shock	129
Fuses	133, 137
Meter	134
Consumer's earth terminal	134

Using professionals

Always be prepared to seek the advice and/or help of a professional electrician if you do not feel competent to handle a particular job yourself, especially if you discover, or even only suspect, that some part of an installation is out of date or dangerous for some other reason.

But make sure that any professional you hire is fully qualified. Check whether he or she is registered with the NICEIC (National Inspection Council for Electrical Installation Contracting). To be a member of this association an electrician must be fully cognizant of, and must comply with, the Regulations for Electrical Installations, the code of practice published by the Institution of Electrical Engineers.

Testing an installation

Any significant rewiring, especially new circuits, must be tested by a competent electrician – indeed, when you apply for connection to the mains supply you have to submit a certificate to the Electricity Board confirming that the new wiring complies with the Wiring Regulations. For a fee, the Electricity Board will test DIY wiring at the time of connection. Never attempt to make connections to the meter or Board's earth terminal yourself. Your local Electricity Board will tell you whether new wiring requires testing.

IS THE POWER OFF?

Having turned off the power you can make doubly sure that a particular outlet is safe to work on by plugging into it some appliance that you know to be in working order – a table lamp, for instance, which you have tested before switching off.

As a further precaution you should check on whether actual terminals or wires are live before tampering with them. Use an electronic mains tester, of the kind in the form of a screwdriver. With your fingertip on its metal cap touch the terminal or wire with the tip of the blade. An indicator in the insulated handle lights up if the terminal or wire is live. Don't use one of the cheap neon testers. Their indicators are not clear in strong light.

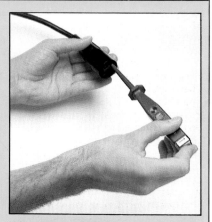

Using an electronic tester
With your finger on the metal cap, touch a terminal with the end of the blade. The terminal is live if the indicator glows.

BATHROOM SAFETY

SEE ALSO

◁ Details for:
Bonding earth	135
Protective multiple earthing	135
Running cable	141-143
Bathroom heaters	153
Shaver sockets	154
Cable	140
Electric shower	159
Close-mounted lights	161
Ceiling switch	163, 165

Water and electricity form a very dangerous combination, for water is a highly efficient conductor of electric current. For this reason bathrooms are potentially the most dangerous areas in terms of electricity. Where there are so many exposed pipes and fittings, combined with wet conditions, stringent regulations must be observed if fatal accidents are to be avoided.

GENERAL SAFETY

● No sockets should be fitted in a bathroom except special ones approved for electric shavers (◁).

● Regulations stipulate that any standard light switches in bathrooms must be out of reach of anyone using a shower, bath or washbasin. The only sure way of complying with this is to fit nothing but ceiling-mounted pull-cord switches.

● Any bathroom heater must comply with IEE Regulations (◁).

● If you have a shower unit in a bedroom it must be at least 2.5m (8ft) from any socket outlet.

● Light fittings must also be out of reach, so fit a close-mounted ceiling light, properly enclosed, rather than a pendant fitting.

● Never use portable fires or other appliances such as hair dryers in a bathroom even if they are plugged into a socket outside.

● **Supplementary bonding in a kitchen**
Supplementary bonding regulations apply to kitchens as well as bathrooms. Bond metal sink units, metallic supply and wastepipes, radiators and central heating pipework. Space and water heaters must be bonded as for bathrooms.

WARNING

Have supplementary bonding tested by a qualified electrician. If you have had no previous experience of wiring and making connections have supplementary bonding installed by a professional.

Supplementary bonding

In a bathroom there are many non-electrical metallic components such as metal baths and basins, supply pipes to bath and basin taps, metal wastepipes, radiators, central heating pipework and so on, all of which could become dangerous if they were to come into contact with a live electrical conductor. To ensure that such an occurrence would blow a fuse in the consumer unit, Wiring Regulations specify that all these metal components must be connected one to another by an earth conductor which itself is connected to a terminal on the earthing block in the consumer unit. This is known as supplementary bonding and is required for new bathrooms even when there is no electrical equipment installed in the room and even though the water and gas pipes are bonded to the consumer's earth terminal near the consumer unit (◁). When electrical equipment like a heater or shower is fitted in a bathroom, that too must be supplementary bonded by connecting its metalwork, such as the casing, to the non-electrical pipework even though the appliance is connected to the earthing conductor in the supply cable.

Supplementary bonding in a bathroom

Making the connections

The Wiring Regulations specify the minimum size of earthing conductor that can be used for supplementary bonding in different situations, so that large-scale electrical installations can be costed economically. In a domestic environment, use 6mm² single-core cable insulated with green-and-yellow PVC for supplementary bonding. This is large enough to be safe in any domestic situation. For a neat appearance, plan the route of the bonding cable to run from point to point behind the bath panel, under floorboards, and through basin pedestals. If necessary, run the cable through a hollow wall or under plaster like any other electrical cable.

Connecting to pipework
Use an earth clamp (**1**) to make connections to pipework. Clean the pipe locally with wire wool to make a good connection between the pipe and clamp, and scrape or strip an area of paintwork if the pipe has been painted.

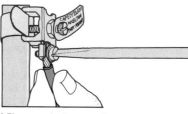

1 Fit an earth clamp to pipework

Connecting to a bath or basin
Metal baths or basins are made with an earth tag. Connect the earth cable by trapping the bared end of the conductor under a nut and bolt with metal washers (**2**). Make sure the tag has not been painted or enamelled.

If an old bath or basin has not been provided with an earth tag, drill a hole through the foot of the bath or to the rim at the back of the basin and connect the cable with a similar nut and bolt.

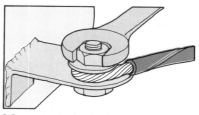

2 Connect to bath or basin earth tag

Connecting to an appliance
Connect the earth to the terminal provided in an electrical appliance (**3**) and run it to a clamp on a metal supply pipe nearby.

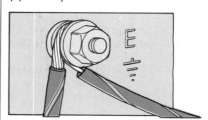

3 Fix to an appliance earth terminal

DEALING WITH ELECTRIC SHOCK

If someone in your presence receives an electric shock and is still in contact with its source, turn off the current at once either by pulling out the plug or by switching off at the socket or consumer unit. If this is not possible, don't take hold of the person – or the current may pass through you too. Pull the victim free with a scarf or dry towel or something like that, or knock their hand free of the electrical equipment with a piece of wood. As a last resort, free the victim by taking hold of their loose clothing – but without touching the body.

Don't attempt to move anyone who has fallen as a result of electric shock – except to place them in the recovery position (see right) – as they may have sustained other injuries. Wrap them in a blanket or coat to keep them warm until they can move themselves.

Once the person can move and is no longer in contact with the electrical equipment, treat their electrical burns by reducing the heat of the injury under slowly running cold water. Apply a dry dressing and seek professional medical advice.

Isolating the victim
If a person sustains an electric shock, turn off the supply of electricity immediately, either at the consumer unit or at a socket (**1**). If this is not possible, pull the victim free with a dry towel, or knock their hand free of the electrical equipment (**2**) with a piece of wood or a broom.

ARTIFICIAL VENTILATION

Severe electric shock can make a person stop breathing. Once you have freed them from the electricity supply, revive them by means of artificial ventilation.

Clear the airway
First, clear the victim's airway. To do this, loosen the clothing round the neck, chest and waist, make sure that the mouth is free of food, and remove loose dentures (**1**).

1 Clear the mouth of food or loose dentures

Lay the person on his or her back and carefully tilt the head back by raising the chin (**2**). This prevents the victim's tongue blocking the airway and may in itself be enough to restart the person's breathing. If it doesn't succeed in doing so quickly, try more direct methods of artificial ventilation.

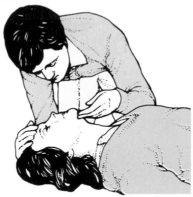

2 Tip the head back to open the airway

Mouth-to-mouth
Keeping the victim's nostrils closed by pinching them between thumb and forefinger, cover the mouth with your own, making a seal all round (**3**). Blow firmly and look for signs of the chest rising. Remove your lips and allow the chest to fall. Repeat this procedure, breathing into the mouth every six seconds. After ten breaths, phone the emergency services. Continue the treatment till normal breathing resumes or expert help arrives.

Mouth-to-nose
If injuries to the face make mouth-to-mouth ventilation impossible, follow a similar procedure but keep the victim's mouth covered with one hand and blow firmly into the nose (**4**).

3 Mouth-to-mouth   **4 Mouth-to-nose**

Reviving a baby
If the victim is a baby or small child, cover both the nose and the mouth at the same time with your own mouth (**5**) and proceed as for mouth-to-mouth ventilation (see left), but breathe every three seconds.

5 Cover a baby's nose and mouth

Recovery
Once breathing has started again, put the victim in the recovery position. Turn him or her face down with the head turned sideways and tilted up slightly. This keeps the airway open and will also prevent vomit being inhaled if the person is sick.

Lift one leg out from the body and support the head by placing the person's left hand, palm down, under his or her cheek (**6**). Keep the casualty warm with blankets until help arrives.

6 Recovery position

SEE ALSO

Details for: ▷
Safety tips   127

129

SIMPLE REPLACEMENTS

You can carry out many repairs and replacements without having to concern yourself with the wiring system installed in your home. Many light fittings and appliances are supplied with electricity through flexible cords that simply plug into the system and are easily disconnected, so there can be no risk of getting an electric shock while you are working on them.

SEE ALSO

◁ Details for:
Colour coding	126
Switching off	134
Fabric-covered flex	160

WARNING

Never attempt to carry out electrical repairs without first disconnecting the appliance or switching off the power supply at the consumer unit (◁).

Flexible cord

All portable appliances and some of the smaller fixed ones, as well as pendant and portable light fittings, are connected to the permanent wiring system by means of conductors of flexible cord, normally called 'flex'. Each conductor in any type of flex is made up of many fine wires twisted together, and each one is insulated from the others with a covering of non-conductive material to contain the current. Insulation material is usually colour-coded to identify live, neutral and earth conductors – brown = live; blue = neutral; green/yellow = earth.

Further protection is provided on some flexible cords in the form of an outer sheathing of insulating material enclosing all the inner conductors.

Heat-resistant flex is available for enclosed light fittings ar.d appliances whose surfaces will become hot.

COILED FLEX

A coiled flex which stretches and retracts is ideal for a portable lamp or appliance.

Coiled flex is sold as a standard length

TYPES OF ELECTRICAL FLEX

PARALLEL TWIN

Parallel twin flex has two conductors insulated with PVC running side by side. The insulation is joined between the two conductors along the length of the flex. This kind of flex should only be used for extra-low-voltage (bell) wiring or inside certain types of light fitting. The wires are hardly ever colour-coded.

TWISTED TWIN

Twisted twin flex is similar to parallel twin, but the PVC-insulated conductors are twisted together for extra strength to support hanging light fittings and shades. However, it is better to use a two-core sheathed flex when wiring up pendant lights. Any old rubber-insulated flex with braided cotton covering still found in some homes should be replaced.

FLAT TWIN SHEATHED

Flat twin sheathed flex has colour-coded live and neutral conductors inside a PVC sheathing. This flex is used for double-insulated light fittings and small appliances.

TWO-CORE CIRCULAR SHEATHED

This has colour-coded neutral and live conductors inside a PVC sheathing that is circular in its cross section. It is used for wiring pendant lights and some double-insulated appliances.

THREE-CORE CIRCULAR SHEATHED

This is like two-core circular sheathed flex but it also contains an insulated and colour-coded earth wire. This flex is perhaps the most commonly used for all kinds of appliances.

UNKINKABLE BRAIDED

This flex is used on appliances like kettles and irons, which are of a high wattage and whose flex must stand up to movement and wear. The three rubber-insulated conductors are strengthened by textile cords running parallel with them, all contained in a rubber sheathing bound outside with braided material.

This type of flex can be wound round the handle of a cool electric iron.

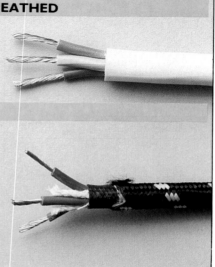

Though the spacing of terminals in plugs and appliances varies, the method of stripping and connecting the flex is the same.

Stripping the flex

If the flex is sheathed slit the sheath lengthwise with a sharp knife **(1)**, being careful not to cut into the insulation covering individual conductors. Divide the conductors of parallel twin flex by pulling them apart before you expose their ends.

Peel the sheathing from the conductors, fold it back over the knife blade and cut it off **(2)**.

Separate the conductors, crop them to length and with wire strippers remove about 12mm (½in) of insulation from the end of each one **(3)**.

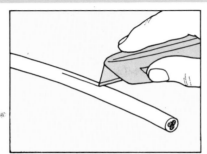
1 Slit sheathing lengthwise

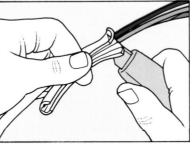
2 Fold sheathing over blade and cut it off

3 Strip insulation from conductors

MULTI-PURPOSE TOOL

A multi-purpose tool will crop and strip any size of cable or flex.

Stripping flex with a multi-purpose tool

Connecting the conductors

Twist together the individual filaments of each conductor to make them neat.

If the plug or appliance has the post type of terminals fold the bared end of wire **(1)** before pushing it in the hole. The insulation should butt against the post. Tighten the clamping screw, then pull gently on the wire to be sure it is held quite firmly.

SEE ALSO

Details for: ▷
Measuring electricity   127

1 Post terminal

When connecting to clamp-type terminals you wrap the bared wire round the post clockwise **(2)**, then screw the clamping nut down tight on the wire and check that the conductor has been securely held.

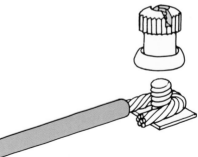
2 Clamp terminal

To attach the wire to a snap-fastening terminal swing open the back of the locking clip, insert the bared end of wire **(3)** and snap the clip back to grip the wire firmly.

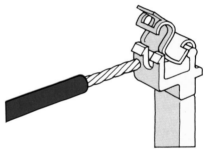
3 Snap-fastening terminal

CHOOSING A FLEX

Not only the right flex for the job is important; the size of its conductors must suit the amount of current that will be used by the appliance.

Flex is rated according to the area of the cross section of its conductors, 0.5mm² being the smallest for normal domestic wiring. Any required size is determined by the flow of current that it can handle safely. Excessive current will make a conductor overheat, so the size of the flex must be matched to the power (wattage) of the appliance which it is feeding.

Manufacturers often fit 1.25mm² flex to appliances of up to 3000W (3kW) because it is safer to use a larger conductor than necessary if a smaller flex might be easily damaged. Adopt the same procedure to replace flex.

Conductor	Current rating	Appliance
0.5 mm²	3 amps	Light fittings up to 720W
0.75 mm²	6 amps	Light fittings and appliances up to 1440W
1.0 mm²	10 amps	Appliances up to 2400W
1.25 mm²	13 amps	Appliances up to 3120W
1.5 mm²	15 amps	Appliances up to 3600W
2.5 mm²	20 amps	Appliances up to 4800W
4.0 mm²	25 amps	Appliances up to 6000W

EXTENDING FLEXIBLE CORD

SEE ALSO

◁ Details for:

Positioning sockets	146
Flex	130
Connecting flex	131

When you plan the positions of socket outlets (◁) make sure there will be enough, all conveniently situated, so that it is never necessary to extend the flexible cord of a table lamp or other appliance. But if you do find that a flex will not reach a socket extend it so that it cannot be pulled tight, which can cause an accident. Never join two lengths of flex by twisting the bared ends of wires together, even if you bind them with insulating tape. People do this as a temporary measure, intending to make a proper connection later, but often forget to, and this can have fatal consequences eventually.

Flex connectors

Ideally you should fit a new length of flex, wiring it into the appliance itself. If you can't do this, or don't wish to dismantle the appliance, use a flex connector, a two- or three-terminal one, according to the type of flex.

Strip off just enough sheathing so that the conductors can reach the terminals and the sheathed part of each cord will be secured under the cord clamp at each end of the connector.

Cut the conductors to length with engineers' pliers and strip and connect them, the live conductor to one of the outer terminals, the neutral to the other and the earth wire (if present) to the central one. Make sure that matching conductors of the two cords are connected to the same terminals, then tighten the cord clamps and screw the cover in place.

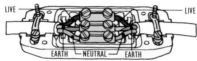

Wiring a flex conductor

In-line switches

If you plan to fit a longer continuous length of flex you can install an in-line switch that will allow you to control the appliance or light fitting from some distance away – a great advantage for the elderly or bed-ridden. Some in-line switches are fluorescent.

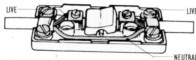

Wiring an in-line switch

Extension leads

If you fit a long flexible cord to a power tool it will inevitably become tangled and one of the conductors will eventually break, perhaps causing a short circuit. The solution is to buy or make an extension lead into which you can plug any tool or appliance you need.

The best type of extension lead to be had commercially is wound on a drum. There are 5amp ones, but it is safer to buy one rated at 13amps so that you can run a wider range of equipment with no danger of overloading it. If you use such a lead while it is wound on the drum it can overheat, so develop the habit of fully unwinding it each time.

The drums of these leads have a built-in 13amp socket to take the plug of the appliance. The plug on the lead is connected to the ordinary wall socket.

You can make an extension lead from a length of 1.5mm^2 three-core flex with a standard 13amp plug on one end and a trailing socket on the other. Use those with unbreakable rubber casings. A trailing socket is wired similarly to a 13amp plug (See opposite). Its terminals are marked to indicate which conductors connect to them.

'Multi-way' trailing sockets will take more than one plug and are ideal for hi-fi systems with individual components that must be connected to mains supply. With a multi-way socket in the cabinet the whole system is supplied from one plug in the wall socket.

Alternatively you can use a lightweight two-part flex connector. One half has three pins which the other half receives.

Unwind a lead
Always fully unwind a 13amp extension lead before you plug in an appliance rated at 1kW or more.

WARNING

When wiring a two-part flex connector never attach the part with the pins to the extension lead. The exposed pins will become live – and dangerous – when the lead is plugged into the socket. In fact nothing electrical should ever be wired so that a plug can become live other than when its pins are concealed in a socket.

TYPES OF FLEX EXTENDER

Below are illustrated four of the devices available for extending the flexible cords of electrical appliances (See left).

Drum-type extension lead

13amp plug and trailing socket

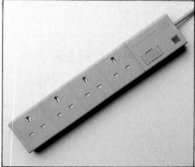

Multi-way trailing socket

Two-part flex connector

WIRING A PLUG

In the past there were many types of plug. Nowadays there are standard ones for all light fittings and portable appliances – 13amp square-pin plugs. They are available with rigid plastic or unbreakable rubber casings. Some have integral neon indicators to show when they are live, and pins insulated for part of their length now prevent the user getting a shock from a plug pulled partly from the socket.

Safety standards and fuses
Use only plugs marked BS 1363, which means conformity to British Standards and therefore safety in use. All square-pin plugs have a small cartridge fuse to protect the appliance – 3amp (red) for appliances of up to 720W or 13amp (brown) for those of from 720 to 3000W. There are 2, 5 and 10 amp fuses but they are rarely used in the home.

Wiring a 13amp plug

Loosen the large screw between the pins and remove the cover. Position the flex on the open plug to determine how much sheathing to remove, remembering that the cord clamp must grip sheathed flex, not the conductors.

Strip the sheathing and again position the flex on the plug so that you can cut the conductors to the right length.

These should take the most direct routes to their terminals and lie neatly in the channels of the plug.

Strip and prepare the ends of the wires, then secure each to its terminal. If you are using two-core flex, wire to the live and neutral terminals, leaving the earth terminal empty.

Tighten the cord clamp to grip the end of the sheathing and secure the flex. One type of plug has a sprung cord grip that tightens if the flex is pulled hard.

Check that a fuse of the correct rating is fitted.

Replace the plug's cover and tighten up the screw.

Wiring older plugs

If your home still has old round-pin sockets you must go on using round-pin plugs, which are not fused. Use the small 2amp one for lighting only, a 5amp one for appliances of up to 1000W and a 15amp one for anything between 1000W and 3000W. You should have your wiring upgraded as soon as possible so that you can use modern fused square-pin plugs.

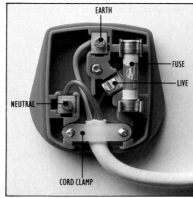
Post-terminal plug

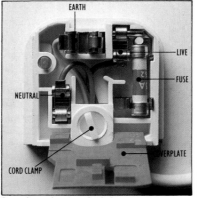
Clamp-terminal plug

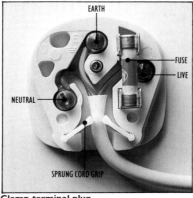
Snap-fastening terminal plug

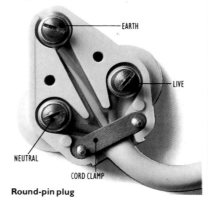
Round-pin plug

REPLACING A PENDANT LAMPHOLDER

Because they are not easy to inspect damaged lampholders can go unnoticed. You should check their condition every so often and replace any suspect ones before they become dangerous.

Pendant lampholders, which hang on flex from the ceiling, are in a stream of hot air rising from the bulb, and in time this can make plastic holders brittle and more easily cracked or broken. On a metal lampholder the earth wire can become detached or corroded so that the fitting is no longer safe.

Types of lampholder
Plastic lampholders are the most common. These have a threaded skirt that screws onto the actual holder, the part that takes the bulb, and some versions have an extended skirt for fitting in bathrooms. You should fit heat-resistant plastic holders if you use a close-fitting or badly ventilated shade.

Plastic holders are designed to take only two-core flex. Don't fit one on a three-core flex as it will have no place to attach the earth wire.

Metal lampholders are similar in their construction but they must be wired with three-core flex so that they can be connected to earth. Never fit a metal lampholder in a bathroom, and never attach one to a two-core flex, which has no earth conductor.

Fitting a lampholder
Before you start remove the fuse for the circuit or switch off the circuit breaker at the consumer unit (▷) so that no-one can turn the power on.

Unscrew the old holder's cap – or the retaining ring if it's a metal one – and slide it up the flex to expose the terminals. Loosen their screws and pull the wires out. If some wires are broken or brittle cut back slightly to expose sound wire before fitting the holder.

Slide the cap of the new fitting up the flex and attach it temporarily with adhesive tape.

Fit the live or neutral wire into either terminal and twist the conductors round the supporting lugs of the holder to take the weight off the terminals, then screw the cap down.

On a metal holder pass the earth wire through the hole in the cap before you screw it down. Wrap the wire clockwise round the fixing screw and tighten it. Screw down the retaining ring to secure the cap.

SEE ALSO

Details for: ▷	
Switching off	134, 138
Flex	130
Connecting flex	131

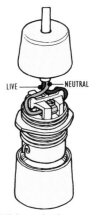
Wiring a plastic pendant lampholder

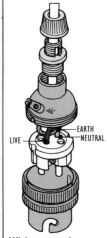
Wiring a metal pendant lampholder

MAIN SWITCH EQUIPMENT

Electricity flows because of a difference in pressure between the live wire and the neutral one, and this difference in the pressures is measured in volts.

Domestic electricity is supplied at 240 volts (240V) 'alternating current' by way of the Electricity Board's service cable, which enters your house underground, though in some areas power is distributed by overhead cables.

SEE ALSO

◁ Details for:

Circuit breakers	**138**
Cheap electricity	124
Consumer unit	136
Fuses/circuit breakers	137
Switchfuse unit	156

The sealing chamber

The main cable terminates at the service head, or sealing chamber, which contains the service fuse. This fuse prevents the neighbourhood being affected if there should be a serious fault in your circuitry. A cable connects the sealing chamber to the meter, which registers how much power is used. The meter and sealing chamber belong to the Electricity Board and must not be tampered with. The meter is sealed to detect interference.

If you use the cheap night-time power for storage heaters and hot water a time switch will be mounted somewhere between the sealing chamber and the meter.

Consumer units

Electricity is fed to and from the consumer unit by 'meter leads', thick single-core cables made up of several wires twisted together. The consumer unit is a box that contains the fuseways which protect the individual circuits in the house. It also incorporates the main isolating switch with which you can cut off the supply of power to the whole of the house.

In a house where several new circuits have been installed over the years the number of circuits may exceed the number of fuseways in the consumer unit, so an individual switchfuse unit – or more than one – may have to be mounted alongside the main unit. Switchfuse units comprise a single fuseway and a.ı isolating switch. They too are connected to the meter by means of meter leads.

If your home is heated by storage heaters you will probably have a separate consumer unit for the circuits that supply the heaters.

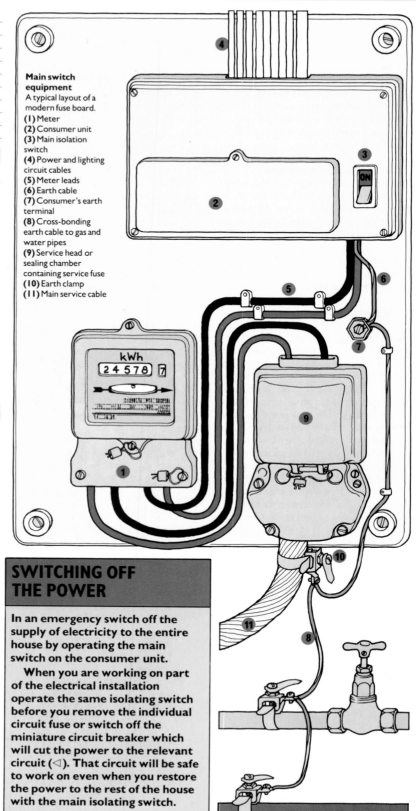

Main switch equipment
A typical layout of a modern fuse board.
(1) Meter
(2) Consumer unit
(3) Main isolation switch
(4) Power and lighting circuit cables
(5) Meter leads
(6) Earth cable
(7) Consumer's earth terminal
(8) Cross-bonding earth cable to gas and water pipes
(9) Service head or sealing chamber containing service fuse
(10) Earth clamp
(11) Main service cable

kWh
2 4 5 7 8 7

SWITCHING OFF THE POWER

In an emergency switch off the supply of electricity to the entire house by operating the main switch on the consumer unit.

When you are working on part of the electrical installation operate the same isolating switch before you remove the individual circuit fuse or switch off the miniature circuit breaker which will cut the power to the relevant circuit (◁). That circuit will be safe to work on even when you restore the power to the rest of the house with the main isolating switch.

EARTHING SYSTEMS

The earthing system

All of the individual earth conductors of the various circuits in the house are connected to one heavy earth cable in the consumer unit. This cable is sheathed in green or green/yellow and runs from the unit to the consumer's earth terminal. In most town houses the earth cable continues from the earth terminal to a clamp on the metal sheath of the main service cable just below the sealing chamber. This is an effective path to earth. The current will pass along the sheath to the Electricity Board's substation, where it is solidly connected to earth.

Until recently most electrical installations were earthed to the cold water supply so that earth-leakage current passed out along the metal water pipes into the ground in which they were buried. But more and more water systems now use non-metallic, non-conductive pipes, so that means of earthing is no longer reliable. Despite this you will find that your pipework is connected to the earth terminal in case one of the live conductors in the house should touch a pipe at some point. The same earth cable is usually clamped to a nearby gas pipe on the house side of the meter before running on to the consumer's earth terminal. This ensures that both water and gas piping systems are cross-bonded so that earth-leakage current passing through either system will run without hindrance to the clamp on the service cable sheath and so to earth. The clamps must never be interfered with.

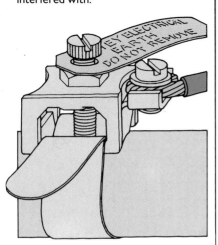

Earth clamp
The earthing system of the house finally connects to the main service cable with this type of clamp. It should not be removed under any circumstances.

PME

Sometimes, especially in country areas, the Electricity Board provides a different method of earthing the system, called 'protective multiple earth' (PME), by which earth-leakage current is fed back to the substation along the neutral return wire, and so to earth.

Regulations regarding the earthing of this system are particularly stringent. Cross-bonding cables to gas and water services are generally required to be larger with PME. Check this with your Electricity Board.

RCCBs

Though the Electricity Board normally provides effective earthing, actually it is the consumer's responsibility. It is often achieved by installing a 'residual-current circuit breaker' or RCCB, into the house circuitry.

Under normal conditions the current flowing out through the neutral conductor is exactly the same as that flowing in through the live one. Should there be an imbalance between the two caused by an earth leakage the RCCB will detect it immediately and isolate the system.

An RCCB can be either installed as a separate unit or incorporated into the consumer unit together with the main isolating switch.

A separate unit containing an RCCB

RECOGNIZING AN OLD FUSE BOARD

Domestic wiring was once very different from a modern system. Beside lighting, water-heating and cooker circuits, each individual socket outlet had its own circuit and fuse, while further circuits would usually be installed from time to time as the needs of the household changed.

Consequently an old house may have a mixture of 'fuse boxes' attached to a fuse board along with the meter. The wiring itself may be haphazard and badly labelled, with the constant risk that you have not safely isolated the circuit you wish to work on. Further, you will be unable to tell if a given fuse is correctly and safely rated unless you know what type of circuit it is protecting.

If your home still has such an old-style fuse board have it inspected and tested by a qualified electrician before you attempt to work on any part of the system. He can advise you on whether to replace the installation with a modern consumer unit or, if the system is in good working condition, he can at least label the various circuits clearly to help you in the future.

SEE ALSO

Details for: ▷
Supplementary bonding 128

An old-fashioned fuse board
This type of installation is out of date. A professional electrician may advise you to replace at least some of the components.

● **RCCB**
An RCCB may be referred to as an RCD – residual-current device. It was formerly known as an ELCB – earth-leakage circuit breaker.

THE CONSUMER UNIT

The consumer unit is the heart of your electrical installation, for every circuit in the house must pass through it. There are several different types and styles of consumer unit but they are all based on similar principles.

SEE ALSO

◁ Details for:
RCCB	135
Ring circuit	139
Main switch equipment	134

Every unit has a large main switch that can turn off the whole installation. On some, more expensive units the switch is in the form of an RCCB (◁) which can be operated manually but will also 'trip' automatically, isolating the entire household system, should any serious fault occur, and much more quickly than the Electricity Board's fuse would take to blow in a similar emergency.

Some consumer units are designed so that it is impossible to remove the outer cover without first turning off the main switch. Even if yours is not of this type you should always switch off before exposing any of the elements within the consumer unit.

Having turned off the main switch, remove the cover or covers so that you can see how the unit is arranged. The cover must be replaced before the unit is switched on again — and remember: even when the unit is switched off the cable connecting the meter to the main switch is still live, so take care.

Take note of the cables that feed the various circuits in the house. Ideally they should all enter the consumer unit from the same direction.

The black-insulated neutral wires run to a common neutral block where they are attached to their individual terminals. Similarly the green earth wires run to a common earthing block. The red-covered live conductors are connected to terminals on individual fuseways or circuit breakers.

Some wires will be twisted together in one terminal. These are the two ends of a ring circuit (◁) and that is how they should be wired.

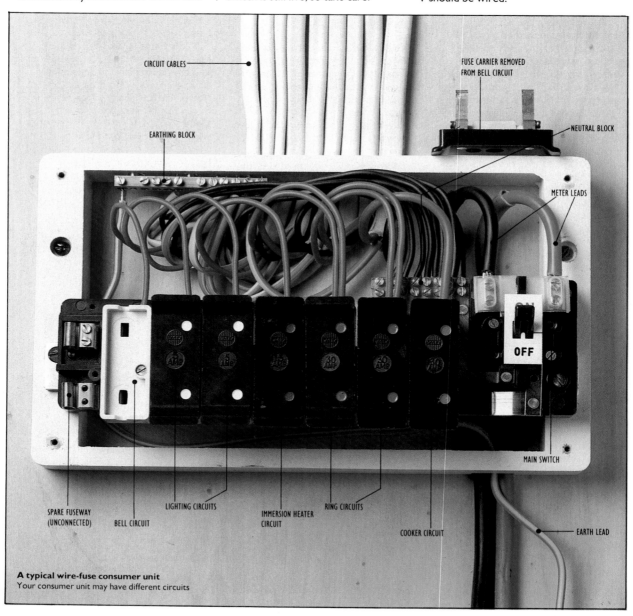

CIRCUIT CABLES

FUSE CARRIER REMOVED
FROM BELL CIRCUIT

EARTHING BLOCK

NEUTRAL BLOCK

METER LEADS

MAIN SWITCH

SPARE FUSEWAY
(UNCONNECTED)

BELL CIRCUIT

LIGHTING CIRCUITS

IMMERSION HEATER
CIRCUIT

RING CIRCUITS

COOKER CIRCUIT

EARTH LEAD

A typical wire-fuse consumer unit
Your consumer unit may have different circuits

FUSES: TYPES AND RATINGS

Into the fuseway of each circuit is plugged a fuse carrier, which is essentially a bridge between the main switch and that particular circuit. When the fuse carrier is removed from the unit current cannot pass across the gap.

Identifying a fuse

Pull any individual fuse carrier out of the unit to see what kind of fuse it contains. At each end of the carrier is a single- or double-bladed contact. A rewirable carrier will have a thin wire running from one contact to the other, held by a screw terminal at each end. The fuse wire is available in different thicknesses, carefully calculated to melt at given temperatures when a circuit is substantially overloaded, breaking the 'bridge' and isolating the circuit.

Alternatively the carrier may contain a cartridge fuse like those used in 13amp plugs, though circuit fuses are larger, varying in size according to their rating. The cartridge is a ceramic tube containing a fuse wire packed in fine sand. The wire is connected to metal caps at the ends of the cartridge which snap into spring clips on the contacts of the fuse carrier. Cartridge fuses provide better protection, as they blow faster than ordinary fuse wire.

Fuse ratings

Whatever the type of fuses used in the consumer unit they are rated in the same way. Cartridge fuses are colour-coded and marked with the appropriate amp rating for a certain type of circuit. Fuse wire is bought wrapped round a card which is clearly labelled.

Never insert fuse wire that is heavier than the gauge intended for the circuit. To do so would mean that a dangerous fault could go unnoticed because of the fuse failing to melt. It is even more dangerous to substitute any other type of wire or metal strip; these will give no protection at all.

When changing a fuse do not replace it automatically with one of the same rating without checking that it is the correct one for the circuit.

The fuse carrier should be marked and/or colour-coded. You can also check the list of circuits on the inside of the consumer unit cover to identify the carriers and their required ratings.

Keep spare fusewire or cartridge fuses in or close to the consumer unit.

FUSE RATINGS

Circuit	Fuse	Colour coding
Doorbell	5amp	White
Lighting	5amp	White
Immersion heater	15amp	Blue
Storage heater	15amp	Blue
Radial circuits – 20sq m maximum floor area	20amp	Yellow
50sq m maximum floor area	30amp	Red
Ring circuits – 100sq m maximum floor area	30amp	Red
Shower unit	45amp	Green
Cooker	30amp	Red

fuse wire
ref. 480
5 AMP For lights and small plug circuits
15 AMP For large plug circuits
30 AMP For cookers and ring mains

A selection of circuit fuses and fuse wire
From left to right: fuse wire, 45amp fuse, 30amp fuse, 20amp fuse, 15amp fuse, 5amp fuse.

FUSE CARRIERS AND MCB'S

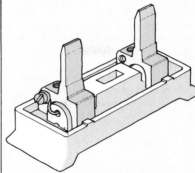

Single-bladed carrier with wire fuse

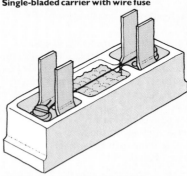

Double-bladed carrier with wire fuse

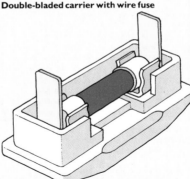

Cartridge fuse carrier

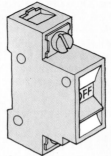

Switch-operated miniature circuit breaker (▷)

Button-operated miniature circuit breaker (▷)

SEE ALSO

Details for: ▷
Circuit breakers   138

● **MCB ratings**
In order to conform to European standards, MCB ratings tend to vary slightly from circuit-fuse ratings. (See CIRCUITS: MAXIMUM LENGTHS.) However, it is perfectly acceptable if you have MCBs that match the slightly smaller ratings shown for circuit fuses.

CHANGING A FUSE

SEE ALSO

◁ Details for:
Consumer unit	136
Fuses/ratings	137
Circuit breakers	137

When everything on a circuit stops working your first step is to check the fuse on the circuit and see if it has blown. Turn off the main switch on the consumer unit, remove the cover and look for the failed fuse. The fuse will be easier to find if you know which circuit is affected, so check the list of circuits inside the unit's cover. If there is no list you will have to inspect all likely circuits. For instance, if the lights 'blew' when you switched them on you need check only the lighting circuits. These are colour-coded white.

Checking a cartridge fuse

The simple way to check a suspect cartridge fuse is to replace it with a new one and see if the circuit works. Or you can check the fuse with a metal-cased torch. Remove the bottom cap of the torch and touch one end of the fuse to the base of the battery while resting its other end against the battery's metal casing. If the battery bulb lights up the fuse is sound.

Testing a cartridge fuse
With the torch switched on, hold the fuse against the battery and the metal casing.

Checking a rewirable fuse

On a blown rewirable fuse a visual check will usually detect the broken wire and scorch marks on the fuse carrier. If the fuse is one on which you cannot see the whole length of the fuse wire you should pull gently on each end of the wire with the tip of a screwdriver to see if it is intact.

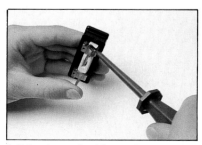

Pull the wire gently with a small screwdriver

HOW TO REPLACE FUSE WIRE

To replace a blown fuse wire loosen the two terminals holding the fuse and extract the broken pieces. Wrap one end of a new length of wire clockwise round one terminal and tighten the screw on it **(1)**, then run the wire across to the other terminal, leaving it slightly slack, attach it in the same way **(2)** and cut off any excess from the ends.

If the wire passes through a tube in the fuse carrier it has to be inserted before either terminal is tightened **(3)**.

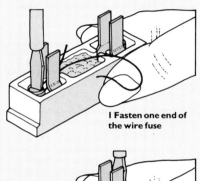

1 Fasten one end of the wire fuse

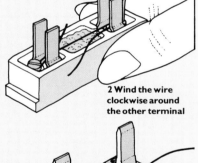

2 Wind the wire clockwise around the other terminal

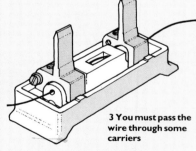

3 You must pass the wire through some carriers

IF THE FUSE BLOWS AGAIN

If a replaced fuse blows again as soon as the power is switched on there is a fault or an overload – too many appliances plugged in – on that circuit and it must be detected and rectified before another fuse is inserted.

Circuit breakers

In some consumer units you will find miniature circuit breakers (MCBs) instead of fuse carriers. Their current ratings tend to differ very slightly from fuse ratings, but the main difference is that circuit breakers switch to the 'off' position automatically, so a faulty circuit is obvious as soon as you inspect the consumer unit.

Turn the consumer unit's main switch off, then simply close the switch on the miniature circuit breaker to reset it. There is no fuse to replace. If the MCB switch or button will not stay in the 'on' position when power is restored, then there is still a fault on the circuit which must be rectified.

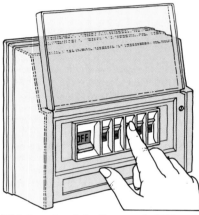

With the main switch off, turn on the MCB

Checking out a fault

An electrician can test a circuit for you with special equipment, but first carry out some simple tests yourself.

Before inspecting any part of the circuit turn off the consumer unit's main switch, remove the relevant fuse holder and keep it in your pocket so that no one can replace it while you work. If you have circuit breakers instead of fuses fix the switch at 'off' with bright adhesive tape and leave a note on the consumer unit.

Unplug all appliances on the faulty circuit to make sure that it is not simply overloaded, then switch on again. If the circuit is still faulty switch off again and inspect the socket outlets and light fittings to see if a conductor has worked loose and is touching one of the other wires, terminals or outer casing, causing a short circuit.

If none of this enables you to find the fault call in an electrician.

TYPES OF DOMESTIC ELECTRICAL CIRCUITS

Running from the consumer unit are the cables which supply the various fixed wiring circuits in your home. Not only are the sizes of the cables different ($\triangleright$); the circuits themselves also differ, depending on what they are used for and also, in some cases, how old they happen to be.

RING CIRCUITS

The most common form of 'power' circuit for feeding socket outlets is the ring circuit, or 'ring main'. With this method of wiring, a cable starts from terminals in the consumer unit and goes round the house, connecting socket to socket and arriving back at the same terminals. This means that power can reach any of the socket outlets or fused connection units from both directions, which reduces the load on the cable.

Ring mains are always run in 2.5mm^2 cable and are protected by 30amp fuses or 32amp MCBs. Theoretically there is no limit to the number of socket outlets or fused connection units that can be fitted to one ring circuit provided that it does not serve a floor area of more than 100sq m (120sq yd) – a limit based on the number of heaters which would be adequate to warm that space. However, in practice two-storey houses usually have one ring main for the upper floor and another one for downstairs.

Spurs

The number of sockets on a ring main can be increased by adding extensions or 'spurs'. A spur can be either a single 2.5mm^2 cable connected to the terminals of an existing socket or fused connection unit or it can run from a junction box inserted in the ring.

It is good practice to have each spur serving one fused connection unit for a fixed appliance or one single or double socket outlet. You can have as many spurs on a ring circuit as there were sockets on it originally, and for this calculation a double socket is counted as two. The 30amp fuse that protects the ring main remains unchanged, no matter how many spurs are connected to the circuit.

Ring circuit

Ring circuit with spurs

RADIAL CIRCUITS

A radial power circuit feeds a number of sockets or fused connection units but, unlike a ring circuit, its cable terminates at the last outlet. The size of cable and the fuse rating depend on the size of the floor area to be supplied by the circuit. In an area of up to 20sq m (24sq yd), the cable should be 2.5mm^2, protected by a 20amp MCB or a 20amp fuse of any type. For a larger area, up to 50sq m (60sq yd), you should use 4mm^2 cable with a 30amp cartridge fuse or 32amp MCB; a rewirable fuse is not permitted.

Any number of socket outlets can be supplied by one of these circuits, and spurs can be added if required. The circuits are known as multi-outlet radial circuits, but a powerful appliance such as a cooker or shower unit must have its own radial circuit.

Radial circuit

LIGHTING CIRCUITS

Domestic lighting circuits are of the radial kind, but there are two systems currently in use.

The loop-in system simply has a single cable that runs from ceiling rose to ceiling rose, terminating at the last one on the circuit. Single cables also run from the ceiling roses to the various light switches.

The older system – known as the junction-box system – incorporates a junction box for each light. The boxes are situated conveniently on the single supply cable. A cable runs from each junction box to the ceiling rose, and another from the box to the light switch. In practice, most lighting systems are a combination of the two methods.

A single circuit of 1mm^2 cable can serve the equivalent of twelve 100W light fittings. Check the load by adding together the wattage of all the light bulbs on the circuit. If it comes to more than 1200W, the circuit should be split. In any case, it makes sense to have two or more separate lighting circuits running from the consumer unit. If your house is large, requiring very long cable runs, use 1.5mm^2 two-core-and-earth cable instead of 1mm^2.

Lighting circuits must be protected by 5amp fuses or 6amp MCBs.

Loop-in system

Junction-box system

SEE ALSO

Details for: $\triangleright$	
Cables	140
Socket outlets	146
Fused connection units	152
Cooker circuit	155
Shower circuit	159
Fuse ratings	137

CABLE: TYPES

Two-core and earth

Cable for the fixed wiring of electrical systems normally has three conductors: the insulated live and neutral ones and the earth conductor lying between them, uninsulated except for the sheathing that encloses all three. Cable up to 2.5mm^2 has solid, single-core conductors, but larger sizes, up to 10mm^2, would be too stiff with solid conductors so each one is made up of seven strands. The live conductor is insulated with red PVC and the neutral

one with black. When an earth conductor is exposed, as in a socket outlet, it should be covered with a green and yellow sleeve. You can buy this from any electricians' supplier. The PVC sheathing on the outside of the cable is usually white or grey.

Heat-resistant cable is available for use in a situation where extra heat may be generated, and there is heat-resistant sleeving for the conductors in enclosed light fittings.

Two-core and earth cable: solid conductors

Two-core and earth cable: stranded conductors

Three-core and earth

This type of cable is used in two-way lighting systems, which can be switched on and off at different switches. It

contains three insulated conductors and a bare earth wire. The conductors have red, yellow and blue coverings.

Three-core and earth cable

Single-core cable

Insulated single-core cable is used in buildings where the electrical wiring is run in metal or plastic conduit – a type of installation rarely found in domestic buildings. The cable is colour-coded in the normal way: red for live, black for neutral, and green-and-yellow for earth.

Single-core 16mm^2 cable insulated in

a green-and-yellow PVC covering is used for connecting the consumer unit to the earth. Single-core cable of the same size is used for connecting the consumer unit to the meter. The meter leads are insulated and sheathed in red for the live conductor and black for the neutral one.

Insulated single-core cable

Insulated and sheathed single-core cable

SEE ALSO
◁ Details for:
Meter leads   134
Earth cable   134

OLD CABLE

Houses which were wired before World War II may still have old rubber-sheathed and -insulated cable, and some old cable may even be sheathed in lead.

Rubber sheathing is usually a matt black. It is more flexible than the modern PVC insulation unless it has deteriorated, when it will be crumbly.

This type of cable may be dangerous

● **Cable sizes**
The chart on the right gives the basic sizes of cables used for wiring domestic circuits. For details of the maximum permitted lengths for circuits, see CIRCUITS: MAXIMUM LENGTHS.

If the Electricity Board fuse is larger than 60amps, 25mm^2 meter leads are required, but consult your local Electricity Board for advice.

CIRCUIT-CABLE SIZES

Circuit	Size	Type
Fixed lighting	1.0mm^2 & 1.5mm^2	Two-core-and-earth
Bell or chime transformer	1.0mm^2	Two-core-and-earth
Immersion heater	2.5mm^2	Two-core-and-earth
Storage heater	2.5mm^2 & 4.0mm^2	Two-core-and-earth
Ring circuit	2.5mm^2	Two-core-and-earth
Spurs	2.5mm^2	Two-core-and-earth
Radial – 20amp	2.5mm^2	Two-core-and-earth
Radial – 30amp	4.0mm^2	Two-core-and-earth
Shower unit	10.0mm^2	Two-core-and-earth
Cooker	4.0mm^2 & 6.0mm^2	Two-core-and-earth
Consumer earth cable	16.0mm^2	Single core
Meter leads	16.0mm^2	Single core

STRIPPING CABLE

When cable is wired up to an accessory some of the sheathing and insulation must be removed.

Slit the sheathing lengthwise with a sharp knife, peel it off the conductors, fold it over the blade and cut it off.

Take about 12mm (½in) of insulation off the ends of the conductors using wire strippers.

Cover the uninsulated earth wire with a green/yellow sleeve, leaving 12mm (½in) of the wire exposed for connecting to the earth terminal.

If more than one conductor is to be inserted in the same terminal twist the exposed ends together with strong pliers to ensure the maximum contact for all of the wires.

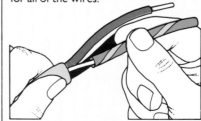

Slip colour-coded sleeving over the earth wire

INSIDE A HOLLOW WALL

For a short cable run on a lath-and-plaster wall, hack the plaster away, fix the cable to the studs and then plaster over again in the normal way.

While you can run cable through the space between the two claddings of a stud partition wall there is no way of doing this without some damage to the wall and the decoration. Drill a 12mm (½in) hole through the top wall plate above the position of the switch, then tap the wall directly below the hole to locate the nogging (▷). Cut a hole in the lath and plaster to reveal the top of the nogging and drill a similar hole through it.

Pass a lead weight on a plumb line through both of the holes and down to the location of the switch. Tie the cable to the line and pull it through.

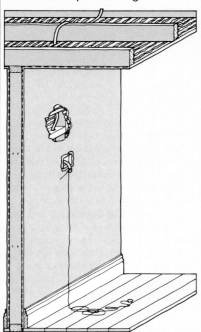

Running cable through a hollow wall
If a nogging prevents you running cable directly to a switch, cut away some laths and plaster to drill a hole through the timber.

RUNNING CABLE

Long runs of cable are necessary to take power from the consumer unit to all the sockets, light fittings and fixed appliances in the home.

The cable must be fixed securely to the structure of the house along its route except in confined spaces to which there is normally no access, such as voids between floors and inside hollow walls. There are accepted ways of running and fixing cable, depending on particular circumstances.

Surface fixing

PVC-insulated and -sheathed cable can be fixed directly to the surface of a wall or ceiling without any further protection. Fix it with plastic cable clips **(1)** or metal buckle clips **(2)** every 400mm (1ft 4in) on vertical runs and every 250mm (10in) on horizontal runs. Keep the runs as straight and neat as possible, and when several cables run in the same direction group them together. Avoid kinks in the cable by keeping it on the drum as long as possible, but if you do have to get any kinks out pull the cable round a thick dowel held in a vice.

If a cable seems vulnerable you can cover it with an impact-resistant plastic channel **(3)** . Having secured the cable with clips, you simply nail the channel in place over it.

1 **Plastic cable clip**

2 **Metal buckle clip**

Concealed fixing

While surface-fixed cable is quite acceptable in cellars, under stairs and in workshops and garages, few people want to see it running across their living room walls or ceilings. It's better to bury it in the plaster or hide it in a wall void. Sheathed cable can be buried without further protection.

Wherever possible cable should run vertically to switches or sockets, to avoid dangerous clashes with wall fittings or fixtures installed later. Most people allow for it to run this way. If you must run horizontal cable confine it to within 150mm (6in) of the ceiling or 300mm (1ft) of the floor. Never run a buried cable diagonally across a wall.

Some people cover all buried cable with a channel, but it isn't required by the IEE Regulations.

Cable buried in light plastic conduit can be withdrawn later, if necessary, without disturbing decorations, but the need is so rare in a house as to be hardly worth considering.

Mark out your cable runs on the plaster, allowing a channel about 25mm (1in) wide for single cable. Cut both sides with a bolster and club hammer and hack out the plaster between the cuts with a cold chisel. Normally plaster is thick enough to conceal cable, but you may have to chop out some brickwork to get the depth. Clip the cable in the channel **(1)** and, when you have checked that the installation is working, plaster over it. To avoid electric shock ensure that the power to that circuit is turned off before you use wet plaster round a switch or socket outlet **(2)** .

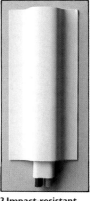

3 **Impact-resistant plastic channel**

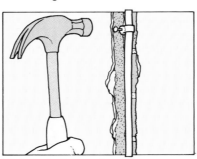

1 **Nail plastic clips over the cable**

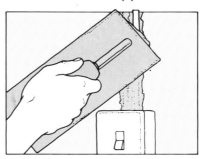

2 **Repair the plaster up to the switch**

SEE ALSO

Details for: ▷

Nogging	147
Repairing plaster	31
Switching off	134

RUNNING CABLE UNDER FLOORS

SEE ALSO

◁ Details for:
Protective channel	141
Spur cables	149

Power and lighting circuits are often concealed beneath floors if access is possible. It isn't necessary to lift every floorboard to run a cable from one side of a room to the other; by lifting a board every 2m (6ft) or so you should be able to pass the cable from one gap to the next with the help of a length of stiff wire bent into a hook at one end. Look for boards that have been taken up before, as they will be fairly easy to lift and you will damage fewer boards.

Lifting floorboards

Lifting square-edged boards

Drive a wide bolster chisel between two boards about 50mm (2in) from the cut end of one of them (**1**). Lever that board up with the bolster, then do the same on its other edge, working along the board until you have raised it enough to wedge a cold chisel under it (**2**). Proceed along the board, raising it with the chisel, until the board is loose.

Full-length boards

If you have to lift a board that runs the whole length of the floor, from one skirting to the other, start somewhere near the middle of the board and close to a floor joist. The nail heads indicate the positions of joists. Lever the board up and make a saw cut through it centred on the joist, then lift the board in the normal way.

Lifting tongued and grooved boards

You cannot lift a tongued and grooved floorboard until you have cut through the tongues along both sides of the board, either with a special floorboard saw, which has a blade with a rounded tip, or with a power jigsaw.

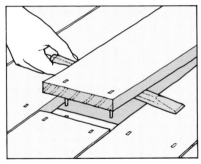

Cutting a full-length board
Cut a full-length board in two directly over a floor joist.

1 Prise up the floorboard with a bolster

2 Wedge the raised end with a cold chisel

CUTTING A BOARD NEXT TO A SKIRTING

Should you need to cut through a board that lies close to a wall it may not be possible to lift it without damaging the bottom edge of the skirting board. In such a case drill a starting hole through the board alongside the joist nearest to the wall, insert the blade of a padsaw or power jigsaw in the hole and cut across the board flush with the side of the joist (**1**). To support the cut end afterwards nail a length of 50 x 50mm (2 x 2in) softwood to the joist. Hold it up tightly against the undersides of the adjacent floorboards while fixing it to ensure that the cut board will lie flush with the others (**2**).

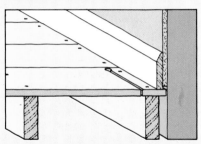

1 Cut through a trapped board with a jigsaw

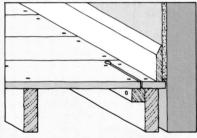

2 Support the cut board with a nailed batten

Solid floors

In a new concrete floor you can lay conduit and run cable through it before the concrete is poured.

In an existing solid floor you can cut a channel for conduit – hard work without an electric hammer and chisel bit – but if the floor is tiled you will not want to spoil it for one or two socket outlets. An alternative is to drop spur cables, buried in the wall plaster, from the ring circuit in the upper floor. Another way is to run cable through the wall from an adjacent area and channel it horizontally in the plaster just above the skirting. Yet another is to remove the skirting, clip the cable to the wall and cover it with protective channel. Note the position of the cable to avoid piercing it when you nail back the skirting board.

In the roof space

In the roof space all wiring can be surface-run, but as people may enter it occasionally you must see that the cable is clipped securely to the joists or rafters. You can even run cable along the tops of joists in some areas, but run it through holes in the normal way where joists are to be boarded over or in areas of access such as round water tanks and the entrance hatch itself.

Wiring overlaid by roof insulation has a slightly higher chance of heating up. Ring mains and lighting circuits do not present a problem , but circuits to heaters, cookers or shower units are more critical. Wherever possible run cable over thermal insulation. If you cannot avoid running it under the material you should use a heavier cable to be on the safe side.

When expanded-polystyrene insulation is in contact with electric cable for a long time it affects the plasticizer in the PVC sheathing on the cable. The plasticizer moves to the surface of the sheathing, reacts with the polystyrene and forms a sticky substance on the cable. This becomes a dry crust which cracks if the cable is lifted out of the roof insulation and bent. It gives the impression that the cable insulation is cracking, but scientific testing has shown that the cracking is merely in the surface crust. On balance it is best to keep cable away from polystyrene.

Running cable through the house structure
Use the most convenient method to run cable to sockets and switches.
1 Clip cable to roof timbers in loft.
2 Junction boxes must be fixed securely.
3 Run cable through holes in the joists near the hatch.
4 Run cable over loft insulation.
5 To avoid damaging a finished floor you can run a short spur through the wall from the next room.
6 When cable runs across the line of joists drill holes 50mm (2in) below the top edges.
7 Cable running parallel to joists can lay on the ceiling below.
8 Let cable drape onto the base below a suspended floor.
9 When you cannot run cable through a concrete floor you can drop a spur from the floor above.
10 Take the opportunity to bury conduit for cable in a new concrete floor.

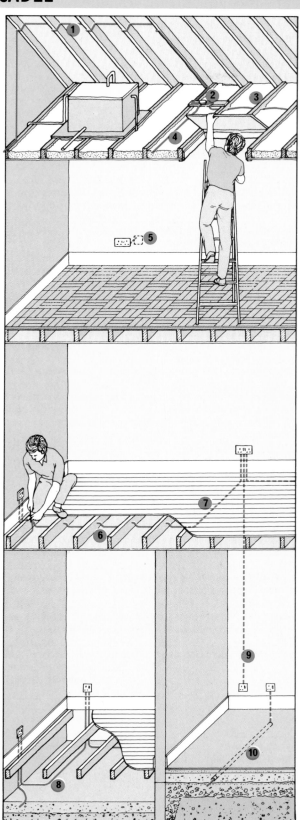

Running the cable

On the ground floor the cable can rest on the earth or on the concrete platform below the joists, provided the space is not open to access. Allow enough slack, so that the cable is not suspended above the platform, which might put a strain on fixings to junction boxes or socket outlets. For the same reason, secure cable with clips to the side of the joist beside junction boxes or other accessories. Never attach circuit cable to gas or water pipes or run it next to heating pipes, as the heat could melt the insulation.

When laying cable between a floor and the ceiling below, it can rest on the ceiling without any other fixing provided it runs parallel with the joists. If it runs at right angles to the joists, drill a series of 12mm (½in) holes, one through each joist along the intended cable run. The holes must be at least 50mm (2in) below the tops of the joists, so that floorboard nails cannot at some time be hammered through the cable. Similarly holes must be at least 50mm (2in) from the bottom edge of ceiling joists, to be certain nails driven from below cannot pierce the cable. The space between the joists is limited, but you can cut down a spade bit and use it in a power drill.

Mark out the position of a socket or fused connection unit and cut a channel from it down to the skirting board. With an extra-long masonry drill in a power tool, remove the plaster from behind the skirting board. By using the drill at a shallow angle you can loosen much of the debris, but you will probably have to finish the job with a slim cold chisel. Use the same chisel to rake the debris out from below.

Pass a length of stiff wire with one end formed into a hook down behind the skirting board. Hook the cable and pull it through, at the same time feeding it from below with your other hand.

Preventing the spread of fire
Every time you cut an opening in the structure of the house for a cable, you are creating a potential route for fire to spread. After you have installed the cable, fill any holes between floors or rooms using plaster or some other non-flammable material (not asbestos). Even where you pass a cable into a mounting box you must fit a 'blind' grommet and cut a hole through it that is only just large enough for the cable.

SEE ALSO

Details for: ▷	
Cable clips	141
Concealing cable	141
Running a spur	149

Drilling the joists
Shorten a spade bit so that your drill fits between the joists.

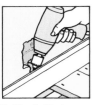

Drilling behind skirting
Use a long masonry drill to remove the plaster behind a skirting board.

143

ASSESSING YOUR INSTALLATION

Inspect your electrical system to ensure that it is safe and adequate for your future needs. But remember, you should never examine any part of it without first switching off the power at the consumer unit (◁).

If you are in doubt about some aspect of the installation you should ask a qualified electrician his opinion. If you get in touch with your Electricity Board they will arrange for someone to test the whole system for you.

SEE ALSO

◁ Details for:
Switching off	134
Earth	
connection	134-135
Old fuse boxes	135
RCCB	135
Fuse ratings	137
Old cable	140
Replacing fuses	138
Running cable	141-143
Replacing sockets	148
Converting radial circuit	151
Replacing switches	164

QUESTIONS	ANSWERS
Do you have a modern consumer unit or a mixture of old 'fuse boxes' (◁)?	Old fuse boxes can be unsafe and should be replaced with a modern unit. Seek professional advice on this.
Is the consumer unit in good condition?	Replace broken casing or cracked covers and check that all fuse carriers are intact and that they fit snugly in the fuseways.
Are the fuse carriers for the circuits clearly labelled?	If you cannot identify the various circuits, have an electrician test the system and label the fuses.
Are all your circuit fuses of the correct ratings (◁)?	Replace any fuses of the wrong rating. If an unusually large fuse is protecting one of the circuits get professional advice before changing it. It may have a special purpose. Any wire other than proper fuse wire found in a fuse should be replaced at once.
Are the cables that lead from the consumer unit in good condition?	The cables should be fixed securely, with no bare wires showing. If the cables seem to be insulated with rubber (◁) have the whole of the insulation checked as soon as possible. Rubber insulation has a limited life, so yours could already be dangerous.
Is the earth connection from the consumer unit intact and in good condition (◁)?	If the connection seems loose or corroded have the Electricity Board check on whether the earthing is sound. You can check an RCCB (◁) by pushing the test button to see if it is working mechanically.
What is the condition of the fixed wiring between floors and in the loft or roof space?	If the cables are rubber-insulated have the system checked by a professional, but first examine each of the circuits, as they may not all have been renewed at the same time. If cable is run in conduit it can be hard to check on its condition, but if it looks doubtful where it enters accessories have the circuit checked professionally. Wiring should be fixed securely and sheathing should run into all accessories, with no bare wire in sight. Junction boxes on lighting circuits should be screwed firmly to the structure and should have their covers in place.
Is the wiring discreet and orderly?	Tidy all surface-run wiring into straight properly-clipped runs. Better still, bury the cable in the wall plaster or run it under floors and inside hollow walls.
Are there any old round-pin socket outlets?	See that their wiring is adequate, though old radial circuits should be replaced with modern ring circuits and 13amp square-pin sockets.
Are the outer casings of all accessories in good condition and fixed securely to the structure?	Replace any cracked or broken components and secure any loose fittings.
Do switches on all accessories work smoothly and effectively?	Where not, replace the accessories.
Are all the wires inside accessories attached securely to their terminals?	Tighten all loose terminals and ensure that no bare wires are visible. Fit sleeves to earth wires where missing.

QUESTIONS	ANSWERS
Is the insulation round wires dry and crumbly inside any accessories?	If so it is rubber insulation in advanced decomposition. Replace the covers carefully and have a professional check the system as soon as possible.
Do any sockets, switches or plugs get warm when live? Is there a smell of burning, or scorch marks on sockets or round the bases of the pins of plugs? Do sockets spark when you remove a plug, or switches when you operate them?	These things mean loose connections in the accessory or plug, or a poor connection between plug and socket. Tighten loose connections and clean all fuse clips, fuse caps and the pins of plugs with fine wire wool. If the fault persists try a new plug; lastly replace the socket or switch.
Is it difficult to insert a plug in a socket?	The socket is worn and should be replaced.
Are your sockets in the right places?	Sockets should be placed conveniently round a room so that you need never have long flexes trailing across the floor or under carpets. Add sockets to the ring circuit by running spurs.
Do you have enough sockets?	If you have to use plug adaptors you need more sockets. Replace singles with doubles, add spurs or extend the ring circuit.
Is there old, braided, twin flex hanging from some ceiling roses?	Replace it with PVC-insulated flex (▷). Also check that the wiring inside the rose is PVC-insulated.
Are there earth wires inside your ceiling roses?	If not get professional advice on whether to replace the lighting circuits.
Is your lighting efficient (▷)?	Make sure you have two-way switching on stairs, and consider extra sockets or different light fittings to make the lighting more effective or atmospheric.
Is there power in the garage or the workshop?	Outbuildings separate from the house need their own power supply.

SEE ALSO

Details for: ▷	
Flex	130
Replacing fuses	138
Replacing sockets	148
Running a spur	149
Extending ring circuit	150
Replacing switches	164

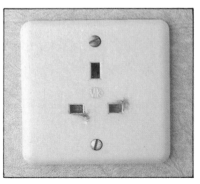

From left to right:

Scorch marks
Scorch marks on a socket or round the base of plug pins indicates poor connections.

Overloaded socket
If you have to use an adaptor to power your appliances fit extra sockets.

Unprotected connections
Make sure covers or faceplates are fitted to all accessories.

From left to right:

Incorrect fuse
Replace improper wire with fuse wire.

Round-pin socket
Replace a round-pin socket with a 13amp square-pin version.

Damaged socket
Replace cracked or broken faceplate.

POWER CIRCUITS: SURFACE-MOUNTING SOCKET OUTLETS

SEE ALSO

◁ Details for:
Wiring a socket	148
Switching off	134
Wiring kitchen appliances	154

Whatever the type of circuits in your home, use only standard 13amp square-pin sockets. All round-pin sockets are now out of date, and though they may not be actually dangerous at the moment you should have them checked and consider changing the wiring to accommodate new 13amp socket outlets.

Before you start work on any socket switch the power off at the consumer unit and remove the fuse for that circuit, then test the socket with an appliance that you know to be working so as to be sure that the socket has been properly switched off.

TYPES OF 13AMP SOCKET

Though all sockets are functionally very similar there are several variations on the basic component.

There are single and double sockets, and both are available either switched or unswitched and with or without neon indicators which tell you at a glance whether the socket is switched on. All these sockets are wired in the same way.

Another basic difference is in how sockets are mounted. They can be surface-mounted – screwed to the wall in a plastic box or pattress – or flush-mounted in a metal box buried in the wall with only its faceplate visible.

Triple sockets
Triple sockets are useful in a situation where several electrical appliances are grouped together.

Switched single | Unswitched single

Switched double

Single switched with indicator

Positioning sockets

Decide on the most convenient positions for television, hi-fi, table lamps and so on and position sockets accordingly. To avoid using adaptors or long leads distribute the sockets evenly round the living room and bedrooms, and wherever possible fit doubles rather than singles. Don't forget sockets for running the vacuum cleaner in hallways and on landings.

The optimum height for a socket is 225 to 300mm (9in to 1ft) above the floor. This will clear most skirting boards and leave ample room for flexible cord to hang from a plug, while being high enough to be in no danger of getting struck by the vacuum cleaner. In the kitchen fit at least four double sockets 150mm (6in) above the worktops, more if you have a lot of small appliances. In addition fit sockets for floor-standing appliances like the refrigerator and dishwasher.

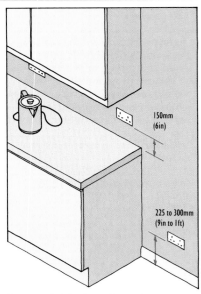

150mm (6in)

225 to 300mm (9in to 1ft)

Optimum heights for socket outlets

Fixing to masonry

First break out the thin plastic webs that cover the fixing holes in the back of the pattress. The best tool for this is an electrician's screwdriver. Two fixings should be sufficient. The fixing holes are slotted to allow for adjustment.

Hold the pattress against the wall, levelling it at the same time with a small spirit level, and mark the fixing holes on the wall with a bradawl through the holes in the pattress. Drill and plug the holes with No 8 wall plugs.

With a larger screwdriver and pliers break out the plastic web covering the most convenient cable-entry hole in the pattress. For surface-run cable this will be in the side; for buried cable it will be the one in the base.

Feed the cable into the pattress to form a loop about 75mm (3in) long **(1)**, then fix the box to the wall with 32mm (1¼in) countersunk woodscrews.

Finally wire and fit the socket (◁).

Fixing to a hollow wall

On a dry partition or lath-and-plaster wall a surface-mounted pattress is fixed with any of the standard fixings for use on hollow walls, though you can use ordinary woodscrews if you can position the pattress over a stud. In the latter case be sure you can feed the cable into the pattress past the stud **(2)**.

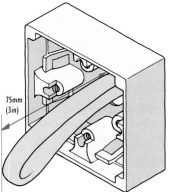

75mm (3in)

1 Leave a 75mm (3in) loop of cable at the box

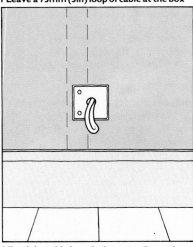

2 Feed the cable into the box past the stud

FLUSH-MOUNTING SOCKET OUTLETS

Fixing to masonry

Hold the metal box against the wall and draw round it with a pencil **(1)**, then mark a 'chase' or channel running up from the skirting to the box's outline.

With a bolster and cold chisel cut away the plaster, down to the brickwork **(2)**, within the marked area.

With a masonry drill bore several rows of holes down to the required depth **(3)** across the recess for the box, then with a cold chisel cut away the brick to the depth of the holes so that the box will lie flush with the plaster.

Try the box in the recess. If it fits in snugly mark the wall through the fixing holes in its back, then drill the wall for the screw plugs. If you have made the recess too deep, or the box rocks from side to side, apply some filler in the recess and press the box into it, flush with the wall and properly positioned. After about 10 minutes ease the box out carefully and leave the filler to harden so that you can mark, drill and plug the fixing holes through it.

Knock out one or more of the blanked-off holes in the box to accommodate the cable. Fit a grommet into each hole to protect the cable's sheathing from the metal edges **(4)**, feed the cable into the box and screw the box to the wall.

Plaster up to the box and over the cable chased into the wall, and when the plaster has hardened wire and fit the socket (▷).

Fixing to plasterboard

To fit a flush socket to a wall made of plasterboard over wooden studs trace the outline of the box in position on the wall, then drill a hole in each corner of the shape with a brace and bit and cut out the waste with a padsaw.

Punch out the blanked-off entry holes in the box, fit rubber grommets and feed the cable into the box.

Clip dry-wall fixing flanges to the sides of the box **(5)**. These will hold it in place by gripping the wall from inside. Ease one side of the box, with flange, into the recess and then, holding the screw fixing lugs so as not to lose the box, manoeuvre it until both flanges are behind the plasterboard and the box sits snugly in the hole.

Now wire and fit the socket (▷). As you tighten the fixing screws the plasterboard will be gripped between the flanges and the faceplate.

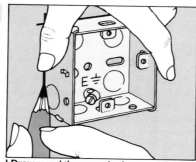
1 Draw round the mounting box

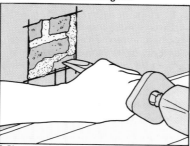
2 Chop away the plaster with a cold chisel

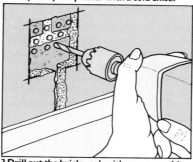
3 Drill out the brickwork with a masonry bit

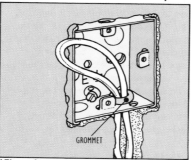
4 Fit a soft grommet in the cable-entry hole

GROMMET

5 Dry-wall fixing flanges clipped to a box

FLUSH MOUNTING TO LATH AND PLASTER

If you wish to fit a flush socket in a lath-and-plaster wall try to locate it over a stud or nogging.

Mark the position of the box, cut out the plaster and saw away the laths with a padsaw. Try the box for fit and, if necessary, chop a notch in the woodwork until the box lies flush with the wall surface **(1)**. Feed in the cable and screw the box to the stud before wiring and fitting the socket (▷).

If you cannot position the socket on a stud, cut away enough plaster and laths to make a slot in the wall running from one stud to the next. Between the studs screw or skew-nail a softwood nogging to which you can fix the box. Set the batten back from the front edges of the studs if that is necessary to make the box lie flush with the wall surface **(2)**. Feed the cable into the box and make good the surrounding plaster before you wire and fit the socket.

SEE ALSO

Details for: ▷	
Running a cable	141-143
Wiring a socket	148

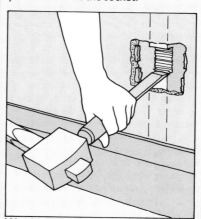
1 Notch a wall stud for a mounting box

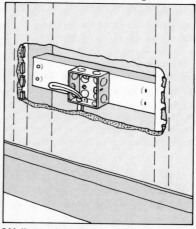
2 Nail a nogging between studs
Cut away wall plaster and laths when you have to fix a mounting box between wall studs.

REPLACING SOCKET OUTLETS

If you have a socket outlet that needs to be replaced because it is faulty or *broken you should consider some options before undertaking the job.*

SEE ALSO

◁ Details for:
**Recessing metal
box**   147
Flush-mounted box   147
Cutting brickwork   147
**Mounting to a
hollow wall**   147
Switching off   134
Stripping cable   140
Types of socket   146

Simple replacement

Replacing a damaged socket with a similar one is quite straightforward. Any style will fit a flush-mounted box, but look carefully when you substitute a socket that screws to a surface-mounted pattress. Though it will fit and function perfectly well, square corners and edges on either will not suit rounded ones on the other. In such a case you may also have to buy a new, matching pattress.

An unswitched socket can be replaced with a switched one without any change to the wiring or fixing.

Switch off the power supply to the circuit, then remove the fixing screws holding the faceplate and pull the socket out of the box.

Loosen off the terminals and free the conductors. Check that all is well inside the pattress, then connect the conductors to the terminals of the new socket. Fit the faceplate, using the original screws if those supplied with the new socket don't match the thread in the pattress.

Surface to flush mounted

If you have to renew a socket for some reason you can use the occasion to replace a surface-mounted pattress with a flush box.

Turn off the power, remove the old socket and recess the metal box into the wall (◁), taking care not to damage the fixed wiring in the wall.

Replacing a single socket with a double

One way to increase the number of sockets in a room is to substitute doubles for singles. Any single socket on a ring circuit can be replaced with a double with no change to the wiring. You can similarly replace a single socket on a spur. Consider using the safer, switched sockets. The wiring is identical.

Surface to surface

Replacing a surface-mounted single unit with a surface-mounted double is quite easy. Having removed the old socket, simply fix the new, double pattress to the wall in the same place.

Flush to surface

Though flush-mounted sockets are neater, you may not want the disturbance to decor of installing a double one. Instead you can fit a double surface-mounted socket over the buried box of the single one (**1**). Turn off the power and remove the socket, leaving the metal box and the wiring in place. Knock out the cable-entry hole in the plastic double pattress and feed the

cable through it. When the pattress is centred over the old box (◁) two fixing holes will line up with the fixing lugs on the buried box. Break out the plastic webs and fix the new pattress to the lugs with the screws that held the old socket in place. Wire up the new double socket and fit it.

Flush to flush

Switch off the power to the circuit, remove the old socket at its metal box, then try the new double box over the hole. You can centre the box over the hole or align it with one end (**2**), whichever is the more convenient. Trace the outline of the box on the wall and cut out the brickwork (◁).

To substitute a double socket in a hollow wall use a similar procedure, installing the socket by whichever method is most convenient (◁).

Surface to flush

To replace a single surface-mounted socket with a flush double one proceed as described above.

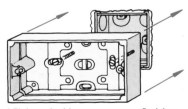
1 Fixing a double pattress over a flush box

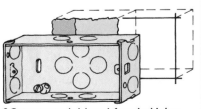
2 Cut out extra brickwork for a double box

CONNECTING UP TO A SOCKET

When a single cable is involved strip off the sheathing in the ordinary way and connect the wires to the terminals: the black wire to neutral – N, the red one to live – L and the earth wire, which you should insulate yourself with a sleeve, to earth – E (**1**). If necessary fold the stripped ends over so that no bare wire protrudes from a terminal.

When connecting to a ring circuit you can cut through the loop of cable, strip the sheathing from each half and twist together the bared ends of matching wires – live with live and so on – after slipping sleeves on the earth wires (**2**). Alternatively you can slit the sheathing lengthwise and peel it off, leaving the wires unbroken (**3**), bare a part of each wire by cutting away insulation, then pinch the exposed part of each wire into a tight fold with the pliers so that it will fit into its terminal. The second method ensures perfect contact, as the ring circuit is uninterrupted. You may have to cut the earth wire to slip sleeves over the halves.

Cable is stiff, and can make it hard to close the socket faceplate, so bend each conductor so that it will fold into the box or pattress. Locate both fixing screws and tighten them gradually in turns until the plate fits firmly in place against the wall or pattress.

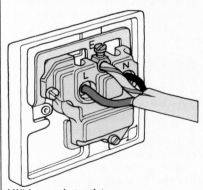
1 Wiring a socket outlet

2 Twist cut wires together

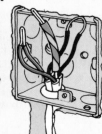
3 Crimp continuous wires with pliers

ADDING A SPUR TO A RING CIRCUIT

If you need more sockets in convenient positions round a room you can run 2.5mm² spur cables from a ring circuit *and have as many spurs as there are sockets already on the ring, each spur feeding a single or double socket.*

A spur cable can be connected to any socket – or fused connection unit – on the ring, or to a junction box inserted in the ring, whichever is the easier. If running cable from one of the present sockets would mean disturbing the plaster it is more convenient to use a junction box, and if there is no socket within easy reach of the proposed new one using a junction box will save cable.

If cable is surface-run and you want to extend a row of sockets – behind a workbench, for example – it is simpler to connect the spur to a socket.

Examine the socket. If there is one cable feeding it, it is already on a spur; if there are three cables in the socket it is already feeding a spur itself. In either case you cannot connect a new spur, so look for a socket with two cables.

Connecting to an existing socket

Fix the new socket, wire it up in the ordinary way (See opposite) and run its spur cable to the existing socket. Switch off power and remove the existing socket. You may have to enlarge the entry hole in the pattress or knock out another to take the spur cable. Feed the cable into the pattress, prepare the conductors and twist their bared ends together with those of the matching conductors of the ring circuit. Insert the wires in their terminals: red – L, black – N and green/yellow – E and replace the socket. Switch the power back on and test the new spur socket.

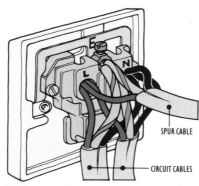

SPUR CABLE

CIRCUIT CABLES

Taking a spur from an existing socket outlet

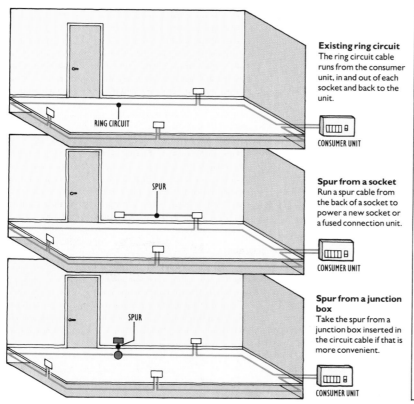

RING CIRCUIT

CONSUMER UNIT

SPUR

CONSUMER UNIT

SPUR

CONSUMER UNIT

Existing ring circuit
The ring circuit cable runs from the consumer unit, in and out of each socket and back to the unit.

Spur from a socket
Run a spur cable from the back of a socket to power a new socket or a fused connection unit.

Spur from a junction box
Take the spur from a junction box inserted in the circuit cable if that is more convenient.

CONNECTING TO A JUNCTION BOX

You will need a 30amp junction box with three terminals to connect to a ring circuit. It will have either knock-out cable-entry holes or a special cover that rotates to blank off unneeded holes. The cover must be screw-fixed.

Lift a floorboard close to the new socket and where you can connect to the ring circuit cable without having to stretch it.

Fix a platform for the box by nailing battens near the bottoms of two joists (See right) and screwing a 100 x 25mm (4 x 1in) strip of wood between the joists and resting on the battens. Loop the ring circuit cable over the platform before fixing it so that the cable need not be cut for connecting up. Remove the cover, screw the junction box to the platform and break out two cable-entry holes. If you do forget to loop the cable over the platform, just cut the cable when you come to connect it up.

Turn off the power at the consumer unit, then rest the ring circuit cable across the box and mark the amount of sheathing to remove. Slit it lengthwise and peel it off the conductors. Don't cut the live and neutral conductors, but slice away just enough insulation on each to expose a section of bare wire that will fit into the terminal (See right). Cut the earth wire and put insulating sleeves on the two ends.

Remove the screws from the terminals and lay the wires across them, the earth wire in the middle terminal and the live and neutral ones on the ends. Push the wires home with a screwdriver.

Having fitted and wired the new spur socket, run its cable to the junction box, cut and prepare the ends of the wires and break out an entry hole so that the spur wires can be fitted to the terminals of the box (See right). Take care that only colour-matched wires from both cables share terminals.

Replace the fixing screws, starting them by hand as they easily cross-thread, then tighten them with a screwdriver. Check that all the wires are secured and that the cables fit snugly in their entry holes with the sheathing running into the box, then fit the cover on the box.

Fix each cable to a nearby joist with cable clips, to take the strain off the terminals, then replace the floorboards.

Switch the power back on and test the new socket.

SEE ALSO

Details for: ▷

Switching off	134
Cables	140
Stripping cable	140
Running cable	141-143
Lifting floorboards	142

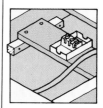

Make a wooden platform for a junction box

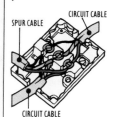

CIRCUIT CABLE

SPUR CABLE

CIRCUIT CABLE

Taking a spur from a junction box

EXTENDING A RING CIRCUIT

There are situations in which it is better to extend a ring circuit than to fit spurs. For instance, you may want to wire a room that was not adequately serviced before, or perhaps all of the conveniently placed sockets already have spurs running from them.

There are two ways of breaking into the ring: at an existing socket or via junction boxes. Whichever method you decide on, switch off the power to the circuit before you break into it.

SEE ALSO

◁ Details for:
Running cable	141-143
Mounting boxes	146-147
Switching off	134
Ring-circuit regulations	139
Positioning sockets	146
Wiring sockets	148
Junction box	149

Using an existing socket

Disconnect one in-going cable from a socket on the ring circuit and take this to the first new socket. Do it via a junction box if the cable will not reach otherwise. Continue the extension with a new section of cable from socket to socket, finally running it from the last one back to the socket where you broke into the ring. Joining the new cable to the old one within the socket completes the circuit.

Using junction boxes

Cut the ring cable and connect each cut end to a junction box, then run a new length of cable from one box to the other, looping it into the new sockets.

Running the extension

No matter how you plan to break into the ring always install the new work first and connect it up to the circuit only at the last moment. This allows you to use power tools on the extension. Switch the power off just before connecting up.

Decide on the positions of the new sockets and plan your cable run: an easy route is better than a difficult shorter one. Allow some slack in the cable.

Cut out the plaster and brickwork for sockets and cable and fit the boxes (◁). Now run the cable, leaving enough spare for joining to the ring circuit (◁), and take it up behind the skirting to the first socket. Leave a loop hanging from the box (See right), then take the cable on to the next, and so on until all the new sockets are supplied. Take the excess cable on to the point where you plan to join the ring.

Make good the plasterwork and fit the new sockets. Switch off the power, break into the ring and connect the extension to it. Switch the power on and test the new sockets separately.

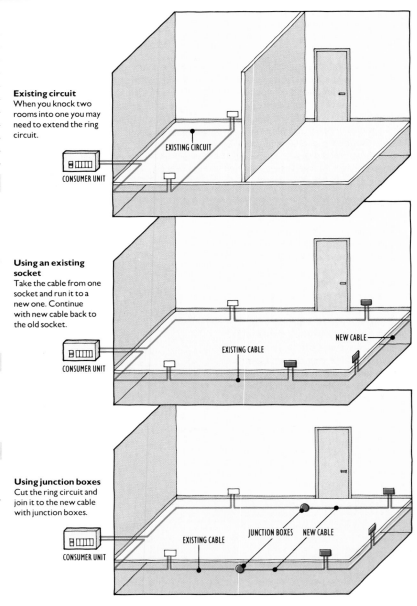

Existing circuit
When you knock two rooms into one you may need to extend the ring circuit.

EXISTING CIRCUIT

CONSUMER UNIT

Using an existing socket
Take the cable from one socket and run it to a new one. Continue with new cable back to the old socket.

CONSUMER UNIT

EXISTING CABLE

NEW CABLE

Using junction boxes
Cut the ring circuit and join it to the new cable with junction boxes.

CONSUMER UNIT

EXISTING CABLE

JUNCTION BOXES

NEW CABLE

LEAVE SOME SLACK IN THE CIRCUIT

Don't pull the cable too tight when you are running a new circuit: it puts a strain on the connections and makes it difficult to modify the circuit at a later stage should it become necessary.

Leave a generous loop of cable at each new socket position until you have run the complete circuit. At that stage you can pull the loop back ready for connecting to the socket.

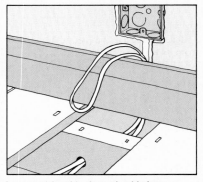

Leave ample cable above the skirting

CONVERTING A RADIAL CIRCUIT TO A RING CIRCUIT

If, when you examine your installation, you find that the power circuit is radial you may decide to convert it to a ring circuit, particularly if you wish to supply a larger area (▷).

Checking cable and fuse

If the radial circuit is wired with 2.5mm^2 cable (solid conductors) continue the circuit back to the consumer unit with the same size cable but change the 20amp circuit fuse for a 30amp fuse and fuseway. If it is wired with 4mm^2 (stranded conductors) you can complete the ring with 2.5mm^2 cable and leave the 30amp circuit fuse alone.

The additional cable is run in exactly the same way as described for extending a ring circuit (See opposite). Join the new cable at the last socket on the radial circuit and run it to all the new sockets. From the last one run it to the consumer unit. Turn off the power.

Connecting to consumer unit

You should examine your consumer unit and familiarize yourself with it (▷). Even when the unit is switched off, the cable that connects the meter to the main switch is still live – so take care.

First locate the terminals to which the radial circuit is connected. The live (red wire) terminal is on the fuseway (or MCB) from which you removed the circuit fuse before starting the work. The neutral (black wire) terminal is on the neutral block, to which all of the black wires are connected. You can usually trace the black wire you're looking for by working along from the sheathed part of the cable, and the earth terminal similarly, by tracing the green-insulated conductor.

Pass the end of the new cable into the consumer unit as closely as possible to the original radial circuit cable. Cut it to length, strip off the sheathing and prepare the ends of the conductors.

Disconnect the live (red) conductor from its terminal and twist its end together with that of the red wire from the new cable, then reconnect both wires in the same terminal. Do the same for the black wires and then the green ones, but first slip a length of insulating sleeving over the new earth wire. Replace the cover.

Check that the circuit fuse is of the correct rating and then replace the fuse carrier. Close the consumer unit, switch on the power and test the circuit.

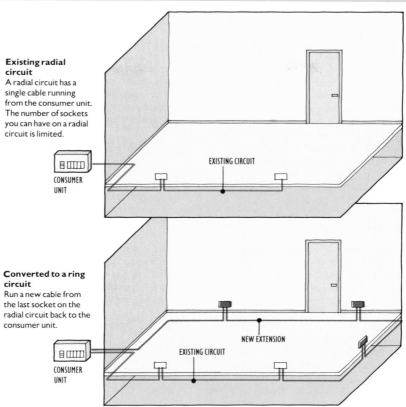

Existing radial circuit
A radial circuit has a single cable running from the consumer unit. The number of sockets you can have on a radial circuit is limited.

EXISTING CIRCUIT

CONSUMER UNIT

Converted to a ring circuit
Run a new cable from the last socket on the radial circuit back to the consumer unit.

NEW EXTENSION

EXISTING CIRCUIT

CONSUMER UNIT

SEE ALSO

Details for: ▷	
Consumer unit	136
Radial-circuit regulations	139
Switching off	134
Fuse ratings	137
Cable	140
Running cable	141-143
Positioning sockets	146
Wiring sockets	148

CONNECTING TO THE CONSUMER UNIT

RADIAL CIRCUIT CABLE

NEW CABLE

EARTH BLOCK

NEUTRAL BLOCK

FUSEWAY

Wire the new cable and radial circuit cable into the same terminals

FIXED APPLIANCES

A 13amp socket is designed to be flexible in use, enabling appliances to be moved from room to room and one socket to be used for different appliances at different times. But many appliances, large and small, are fixed to the structure of the house, or stand in one position permanently. Such appliances may just as well be wired permanently into the electrical installation. For some there is no alternative, and they may even require individual radial circuits direct from the consumer unit.

SEE ALSO

◁ Details for:
Mounting boxes	146-147
Stripping flex	131
Switching off	134
Power circuits	139
Stripping cable	140

FUSED CONNECTION UNITS

A fused connection unit is basically a device for joining circuit wiring to the flex – or sometimes cable – of an appliance. The junction incorporates the added protection of a cartridge fuse like that found in a 13amp plug. If the appliance is connected by a flex, choose a unit with a cord outlet in the faceplate.

Some fused connection units are also switched, with or without a neon indicator that shows when the switch is on. The switched connection unit allows you completely to isolate the appliance from the mains.

All fused connection units are single – there are no double ones – with square faceplates that fit the standard plastic surface-mounted pattresses or the metal boxes for flush mounting.

Changing a fuse
With the power off, remove the retaining screw in the face of the fuse holder. Take the holder from the unit, prise out the old fuse and fit a new one. Replace the fuse holder.

Fused connection units
1 Unswitched connection unit
2 Switched unit with cord outlet and indicator
3 Connection unit and socket in a dual box

Small appliances

All small electrical appliances with ratings of up to 3000W (3kW) – wall heaters, cooker hoods, heated towel rails and so on – can be wired into a ring or radial circuit by means of fused connection units. They could also be connected by 13amp plugs to sockets, but the electrical contact is not so good and there is some risk of fire with that type of permanent installation.

Always remember to switch off the power at the consumer unit before wiring a fused connection unit to the house circuitry.

Mounting a fused connection unit

A fused connection unit is mounted in the same type of box as an ordinary socket outlet, and the box is fixed to the wall in the same way (◁). The unit can also be mounted in a dual box which is designed to hold two single units – for example, a standard socket outlet next to a connection unit. The socket is wired to the ring circuit and the two units are linked together inside the box by a short 2.5mm² spur.

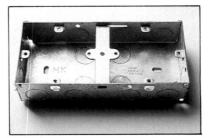

A dual mounting box

Wiring a fused connection unit

Fused connection units can be supplied by a ring circuit, a radial circuit or a spur.

Some appliances are connected to the unit by a length of flex while others are wired up with cable but the wiring arrangements inside the units are the same. Units with cord outlets have clamps to secure the connecting flex.

An unswitched connection unit has two live (L) terminals, one marked 'Load' for the brown wire of the flex, and the other marked 'Mains' for the red wire from the circuit cable. The blue wire from the flex and the black wire from the circuit cable go to similar neutral (N) terminals and both earth wires are connected to the E terminal or terminals (**1**).

A switched connection unit

A fused connection unit with a switch has two sets of terminals. Those marked 'Mains' are for the spur or ring cable that supplies the power; the terminals marked 'Load' are for the flex or cable from the appliance.

Wire up the flex side first, connecting the brown wire to the L terminal and the blue one to the N terminal, both on the Load side. Connect the green/yellow wire to the E terminal (**2**) and tighten the cord clamp.

Attach the circuit conductors to the Mains terminals – red to L and black to N, then sleeve the earth wire and take it to the E terminal (**2**).

If the fused connection unit is on a ring circuit you must fit two circuit conductors into each Mains terminal and the earth terminal.

Before securing the unit in its box with the fixing screws make sure the wires are held firmly in the terminals and that they can fold away neatly.

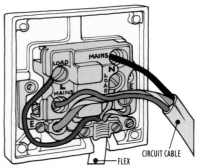

1 Wiring a fused connection unit

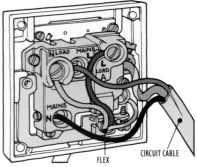

2 Wiring a switched fused connection unit

WIRING HEATERS

When installing a skirting heater, wall-mounted heater or oil-filled radiator, wire the appliance to a fused connection unit mounted nearby at a height of about 150 to 300mm (6in to 1ft) from the floor. Whether the connection to the unit is by flex or cable will depend on the type of appliance. Follow the manufacturer's instructions for wiring, and fit the appropriate fuse in the connection unit.

In a bathroom, a fused connection unit must be mounted out of reach. Any heater that is mounted near the floor of a bathroom must therefore be wired to a connection unit installed outside the room. If the appliance is fitted with flex, mount a flexible-cord outlet (**1**) next to the appliance – and then run a cable from the outlet to the fused connection unit outside the bathroom and connect it to the 'Load' terminals in the unit.

The flexible-cord outlet is mounted on a standard surface-mounted box or flush on a metal box. At the back of the faceplate are three pairs of terminals to take the conductors from the flex and the cable (**2**).

Radiant wall heaters for use in bathrooms must be fixed high on the wall, out of reach from the bath or shower. A fused connection unit fitted with a 13amp fuse (or a 5amp fuse for a heater of 1kW or less) must be mounted at the same level, and the heater must be controlled by a double-pole pull-cord switch (the type that works by breaking both live and neutral contacts). Many heaters have a built-in double-pole switch; otherwise you must fit a ceiling-mounted 15amp double-pole switch between the fused connection unit and the heater. Switch terminals marked 'Mains' are for the cable on the circuit side of the switch; those marked 'Load' are for the heater side. The earth wires are connected to a common terminal on the switch box.

If it is not possible to run a spur to the fused connection unit from a socket outside the bathroom, don't be tempted to connect a radiant wall heater to the lighting circuit. Instead, run a separate radial circuit from the connection unit to a 15amp fuseway in the consumer unit, using 2.5mm² cable.

Heated towel rail

The Regulations covering other kinds of heater apply to a heated towel rail if it is situated in a bathroom. As it is mounted near the floor, run a flex from it to a flexible-cord outlet which is in turn wired to a fused connection unit outside the bathroom.

Fit a 13amp fuse, or, for a heater of 1kW or less, a 5amp fuse.

If a heated towel rail is installed in a bedroom the fused connection unit can be mounted alongside it.

Heat/light unit

Heat/light units, which are sometimes fitted in bathrooms, incorporate a radiant heater and a light fitting in the one appliance. Although they are ceiling-mounted, usually in the position of the ceiling rose, these units must never be connected to lighting circuits.

To install a heat/light unit in this position, turn off the power and, having identified the lighting cables, remove the rose and withdraw the cables into the ceiling void. Fit a junction box to a nearby joist and terminate the lighting cables at that point (**3**). Don't connect the switch cable, as it won't be needed.

Run a 2.5mm² two-core-and-earth spur cable from an unswitched fused connection unit mounted outside the bathroom to a ceiling-mounted 15amp double-pole switch, and from there to the heat/light unit.

Connect up to the fused connection unit (see opposite), then wire the heat/light unit according to the maker's instructions and fit a 13amp fuse in the connection unit.

SEE ALSO

Details for: ▷

Double-pole ceiling switch	159
Ceiling-rose connections	160
Switching off	134
Running cable	141-143

1 Flexible cord outlet

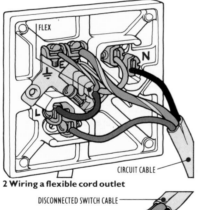
2 Wiring a flexible cord outlet

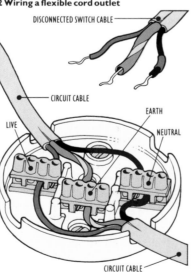
3 Terminating the lighting cables
Join the circuit cables in a junction box. Label the switch wire for future reference.

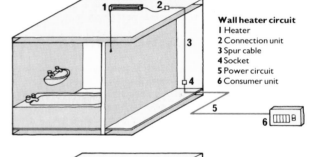
Wall heater circuit
1 Heater
2 Connection unit
3 Spur cable
4 Socket
5 Power circuit
6 Consumer unit

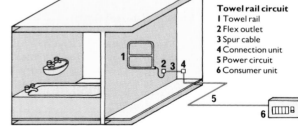
Towel rail circuit
1 Towel rail
2 Flex outlet
3 Spur cable
4 Connection unit
5 Power circuit
6 Consumer unit

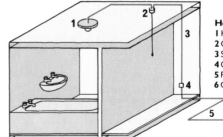
Heat/light circuit
1 Heat/light unit
2 Ceiling switch
3 Spur cable
4 Connection unit
5 Power circuit
6 Consumer unit

WIRING SMALL APPLIANCES

SHAVER SOCKETS

Extractor fan

To install an extractor fan in a kitchen mount a fused connection unit 150mm (6in) above the worktop and run a cable to the fan or to a flex outlet next to it. If the fan has no integral switch use a switched connection unit to control it. Fit a 3 or 5amp fuse as recommended by the maker.

If the fan's speed and direction are controllable it may have a separate control unit, in which case wire the connection unit to it following the manufacturer's instructions.

To fit an extractor fan in a bathroom mount the fused connection unit outside and run the cable to the fan or its flex outlet via a ceiling-mounted double-pole pull-switch.

SEE ALSO

◁ Details for:
Wiring a shower	159
Fitting a fan	121-122
Fitting a cooker hood	120
Running a spur	149
Fused connection unit	152
Flex outlet	153

Fridges, dishwashers and washing machines

There is no reason why you cannot plug an appliance like a fridge, dishwasher or washing machine into a standard socket outlet except that in modern kitchens such appliances fit snugly under worktops, and sockets mounted behind them are hard to reach.

To control an appliance conveniently first mount a switched fused connection unit 150mm (6in) above the worktop and connect it to the ring circuit, then run a spur, using 2.5mm² cable, from the connection unit to a socket outlet mounted behind the appliance.

Cooker hood

Mount a fused connection unit, using a 3amp fuse, close to the cooker hood itself, or mount the connection unit at worktop height, then run a 1mm² cable from the unit to a flex outlet beside the cooker hood.

Instantaneous water heater

You can install an instantaneous water heater above a sink or washbasin to provide on-the-spot hot water. Join a 3kW model by heat-resistant flex to a switched fused connection unit mounted out of reach of anyone using the water.

If the heater is used in a bathroom wire it via a flex outlet to a ceiling pull-switch, then to the connection unit outside the bathroom. Lastly fit a 13amp fuse in the connection unit.

Wire a 7kW water heater like a shower (◁). If it is in the kitchen you can use a double-pole wall switch to control it.

Waste disposal unit

The waste disposal unit is housed in the sink base unit. Mount a switched fused connection unit 150mm (6in) above a worktop near the sink but out of reach of those using it and of small children.

From the unit run a 1mm² cable to a flex outlet next to the disposal unit.

Clearly label the connection unit 'disposal' to avoid accidents.

Finally fit a 13amp fuse.

Special shaver outlets are the only sockets allowed in bathrooms. They contain transformers which isolate the user side of the units from the mains, so they cannot cause an electric shock.

A shaver unit can be wired to a spur from a ring circuit or to a junction box on an earthed lighting circuit. Connect the conductors to the shaver unit: red to L, black to N and earth to E (1).

This type of socket conforms to the exacting British Standard, BS 3535, but there are shaver socket outlets which do not have isolating transformers. These are quite safe to install and use in a bedroom but must not be fitted in a bathroom. Wire such an outlet from the lighting circuit or from a fused connection unit on a ring circuit spur. Fit a 3amp fuse.

Shaver unit for use in a bathroom

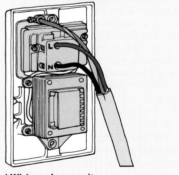

1 Wiring a shaver unit

Kitchen equipment circuits
1 Connection units
2 Flex outlets
3 Socket outlets

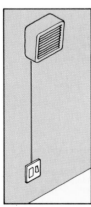

Wall-mounted fan
Run a 1.5mm² cable from a fused connection unit to a wall-mounted extractor fan.

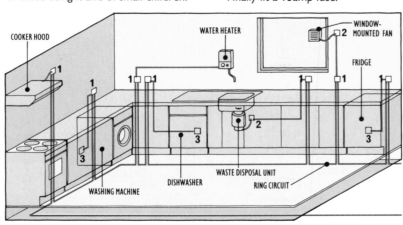

COOKER HOOD

WATER HEATER

WINDOW-MOUNTED FAN

FRIDGE

WASHING MACHINE

DISHWASHER

WASTE DISPOSAL UNIT

RING CIRCUIT

LARGER APPLIANCES: WIRING A COOKER

Powerful appliances such as cookers, with a power load greater than 3000W (3kW), must have their own radial circuits connected directly to the consumer unit, with separate fuses protecting them.

Cookers

Some small table cookers and separate ovens, which rate no more than 3000W (3kW), can consequently be connected to a ring circuit by a fused connection unit, or even by means of a 13amp plug and socket. But most domestic cookers are much more powerful, and must be installed on their own circuits.

The radial circuit
Cookers up to 14kW can be connected on a 30amp radial circuit. Provided that the cooker control unit does not include a 13amp socket outlet, cookers up to 18kW can be connected to a similar circuit. Depending on the length of the relevant circuit, you can use 4mm² or 6mm² two-core-and-earth cable (see CIRCUITS: MAXIMUM LENGTHS).

A separate radial circuit has to have its own fuseway. You can either use a spare fuseway in your consumer unit or fit an individual switchfuse unit – which performs a similar function to the consumer unit but for a single appliance. Ideally buy a switchfuse unit with a 32amp MCB; failing that, one with a 30amp cartridge fuse.

Cooker control units
The cable from the consumer unit runs to a cooker control unit situated within 2m (6ft 6in) of the cooker.

The control unit is basically a double-pole isolating switch, but it may also incorporate a single 13amp switched socket outlet that can be used for an appliance such as an electric kettle. Now that more homes have a number of sockets installed at worktop height the additional one on the cooker control unit is not so important, and in fact it's better not to have one if it is to

be situated above the cooker, from where a flex could trail across one of the hotplates.

The control unit must not only be within reach of the cooker but easily accessible, so don't install it inside a cupboard or under a worktop.

A single control unit can serve both parts of a split-level cooker, with separate cables running to the hob and the oven, provided the control unit is within 2m (6ft 6in) of both. If this is not possible in your case you will have to install a separate control unit for each part. The connecting cables must be of the same size as the cable used in the radial circuit.

Cooker control units can be surface- or flush-mounted.

Because a free-standing cooker has to be moved from time to time for cleaning round and behind it, it should be wired with enough cable to allow it to be moved well out from the wall. The cable is connected to a terminal outlet box which is screwed to the wall about 600mm (2ft) above floor level. A fixed cable runs from the outlet box to the cooker control unit.

Above ▲
1 Control unit with socket
2 Basic control unit
3 Terminal outlet box

Cooker circuit
1 Cooker
2 Terminal outlet box
3 Control unit
4 Radial circuit
5 Consumer unit

WIRING THE CONTROL UNIT

Having decided on the position for the cooker control unit knock out the cable-entry holes in the pattress and screw it to the wall. If your unit is to be flush-mounted cut a hole in the plaster and brickwork for the metal box (▷).

Running cable
Run and fix the cable, taking the most economical route to the cooker from the switchfuse unit or the consumer unit (▷). Cut a channel in the wall up to the control unit if you intend to bury the cable in the plaster, then cut similar channels for cables running to the separate hob and oven of a split-level cooker or for a single cable running to a terminal outlet box.

Connecting up the control unit
Feed the circuit cable and cooker cable into the control unit, then strip and prepare the conductors for connection. There are two sets of terminals in the control unit, one marked 'Mains' for the circuit conductors, and the other marked 'Load', for the cooker cable.

Run the red wires to the L terminals and the black ones to the terminals marked N. Put insulating sleeves on both earth conductors and connect them to the E terminals (**1**). Fold the wires to fit into the box and screw on the faceplate.

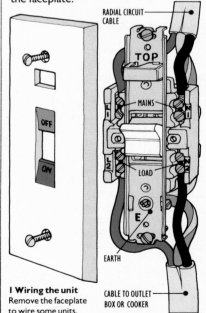

1 Wiring the unit
Remove the faceplate to wire some units.

Labels: RADIAL CIRCUIT CABLE, TOP, MAINS, LOAD, E, EARTH, CABLE TO OUTLET BOX OR COOKER

SEE ALSO

Details for: ▷

Running cable	141-143
Flush mounting	147
Circuit fuses	137
Stripping cable	140
Switchfuse unit	156

CONNECTING THE COOKER

IMMERSION HEATERS

Wiring to the cooker

Connect the cable to the hob and the oven following the manufacturer's instructions exactly.

For a free-standing cooker run the cable down the wall from the control unit to the terminal outlet box, which has terminals for connecting both cables. Strip and insert the wires of the control unit cable in the terminals (**1**), then take the cooker cable and insert its wires in the same terminals, matching colour for colour, and secure it with the clamp. Screw the plastic faceplate onto the outlet box.

SEE ALSO

◁ Details for:
Consumer unit	136
Switching off	134
Circuit fuses	137
Cables	140
Stripping cable	140
Running cable	141-143

Wiring the switchfuse unit

If you are wiring to a fuseway in your consumer unit, run the red wire to the terminal on the fuseway, the black one to the neutral block, and – having first sleeved it – the earth wire to the earth block. All other connections will already have been made. Don't forget to switch off the power before starting this work, and remember that even then the cable connecting the meter to the main switch is still live.

Here we will assume that the cooker circuit is to be run from a switchfuse unit. Screw the unit to the wall close to the consumer unit, feed the cooker-circuit cable into it, and prepare the conductors for connection. Fix the red wire to the live terminal on the fuseway or MCB, the black wire to the neutral terminal, and the sleeved earth wire to the earth terminal (**2**).

Prepare the meter leads, one black and one red, from PVC-sheathed-and-insulated 16mm² single-core cable. (Use 10mm² cable if 16mm² cable is too thick for the switchfuse-unit terminals, but keep the meter leads as short as possible.) Bare about 25mm (1in) of each cable and connect them to their separate terminals on the main isolating switch, red to L and black to N (**2**). For an earth lead, prepare a similar length of the same size single-core cable sheathed in green-and-yellow PVC and attach it to the earth terminal in the switchfuse unit (**2**), for connection to the consumer's earth terminal. Don't make the connection to the Board's earth yourself.

Fit the appropriate fuse, then plug in the fuse carrier. Finally, label the carrier to indicate which circuit is run from the unit and fit the cover.

1 Wiring a terminal outlet box

CABLE FROM CONTROL UNIT
L E ⏚ N
COOKER CABLE

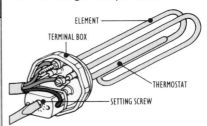

METER LEADS — CIRCUIT CABLE — LIVE

OFF

NEUTRAL — EARTH LEAD

2 Wiring switchfuse unit for the cooker

CONNECTING TO THE MAINS

A new circuit must be tested by a competent electrician and a certificate stating that the wiring complies with the Wiring Regulations must be submitted to the Electricity Board to apply for mains connection. Do not try to make this connection yourself.

It may not be possible to attach both sets of meter leads – from consumer unit and switchfuse unit – to the meter, and you may have to install a connector block that has enough terminals to accommodate all the conductors. It's as well to consult the Electricity Board on these matters before starting.

Water in a storage cylinder is heated by an electric immersion heater, providing a central supply of hot water for the whole house. The heating element, rather like a larger version of the one that heats an electric kettle, is normally sheathed in copper, but more expensive sheathings of incoloy or titanium will increase the life of an element in hard water areas.

Adjusting the water temperature

A thermostat to control the maximum temperature of the water is set by adjusting a screw inside the plastic cap that covers the terminal box (**1**).

Types of immersion heater

An immersion heater can be installed from the top of the cylinder or from the side, and top-entry units can have single or double elements. In the single-element top-entry type of heater the element extends down almost to the bottom of the cylinder, so that the whole of its contents is heated whenever the heater is switched on (**2**). For economy one element in the double-element type is a short one that heats only the top half of the cylinder while the other element is a full-length one that is switched on when greater quantities of hot water are needed (**3**).

A double-element heater with a single thermostat is called a twin-element heater. One with a thermostat for each element is known as a dual-element heater.

Side-entry heaters are the same length, one being positioned near the bottom of the cylinder and the other a little above half way (**4**). This is a more efficient arrangement for heating water and controlling its temperature.

ELEMENT
TERMINAL BOX
THERMOSTAT
SETTING SCREW

1 Adjusting the thermostat

2 Single element **3 Double element** **4 Side-entry elements**

HEATING WATER ON THE NIGHT RATE

If you agree to have a special meter installed the Electricity Board will supply you with power at a cheap rate for seven hours between midnight and 8.00 a.m., the hours varying with the time of year.

The scheme is called Economy 7 (▷). Providing you have a cylinder of big enough capacity to store hot water for a day's requirements you can benefit by producing all your hot water during the Economy 7 hours. Even if you heat your water electrically only in the summer it can be worth considering the scheme. For the water to retain its heat all day you must have an efficient insulating jacket fitted to the cylinder or a cylinder already factory-insulated with a layer of heat-retaining foam (▷).

If your cylinder is already fitted with an immersion heater you can use its wiring by fitting an Economy 7 programmer, a device which will switch your immersion heater on automatically at night and heat up the whole cylinder. If you should occasionally run out of hot water during the day you can adjust the programmer's controls to boost the temperature briefly on the more expensive daytime rate.

You can make even greater savings if you have two side-entry immersion heaters or a dual-element one. The programmer will switch on the longer element – or the bottom one – at night, but should you need daytime water-heating only the upper element is used.

You can have a similar arrangement without a programmer by wiring two separate circuits for the elements. The upper element is wired to the daytime supply and the lower one is wired to its own switchfuse unit and operated by the Electricity Board's Economy 7 timeswitch during the hours of the night-time tariff only. A setting of 75°C (167°F) is recommended for the lower element and 60°C (140°F) for the upper one. If you live in a soft water area or have heater elements sheathed in incoloy or titanium you can raise the temperatures to 80°C (175°F) and 65°C (150°F) respectively without reducing lives of the elements.

To ensure that you never run short of hot water leave the upper unit switched on permanently. It will start heating up only when the thermostat detects a temperature of 60°C (140°F), which should happen only rarely if you have a large and properly insulated cylinder.

WIRING THE IMMERSION HEATER

The circuit

Immersion heaters are mostly rated at 3kW. Although you can wire most 3kW appliances to a ring circuit, an immersion heater is regarded as using 3kW continuously, even though rarely switched on all the time. A continuous 3kW load would greatly reduce a ring circuit's capacity, so immersion heaters must have their own radial circuits.

The circuit needs to be run in 2.5mm² two-core-and-earth cable protected by a 15amp fuse. Each element must have a two-pole isolating switch mounted near the cylinder; the switch should be marked 'WATER HEATER' and have a neon indicator (1). A 2.5mm² heat-resistant flex runs from the switch to the immersion heater.

If the cylinder is situated in a bathroom, the switch must be inaccessible to anyone who may be using the washbasin, bath or shower. If this precludes a normal water-heater switch, you should use a 20amp ceiling-mounted pull-switch with a mechanical ON/OFF indicator.

Wiring two side-entry heaters

For simplicity use two switches, one for each heater and marked accordingly.

Wiring the switches
Fix the mounting boxes to the wall, feed a circuit cable to each and wire them in the same way. Strip and prepare the wires, connect them to the 'Mains' terminals – red to L, black to N–sleeve the earth wire and fix it to the common earth terminal (2). Prepare a heat-resistant flex for each switch. At each take the green/yellow earth wire to the common earth terminal, the other wires to the 'Load' terminals– brown to L and blue to N (2) – tighten the flex clamps and screw on the faceplates.

Wiring the heaters
The flex from the upper switch goes to the top heater and that from the lower switch to the bottom one. At each one feed the flex through the hole in the cap and prepare the wires. Connect the brown wire to one terminal on the thermostat (the other terminal on the thermostat is already connected to the wire running to the L terminal of the heating element). Connect the blue wire to the N terminal and green/yellow wire to the E terminal (3) and replace the caps on the terminal boxes.

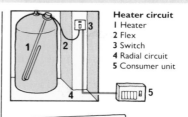

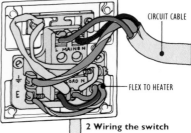

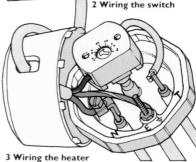

Heater circuit
1 Heater
2 Flex
3 Switch
4 Radial circuit
5 Consumer unit

CIRCUIT CABLE

FLEX TO HEATER

2 Wiring the switch

3 Wiring the heater

Running the cable
Run the circuit cables from the cylinder cupboard to the fuseboard and, with the power off, connect the cable from the upper heater to a spare fuseway in the consumer unit. Though the consumer unit is switched off the cable between main switch and meter is live, so take care. Wire the other cable to its own switchfuse unit – or storage-radiator consumer unit if you have one – ready for connecting to the Economy 7 timeswitch. Make the connections as described for a cooker circuit. (▷).

WIRING A DUAL-ELEMENT HEATER

Wire the circuit as described above, but feed the flex from both switches into the cap on the heater. Connect the brown wire from the upper switch to the L2 terminal on one thermostat and the other brown wire to the L1 terminal on the second thermostat (4). Connect the blue wires to the respective neutral terminals (4), and both earth wires to E terminal.

SEE ALSO

Details for: ▷	
Insulation	109
Economy 7	124
Cooker circuit	155-156
Switching off	134
Consumer unit	136, 156

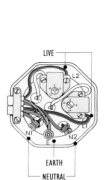

1 20amp switch for immersion heater

LIVE

L2

L1

N1

N2

EARTH

NEUTRAL

4 Make sure your heater is fitted with two thermostats as shown.

157

DOORBELLS, BUZZERS AND CHIMES

Whether you choose a doorbell, a buzzer or a set of chimes there are no practical differences to affect the business of installing them.

SEE ALSO

◁ Details for:
Consumer unit	136, 156
Running cable	141-143
Running a spur	149
Connecting to light circuit	165

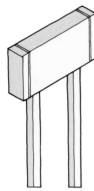

Chimes
A set of chimes has two tubes, each tuned to a different note.

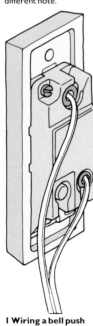

I Wiring a bell push

Bells

Most doorbells are of the 'trembler' type. When electricity is supplied to the bell – that is when someone presses the button at the door – it activates an electro-magnet which causes a striker to hit the bell. But as the striker moves to the bell it breaks a contact, cutting off power to the magnet, so the striker swings back, makes contact again and repeats the process, going on for as long as the button is depressed. This type of bell can be operated by battery or by a mains transformer. Other types of doorbells, known as AC bells, can be used only with mains power.

Buzzers

A buzzer operates on exactly the same principle as a trembler bell but in the buzzer the striker hits the magnet itself instead of a bell.

Chimes

A set of ordinary door chimes has two tubes or bars tuned to different notes. Between them is a solenoid, a wound coil that acts like a magnet when it is energized. When the button is pressed a spring-loaded plunger inside the solenoid is thrown against one tube, sounding a note. When the button is released the spring throws the plunger against the other tube, sounding the other note before returning to its point of rest. Other chimes have a programmed microprocessor that gives a choice of tunes when operated by the bell push. Most chimes can be run from a battery or a transformer.

Bell pushes

When the bell push at the door is pressed it completes the circuit that supplies power to the bell. It is a switch that is on only when held in the 'on' position. Inside it are two contacts to which the circuit wires are connected. One contact is spring-loaded, touching the other when the push is depressed, to complete the circuit, and springing back when the push is released (**1**).

Illuminated bell pushes incorporate a tiny bulb which enables you to see the bell push in the dark. These must be operated from mains transformers, as the power to the bulb, though only a trickle, is on continuously and would soon drain a battery. Luminous types glow at night without a power supply.

Batteries or transformer?

Some doorbells and chimes house batteries inside their casings, while others incorporate built-in transformers that reduce the 240-volt mains electricity to the very low voltages needed for this type of equipment. For many bells or chimes you can use either method. Most of them use two or four 1½ volt batteries, but some require a 4½ volt battery, housed separately. Transformers sold for use with doorbell systems have three low-voltage tappings – 3 volt, 5 volt and 8 volt – to meet various needs. Usually 3 volt and 5 volt connections are suitable for bells or buzzers, and the 8 volt tapping is enough for many sets of chimes.

Some other chimes need higher voltages, and for these you will need a transformer with 4 volt, 8 volt and 12 volt tappings. A bell transformer must be designed so that the full mains voltage cannot cross over to the low-voltage wiring.

Circuit wiring

The battery, bell push and bell are all connected by two-core insulated 'bell wire'. This fine wire is usually surface run, fixed with small staples, but it can be run under floors and in cupboards too. Bell wire is also used to connect a transformer to a bell and bell push.

Connect a BS 3535 Class 2 double-insulated transformer to a junction box or ceiling rose on a lighting circuit with 1mm² two-core-and-earth cable. As no earth is required for a double-insulated transformer, cut and tape back the cable's earth wire at the transformer end. Alternatively, run a spur from a ring circuit in 2.5mm² two-core-and-earth cable to an unswitched fused connection unit fitted with a 3amp fuse; and then run a 1mm² two-core-and-earth cable from the unit to the transformer's 'Mains' terminals. Or you could run 1mm² two-core-and-earth cable directly from a spare 5amp fuseway in your consumer unit.

INSTALLING A SYSTEM

The bell itself can be installed in any convenient position except over a source of heat. The entrance hall is usually best as a bell there can be heard in most parts of the house. Keep the bell wire runs to a minimum, especially for a battery-operated bell. With a mains-powered bell you will not want long and costly runs of cable, so place the transformer where it can be wired simply. A cupboard under the stairs is a good place, especially if it is near the consumer unit.

Drill a small hole in the door frame and pass the bell wire through to the outside. Fix the conductors to the terminals of the push, then screw it over the hole.

If the battery is in the bell casing there will be two terminals for attaching the other ends of the wires. Either wire can go to either terminal. If the battery is separate from the bell run the bell wire from the push to the bell. Separate the conductors, cut one of them and join each cut end to a bell terminal. Run the wire on to the battery and attach it to the terminals (**1**).

When you wire to a transformer proceed as above but connect the bell wire to whichever two of the three terminals combine to give you the required voltage (**2**). Some bells and chimes need separate lengths of bell wire, one from the bell push and another from the transformer. Fix the wires to terminals in the bell housing following manufacturers' instructions.

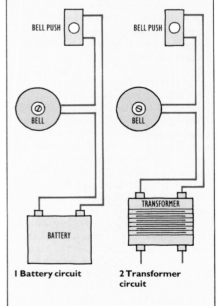

I Battery circuit

2 Transformer circuit

WIRING A SHOWER UNIT

An electrically heated shower unit is plumbed into the mains water supply. The flow of water operates a switch to energize an element that heats the water on its way to the sprayhead. As there is little time to heat the water, instantaneous showers use a heavy load, from 6 to 9.6kW, and the shower unit must have a separate radial circuit protected by a 30 milliamp RCD.

The circuit cable needs to be $10mm^2$ two-core-and-earth, protected by a 40amp MCB or a 45amp fuse in a spare fuseway at the consumer unit or in a separate 45amp switchfuse unit. The cable runs directly to the shower unit, where it must be wired according to the manufacturer's instructions.

The shower unit has its own on/off switch. There must also be a separate isolating switch in the circuit, inaccessible to anyone using the shower, so install a ceiling-mounted 45amp double-pole pull-switch with a contact gap of at least 3mm, and preferably a neon 'on' indicator. Fix the backplate of the switch to the ceiling, sheathe the earth wires with green-and-yellow sleeving and connect them to the E terminal on the switch. Connect the conductors from the consumer unit to the switch's 'Mains' terminal, and those of the cable to the shower to the 'Load' terminals (**1**).

The shower unit and all metal pipes and fittings must be bonded to earth.

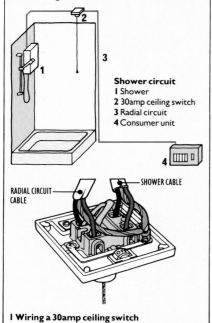

Shower circuit
1 Shower
2 30amp ceiling switch
3 Radial circuit
4 Consumer unit

RADIAL CIRCUIT CABLE

SHOWER CABLE

1 Wiring a 30amp ceiling switch

LIGHTING CIRCUITS

Every lighting system needs a feed cable to supply power to all the lighting points, and a switch that can interrupt the supply to each point. There are two ways of meeting these requirements in your home: the junction-box system and the loop-in system. Your house may be wired with either one, though it is quite likely that there will be a combination of the two systems.

The junction-box system
In the junction-box system a two-core and earth feed cable runs from a fuseway in the consumer unit to a series of junction boxes, one for each lighting point. From each junction box a separate cable runs to a light and another runs to its switch.

The loop-in system
In the loop-in system the ceiling rose takes the place of the junction box. The cable from the consumer unit runs into each rose and out again, then on to the next. The switch cable and the flex to the bulb are connected at the rose.

Combined system
The loop-in system is now the most widely used as it entails fewer connections as well as saving on the cost of junction boxes. However, lights at some distance from a loop-in circuit are often run from a junction box on the circuit to save cable, and lights added after the circuit has been installed are often wired from junction boxes.

The circuit
Both the junction-box and the loop-in systems are, in effect, multi-outlet radial circuits. The cable runs from the consumer unit, looping in and out of the ceiling roses or junction boxes and terminating at the last one. It does not return to the consumer unit.

Lighting circuits require $1mm^2$ or $1.5mm^2$ two-core-and-earth cable, and each circuit is protected by a 5amp circuit fuse or 6amp MCB. A maximum of twelve 100W bulbs or their equivalent can thus use the circuit.

In the average two-storey house it's usual to have two separate lighting circuits – one for the ground floor and another for upstairs.

SEE ALSO	
Details for: ▷	
Bonding to earth	128
Fixing to ceiling	161
Plumbing a shower	202
Consumer unit	136, 156
Circuit fuses	137
Cables	140
Running cable	141-143
Switchfuse unit	156

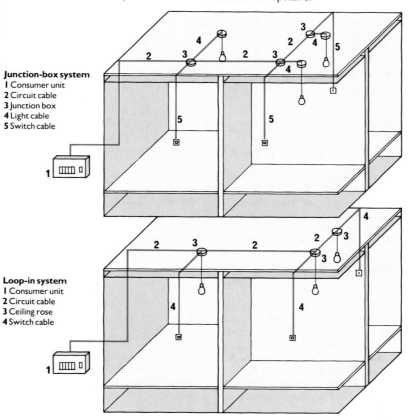

Junction-box system
1 Consumer unit
2 Circuit cable
3 Junction box
4 Light cable
5 Switch cable

Loop-in system
1 Consumer unit
2 Circuit cable
3 Ceiling rose
4 Switch cable

IDENTIFYING THE CONNECTIONS

Loop-in system

A modern loop-in ceiling rose has three terminal blocks arranged in a row. The live (red) conductors from the two cut ends of the circuit-feed cable run to the central live block, and the neutral (black) conductors run to the neutral block on one side. The earth conductors run to a common earth terminal **(1)** .

The live (red) conductor from the switch cable is connected to the remaining terminal in the central live block. Power runs through this conductor to the switch and back to the ceiling rose through the black conductor, the 'switch-return wire', and this is connected to the third terminal block in the ceiling rose, the 'switch-wire block'. When the light is 'on' the switch-return wire is live, so it should

be identified with a piece of red tape wrapped round it to distinguish it from the other black wires, which are neutral. The earth conductor in the switch cable goes to the common earth terminal **(1)** .

The brown conductor from the pendant-light flex connects to the remaining terminal in the switch block while the blue conductor runs to the neutral block. If three-core flex is used the green/yellow earth conductor runs to the common earth terminal **(1)** .

When the circuit-feed cable terminates at the last ceiling rose on the circuit only one set of cable conductors is connected **(2)** . Switch cable and light flex are connected like those in a normal loop-in rose.

SEE ALSO

◁ Details for:
Lighting circuits   159

Junction-box system

The junction boxes on a lighting circuit normally have four unmarked terminals, for live, neutral, earth and switch connections. The live, neutral and earth conductors from the circuit feed cable go to their respective terminals **(3)** .

The live conductor from the cable that runs to the ceiling rose is connected to the switch terminal, the black wire to the neutral terminal and the earth conductor to the earth terminal **(3)** .

The red wire from the switch cable is connected to the live terminal, the earth conductor to the earth terminal and the black return wire from the switch goes to the switch terminal **(3)** .

This last conductor should be identified by having a piece of red tape wrapped round it.

At the ceiling rose the live cable conductor is connected to one of the outer terminal blocks, the neutral conductor to the other and the central block left empty. The earth conductor goes to the earth terminal **(4)** .

The flex conductors are wired up to match those from the cable. The brown wire is connected to the same terminal block as the red conductor and the blue wire goes to the block holding the black conductor. If the flex has a yellow/green earth wire it is connected to the common earth terminal **(4)** .

Checking an old light circuit

Switch off the power at the consumer unit, remove the circuit fuse and examine ceiling roses and light switches for any signs of deterioration. Pre-World War II wiring will have been carried out in rubber-insulated and -sheathed cable. If the insulation seems dry and crumbly it is no longer safe. The circuit should be rewired. If you detect any signs at all that the circuitry is out of date, and perhaps dangerous, consult a professional electrician.

An old installation may have loop-in or junction-box lighting circuits, though the junction-box system is more likely. It may also lack any earth conductors, another good reason for renewing it.

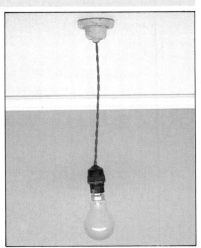

Old fabric-covered flex should be replaced

CONNECTIONS FOR LOOP-IN AND JUNCTION-BOX SYSTEMS

SWITCH CABLE   CIRCUIT CABLES

LIGHT FLEX

1 Loop-in ceiling rose

SWITCH CABLE   CIRCUIT CABLE

LIGHT FLEX

2 Last rose on a loop-in system

EARTH   SWITCH CABLE
CIRCUIT CABLE   SWITCH
NEUTRAL   LIVE
LIGHT CABLE   CIRCUIT CABLE

3 Lighting junction box

LIGHT CABLE

LIGHT FLEX

4 Ceiling rose on a junction-box system

LIGHT FITTINGS

There is now a vast range of lighting fittings that can be used in the home, and though they may differ greatly in *their appearance they can be grouped roughly in about eight basic categories according to their functions.*

Types of light fitting

Pendant lights
The pendant light is probably the most common light fitting. It comprises a lamp-holder with bulb, usually with some kind of shade, suspended from a ceiling rose by a length of flex. The flex is connected to the power supply through terminals inside the ceiling rose (See opposite).

Decorative pendant lights
Most decorative pendant light fittings are designed to take several bulbs, and are consequently much heavier than standard pendant lights. Because of its weight this type of fitting is attached to the ceiling by a rigid tube. The flex that conducts the power to the bulbs passes through the tube to the lighting circuit.

Close-mounted ceiling lights
A close-mounted ceiling light is screwed directly to the ceiling, dispensing with a ceiling rose, by means of a backplate that houses the lampholder or holders. The fitting is usually enclosed by some kind of rigid light-diffuser that is also attached to the backplate.

Recessed ceiling lights
In this type of light fitting the lamp housing itself is recessed into the ceiling void and the diffuser lies flush with, or projects only slightly below, the ceiling. Lights of this type are ideal for rooms with low ceilings; they are often referred to as downlighters.

Track lights
Several individual light fittings can be attached to an aluminium track which is screwed to the ceiling or wall. Because a contact runs the length of the track, lights can be fitted anywhere along it.

Fluorescent light fittings
A fluorescent light fitting uses a glass tube containing mercury vapour. The power makes electrons flow between electrodes at the ends of the tube and bombard an internal coating, which fluoresces to produce the light. The fitting, which also contains a starter mechanism, is usually mounted directly on the ceiling, though as they produce very little heat fluorescent lights are used for under-cupboard lighting.

Wall lights
A light fitting adapted for screwing to a wall instead of a ceiling can be supplied from the lighting circuit in the ceiling void or from a spur off the ring circuit. Various kinds of close-mounted fittings or adjustable spotlights are the most popular wall lights.

Batten holders
A batten holder is a basic fitting with a lamp-holder mounted on a plate that fixes directly to wall or ceiling. Straight, angled and swivel versions are available. Batten holders are for use in areas – such as lofts or cellars – where appearance is not important.

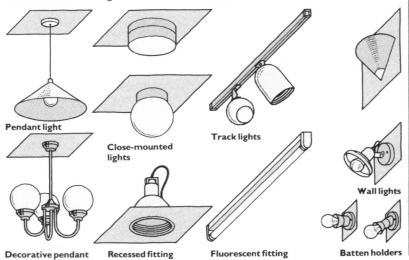

Pendant light

Close-mounted lights

Track lights

Decorative pendant

Recessed fitting

Fluorescent fitting

Wall lights

Batten holders

REPLACING A CEILING ROSE

Turn off power at the consumer unit and remove the circuit fuse. Switching off at the wall is not enough.

Unscrew the rose's cover and inspect the connections so that you can wire the new ones to work in the same way. A modern loop-in rose will be wired by one of the methods shown opposite. Identify the switch-return wire with tape if it is not already marked. If there is only one red and one black conductor the rose is on a junction-box system and will have no switch cable.

In an old rose you may have to identify the wires. If there are wires running into three terminal blocks look first for the one with all red wires and no flex wires. That is the live block, containing live circuit-feed wires and a live switch wire. The neutral terminal block contains the black neutral circuit feed wires and the blue flex wire. The third block will contain the brown flex wire plus a black conductor – the switch return wire – which should be marked with red tape, and may even be sheathed in red PVC.

All earth wires will run to one terminal on the backplate, but an old system may have no earth wires. In this case reconnect the other conductors temporarily but get expert advice on rewiring the circuit.

Fixing the new rose
Disconnect the wires from the terminals and separate any that are twisted together, but identify them with tapes. Unscrew the old backplate from the ceiling. Knock out the entry hole in the new backplate, thread the cables through it and fix the backplate to the ceiling, using the old screws and fixing points if possible. If the old fixings are not secure nail a piece of wood between the joists above the ceiling (See right) and drill a hole through it from below for cable access. Screw the new rose backplate to the wood through the ceiling.

Make sure that the ends of the conductors are clean and sound, then wire the ceiling rose, following the diagrams opposite.

Slip the new cover over the pendant flex and connect the flex wires to the terminals in the rose, looping the wires over the rose's support hooks to take the weight off the terminals. Screw the cover onto the backplate, switch on the power and test the light.

SEE ALSO

Details for: ▷	
Lampholders	133
Switching off	134
Close-mounted light	162
Track light	162
Fluorescent light	163

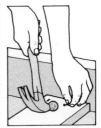

Fixing a platform
Skew-nail a board between the joists to support a ceiling rose.

FITTING A CLOSE-MOUNTED LIGHT

Some close-mounted light fittings have a backplate that screws directly to the ceiling in place of a ceiling rose. To fit one, first switch off the power for the circuit at the consumer unit and take out the fuse, then remove the ceiling rose and fix the backplate to the ceiling (◁).

◁ Details for:

Junction box	160
Fixing to ceiling	161
Switching off	134
Loop-in system	159, 160
Close-mounted lights	161
Track lights	161
Recessed lights	161

If only one cable feeds the light attach its conductors to the terminals of the lampholder and the earth wire to the terminal on the backplate.

As more heat will be generated in an enclosed fitting, slip heat-resistant sleeving over the conductors before attaching them to their terminals.

If the original ceiling rose was wired into a loop-in system the light fitting will not accommodate all the cables. Withdraw them into the ceiling void and wire them into a junction box (◁) screwed to a length of 100 x 25mm (4 x 1in) timber nailed between the joists, then run a short length of heat-resistant cable from the junction box to the close-mounted light fitting.

1 BESA box
Use a BESA box to house the connections when a light fitting is supplied without a backplate.

FITTING A PLASTIC BESA BOX

Fit a platform between the joists to support a junction box and BESA box.

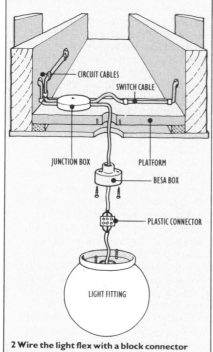

CIRCUIT CABLES

SWITCH CABLE

JUNCTION BOX

PLATFORM

BESA BOX

PLASTIC CONNECTOR

LIGHT FITTING

2 Wire the light flex with a block connector

Fittings without backplates

Sometimes close-mounted lights are supplied without backplates.

Wiring Regulations recommend that all unsheathed conductors and terminals must be enclosed in a non-combustible housing, so if you use a fitting with no backplate you must find a means of complying. The best way is to fit a BESA box **(1)**, a plastic or metal box that is fixed into the ceiling void so as to lie flush with the ceiling.

Screw-fixing lugs on the box should line up with the fixing holes in the light fitting's coverplate, but check that they do so before buying the box. You will also need two machine screws of the right thread for attaching the light to the BESA box.

Check that there is no joist right above where you wish to fit the light. If there is one, move the light to one side until it fits between two joists. Hold the box against the ceiling, trace round it and with a padsaw carefully cut the traced shape out of the ceiling.

Cut a fixing board from 25mm (1in) thick timber to fit between the joists and place it directly over the hole in the ceiling while an assistant marks out the position of the hole on the board from below, then drill a cable-feed hole centrally through the marked-out shape of the ceiling aperture on the board. This hole must also be able to take any boss on the back of the BESA box. Position the box and screw it securely to the board.

Have your assistant press some kind of flat panel against the ceiling and over the aperture. Fit the BESA box into the aperture from above so that it rests on the panel, mark the level of the fixing board on both joists, then screw a batten to each joist to support the board at that level.

Fix the board to the battens and feed the cable through the hole in the centre of the BESA box. The light fitting will probably have a plastic connector for attaching the cable conductors **(2)**, and this may have three terminals. Alternatively, a separate terminal for the earth conductor may be attached to the coverplate.

When the conductors are secured fix the coverplate to the BESA box with the machine screws.

If the original ceiling rose was fed by more than one cable, connect them to a junction box in the ceiling void as described above left.

FITTING A DOWNLIGHTER

Decide where you want the light, check from above that it falls between joists, then use the cardboard template supplied with all downlighters to mark the circle for the aperture on the ceiling. Drill a series of 12mm (½in) holes just inside the perimeter of the marked circle to remove most of the waste, then cut it out with a padsaw.

Bring a single lighting circuit cable from a junction box (◁) through the opening and attach it to the downlighter, following the manufacturer's instructions. You may have to fit another junction box into the void to connect the circuit cable to the heat-resistant flex attached to the light fitting.

Fit the downlighter into the opening and secure it there by adjusting the clamps that bear on the upper, hidden surface of the ceiling.

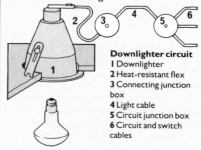

Downlighter circuit
1 Downlighter
2 Heat-resistant flex
3 Connecting junction box
4 Light cable
5 Circuit junction box
6 Circuit and switch cables

FITTING TRACK LIGHTING

Ceiling fixings are supplied with all track lighting systems. Mount the track so that the terminal block housing at one end is situated where the old ceiling rose was fitted. Pass the circuit cable into the fitting and wire it to the cable-connector provided.

If the circuit is a loop-in system mount a junction box in the ceiling void (◁) to connect the cables.

Make sure that the number of lights you intend to use on the track will not overload the lighting circuit, which can supply a maximum of twelve 100W lamps or the equivalent.

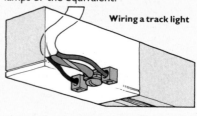

Wiring a track light

Fluorescent lights

Fluorescent light fittings are supplied with terminal blocks for connection to the mains supply.

With the ceiling rose removed screw the fitting to the ceiling, positioned so that the circuit cable can be fed into it conveniently. The terminal block will take only three conductors, so the fitting must be connected to a junction-box system, or a junction box must be installed in the ceiling void to accommodate loop-in wiring as for a close-mounted light (See opposite).

Fluorescent lights normally need earth connections, so they cannot be used on old systems that have not got earth conductors.

You can mount a fluorescent unit by screwing directly into ceiling joists or into boards nailed between joists to provide secure fixings.

Wiring a fluorescent light fitting
A simple plastic block connector is fitted inside a fluorescent light fitting for the circuit cable.

FLUORESCENTS UNDER CUPBOARDS

You can fit fluorescent lighting under kitchen cupboards to illuminate the work surfaces below, the power being supplied from a switched fused connection unit (▷) fitted with a 3amp cartridge fuse.

You can install a second fluorescent light fitting and supply its power by wiring it into the terminal block of the first one.

LIGHT SWITCHES

The commonest type of switch for controlling lighting is the plateswitch. It has a switch mechanism mounted behind a square faceplate that may have one, two or three rockers. Though these are usually quite adequate for domestic use there are also double faceplates with four or six rockers.

A one-way switch simply turns a light on and off, but two-way switches are wired in pairs so that the light can be controlled from two places – typically, the head and foot of a staircase. There is also an intermediate switch that allows a light to be controlled from three places.

Any switch can be flush-mounted in a metal box that is buried in the wall, or surface-mounted in a plastic pattress. Boxes 16 and 25mm (⅝ and 1in) deep are available to accommodate switches of different depths.

Where there is not enough room for a standard switch a narrow architrave switch can be used. There are single ones and double versions that have their rockers one above the other.

A dimmer switch is a device by which the intensity of light can be controlled as well as switching on and off. In some versions a single knob works as both switch and dimmer. Others have a separate one for switching so that the light level does not have to be adjusted each time the light is switched on.

A conventional switch cannot be mounted within reach of a bath or shower unit, and in such situations ceiling-mounted double-pole switches with pull-cords are installed.

Fixing and cable runs
Lighting cable is run underneath floorboards or within the hollow of cavity walls, or is buried in wall plaster (▷). The mounting boxes and switches are fixed to various walls by exactly the same methods as used for sockets (▷).

Light switches must be installed in relatively accessible positions, which normally means at about adult shoulder height for a wall switch and just inside the door of a room.

TYPES OF SWITCHES

Most light switches are made from white plastic but there are some more striking finishes to compliment your decorative scheme. Bright primary-coloured switches can be matched with coloured flex, plugs and socket outlets to make an unusual and attractive feature. Brass antique-reproduction switches suit traditional interiors.

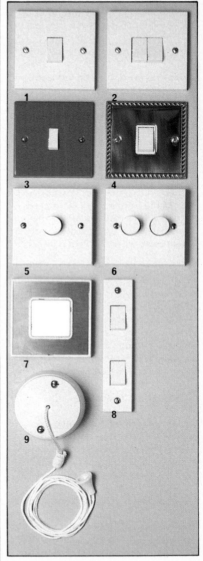

Selection of light switches
1 One-gang rocker
2 Two-gang rocker
3 Switches are made in a range of colours
4 Reproduction antique switch
5 One-gang dimmer
6 Two-gang dimmer
7 Touch dimmer
8 Two-gang architrave switch
9 Ceiling switch

SEE ALSO

Details for: ▷

Running cable	141-143
Mounting boxes	146-147
Fused connection unit	152
Switching off ·	134
Junction box	160
Fluorescent lights	161
Fixing to ceiling	161
Wiring switches	164

REPLACING SWITCHES

SEE ALSO

◁ Details for:
Flush mounting	147
Switches	163
Switching off	134
Cables	140

Replacing a damaged switch is a matter of connecting the existing wiring to the new switch in exactly the same way as it was connected to the old one.

Always turn off the power and remove the fuse before you take off the faceplate to inspect the wiring.

In the case of a surface-mounted switch make sure that a new faceplate will fit the existing pattress; otherwise you will have to replace both parts. If you do use the old pattress, also use the old machine screws for fixing on the faceplate. In this way you know that you have matching threads on the screws.

To replace a surface-mounted switch with a flush-mounted one remove the old switch, then hold the metal box over the position of the original switch and trace round it. Cut away the plaster to the depth of the box and screw it to the brickwork (◁). Take great care not to damage the existing wiring while you are working.

HOW SWITCHES ARE WIRED

It is very easy to replace a damaged switch or swap one for a switch of a different nature (◁). The illustrations below show four common methods of wiring switches. If your switch is wired differently it is probably part of a two- or three-way lighting system (◁). Replace the switch as described left.

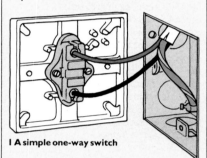

Replacing a one-way switch

A one-way switch will be serviced by a two-core and earth cable, and the earth conductor, where there is one, will be connected to an earth terminal on the mounting box. The red and black wires will be connected to the switch itself.

A true one-way switch has only two terminals, one above the other, and the red or black conductors can be connected to either terminal (1) . The back of the faceplate will be marked 'top' to ensure that you mount the switch right way up, so that the rocker is depressed when the light is on. The switch would work just as well upside down but the 'up for off' convention is a good one as it tells you that a switch is on or off even when a bulb has failed.

Occasionally you will find a switch that is fed by a two-core and earth cable and operates as a one-way switch, yet has three terminals (2) . This is a two-way switch wired up for a one-way function, something that is fairly common and perfectly safe. With the switch mounted right way up the red and black wires should be connected to the 'Common' and 'L2' terminals.

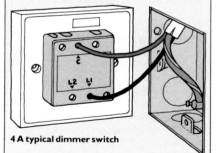

1 A simple one-way switch

2 Two-way switch wired for one-way function

Replacing a two-way switch

A two-way switch will have at least one conductor in each of its three terminals. Without going into the complexities of two-way wiring at this stage, the simplest method for replacing a damaged two-way switch is to write down a note of which wires run to which terminals before disconnecting them. Another way is to detach the conductors from their terminals one at a time and connect each one to the corresponding terminal on the new two-way switch before dealing with the next conductor.

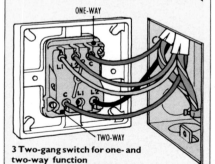

3 Two-gang switch for one- and two-way function

Two-gang switches

A two-gang switch is two single switches mounted on one faceplate. Each switch may be wired differently. One may be working as a one-way switch and the other as a two-way (3) .

Use one of the methods described above, for replacing a two-way switch, to transfer the wires from the old to the new terminals, working on one switch at a time.

Replacing a rocker switch with a dimmer switch

Examine the present switch to determine the type of wiring that feeds it and buy a dimmer switch that will accommodate it. The manufacturers of dimmer switches provide instructions with them, but the connections are basically the same as for ordinary rocker switches (4).

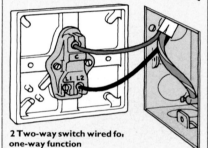

4 A typical dimmer switch

ADDING NEW SWITCHES AND CIRCUITS

When you want to move a switch or install one where none existed before you will have to modify the circuit — *cables or run a new spur cable from the existing lighting circuit to take the power to where it is needed.*

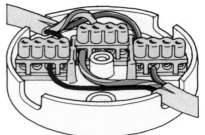

I Link the switch cable with a junction-box

Replacing a wall switch with a ceiling switch

Light switches must be out of reach of anyone using a bath or shower. If your bathroom has a wall switch that breaks this rule replace it with a ceiling switch that operates by a pull-cord.

Turn the power off at the consumer unit and remove the old switch. If the cable running up the wall is surface-mounted or in a plastic conduit you can pull it up into the ceiling void. It should be long enough to reach the point where the new switch is to be.

If the switch cable is buried in the wall trace it in the ceiling void and cut it, then wire the part that runs to the light into a three-terminal junction box fixed to a joist or to a piece of wood nailed between two joists (▷). Connect the conductors to separate terminals **(1)**,

and from those terminals run matching 1mm² two-core and earth cable to the site of the ceiling switch.

Bore a hole in the ceiling to pass the cable through to the switch. Screw the switch to the joist if the hole is close enough; otherwise fix a support board between joists.

Knock out the entry hole in the switch backplate, pass the cable through it and screw the plate to the ceiling.

Strip and prepare the ends of the conductors, connecting the earth to the terminal on the backplate. Connect the red and black conductors to the terminals on the switch – either wire to either terminal **(2)** – then attach the switch to the backplate and make good any damage done to the plasterwork.

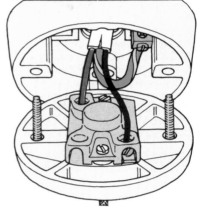

2 Wiring a ceiling switch

SEE ALSO	
Details for: ▷	
Cutting a chase	141
Running a cable	141-143
Wiring a rose	
(last on loop-in)	160
Nail-fixed wood	161
Wiring	
one-way switch	164
Wiring two-way	
as one-way	164
Switching off	134
Connecting to junction box	149

Adding a new switch and light

Turn the power off at the consumer unit and check your lighting circuit to see if it is earthed. If there is no earth wire get expert advice before you try to install a new light.

Decide on where you want the fitting and bore a hole through the ceiling for the cable. Screw a ceiling rose to a nearby joist or nail a board between two joists to provide a strong fixing for the rose (▷).

Bore another hole in the ceiling right above the site of the new switch and as close to the wall as possible. Push twists of paper through both holes so that you can find them easily from above.

Screw the switch mounting box to the wall and cut a chase in the plaster for the cable up to the hole already bored in the ceiling (▷).

Your new light can be supplied from a nearby junction box, from a ceiling rose that is already on the lighting circuit or, if it is more convenient that way, from a new junction box wired into the lighting circuit cable.

From whichever of these sources you choose run a length of 1mm² two-core and earth cable to the new light position, but do not connect the circuit until the whole of the installation is complete. Push the end of the cable through the hole in the ceiling and identify it with tape **(1)**. Write 'Mains' on the tape to be absolutely sure. Now

run a similar cable from the switch to the same lighting point (▷).

Strip and prepare the cable at the switch, connecting the earth wire to the terminal on the mounting box, and connect the red and black wires, either wire to either terminal (▷) if it is a one-way switch. If you can get only a two-way switch connect the wires to its 'Common' and 'L2' terminals (▷). It will work just as well. Now screw the switch to the mounting box.

Knock out the entry hole in the ceiling rose, feed both cables through it and screw the rose to the ceiling.

Take the cable marked 'Mains' and connect its red conductor to the central live block, its black one to the neutral block. Slip a green/yellow sleeve over the earth wire and connect it to the earth terminal (▷).

Connect the red wire of the switch cable to the live block and the black wire to the switch-wire block after marking the black wire with red tape. Connect the switch earth wire to the same earth terminal (▷). Screw the cover on the rose.

Make sure that the power is switched off and connect the new light circuit to the old one at the rose or junction box. The new conductors will have to share terminals already connected: red to live, black to neutral and earth to earth **(2)**.

Switch on and test the new circuit.

I Identify the cables

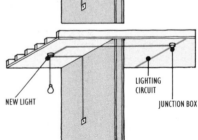

Circuit for a new light ▶
Take the power for a new light from an existing ceiling rose, or insert a new junction box into the existing lighting circuit.

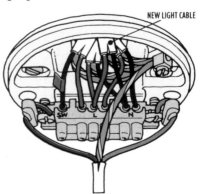

2 Lighting cable connected to a loop-in rose

COMPLETE REWIRING

Planning ahead

Before deciding to take on the complete rewiring of your house yourself, it is advisable to consider the time factor very carefully. When you are working on only one circuit, the rest of the household can function normally, but to renew all the circuits running to the consumer unit means that eventually every part of your home will be affected by the work.

A full-time professional can cope with all this in such a way that the level of inconvenience and disruption to the household is kept to a minimum. But the amateur, perhaps obliged to work only at weekends, will almost certainly have to think in terms of a time span lasting several weeks – especially since it is very important not to work hastily on such installations, as hurried work can lead to dangerous mistakes.

So unless you are very experienced and are able to make the installation a full-time commitment for a week or two, you would be well advised to employ a fully qualified electrician to undertake this time-consuming job.

He or she may perhaps be willing to work alongside you, enabling you to save considerably on the cost by doing some of the jobs that have nothing to do with electrical work – such as running cable under floors and channelling out plaster and brickwork.

SEE ALSO

◁ Details for:
Hiring an
electrician 127
RCCB 135
Consumer unit/fuses 136-137
Power circuits 139
Lighting circuits 139
Fixed appliances 152-154
Larger appliances 155-159

Circuits: maximum lengths

The maximum length of a circuit is limited by the permitted voltage drop and the time it takes to operate the fuse or MCB in the event of a fault.

The method for calculation given in the Wiring Regulations is extremely complicated, but the table below will provide you with a simple method for determining the maximum cable lengths for common domestic circuits.

If necessary, split up your circuits so that none of the indicated cable lengths are exceeded. If your requirements fall outside the limits of this chart, then ask an electrician to make the calculations.

Rewirable fuses are not included as they are subject to special restrictions, which make them an unwise choice.

Most two-core-and-earth cables have a standard-size protective circuit conductor (earth wire). In each case, the chart shows the size of earth wire used in the calculations.

The maximum circuit lengths given in the chart are based on the assumption that you won't install any cables where the ambient temperature exceeds 30°C (86°F), that no more than two cables will be bunched together, and that you will not cover any of the cables with thermal insulation. The shower-circuit lengths assume that a 30 milliamp RCD is used in the circuit.

MAXIMUM LENGTHS FOR DOMESTIC CIRCUITS

TYPE OF CIRCUIT		Max. floor area	Cable size in mm²	Size of earth wire in mm²	Current rating of circuit fuse	Max. cable length using cartridge fuse	Current rating of MCB	Max. cable length using MCB
					USING FUSES		USING MCBs	
RING CIRCUIT	100sq m	2.5	1.5	30amp	60m	32amp	50m
RADIAL CIRCUIT	20sq m	2.5	1.5	20amp	35m	20amp	33m
	50sq m	4	1.5	30amp	38m	32amp	15m
COOKER with socket outlet		4	1.5	30amp	20m	32amp	15m
		6	2.5	30amp	38m	32amp	24m
IMMERSION HEATER up to 3kW		2.5	1.5	15amp	40m	16amp	38m
SHOWER up to 9.6kW		10	4	45amp	20m	40amp	20m
STORAGE HEATER		2.5	1.5	15amp	35m	16amp	30m
STORAGE FAN HEATER		4	1.5	30amp	24m	32amp	34m
FIXED LIGHTING excluding switch drops		1	1	5amp	95m	6amp	95m
		1.5	1	5amp	110m	6amp	110m

DESIGNING YOUR SYSTEM

Before discussing your requirements with a professional, you need to form clear ideas about the kind of installation you want. Although you may eventually decide between you to change some of the details, a proper specification can help the electrician considerably and will also enable you to avoid expensive additions and modifications.

Choosing the best consumer unit

It is worth installing the best consumer unit you can afford. Choose one that has cartridge fuses or miniature circuit breakers (MCBs), and make sure it has enough spare fuseways for possible additional circuits.

Residual current devices

Ask the electrician about the value of installing a residual current device (sometimes called RCCB). One could be built into your consumer unit.

Power circuits

Ring circuits are better than radial circuits for supplying socket outlets. Provided that the floor area in question does not exceed 100sq m (120sq yds), you can have as many sockets as you like – so make sure your plan includes enough outlets to meet your present and likely future needs. Economizing on the cost of a few sockets now could cause you considerable inconvenience in the future, if you have to start adding spurs to the system.

Lighting circuits

Modern domestic lighting circuits are normally designed round a loop-in system; but remember that, if expedient, individual light fittings can be supplied from a junction box.

You should insist on a lighting circuit for each floor – so that you will never be left totally without electric lights if a fuse should blow.

In the interests of safety, make sure that you have two-way or three-way switches installed for lights in passage-ways and on landings and staircases.

Additional circuits

If you are having your whole house rewired, consider installing extra radial circuits for appliances such as immersion heaters and electrically heated showers.

5

PLUMBING SYSTEMS	168
EMERGENCY REPAIRS	171
TAPS:REPAIRS	172
CISTERNS:MAINTENANCE	174
DRAINAGE	177
PIPEWORK	181
WC	190
WASH BASINS	193
BATHS	197
SHOWERS	199
BIDETS	203
SINKS	204
WASTE DISPOSAL UNITS	205
WASHING MACHINES	206
STORAGE CISTERNS	208

PLUMBING

PLUMBING – UNDERSTANDING THE SYSTEM

SEE ALSO

◁ Details for:
Earthing   128, 135

Over recent years, house owners and tenants have demonstrated a willingness, indeed a preference, to tackle their own plumbing repairs. As manufacturers responded to these demands by supplying hardware specially designed for them, householders in turn became even more ambitious, stimulating a growing industry aimed directly at the DIY market. Almost every aspect of home plumbing repair and improvement has been catered for with lightweight, attractive fittings which can be plumbed in quickly and confidently with traditional metal or modern plastic pipework. As usual, the need to save money has been the main incentive for the increased interest in DIY plumbing.

Materials alone are relatively expensive but the price of professional labour constitutes the greater part of any bill you incur, especially if it is necessary to call out a plumber at weekends or at an inconveniently late hour. Furthermore, stopping a leak quickly can save the expense and disappointment of ruined decorations or even the replacement of rotted household timbers. Even if you are insured against plumbing failures, it does not compensate for the disruption caused by major refurbishment. Lastly, there is the cost of water itself. A dripping tap wastes gallons of water a day, and if it's a hot water tap, there is the additional expense of heating it literally down the drain. The few pence spent on a washer can save you pounds.

Direct and indirect systems

You should familiarize yourself with the plumbing system in your own house so that you can isolate the relevant sections and drain the water during an emergency or prior to repairs and rerouting pipework.

Direct system
In many older properties, mains pressure is supplied to all cold water taps and WCs. Hot water is fed indirectly from the storage cistern via the hot water cylinder. The only advantage with this direct system is that drinking water can be drawn from any cold water tap in the house.

Indirect system
Most homes, and certainly modern houses, are plumbed with an indirect system. Water under mains pressure enters the house through a service pipe and proceeds via the rising main directly to the cold water storage cistern, normally situated in the roof space. A branch pipe from the rising main delivers drinking water to the kitchen sink, and possibly to a garden tap

through another pipe. All other cold water taps and appliances are fed indirectly, that is, under gravity pressure only, from the storage cistern. The hot water storage cylinder is also supplied with cold water from the same cistern. There it is heated either indirectly by the central heating system, or by electric immersion heaters, then drawn off from the top of the cylinder to hot water taps in the bathroom, kitchen and some of the bedrooms.

An indirect system provides several advantages to the householder and the water authority. Firstly, there is adequate water stored in the cistern to flush sanitary ware during a temporary mains failure. Also, as the major part of the supply is under relatively low pressure, an indirect system is reasonably quiet. (High mains pressure can cause 'water hammer' as the water tries to negotiate tight bends.) As few outlets are connected to the mains, there is less likelihood of impure water being siphoned back into the mains supply – an important consideration with regard to hygiene.

Drainage

Waste water is drained from either system in one of two ways. Up until the late 1940s or 50s, water was drained from baths, sinks and basins into a wastepipe which fed into a trapped gully at ground level. Toilet waste fed separately into a large diameter soil pipe running directly to the underground main drainage network.

A single stack waste system is used on later buildings where all waste drains into a single soil pipe. The only possible exception is the kitchen sink which still drains into a gully.

Rainwater always feeds into a separate drain so that the house drainage system will not be flooded in the event of a storm.

PLUMBING REGULATIONS

Your local water authority insists that certain regulations are observed whenever you alter existing installations or install new plumbing. The regulations are intended to preserve the health of the community and to reduce unnecessary waste. Except for straightforward replacements, you should seek the advice of the appropriate authority on your local council. The methods described in this chapter comply with the regulations but a telephone call to the Town Hall will put you in touch with someone who can help you with queries about local requirements.

At the same time make sure that you do not contravene electrical regulations. All metal plumbing must be bonded to the Electricity Board's earth terminal near your meter. If you replace a section of metal plumbing with plastic, you may break the path to earth. Make sure that you reinstate the link (◁). If in doubt, consult a qualified electrician.

THE DIRECT SYSTEM
1. Water authority's stopcock
2. Service pipe
3. Main stopcock
4. Rising main Supplies water to storage cylinder as well as cold water taps and WCs.
5. Cold water storage cistern
6. Hot water cylinder
7. Wastepipe Surmounted by hopper head collects water from basin and bath.
8. Soil pipe Separate pipe takes toilet waste to main drains.
9. Kitchen wastepipe Kitchen sink drains into same gully as wastepipe from upstairs.
10. Trapped gully

Indirect system

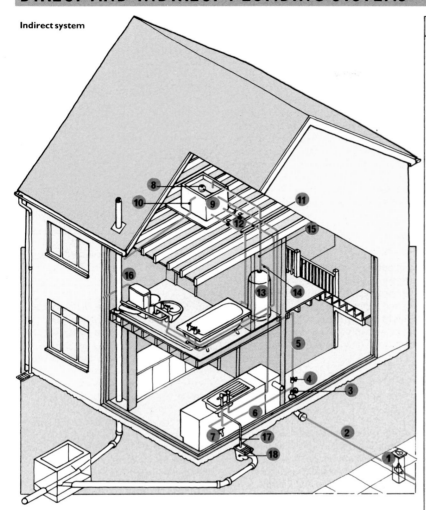

THE INDIRECT SYSTEM

1 Water authority's stopcock
Water from the public main can be turned off at this stopcock. It works like a tap but also acts as a non-return valve so that, should mains pressure drop, water will not be siphoned from the household plumbing to contaminate the public supply.

2 Service pipe
From the stopcock onwards, the plumbing becomes the responsibility of the householder. The service pipe enters the house through a drainpipe packed with insulant to prevent water freezing.

3 Main stopcock
The water supply to the whole house is shut off at this point.

4 Draincock
A draincock here allows you to drain water from the rising main.

5 Rising main
Mains pressure water passes to the cold water cistern.

6 Drinking water
Drinking water is drawn off the rising main to the kitchen sink.

7 Garden tap
The water authority allows a garden tap to be supplied with mains pressure.

8 Float valve
Shuts off the supply from the rising main when the cistern is full.

9 Cold water storage cistern
Stores 230 to 360 litres (50 to 80 gallons) of water. Positioned in the roof, it provides sufficient 'head' or pressure to feed the whole house.

10 Overflow pipe
Also known as a warning pipe, it prevents an overflow by draining water to the outside of the house should the float valve fail to operate.

11 Cold feed pipes
Water is drawn off to the bathroom and to the hot water cylinder from the base of the storage cistern.

12 Cold feed valves
Valves at these points allow you to drain the cold water in the feed pipe without having to drain the whole cistern as well. Alternatively, they may be placed in the airing cupboard.

13 Hot water cylinder
There may be a draincock in this position to empty the cylinder.

14 Hot feed pipe
All hot water is fed from this point.

15 Vent pipe
A vent pipe drains into the cistern to allow for expansion of heated water and to vent air from the system.

16 Single stack soil pipe

17 Sink waste
Drains into trapped gully.

18 Trapped gully

Direct system

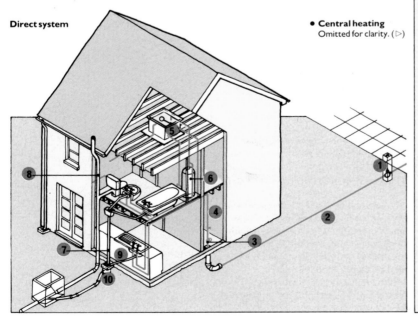

● **Central heating**
Omitted for clarity. (▷)

DRAINING THE SYSTEM

You will have to drain at least part of any plumbing system before you can work on it, and if you detect a leak, you will have to drain the relevant section quickly, so find out where the valves, stopcock and drain cocks are situated before you are faced with an emergency.

SEE ALSO

◁ Details for:
Cylinder vent pipe 169

Draining cold water taps and pipes

● Turn off the main stopcock on the rising main to cut off the supply to the kitchen tap. (And every other cold tap on a direct system.)
● Open the tap until the water ceases to flow.
● To isolate bathroom taps, close the valve on the appropriate cold feed pipe from the storage cistern and open all taps on that section. If you can't find a valve, rest a wooden batten across the cistern and tie the arm of the float valve to it. This will shut off the supply to the cistern so you can empty it by running all the cold taps in the bathroom. If you can't get into the loft, turn off the main stopcock, then run the cold taps.

Draining hot water taps and pipes

● Turn off immersion heaters or boiler.
● Close the valve on the cold feed pipe to the cylinder and run the hot taps. Even when the water stops flowing, the cylinder will still be full.
● If there is no valve on the cold feed pipe, tie up the float valve arm, then turn on bathroom cold taps to empty the storage cistern. (If you run the hot taps first, the water stored in the cistern will flush out all your hot water from the cylinder.) When cold taps run dry, open the hot taps. In an emergency, run the hot and cold taps together to clear the pipes as quickly as possible. (With a direct system you have no choice but to drain the system via the hot taps.)

Draining a WC cistern

● To merely empty the cistern itself, tie up the float valve arm (See above) and flush the WC.
● To empty the pipe supplying the cistern, either turn off the main stopcock on a direct system, or, on an indirect system, close the valve on the cold feed from the storage cistern. Alternatively, tie up the float valve arm and empty the storage cistern through the cold taps. Flush the WC until no more water enters its cistern.

Draining the cold water storage cistern

● To drain the storage cistern in the roof, close the main stopcock on the rising main then open all the cold taps in the bathroom. (Hot taps on a direct system.) Bail out the residue of water at the bottom of the cistern.

Draining the hot water cylinder

If the cylinder springs a leak, or you intend to replace it, first turn off immersion heaters or boiler, then shut off its cold water supply or drain the cold water cistern (See above). Run hot water from taps.
● If the water is heated by immersion heaters only, there should be a draincock on the cold feed pipe just before it enters the cylinder. Attach a hose to it and drain the water still in the cylinder into the nearest drain or sink at a lower level.
● If the water is heated by a boiler which is not part of a central heating system, empty the cylinder with a hose from the draincock on the return pipe next to the boiler.
● When a boiler heats the water and the central heating system, empty the cylinder from the draincock on its cold feed pipe from the storage cistern. (The primary circuit, which heats the radiators and the heat exchanger in the cylinder, is still filled with water. That circuit is drained when necessary from the draincock next to the boiler. Close both valves on radiators if you do not need to empty them.)
● If no draincocks are provided, disconnect the vent pipe (◁) and siphon the cylinder with a hosepipe.

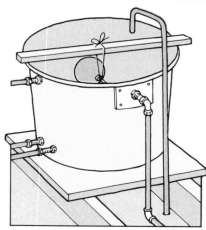

Closing a float valve
Cut off the supply of water to a storage cistern by tying the float arm to a batten.

ADDING EXTRA VALVES

You will have to drain off a substantial part of a typical plumbing installation even for a simple washer replacement unless you divide the system into relatively short pipe runs with valves.
● Install a gate valve on both cold feed pipes running from the cold water storage cistern. This will save you having to drain gallons of water in order to isolate pipes and appliances on the low-pressure cold and hot-water supply.
● When you are fitting new taps, take the opportunity to fit miniature valves on the supply pipes just below the sink or basin. In future, you will be able to isolate an individual tap in moments when you have to repair it.

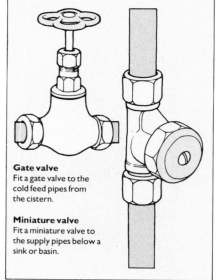

Gate valve
Fit a gate valve to the cold feed pipes from the cistern.

Miniature valve
Fit a miniature valve to the supply pipes below a sink or basin.

DRAINING AND REFILLING THE WHOLE SYSTEM

Drain the complete plumbing system when you intend to leave the house unoccupied for a long period during the winter, otherwise you run the risk of a 'freeze up' which may burst pipes or force joints apart. Drain the system in the following order.

• Switch off the boiler or immersion heaters. Rake out a solid fuel boiler and allow it to cool.
• Turn off the main stopcock on the rising main, and run off the water from all cold and hot taps.
• If there is a draincock on the rising main, drain what water is left in the pipe from that point.
• Flush the WCs.
• Drain the hot water cylinder.
• Don't bother to drain the water from the central heating system, but make sure it contains antifreeze.
• Place a note prominently to remind yourself to fill the system before lighting the boiler or switching on the immersion heater.
• If you can expect very low temperatures where you live, pour some salt into the WC pan to stop the water freezing in the trap. Treat other traps similarly.

Refilling the system
To refill the system, close all taps and draincocks, then open the main stopcock. As the system fills, check that float valves are operating smoothly. Air trapped in the system may cause taps to splutter for a while. If it doesn't clear naturally, flush it out with mains pressure (See below).

CURING AN AIR LOCK

Air trapped in the system can cause a tap to splutter or fail completely. Force the air out using mains water pressure.

Attach a length of hosepipe between the affected tap and the cold water tap over the kitchen sink. (Any cold water tap on a direct system.) Leave both taps open for a short while and try the air-locked tap again. If necessary, repeat the procedure until water runs freely.

If you have to use a long hose, it will contain a lot of water so drain it into the kitchen sink before you move it.

EMERGENCY REPAIRS

Every householder should master the simple techniques for coping with emergency repairs in order to avoid unnecessary damage to property, and the high cost of calling out a plumber at short notice. All you need is a simple tool kit and a few spare parts.

Thawing frozen pipes

Insulate your pipework and fittings, particularly those in the loft or under the floor (▷), to stop them freezing. If you leave the house unheated for a long time during the winter, drain the system (See left). Cure dripping taps so that leaking water does not freeze in your drainage system overnight.

If water will not flow from a tap or a cistern refuses to fill in cold weather, a plug of ice may have formed in one of the supply pipes. The plug cannot be in a pipe supplying those taps or float valves which are working normally, so you should be able to trace the blockage fairly quickly. In fact, freezing usually occurs first in the roof space.

As copper pipework transmits heat readily, use a hairdryer to warm the suspect pipe, starting as close as possible to the tap or valve, then work along it. Leave the tap open so that water can flow normally as soon as the ice thaws. If you cannot heat the pipe with a hairdryer, wrap it in a hot towel or hang a rubber hot water bottle over it.

Dealing with a nailed pipe

Unless you are absolutely sure where your pipes run, it is all too easy to nail through one of them when fixing a loose floorboard. You may be able to detect a hissing sound as water escapes under pressure, but more than likely you won't notice your mistake until a wet patch appears on the ceiling below or some problem associated with damp occurs at a later date. With the nail in place, water will leak relatively slowly so don't pull it out until you have drained the pipework and can repair the leak. If you pull it out by lifting a floorboard, put it back immediately.

If you plan to lay fitted carpet, you can paint pipe runs on the floorboards to avoid a similar accident.

Patching a leak

During freezing conditions, water within a pipe will turn to ice which expands until it eventually splits the walls of the tube or forces a joint apart. Copper pipework is more likely to split than lead which can stretch to accommodate the expansion, taking a few hard winters before reaching breaking point. Patch either pipe as described right but close up a split in lead beforehand using gentle taps with a hammer. Repairing lead permanently is not easy, so hire a plumber as soon as you have contained the leak.

The only other reason for leaking plumbing is mechanical failure, either through deterioration or because the plumber failed to make a completely waterproof joint.

If you can, make a permanent repair by inserting a new section of pipe or replace a leaking joint. If it is a compression joint that has failed, try tightening it first (▷). However, you may have to make an emergency repair for the time being. Always drain the pipe first unless it is frozen, in which case make the repair before it thaws.

Using a hose and Jubilee clips
Cut a length of garden hose to cover the leak, and slit it lengthwise so that you can slip it over the pipe. Bind the hose with two or three Jubilee clips. (Normally used to attach hoses on a car engine.) If you cannot obtain clips, twist wire loops around the hose with pliers.

Patching with epoxy putty
The putty is supplied in two parts which begin to harden as soon as they are mixed, giving you about 20 minutes to complete the repair. The putty will adhere to most metals and hard plastic. Although it is better to insert a new length of pipe, epoxy putty will produce a fairly long-term repair.

Use abrasive paper or wire wool to clean a 25 to 50mm (1 to 2in) length of pipe on each side of the leak. Mix the putty thoroughly and press it into the hole or around a joint, building it to a thickness of 3 to 6mm (⅛ to ¼in). It will cure to full strength within 24 hours, but you can run low pressure water immediately if you bind the putty with self-adhesive tape.

SEE ALSO

Details for: ▷	
Insulating pipes	109
Compression joints	184
Joining pipes	182–189

Thawing a frozen pipe
Play a hairdryer along a frozen pipe working away from the blocked tap or valve.

Binding a split pipe
Bind a length of hosepipe around a split pipe with hose clips.

Smoothing epoxy putty
When you have patched a hole with epoxy putty, smooth it with a damp, soapy cloth for a neat finish.

REPAIRING A LEAKING TAP

A tap may leak for a number of reasons but none of them are difficult to deal with. When water drips from a spout, for instance, it is most likely caused by a faulty washer, or if the tap is old, the seat against which the washer is compressed may be worn also. If water leaks from beneath the head of the tap when it's in use, the gland packing or 'O' ring needs replacing.

When working on taps, insert the plug and lay a towel in the bottom of the sink or bath to catch small objects.

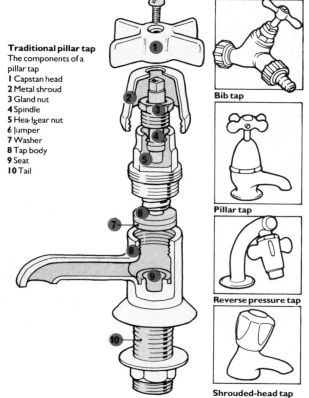

Traditional pillar tap
The components of a pillar tap
1 Capstan head
2 Metal shroud
3 Gland nut
4 Spindle
5 Headgear nut
6 Jumper
7 Washer
8 Tap body
9 Seat
10 Tail

Bib tap

Pillar tap

Reverse pressure tap

Shrouded-head tap

REMOVING A SHROUDED HEAD

On most modern taps the head and cover is in one piece. You will have to remove it to expose the headgear nut. Often a retaining screw is hidden beneath the coloured hot/cold disc in the centre of the head. Prise it out with the point of a knife. If there is no retaining screw, the head will pull off, or remove it by continuing to unscrew the head as if you were turning the tap on in the normal way.

Replacing a washer

To replace the washer in a traditional bib or pillar tap, first drain the supply pipe, then open the valve as far as possible before dismantling either of the taps.

If the tap is shrouded with a metal cover, unscrew it, by hand if possible, or tape the jaws of a wrench to protect the chrome finish.

Lift up the cover to reveal the headgear nut just above the body of the tap. Slip a narrow spanner onto the nut and unscrew it (**1**) until you can lift out the entire headgear assembly.

The jumper, to which the washer is fixed, fits into the bottom of the headgear. With some taps, the jumper is removed along with the headgear (**2**) but in other cases it will be lying inside the tap body.

The washer itself may be pressed over a small button in the centre of the jumper (**3**), in which case, prise it off with a screwdriver. If the washer is held in place by a nut, it can be difficult to remove. Allow penetrating oil to soften any corrosion, then, holding the jumper stem with pliers, unscrew the nut with a snug-fitting spanner (**4**). (If the nut will not budge, replace the whole jumper and washer.) Fit a new washer and retaining nut, then reassemble the tap.

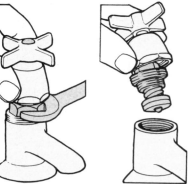

1 Loosen headgear nut   **2 Lift out headgear**   **3 Prise off washer**   **4 Or undo fixing nut**

Replacing a washer in a reverse-pressure tap

The distinctive reverse-pressure tap is like an upside down version of a conventional tap – the washer is screwed upwards against the seat. When replacing a washer, there is no need to shut off the water because an integral check valve closes automatically as the body is removed.

Loosen the retaining nut above the tap body (**1**), then unscrew the body itself as if you were opening the tap. Water will run until the check valve

operates, but continue to unscrew the body (**2**) until it drops into your hand.

Tap the nozzle on the floor (**3**), not on a ceramic basin, then turn the body upside down to tip out the finned, anti-splash device. Prise the combined jumper and washer from the end of the anti-splash device (**4**) and replace it.

Reassemble the tap in the reverse order, remembering that the body is screwed back clockwise when viewed from above.

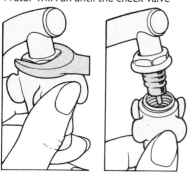

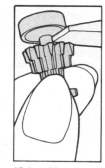

1 Loosen retaining nut   **2 Remove tap body**   **3 Tap nozzle on floor**   **4 Prise off jumper**

REPLACING 'O' RINGS ON MIXER TAPS

Each valve on a mixer tap is fitted with a washer like a conventional tap but in most mixers, the gland packing has been replaced by a rubber 'O' ring.

Having removed the shrouded head, take out the circlip holding the spindle in place (1). Remove the spindle, and slip the old 'O' ring out of its groove (2). Replace it with a new one and reassemble the tap.

 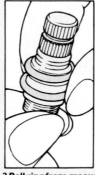

| **1 Remove circlip** | **2 Roll ring from groove** |

The base of a mixer's swivel spout is sealed with a washer or 'O' ring. If water seeps from that junction, turn off both valves and unscrew the spout, or remove the retaining screw (3) on one side. Note the type of seal and buy a matching replacement.

3 Remove screw to release mixer spout

MAINTAINING STOPCOCKS AND VALVES

Stopcocks and gate valves are used rarely so their maintenance is often neglected, but, if they fail to work just when you need them, you could have a serious problem on your hands.

Make sure they are operating smoothly by closing and opening them from time to time. If the spindles move stiffly, lubricate them with a little penetrating oil. Unlike a gate valve, a stopcock is fitted with a standard washer but as it is hardly ever under pressure, it is unlikely to wear. However, the gland packing on both the gate valve and stopcock may need attention (See right).

REPAIRING SEATS AND GLANDS

Regrinding the seat

If a tap continues to drip after you have replaced the washer, the seat is probably worn and water is leaking past the washer.

One way to cure it is to grind the seat flat with a specialized reseating tool rented from a hire company. Remove the headgear and jumper so that you can screw the tool into the body of the tap.

Adjust the cutter until it is in contact with the seat then turn the handle to smooth the seat (1). Alternatively, cover the old seat with a nylon substitute, sold with a matching jumper and washer (2). Drop the seating component over the old seat, replace the jumper and assemble the tap. Close the tap to force the seat in position.

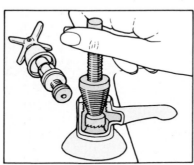

1 Revolve the tool to smooth the seat

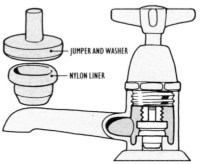

JUMPER AND WASHER

NYLON LINER

2 Repair a worn seat with a nylon liner

Curing a leaking gland

The head of a tap is fixed to a shaft or spindle which is screwed up or down to control the flow of water. The spindle passes through a gland, also known as a stuffing box, on top of the headgear assembly (▷). A watertight packing is forced into the gland by a nut to prevent water leaking past the spindle when the tap is turned on. If water drips from under the head of the tap, the gland packing has failed and should be replaced.

Some taps incorporate a rubber 'O' ring which slips over the spindle to perform the same function as the packing (See left).

Replacing the gland packing
There is no need to turn off the supply of water to replace gland packing; just make sure the tap is turned off fully.

To remove a cross or capstan head,

expose a fixing screw by picking out the plastic plug in the centre of the head, or look for a screw holding it at the side. Lift off the head by rocking it from side to side, or tap it gently from below with a hammer.

If the head is stuck firmly, open the tap as far as possible, unscrew the cover and wedge wooden packing between it and the headgear (1). Closing the tap jacks the head off the spindle.

Lift off the head and cover, then attempt to seal the leak by tightening the gland nut. If that fails, remove the nut and pick out the old packing with a small screwdriver.

To replace the packing, use special impregnated twine from a plumbers' merchant or twist a thread from PTFE (polytetrafluorethylene) tape (▷). Wind it around the spindle and pack it into the gland with a screwdriver (2).

1 Jack the head off a tap with wooden packing

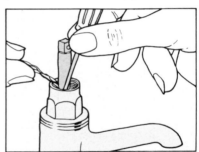

2 Stuff a thread of PTFE tape into the gland

SEE ALSO

Details for: ▷	
Tap mechanisms	172,194
PTFE tape	184
Gate valve	182
Stopcock	186

GLAND PACKING

Gland packing
Older style taps are sealed with a watertight packing around the spindle.

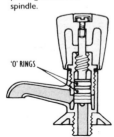

'O' RINGS

'O' ring seal
More modern taps are sealed with rubber rings in place of the gland packing.

MAINTAINING WC AND STORAGE CISTERNS

There is no reason why anyone should have to call out a plumber to service a WC cistern. Most of them are situated directly behind the WC pan so they are readily accessible, but even an old-fashioned, high-level cistern can be reached from a stepladder. The design of a cistern mechanism varies so little that components are available from the stock of any plumbers' merchant and many DIY outlets.

The water storage cistern in the loft is simply a container. Apart from a leak, which is unlikely to occur with a modern cistern, the only problems to arise are as a result of float valve failure. The float valve in a storage cistern is basically the same as that used for the WC cistern.

SEE ALSO

◁ Details for:
Float arm ... 176

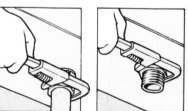

Direct action cistern
The components of a typical direct action WC cistern.
1 Overflow
2 Float
3 Float arm
4 Float valve
5 Siphon
6 Wire link
7 Flushing lever
8 Flap valve
9 Perforated plate
10 Sealing washer
11 Retaining nut
12 Flush pipe connector

DIRECT ACTION WC CISTERN

Most modern WCs are washed down with direct flushing cisterns. Water enters an empty cistern through a valve which is opened and closed by the action of a hollow float attached to one end of a rigid arm. As the water rises in the cistern, it lifts the float until the other end of the arm eventually closes the valve and shuts off the supply.

Flushing is carried out by depressing a lever which lifts a perforated metal plate at the bottom of an inverted 'U' bend tube (siphon). As the plate rises, the perforations are sealed by a flexible plastic diaphragm (flap valve) so that the plate can displace a body of water over the 'U' bend to promote a siphoning action. The resulting water pressure behind the diaphragm lifts it again so that the contents of the cistern flow up through the perforations in the plate, over the 'U' bend, and down the flush pipe. As the water level in the cistern drops, so does the float, opening the float valve to refill the cistern.

There are few problems associated with this type of cistern and all of them can be solved with regular maintenance. A faulty float valve or poorly adjusted arm allows water to leak into the cistern until it drips from the overflow pipe running to the outside of the house. Slow or noisy filling is often rectified by replacing the float valve. If the cistern will not flush until the lever is operated several times, the flap valve is probably worn and needs replacing.

Tying up a float arm
Tie the arm to a batten placed across the cistern when you need to shut off the supply of water.

Replacing the flap valve

If the WC cistern will not flush first time, take off the lid and check that the lever is actually operating the mechanism. If it is working normally, replace the flap valve in the siphon. Shut off the water by tying up the float valve arm (◁), and flush the cistern.

Use a large wrench to unscrew the nut holding the flush pipe to the underside of the cistern (1). Move the pipe to one side.

Release the remaining nut which clamps the siphon to the base of the cistern (2). A little water will run out as you loosen the nut so have a bucket handy. (It's just possible that the siphon is bolted to the base of the cistern instead of being clamped by one large retaining nut.)

Disconnect the flushing arm and ease the siphon out of the cistern. Lift the diaphragm off the metal plate (3) and substitute one of the same size. Reassemble the flushing mechanism in the reverse order and attach the flush pipe to the cistern.

1 Release flush pipe   2 Loosen retaining nut   3 Lift off flap valve

Making a new link

If the flushing lever feels slack and the cistern will not even attempt to flush, look to see if the wire link at the end of the flushing arm is intact.

Retrieve the broken pieces from the cistern and bend a new link from a piece of thick wire. If you have thin wire only, twist the ends together with pliers to make a temporary repair until you can buy a new link.

Curing continuous running water

If you notice water continuously trickling into the pan from the flush pipe, lift out the siphon as described above and renew the washer which seals the siphon to the base of the cistern. Make sure the replacement is identical.

DIAPHRAGM VALVES

The pivoting end of the float arm on a diaphragm valve presses against the end of a small plastic piston which moves the large rubber diaphragm to seal the water outlet.

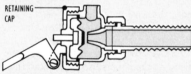

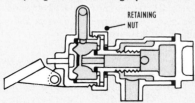

1 Diaphragm valve: retaining cap to the front

2 Diaphragm valve: retaining nut to the rear

Replacing the diaphragm

Turn off the water supply then unscrew the large retaining cap. Depending on the model, the nut may be screwed onto the end of the valve (1) or it may be behind it (2).

With the latter type of valve, slide out the cartridge inside the body (3) to find the diaphragm behind it. With the former, you will find a similar piston and diaphragm immediately behind the retaining cap (4).

Wash out the valve before assembling it along with the new diaphragm.

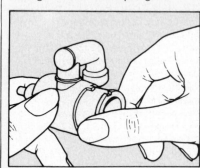

3 Slide out piston to release the diaphragm

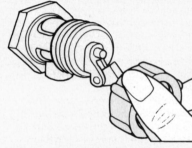

4 Remove cap and pull float arm to find valve

RENOVATING FLOAT VALVES

A faulty float valve is responsible for most of the difficulties that arise with WC and water storage cisterns. Traditionally, the water outlet in the valve is sealed with a washer, but later patterns of valve utilize a large diaphragm instead, designed to protect the mechanism from scale deposits. Both

types of valve are still widely available. If the outlet isn't sealed properly, water continues to feed into the cistern until it escapes to the outside via the overflow pipe. You may be able to solve the problem by simply adjusting the float arm, but more than likely, the washer or diaphragm is worn.

Portsmouth pattern valves

In a Portsmouth pattern valve, a piston moves horizontally inside the hollow metal body. The float arm, pivoting on a split pin, moves the piston back and forth to control the flow of water. A washer trapped in the end of the piston finally seals the outlet by pressing against the valve seat.

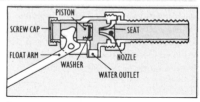

Portsmouth pattern valve

Replacing a washer

If you have to force the valve closed to stop water dripping, replace the washer. Cut off the supply of water to the cistern (▷), and although it is not essential, flush the cistern in case you drop a component into the water. Remove the split pin from beneath the valve and detach the float arm.

If there is a screw cap on the end of the valve body, remove it (1). You may have to apply a little penetrating oil to ease the threads, and grip the cap with slip-joint pliers.

Insert the tip of a screwdriver in the slot beneath the valve body and slide the piston out (2).

To remove the captive washer, unscrew the end cap of the piston with pliers. Steady the piston by holding a

screwdriver in its slot (3).

Pick the old washer out of the cap (4) but before replacing it, clean the piston with fine wire wool. Some pistons do not have a removable end cap, and the washer must be dug out with a pointed knife. Take care when replacing this type of washer which is a tight fit within a groove in the piston.

Use wet and dry paper wrapped around a dowel rod to clean inside the valve body but take care not to damage the valve seat at the far end.

Reassemble the piston and smear it with a light coating of petroleum jelly. Rebuild the valve and connect the float arm. Restore the supply of water and adjust the arm to regulate the water level in the cistern (▷).

SEE ALSO
Details for: ▷
Turning off water 170
Adjusting float arm 176

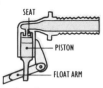

Croydon pattern valve
Only old fashioned cisterns will be fitted with this valve. The piston travels vertically to close against the seat. Replace the washer as described left.

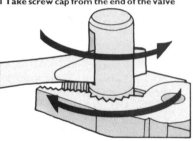

1 Take screw cap from the end of the valve

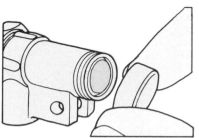

3 Split the piston into two parts

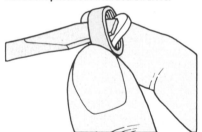

2 Slide the piston out with a screwdriver

4 Pick out the washer with a screwdriver

RENOVATING VALVES AND FLOATS

Adjusting the float arm

Adjust the float to maintain the optimum level of water which is about 25mm (1in) below the outlet of the overflow pipe.

The arm on a Portsmouth valve is a solid metal rod. Bend it downward slightly to reduce the water level or straighten it to admit more water (1).

The arm on a diaphragm valve is fitted with an adjusting screw which presses on the end of the piston. Release the lock nut and turn the screw towards the valve to lower the water level or away from it to allow the water to rise (2).

SEE ALSO

◁ Details for:
Supporting pipes 185

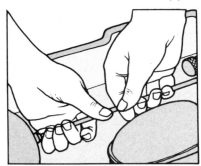

1 Straighten or bend a metal float arm

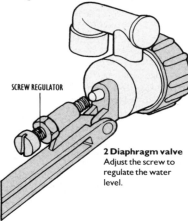

SCREW REGULATOR

2 Diaphragm valve
Adjust the screw to regulate the water level.

Replacing the float

Modern plastic floats rarely leak but old style metal floats do corrode eventually, allowing water to seep into the ball. It gradually sinks until it won't ride high enough to close the valve.

Unscrew the float and shake it to test whether there is water inside. If you can't replace it for several days, lay the ball on a bench and enlarge the leaking hole with a screwdriver, then pour out the water. Replace the float and cover it with a plastic bag, tying the neck tightly around the float arm.

Curing noisy cisterns

Cisterns that fill noisily can be a real source of annoyance, particularly if the WC is situated right next to a bedroom. It was once permitted to screw a pipe into the outlet of a valve so that it hung vertically below the level of the water. It solved the problem of water splashing into the cistern but water authorities were alarmed at the possibility of water 'back-siphoning' through the silencer tube into the mains supply. Although rigid tubes are banned nowadays, you are permitted to fit a valve with a flexible plastic silencer tube because it will seal itself by collapsing should back-siphonage occur.

A silencer tube can also prevent water hammer – a rythmic thudding that reverberates along the pipework. It is largely the result of ripples on the surface of the water in a cistern, caused by a heavy flow from the float valve. As the water rises, the float arm, bouncing on the ripples, hammers the valve and the sound is amplified and transmitted along the pipes. A flexible plastic silencer tube will eliminate ripples by introducing water below the surface.

If the water pressure through the valve is too high, the arm oscillates as it tries to close the valve – another cause of water hammer. Cure it by fitting an equilibrium valve. As water flows through the valve, some of it is introduced behind the piston or diaphragm to equalize the pressure on each side so that the valve closes smoothly and silently.

Before swapping your present valve, check that the pipework is clipped securely (◁) to cut down vibration.

Float valve with flexible silencer tube

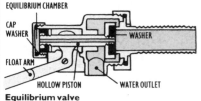

EQUILIBRIUM CHAMBER

CAP
WASHER

WASHER

FLOAT ARM

HOLLOW PISTON   WATER OUTLET

Equilibrium valve

Changing a float valve

Turn off the supply of water to the cistern and flush the pipework, then use a spanner to loosen the tap connector joining the supply pipe to the float valve stem. Remove the float arm, then unscrew the fixing nut on the outside of the cistern and pull out the valve.

Fit the new valve and, if possible, use the same tap connector to join it to the supply pipe. Adjust and tighten the fixing nuts to clamp the new valve to the cistern, then turn on the water and adjust the float arm.

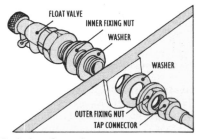

FLOAT VALVE

INNER FIXING NUT

WASHER

WASHER

OUTER FIXING NUT
TAP CONNECTOR

Replacing a float valve
Clamp a valve to the cistern with fixing nuts.

CHOOSING THE RIGHT PRESSURE

Float valves are made to suit different water pressures: low, medium and high (LP, MP, HP). It is important to choose a valve of the correct pressure or it may take a long time to fill. Conversely, the water pressure may be so high that the valve leaks continuously. Those fed direct from the mains should be HP valves, whereas most domestic WC cisterns require an LP valve. If the head (the height of the cistern above the float valve) is greater than 13.5m (45ft), fit an MP valve. In rare cases where the head exceeds 30m (100ft), fit an HP valve. In an apartment using a packaged plumbing system (a storage cistern built on top of the hot water cylinder, the pressure may be so low that you will have to fit a 'full way' valve to the WC cistern to get it to fill quickly. If you live in an area where water pressure fluctuates a great deal, it pays to fit an equilibrium valve (See left).

To alter the pressure, replace the nozzle inside a modern Portsmouth or diaphragm valve. If the valve is a very old pattern, you will have to swap it for another one of a different pressure.

MAINTAINING A DRAINAGE SYSTEM

A drainage system is designed to carry dirty water and WC waste from the various appliances to underground drains leading to the main sewer. The different branches of the waste system are protected by 'U' bend traps full of water to stop drain smells fouling the house. Depending on the age of your house, it will have a two-pipe system or a single stack. Because the two-pipe system has been in use for very much longer, it is still the more common of the two. Use similar methods to maintain either system.

Two-pipe system

The wastepipes of older houses are divided into two separate systems. WC waste is fed into a large diameter, vertical soil pipe which leads directly to the underground drains. To discharge drain gases at a safe height, and to make sure that back-siphoning cannot empty the WC traps, the soil pipe is vented to the open air above the guttering.

Individual branch pipes, leading from upstairs wash basins and baths, drain into an open hopper which funnels the water into another vertical wastepipe. Instead of feeding directly into the underground drains, this wastepipe terminates over a yard gully – another trap covered by a grid. A separate wastepipe from the kitchen sink normally drains into the same gully.

The yard gully and soil pipe discharge into an underground inspection chamber, or manhole. These chambers provide access to the main drains for clearing blockages, and you will find one wherever the drain changes direction on its way to the sewer. At the last inspection chamber, just before the drain enters the sewer, there is an interceptor trap, the final barrier to drain gases, and in this case, sewer rats.

Single stack system

Since the 1960s, most houses have been drained using a single stack system. Waste from basins, baths and WCs is fed into the same vertical soil pipe or stack, which, unlike the two-pipe system, is often built inside the house. A single stack system must be designed carefully to prevent a heavy discharge of waste from one appliance siphoning the trap of another, and to avoid the possibility of WC waste blocking other branch pipes. The vent pipe of the stack terminates above the roof and is capped with an open cage to prevent birds sealing the pipe by nesting in it.

The kitchen sink can be drained through the same stack but it is still common practice to drain sink waste into a yard gully. Nowadays, wastepipes must pass through the grid, stopping short of the water in the gully trap so that even when the grid becomes blocked with leaves, the waste can discharge unobstructed into the gully. Alternatively, it will be a back-inlet gully with the waste pipe entering below ground level.

A downstairs WC is sometimes drained through its own branch drain to an inspection chamber.

RESPONSIBILITY FOR THE DRAINS

Where a house is drained individually, the whole system up to where it joins the sewer is the responsibility of the householder. Where a house is connected to a communal drainage system linking several houses, the arrangement for maintenance, including the clearance of blockages, is not so straightforward.

If the drains were constructed prior to 1937, the local council is responsible for cleansing but can reclaim the cost of repairing any part of the communal system from the householders. After that date, the entire responsibility falls upon the householders collectively, so that they are required to share the cost of both repair and cleansing of the drains up to the sewer, no matter where the problem occurs. Contact the Environmental Health Officer of your local council to find out who is responsible for your drains.

SEE ALSO

Details for: ▷	
Plumbing systems	169
Yard gully	179
Blocked soil pipe	179
Blocked drains	180

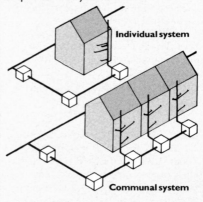

Individual system

Communal system

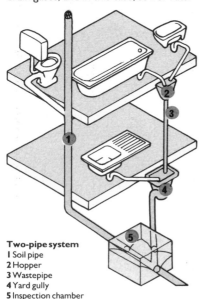

Two-pipe system
1 Soil pipe
2 Hopper
3 Wastepipe
4 Yard gully
5 Inspection chamber

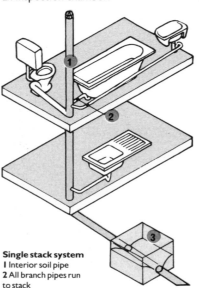

Single stack system
1 Interior soil pipe
2 All branch pipes run to stack
3 Inspection chamber

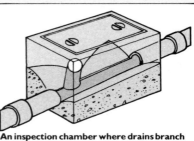

An inspection chamber where drains branch

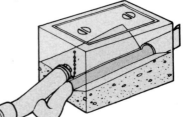

A chamber with interceptor trap

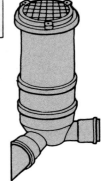

Pre-fabricated chamber
The inspection chambers of a modern drainage system may be cylindrical pre-fabricated units. There may not be an interceptor trap in the chamber before the sewer.

177

CLEARING A BLOCKED WASTE SYSTEM

SEE ALSO

◁ Details for:
Frozen pipes   171

Don't ignore the early signs of an imminent blockage of the wastepipe from a sink, bath or basin. If the water drains away slowiy, use a chemical cleaner to remove a partial blockage before you are faced with clearing a serious obstruction. If a wastepipe blocks without warning, try a series of measures to locate and clear the obstruction.

Cleansing the wastepipe

Grease, hair and particles of kitchen debris build up gradually within the traps and wastepipes. Regular cleaning with a proprietary chemical drain cleaner will keep the waste system clear and sweet smelling.

If water drains sluggishly, use a cleaner immediately, following the manufacturer's instructions with particular regard to safety. Always wear protective gloves when handling chemical cleaners and keep them out of the reach of children.

If unpleasant odours linger after you have cleaned the waste, pour a little disinfectant into the basin overflow.

USING COMPRESSED AIR TO CLEAR A SINK

Clear a blocked waste with compressed air using a simple hand operated tool. Three strokes of the hand pump builds a low pressure which will clear most blockages without blowing apart push-fit joints. Place the rubber nozzle of the tool into the waste outlet and squeeze the trigger. If the blockage persists, increase the pressure gradually.

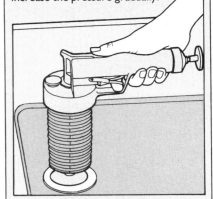

Using a compressed air gun
The tool is supplied with a range of soft adaptor nozzles to fit different sizes of sink plug. Press the nozzle into the waste and squeeze the trigger to clear a blockage.

Using a plunger

If a basin fails to empty while others are functioning normally, the blockage must be somewhere along its individual branch pipe. Before you attempt to locate the blockage, try forcing it out of the pipe with a sink plunger. Smear the rim of the rubber cap with petroleum jelly, then lower it into the blocked basin to cover the waste outlet. Make sure there is enough water in the basin to cover the cup. Hold a wet cloth in the overflow with one hand while you pump the handle of the plunger up and down a few times. The waste may not clear immediately if the blockage is merely forced further along the pipe, so repeat the process until the water drains away. If it will not clear after several attempts, try clearing the trap, or use compressed air to clear the pipe (**See left**).

Clearing the trap

The trap, situated immediately below the waste outlet of a sink or basin, is basically a bent tube designed to hold water to seal out drain odours. Traps become blocked when debris collects at the lowest point of the bend. Place a bucket under the basin to catch the water then use a wrench to release the cleaning eye at the base of a standard trap. Alternatively, remove the large access cap on a bottle trap by hand. If there is no provision for gaining access to the trap, unscrew the connecting nuts and remove the entire trap. (Take the opportunity to scrub it out with detergent before replacing it.)

Let the contents of the trap drain into the bucket, then bend a hook on the end of a length of wire to probe the section of wastepipe beyond the trap. If the pipe is clear but the blockage is still intact, it must be in the branch running to the soil stack or outside to the hopper and vertical wastepipe.

Cleaning the branch pipe

Quite often, a vertical pipe from the trap joins a virtually horizontal section of the wastepipe. There should be an access plug built into the joint so that you can clear the horizontal pipe. Have a bowl ready to collect any trapped water then unscrew the plug by hand. Use a length of hooked wire to probe the branch pipe. If you locate a blockage which seems very firm, rent a drain auger from a tool-hire company to clear the pipework.

If there is no access plug, remove the trap and probe the pipe with an auger. If the wastepipe is constructed with push-fit joints, you can dismantle it.

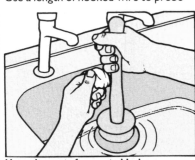
Use a plunger to force out a blockage

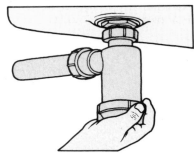
Unscrew the access cap on a bottle trap

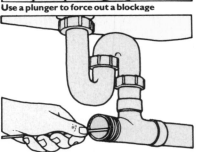
Use hooked wire to probe a branch pipe

Tubular trap
If the access cap to the cleaning eye is stiff, remove it with a wrench.

Bottle trap
A bottle trap can be cleared easily because the whole base unscrews by hand.

CLEARING A STACK OR GULLY

If several fittings are draining poorly the vertical stack itself is probably obstructed. The hopper and downpipe as well as the yard gully are frequently blocked with leaves in the autumn. It may not be obvious when you empty a hand basin, but the contents of a bath will almost certainly cause the hopper or gully to overflow. Clear the blockage urgently to avoid penetrating damp (▷).

Cleaning out the hopper and drainpipe

Wearing protective gloves, scoop out the debris from the hopper then gently probe the drainpipe with a cane to check that it is free. Clear the bottom end of the pipe with a piece of bent wire. If an old cast iron wastepipe has been replaced with a modern plastic type, you may find cleaning eyes or access plugs at strategic points for clearing a blockage.

While you are on the ladder, scrub the inside of the hopper and disinfect it to prevent stale odours entering a nearby bathroom.

Unblocking a yard gully

Unless you decide to hire an auger, there is little option but to clear a blocked gully by hand, but by the time it overflows, the water in the gully will be quite deep so try bailing some of it out with a small disposable container. Wearing rubber gloves, scoop out the debris from the trap until the remaining water disperses.

Rinse the gully with a hose and cleanse it with disinfectant. Scrub the grid as clean as possible or alternatively, burn off accumulated grime from a metal grid with a gas torch (▷).

If a flooded gully appears to be clear, and yet the water will not drain away, try to locate the blockage at the nearest inspection chamber (▷).

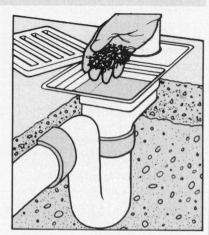
Bail out the water then clear a gully by hand

Unblocking the soil pipe

Unblocking the soil pipe is an unpleasant job and it's worth hiring a professional cleaning company, especially if the pipe is made of cast iron because it will almost certainly have to be cleared via the vent above the roof.

You can clean a modern plastic stack yourself because there should be a large hinged cleaning eye or other access plugs wherever the branch pipes join the stack. If the stack is inside the house, lay large polythene sheets on the floor and be prepared to mop up trapped sewage when it spills from the pipe.

Unscrew and open the cleaning eye to insert a hired drain auger. Pass the auger into the stack until you locate the obstruction then crank the handle to engage it. Push or pull the auger until you can dislodge the obstruction to clear the trapped water, then hose out the stack. Wash and disinfect the surrounding area.

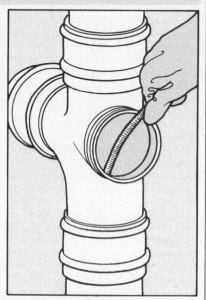
Use a hired auger to clear a soil stack

BLOCKED TOILETS

Unblocking a WC pan

If the water in a WC pan rises when you flush it, there is a blockage in the vicinity of the trap. A partial blockage allows the water level to fall slowly.

Hire a larger version of the sink plunger to force the obstruction into the soil pipe. Position the rubber cap of the plunger well down into the 'U' bend and pump the handle several times. When the blockage clears, the water level will drop suddenly accompanied by an audible gurgling.

If the trap is blocked solidly, hire a special WC auger. Pass the flexible clearing rod as far as possible into the trap, then crank the handle to dislodge the blockage. Wash the auger in hot water and disinfect it before returning the tool to the hire company.

SEE ALSO

Details for: ▷	
Penetrating damp	26
Inspection chambers	180
Gas torch	183

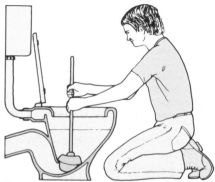
Use a special plunger to pump a blocked WC

Alternatively, clear it with a WC auger

RODDING THE DRAINS

The first sign of a blocked underground drain could be an unpleasant smell from an inspection chamber, but a severe blockage can cause sewage to back up until it begins to overflow from a gully or from beneath the cover of an inspection chamber. Hire a set of drain rods – short, flexible components made of plastic, cane or wire, screwed end to end – to clear a blocked drain. Metal screws or a rubber plunger are threaded onto the rods.

SEE ALSO

◁ Details for:
Inspection chambers   177

Locating the blockage

Lift the cover from the inspection chamber nearest the house. If it is stuck firmly, or the handles have rusted away, scrape the dirt from around its edges and prise it up with a garden spade.

● If the chamber contains water, check the one nearer the road or boundary. If that chamber is dry, the blockage is between the two chambers.
● If the chamber nearest the road is full, the blockage will be in the interceptor trap or in the pipe beyond leading to the sewer.
● If both chambers are dry and yet either a yard gully or downstairs WC will not empty, check for blockages in the branch drains joining the first inspection chamber.

Rodding points
A modern drainage system could be fitted with rodding points to provide access to the drain. They are sealed with small oval or circular covers.

Rodding a drain

Screw two or three rods together and attach a corkscrew fitting to the end. Insert the rods into the drain at the bottom of the inspection chamber in the direction of the suspected blockage. If the chamber is full of water, use the end of a rod to locate an open channel running across the floor, leading to the mouth of the drain.

As you pass the rods along the drain, attach further lengths until you reach the obstruction, then twist the rods clockwise to engage the screw. (Never twist the rods anti-clockwise or they will become detached.) Pull and push the obstruction until it breaks up, allowing the water to flow away. Extract the rods, flush the chamber with a hose and replace the lid.

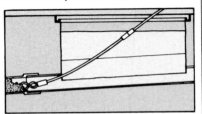

Use a corkscrew fitting to clear a drain

Clearing an interceptor trap

Screw a rubber plunger to the end of a short length of rods and locate the channel leading to the base of the trap. Push the plunger into the opening of the trap, then pump the rods a few times to expel the blockage.

If the water level does not drop after several attempts, try clearing the drain leading to the sewer. Access to this drain is through a cleaning eye above the trap. It will be sealed with a stopper which you will have to dislodge with a drain rod unless it is attached to a chain stapled to the chamber wall. Make sure the stopper doesn't fall into the channel and block the interceptor trap. Rod the drain to the sewer using the corkscrew fitting then hose out the chamber before replacing the stopper and cover.

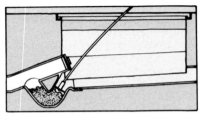

Fit a plunger to rod an interceptor trap

CESSPOOLS AND SEPTIC TANKS

Houses built in the country or on the outskirts of a town are not always connected to a public sewer. Instead, waste is drained into a cesspool or septic tank. A cesspool is simply a collection point for sewage until it can be pumped out by the local council. A septic tank is a complete waste disposal system in which sewage is broken down by bacterial action before the water is discharged into a local waterway or distributed underground.

Cesspools

Current building regulations stipulate that cesspools should have a minimum capacity of 18 cu m (4,000 gallons) but many existing cesspools accommodate far less, and require emptying perhaps once every two weeks. It would be worth checking on the capacity of a cesspool before you buy a country home to ensure it will cope with your needs. Water authorities estimate the **disposal** of approximately 115 litres (25 gallons) per person per day.

Most cesspools are cylindrical pits lined with brick or concrete. Modern ones are sometimes prefabricated in glass-reinforced plastic. Access is via a manhole cover.

Septic tanks

The sewage in a septic tank separates slowly, heavy sludge falling to the bottom leaving relatively clear water with a layer of scum floating on the surface. A dip-pipe discharges waste below the surface so that incoming water does not stir up the sewage. Bacterial action takes a minimum of 24 hours so the tank is divided into chambers by baffles to slow down the movement of sewage through the tank.

The partly treated waste passes out of the tank through another dip-pipe into some form of filtration system which allows further bacterial action to take place. It may be another chamber containing a deep filter bed or alternatively, the waste may flow underground through a network of drains which disperses the water over a wide area to filter through the soil.

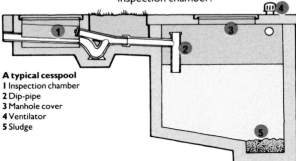

A typical cesspool
1 Inspection chamber
2 Dip-pipe
3 Manhole cover
4 Ventilator
5 Sludge

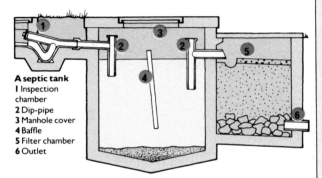

A septic tank
1 Inspection chamber
2 Dip-pipe
3 Manhole cover
4 Baffle
5 Filter chamber
6 Outlet

INSTALLING PIPES

The ability to install a run of pipework, make watertight joints and connect up to fittings are the basic requirements of plumbing. Without those skills, a householder is restricted to simple maintenance. When lead piping was universal, plumbing was a trade requiring years of experience, but modern materials and technology has made it possible for anybody who is prepared to master a few techniques to upgrade and extend household plumbing without having to hire a professional.

Metric and imperial pipes

Copper and stainless steel pipes are now made in metric sizes whereas a lot of pipework already installed in a house will be of the old imperial measurements. If you compare the equivalent dimensions; 15mm – ½in, 22mm – ¾in, and 28mm – 1in; the difference seems obvious, but metric pipe is measured externally while imperial pipe is measured internally. In fact, the difference is very small, but enough to cause some problems when joining one type of pipe to the other.

An exact fit is essential when making soldered joints so imperial to metric adaptors are used for all sizes of pipe. Adaptors are not necessary when joining 15mm and 28mm pipes to their imperial equivalents with compression joints but you will have to use them for joining 22mm to ¾in pipes.

Use 22mm pipes for the main runs and 15mm for most branch pipes. 28mm pipe is for the primary flow and return pipes connected to a boiler.

Electro-chemical action

If you live in a soft water area, take care when joining copper to galvanized steel (iron) pipes or storage tanks. The two metals in combination with a weak acidic solution produce the conditions of an electric cell which gradually dissolve the zinc coating on the steel.

Brass can corrode in a similar way due to the zinc content of the metal. Use corrosion-resistant brass or gunmetal fittings and special copper to steel connectors where these conditions are likely to occur. Check with your water authority for advice.

TYPES OF METAL PLUMBING

Over the years, most household plumbing systems have undergone some form of improvement or alteration. As a result you may find any of a number of metals used, perhaps in combination, depending on the availability of materials at the time it was installed, or the preference of an individual plumber.

COPPER

Half-hard tempered copper tubing is by far the most widely used material for pipework. It is lightweight, solders well and can be bent easily, even by hand with the aid of a bending spring. It is used for both hot and cold water supply as well as central heating systems. Invariably, three sizes of pipe are used for general domestic plumbing: 15mm (½in), 22mm (¾in) and 28mm (1in).

STAINLESS STEEL

Stainless steel tubing is not as common as copper but is available in the same sizes. You may have to order it from a plumbers' merchant. Stainless steel offers few advantages to a DIY plumber. It is harder than copper so cannot be bent as easily and it is difficult to solder. For both reasons, use compression joints to connect stainless steel pipes, but tighten them slightly more than you would when joining copper. Alternatively, use a special adhesive. However, stainless steel does not react adversely with galvanized steel (iron) pipes which may have been installed previously. (See electro-chemical action, left)

LEAD

Lead is never used for new plumbing but thousands of houses still have a lead rising main connected to a modernized system. This is perfectly acceptable, but extensive lead plumbing still in use must be nearing the end of its useful life so replace it whenever the opportunity arises. When drinking water lies in a lead pipe for some time, it absorbs toxins from the metal. If you have a lead pipe supplying your drinking water, always run off a little water before you use any.

GALVANIZED STEEL (IRON)

Galvanized steel was used to provide strong pipework where lead might easily have been damaged. It can still be obtained but there is no longer any point in using it for general plumbing especially as the ends of straight lengths have to be threaded before you can make a joint. Take care when joining copper to existing galvanized steel pipes. (See electro-chemical action, left)

CAST IRON

All old soil pipes are made of cast iron but the metal is very prone to rusting. In fact it is only the relatively thick walls of the pipes that have preserved them for so long. Should you need to replace one, ask for one of the plastic alternatives.

BRASS

Because it machines and casts so well, brass is used to make compression joints, taps, stopcocks and other fittings. Corrosion-resistant brass is used to avoid electro-chemical action between zinc content of brass and copper pipes.

GUNMETAL

Gunmetal connectors are manufactured for joining copper pipework to galvanized steel where standard brass fittings would be corroded.

SEE ALSO

Details for: ▷

Soldered joints	183

● **Gluing stainless steel**
Stainless-steel plumbing can be glued with a special adhesive and activator such as Loctite 638 (Activator 'N') or Permabond A128 ('Speed' primer). Key end of tube and inside of fitting. Spray activator onto both surfaces. After 30 seconds apply a ring of glue to the leading edge of the fitting and to the end of the tube. Assemble joint and leave it to harden for at least two minutes.

METAL PIPE JOINTS

As most domestic plumbing is carried out in copper, the methods described on the next few pages are primarily for joining copper pipes. You can use the same techniques for stainless steel plumbing but, because it is harder than copper, you will find it easier to cut the metal with a hacksaw and use an active flux for soldering joints. Join copper to galvanized steel or plastic plumbing with specially designed couplings.

SEE ALSO

◁ Details for:
Metal plumbing   181

Compression & capillary joints

It would be impossible to make strong, watertight joints by simply soldering two lengths of copper pipe end to end. Instead, plumbers use capillary or compression joints.

Capillary joints

Capillary joints are made to fit snugly over the ends of the pipe. The very small space between the pipe and sleeve is filled with molten solder which solidifies on cooling to hold the joint together and make it watertight. Capillary joints are neat and inexpensive but, because you need to heat the metal with a blow torch, there is a slight risk of fire when working in confined spaces under floors and in the loft.

Compression joints

Compression joints are very easy to use but are more expensive than capillary joints. They are also more obtrusive, and you will find it impossible to manoeuvre a wrench where space is restricted. When the cap-nut is tightened with a wrench, it compresses a ring of soft metal, known as an olive, to fill the joint between fitting and pipe.

Capillary joints
Solder is introduced to the mouth of the assembled end-feed joint (top) and flows by capillary action into the fitting. The ring pressed into the sleeves of an integral ring fitting (above) contains the exact amount of solder to make a perfect joint.

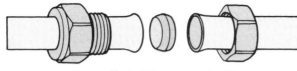

Manipulative compression joint
The ends of the pipes are flared to accept a soft copper cone. When the nut is tightened, the cone is compressed to seal the joint.

Non-manipulative compression joint
This is the simplest and most widely used compression joint. The end of each pipe is cut square before the joint is assembled.

METAL JOINTS AND FITTINGS

Capillary and compression joints are made to connect pipes at different angles and in various combinations. There are adaptors for joining metric and imperial pipes and for connecting one material to another. You will have to consult manufacturers' catalogues to see every variation, but the examples below illustrate a range of typical joints and fittings.

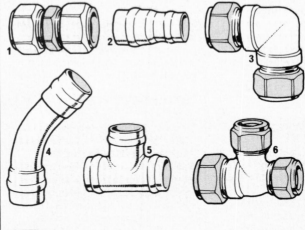

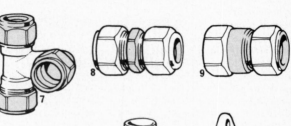

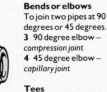

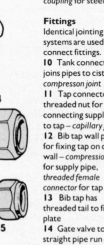

Straight connectors
To join two pipes end to end in a straight line.
1 For pipes of equal diameter – *compression joint*
2 Reducer to connect 22mm (¾in) and 15mm (½in) pipes – *capillary joint*

Bends or elbows
To join two pipes at 90 degrees or 45 degrees.
3 90 degree elbow – *compression joint*
4 45 degree elbow – *capillary joint*

Tees
To join three pipes.
5 Equal tee to join three pipes of the same diameter – *capillary joint*
6 Unequal tee to reduce size of pipe run and join a branch pipe – *compression joint*
7 Off-set tee joins branch pipe to one side of main pipe run – *compression joint*

Adaptors
To join dissimilar pipes.
8 Straight coupling to join 22mm and ¾in pipes – *compression joint*
9 Copper to galvanized steel connector – *compression joint* for copper, *threaded female coupling* for steel

Fittings
Identical jointing systems are used to connect fittings.
10 Tank connector joins pipes to cisterns – *compresson joint*
11 Tap connector with threaded nut for connecting supply pipe to tap – *capillary joint*
12 Bib tap wall plate for fixing tap on outside wall – *compression joint* for supply pipe, *threaded female connector* for tap
13 Bib tap has threaded tail to fit wall plate
14 Gate valve to fit in straight pipe run – *compression joint*
15 Drain cock to empty a pipe run – *compression joint*

MAKING SOLDERED JOINTS

Soldering pipe joints is very simple once you have had a little practice. The fittings are relatively cheap so try out the techniques before you install actual pipework. Your basic equipment is a gas torch to apply heat, some flux to clean the metal and solder to make the joint.

CUTTING METAL PIPE

Calculate the length of pipe you need, allowing enough to fit into the sleeve of the joint at each end. Whatever type of joint you use, it is essential to cut the end of every length of pipe square.

To ensure a perfectly square cut each time, use a tube cutter. Align the cutting wheel with your mark, and adjust the handle of the tool to clamp the rollers against the pipe (1). Rotate the tool around the pipe, adjusting the handle after each revolution to make the cutter bite deeper into the metal.

Use the pointed reamer on the end of the tool to clean the burr from inside the cut pipe (2). A tube cutter makes a clean cut on the outside of the pipe automatically.

If you want to use a hacksaw, make sure the cut is square by wrapping a piece of paper with a straight edge around the pipe. Align the wrapped edge and use it to guide the saw blade (3). Remove the burr, inside and out, with a file.

1 Clamp cutter on pipe

2 Clean off the burr

3 Wrap notepaper around a pipe to guide a saw

Gas torches

To heat the metal sufficiently to make a good soldered joint, most plumbers use a gas torch. Gas, liquefied under pressure, is contained in a disposable metal canister. When the control valve of the torch is opened, gas is vapourized to combine with air to make a highly combustible mixture. Once ignited, the flame is adjusted until it burns with a clear, blue colour.

Many professional plumbers use a propane torch connected by a hose to a metal gas bottle. The average householder does not need such expensive equipment, but if you happen to own a propane torch, perhaps for car repairs, you can use the same tool to solder plumbing joints.

Using integral ring joints

Clean the ends of each pipe and the inside of the joint sleeves with wire wool or abrasive paper until the metal is shiny. Brush flux onto the cleaned metal and push the pipes into the joint, twisting them to spread the flux evenly. Make sure each pipe is up against the integral stop in the joint. Wipe off excess flux with a cloth.

If you are using elbows or tees, mark the pipe and joint with a pencil to make sure they do not get misaligned during the soldering.

Slip a ceramic tile or plumbers' fibreglass mat behind the joint to protect any flammable materials, then apply the flame of a gas torch over the area of the joint to heat it evenly (1).

Using end-feed joints

Clean and assemble an end-feed joint like an integral ring type, then heat the area of the joint evenly. When the flux begins to bubble, remove the flame and touch the end of the solder wire to two

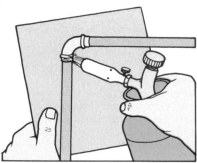

1 Heat the joint to melt the captive solder

Solder and flux

Solder is a soft alloy of tin and lead manufactured with a melting point lower than that of the metal it is joining. Plumbers' solder is sold as wound wire.

Copper must be spotlessly clean and grease-free to produce a properly soldered joint. Even when you have cleaned it mechanically with wire wool, copper begins to oxidize immediately, so a chemical cleaner known as flux is painted onto the metal to provide a barrier against oxidation until the solder is applied. A non-corrosive flux in the form of a paste is the best one to use, but for stainless steel use a highly efficient active flux but wash it off with warm water after the joint is made or the metal will corrode.

When a bright ring of solder appears at each end of the joint, remove the flame and allow the metal to cool for a couple of minutes before disturbing it.

Repairing a weeping joint
When you fill a new installation with water for the first time, check every joint to make sure it is watertight. If you notice water 'weeping' from a soldered joint, drain the pipe and allow it to dry. Heat the joint and apply some fresh solder to the edge of each mouth. If it leaks a second time, heat the joint until you can pull it apart with gloved hands. Use a new joint, or clean and flux all surfaces and reuse the same joint as an end-feed fitting.

or three points around the mouth of each sleeve (2). You will know that the joint is full of solder when a bright ring appears around each sleeve. Allow it to cool. Mend a weeping joint as above.

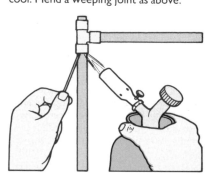

2 Introduce solder to a heated end-feed joint

SEE ALSO

Details for: ▷
Pipe fittings   182

Gas torches
A gas torch is used to heat soldered joints. A simple torch (top) is available from any DIY outlet. The propane torch (above) is used by professional plumbers.

MAKING COMPRESSION JOINTS

SEE ALSO

◁ Details for:
Plumbing adaptors   182

Using non-manipulative joints is so straightforward that you will be able to make watertight joints without any *previous experience. There is no advantage in using a manipulative joint unless it will be under tension.*

Using non-manipulative joints

Cut the ends of each pipe square and clean them, along with the olives, with wire wool. Dismantle the joint and slip a cap-nut onto a pipe followed by an olive (**1**) . Look carefully to see if the sloping sides of the olive are equal in length. If one is longer than the other, that side should face away from the nut.

Push the pipe firmly into the joint body (**2**) , twisting it slightly to ensure it is firmly against the integral stop. Slide the olive up to the body then hand tighten the nut.

The olive must be compressed the right amount to ensure a watertight joint. As a guide, use a pencil to mark one face of the nut and the opposing face on the joint body then, holding the body steady with a spanner, use another to turn the nut one complete revolution (**3**). Assemble the other half of the joint in the same way.

To make absolutely sure the joint is watertight, some plumbers prefer to smear a little jointing compound onto the olive before tightening the nut, but a properly tightened compression joint should be watertight without it.

Repairing a weeping joint

Having filled the pipe with water, check each joint for leaks. Make one further quarter turn on any nut that appears to be weeping.

Crushing an olive by overtightening a compression joint will cause it to leak. Drain the pipe and dismantle the joint. Cut through the damaged olive with a junior hacksaw taking care not to damage the pipe. Remake the joint with a new olive, restore the supply of water and check for leaks once more.

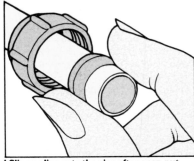

1 Slip an olive onto the pipe after a cap-nut

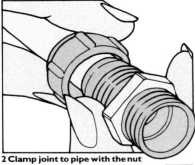

2 Clamp joint to pipe with the nut

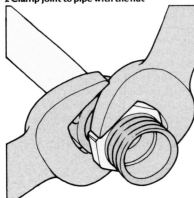

3 Tighten the joint with two spanners

Using manipulative joints

Whatever type of manipulative compression joint you use, the ends of the tubing must be shaped (manipulated) to fit the joint. There are special flaring tools to produce the effect, or drive a steel drift into the end of the pipe. Follow the manufacturer's instructions for individual joints, but the following example demonstrates the principle.

Having cut and cleaned the pipes, slip the cap-nut onto one tube and the joint

body onto the other. Insert the drift into one pipe and strike it with a hammer until the cone of the drift flares the pipe (**1**) . Flare the other pipe in the same way. Sandwich a copper compression ring or 'cone' between the flared pipes and smear the area with jointing compound. Hand-tighten the cap-nut then use two spanners to complete the joint.

1 Manipulative joint
Flare the pipe by driving a metal drift into one end.

MAKING COPPER TO STEEL CONNECTIONS

Galvanized steel pipe is connected by threaded joints so if you plan to extend old pipework using the same material, you will need a pipe die to cut the threads on the end of each length of new pipe. You can hire the tool but it would be simpler to continue the run in copper using an adaptor to connect one system to another. One end of the adaptor has a capillary or compression joint for the copper pipework. The other end has a male or female threaded connector for the galvanized steel.

Use two stilson wrenches to unscrew the joint on the old pipework where you intend to connect up to copper. Grip the joint with one wrench and the pipe with the other, pushing and pulling in the direction the jaws face (**1**) . If the joint is stiff, use penetrating oil or play the flame of a gas torch along it.

Threaded connections leak unless they are made watertight with plumbers' hemp or PTFE tape. To use hemp, smear some jointing compound (a waterproofing paste sold by plumbers' merchants) around the male thread. Tease out a short length of hemp and wrap it clockwise around the thread. Leave about one third of the thread free at the end of the pipe to engage the connector accurately before it encounters the hemp (**2**) . Tighten the joint with a spanner.

PTFE tape is bound over the threads instead of the hemp. No jointing compound is required. Wrap the tape clockwise two or three times around the pipe (**3**), engage and tighten the nut.

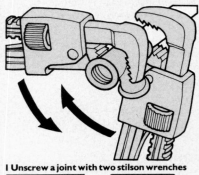

1 Unscrew a joint with two stilson wrenches

2 Wrap with hemp   **3 Or use PTFE tape**

MAKING COPPER-TO-LEAD CONNECTIONS

When replacing old lead plumbing with copper, a plumber would formerly make the connection to the lead rising main with solder and a blowlamp. Such joints are now illegal, and it is also far simpler to use a special lead-to-copper compression joint. The connection can be made with water still in the pipe.

Joints are manufactured to fit different size lead pipes and for 15 and 22mm (½ and ¾in) copper pipes. You can use the same joints for plastic plumbing provided you reinforce the plastic pipe with metal inserts. Although the connectors are specified according to the bore of lead pipework, measure the outside diameter of your rising main and ask a plumbers' merchant to provide a suitable compression joint.

Making the connection
Select a straight length of lead pipe that is as round as possible. It must also be in good condition: the O-ring inside the fitting will not make a watertight seal if the lead is dented or scored.

If possible, turn off the water. Cut the lead pipe with a hacksaw, chamfer the outside edge and remove the burr from inside. Dismantle the compression joint and check that the large thrust nut makes a good sliding fit on the pipe. You can scrape back a slightly oversize pipe to fit, keeping it as round as possible.

Slide the thrust nut onto the pipe, then the two metal rings and the rubber O-ring (1). Slide the threaded coupling body onto the end of the pipe and push it against the internal end stop. Tighten the coupling (2) until you feel resistance, but don't force it.

The other end of the coupling body carries a conventional compression joint for the copper pipe.

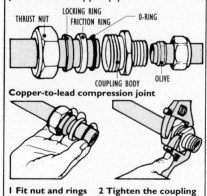

THRUST NUT — LOCKING RING — FRICTION RING — O-RING — COUPLING BODY — OLIVE

Copper-to-lead compression joint

1 Fit nut and rings   2 Tighten the coupling

BENDING PIPES

You can change the direction of a pipe run by using an elbow joint but there are occasions when bending the pipe itself will produce a neater or more accurate result. If you want to carry a pipe over a small obstruction, like another pipe for instance, a slight kink in the pipe will be less of an obstruction to the flow of water than two joints within a few centimetres of each other. It is also cheaper. You might want to run pipes into a window alcove where the walls meet at an unusual angle. Bending the pipes accurately will allow you to fit the pipes neatly against the walls of the alcove.

Using a bending spring

A bending spring is the cheapest and easiest tool for making bends in small pipe runs. It is a hardened steel coil spring which supports the walls of copper tube to stop it kinking. Most bending springs are made to fit inside the pipe but some slide over the tube.

Slide the spring into the tube to support the area you want to bend. Hold the tube against your knee and bend it to the required angle (1).

A bent tube grips the spring but if you slip a screwdriver into the ring at one end and twist it anti-clockwise, it reduces the diameter of the spring so that you can pull it out. If you make a bend some distance from the end of a tube, you can't withdraw the bending spring in the normal way. Either use an external spring, or tie a length of twine to the ring and lightly grease the spring with petroleum jelly before you insert it. Slightly overbend the tube and open it out to the correct angle to release the spring, then pull it out with the twine.

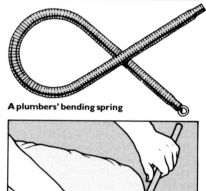

A plumbers' bending spring

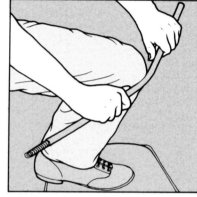

1 Bend the pipe against your knee

Using a pipe bender

Although you can hire bending springs to fit the larger pipes, it isn't easy to bend 22mm or 28mm (¾ or 1in) tube over your knee. It is well worth hiring a pipe bender.

Hold the pipe against the radiused former and insert the straight former to support it. Pull both levers towards each other to make the bend, then open up the bender to remove the pipe.

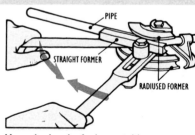

PIPE — STRAIGHT FORMER — RADIUSED FORMER

Use a pipe bender for larger tubing

Getting the bends in the right place

To make sure a bend is in the right place along a pipe, bend the tube before you cut it to length.

It is difficult to position more than two bends along one length of pipe. If you want to fit an alcove for instance, bend two tubes, one to fit each side, then cut the tubes where they overlap and insert a joint.

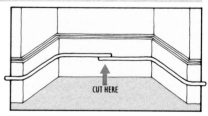

CUT HERE

Bend two separate tubes to fit an alcove

Supporting pipe runs
Place a plastic or metal clip every metre (yard) along a horizontal run of 15mm (½in) pipe, but increase the spacing to every 1.5m (4ft 6in) on a vertical run. For larger pipes, increase the spacing a little more.

Notching floorboards
When you run pipes under floorboards, notch each joist to receive the pipe. Cut the notch to align with the centre of a floorboard and drive a nail on each side when replacing the board.

185

PLASTIC PLUMBING

The introduction of plastics is probably the most innovative development in plumbing since copper was first used. Plastic plumbing is cheap, lightweight and extremely easy to construct. It does not freeze, corrode or adversely affect other materials, and depending on the type of plastic, it can be used for hot and cold water including central heating pipework. It is already used universally for waste systems and is becoming increasingly popular for supply pipes.

SEE ALSO

◁ Details for:
Solvent joints	188
Push-fit joints	188-189

Being a comparatively recent development, plastic plumbing is not yet standardized. As a result, it is advisable to use one manufacturer's range of equipment and materials to ensure that every component is compatible.

Some plastics are still being tested by water authorities, and may not be officially approved for certain applications. Use manufacturers' catalogues as a guide or seek the advice of your supplier.

Most plastic systems can be connected to existing metal pipe with special adaptors.

Plastic pipe: standard sizes

Plastic pipes are made to more or less standard sizes, but there may be slight variation from one manufacturer's stock to another. As with metal pipework, most metric dimensions refer to the outside diameter of the tube and imperial dimensions to the inside, but not all manufacturers specify their pipes in the same way. Check that pipes and fittings are compatible with existing plumbing before you buy them. The following list is a guide to the available sizes of plastic pipe.

PLASTIC PIPEWORK	
General pipework	15mm (½in); 22mm (¾in); 28mm (1in)
Overflow pipes	21mm (¾in)
Wash basin waste pipes	36mm (1¼in)
Bath/sink waste pipes	43mm (1½in)
Soil pipe	100mm (4in)

PLASTIC JOINTS AND FITTINGS

Most plastic joints and fittings are similar to those used for metal plumbing but in addition, there are easy-flow bends and tees for drainage systems. These joints frequently have cleaning eyes or access plugs for removing blockages in the pipe. Joints and pipes are normally made from the same material, but there are several specialized connectors with metal couplings for joining plastic plumbing to taps, valves and existing metal plumbing.

You will have to browse through different manufacturers' catalogues to see the huge variety of plastic joints for both supply and waste systems, but the selection illustrated below shows the main categories of joint with examples of the different types of coupling.

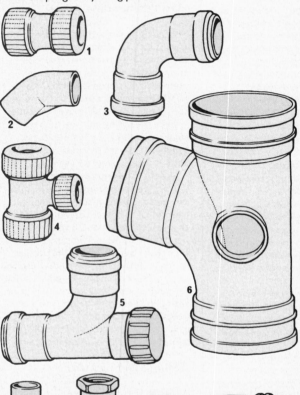

Straight connectors
To join two pipes end to end in a straight line.
1 For pipes of equal diameter – *push-fit*: supply

Bends or elbows
To join two pipes at an angle.
2 45 degree elbow – *solvent weld*: supply
3 Easy-flow bend – *push-fit*: waste

Tees
To join three pipes.
4 Unequal tee to join 15mm (½in) branch pipe to main pipe run – *push-fit*: supply
5 Swept tee with access plug – *push-fit*: waste
6 Branch tee to WC – *solvent weld*: soil pipe

Adaptors
To join dissimilar pipes.
7 Plastic to copper connector – *solvent weld* and *compression joint*: supply
8 Plastic to galvanized steel connector – *push-fit* and *threaded female coupling*: supply

Fittings
Specialized connections are available to join plastic plumbing to fittings. Each manufacturer will supply items like taps and valves to match their particular range.
9 Tap connector with threaded nut for connecting supply pipe to tail of tap – *solvent weld*: supply
10 Tank connector joins pipes to storage cisterns – *push-fit*: supply
11 Stop cock – *push-fit*: supply
12 Sink trap – *compression joint*: waste

JOINING PLASTIC PIPES

Plastics are complex materials, each with its own properties. A technique or material that is suitable for joining one plastic might be quite useless for another. To make sure joints are watertight, it is important to follow each manufacturer's instructions carefully, and to use the solvents and lubricants they recommend. The following examples illustrate the common methods used to connect plastic plumbing.

Solvent weld joints

Lengths of pipe are linked by simple socketed connectors. As they are assembled, a solvent is introduced to the joint which dissolves the surfaces of the mating components. As the solvent evaporates, the joint and pipes are literally fused together into one piece of plastic. Solvent weld joints are used for supply and waste pipes.

Push-fit joints – waste systems

Because a waste system is never under pressure, a pipe run can be constructed by simply pushing plain pipes into the sockets of the joints. A captive rubber seal in each socket holds the pipe in place and makes the joint watertight.

Push-fit joints – supply systems

Polybutylene pipes are connected with a unique push-fit joint. When the pipe is inserted, an 'O' ring seals in the water in the normal way, but a metal grab ring behind the seal has one-way barbed teeth to prevent the pipe being pulled out again. The joints can be dismantled, but only by removing the retaining cap and crushing the grab ring. The joints are more obtrusive than welded types but the speed and simplicity with which you can assemble them more than compensates.

Compression joints

So that they can be dismantled easily, sink, bath and basin traps are often connected to the pipework by compression joints incorporating a rubber ring or washer to make the joint watertight.

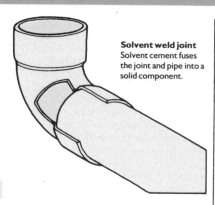

Solvent weld joint
Solvent cement fuses the joint and pipe into a solid component.

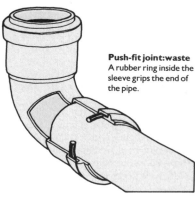

Push-fit joint: waste
A rubber ring inside the sleeve grips the end of the pipe.

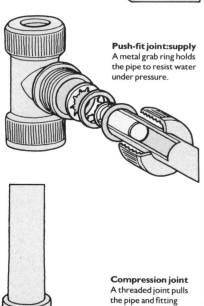

Push-fit joint: supply
A metal grab ring holds the pipe to resist water under pressure.

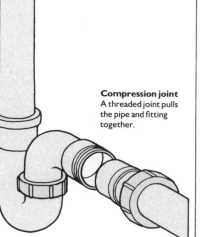

Compression joint
A threaded joint pulls the pipe and fitting together.

TYPES OF PLASTIC

The technology of plastics is such that new or modified materials are being introduced all the time, but the plastics described below are widely available.

Unplasticized polyvinyl chloride

UPVC
A hard, rigid plastic used for waste systems and cold water supply.

Modified polyvinyl chloride

PVC
A similar plastic to UPVC but it is slightly more flexible and therefore shock resistant.

Chlorinated polyvinyl chloride

CPVC
A versatile plastic suitable for hot and cold water supply. It can even withstand the temperatures required for central heating systems.

Polypropylene

PP
A slightly flexible plastic with a somewhat greasy feel. It is used for hot and cold waste systems but expands when heated. It is impossible to glue PP so it's never welded with solvent.

Acrylonitrile butadiene styrene

ABS
A very tough plastic equally suited to hot and cold waste.

Polybutylene

PB
A tough, flexible plastic used for hot and cold water supply – even central heating. Available in standard lengths or continuous coils.

SEE ALSO

Details for: ▷
Solvent joints	188
Push-fit joints	188-189

MAKING JOINTS IN PLASTIC PIPES

You should follow the detailed advice supplied with any specific make of pipe or fitting, but the instructions below and on the facing page demonstrate the basic methods used to connect plastic pipework. Do not inhale solvent fumes, and especially avoid smoking when welding joints. Some solvents give off fumes which become toxic when inhaled through a cigarette. Keep solvents away from children. Work carefully to avoid spilling solvent cement as it will etch the surface of the pipework and certain other plastics as well.

JOINING PUSH-FIT WASTE PIPES

Cut the pipe to length and chamfer the end as for solvent weld joints. Wipe the inside of the socket with the recommended cleaner and lubricate the pipe with a little of the silicone lubricant supplied with it.

Push the pipe into the joint right up to the stop and mark the edge of the socket on the pipe with a pencil **(1)**.

Withdraw the pipe about 10mm (⅜in) **(2)** to allow the pipe to expand when subjected to hot water.

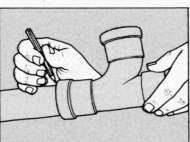

1 Mark the edge of the socket on the pipe

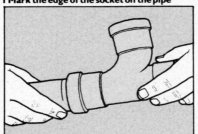

2 Withdraw the pipe about 10mm (⅜in)

Repairing a weeping joint
If a push-fit joint is leaking, the rubber seal has been pushed out of position, probably because the socket is out of line with the pipe. Dismantle the joint and check the condition of the seal.

6 Expansion loop
Build a loop into a long pipe run to allow for expansion using short lengths of tube and elbows.

Making solvent weld joints

Cut the pipe to length with a saw allowing for the depth of the joint socket. When working with large diameter pipes, make sure your cut is square by winding a piece of note paper around the tube, aligning the wrapped edge carefully as a guide for the saw **(1)**.

Revolve the pipe away from you as you cut it. Smooth the cut edge with a file.

Chamfer the pipe with a file to make it easier to push into the socket **(2)**.

Welding the joint
Push the pipe into the socket to test the fit then mark the end of the joint on the pipe with a pencil **(3)**. This will act as a guide for applying the solvent. You must key the outside of the pipe up to this line, and the inside of the socket, with fine abrasive paper before using some solvents. Check the manufacturer's instructions.

When using elbows and tees, scratch the pipe and joint with a knife **(4)** before dismantling to align them correctly when you reassemble the components.

Use a clean rag to wipe the surface of pipe and fitting with the recommended spirit cleaner.

Paint solvent evenly onto both components **(5)** and immediately push home the socket. (Some manufacturers recommend that you twist the joint to spread the solvent.) Align the joint properly and leave it for 15 seconds.

The pipe is ready for use with cold water after one hour. Do not pass hot water through the system until at least four hours has elapsed, preferably longer, according to manufacturer's recommendations.

Allowing for expansion
Plastic pipes expand when subjected to hot water but this is only a problem over a long, straight run.
● If a waste run exceeds 1.8m (6ft), incorporate an expansion coupling with a push-fit rubber seal at one end,.
● For supply pipes over 10m (33ft) in length, form an expansion loop in the run by joining three 150mm (3in) lengths of pipe with elbows **(6)**.

Repairing a weeping joint
If a joint leaks when the system is filled with water, drain it again and allow it to dry out. Apply a little more solvent cement to the mouth of the socket allowing it to flow into the joint by capillary action.

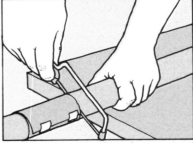

1 Use paper as a guide to keep the cut square

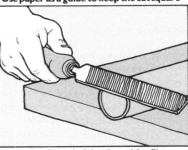

2 Chamfer the end of the pipe with a file

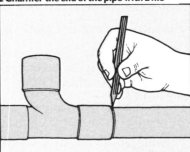

3 Assemble the joint and mark the socket

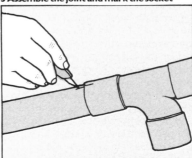

4 Scratch pipe and joint to realign them

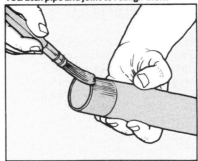

5 Paint solvent up to pencil mark

MAKING JOINTS IN PLASTIC PIPES

Joining push-fit supply pipes

Cut polybutylene pipe to length with special shears supplied by the manufacturer (1), or use a sharp craft knife. As long as the cut is reasonably square, the joint will be watertight.

Push a metal support sleeve into the pipe (2), then use a fingertip to smear a little silicone lubricant around the end of the pipe and inside the socket (3).

Push the prepared pipe firmly into the socket a full 25mm (1in) (4). As the joint can revolve freely around the pipe after connection without breaking the seal, there is no problem when aligning tees and elbows with other pipe runs.

1 Cut pipe to length

2 Insert metal sleeve

3 Apply lubricant

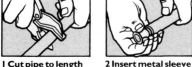
4 Push pipe into joint

Dismantling a joint

If you need to dismantle a joint to alter a system, release the cap with mole grips and unscrew it by hand. Pull out the pipe, slide the rubber ring and washer along the pipe then crush the metal grab ring with pliers (5) to remove it.

Drop a new grab ring into the socket – teeth facing into the fitting – and replace first the washer, then the rubber ring.

Screw back the cap hand-tight then use mole grips to turn it 2mm (1/8in) further. Overtightening will render the joint ineffective.

Connect to the pipe as described above. Never attempt to assemble the fitting like a compression joint or it will blow out under pressure.

Repairing a weeping joint
The only reason why a supply push-fit joint should leak is the failure to push home the pipe fully.

5 Crush the metal grab ring to dismantle joint

Bending plastic pipes

It isn't practical to bend plastic wastepipes especially when you can use easy-flow joints instead.

It is possible to bend a rigid supply pipe by heating it gently. Pass the flame of a gas torch over the area you wish to bend. Keep the flame moving and revolve the pipe all the time. When the pipe is soft enough, bend it by hand on a flat surface (1) and hold it still until the plastic hardens again.

Polybutylene pipe can be bent cold to a minimum radius of eight times the pipe diameter. Use a pipe clip at each side of the bend to hold the curve, or use the manufacturer's special clamp (2). Because the pipe is flexible, long gentle curves can be made by simply threading it around obstacles. Running this type of pipe under floorboards is very easy.

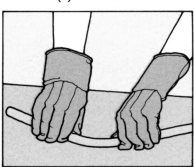
1 Bend the softened pipe on a flat surface

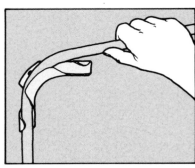
2 Hook flexible pipe into a metal clamp

MAKING COMPRESSION JOINTS TO TRAPS

With some traps, a short threaded pipe is located in the outlet of the trap and secured by a large compression nut. The other end of the pipe is connected to the rest of the waste system with a push-fit or solvent weld joint.

Other traps connect directly to a plain wastepipe. Slip the threaded nut onto the pipe followed by the washer and then the rubber ring.

Push the pipe into the socket of the trap and tighten the compression nut.

CONNECTING PLASTIC TO METAL PLUMBING

To connect most plastic pipes to copper or galvanized steel plumbing, use special adaptor couplings (▷).

To join polybutylene pipe to copper, insert the usual support sleeve then use a standard brass compression joint. Alternatively, you can joint copper to a polybutylene run using the push-fit joint. Cut and deburr the copper pipe carefully and lubricate it before pushing it into the joint.

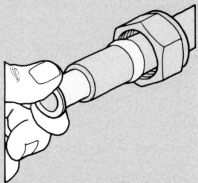
Joining plastic pipe with compression fitting Insert support sleeve before tightening joint.

SUPPORTING PIPE RUNS

Plastic pipework should be supported with clips or saddles similar to those used for metal pipe, but because it is more flexible, you will have to space the clips closer together. Check with manufacturers' literature for exact dimensions.

If you plan to surface-run flexible pipes, consider ducting or boxing-in because it's difficult to make a really neat installation.

SEE ALSO

Details for: ▷
Adaptor couplings	186
Supporting pipes	185
Push-fit joints	187

REPLACING A WC SUITE

Low-level cistern
This type of cistern is
very common. It is
made in plastic or glazed
ceramic.

Compact cistern
A very slim plastic
cistern for use where
space is limited.

Concealed cistern
A cheap plastic cistern
which is hidden behind
panelling.

**Close-coupled
cistern**
This type of cistern is
designed as part of the
WC pan.

When remodelling a bathroom, you may decide to relace an old-style, high-level WC cistern with one of the more compact and less obtrusive low-level versions. In many cases this can be achieved without having to renew the pan at the same time, but if that too is old and unsightly, or if the joint with the soil pipe is leaking, take the opportunity to install a completely new suite. If you connect to the existing branch of the soil pipe, it is a relatively simple operation, but if you plan to move the WC or even install a second convenience elsewhere, you will have to break into the main soil pipe itself or run the waste directly into the underground drainage system. In either case, hire a professional plumber to make the installation.

SEE ALSO

◁ Details for:
WC cisterns   174
Installing a WC suite 192

Choosing the equipment

There was a time when more or less every WC looked identical and worked in the same way, but you have now a choice of compact and colourful appliances which perform their functions more quietly and efficiently than their predecessors.

Types of cistern

Space for a WC
You will need a space in front of the pan of at least 600mm (2ft) square.

Most WCs are fitted with a direct action cistern (◁) but this basic design is available in various models.

High-level cistern
If you simply want to replace an existing high-level cistern without having to modify the plumbing, comparable cisterns are still widely available.

Standard low-level cistern
Most people prefer a cistern mounted on the wall just above the WC pan. A short flush pipe from the base of the cistern connects to the flushing horn on the rear of the pan, while inlet and overflow pipes can be fitted to either side of the cistern. Most low-level cisterns are made from the same vitreous china as the pan.

Compact low-level cistern
Where space is limited, use a plastic cistern which is only 114mm (4½in)

from front to back. This type of cistern is operated by a push-down knob on top.

Concealed cistern
A low-level cistern can be concealed behind panelling. Supply and overflow connections are identical to other cisterns but the flushing lever is mounted on the face of the panel. These plastic cisterns are utilitarian in character with no concession to fashion or style, and are therefore relatively inexpensive. You must provide access for servicing.

Close-coupled cisterns
A close-coupled cistern is bolted directly to the pan forming an integral unit. Both the inlet and overflow connections are made at the base of the cistern. An internal standpipe rises vertically from the overflow connection to protrude above the level of the water in the cistern.

Types of WC pan

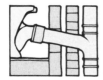

Floor exit trap
Use an 'S' trap when the soil pipe passes through the floor.

Wall exit trap
Use a 'P' trap when the pipe passes through the wall behind the pan.

When you visit a showroom you are confronted with many apparently different WC pans to choose from, but in fact, there are two basic patterns, a washdown or syphonic pan.

Siphonic pans
Siphonic pans need no heavy fall of water to cleanse them and are much quieter as a result. A single trap pan has a narrow outlet immediately after the bend to slow down the flow of water from the pan. The body of water expels air from the outlet to promote the siphonic action. A double trap pan is more sophisticated and exceptionally

quiet. A small vent pipe connects the space between two traps to the inlet running between the cistern and pan. As water flows along the inlet, it sucks air from the trap system through the vent pipe. A vacuum is formed between the traps, and water in the pan is forced by atmospheric pressure into the soil pipe.

Washdown pans
If your existing pan is old enough to need replacing, it will be a standard washdown model. It is the most straightforward and least expensive pan. The contents are washed out by the water falling from the cistern.

CHOOSING A WC PAN

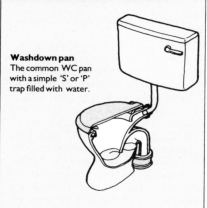

Washdown pan
The common WC pan with a simple 'S' or 'P' trap filled with water.

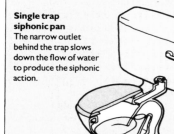

Single trap siphonic pan
The narrow outlet behind the trap slows down the flow of water to produce the siphonic action.

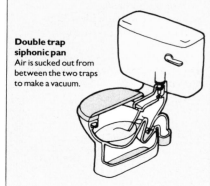

Double trap siphonic pan
Air is sucked out from between the two traps to make a vacuum.

Wall-hung pan
A wall-mounted pan, connected to a concealed cistern, leaves the floor clear for cleaning. Unless it is built into the masonry, the pan is supported by a metal bracket/stand.

REMOVING THE OLD WC

Cut off the water supply (▷) then flush the cistern to empty it. If you are merely renewing a cistern, you will have to disconnect the supply and overflow pipes with a wrench and loosen the large nut connecting the flush pipe to the base of the cistern. These connections are often corroded and painted, so it is easier to hacksaw through the pipes close to the connections if you intend to replace the entire suite.

Having lifted the cistern off its support brackets, try freeing the fixing screws. In all probability, they will be corroded, so lever the brackets off the wall with a crow bar.

Cut the overflow pipe from the wall with a cold chisel. Repair the plaster when you decorate the bathroom.

If the old pan is screwed to a wooden floor, it will probably have a 'P' trap connected to a nearly horizontal branch soil pipe. Remove the floor fixing screws and scrape out the old putty around the pipe joint. Attempt to free the pan by pulling it towards you while rocking it slightly from side to side.

If the joint is fixed firmly, smash the pan outlet just in front of the soil pipe with a club hammer (1). Protect your eyes with goggles. Stuff rags into the soil pipe to prevent debris falling into it, then chip out the remains of the pan outlet with a cold chisel (2). Work carefully to preserve the soil pipe.

Smash an 'S' trap in the same way, and if the pan is cemented to a solid floor, drive a cold chisel under its base to break the seal. Chop out the broken fragments as before and clean up the floor with a cold chisel.

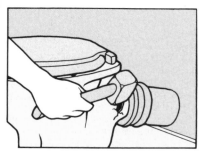

1 Break the outlet of the pan with a hammer

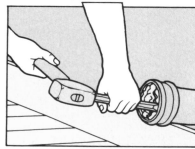

2 Use a cold chisel to cut out the remnants

Cutting the soil pipe

If you break the soil pipe while chipping out the pan outlet, cut the pipe square with a hired chain-link pipe cutter. Clamp the chain of cutters around the pipe and work the shaft back and forth to sever it. Ratchet-action cutters enable you to work in a confined space. When you buy a push-fit pan connector (see below), make sure it is long enough to reach the severed pipe.

Pan to soil pipe connection

Before you install the new suite, choose a push-fit flexible connector to join the pan to the soil pipe. Connectors of different angles are available to suit any situation, even if the two elements are slightly misaligned. You can even choose a colour to match the suite. Make a note of the following dimensions when selecting a connector: the external diameter of pan outlet; the internal diameter of soil pipe; the distance between the outlet and pipe when the pan is installed.

SEE ALSO

Details for: ▷	
Turning off water	170
WC cistern	174

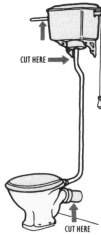

CUT HERE

CUT HERE

Removing an appliance
If fittings are corroded, remove the appliance by cutting the flush pipe, overflow and pan outlet.

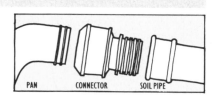

Cutting a soil pipe
Use a chain-link cutter to sever a broken soil pipe.

PAN   CONNECTOR   SOIL PIPE

OFF-SET   CRANKED   BENT

Push-fit flexible pan connectors

SEE ALSO

◁ Details for:

**Fused
connection unit** 152
Flex outlet 153
Float valves 175
**Adjusting
float valve** 176
Tank connector 182, 186
Running pipework 185
Waste boss 196
Overflow unit 198
Connecting pipes 182–189
WC cisterns 190
WC pans 191

INSTALLING A NEW WC SUITE

To install a new WC, begin by pushing the plastic connector onto the pan outlet. Check that the inside of the soil pipe is clean and smooth. Smear a rough surface with a lubricant supplied by the manufacturer then push the pan and connector firmly into the soil pipe.

Don't fix the pan at this stage, but if the floor is made of concrete, you will have to drill holes and plug the fixing holes. Level the pan using a spirit level, adjusting it with scraps of veneer or vinyl floor covering. (Trim them with a knife when the installation is complete.)

Stand a close-coupled cistern on the pan, or connect the flush pipe and hold the cistern against the wall to mark the fixing holes. Fix the cistern to the wall with non-corroding screws and washers making sure it is level, then tighten the flush pipe connection under the cistern.

Screw the pan to the floor, tightening the screws carefully in rotation to avoid cracking the pan.

Run the new 15mm (½in) supply pipe to the float valve (◁), fit a tap connector and tighten it with a wrench.

Use a tank connector (◁) to attach the 21mm (¾in) overflow pipe. Drill a hole through the nearest outside wall where an overflow will be detected prompty. Slope the pipe a few degrees and let it project from the outer face of the wall at least 150mm (6in).

When there is no external wall nearby, you can run the WC overflow pipe to a special combined waste and overflow unit on the bath (◁).

Turn on the supply of water and adjust the float valve (◁).

Small bore waste system

The siting of a WC is normally limited by the need to use a conventional 100mm (4in) soil pipe, and to provide sufficient fall to discharge the waste into the soil stack. By using an electrically driven pump and shredder, you can discharge WC waste through a 22mm (¾in) pipe up to 50m (55yd) away from the stack. The shredder will even pump vertically to a maximum of 4m (4yd). You can run the small-bore pipework through the narrow space between a floor and ceiling (◁). Consequently, a WC can be installed as part of an en-suite bathroom, under the stairs or even in a basement providing the space is adequately ventilated.

The unit, which accepts any conventional 'P' trap WC pan, is activated automatically by flushing the cistern and switches off about 18 seconds later. It must be wired to a fused connection unit, but via a suitable flex outlet if installed in a bathroom (◁). The wastepipe is connected to the soil stack using any standard 36mm (1¼in) waste boss (◁) so long as the manufacturer supplies a 22-36mm (¾-1¼in) adaptor. A WC waste must be connected to the stack at least 200mm (8in) above other waste connections.

Check that the system is approved by your local water authority before installation.

Plumbing a WC
1 Bent plastic tank connector
2 21mm (¾in) overflow
3 Cistern
4 Float valve
5 Tap connector
6 15mm (½in) supply pipe
7 Flush pipe connector
8 Flush pipe
9 Push-fit flexible connector
10 WC pan outlet
11 Flexible outlet connector
12 Soil pipe

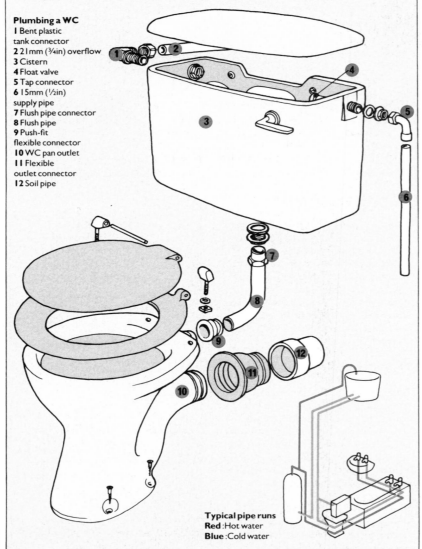

Typical pipe runs
Red : Hot water
Blue : Cold water

Small bore waste system for a WC
The shredding unit fits neatly behind a 'P' trap WC pan. When it is situated in a bathroom, the unit must be wired to a flex outlet as shown above (◁), otherwise it can be connected directly to a fused connection unit (◁).

FITTING A WASH BASIN

Whether you are modifying existing plumbing or running new pipework to a different location, fitting a wash basin in a bathroom or guest room presents few difficulties so long as you give some *thought to how you will run the waste to the vertical stack. The waste must have a minimum fall or slope of 6mm (¼in) for every 300mm (1ft) of pipe run. It should not exceed 3m (10ft) in length.*

Choosing a wash basin

Wall-hung and pedestal basins are made from vitreous china, but basins supported all round by a vanity unit counter-top are also made in pressed steel or plastic. Select the taps at the same time to ensure that the basin of your choice has holes at the required spacing to receive the taps, or no holes at all if the taps are to be wall-mounted.

Make sure the basin has sufficient space on each side or to the rear for soaps, shampoo or other toiletries otherwise you will have to provide a separate shelf or cabinet.

Pedestal basins
Although the hollow pedestal provides some additional support to the basin, its main purpose is to conceal unsightly supply pipes.

Wall-hung basin
Older wall-mounted basins are supported on large, screw-fixed brackets but a modern concealed wall mounting is just as strong and provides a far more attractive fixture.

Check that you can fix securely to the studs of a timber-frame wall or hack off the plaster and install a mounting board. (Use the same method to secure an existing basin with loose wall fixings.)

If you want to hide supply pipes, consider some form of panelling.

Corner basin
Hand basins which fit into the corner of a room are popular because supply and wastepipes can be run conveniently through adjacent walls or concealed by boxing them in across the corner.

Recessed basin
A small hand basin can be recessed into a wall of a cloakroom or WC where space is limited.

Counter-top basins
In a large bathroom or bedroom, you can fit a wash basin into a counter-top as part of a built-in vanity unit. The cupboards below provide ample storage for towels and toiletries while hiding the plumbing at the same time.

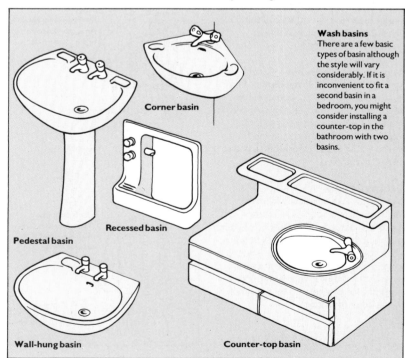

Wash basins
There are a few basic types of basin although the style will vary considerably. If it is inconvenient to fit a second basin in a bedroom, you might consider installing a counter-top in the bathroom with two basins.

Corner basin

Recessed basin

Pedestal basin

Wall-hung basin

Counter-top basin

CONCEALING PIPEWORK

The manufacturers of appliances and fittings are aware that most people find visible plumbing unattractive, and as a result, supply fitments such as sink units, panelled baths, shower cubicles, concealed cisterns, pedestal and counter-top basins, all of which are designed to hide their supply pipes and drainage. With careful selection and intelligently designed pipe runs, it should be possible to plumb your house without a single visible pipe. In practice, however, there are always situations where you have no option but to surface-run at least some pipes, especially when you cannot take them under floorboards. You can minimize the effect by taking special care to group pipes together neatly, and keep runs both straight and parallel. When painted to match the skirtings or walls, such pipes are practically invisible.

Alternatively, you can construct ducting to conceal pipes completely. Make your own ducting with softwood battens and plywood to bridge the corner of a room, or construct a false skirting deep enough to contain the pipes. It is a wise precaution to make at least part of the ducting removable to gain access to joints or other fittings in case you need to service them at a later date. For total accessibility, use proprietary ducting made from PVC. It is manufactured in a range of sizes to contain grouped or individual pipes. With right-angle and tee-piece joints, you can construct a system of ducting to cover any new or existing installation. Optional foam liners insulate hot water or central heating pipes.

Clip pipes into plastic ducting

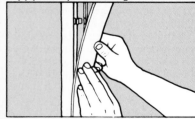

Snap on the matching cover-strips.

SEE ALSO

Details for: ▷
Running pipework   185

Space for a basin
Allow extra elbow room for washing hair. A space 1100mm (3ft 8in) x 700mm (2ft 4in) should be sufficient. To suit most people, position the rim of a basin 800mm (2ft 8in) from the floor.

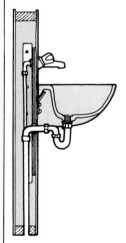

Mounting a basin
Fix a wall-mounted hand basin and taps to an exterior-grade plywood board.

SELECTING TAPS FOR A BASIN

Most taps are made of chromium plated or enamelled brass although there is a limited range of plastic-bodied taps. Plastic taps are not as durable as metal ones but they are considerably cheaper. All basin taps have a 15mm (½in) threaded inlet known as the tail for attaching the supply pipe.

SEE ALSO

◁ Details for:
Repairing taps   172-173

Types of tap

Individual taps
The majority of wash basins are fitted with individual taps for the hot and cold water supply. Cross or capstan head taps are still manufactured for traditionally-styled bathrooms but most taps have a metal or plastic shrouded head. A lever head tap turns the tap from off to full on with one quarter turn only. They are especially convenient for the elderly or disabled.

Individual wall-mounted taps are known as bib taps while those fixed directly to the basin itself are called pillar taps.

Mixer taps
A mixer tap has a hot and cold valve linked to a common spout. Water is provided at the required temperature by adjusting the two valves simultaneously.

Basin mixer taps often incorporate a pop-up waste. A series of inter-linking rods, operated by a button on the centre of the mixer, open and close the waste plug in the basin.

Normally, the body of the tap which connects the valves and spout, rests on the upper surface of the basin. The tails only protrude through holes in the basin to meet the supply pipes. This is a two-hole mixer with tails spaced 100mm (4in) apart.

A three-hole mixer appears to have separate valves and spout but they are linked by a tube below the basin. The tube is cut to length to accommodate the distance between the holes in the basin which may be from 200 to 250mm (8 to 10in) apart.

Both inlets of a one-hole mixer pass through the same hole.

An entire mixer set can be mounted on a wall above the basin. Alternatively, the valves can be mounted on the basin yet still divert hot and cold water to a wall-mounted spout.

Shrouded-head tap

Lever-head tap

Two-hole mixer

Three-hole mixer

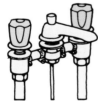

One-hole mixer

TAP MECHANISMS

Over recent years there have been revolutionary changes in tap design, and not just in their appearance or styling. Entirely new thinking about the function of a tap has provided the consumer with taps that are easier to operate, more hard-wearing and simpler to maintain.

Rising-spindle taps
Within a traditionally designed tap, the entire spindle, jumper and washer move up and down, turning along with the head when you operate the tap.

Non-rising head taps
Outwardly, these taps resemble a rising-spindle tap but when the head turns, it does not move up and down. Instead, it causes a threaded spindle and washer unit to rise vertically without turning. Because the washer is not twisted against the seat as the valve is closed, neither the washer nor seat wear as quickly as those in a conventional tap.

Ceramic disc taps
Precision ground ceramic discs replace the traditional washer, but instead of separating, one disc rotates on the other so that waterways through them gradually align with each other allowing water to flow. There is virtually no wear as hard water scale or other debris cannot interfere with the fit of the discs. If a problem develops, the whole mechanism is replaced.

Reverse-pressure taps
An original concept in tap design. The head and spout hang from the water inlet and move as one unit forcing the washer upwards against the seat. A unique check valve inside the tap shuts off the water as the tap is dismantled to change a washer.

Electronic taps
Water flows automatically from an electronic tap as soon as an integral photo-cell detects the presence of your hands under the spout. It stops flowing when you remove your hands. The tap is powered by a transformer mounted beneath the basin or vanity unit. Water temperature is regulated by a control on the body of the tap.

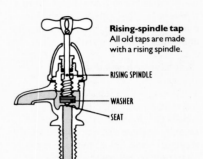

Rising-spindle tap
All old taps are made with a rising spindle.

RISING SPINDLE

WASHER

SEAT

Non-rising head tap
A spindle which does not revolve reduces wear on the washer.

SPINDLE

WASHER

SEAT

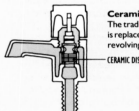

Ceramic disc tap
The traditional washer is replaced with revolving ceramic discs.

CERAMIC DISCS

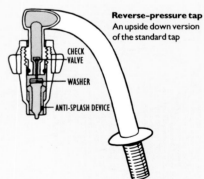

Reverse-pressure tap
An upside down version of the standard tap

CHECK VALVE

WASHER

ANTI-SPLASH DEVICE

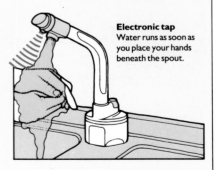

Electronic tap
Water runs as soon as you place your hands beneath the spout.

REPLACING OLD TAPS

When replacing taps, you will want to use the existing plumbing if possible but it can be difficult to disconnect old corroded fittings. Apply penetrating oil to the tap connectors and to the back-nuts clamping the tap to the basin. While the oil takes effect, shut off the cold and hot water supply.

Applying heat with a gas torch can break down corrosion by expanding metal fittings, but wrap a wet cloth around nearby soldered joints or you may melt the solder. Take care that you do not damage a plastic waste and trap, and protect flammable surfaces with a ceramic tile. Too much heat may crack a ceramic basin.

It is not always possible to engage the nuts with a standard wrench. Instead, hire a special cranked spanner designed to reach into the confined spaces below a basin or bath. You can apply extra leverage to the spanner by slipping a stout metal bar or wrench handle into the other end.

Having disconnected the pipework, tap the bottom of the tap tails with a wooden mallet to break the seal of plumbers' putty under the taps. Clean the remnants of putty from around the taps holes and fit new taps. If the tap tails are shorter than the originals, or the threads do not match the tap connectors, check a manufacturer's catalogue for various adaptors.

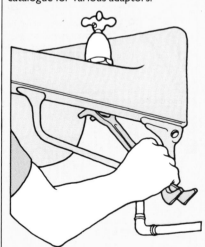

Releasing a tap connector
Use a special cranked spanner to release the fixing nut of a tap connector.

A cranked spanner fits basin and bath taps

FIXING A WALL-HUNG BASIN

Turn off the supply of water to an old basin before you disconnect it (▷). However, you can save some time by *fitting the new taps to its replacement beforehand so that you are not without water in the meantime.*

Removing the old basin

If you want to use existing plumbing, loosen the compression nuts on the tap tails (see left) and trap, otherwise cut through the waste and supply pipes at a point where you can most easily connect new plumbing (1).

Remove any fixings holding the basin to its support brackets or pedestal and lift it from the wall. Apply penetrating oil to the bracket wall fixings in an attempt to remove them without damaging the plaster, but as a last resort, lever the brackets off the wall. Take care not to break cast iron fittings as they can be quite valuable.

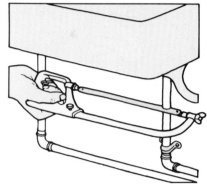

1 Cut through old supply pipes with a hacksaw

Fitting new taps

Fit new taps to the basin before fixing it to the wall. Slip a plastic washer supplied with the tap onto its tail, then pass the tail through the hole in the basin. If no washer is supplied, spread some plumbers' putty around the top of the tail and beneath the base of the tap.

With the basin resting on its rim, slip a second washer onto the tail then hand tighten the back-nut to clamp the tap onto the basin (2). Check that the spout faces into the basin then tighten the back-nut carefully with a cranked spanner (See left).

Wipe excess putty from the basin then fit the second tap.

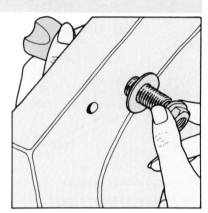

2 Slip the back-nut onto the tail of the tap

Fixing the basin to the wall

Have an assistant hold the basin against the wall at the required height and check it is horizontal with a spirit level, then mark the fixing holes for the wall bracket (3). Lay the basin to one side while you drill and plug the fixing holes.

Screw the bracket securely to the wall and bolt the basin to it with whatever fixings are supplied by the manufacturer. Connect the plumbing to the taps and fit the waste system (▷).

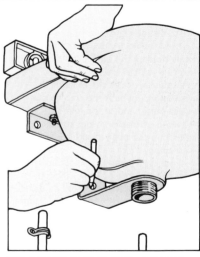

3 Mark the bracket fixing holes on the wall

SEE ALSO

Details for: ▷
Turning off water   170
Connecting pipes 182-189

CONNECTING A WALL-HUNG BASIN

Once you have fitted new taps and mounted the basin on the wall (◁), finish the installation by connecting the waste system along with the hot and cold supply pipes.

SEE ALSO

◁ Details for:	
Draining system	170
Connecting pipes	182-189
Fitting taps	195
Mounting a basin	195
Waste units	198
Cranked spanner	195
Soil pipes	169
Pipe clips	185

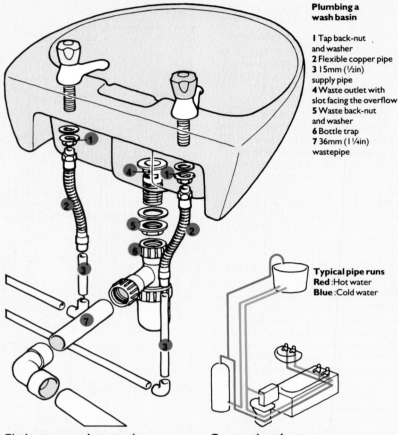

Plumbing a wash basin

1 Tap back-nut and washer
2 Flexible copper pipe
3 15mm (½in) supply pipe
4 Waste outlet with slot facing the overflow
5 Waste back-nut and washer
6 Bottle trap
7 36mm (1¼in) wastepipe

Typical pipe runs
Red :Hot water
Blue :Cold water

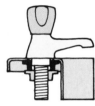

A pressed-metal basin
When you fit taps to a pressed-metal basin, slip built-up 'top hat' washers onto the tails to cover the shanks. The basin itself may be supplied with a rubber strip to seal the joint with the counter-top. It will need a combined waste and overflow like a bath (◁).

● **Counter-top basin** Manufacturers supply a template for cutting the hole in a counter-top to receive the basin. Run mastic around the edge to seal a ceramic basin, and clamp it with the fixings supplied.

Fitting trap and wastepipe
Fit the waste outlet into the bottom of the basin as for taps using washers or plumbers' putty to form a watertight seal. The basin will probably have an integral overflow running to the waste, in which case ensure that the slot in the waste outlet aligns with the overflow. Tighten the back-nut under the basin while holding the outlet still by gripping its grille with pliers.

If you can utilize the existing wastepipe, connect the trap to the waste outlet and to the end of the pipe. A two-part trap provides some adjustment to align it with the old wastepipe.

If necessary, run a new 36mm (1¼in) wastepipe, cutting a hole through the wall with a masonry drill and cold chisel. Run the pipe, with sufficient fall – 6mm (¼in) per 300mm (1ft) run – to terminate over the hopper on top of the vertical wastepipe. Fix the pipe to the wall with saddle clips.

Connecting the taps
You can run standard 15mm (½in) copper or plastic pipes to the taps and join them with tap connectors, but it is easier to use short lengths of flexible, corrugated copper pipe specially designed for tap connection. They can be bent by hand to allow for any slight misalignment between the supply pipes and tap tails. Each corrugated pipe has a tap connector at one end, and at the other, a compression or capillary joint.

Connect the corrugated pipes to the tap tails but leave them hand tight only, then run new branch pipework to meet them. Make soldered or compression joints to connect the pipes (◁). Tighten the tap connectors with a cranked spanner (◁).

Turn on the water supply and check the pipes for leaks. Drain the system to repair a weeping joint (◁).

Connecting waste to soil pipe

Connect a basin wastepipe to a single stack, plastic soil pipe with a proprietary pipe boss. A boss may be connected by other methods, but is often clamped to the soil pipe with a strap.

Mark where the basin waste meets the soil pipe and cut a hole of the recommended diameter with a hole saw (**1**) . Smooth the edge of the hole with abrasive paper.

Wipe both contacting surfaces with the manufacturer's cleaner, then apply gap-filling solvent cement around the hole. Strap the boss over the hole and tighten the bolt (**2**) .

Insert the rubber lining in the boss in preparation for the wastepipe (**3**) .

Lubricate the end of the pipe and push it firmly into the boss (**4**) . Clip the pipe to the wall.

1 Cut a hole in the pipe with a hole saw

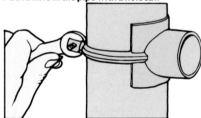

2 Strap the boss over the hole

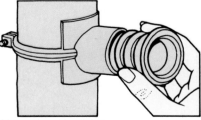

3 Insert the rubber lining

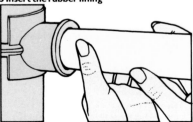

4 Push the wastepipe into the boss

INSTALLING A NEW BATH

There are companies who will re-enamel your old bath – some will even spray it in-situ. If you own an attractive, antique cast iron bath it would be worth asking for quotations before you make up your mind to discard it. Even if you don't want the bath yourself, you may *be able to sell it to a company who specializes in bath restoration. On the other hand, most old baths are simply too ugly to restore, and it may prove to be more economical to replace one that is badly chipped or stained. If a bath is cracked, it is beyond repair.*

Choosing a bath

You can buy reproduction or even restored Victorian baths in cast iron from specialist suppliers but they are likely to be expensive. In practical terms, a cast iron bath is far too heavy for one person to handle: even two people would have difficulty carrying one to an upstairs bathroom. A cast iron bath can look splendid when left freestanding in a room, but it can be virtually impossible to clean behind one, and panelling-in the curved and sometimes tapering shape is rarely successful.

Nowadays, the majority of baths are made from enamelled pressed steel, acrylic or glass-reinforced plastic. Two people can handle a steel bath with ease and you could carry a plastic bath on your own. Although modern plastic baths are strong and durable, some are harmed by abrasive cleaners, bleach and especially heat. It is not advisable to use a gas torch near a plastic bath.

When it comes to style and colour, there is no lack of choice in any material, although the more unconventional baths are likely to be made of plastic. Nearly every bath comes with matching panels and optional features like hand grips and dropped sides to make it easier to step in and out. Taps do not have to be mounted at the foot of the bath. Many manufacturers offer alternative corner or side mounting facilities. Some will even cut tap holes to order.

You can order a bath in any style to double as a jacuzzi, but the plumbing is somewhat complicated so you will need to have it professionally installed.

Rectangular bath

A standard, rectangular bath is still the most popular and economical design. Baths vary in size from 1.5 to 1.8m (5 to 6ft) in length, with a choice of widths from 700 to 800mm (2ft 4in to 2ft 8in)

Corner bath

A corner bath occupies more actual floor area than a rectangular bath of the same capacity, but because the tub itself is turned at an angle to the room, it may take up less wall-space. A corner bath always provides generous shelf space for essential toiletries.

Round bath

A round bath would prove to be impractical in most bathrooms, but if you are converting a spare bedroom, you may decide to make the bath a feature of interior design as well as a practical appliance.

Selecting taps for a bath

The basic design and style of bath taps are identical to basin taps (▷), but they are proportionally larger with 22mm (¾in) tails. Individual hot and cold taps or mixers are made to fit a bath with hole centres 180mm (7⅛in) apart.

Some bath mixers are designed to supply water to a shower head, either mounted telephone-style on the mixer itself, or hung from a bracket mounted on a wall above the bath (▷).

SUPPORTING A PLASTIC BATH

A metal frame is supplied to cradle a flexible plastic bath. Without it, the bath would distort and possibly crack.

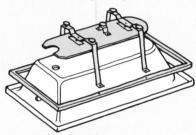

Assembling the cradle
Turn a bath on its rim to fit the cradle.

TYPES OF BATH

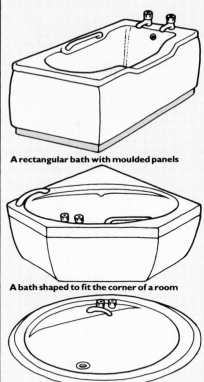

A rectangular bath with moulded panels

A bath shaped to fit the corner of a room

A circular bath fits flush with the floor

RENOVATING BATH ENAMEL

You can buy two-part paints prepared specifically to restore the enamel surface of an old bath, sink or basin. To achieve a first-class result, the bath must be scrupulously clean and dry, so tape plastic bags over the taps to prevent water dripping into the bath and work in a warm atmosphere where condensation will not occur. Wipe the surface with a cloth dampened with white spirit to remove traces of grease, then paint the bath from the bottom upwards in a circular direction. This type of paint is self-levelling so don't brush it out too much. Pick up runs or tears immediately and work fairly quickly to keep the wet edge fresh.

For a professional finish, hire a company which will send an operator to spray a stained bath in-situ. The whole process should take no longer than two to three hours. The bath is cleaned chemically before a grinder is used to key the surface and remove heavy stains. Chipped enamel can be repaired at the same time. Finally, surrounding areas are masked before the bath is sprayed.

SEE ALSO

Details for: ▷	
Selecting taps	194
Shower mixer	200
Plumbing a bath	198
Panelling a bath	199

Access to the bath
Allow a space of 1100 × 700mm (3ft 8in × 2ft 4in) beside the bath to climb in and out safely, and for bathing younger members of the family.

PLUMBING THE BATH

Once a bath is fitted close to the walls of a bathroom, it can be difficult to make the joints and connections, so fit the taps, overflow and trap before you push the new bath into position and prior to removing the existing bath.

Fit adjustable feet to the new bath or suspend a plastic bath in its supporting cradle according to the manufacturer's instructions.

SEE ALSO

◁ Details for:
Draining system	170
Connecting pipes	182–189
Fitting taps	195
Top-hat washers	196
Stack connection	196

Waste/overflow units
A flexible tube takes overflow water to the trap.

Compression unit
Runs to cleaning eye on the trap.

Banjo unit
Slips over tail of waste outlet.

WC and bath overflow
Overflow from a WC joins the bath unit.

Shallow-seal trap
Use this type of trap when space is limited but it must discharge to a yard gully.

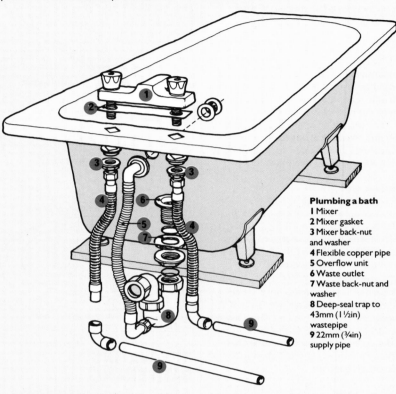

Plumbing a bath
1 Mixer
2 Mixer gasket
3 Mixer back-nut and washer
4 Flexible copper pipe
5 Overflow unit
6 Waste outlet
7 Waste back-nut and washer
8 Deep-seal trap to 43mm (1½in) wastepipe
9 22mm (¾in) supply pipe

Fitting the taps

Fit individual hot and cold taps as for a wash basin (◁). Fitting a mixer is a similar procedure, but most units are supplied with a long sealing gasket which slips over both tails. Drop the tails through the holes in the rim, slip top-hat washers onto them (◁) and tighten both back-nuts to clamp the mixer to the bath.

Fit a flexible 22mm (¾in) copper pipe (similar to those used for washbasin taps) onto each tail. As an alternative, you can attach short lengths of standard 22mm (¾in) copper or plastic pipe with tap connectors in preparation for jointing to the pipe run, but the flexible pipes allow for adjustment in case joints are slightly misaligned.

Fitting waste and overflow

Fit a combined waste and overflow unit. A flexible plastic hose takes water from the overflow outlet in the end of the bath to the waste outlet or trap. If you use a 'banjo' unit, you must fit the overflow before the trap, but the flexible pipe of a compression fitting unit connects to the trap itself. (See left.)

Spread a layer of plumbers' putty under the rim of the waste outlet, or fit a circular rubber seal. Before inserting its tail into the hole in the bottom of the bath, seal the thread with PTFE tape. On the underside, add a plastic washer then tighten the large back-nut, bedding the outlet down onto the putty or rubber seal. Wipe off excess putty before it sets.

Connect the bath trap (see left) to the tail of the waste outlet with its own compression nut. (Fit a banjo overflow unit at the same time.)

Pass the threaded boss of the overflow hose through the hole in the end of the bath. Slip a washer seal over the boss, then use a pair of pliers to screw on the overflow outlet grille. If you are using a compression fitting overflow, connect the nut on the other end of the hose to the cleaning eye of the trap.

Removing the old bath

Turn off the hot and cold water supply, then drain the system (◁).

Have a shallow bowl ready to catch any trapped water, then use a junior hacksaw to cut through the old supply and wastepipes. As the overflow from an old bath will almost certainly exit through the wall, saw through it at the same time.

If adjustable feet are fitted to the bath, lower them, pushing down on the bath to break the mastic seal between the rim and bathroom walls. Pull the bath away from the wall.

If you don't want to preserve a cast iron bath, it will be easier to break it up in the bathroom and carry it out in pieces. Wear protective goggles and ear protectors, drape a dust sheet over the bath then smash it with a heavy hammer.

Hack the old overflow from the wall with a cold chisel, fill the hole with mortar, and repair the plasterwork.

Installing the new bath

Run new 22mm (¾in) supply pipes, or attach spurs to the existing ones, ready for connection to the flexible pipes already fitted on the bath taps.

Cut two boards to support the feet of the bath and spread the point load over a wider area. Slide the bath into position and adjust the height of the feet with a spanner. Use a spirit level to check that the rim is horizontal.

Adjust the flexible tap pipes and join them to the supply pipes (◁).

Connect a 43mm (1½in) wastepipe to the trap and run it to the external hopper or soil stack as for a wash basin (◁). Restore the water supply and check for leaks before you fix the bath panels.

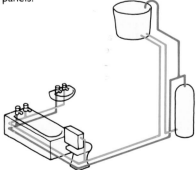

Typical bathroom pipe runs
Red: Hot water – **Blue**: Cold water.

Panelling a bath

In all probability, your bath will be supplied with moulded polystyrene panels to hide the plumbing and facilitate cleaning.

You can panel a basic rectangular bath with a softwood framework supporting a sheet of hardboard or plywood. The finish is a matter of personal choice. You can paint a standard plain hardboard or apply a wall covering to match or contrast with the bathroom decor. Alternatively, use a melamine-faced board – a practical, easy-to-clean surface – or add a texture with an embossed hardboard. You could continue the floorcovering up the panel using an adhesive to attach carpet, vinyl or cork tiles. If you want to use ceramic tiles, provide a small removable panel at the end of the bath so that you can service the plumbing. Design the panel to break between two rows of tiles.

When a bath does not fit against a wall at both ends, either continue the panelling around the exposed end, or make a fixed shelf of tiled marine plywood to fit behind the head or taps, and run the panelling from wall to wall.

Make the framework of 50mm x 25mm (2in x 1in) sawn softwood. Simple butt joints held together with timber connectors will suffice as the fixed sheet will make the frame rigid.

Scribe the sheet to fit under the rim of the bath and to fit the wall at each end, then pin and glue it to the framework. If pinning would spoil the surface, use planed timber for the frame and attach the sheet with adhesive.

Screw a vertical batten to the wall at each end of the bath to support the panelled frame and nail one or two softwood blocks to the floor for the frame to rest against. Screw the finished panel to the battens with brass screws and screw caps. Alternatively, use magnetic catches and fit small knobs or handles to the panel.

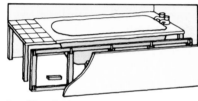

Panelling a bath
This example shows wall-to-wall panelling with a tiled shelf to fill the gap, but you can use a similar construction to fit any situation.

Soaking in a bath tub is very relaxing but taking a shower is more invigorating and hygienic while using far less hot water. A shower cubicle occupies a 750mm (2ft 6in) square of floor space so it is quite possible to locate one somewhere other than the bathroom. The corner of a bedroom is an obvious choice but you may prefer to convert a downstairs cloakroom or install a shower in a utility room along with the washing machine and tumble dryer. A separate shower can be a boon to a busy family who would otherwise queue for a single bathroom before leaving for work or school.

IMPORTANT CONSIDERATIONS

A shower must comply with certain requirements to satisfy the water authority and provide you with a facility which is both safe and comfortable.

Equal water pressure

The hot and cold water supply to a shower must be under equal pressure. You must never mix hot water from a cylinder with mains pressure cold water. The cold water must be supplied from the storage cistern. It is against water authority regulations to mix mains and stored water and, in any case, it would be difficult to maintain a comfortable temperature at the shower.

Sufficient pressure

Unless the water pressure is high enough, the performance of your shower will never be satisfactory. Apart from a mains pressure instantaneous shower, water pressure is determined by the height of the cold water storage cistern. The bottom of the cistern should be 1.5m (5ft) or more above the shower head. A shower can work satisfactorily when the shower head is only 900mm (3ft) below the cistern but only if the pipe run is short and straight.

Hot water pressure is unaffected by the position of the cylinder as it is supplied initially from the same cold water cistern and therefore its pressure is equal to the cold water supply.

When the pressure is insufficient, you can either raise the cistern on a strong wooden frame which means lengthening all the existing pipes, or you can fit a pump to boost the shower pressure.

Independent supply

If your shower is fed by branch pipes connected to the rest of the bathroom plumbing, there is a risk that water pressure will drop if someone draws water at another appliance. If it is the pressure on the hot supply that drops, then your shower will suddenly run cold which is merely unpleasant, but if pressure drops on the cold supply, the shower could become dangerously hot.

Ideally, the cold supply should be a 15mm (1/2in) pipe run independently from the storage cistern, and the hot supply should be a 15mm (1/2in) branch pipe taken directly from the vent pipe above the cylinder. Independent pipe runs are not essential if you install a thermostatic shower which can cope with slight variations in pressure.

Drainage

Because a shower tray stands on the floor, it can be difficult to obtain the minimum fall of 6mm (1/4in) per 300mm (1ft) run of wastepipe. You may be able to run the waste under floorboards, but only if the joists run in the same direction as the pipe. Sometimes it is necessary to raise the tray on a plinth.

SEE ALSO

Details for: ▷	
Shower units	200
Booster pumps	200

SHOWER UNITS

Installing an independent shower cubicle with its own supply and waste system requires some previous experience of plumbing but if you utilize an existing bath as a shower tray, fitting a shower unit can involve little more than replacing the taps.

SEE ALSO

◁ Details for:
Fused	
connection unit	152
Wiring a shower	159
Fitting a mixer	198
Shower requirements	199
Plumbing showers	202

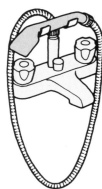

Bath/shower mixer
Fit this type of shower unit like an ordinary bath mixer.

Thermostatic mixer
This unit has separate controls for flow and temperature.

Bath/shower mixer

This type of shower is the simplest to install. It is connected like a standard bath mixer to the existing 22mm (¾in) cold and hot water pipes, while the bath waste system takes care of the drainage. Having obtained the required temperature at the spout by adjusting the hot and cold valves, lifting a button on the mixer diverts the water, via a flexible hose, to the shower head. The shower head can be hand-held for washing hair, or hung from a wall-mounted bracket to provide a conventional shower.

You must not fit a bath/shower mixer when cold water is supplied under mains pressure to the bath tap. As the supply pipes are already part of the bathroom plumbing network, it is impossible to guard against fluctuating pressure unless the mixer is fitted with a thermostatic valve. If the pressure is insufficient, fit a booster pump.

Thermostatic shower mixer

A thermostatic mixer is similar in design to a manual version but another control is incorporated to pre-set the water temperature. If the pressure drops on either the hot or cold supply, the thermostatic valve compensates by lowering the pressure on the other side. Consequently, you can supply a thermostatic shower with branch pipes from the bathroom plumbing but try to join them as near as possible to the cold cistern and hot cylinder.

The mixer cannot raise the pressure of the supply: you still need a booster pump if it is low. Neither will it compensate for the considerable difference in pressure between mains and gravity fed water.

Manual shower mixer (near right)
A unit with a single control to regulate the rate of flow and the temperature of the water.

Booster pump (far right)
The simplest type of pump is mounted to the shower wall between the mixer and shower head.

Manual shower mixer

A manual shower mixer can be mounted on the wall above a bathtub, but with its own supply of hot and cold water, or it can be situated in a separate shower cubicle. Simple mixers have individual hot and cold valves, but most manual shower mixers have a single control which regulates flow and water temperature. A manual mixer must have independent hot and cold supply.

Booster pump

If your existing shower installation is unsatisfactory due to low pressure, you can improve its performance by adding an electric booster pump. Some pumps are designed for remote installation, usually in an airing cupboard next to the hot water cylinder. Hot and cold pipes are fed to the pump, then out again to the shower mixer.

So long as you don't object to it being visible, it is simpler to mount a pump in the shower cubicle or over the bath. No extra plumbing is required as the pump is connected to the shower mixer by a flexible metal hose. A two core and earth electrical cable runs from the pump to a switched, fused connection unit (◁) which must be clearly identified and accessible, but out of reach of anyone using the shower or bath.

If you want to install a new shower where water pressure is low, buy a shower unit with an integral pump.

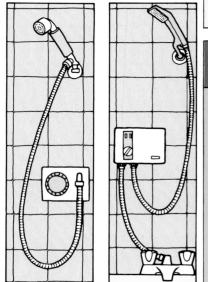

Manual shower mixer   **Booster pump**

INSTANTANEOUS SHOWER

An instantaneous shower solves many problems associated with other types of shower. It is designed specifically for connection to the mains water supply with one 15mm (½in) branch pipe from the rising main. Because the rising main passes through every floor of the house, you can install an instantaneous shower practically anywhere so long as drainage is feasible. Incoming water is heated within the unit so there is no separate hot water supply to balance. The shower is thermostatically controlled to prevent fluctuations in pressure affecting the water temperature – in fact it switches off completely if there is a serious failure of pressure.

Most instantaneous showers are electrically powered and require their own circuit from the consumer unit. A ceiling-mounted, 45 amp, double-pole switch must be connected to the circuit to turn the appliance on and off. Gas-heated showers are available but they should be installed by a qualified fitter.

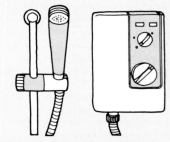

An instantaneous shower control unit
A detachable shower head is connected to the control unit by a flexible hose.

ELECTRICAL INSTALLATIONS

Electrical installations in a bathroom are dangerous unless they conform to the current Institute of Electrical Engineers wiring regulations. Read the electrical section in this book and manufacturers' instructions carefully to make sure you understand thoroughly the requirements for wiring in a bathroom before undertaking the work. If you are in any doubt, or have had no previous experience, hire a qualified electrician.

Without doubt, the simplest way to acquire a shower cubicle is to install a factory-assembled cabinet, complete with tray and shower mixer, together with waterproof doors or a curtain to contain the spray from the shower head. Having run supply pipes and drainage, the installation is complete. However, the cabinets are expensive. The alternative is to construct a purpose-made shower cubicle to fit exactly the space you have allocated.

SHOWER TRAYS

Shower trays are made from enamelled cast iron or steel, ceramics or glass-reinforced plastic. Metal or ceramic trays are substantial but heavy, and may require two people to move them into position. Plastic trays are lightweight and cheap but they have a tendency to flex slightly in use so it is particularly important to seal the edges carefully with a flexible mastic instead of relying on grout. Whatever material you choose, you should have no problem finding a colour to match other bathroom appliances.

Trays are between 750mm (2ft 6in) and 900mm (3ft) square. Most are designed to stand on the floor with a surrounding apron about 150mm (6in) in height. Some have adjustable feet to level the tray, or even a metal underframe to raise it off the floor to provide a fall for the waste-pipe. A plinth screwed across the front of the tray hides the underframe and plumbing while providing access to the trap for servicing. Some trays are intended to be flush with the floor.

A round waste outlet fits in the bottom of the tray much like a bath but it is not slotted to accommodate an overflow. Fit a space-saving, shallow-seal trap to the outlet.

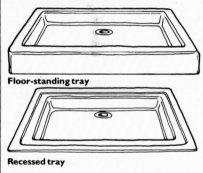

Floor-standing tray

Recessed tray

Choosing the site

When you are deciding upon the location of your shower, consider how you are going to build the walls of the cubicle. Some sites will involve more work than others.

Free-standing
You can place the shower tray against a flat wall and either construct a stud partition (▷) on each side, or surround the tray with a proprietary shower enclosure.

Corner site
If you place the tray in a corner of a room, two sides of the cubicle are ready-made. Either run a curtain around the tray or install a corner-entry enclosure with sliding doors. Alternatively, build a fixed side wall yourself and place a door or curtain across the entrance.

Built-in cupboards
Blend a shower cubicle into a bedroom by placing it into a corner as described above, then construct a built-in wardrobe unit between the shower and the opposite wall.

Concealing the plumbing

A shower with exposed pipework will work perfectly well but it spoils the appearance of the cubicle. You could install a proprietary rigid plastic pillar in the corner of the cubicle to cover the pipework and house the mixer and shower head.

If you erect a stud partition on one side, you can run the plumbing between the studs. Screw and glue exterior-grade plywood on the inside of the frame as a mounting board for the shower mixer and spray head. Connect the plumbing to the mixer before you panel the outside of the framework.

Cover the plywood panel with ceramic tiles or, alternatively, use a melamine-faced board, attaching it to the framework with metal angle-brackets. Prime the edges of the board and apply a mastic seal where it meets the wall and tray.

Running plumbing through a partition ▷
Conceal pipework in a simple timber partition covered with plywood and ceramic tiles.

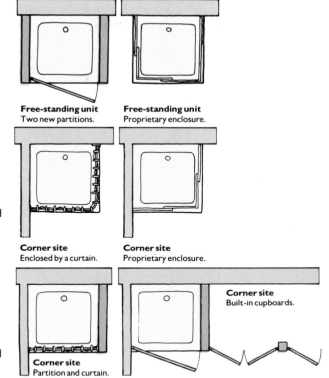

Free-standing unit
Two new partitions.

Free-standing unit
Proprietary enclosure.

Corner site
Enclosed by a curtain.

Corner site
Proprietary enclosure.

Corner site
Partition and curtain.

Corner site
Built-in cupboards.

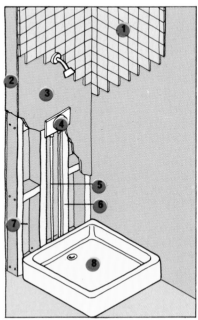

Proprietary unit to conceal plumbing
The plastic corner pillar, shower set, tray and curtain are designed as a complete system.

1 Ceramic tiles
2 Timber cover strip
3 Exterior-grade plywood
4 Shower mixer
5 Pipework
6 Timber frame
7 Plasterboard
8 Shower tray

SEE ALSO

◁ Details for:
Tiling	69-74
Wiring a shower	159
Connecting pipes	182-189
Leaking joints	183,184
Leaking joints	188,189
Strap boss	196
Waste outlet	198
Shallow-seal trap	198
Building partition	201
Turning off water	170

PROCEDURE FOR INSTALLING A SHOWER

Use the procedure below as a guide to the stage by stage installation of a shower and cubicle. Follow the instructions on fitting plastic or copper supply pipes and drainage (◁), and take note of the manufacturer's recommendations for the particular shower unit you are installing.

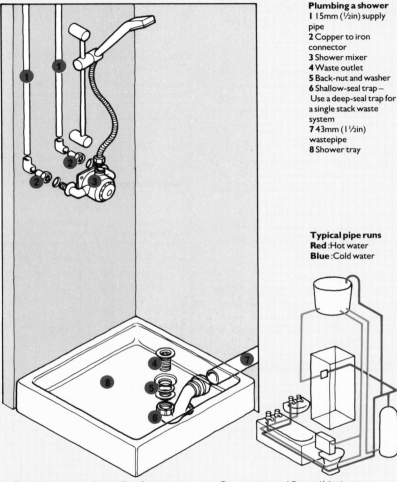

Plumbing a shower
1 15mm (½in) supply pipe
2 Copper to iron connector
3 Shower mixer
4 Waste outlet
5 Back-nut and washer
6 Shallow-seal trap – Use a deep-seal trap for a single stack waste system
7 43mm (1½in) wastepipe
8 Shower tray

Typical pipe runs
Red : Hot water
Blue : Cold water

● Fit the waste outlet in the shower tray and connect a shallow-seal trap as for a bath (◁).

● Install the tray and run a 43mm (1½in) wastepipe to the outside hopper. **To connect it to a waste stack with a strap boss** (◁), **use a deep-seal trap.**

● To enclose a shower, construct a stud partition on one side and line the inner surface with exterior-grade plywood.

● Cut a hole in the board for a flush-mounted shower mixer, or drill holes for the supply pipes to a surface-mounted version.

● Assemble the shower mixer and head according to the manufacturer's instructions.

● Connect it to 15mm (½in) pipes, running them back to the supply (◁). Turn off the water and join the pipes to the supply. Turn the water on again then test the installation for leaks (◁).

● Panel or plasterboard the outside of the stud partition and tile the inside of the cubicle using waterproof adhesive and grout (◁).

● Erect the shower enclosure or fit a shower rail and curtain.

● Seal around the edges of the tray with a flexible mastic.

Instantaneous showers

If you want to install an instanteous shower in the cubicle, run the electrical supply cable, and a single 15mm (½in) pipe from the rising main, through the stud partition (◁). Drill two holes in the wall behind the shower unit for the pipe and cable. Join a threaded or compression connector to the supply pipe, whichever is appropriate for the water inlet built into the shower unit. Make the electrical connections to the shower as recommended by the manufacturer and read the instructions for wiring a shower (◁).

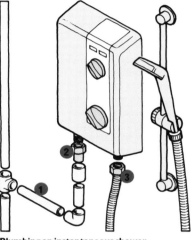

Plumbing an instantaneous shower
1 15mm (½in) pipe from rising main
2 Tap connector
3 Hose to shower head

Enclosing the shower

Showers in cubicles and over bath tubs must be provided with some means of preventing water spraying out onto the floor. Hanging a plastic curtain across the entrance is the simplest and cheapest method. Fit a ceiling-mounted curtain track or a tubular shower rail.

Even when a curtain is tucked into the shower tray, water always seems to escape around the sides of the curtain, or at least drips onto the floor when it is drawn aside. Make a more satisfactory enclosure with metal-framed glass or plastic panels. Hinged, sliding or concertina doors operate within an adjustable frame fixed to the top edge of the tray and the side walls. Bed the lower track onto mastic to make a waterproof joint with the tray and, having completed the enclosure, run a bead of mastic between the framework and the tiled walls of the cubicle.

PLUMBING A BIDET

Although a bidet is primarily for washing the lower parts of the body and genitals, it can double as a footbath for the elderly and small children. Due to the stringent requirements of the water authority, installing a bidet can be an expensive and time consuming procedure. However, if you opt for the simpler version, it is just like plumbing a wash basin.

Over-rim supply bidet

This type of bidet is simply a low level basin. It is fitted with individual hot and cold taps or a basin mixer, and has a built-in overflow running to the waste outlet in the basin. There's only one disadvantage with an over-rim bidet: it is cold when you sit astride it.

Rim supply bidet

A more sophisticated bidet delivers warm water to the basin via a hollow rim. Consequently the rim is pre-heated and comfortable to sit on. A special mixer set with a douche spray is fitted to this type of bidet. It incorporates the normal hot and cold valves but a control in the centre of the mixer diverts water from the rim to the spray head mounted in the bottom of the basin. Because the spray head is submerged when the basin is full, water authority regulations stipulate that a rim supply bidet must take its cold water directly from the storage cistern and there must be no other connections to that pipe. Similarly, the hot water supply must be completely independent and connected to the vent pipe immediately above the cylinder. Check with your water authority before you install a bidet to make sure you comply with local regulations.

INSTALLING A BIDET

When plumbing an over-rim supply bidet, use exactly the same procedures, pipes and connectors described for plumbing a washbasin (▷). Fit the taps, waste outlet and trap, then use a spirit level to position the bidet before fixing it to the floor with non-corrosive screws and washers. Supply the taps with branch pipes from the existing bathroom plumbing and take the wastepipe to the hopper or stack.

Attach the bidet set and trap to a rim supply appliance following the manufacturer's instructions. Screw the bidet to the floor before running 15mm (½in) supply pipes and a 36mm (1¼in) waste according to the water authority regulations (see left). Connect the cold supply to the cistern at the same level as the existing supply pipe.

Plumbing an over-rim supply bidet
1 Tap
2 Tap back-nut and washer
3 Tap connector
4 15mm (½in) supply pipe
5 Waste outlet
6 Waste back-nut and washer
7 Trap
8 36mm (1¼in) wastepipe

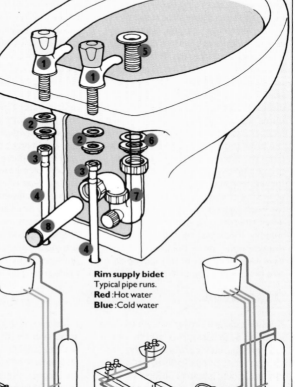

Over-rim supply bidet
Typical pipe runs.
Red: Hot water
Blue: Cold water

Rim supply bidet
Typical pipe runs.
Red: Hot water
Blue: Cold water

BIDETS
INSTALLATION

SEE ALSO

Details for: ▷	
Wash basin	195-196
Cistern supply	208
Connecting pipes	182-189
Taps	194
Strap boss	196

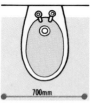

700mm

Space for a bidet
When planning the position of a bidet, allow enough knee room on each side – about 700mm (2ft 3in) overall

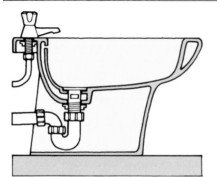

Over-rim supply bidet
This type of bidet is simple to install, just like any wash basin.

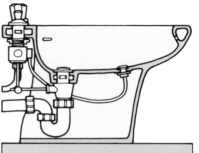

Rim supply bidet
The installation of this type of bidet is complicated by the submerged douche spray. Independent plumbing is essential, and you will need a special mixer set.

FITTING A NEW SINK

SEE ALSO

◁ Details for:

| Taps | 194 |
| Kitchen decor | 18 |

A house that has not been improved substantially for perhaps fifty years or more may well have an old fashioned, glazed stoneware sink in the kitchen. Even if you wanted to, it is virtually impossible to incorporate this type of sink into a modern range of kitchen fitments. As it happens, most stoneware sinks were replaced years ago by a stainless steel sinktop incorporating a bowl and drainer in a single pressing, but that too might look somewhat outdated when compared with the present-day colourful alternatives.

Choosing a kitchen sink

Choose the sink to make the best use of available space, to suit the style of the kitchen, and according to how many other appliances you plan to install which will relieve the sink area of certain functions. Unless your kitchen is fitted with an automatic dishwasher, for instance, the sink must be large enough to cope with a considerable volume of washing-up, and not just the obvious dishes. Don't forget to allow for larger items like baking trays, oven racks and freezer baskets. In addition, check that the bowl is deep enough to fill a bucket from the kitchen tap. If space allows, select a unit with two bowls, primarily for washing and rinsing dishes but also to ensure that one bowl is always free for washing vegetables and salads even when the second is occupied by soaking laundry. If you plan to install a waste disposal unit, one of the bowls must have a waste outlet of the appropriate size (See opposite), or choose a sink unit with a small bowl reserved especially for waste disposal. A double drainer is another useful feature, but if space is limited, allow at least some space to the side of the bowl to avoid piling soiled and clean crockery on a single drainer.

One-piece sinktops are made to modular sizes to fit standard kitchen base units, but sinks which are designed to be set into a continuous work surface offer greater flexibility in size, shape and above all, positioning. What's more, you can set individual bowls or drainers into the worktop to design the layout to suit yourself, and even add a second bowl at a later stage if the need arises. If you opt for this type of installation, choose a drainer equipped with its own waste outlet to drain surface water into the trap beneath the bowl.

Stainless and enamelled steel are still the most popular materials for sinktops, but inset sinks in particular are also made from plastics and ceramic.

Kitchen taps

Kitchen taps are similar in style to those used for wash basins (◁), and there is a kitchen version incorporating the various types of mechanism, but a kitchen mixer has an additional feature. Cold drinking water is supplied from the rising main whereas the hot water at a sink comes from the same storage cylinder that supplies all the other hot taps in the house. As it is against water authority regulations to mix mains and stored water within a fitting, a sink mixer has separate waterways to isolate one supply from the other until the water emerges from the spout. If you are fitting a double-bowl sink, choose a mixer with a swivelling spout. Some sink mixers have an additional hot rinse attachment with a lever-operated spray and detachable brush head for removing stubborn food scraps from crockery and saucepans. Alternatively, you can install an individual attachment supplied by a flexible hose plumbed into the hot water supply pipe below the sink. Make sure the sink you choose is supplied with a hole in the rim to accept the attachment holder.

Individual kitchen taps resemble basin taps in every respect except for their extended pillars to make it possible to fill a bucket in the sink. Sink taps and mixers are provided with 15mm (½in) tails for connecting to the pipes.

Accessories for a kitchen sink

There is a range of accessories designed to fit most kitchen sinks, typically a hardwood or laminated plastic chopping board which drops into the rim of the bowl or drainer, and a selection of plastic-dipped wire baskets for rinsing vegetables or draining crockery and cutlery. Pump-action dispensers for soap and washing-up liquid rid the sink of unsightly plastic bottles and soap dishes.

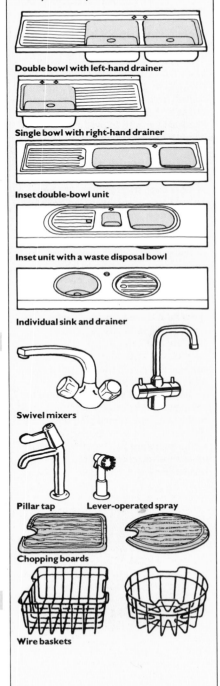

SINK UNITS, TAPS AND ACCESSORIES

There is a wide variety of kitchen sinks, taps and accessories for the domestic market. Steel, enamel, plastic, double, single, plain and coloured: a bewildering choice when planning your kitchen. Shown below is a cross section of popular sinks, accessories and taps to assist you with your decision.

Double bowl with left-hand drainer

Single bowl with right-hand drainer

Inset double-bowl unit

Inset unit with a waste disposal bowl

Individual sink and drainer

Swivel mixers

Pillar tap **Lever-operated spray**

Chopping boards

Wire baskets

INSTALLING A SINK

The installation of a kitchen sink is essentially the same as fitting a wash basin or vanity unit (▷). All except a ceramic sink will require a combined overflow/waste outlet like a bath (▷). Fit a tubular trap to a sink because a bottle trap blocks too easily.

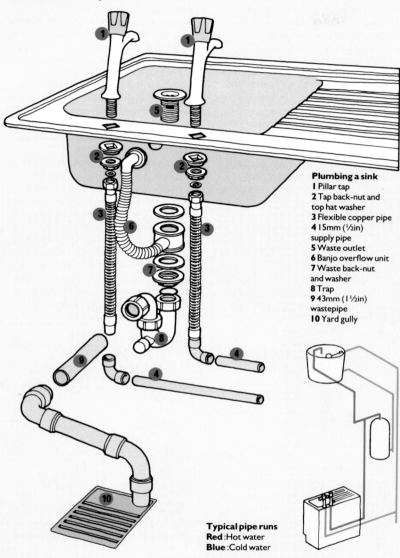

Plumbing a sink
1 Pillar tap
2 Tap back-nut and top hat washer
3 Flexible copper pipe
4 15mm (½in) supply pipe
5 Waste outlet
6 Banjo overflow unit
7 Waste back-nut and washer
8 Trap
9 43mm (1½in) wastepipe
10 Yard gully

Typical pipe runs
Red : Hot water
Blue : Cold water

• Fit the taps, overflow and waste outlet to the sink before you place it in position.

• Turn off the hot and cold supply then remove the old sink by dismantling the plumbing. Hack the old pipes from the wall unless you plan to adapt them.

• Clamp the new sink to its base unit or worktop with the fittings provided, then run a 15mm (½in) cold supply from the rising main and a branch pipe of the same size from the nearest hot water pipe. Connect the pipes to the taps with flexible copper tap conectors (▷). If you prefer to use standard pipe and tap connectors, attach short spur pipes to each tap tail before you install the sink.

• Fit the trap and run a 43mm (1½in) wastepipe through the wall behind the base unit to the yard gully. According to current regulations, the pipe should pass through the grid covering the gully but stop short of the water in the gully trap. Adapt an existing grid by cutting out one corner with a hacksaw.

WASTE DISPOSAL

Waste disposal units

A waste disposal unit provides an hygienic method of dealing with soft food scraps, reserving the kitchen wastebin for dry refuse and bones. The unit houses an electric motor which drives steel cutters for grinding food scraps into a fine slurry which is washed into the yard gully or soil stack. A continuous-feed disposal unit is operated by a manual switch, then, with the cold tap running, scraps are fed into it. To prevent the unit being switched on accidentally, a batch-feed model cannot be operated until a removable plug is inserted in the sink waste outlet.

Most disposal units are designed to fit an 89mm (3½in) outlet in the base of the sink bowl. A special cutter can be hired to adapt a standard stainless steel or plastic sink.

With a sink waste outlet and seal in position (▷), clamp a retaining collar to the outlet from under the sink. Bolt or clip the unit housing to the collar: every unit is supplied with individual instructions.

The waste outlet from the unit itself fits a standard sink trap (not a bottle trap) and wastepipe. If the wastepipe runs to a yard gully, make sure it passes through the covering grid (see left). Wire the unit to a switched, fused connection unit (▷) mounted above the worktop where it is out of the reach of children. Identify the switch to avoid accidental operation.

SEE ALSO

Details for: ▷

Fused connection unit	152
Wash basin	195-196
Tap connectors	196
Fitting sink waste	196
Overflow/waste	198
Earthing	128
Connecting pipes	182-189

Cutting a hole for a waste disposal unit
The supplier of the waste disposal unit, or possibly a tool hire company, will rent you a special cutter to convert an existing sink. The cutter cannot be used on a ceramic sink.

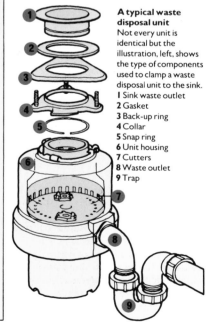

A typical waste disposal unit
Not every unit is identical but the illustration, left, shows the type of components used to clamp a waste disposal unit to the sink.
1 Sink waste outlet
2 Gasket
3 Back-up ring
4 Collar
5 Snap ring
6 Unit housing
7 Cutters
8 Waste outlet
9 Trap

205

PLUMBING A DISHWASHER AND WASHING MACHINE

The full potential of a dishwasher or washing machine as a labour-saving appliance is somewhat limited if you have to pull it out from under a worksurface before attaching flexible hoses to the kitchen sink. If at all possible, provide any automatic machine with permanent supply and waste systems. Dishwashers need a cold supply only whereas washing machines may be hot and cold fill. Washing machines supplied with hot water provide a faster washing cycle and may be more economical to run depending on how you heat your water. Any retailer will be happy to advise you.

Instructions supplied with the machine should state what water pressure is required. If the machine is installed upstairs, make sure the storage cistern is high enough to provide the required pressure (◁). In a downstairs kitchen or utility room, there is rarely a problem with pressure, especially if you can take the cold water from the mains supply at the sink. However, check with your water authority if you want to connect more than one machine.

SEE ALSO

◁ Details for:
Draining system	170
Compression joints	184
Storage cistern	199, 208
Connecting pipes	182-189

Appliance valves
Typical valves used to connect washing machines or dishwashers to the water supply.

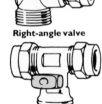

In-line valve

Right-angle valve

Tee-piece valve

Plumbing a washing machine
1 15mm (½in) supply pipe
2 Appliance valve
3 PVC inlet hose
4 Machine inlets
5 Outlet hose
6 Standpipe
7 Trap
8 43mm (1½in) wastepipe to gully

Running the supply

Washing machines and dishwashers are supplied with PVC hoses to link the water inlets at the back of each appliance to special miniature valves connected to the household plumbing. Using these valves, you can turn off the water to service a machine without disrupting the supply to the rest of the house. There are a number of valves to choose from. Select the type which provides the most practical method of connecting to the plumbing depending on the location of the machine in relation to existing pipework.

Self-bore valves

When 15mm (½in) cold and hot water pipes run conveniently behind or alongside the machine, use a valve which bores a hole in the pipe without having to turn off the water supply and drain the system. Each valve is colour coded for hot or cold, and has a threaded outlet for the standard machine hose. Self-bore valves are not approved by all water authorities because the small disc of metal they cut from the pipe may restrict the flow of water. In practice, this hardly ever happens.

To fit a valve, screw the backplate to the wall behind the pipe. Place the saddle with its rubber seal over the pipe. Ensure that the holes in the seal and saddle are aligned before screwing the saddle to the backplate (1).

Make sure the valve is turned off then screw it to the saddle (2). As you insert the valve, the integral cutter bores a hole in the pipe. With the valve in the vertical position, tighten the adjusting nut with a spanner (3). Connect the hose to the valve outlet (4).

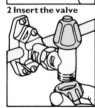

1 Fit the saddle   2 Insert the valve

3 Tighten the nut   4 Attach the hose

Running branch pipes

If you have to extend the plumbing to reach the machine, take branch pipes from the hot and cold pipes supplying the kitchen taps. Terminate the pipes at a convenient position close to the machine and fit a small appliance valve (See left) with a standard compression joint (◁) for connecting to the pipework and a threaded outlet for the hose. When you are fitting this type of valve, turn off the water and drain the system in the normal way (◁). When the supply is restored, open the valve by turning the control level to align with the outlet.

Washing machines and dishwashers are supplied with an outlet hose which must be connected to a waste system to discharge dirty water into a yard gully or single waste stack.

Standpipe and trap

The standard method, approved by all water authorities, employs a vertical 43mm (1½in) plastic standpipe attached to a deep-seal trap. Most plumbing suppliers stock the standpipe, trap and wall fixings as a kit. The machine hose fits loosely in the open-ended pipe to avoid the possibility of dirty water being siphoned back into the machine. Check with the machine manufacturer's instructions regarding the position of the standpipe, but in the absence of other advice, ensure that the open end is at least 600mm (2ft) above the floor.

Cut a hole through the wall to the outside and run the wastepipe to the gully, or attach it to a drainage stack with a strap boss (▷). Allow a minimum fall of 6mm (¼in) for every 300mm (1ft) of pipe run.

Anti-siphon devices

The standpipe and trap method of draining domestic appliances prevents back-siphonage by venting the pipe to the air. There are other ways of dealing with the problem, but you should check with your local water authority to ensure that such methods meet with their approval. If an existing 36 or 43mm (1¼ or 1½in) wastepipe runs behind the machine, you can attach a hose connector which incorporates a non-return valve to eliminate reverse flow. Connectors are available with short spigots (**1**) or as a standpipe. Double standpipes (**2**) permit two appliances to drain into the same connector.

Clamp the saddle over the wastepipe (**3**), then use the cutter supplied with the fitting to bore a hole in the pipe using the saddle as a guide (**4**).

You can drain a washing machine to a sink trap which has a built-in connector for the hose, but you should insert an in-line anti-siphon return valve in the appliance drain hose. It is a small plastic device with a hose connector at each end (**5**).

PREVENTING A FLOOD

Anyone who has had the misfortune of a flooded kitchen caused by a split hose or some mechanical breakdown within a machine will be only too aware of the possible extent of the damage. If the machine is unattended, water continues to flow at mains pressure, ruining floor coverings and furnishings. The consequences can be even worse if the machine is installed upstairs. Once the ceiling beneath becomes thoroughly waterlogged, it collapses, dumping the flood water into the room below.

An overflow safety valve, fitted into the supply, measures the amount of water passing through. If a fault occurs, and the volume of water exceeds a predetermined setting, the valve shuts off the supply immediately. The valve is set before installation to allow for the capacity of the machine it is monitoring plus a small safety margin to avoid excessive sensitivity. Setting instructions are provided by the manufacturer. If a flood occurs, some damage is inevitable, but the valve will avert a disaster. Once the fault is repaired, the valve is reset by pressing a button inside the outlet.

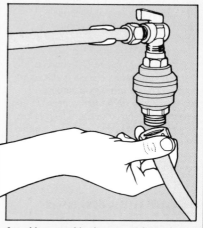

Attaching a machine hose to a safety valve

SEE ALSO

Details for: ▷	
Strap boss	196
Cutting wall	122
Connecting pipes	182-189

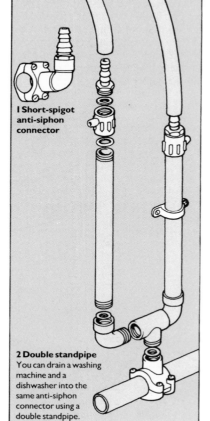

1 Short-spigot anti-siphon connector

2 Double standpipe
You can drain a washing machine and a dishwasher into the same anti-siphon connector using a double standpipe.

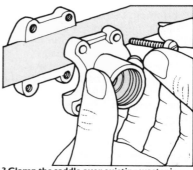

3 Clamp the saddle over existing wastepipe

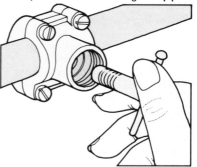

4 Bore a hole with the special cutter

5 An in-line anti-siphon hose valve

STORAGE CISTERNS

PLUMBING A NEW CISTERN

The cold water storage cistern, normally situated in the roofspace, supplies the hot water cylinder and all the cold taps in the house other than the one used for drinking water in the kitchen. An old house may still be fitted with a heavy, galvanized steel cistern which has probably been in service since the house was built. Eventually it will corrode and although it can be patched up temporarily with an epoxy filler, it makes sense to replace it before a serious leak develops.

A circular, 227 litre (50 gallon) capacity, polythene cistern is the most popular choice as a replacement because it can be folded to pass through a narrow hatchway to the loft. It is also very much lighter and easier to handle than the old style cistern. Make sure the new cistern is supplied with a lid to keep the water clean.

SEE ALSO

◁ Details for:
Insulation	109, 114
Float valves	175-176
Tap connector	176
Adjusting float arm	176
Gate valve	182
Compression joint	184

Tank cutters
Hire a tank cutter to bore holes in a cistern for pipework. Some cutters are adjustable to drill holes of different diameters. Alternatively, use a hole saw clamped to a drill.

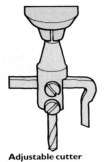

Adjustable cutter

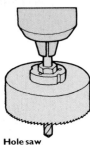

Hole saw

Removing the old cistern

Switch off water-heating appliances, then close the stopcock on the rising main and drain the cistern by opening the bathroom cold taps.

Bail out the remaining water in the bottom of the cistern, then use a spanner to disconnect the fittings connecting the float valve, distribution pipes and overflow, to the cistern. Use a little penetrating oil if the fittings are stiff with corrosion. The cistern may have been built into the house before the roof was completed, so it is unlikely to pass through the loft hatch. In any case it is very cumbersome, so just pull it to one side.

Installing the new cistern

You may be able to use the existing fittings although the pipework is unlikely to fit the new cistern without some modification. If the fittings are badly corroded, buy new replacements.

Prepare a firm base for the cistern by nailing stout planks across the joists or build a platform with 18mm (¾in) thick chipboard or plywood.

Connecting the float valve
A float valve shuts off the flow of water from the rising main when the cistern is full. Cut a hole for the float valve 75mm (3in) below the top of the cistern. Slip a plastic washer onto the tail of the float valve and pass it through the hole. Slide the reinforcing plate onto the tail, followed by another washer and a fixing nut, then tighten the fitting with the aid of two spanners.

Screw a tap connector onto the valve, ready for connecting to the 15mm (½in) rising main.

Connecting the distribution pipes
The 22mm (¾in) pipes running to the cylinder and cold taps are attached to the cistern with tank connectors – threaded inlets with a compression fitting for the pipework. Drill a hole for each tank connector about 50mm (2in) above the bottom of the cistern. Push a tank connector through each hole with one polyethylene washer on the inside. Wrap a couple of turns of PTFE tape around the threads and fit the other washer. Screw on the nut, holding the tank connector to stop it turning. Do not overtighten the nut or you will damage the washer and cause it to leak.

Take the opportunity to fit a gate valve to each distribution pipe so that you can cut off the supply of water without having to empty the cistern.

Connecting the overflow
Drill a hole 25mm (1in) below the level of the float-valve inlet for the threaded connector on the overflow-pipe assembly. Pass the connector through the hole, fit a washer and tighten its fixing nut on the inside of the cistern. Fit the dip pipe and insect filter.

Attach a 21mm (¾in) plastic overflow pipe to the assembly. Run the pipe to the floor then to the outside of the house, maintaining a continuous fall. The pipe must emerge in a conspicuous position so that an overflow can be detected immediately. Clip the pipe to the roof timbers.

Connecting the plumbing
Modify the rising main and distribution pipes to align with their fittings, then connect them with compression fittings. (Don't use soldered joints near a plastic cistern.) Clip all the pipework securely to the joists.

Open the main stopcock and check for leaks as the cistern fills. As the water level approaches the top, adjust the float arm to maintain the level 25mm (1in) below the overflow outlet.

Adapt the vent pipe from the hot-water cylinder to pass through the hole in the lid. Finally, insulate the cistern and pipework, but make sure there is no loft insulation under the cistern as this will prevent warmth rising from below.

Plumbing a cistern.
1 Float valve
2 Reinforcing plate
3 Tap connector
4 Rising main
5 Tank connector
6 Gate valve
7 22mm (¾in) distribution pipe
8 Pipe clip
9 Overflow-pipe assembly
10 Overflow pipe
11 Vent pipe

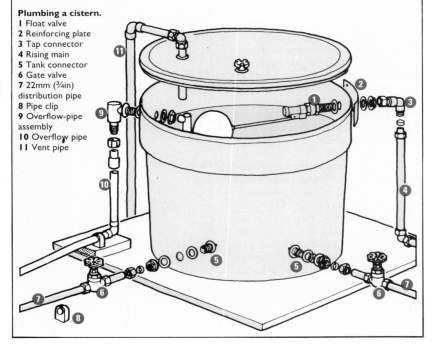

6

FENCES	210
MASONRY	215
BRICKWORK	216
BLOCKWORK	223
PATHS/DRIVES/PATIOS	224
CONCRETE	224
LAYING PAVING	232

WORKING OUTDOORS

FENCES: TYPES OF POST

Whatever type of fence you plan to erect, its strength and durability rely on good-quality posts set solidly in the ground. Buy the best posts you can afford, and erect them carefully. It is worth taking longer over its construction to avoid having to dismantle and repair a fence in the future.

SEE ALSO
◁ Details for:
Preservatives   47

TYPES OF POST

In some cases the nature of the fencing will determine the choice of post. Concrete fencing, for instance, must be supported by compatible concrete posts, but, in the main, you can choose the material and style of post which suits the appearance of the fence.

TIMBER POSTS

Most fences are supported by square-section timber posts. Standard sizes are 75mm and 100mm (3in and 4in) square, but 125mm, 150mm and even 200mm (5in, 6in, 8in) square gate posts are available. Most timber merchants supply pre-treated softwood posts unless you ask specifically for hardwood.

CONCRETE POSTS

A variety of 100mm (4in) square, reinforced-concrete posts exists to suit different styles of fence: drilled for chain link, mortised for rails and recessed or grooved for panels. Special corner and end posts are notched to accommodate bracing struts for chain link fencing.

METAL POSTS

Angle iron or plastic-coated steel posts are made to support chain link or plastic fences. Although angle iron posts are very sturdy, they do not make for a very attractive garden fence.

PLASTIC POSTS

PVC posts are supplied with plastic fencing but most have to be reinforced internally by a timber insert for fences over 750mm (2ft 6in) in height.

Preserving fence posts

Even when a timber post is pre-treated to prevent rot, provide additional protection by soaking the base of each post in a bucket of chemical preservative for at least ten minutes, and longer if possible (◁).

● **Capping fence posts**
If you simply cut the end of a timber post square, the top of the post will rot relatively quickly. The solution is to cut a single or double bevel to shed the rainwater, or nail a wooden or galvanized metal cap over the end of the fence post.

Square timber post

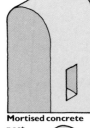

Drilled concrete post   **Mortised concrete post**

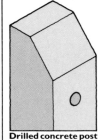

Grooved concrete post   **Notched end post**

Angle iron post   **Tubular steel post**

Capped plastic post

REMOVING OLD FENCE POSTS

Fixing posts in virgin soil is straightforward, but if you are replacing a fence you may want to put the new posts in the same positions as the old ones. Remove the topsoil from around each post to loosen the grip of the soil. If one is bedded firmly, or sunk into concrete, lever it out with a stout batten. Drive large nails in two opposite faces of the post, about 300mm (1ft) from the ground. Bind a length of rope around the post just below the nails, and tie the ends to the tip of the batten. Build a pile of bricks close to the post and use it as a fulcrum to lever the post out of the ground.

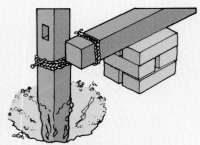

Levering a rotted fence post
Use a pile of bricks as a fulcrum to lift the post.

FIXING TO A WALL

If a fence runs up to the house, fix the first post to the wall with three expanding masonry bolts. Place a washer under each bolt head to stop the wood being crushed. Check the post is vertical with a spirit level, driving packing between the post and wall to make slight adjustments.

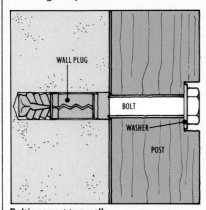

WALL PLUG

BOLT

WASHER

POST

Bolting a post to a wall
If you are fitting a pre-fabricated panel against a wall-fixed post, counter-bore the bolts so that the heads lie flush with the surface of the wood.

USING METAL SPIKES

Instead of anchoring fence posts in concrete, you can plug the base of each post into the square socket of a metal spike driven into firm ground. Use a 600mm (2ft) spike for fences up to 1.2m (4ft) high but use a 750mm (2ft 6in) spike for a 1.8m (6ft) high fence.

Place a scrap of hardwood post into the socket to protect the metal, then drive the spike partly into the ground with a sledgehammer. Hold a spirit level against the socket to make certain the spike is upright (1). Continue to hammer the spike into the ground until only the socket is visible. Insert the post and secure it by screwing through the side of the socket or by tightening clamping bolts (2), depending on the design of the spike you are using.

If you are erecting a panel fence, use the edge of a fixed panel to position the next spike (3).

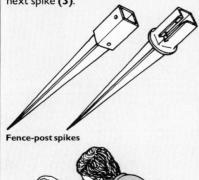

Fence-post spikes

1 Check a spike is vertical with a spirit level

2 Fix the post   3 Position next spike

ERECTING FENCE POSTS

The type of fence often dictates whether you erect all the posts first or one at a time along with the other components. When building a pre-fabricated panel fence, for instance, fix the posts in the ground as you erect the fence, but complete the run of posts before you install chain link fencing.

Marking out

Drive a peg into the ground at each end of the fence run and stretch a line between. If possible, adjust the spacing of the posts to avoid obstructions such as large tree roots. If one or more posts have to be inserted across a paved patio, lift enough slabs to dig the necessary holes. You may have to break up a section of concrete beneath the slabs using a cold chisel and hammer.

SEE ALSO

Details for: ▷	
Straining wires	212
Intermediate posts	212
Mixing concrete	224-225
Chain link fencing	212
Erecting a panel fence	214

Erecting the posts

Digging the hole
Bury one quarter of each post to provide a firm foundation. For a 1.8m (6ft) high fence, dig a 600mm (2ft) hole to take a 2.4m (8ft) post. You can hire a post hole auger to remove the central core of earth. Twist the tool to drive it into the ground (1) and pull it out after every 150mm (6in) to remove the soil. When you have reached a sufficient depth, taper the sides of the hole slightly so that you can pack hardcore and concrete around the post.

Anchoring the post
Ram a layer of hardcore (broken bricks or small stones) into the bottom of the hole to support the base of the post and provide drainage. Get someone to hold the post upright while you brace it with battens nailed to the post and to stakes driven into the ground (2). Use a spirit level to check that it is vertical. (Use guy ropes to support a concrete post.)

Ram more hardcore around the post, leaving a hole about 300mm (1ft) deep for filling with concrete. Mix some concrete to a firm consistency using the proportions 1 part cement: 2 parts sand: 3 parts aggregate (▷). Use a trowel to drop concrete into the hole all round the post and tamp it down with the end of a batten (3). Build the concrete just above the level of the soil and smooth it to slope away from the post (4). This will help shed water and prevent rot. Leave the concrete to harden for about a week before removing the struts. To support a panel fence temporarily, wedge struts against the posts.

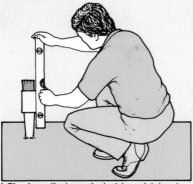
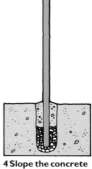

1 Dig the post hole   2 Brace the post   3 Fill with concrete   4 Slope the concrete

Supporting end posts

Chain link fence posts must resist the tension of the straining wires (▷). Brace each end post (and some intermediate posts (▷) over a long run) with a strut made from a length of fence post. Shape the end of the strut to fit a notch cut into the post (1) and nail it in place. Order special posts and pre-cast struts for concrete components .

Anchor the post in the ground in the normal way, but dig a 450mm (1ft 6in) deep trench alongside for the strut. Wedge a brick under the end of the strut before ramming hardcore around the post and strut. Fill the trench up to ground level with concrete (2).

Support a corner post with two struts set at right angles. Where a fence adjoins a masonry wall, fix as described in the box on the opposite page.

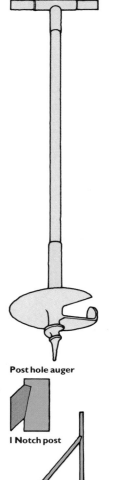

Post hole auger

1 Notch post

2 Concreting end post

211

ERECTING A CHAIN LINK FENCE

Set out a complete row of timber, concrete or angle iron posts to support chain link fencing, spacing them no more than 3m (10ft) apart. Brace the end posts with struts (◁) to resist the pull of the straining wires. A long run of fencing will need a braced intermediate post every 70m (225 ft) or so.

SEE ALSO

◁ Details for:
| Bracing struts | 211 |
| Fence posts | 210-211 |

Using timber posts

Support the chain link fencing on straining wires (See right). As it is impossible to tension this heavy-gauge wire by hand, use large straining bolts to stretch it between the posts. Mark the height of each wire on the posts: one to coincide with the top of the fencing, one about 150mm (6in) from the ground, and the third, midway between. Drill 10mm (⅜in) diameter holes right through the posts, insert a bolt into each hole and fit a washer and nut, leaving enough thread to provide about 50mm (2in) of movement once you begin to apply tension to the wire (**1**).

Pass the end of the wire through the eye of a bolt and twist it around itself with pliers (**2**). Stretch the wire along the run of fencing, stapling it to each post and strut, but leave enough slack for the wire to move when tensioned (**3**). Cut the wire to length and twist it through the bolt at the other end of the fence. Tension the wire from both ends by turning the nuts with a spanner (**4**).

Standard straining bolts provide enough tension for the average garden fence, but over a long run (70m (225ft) or more) use a turnbuckle for each wire, applying tension with a metal bar (See left).

Using concrete posts

Fix straining wires to concrete posts using a special bolt and cleat (See right). Bolt a stretcher bar to the cleats when putting on the wire netting.

Tie the straining wire to intermediate posts with a length of galvanized wire passed through the pre-drilled hole.

Using angle iron posts

Winding brackets are supplied with angle iron fence posts to attach stretcher bars and to apply tension to the straining wires (See right).

As you pass the straining wire from end to end, pass it through the pre-drilled hole in every intermediate post.

Using a turnbuckle
Apply tension by turning the turnbuckle with a metal bar.

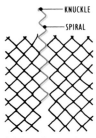
Joining wire mesh
Chain link fencing is supplied in 25m (82ft) lengths. To join one roll to another, unfold the knuckles at each end of the first wire spiral, then turn the spiral anticlockwise to withdraw it from the mesh. Connect the two rolls by re-threading the loose spiral in a clockwise direction through each link of the mesh. Bend over the knuckle at the top and bottom.

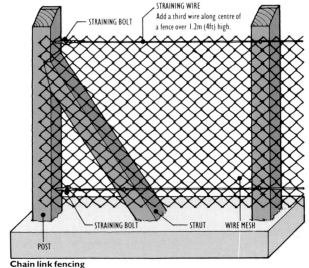

Chain link fencing

Attaching the mesh Staple each end link to the post. Unroll the mesh and pull it taut. Tie it to straining wires every 300mm (1ft) with galvanized wire. Fix to post at other end.
Staple mesh to post
Tie with wire loops

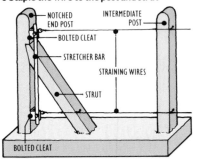
1 Insert a straining bolt in the end post
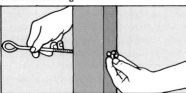
2 Attach a straining wire to the bolt
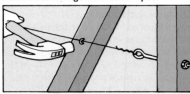
3 Staple the wire to the post and strut
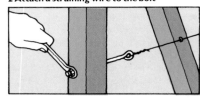
4 Tension the bolt at far end of fence

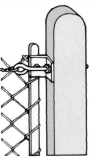
Concrete fence posts

Cleat and stretcher bar **Tie wire to post**

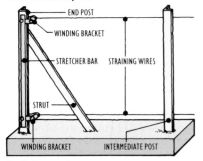
Angle iron posts

Winding bracket

Pass wire through post

ERECTING A CLOSEBOARD FENCE

The featherboards used to panel the fence are nailed to triangular-section rails known as arris rails. The arris rails are mortised into the fence posts. Concrete, and some wooden, posts are supplied ready-mortised, but if you buy standard timber posts you will have to cut the mortises. The unprotected end grain of the featherboards is liable to rot, especially if they are in contact with the ground, so fix horizontal 150 x 25mm (6 x 1in) gravel boards at the foot of the fence, and nail wooden capping strips across the tops of the featherboards. Space the fence posts no more than 3m (10ft) apart.

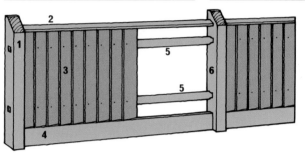

Closeboard fencing
1 End post
2 Capping strip
3 Featherboards
4 Gravel board
5 Arris rail
6 Intermediate post

Erecting the framework

If you are using plain wooden posts, mark and cut 50 x 22mm (2 x ⅞in) mortises for the arris rails about 150mm (6in) above and below the ends of the fixed featherboards. For fencing over 1.2m (4ft) high, cut mortises for a third rail midway between the others. Position the mortises 25mm (1in) from the front face of each post (the featherboarded side of the fence).

As you erect the fence, cut the rails to length and shape a tenon on each end with a coarse rasp or *Surform* file **(1)**. Paint preservative onto the shaped ends and into the mortises before you assemble the rails.

Erect the first fence post and pack hardcore around its base (▷). Get someone to hold the post steady while you fit the arris rails and erect the next post, tapping it onto the ends of the rails with a mallet **(2)**. Check that the rails are horizontal and the posts are vertical before packing hardcore around the second post. Construct the entire run of posts and rails in the same way. If you cannot manoeuvre the last post onto tenoned rails, cut the rails square and fix them to the post with metal brackets (See box right).

Check the whole run once more to ensure that the rails are bedded firmly in their mortises and the framework is true, then secure each rail by driving a nail through the post into the tenon **(3)**. Or drill a hole and insert a wooden dowel. Pack concrete around each post (▷). Leave to harden for about a week.

Fitting the boards

Gravel boards
Some concrete posts are mortised to take gravel boards. In this case they must be fitted with the arris rails. To fit gravel boards to wooden posts, skew-nail treated wooden cleats at the foot of each post, then nail the gravel boards to the cleats **(4)**.

If a concrete post is not mortised for gravel boards, bed wooden cleats into the concrete filling at the base of the post, and screw the board to the cleat when the concrete is set.

Featherboards
Cut the featherboards to length and treat the end grain. Stand the first board on the gravel board with its thick edge against the post. Nail the board to the arris rails with galvanized nails positioned 18mm (¾ in) from the thick edge. Place the next board in position, overlapping the thin edge of the fixed board by 12mm (½ in). Check that it is vertical, then nail it in the same way. Don't drive a nail through both boards or they will not be able to move when they shrink. To space the other boards equally, make a spacer block from a scrap of wood **(5)**. Place the last board to fit against the next post and fix it, this time with two nails per rail **(6)**.

When the fence is completed, nail capping strips across the tops of the featherboards, cut the posts to length and cap them (▷).

REPAIRING A DAMAGED ARRIS RAIL

The arris rails take most of the strain when a closeboard fence is buffeted by high winds. Not surprisingly, they eventually crack across the middle or break where the tenon enters the mortise. You can buy galvanized metal brackets for repairing broken arris rails.

If you wish, you can use end brackets to construct a new fence instead of cutting mortises for the rails. However, it will not be as strong as a fence built with mortise and tenon joints.

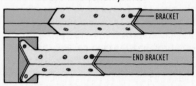

SEE ALSO

Details for: ▷	
Capping posts	210
Erecting posts	211
Preservatives	47

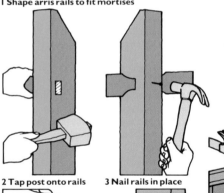

1 Shape arris rails to fit mortises

2 Tap post onto rails   3 Nail rails in place

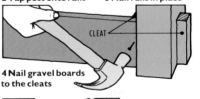

4 Nail gravel boards to the cleats

Capping the fence
Nail a wooden capping strip to the ends of the featherboards to shed rainwater.

5 Position featherboards with a spacer block

6 Fix last board with two nails

ERECTING A PANEL FENCE

To prevent a pre-fabricated panel rotting, either fit gravel boards as for a closeboard fence, or leave a gap at the bottom by supporting a panel temporarily on two bricks while you nail it to the fence posts.

SEE ALSO

◁ Details for:
Capping posts	210
Erecting posts	211
Concrete	211

Using timber posts

Pack the first post into its hole with hardcore (◁), then get someone to hold a panel against the post while you skew-nail through its framework into the post (**1**). If you can work from both sides, drive three nails from each side of the fence. If the frame starts to split, blunt the nails by tapping their points with a hammer. Alternatively, use metal angle brackets to secure the panels (**2**). Construct the entire fence erecting panels and posts alternately.

Nail capping strips across the panels if they have not been fitted by the manufacturer. Finally, cut each post to length and cap it (◁).

Wedge struts made from scrap timber against each post to keep it vertical, then top up the holes with concrete (◁). If you are unable to work from both sides, you will have to fill each hole as you build the fence.

Using concrete posts

Panels are supported by grooved concrete posts without additional fixings (**3**). Recessed posts are supplied with metal brackets for screw-fixing the panels (**4**).

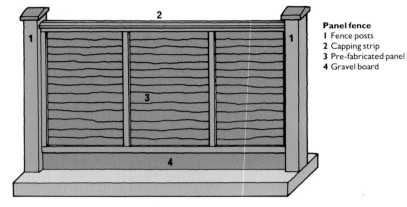

Panel fence
1 Fence posts
2 Capping strip
3 Pre-fabricated panel
4 Gravel board

1 Nail the panel through its framework

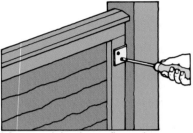

2 Or use angle brackets to fix panel to posts

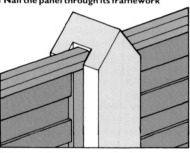

3 A grooved concrete post for a fence panel

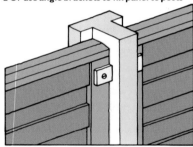

4 A recessed concrete post with fixing bracket

Building a panel fence
Posts and panels are erected alternately. Dig a hole for the post (**1**) and hold it upright with hardcore (◁). Support a panel on bricks (**2**) and have a helper push it against the post (**3**)

while you nail it (**4**). Fit gravel boards (**5**), capping strips (**6**) and cap the posts (**7**). Top up the holes with concrete (**8**) and allow it to set.

WALLS: MIXING MORTAR

When building a wall, mortar is used to bind together the bricks, concrete blocks or stones. The durability of a masonry structure depends on the quality of the mortar used in its construction. If it is mixed correctly to the right consistency, the mortar will become as hard and strong as the masonry itself, but if the ingredients are added in the wrong proportions, the mortar will be weak and prone to cracking. If too much water is used, the mortar will be squeezed out of the joints by the weight of the masonry, and if the mortar is too dry, adhesion will be poor.

BRICKLAYERS' TERMS

Bricklayers use a number of specialized words and phrases to describe their craft and materials. Terms used frequently are listed below while others are described as they occur.

BRICK FACES *The surfaces of a brick.*
Stretcher faces The long sides of a brick.
Header faces The short ends of a brick.
Bedding faces The top and bottom surfaces.
Frog The depression in one bedding face.

COURSES *The individual, horizontal rows of bricks.*
Stretcher course A single course with stretcher faces visible.
Header course A single course with header faces visible.
Coping The top course designed to protect the wall from rainwater.
Bond Pattern produced by staggering alternate courses so that vertical joints are not aligned one above the other.
Stretcher A single brick from a stretcher course.
Header A single brick from a header course.
Closure brick The last brick laid in a course.

CUT BRICKS *Bricks cut with a bolster chisel to even up the bond.*
Bat A brick cut across its width, i.e. half-bat, three-quarter bat.
Queen closer A brick cut along its length.

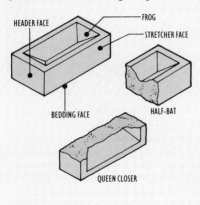

HEADER FACE
FROG
STRETCHER FACE
BEDDING FACE
HALF-BAT
QUEEN CLOSER

The ingredients of mortar

The ingredients of general-purpose mortar are Portland cement, hydrated lime and sand, mixed with enough water to make a workable paste.

Cement is the hardening agent which binds the other ingredients together. The lime slows down the drying process and prevents the mortar setting too quickly. It also makes the mix flow well so that it fills gaps in the masonry and adheres to the texture of blocks or bricks. The sand acts as fine aggregate, adding body to the mortar, and reduces the possibility of shrinkage.

Use fine builders' sand for general-purpose mortar. However, use silver sand if you want a paler mortar to bond white screen blocks.

Plasticizers

If you are laying masonry in cold weather, substitute a proprietary plasticizer for the lime. Plasticizer produces aerated mortar – the tiny air bubbles in the mix allow the water to expand in freezing conditions and reduce the risk of cracking. Pre-mixed masonry cement, with an aerating agent, is ready for mixing with sand.

Ready-mix mortar

Ready-mix mortar contains all the essential ingredients mixed to the correct proportions. You simply add water. It is a more expensive way of buying mortar but convenient to use and is available in small quantities.

Mixing mortar

Mortar must be used within two hours of mixing or be discarded, so make only as much as you can use within that time. An average of about two minutes to lay one brick is a reasonable estimate.

Choose a flat site upon which to mix the materials – a sheet of plywood will do – and dampen it slightly to prevent it absorbing water from the mortar. Make a pile of half the amount of sand to be used, then add the other ingredients. Put the rest of the sand on top, and mix the dry materials thoroughly.

Scoop a depression in the pile and add clean tap water. Never use contaminated or salty water. Push the dry mix from around the edge of the pile into the water until it has absorbed enough for you to blend the mix with a shovel, using a chopping action. Add more water, little by little, until the mortar has a butter-like consistency, slipping easily from the shovel but firm enough to hold its shape if you make a hollow in the mix. If the sides of the hollow collapse, add more dry ingredients until the mortar firms up. Make sure the mortar is not too dry or it won't form a strong bond with the masonry.

If mortar stiffens up while you are working, add just enough water to restore the consistency. Dampen the mixing board again.

Proportions for masonry mixes

Mix the ingredients according to the prevailing conditions at the building site. Use a general-purpose mortar for moderate conditions where the wall is reasonably sheltered, but use a stronger mix for severe conditions where the wall will be exposed to wind and driving rain, or if the site is elevated or near the coast. If you are using plasticizer instead of lime, follow the manufacturer's instructions regarding the quantity you should add to the sand.

SEE ALSO

Details for: ▷
Cutting bricks   218

Correct consistency
The mortar mix should be firm enough to hold its shape when you make a depression in the mix.

● **Estimating quantity**
As a rough guide to estimating how much mortar you will need, allow approximately 1 cu m (1⅓cu yd) of sand (other ingredients in proportion) to lay: 1600 to 1650 bricks; 40 to 45sq m (69 to 70sq yd) average facing blocks; 80 to 85sq m (100 to 105sq yd) screen or structural blocks.

MORTAR MIXING PROPORTIONS

	Cement/lime mortar	Plasticized mortar	Masonry cement mortar
General-purpose mortar (Moderate conditions)	1 part cement 1 part lime 6 parts sand	1 part cement 6 parts sand/ plasticizer	1 part cement 5 parts sand
Strong mortar (Severe conditions)	1 part cement ½ part lime 4 parts sand	1 part cement 4 parts sand/ plasticizer	1 part cement 3 parts sand

SEE ALSO

◁ Details for:

Wall ties	221
Copings	220
Building piers	222

DESIGNING A WALL FOR STABILITY

It is easy enough to appreciate the loads and stresses imposed upon the walls of a house or outbuilding, and therefore the necessity for solid foundations and adequate methods of reinforcement and protection to prevent them collapsing. It is not so obvious, but even simple garden walling requires similar measures to ensure its stability. It is merely irritating if a low dividing wall or planter falls apart, but a serious injury could result from the collapse of a heavy boundary wall.

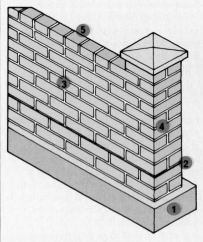

The basic structure of a wall
Unless you design and build a wall in the correct manner, it will not be strong and stable.

1 Footings
A wall must be built upon a solid concrete platform known as a strip footing. The dimensions of the footing vary according to the height and weight of the wall.

2 Damp-proof course
A layer of waterproof material 150mm (6in) above ground level stops water rising from the soil. It is not needed for most garden walling unless it abuts a building with a similar DPC. Not only does it protect the house from damp, but it reduces the likelihood of freezing water expanding and cracking the joints.

3 Bonding
The staggered pattern of bricks is not merely decorative. It is designed to spread the static load along the wall and to tie the individual units together.

4 Piers
Straight walls over a certain height and length must be buttressed at regular intervals with thick columns of brickwork known as piers. They resist the sideways pressure caused by high winds.

5 Coping
The coping prevents frost damage by shedding rainwater from the top of the wall where it could seep into the upper brick joints.

BONDING BRICKWORK

Mortar is extremely strong under compression, but its tensile strength is relatively weak. If bricks were stacked one upon the other so that the vertical joints were continuous, any movement within the wall would pull them apart and the structure would be seriously weakened. Bonding brickwork staggers the vertical joints, transmitting the load along the entire length of the wall. Try out the bond of your choice by dry-laying a few bricks before you embark on the actual building work.

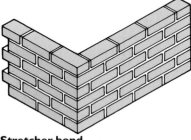

Stretcher bond
The stretcher bond is the simplest form of bonding, used for single-thickness walls, including the two individual leaves of a cavity wall found in the construction of modern buildings. Half-bats are used to make the bond at the end of a straight wall, while a corner is formed by alternating headers and stretchers.

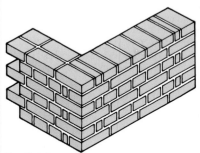

English bond
If you build a 215mm (8½ in) thick wall by laying courses of stretcher-bonded bricks side by side, there would be a weak vertical joint running centrally down the wall. An English bond strengthens the wall by using alternate courses of headers. Staggered joints are maintained at the end of a wall and at a corner by inserting a queen closer before the last header.

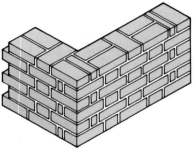

Flemish bond
The Flemish bond is an alternative method to English bond for building a solid, 215mm (8½ in) thick wall. Every course is laid with alternate headers and stretchers. Stagger the joint at the end of a course and at a corner by laying a queen closer before the header.

Decorative bonds
Stretcher, English and Flemish bonds are designed to construct strong walls – decorative qualities are incidental. Other bonds, used primarily for their visual effect, are suitable for low, non-loadbearing walls only, supported by a conventionally bonded base and piers.

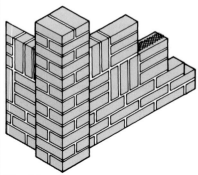

Stack bonding
A basket-weave effect is achieved by stack bonding bricks in groups of three. Strengthen the continuous vertical joints with wall ties (◁).

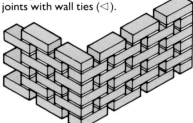

Honeycomb bond
Build an open, decorative screen using a stretcher-like bond with a quarter-bat-size space between each brick. Build the screen carefully to keep the bond regular, and cut quarter-bats to fill the gaps in the top course.

CONSTRUCTING STRIP FOOTINGS

Stringent Building Regulations govern the size and reinforcement required for the footings to support high and especially structural walls, but most garden walls can be built upon concrete footings laid in a straight-sided trench.

Size of footings

The footing must be sufficiently substantial to support the weight of the wall, and the soil must be firm and well drained to avoid possible subsidence. It is unwise to set footings in ground which has been filled recently, such as a new building site. Also, take care to avoid tree roots and drainpipes. If the trench begins to fill with water as you are digging, seek professional advice before proceeding.

Dig the trench deeper than the footing itself so that the first one or two courses of brick are below ground level. This will allow for an adequate depth of soil for planting right up to the wall.

If the soil is not firmly packed when you reach the required depth, dig deeper until you reach a firm level, then fill the bottom of the trench with compacted hardcore up to the lowest level of the proposed footing.

RECOMMENDED DIMENSIONS FOR FOOTINGS			
Type of wall	Height of wall	Depth of footing	Width of footing
One brick thick	Up to 1m (3ft 3in)	100 to 150mm (4 to 6in)	300mm (1ft)
Two bricks thick	Up to 1m (3ft 3in)	225 to 300mm (9in to 1ft)	450mm (1ft 6in)
Two bricks thick	Over 1m up to 2m (Up to 6ft 6in)	375 to 450mm (1ft 3in to 1ft 6in)	450 to 600 mm (1ft 6in to 2ft)
Retaining wall	Up to 1m (3ft 3in)	150 to 300mm (6in to 1ft)	375 to 450mm (1ft 3in to 1ft 6in)

Setting out the footings

For a straight footing, set up two profile boards made from 25mm (1in) thick timber nailed to stakes driven into the ground at each end of the proposed trench but well outside the work area.

Drive nails into the top edge of each board and stretch lines between them to mark the front and back edges of the wall. Then drive nails into the profile boards on each side of the wall line to indicate the width of the footing, and stretch more lines between them (1).

When you are satisfied that the setting out is accurate, remove the lines marking the wall but leave the nails in place so that you can replace the lines when you come to lay the bricks.

Place a spirit level against the remaining lines to mark the edge of the footing on the ground (2). Mark the ends of the footing extending beyond the line of the wall by half the wall's thickness. Mark the edge of the trench on the ground with a spade and remove the lines. Leave the boards in place.

Turning corners
If your wall will have a right-angled corner, set up two sets of profile boards as before, checking carefully that the lines form a true right angle using the 3:4:5 principle (3).

Digging the trench
Excavate the trench, keeping the sides vertical, and check that the bottom is level, using a long, straight piece of wood and a spirit level.

Drive a stake into the bottom of the trench near one end until the top of the stake represents the depth of the footing. Drive in more stakes at 1m (3ft 3in) intervals, checking that the tops are level (4).

Filling the trench
Pour a foundation mix of concrete ($\triangleright$) into the trench, then tamp it down firmly with a stout piece of timber until it is exactly level with the top of the stakes. Leave the stakes in place and allow the footing to harden thoroughly before building the wall.

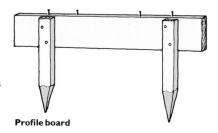
Profile board

FOOTING FOR A SLOPING SITE

When the ground slopes gently, simply ignore the gradient and make the footing perfectly level. If the site slopes noticeably, make a stepped footing by placing plywood shuttering across the trench at regular intervals. Calculate the height and length of the steps using multiples of normal brick size.

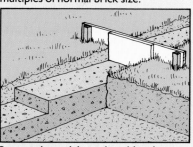
Support plywood shuttering with stakes

Section through a stepped footing
A typical stepped concrete footing with one of the plywood shuttering boards in place.

SEE ALSO

Details for: $\triangleright$
Concrete mixes 227

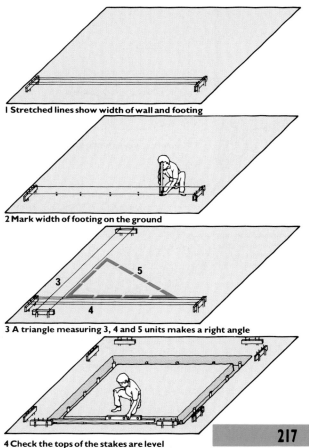
1 Stretched lines show width of wall and footing

2 Mark width of footing on the ground

3 A triangle measuring 3, 4 and 5 units makes a right angle

4 Check the tops of the stakes are level

BRICKLAYING TOOLS

You can make or improvise some builder's tools (◁) but you will have to buy some of the more-specialized bricklayer's tools.

SEE ALSO

◁ Details for:	
Mixing mortar	215
Mortar boards	84

Tools for basic bricklaying
1 Club hammer **2** Spirit level **3** Bolster chisel
4 Pointing trowel **5** Brick trowel.

LAYING BRICKS

Spreading a bed of mortar— throwing a line — requires practice before you can develop speed, so concentrate at first on laying bricks neatly and accurately. Mortar mixed to the right consistency (◁) helps to keep the visible faces of the bricks clean. In hot, dry weather dampen the footings and bricks, but let any surface water evaporate before you begin to lay bricks.

Bricklaying techniques

Hold the brick trowel with your thumb in line with the handle, pointing towards the tip of the blade (**1**).

Scoop a measure of mortar out of the pile and shape it roughly to match the shape of the trowel blade. Pick up the mortar by sliding the blade under the pile, setting it onto the trowel with a slight jerk of the wrist (**2**).

Spread the mortar along the top course by aligning the edge of the trowel with the centre line of the bricks. As you tip the blade to deposit the mortar, draw the trowel back towards you to stretch the bed over at least two to three bricks (**3**).

Furrow the mortar by pressing the point of the trowel along the centre (**4**).

Pick up a brick with your other hand, but don't extend your thumb too far onto the stretcher face or it will disturb the builders' line every time you place a brick in position. Press the brick into the bed, picking up excess mortar squeezed from the joint by sliding the edge of the trowel along the wall (**5**).

With the mortar picked up on the trowel, butter the header of the next brick, making a neat 10mm (³⁄₈in) bed for the header joint (**6**). Press the brick against its neighbour, scooping off excess mortar with the trowel.

Having laid three bricks, check they are horizontal using the spirit level. Make any adjustments by tapping them down with the trowel handle (**7**).

Hold the level along the outer edge of the bricks to check they are in line. To move a brick sideways without knocking it off its mortar bed, tap the upper edge with the trowel at about 45 degrees (**8**).

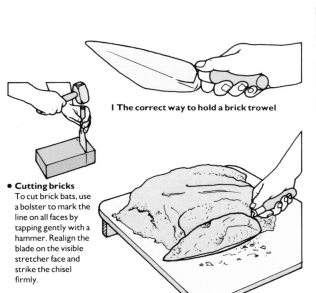

1 The correct way to hold a brick trowel

• Cutting bricks
To cut brick bats, use a bolster to mark the line on all faces by tapping gently with a hammer. Realign the blade on the visible stretcher face and strike the chisel firmly.

2 Scoop a measure of mortar onto the trowel

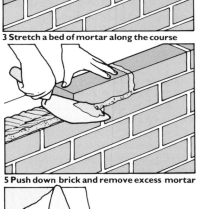

3 Stretch a bed of mortar along the course

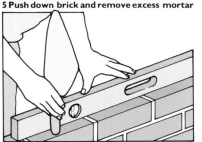

5 Push down brick and remove excess mortar

7 Level the course of bricks with the trowel

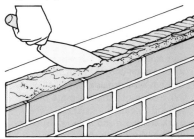

4 Furrow the mortar with the trowel point

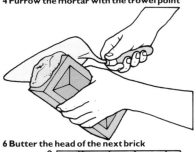

6 Butter the head of the next brick

8 Tap the bricks sideways to align them

BUILDING A STRETCHER-BONDED WALL

A single-width brick wall looks visually mean and, over a certain height, is structurally weak unless it is supported with piers, or changes direction by forming right-angle corners. In any case, the ability to construct strong, accurate corners is a requirement for building most structures, including simple garden planters. Building a wall with another type of bond is a little more complicated in detail (▷) but the basic principles remain the same.

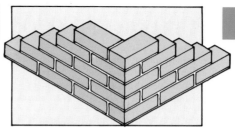

A stepped lead for a corner

SEE ALSO

Details for: ▷	
Bonding brickwork	216
Profile boards	217
Copings	220
Footings	217

Setting out the corners

Mark out the footings and face of the wall by stretching string lines between profile boards (▷). When the footings have been filled and the concrete has set, use a plumb line or hold a level lightly against the line to mark the corners and the face of the wall on the footing (1). Join the marks with a pencil and straight batten, and check the accuracy of the corners with a builder's square. Stretch a line between the corner marks to check the alignment.

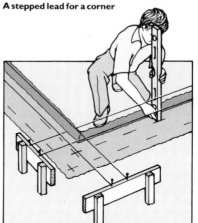

1 Mark the face of the wall on the footing

Building the corners

Build the corners first as a series of steps or 'leads' before filling between. It is essential that they form true right angles, so take your time.

Throw a bed of mortar, then lay three bricks in both directions against the marked line. Check they are level in all directions, including across the diagonal by laying a spirit level between the end bricks (2).

Build the leads to a height of five stepped courses, using a gauge stick to measure the height of each course as you proceed (3). Use alternate headers and stretchers to form the actual point of the corner.

Use a level to plumb the corner, and check the alignment of the stepped bricks by holding the level against the side of the wall (4).

2 Level the first course of bricks

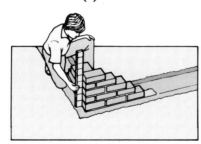

3 Check the height with a gauge stick

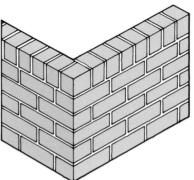

4 Check that the steps are in line

- **Covering the wall**
Cover finished or partly built walls overnight with sheets of polythene or tarpaulin to protect the brickwork from rain or frost. Weight the edges of the covers with bricks.

Building the straight sections

Stretch a builder's line between the corners so that it aligns perfectly with the top edge of the first course (5).

Lay the first straight course of bricks from both ends towards the middle. As you near the middle point, lay the last few bricks dry to make certain they will fit. Then mortar them in, finishing with the central or 'closure' brick. Spread mortar onto both ends of the closure brick and onto the header faces of the bricks on each side. Lay the closure brick very carefully (6), and scoop off excess mortar with the trowel.

Lay subsequent courses between the leads in the same way, raising the builder's line each time. To build the wall higher, raise the corners first by constructing leads to the required height, then fill the spaces between.

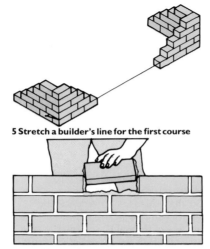

5 Stretch a builder's line for the first course

6 Carefully lay the last or closure brick

- **Building a straight wall**
To build a straight wall without a corner, follow the procedure described left, building end leads – straight stepped sections – at each end of the wall, then fill between with bricks.

Coping the wall
You could finish the wall by laying the last course frog downwards, but a coping of half-bats laid on end looks more professional. Alternatively use proprietary coping bricks or blocks (▷).

POINTING BRICKWORK

Finishing the mortar joints – pointing – compresses the materials to make a packed, watertight joint and enhances the appearance of the wall. Well-struck joints and clean brickwork are essential if the wall is to look professionally built but the mortar must be shaped at the right time for the best results.

SEE ALSO
◁ Details for:
DPC   216

Flush joint

Concave joint

'V' joint

Raked joint

Weather joint

Coloured mortar
You can add coloured powders to your mortar mix. Make a trial batch to test the colour when dry. Rake out the joint and apply with a tray to avoid staining the bricks.

Mortar for pointing work

If the mortar is still too wet the joint will not be crisp and you may drag mortar out from between the bricks. On the other hand, if it is left to harden too long pointing will be hard work and you may leave dark marks on the joint.

Test the consistency of the mortar by pressing your thumb into a joint. If it holds a clear impression without sticking to your thumb the mortar is just right for pointing. Because it is so important you shape the joint at exactly the right moment you may have to point the work in stages before you can complete the wall.

Shape the joints to match existing brickwork or choose one that is suitable for the prevailing weather conditions.

How to make pointing joints

Flush joint
Rub a piece of sacking along each joint to finish the mortar flush with the bricks. This is a utilitarian joint for a wall built with second-hand bricks which are not of a sufficiently good quality to take a crisp joint.

Concave joint
Buy a shaped jointing tool to make a concave joint, or improvise with a length of bent tubing. Flush the mortar first, then drag the tool along the joints. Finish the vertical joints, then do the long, continuous horizontal ones.

Shape the mortar with a jointing tool

'V' joint
Produced in a similar way to the concave joint, the 'V' joint gives a very smart finish to new brickwork and sheds rainwater well.

Raked joint
Use a piece of wood or metal to rake out the joints to a depth of about 6mm (¼in), then compress them again by smoothing the mortar lightly with a piece of rounded dowel rod. Raked joints do not shed water so don't use them on an exposed site.

Weather joint
The angled weather joint is ideal, even in harsh conditions. Use a small pointing trowel to shape the vertical joints (1). They can slope to the left or right, but be consistent throughout the same section of brickwork. Shape the horizontal joints allowing the mortar to spill out slightly at the base of each joint. Professionals finish the joint by cutting off excess mortar with a tool called a Frenchman, similar to a table knife with the tip at 90 degrees. Improvise a similar tool with a strip of bent metal. Align a batten with the bottom of the joint to guide the tool and produce a neat, straight edge to the mortar. Nail two scraps of plywood to the batten to hold it away from the wall (2).

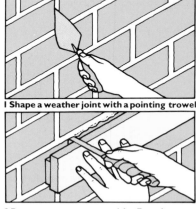

1 Shape a weather joint with a pointing trowel

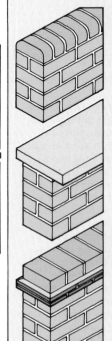

2 Remove excess mortar with a Frenchman

Brushing the brickwork
Let the shaped joints harden a little before you clean scraps of mortar from the face of the wall. Use a medium-soft banister brush, sweeping lightly across the joints so as not to damage them.

COPINGS FOR BRICK WALLS

The coping, which forms the top course of the wall, protects the brickwork from weathering and gives a finished appearance to the wall. Strictly speaking, if the coping is flush with both faces of the wall it is a capping. A true coping projects from the face so that water drips clear and does not stain the brickwork.

You can lay a coping of bricks with their stretcher faces across the width of the wall. Use the same type of brick employed in the construction of the wall or specially shaped coping bricks designed to shed rainwater. Engineering bricks are sometimes used for copings. The dense water-resistant quality of the brick is an advantage and the colour makes a pleasing contrast with regular brickwork.

Stone or cast concrete slabs are popular for garden walling. They are quick to lay and are wide enough to form low, bench-type seating.

On an exposed site, consider installing a damp-proof course (◁) under the coping to reduce the risk of frost attack. Use a standard bituminous felt DPC or lay two courses of plain roof tiles with staggered joints and a brick coping above. Let the tiles project from the face of the wall but run a sloping mortar joint along the top of the projection to shed water.

Brick coping
Specially shaped bricks are made to cope a wall.

Slab coping
Choose a concrete or stone slab that is wider than the wall itself.

Tile and brick coping
Lay flat roof tiles or specially made creasing tiles beneath a brick coping to form a weatherproof layer which allows water to drip clear of the wall.

BRICKWORK PIERS

A pier is a free-standing column of masonry used to support a porch or as an individual gatepost, for instance. When it is built as part of a wall, it is more accurately termed a pilaster. In practice, however, a column often covers either description. Columns bonded into a masonry base but extending up each side of a wooden trellis to support a pergola are typical examples. To avoid confusion, any supporting brick column will be described as a pier. Thorough planning is essential when building piers.

Structural considerations

Any free-standing straight wall over a certain length and height must be buttressed at regular intervals by piers. Sections of walling and piers must be tied together, either by a brick bond or by inserting metal wall ties in every third course of bricks. Any single-width brick wall, whatever its height, would benefit from supporting piers at open ends and gateways where it is most vulnerable; these will also improve the appearance of the wall. Piers over 1m (3ft 3in), and especially those supporting gates, should be built around steel reinforcing rods set in the concrete footings. Whether reinforcing is included or not, allow for the size of piers when designing the footings (◁).

Designing the piers

Piers should be placed no more than 3m (9ft 9in) apart in walls over a certain height (See chart). The wall itself can be flush with one face of a pier but the structure is stronger if it is centred on the column.

Piers should be a minimum of twice the thickness of a 102.5mm (4in) thick wall, but build 328mm (1ft 1in) square piers when reinforcement is required, including gateways, and to buttress 215mm (8½in) thick walls.

INCORPORATING PIERS IN A BRICK WALL

Thickness of wall	Maximum height without piers	Maximum pier spacing
102.5mm (4in)	450mm (1ft 6in)	3m (9ft 9in)
215mm (8½in)	1.35m (4ft 6in)	3m (9ft 9in)

BONDING PIERS

If you prefer the appearance of bonded brick piers, construct them as shown below, but it is easier, especially when building walls centred on piers, to use wall ties to reinforce continuous vertical joints in the brickwork.

Various types of galvanized metal wall ties are available. Wire is bent into a butterfly shape (1). Stamped metal steel strips have forked ends and are known as fish tails (2). Expanded metal mesh is cut in straight strips (3).

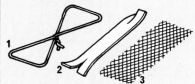

SEE ALSO

Details for: ▷	
Footings	217
Laying bricks	218-219
Reinforced piers	222

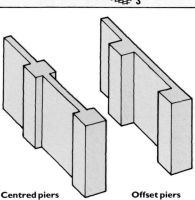

Centred piers **Offset piers**

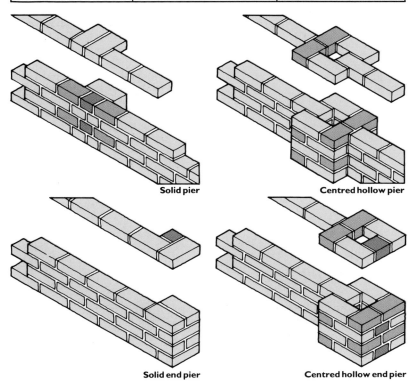

Solid pier **Centred hollow pier** **Offset hollow pier**

Solid end pier **Centred hollow end pier** **Offset hollow end pier**

• **Bonding piers**
It is simpler to tie any wall to a pier with wall ties (See above right) but it is relatively easy to bond a pier into a single-brick width wall.

Colour key
You will have to cut certain bricks to bond a pier into a straight wall. Whole bricks are coloured with a light tone, three-quarter bats with a medium tone, and half-bats with a dark tone.

BUILDING PIERS

Mark out accurately the positions of piers and the face of the wall on the concrete footing (▷). Lay the first course for the piers using a builder's line stretched between two stakes to align them (**1**). Adjust the position of the line if necessary, and fill in between with the first straight course working from both ends towards the middle (**2**). Build alternate pier and wall courses, checking the level and the vertical faces and corners of the piers. At the third course, push metal wall ties into the mortar bed to span the joint between wall and pier (**3**). Continue in the same way to the required height of the wall, then raise the piers to their required height (**4**). Lay a coping along the wall and cap the piers with concrete or stone slabs (**5**).

SEE ALSO

◁ Details for:
Marking out	219
Laying bricks	218-219
Wall ties	221

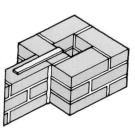

Making a control joint
Tie the pier to the wall with galvanized-metal strips when making a control joint (shown here before it's set in mortar). The mastic is squeezed into the joint between the wall and the pier.

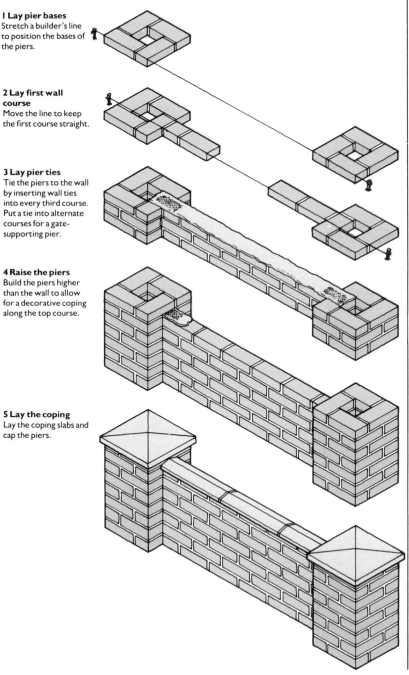

1 Lay pier bases
Stretch a builder's line to position the bases of the piers.

2 Lay first wall course
Move the line to keep the first course straight.

3 Lay pier ties
Tie the piers to the wall by inserting wall ties into every third course. Put a tie into alternate courses for a gate-supporting pier.

4 Raise the piers
Build the piers higher than the wall to allow for a decorative coping along the top course.

5 Lay the coping
Lay the coping slabs and cap the piers.

Incorporating control joints

Although you would never notice, a brick wall is constantly moving due to ground settlement as well as expansion and contraction of the materials. Over short distances, the movement is so slight that it hardly affects the brickwork, but the combined movement of masonry in a long wall can crack the structure. To compensate for this movement, build unmortared, continuous vertical joints into a wall at intervals of about 6m (19ft 6in). These control joints can be placed in a straight section of walling, but it is neater and more convenient to place them where the wall meets a pier. Build the pier and wall as normal, but omit the mortar from the header joints of the wall. Instead of inserting standard wall ties, embed a flat, 3mm (⅛in) thick galvanized strip in the mortar bed. Lightly grease one half of the strip so that it can slide lengthwise to allow for movement yet still key the wall and pier together. When the wall is complete, fill the joint from both sides with mastic.

Incorporating reinforcement

Use 16mm (⅝in) steel reinforcing bars to strengthen brick piers. If the pier is under 1m (3ft 3in) in height, use one continuous length of bar (**1**), but for taller piers, embed a bent 'starter' bar in the footing, projecting a minimum of 500mm (1ft 8in) above the level of the concrete (**2**). As the work proceeds, bind extension bars to the projection with galvanized wire up to within 50mm (2in) of the top of the pier. Fill in around the reinforcement with concrete as you build the pier but pack it carefully, trying not to disturb the brickwork.

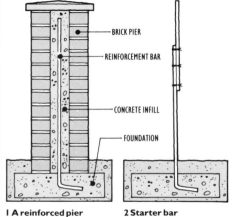

BRICK PIER

REINFORCEMENT BAR

CONCRETE INFILL

FOUNDATION

1 A reinforced pier   **2 Starter bar**

BUILDING A DECORATIVE BLOCK SCREEN

Basic bricklaying techniques and tools (▷) are used to build a pierced concrete screen but because the blocks are stack-bonded – with continuous vertical joints – the wall must be reinforced vertically with 16mm (⅝in) steel bars, and horizontally with galvanized mesh if it is built higher than 600mm (2ft). Build the screen with supporting piers no more than 3m (9ft 9in) apart using matching pilaster blocks. Or, if you prefer the appearance of contrasting masonry, construct a base and piers from bricks or facing blocks.

Constructing the screen

Set out and fill the footings (▷) twice the width of the pilaster blocks. Embed pier-reinforcing bars in the concrete and support them with guy ropes until the concrete sets.

Lower a pilaster block over the first bar, setting it onto a bed of mortar laid around the base of the bar. Check the block is perfectly vertical and level, and that its locating channel faces the next pier. Pack mortar or concrete into its core, then proceed with two more blocks so that the pier corresponds to the height of two mortared screen blocks (1). Construct each pier in the same way. Intermediate piers will have a locating channel on each side.

Allow the mortar to harden overnight, then lay a mortar bed for two screen blocks next to the first pier. Butter the vertical edge of a screen block and press it into the pier locating channel (2). Tap it into the mortar bed and check it is level. Mortar the next block and place it alongside the first.

When buttering screen blocks, take special care to keep the faces clean by making a neat, chamfered bed of mortar on each block (3).

Lay two more blocks against the next pier, stretch a builder's line to gauge the top edge of the first course, and then lay the rest of the blocks towards the centre. Lay the second course in the same way, making sure the vertical joints are aligned perfectly.

Before building any higher, embed a wire reinforcing strip running from pier to pier in the next mortar bed (4). Continue to build the piers and screen up to a maximum height of 2m (6ft 6in), inserting a wire strip into alternate courses. Finally, lay coping slabs at the top of each pier and along the top of the screen (5).

If you don't like the appearance of ordinary mortar joints, rake out some of the mortar and repoint with mortar made with silver sand. A concave joint suits decorative screening (▷).

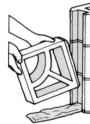

1 Build the piers   **2 Fit block to pier**   **3 Butter edge of block**

4 Lay a wire reinforcing strip into the mortar

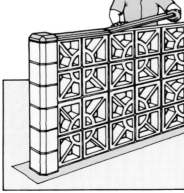

5 Lay coping slabs along the wall

CAVITY WALLS

Cavity walls are used in the construction of habitable buildings to prevent the passage of moisture through the wall to the interior. This is achieved by building two independent leaves of masonry with a clear gap between them. The gap provides a degree of thermal insulation but the insulation value increases appreciably if an efficient insulant is introduced to the cavity. The exterior leaf of most cavity walls is constructed with facing bricks. The inner leaf is sometimes built with interior-grade bricks but more often with concrete blocks. Whatever type of masonry is used, both leaves must be tied together with wall ties spanning the gap. Cavity walls are likely to be loadbearing, so have to be built very accurately – hire a professional to construct them. Make sure the bricklayer includes a DPC in both leaves and avoids dropping mortar into the gap. If mortar collects at the base of the cavity, or even on one of the wall ties, moisture can bridge the gap leading to damp on the inside.

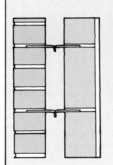

Cavity wall construction
A section through a typical cavity wall built with an exterior leaf of bricks tied to an inner leaf of plastered concrete blocks.

Building a brick base and piers
Build piers and a low base of bricks or facing blocks (▷), including reinforcing bars in the centre of each pier. Lay coping slabs along the wall and continue to build the piers along with the screen. Tie the screen and piers together with reinforcing strips as described left, but insert standard wall ties in alternate courses to provide additional location and support.

SEE ALSO

Details for: ▷	
Footings	217
Laying bricks	218-219
Concave joint	220

PATHS, DRIVES AND PATIOS

For many people, paving of any kind is associated with the old 'back yard' environment, conjuring up an image of a concreted patch devoid of plants, trees and grass – inhuman and unattractive. In reality, introducing paving to a garden provides an opportunity to create surprising contrasts of colour and texture intensified by sunlight and deep shadows. The harshness of a hard, unyielding surface is softened by the addition of foliage, while certain sculptural plants which recede into a background of soil and grass are seen to advantage against stone and gravel.

SEE ALSO

◁ Details for:
Concrete mixes	227
Paving slabs	232
Finishing concrete	231

A paved patio
A paved area surrounded by stone or brick walls makes a perfect suntrap for swimming and relaxing.

Designing paved areas

The marriage of different materials offers numerous possibilities. It may be convenient to define areas of paving as paths, drives and patios, but they are only names to describe the function of those particular spaces in the garden. There is no reason why you cannot blend one area into another using the same material throughout, or use similar colours to link one type of paving with another. On the other hand, you could take a completely different approach and deliberately juxtapose coarse and smooth textures, or use pale and dark tones to make one space stand out from the next.

Having so many choices at your disposal does have its drawbacks. There is a strong temptation to experiment with any and every combination until the end result is a distracting mishmash. A few well-chosen materials which complement the house and its surroundings produce an environment which is not only more appealing in the short term, but actually improves as the garden matures.

Working with concrete

Concrete might not be everybody's first choice for paving a garden, but it is such a versatile material that you may not even be aware of its use. When it is cast into paving slabs (◁), for instance, it can be mistaken for natural stone, or you might be more aware of the geometric pattern created by the combination of individual units rather than the material itself. Even ordinary concrete can be finished with a surprising variety of textures, and is incomparable as a material for the foundations of outbuildings or extensions.

THE INGREDIENTS OF CONCRETE

Concrete in its simplest form consists of cement and fine particles of stone – sand and pebbles – known as aggregate. The dry ingredients are mixed with water to create a chemical reaction with the cement which binds the aggregate into a hard, dense material. The initial hardening process takes place quite quickly. The mix becomes unworkable after a couple of hours depending on the temperature and humidity, but the concrete has no real strength for three to seven days. The process continues for up to a month, or as long as there is moisture present within the concrete. Moisture is essential to the reaction and the concrete must not dry out too quickly in the first few days.

CEMENT

Standard Portland cement, sold in 50kg (110 lb) bags from builders' merchants or DIY outlets, is used in the manufacture of concrete. In its dry condition, it is a fine, grey powder.

SAND

Sharp sand, a rather coarse and gritty material, constitutes part of the aggregate of a concrete mix. Don't buy fine builders' sand used for mortar, and avoid unwashed or beach sand, both of which contain impurities that could affect the quality of the concrete. Sharp sand is sold by the cubic metre (or cubic yard) from a builders' merchant, although it is perhaps more convenient to buy it in large plastic bags if you have to transport it by car or van.

COARSE AGGREGATE

Coarse aggregate is gravel or crushed stone composed of particles large enough to be retained by a 5mm (¼in) sieve up to a maximum size of 20mm (¾in) for normal use. Once again, it can be bought loose by the cubic metre (cubic yard) or in smaller quantities packed in plastic sacks.

PIGMENTS

Special pigments can be added, but it is difficult to guarantee an even colour from one batch of concrete to another.

COMBINED AGGREGATE

Naturally occurring sand and gravel mix, known as ballast, is sold as a combined aggregate for concreting. The proportion of sand to gravel is not guaranteed unless the ballast has been reconstituted to adjust the mix, and you may have to do it yourself. In any case, make sure it has been washed to remove impurities.

DRY-PACKED CONCRETE

You can buy dry cement, sand and aggregate mixed to the required proportions for making concrete. Choose the proportion that best suits the job you have in mind (◁). Concrete mix is sold in various size bags up to 50kg (110 lb). Available from the usual outlets, it is a more expensive way of buying the ingredients, but is a simple and convenient method of ordering exactly the amount you will need. Before you add water to the mix, make sure the ingredients are mixed thoroughly.

WATER

Use ordinary tap water to mix concrete, never river or sea water.

PVA ADMIXTURE

You can buy a PVA admixture from builders' merchants to make a smoother concrete mix which is less susceptible to frost damage. Follow manufacturers' instructions for its use.

MIXING CONCRETE

You can hire small mixing machines if you have to prepare a large volume of concrete, but for the average job it is just as convenient to mix concrete by *hand. It isn't necessary to weigh out the ingredients when mixing concrete. Simply mix them by volume, choosing the proportions that suit the job in hand.*

Mixing by hand

Use large buckets to measure the ingredients, one for the cement and an identical one for the aggregate, in order to keep the cement perfectly dry. Different shovels are also a good idea. Measure the materials accurately, levelling them with the rim of the bucket. Tap the side of the bucket with the shovel as you load it with sand or cement to shake down the loose particles.

Mix the sand and aggregate first on a hard flat surface. Scoop a depression in the pile for the measure of cement, and mix all the ingredients until they form an even colour.

1 Mixing ingredients
Mix the ingredients by chopping the concrete mix with the shovel. Turn the mix over and chop again.

Form another depression and add some water from a watering can. Push the dry ingredients into the water from around the edge until surface water is absorbed, then mix the batch by chopping the concrete with the shovel (**1**). Add more water, turning concrete from the bottom of the pile and chop it as before until the whole batch has an even consistency. To test the workability of the mix, form a series of ridges by dragging the back of the shovel across the pile (**2**). The surface of the concrete should be flat and even in texture, and the ridges should hold their shape without slumping.

2 Testing the mix
Make ridges with the back of the shovel to text the workability of the mix.

Mixing by machine

Make sure you set up the concrete mixer on a hard, level surface and that the drum is upright before you start the motor. Use a bucket to pour half the measure of coarse aggregate into the drum and add water. This will clean the drum after each batch has been mixed. Add the sand and cement alternately in small batches, plus the rest of the aggregate. Add water little by little along with the other ingredients.

Let the batch mix for a few minutes. Then, with the drum of the mixer still rotating, turn out a little concrete into a wheelbarrow to test its consistency (See above). If necessary, return the concrete to the mixer to adjust it.

Storing materials

If you buy sand and coarse aggregate in sacks, simply use whatever you need at a time, keeping the rest bagged up until required. If you buy them loose, store sand and aggregate in piles, separated by a wooden plank if necessary, on a hard surface or thick polythene sheets. Protect the materials from prolonged rain with weighted sheets of plastic.

Storing cement is more critical. It is sold in paper sacks which will absorb moisture from the ground, so pile them on a board propped up on battens. Keep cement in a dry shed or garage if possible, but if you have to store it outdoors cover the bags with sheets of plastic weighted down with bricks. Once open, cement can absorb moisture from the air. Keep a partly used bag in a sealed plastic sack.

MACHINE SAFETY

- Make sure you understand the operating instructions before turning on the machine.
- Prop the mixer level and stable with blocks of wood.
- Never put your hands or shovel into the drum while the mixer is running.
- Don't lean over a rotating drum when you inspect the contents. It is good practice to wear goggles when mixing concrete.

READY-MIXED CONCRETE

If you need a lot of concrete for a driveway or large patio it may be worth ordering a supply of ready-mixed concrete from a local supplier. Always speak to the supplier well before you need the concrete to discuss your particular requirements. Specify the proportions of the ingredients and say whether you will require the addition of a retarding agent to slow down the setting time. Once a normal mix of concrete is delivered, you will have no more than two hours to finish the job. A retarding agent can add up to two hours to the setting time. Tell the supplier what you need the concrete for and accept his advice.

For quantities of less than 6cu m (6cu yd) you might have to shop around for a supplier who is willing to deliver without an additional charge. Discuss any problems of discharging the concrete on site. To avoid transporting the concrete too far by wheelbarrow, have it discharged as close to the site as possible, if not directly into place. The chute on a delivery truck can reach only so far, and if the truck is too large or heavy to drive onto your property you will need several helpers to move the quantity of concrete while it is still workable. A single cubic metre of concrete will fill 25 to 30 large wheelbarrows. If it takes longer than 30 to 40 minutes to discharge the load, you may have to pay extra.

SEE ALSO

Details for: ▷	
Calculating quantities	227
Cleaning equipment	227
Laying concrete	228-231

● **Professional mixing**
There are companies who will deliver concrete ingredients and mix them to your specification on the spot. All you have to do is barrow the concrete and pour it into place. There is no waste as you only pay for the concrete you use. Telephone a local company for details on price and minimum quantity.

Storing sand and aggregate
Separate the piles of sand and aggregate with a wooden plank

Storing cement
Raise bags of cement off the ground and cover them with plastic sheeting.

DESIGNING CONCRETE PAVING

The idea of having to design simple concrete pads and pathways might seem odd, but there are important factors to consider if the concrete is to be durable. At the least, you will have to decide on the thickness of the concrete to support the weight of traffic, and determine the angle of slope required to drain off surface water. When the area of concrete is large or a complicated shape, you must incorporate control joints to allow the material to expand and contract without cracking. If a pad is to support a habitable building, it must include a damp-proof membrane to prevent moisture rising from the ground. Even the proportions of sand, cement and coarse aggregate used in the concrete mix must be considered carefully to suit the function of the paving (see opposite).

SEE ALSO

◁ Details for:
Control joints	230-231
Laying sub-base	229

Deciding on the slope

In theory, a free-standing pad can be laid perfectly level, especially when it is supporting a small outbuilding, but, in fact, a very slight slope or fall prevents water collecting in puddles if you have failed to get the concrete absolutely flat. When a pad is laid directly against a house, it must have a definite fall away from the building, and any parking area or drive must shed water to provide adequate traction for vehicles and to minimize the formation of ice. When concrete is laid against a building, it must be at least 150mm (6in) below the existing damp-proof course.

USE OF PAVING	ANGLE OF FALL
Pathways	Not required
Drive	1 in 40 25mm per metre 1in per yard
Patio Parking space	1 in 60 away from building 16mm per metre ⅝in per yard
Outbuildings	1 in 80 towards the door 12·5mm per metre ½in per yard

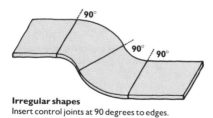

Irregular shapes
Insert control joints at 90 degrees to edges.

RECOMMENDED THICKNESSES FOR CONCRETE

The normal thicknesses recommended for concrete paving assumes it will be laid on a firm subsoil, but if the soil is clay or peat, increase the thickness by about 50 per cent. The same applies to a new site where the soil might not be compacted. Unless the concrete is for pedestrian traffic only, lay a sub-base of compacted hardcore below the paving. This will absorb ground movement without affecting the concrete itself. A sub-base is not essential for a very lightweight structure like a small wooden shed, but as you might want to increase the weight at some time, it is wise to install a sub-base at the outset.

PATHWAYS

For pedestrian traffic only
Concrete: 75mm (3in)
Sub-base: Not needed

PATIOS

Any extensive area of concrete for pedestrian traffic
Concrete: 100mm (4in)
Sub-base: 100mm (4in)

DRIVEWAYS

A drive which is used for an average family car only
Concrete: 100mm (4in)
Sub-base: 100mm (4in)
For heavier vehicles like delivery trucks
Concrete: 150mm (6in)
Sub-base: 100mm (4in)

LIGHT STRUCTURES

A support pad for a wooden shed, coal bunker and so on
Concrete: 75mm (3in)
Sub-base: 75mm (3in)

PARKING SPACES

Exposed paving for parking family car
Concrete: 100mm (4in)
Sub-base: 100mm (4in)

GARAGES

Thicken up the edges of a garage pad to support the weight of the walls
Concrete:
Floor: 100mm (4in)
Edges: 200mm (8in)
Sub-base:
Minimum 100mm (4in)

Allowing for expansion

Change in temperature causes concrete to expand and contract. If this movement is allowed to happen at random, a pad or pathway will crack at the weakest or most vulnerable point. A control joint, composed of a compressible material (◁), will absorb the movement or concentrate the force in predetermined areas where it does little harm. Joints should meet the sides of a concrete area at more or less 90 degrees. Always place a control joint between concrete and a wall, and around inspection chambers.

Positioning control joints
The position of control joints depends on the area and shape of the concrete.

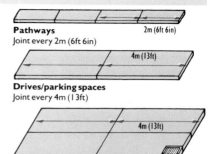

Pathways　　　　　　2m (6ft 6in)
Joint every 2m (6ft 6in)

Drives/parking spaces
Joint every 4m (13ft)

Concrete pads
Joints no more than 4m (13ft) apart and around inspection chambers.

Divide a pad into equal bays if:
● Length is more than twice the width.
● Longest dimension is more than 40 x thickness.
● Longest dimension exceeds 4m (13ft).

CALCULATING QUANTITIES OF CONCRETE

Estimate the amount of materials you require by calculating the volume of concrete in the finished pad, path or drive. Measure the surface area of the site and multiply that figure by the thickness of the concrete.

Estimating quantities of concrete

Use the gridded diagram to estimate the volume of concrete by reading off the area of the site in square metres (square yards) and trace it across horizontally to meet the angled line indicating the thickness of the concrete. Trace the line up to find the volume in cubic metres (cubic yards).

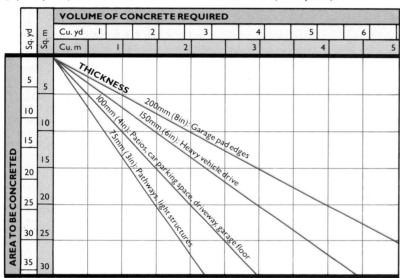

Estimating quantities of ingredients

Use the bar charts to estimate how much cement, sand and aggregate is needed to mix up the volume of concrete worked out by using the chart above.

The figures are based on the amount of ingredients used to mix one cubic metre of concrete using a particular type of mix (See below) plus about 10 per cent for wastage.

CUBIC METRES OF CONCRETE	1.00	1.50	2.00	2.50	3.00	3.50	4.00	4.50	5.00
GENERAL-PURPOSE MIX									
Cement (50kg bags)	7.00	10.50	14.00	17.50	21.00	24.50	28.00	31.50	35·00
Sand (Cubic metres)	0.50	0.75	1.00	1.25	1.50	1.75	2.00	2.25	2.50
Aggregate (Cubic metres)	0.75	1·15	1.50	1.90	2.25	2.65	3.00	3.40	3.75
Ballast (Cubic metres)	0.90	1.35	1.80	2.25	2.70	3.15	3.60	4.05	4.50
FOUNDATION MIX									
Cement (50kg bags)	6.00	9.00	12.00	15.00	18.00	21.00	24.00	27.00	30.00
Sand (Cubic metres)	0.55	0.80	1.10	1.40	1.65	1.95	2.20	2.50	2.75
Aggregate (Cubic metres)	0.75	1.15	1.50	1.90	2.25	2.65	3.00	3.40	3.75
Ballast (Cubic metres)	1.00	1.50	2.00	2.50	3.00	3.50	4.00	4.50	5.00
PAVING MIX									
Cement (50kg bags)	9.00	13.50	18.00	22.50	27.00	31.50	36.00	40.50	45.00
Sand (Cubic metres)	0.45	0.70	0.90	1.15	1.35	1.60	1.80	2.00	2.25
Aggregate (Cubic metres)	0.75	1.15	1.50	1.90	2.25	2.65	3.00	3.40	3.75
Ballast (Cubic metres)	1.00	1.50	2.00	2.50	3.00	3.50	4.00	4.50	5.00

CALCULATING AREAS

Squares and rectangles
Calculate the area of rectangular paving by multiplying width by length :

Example:
2m × 3m = 6 sq m
78in × 117in = 9126 sq in or 7 sq yd

Circles
Use the formula πr^2 to calculate the area of a circle. $\pi = 3.14$. r = radius of circle.

Example
$3.14 \times 2m^2 = 3.14 \times 4 = 12.56$sq m
$3.14 \times 78in^2 = 3.14 \times 6084 = 19104$sq in or 14.75 sq yd

Irregular shapes
Draw an irregular area of paving on squared paper. Count the whole squares and average out the portions to find the approximate area.

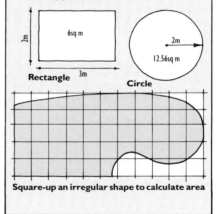

Rectangle 3m   **Circle** 12.56sq m   6sq m   2m

Square-up an irregular shape to calculate area

CLEANING TOOLS AND MACHINERY

Keep the shovel as clean as possible between mixing batches of concrete, and at the end of a working day wash all traces of concrete from your tools and wheelbarrow.

When you have finished using a concrete mixer, add a few shovels of coarse aggregate and a little water, then run the machine for a couple of minutes to scour the inside of the drum. Dump the aggregate, then hose out the drum with clean water.

Shovel unused concrete into sacks ready for disposal at a refuse dump and wash the mixing area with a stiff broom. Never hose concrete or any of the separate ingredients into a drain.

SEE ALSO

Details for: ▷
Mixing concrete   225

LAYING A CONCRETE PAD

Laying a simple pad as a base for a small shed or similar structure involves all the basic principles of concreting: building a retaining formwork, as well as the pouring, levelling and finishing of concrete. As long as the base is less than 2m (6ft 6in) square, there is no need to include control joints.

SEE ALSO

◁ Details for:	
Pad thickness	**226**
Crossfall	**226**
Control joints	226
Finishing concrete	231

Mixing concrete by volume

Mixing the ingredients by volume is the easiest and most accurate way to guarantee the required proportions. Whatever container you use to measure the ingredients – shovel, bucket, wheelbarrow – the proportions remain the same.

MIXING CONCRETE BY VOLUME		
Type of mix	Proportions	For I cu m concrete
GENERAL PURPOSE		
Use in most situations including covered pads other than garage floors	I part cement	6.4 bags (50kg)
	2 parts sand	0.448 cu m
	3 parts aggregate	0.672 cu m
	4 parts ballast	0.896 cu m
FOUNDATION		
Use for footings at the base of masonry walls	I part cement	5.6 bags (50kg)
	2½ parts sand	0.49 cu m
	3½ parts aggregate	0.686 cu m
	5 parts ballast	0.98 cu m
PAVING		
Use for exposed pads such as drives, parking areas or footpaths, but also for garage floors	I part cement	8 bags (50kg)
	1½ parts sand	0.42 cu m
	2½ parts aggregate	0.7 cu m
	3½ parts ballast	0.98 cu m

Excavating the site

Mark out the area of the pad with string lines attached to pegs driven into the ground outside the work area (**1**). Remove them to excavate the site but replace them later to help position the formwork which will hold the concrete in place.

Remove the topsoil and all vegetable matter within the site down to a level which allows for the combined thickness of concrete and sub-base (◁). Extend the area of excavation about 150mm (6in) outside the space allowed for the pad. Cut back any roots you encounter. Put the turf aside to cover the infill surrounding the completed pad. Level the bottom of the excavation by dragging a board across it (**2**), and compact the soil with a garden roller.

Erecting the formwork

Until the concrete sets hard it must be supported all round by formwork. For a straightforward rectangular pad, construct the formwork from 25mm (1in) thick softwood planks set on edge. The planks, which must be as wide as the finished depth of concrete, are held in place temporarily with stout 50 x 50mm (2x2in) wooden stakes. Second-hand or sawn timber is quite adequate. If it is slightly thinner than 25mm (1in), just use more stakes to brace it. If you have to join planks, butt them end to end, nailing a cleat on the outside (**3**).

Using the string lines as a guide, erect one board at the 'high' end of the pad, and drive stakes behind it at about 1m (3ft) intervals or less, with one for each corner. The tops of the stakes and board must be level and correspond exactly to the proposed surface of the pad. Nail the board to the stakes (**4**).

Set up another board opposite, but before you nail it to the stakes, establish the crossfall (◁) with a straightedge and spirit level. Work out the difference in level from one end of the pad to the other. For example, a pad which is 2m (6ft 6in) long should drop 25mm (1in) over that distance. Tape a shim of timber to one end of the straightedge, and with the shim resting on the 'low' stakes, place the other end on the opposite board (**5**). Drive home each low stake until the spirit level reads horizontal. Then nail the board flush with the tops of the stakes.

Erect the sides of the formwork, allowing the ends of the boards to overshoot the corners to make it easier to dismantle them when the concrete has set (**6**). Use the straightedge, this time without the shim, to level the boards across the formwork.

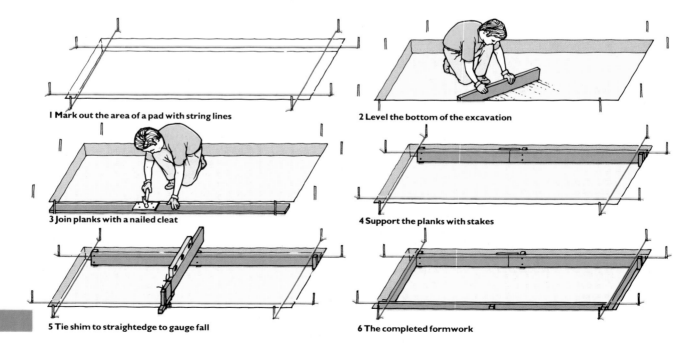

I Mark out the area of a pad with string lines

2 Level the bottom of the excavation

3 Join planks with a nailed cleat

4 Support the planks with stakes

5 Tie shim to straightedge to gauge fall

6 The completed formwork

LAYING A CONCRETE PAD

Laying the sub-base

Hoggin, a mixture of gravel and sand, is an ideal material for a sub-base, but you can use crushed stone or brick as long as you throw out any plaster, scrap metal or similar rubbish. Also remove large lumps of masonry as they will not compact well. Pour hardcore into the formwork and rake it fairly level before tamping it down with a heavy balk of timber (**7**). Break up any stubborn lumps with a heavy hammer. Fill in low spots with more hardcore or sharp sand until the sub-base comes up to the underside of the formwork boards.

Filling with concrete

Mix the concrete as near to the site as is practicable and transport the fresh mix to the formwork in a wheelbarrow. Set up firm runways of scaffold boards if the ground is soft, especially around the perimeter of the formwork. Dampen the sub-base and formwork with a fine spray and let surface water evaporate before tipping the concrete in place. Start filling from one end of the site and push the concrete firmly into the corners (**8**). Rake it level until the concrete stands about 18mm (¾in) above the level of the boards.

Tamp down the concrete with the edge of a 50mm (2in) thick plank long enough to span across the formwork. Starting at one end of the site, compact the concrete with steady blows of the plank, moving it along by about half its thickness each time (**9**). Cover the whole area twice, then remove excess concrete using the plank with a sawing action (**10**). Fill any low spots, then compact and level once more.

Cover the pad with sheets of polythene, taped at the joints to retain the moisture and weighted down with bricks around the edge (**11**). Alternatively, use wet sacking which you must keep damp for three days using a fine spray. Try to avoid laying concrete in very cold weather, but if it is unavoidable, spread a layer of earth or sand on top of the sheeting to insulate the concrete from frost. You can walk on the concrete after three days but leave it for about a week before removing the formwork and erecting a shed or similar outbuilding.

SEE ALSO

Details for: ▷
Mixing concrete   225

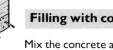

Extending a pad
If you want to enlarge a patio, simply butt a new section of concrete against the existing pad. The butt joint will form a control joint. To add a narrow strip, for a larger shed for instance, drill holes in the edge of the pad and use epoxy adhesive to glue in short reinforcing rods before pouring the fresh concrete.

Finishing the edges
If any of the edges are exposed, the sharp corners might cause a painful injury. Radius the corners with a home-made edging float. Bend a piece of sheet metal over an 18mm (¾in) diameter rod or tube and screw a handle in the centre. Run the float along the formwork as you finish the surface of the concrete.

7 Level hardcore base with a heavy balk of timber

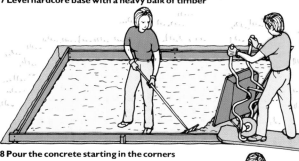

8 Pour the concrete starting in the corners

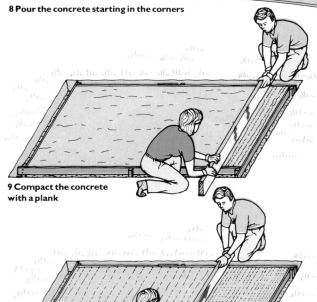

9 Compact the concrete with a plank

10 Use a sawing action to remove excess concrete

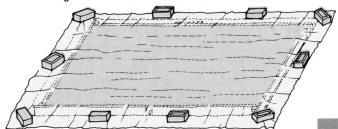

11 Cover the pad with weighted sheets of plastic

LAYING PATHS AND DRIVES

Paths and drives are laid and compacted in the same way as simple rectangular pads, using similar formwork to contain the fresh concrete, but the proportions of most paths and drives necessitate the inclusion of control joints to allow for expansion and contraction (◁). You must install a sub-base beneath a drive, but a footpath can be laid on compacted soil levelled with sharp sand. Establish a slight fall across the site to shed rainwater (◁). Don't use a vehicle on concrete for 10 days after laying.

SEE ALSO

◁ Details for:
Control joints	**226**
Fall across site	**226**
Formwork	**228**
Pad thickness	226
Tamping concrete	229

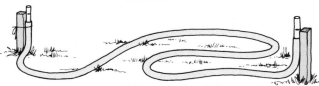
I A water level made from a garden hose

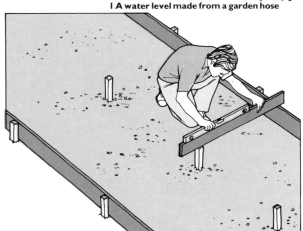
2 Level the formwork using a datum peg

A sloping drive
If you build a drive on a sloping site, make the transition from level ground as gentle as possible. If it runs towards a garage, let the last 2m (6ft) slope up towards the door. Use a pole to impress a drain across the wet concrete at the lowest point.

DRAIN

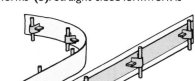
5 Support board with concrete and nails

6 Make a dummy joint with T-section metal

Setting out paths and drives

Excavate the site, allowing for the thickness of sub-base and concrete. Level the bottom of the excavation as accurately as you can, using a board to scrape the surface flat.

Drive accurately levelled pegs into the ground along the site to act as datum points for the formwork. Space them about 2m (6ft 6in) apart down the centre of the pathway. Drive in the first peg until its top corresponds exactly to the proposed surface of the concrete. Use a long straightedge and spirit level to position every other peg or, better still, use a home-made water level. Push a short length of transparent plastic tubing into each end of an ordinary garden hose. Fill the hose with water until it appears in the tube at both ends. As long as the ends remain open, the water level at each end is constant so that you can establish a level over any distance, even around obstacles or corners. Tie one end of the hose to the first datum peg so that the water level aligns with the top of the peg. Use the other to establish the level of every other peg along the pathway (**1**). Cork each end of the hose to retain the water as you move it.

To set a fall with a water level, make a mark on one tube below the surface of the water and use that as a gauge for the top of the peg.

Erecting formwork

Construct formwork from 25mm (1in) thick planks as for a concrete pad (◁). To check it is level, rest a straightedge on the nearest datum peg (**2**).

If the drive or path is very long, timber formwork can be expensive. It might be cheaper to hire metal 'road forms' (**3**). Straight-sided formwork is made from rigid units, but flexible sections are available to form curves.

If you want to bend wooden formwork, make a series of parallel saw cuts across the width of the plank in the area of the curve (**4**). The timber is less likely to snap if you place the saw cuts on the inside of the bend.

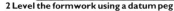
3 Curved and straight road forms

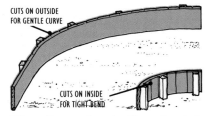
CUTS ON OUTSIDE FOR GENTLE CURVE

CUTS ON INSIDE FOR TIGHT BEND
4 Curved formwork made with wooden planks

Installing control joints

Install a permanent expansion joint every 2m (6ft 6in) for a footpath and every 4m (13ft) along a drive. Cut strips of rot-proof treated hardboard or 12mm (½in) thick softwood to fit exactly between the formwork and to match the depth of the concrete. Before pouring, hold the control joints in place with mounds of concrete and nails on each side of the board driven into the formwork (**5**). Pack more concrete carefully on each side of the joints as you fill the formwork and tamp towards them from both sides so that they are not dislodged.

As the joints are permanent fixtures, make sure they are level with the surface of the concrete. Install similar joints in a patio or use an alternate bay construction (See opposite page).

To prevent concrete cracking between joints on a narrow path, cut 18mm (¾in) deep grooves across the compacted concrete to form dummy joints alternating with the physical ones. The simplest method is to cut a length of T-section metal to fit between the formwork boards. Place it on the surface of the wet concrete and tap it down with a mallet (**6**). Carefully lift the strip out of the concrete to leave a neat impression. If the concrete should move, a crack will develop unnoticed at the bottom of the groove.

Place strips of thick bituminous felt between concrete and an adjoining wall to absorb expansion. Hold the felt in place with mounds of concrete, as described left, before pouring the full amount of concrete.

ALTERNATE BAY METHOD OF CONSTRUCTION

It is not always possible to lay all the concrete in one operation. In such cases it is easier to divide the formwork crosswise with additional planks known as stop ends to form equal-size bays. By filling alternate bays with concrete, you have plenty of time to compact and level each section and more room in which to manoeuvre. It is a convenient way to lay a large patio which would be practically impossible to compact and level in one go, and it is the only method to use for drives or paths butting against a wall which makes it impossible to work across the width. Alternate bay construction is often used for drives on a steep slope to prevent heavy, wet concrete slumping downhill.

There is no need to install physical control joints as the simple butt joint between the bays is sufficient allowance for movement within the concrete

Concreting alternate bays
Stand in the empty bays to compact concrete laid against a wall. When the first bays are set hard, remove the stop ends and fill the gaps, using the surface of the firm concrete as a level.

INSPECTION CHAMBERS

Prevent expansion damaging an inspection chamber by surrounding it with control joints. Place formwork around the chamber and fill with concrete. When set, remove the boards and place felt strips or rot-proof treated softwood boards on all sides.

Surround inspection chamber with formwork

SURFACE FINISHES FOR CONCRETE

The surface finishes produced by tamping or striking off with a sawing action are perfectly adequate for a skid-proof, workmanlike surface for a pad, drive or pathway, but you can produce a range of other finishes using simple handtools once you have compacted and levelled the concrete.

Float finishes
Smooth the tamped concrete by sweeping a wooden float across the surface, or make an even finer texture by finishing with a trowel (steel float). Let the concrete dry out a little before using a float or you will bring water to the top and weaken it, eventually resulting in a dusty residue on the hardened concrete. Bridge the formwork with a stout plank so that you can reach the centre, or hire a skip float with a long handle for large pads.

Make a smooth finish with a wooden float

Brush finishes
Make a finely textured surface by drawing a yard broom across the setting concrete. Flatten the concrete initially with a wooden float, then make parallel passes with the broom held at a low angle to avoid 'tearing' the surface.

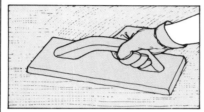

Texture the surface with a broom

Brush-finishing concrete

Exposed-aggregate finish
Embedding small stones or pebbles in the surface makes a very attractive and practical finish but it takes a little practice to be successful.

Scatter dampened pebbles onto the freshly laid concrete and tamp them firmly with a length of timber until they are flush with the surface (**1**). Place a plank across the formwork and apply your full weight to make sure the surface is even. Leave the concrete to harden for a while until all surface water has evaporated, then use a very fine spray and a brush to wash away the cement from around the pebbles until they protrude (**2**). Cover the concrete for about 24 hours, then lightly wash the surface again to clean any sediment off the actual pebbles. Cover the concrete again and leave it to harden thoroughly.

1 Tamp pebbles into the fresh concrete

2 Wash the cement from around the pebbles

Exposed-aggregate finish

SEE ALSO

Details for: ▷	
Preservatives	47
Control joints	226
Tamping concrete	229

PAVING SLABS

If your only experience of paving slabs is the rather bland variety used for public footpaths, then cast concrete paving may not seem a very attractive proposition for a garden. However, manufacturers can supply more pleasing products in a wide range of shapes, colours and finishes.

SEE ALSO

◁ Details for:
Brick pavers   235

Colours and textures

Paving slabs are made by hydraulic pressing or casting in moulds to create the desired surface finish. Pigments and selected aggregates added to the concrete mix create the illusion of natural stone or a range of muted colours. Combining two or more colours within the same area of paving can be very striking.

1 Cobbles or sets
Large slabs resemble an area of smaller cobbles or sets. Careful laying and filling are essential. Sets are 'laid' in straight rows or as curves.

2 Planter
Four planter stones laid in a square leave a circle for a tree or shrub.

3 Exposed aggregate
Crushed stone aggregate has a very pleasing mottled appearance, either exposed to make a coarse gritstone texture or polished flat to resemble terrazzo.

4 Brushed finishes
A brush-finished slab, textured with parallel grooves as if a stiff broom had been dragged across the wet concrete, is practical and non-slip. Straight or swirling patterns are available.

5 Riven stone
The finish resembles that of natural stone. The best-quality slabs are cast from real stone originals in a wide variety of subtle textures. If the texture continues over the edge of the slabs, they can be used for steps and coping.

SHAPES AND SIZES

Although some manufacturers offer a wider choice than others, there is a fairly standard range of shapes and modular sizes. You can carry the largest slabs single-handed, but it is a good idea to have an assistant when manoeuvring them carefully into place.

Square and rectangular
One size and shape make grid-like patterns or, staggered, create a bonded brickwork effect. Rectangular slabs can form a basket-weave or herringbone pattern. Or, combine different sizes to create the impression of random paving.

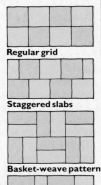

Regular grid

Staggered slabs

Basket-weave pattern

Herringbone pattern   **Random paving**

Hexagonal
Hexagonal slabs form honeycomb patterns. Use half slabs, running across flats or from point to point, to edge areas paved in straight lines.

Half-hexagonal slabs

Hexagonal slab   **Honeycomb pattern**

Tapered slabs
Use tapered slabs to edge ponds, around trees, and for curved paths or steps. Lay them head to toe to make straight sections of paving. Use right- or left-handed half slabs at the ends.

Full and half-tapered slabs

Straight section

Circular
Circular slabs make perfect individual stepping stones across a lawn or flower bed, but for a wide area fill the spaces between with cobbles or gravel.

Butted circular slabs

LAYING PAVING SLABS

Laying heavy paving slabs involves a fair amount of physical labour, but in terms of technique it is no more complicated than tiling a wall. Accurate setting out and careful laying, especially during the early stages, will produce perfect results. Take extra care when laying hexagonal slabs to ensure that the last few slabs fit properly.

CUTTING CONCRETE SLABS

Mark a line across a slab with a soft pencil or chalk. Then, using a bolster and hammer, chisel a groove about 3mm (⅛in) deep following the line (1). Continue the groove down both edges and across the underside of the slab. Place the slab on a bed of sand and put a block of wood at one end of the groove. Strike the block with a hammer while moving it along the groove until a split develops through the slab (2). Clean up the rough edge with a bolster.

For a perfectly clean cut each time, hire an angle grinder fitted with a stone-cutting disc. Score a deep groove on both sides of the slab and across the edges. Tap along the groove with a bolster to propagate a crack.

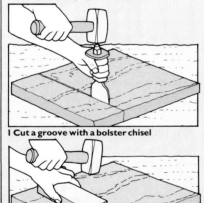

1 Cut a groove with a bolster chisel

2 Strike block over groove with a hammer

Setting out the area of paving

Wherever possible, to eliminate the arduous task of cutting units to fit, plan an area of paving to be laid with whole slabs only. Use a straight wall as a datum line and measure away from it, or allow for a 100 to 150mm (4 to 6in) margin of gravel between the paving and wall if the location dictates that you have to lay slabs towards the house. A gravel margin not only saves time and money by using fewer slabs, but also provides an area for planting climbers and adequate drainage to keep the wall dry. Even so, establish a 16mm per metre (⅝in per yard) slope across the paving so that most surface water will drain into the garden. Any paving must be 150mm (6in) below a damp-proof course to protect the building.

As paving slabs are made to reasonably precise dimensions, marking out an area simply involves accurate measurement, allowing for a 6 to 8mm (¼in) gap between slabs. Some slabs are cast with sloping edges to provide a tapered joint (1) and should be butted edge to edge. Use pegs and string to mark out the perimeter of the paved area, and check your measurements before you excavate.

Preparing a base for paving

Paving slabs must be laid upon a firm, level base, but the depth and substance of that base depends on the type of soil and the proposed use of the paving.

For straightforward patios and paths, remove vegetable matter and topsoil to allow for the thickness of the slabs and a 25mm (1in) layer of sharp sand. Set the paving about 18mm (¾in) below the level of surrounding turf to avoid damaging the lawn mower when you cut the grass. Having compacted the soil using a garden roller, spread the sand with a rake and level it by scraping and tamping with a length of timber (2).

To support heavier loads, or if the soil is composed of clay or peat, lay a sub-base (▷) of firmly compacted hardcore – broken bricks or crushed stone – to a depth of 75 to 100mm (3 to 4in) before spreading the sand to level the surface.

If you plan to park vehicles on the paving, then increase the depth of hardcore to 150mm (6in).

Laying the paving slabs

Set up string lines again as a guide and lay the edging slabs on the sand, working in both directions from a corner. When you are satisfied with their positions, lift them one at a time and set them on a bed of mortar (1 part cement: 4 parts sand). Add just enough water to make a firm mortar. Lay a fist-size blob under each corner and one more to support the centre of the slab (3). If you intend to drive vehicles across the slabs, lay a continuous bed of mortar about 50mm (2in) thick.

Lay three slabs at a time with 6mm (¼in) wooden spacers between. Level each slab by tapping with a heavy hammer, using a block of wood (4). Check the alignment.

Gauge the slope across the paving by setting up datum pegs along the high side (▷). Drive them into the ground until the top of each corresponds to the finished surface of the paving, then use the straightedge to check the fall on the slabs (5). Lay the remainder of the slabs, working out from the corner each time to keep the joints square. Remove the spacers before the mortar sets.

SEE ALSO

Details for: ▷
Paving slope	226
Sub-base	226, 229

1 Tapered joint

2 Level the sand base

3 Lay blobs of mortar

4 Level the slabs

5 Check the fall with a spirit level

Filling the joints

Don't walk on the paving for two to three days until the mortar has set. If you have to cross the area, lay planks across the slabs to spread the load.

To fill the gaps between the slabs, brush a dry mortar mix of 1 part cement: 3 parts sand into the open joints (6). Remove any surplus material from the surface of the paving, then sprinkle the area with a very fine spray of water to consolidate the mortar. Avoid dry mortaring if heavy rain is imminent; it may wash the mortar out.

6 Fill the joints

LAYING CRAZY PAVING

SEE ALSO

◁ Details for:
Mixing mortar	215
Trimming slabs	233

The informal nature of paths or patios laid with irregular-shaped paving stones has always been popular. The random jig-saw effect, which many people find more appealing than the geometric accuracy of neatly laid slabs, is also very easy to achieve. A good eye for shape and proportion is more important than a practised technique.

Materials for crazy paving

You can use broken concrete slabs if you can find enough but, in terms of appearance, nothing compares with natural riven stone. Stratified rock which splits into thin layers of its own accord as it is quarried is ideal for crazy paving, and can be obtained at a very reasonable price if you can collect it yourself. Select stones which are approximately 40 to 50mm (1½ to 2in) thick in a variety of shapes and sizes.

Crazy paving made with broken concrete slabs

SETTING OUT AND LAYING A BASE

You can, if you wish, set out string lines to define straight edges to crazy paving although they will never be as precisely defined as those formed with cast concrete slabs. Or, allow the stones to form a broken irregular junction with grass or shingle, perhaps setting one or two individual stones out from the edge of the paving to blend one area into the other.

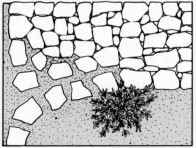

Create an irregular edge to crazy paving

Laying the stones

Arrange an area of stones, selecting them for a close fit but avoiding too many straight, continuous joints. Trim those that don't quite fit with a bolster and hammer. Reserve fairly large stones for the perimeter of the paved area as small stones tend to break away.

Use a mallet or block of wood and a hammer to bed each stone into the sand (**1**) until they are all perfectly stable and reasonably level. Having bedded an area of about 1sq m (1sq yd), use a straightedge and spirit level to true up the stones (**2**). If necessary, add or

1 Bed the stones in the sand base

3 Fill the gaps with small stones

remove sand beneath individual stones until the whole area is level. When the main area is complete, fill in the larger gaps with small stones, tapping them into place with a mallet (**3**).

Fill the joints by spreading more sand across the paving and sweeping it into the joints from all directions (**4**). Alternatively, mix up a stiff, almost dry, mortar and press it into the joints with a trowel, leaving no gaps.

Use an old paintbrush to smooth the mortared joints and wipe the stones clean with a damp sponge.

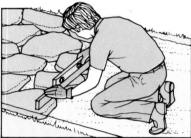

2 Check the level across several stones

4 Sweep dry sand into the joints

Laying stepping stones

Place individual stones or slabs across a lawn to form a row of stepping stones. Cut around the edge of each stone with a spade or trowel and remove the area of turf directly beneath. Scoop out the earth to allow for a 25mm (1in) bed of sharp sand plus the stone, which must be about 18mm (¾in) below the level of the surrounding turf. Tap the stone into the sand until it no longer rocks when you step on it.

Cut around a stepping stone with a trowel

Stepping stones preserve a lawn

BRICK PATTERNS

Concrete bricks have one surface face with chamfered edges all round, and spacers moulded into the sides to form accurate joints. Housebricks can be laid on edge or face down showing the wide face normally unseen in a wall.

Unlike brick walls, which must be bonded in a certain way for stability (▷), brick paths can be laid to any pattern that appeals to you.

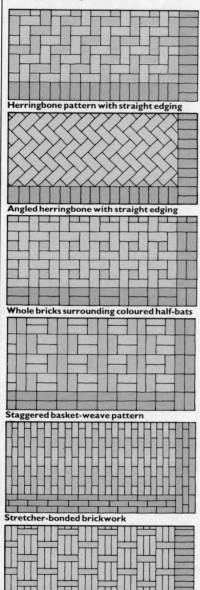

Herringbone pattern with straight edging

Angled herringbone with straight edging

Whole bricks surrounding coloured half-bats

Staggered basket-weave pattern

Stretcher-bonded brickwork

Cane-weave pattern

PAVING WITH BRICKS

Bricks make charming and attractive paths. The wide variety of textures and colours available gives endless *possibilities of pattern, but choose the type of brick carefully, bearing in mind the sort of use your paving can expect.*

Materials for brick paving

Ordinary housebricks are often selected for paths, and also small patios, even though there is the risk of spalling in freezing conditions unless they happen to be engineering bricks. The slightly uneven texture and colour are the very reasons why second-hand bricks in particular are so much in demand for garden paving, so a little frost damage is usually acceptable.

Housebricks are not really suitable if the paved area is to be a parking space or drive, especially if it is to be used by heavy vehicles. For a durable surface, even under severe conditions, use concrete bricks. They are slightly smaller than standard housebricks, being 200 x 100 x 65mm (8 x 4 x 2½in). Red or grey are widely available and you can obtain other colours by special order.

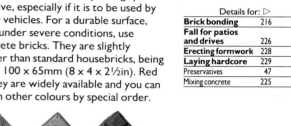

Providing a base for brick paving

Lay brick footpaths and patios on a 75mm (3in) hardcore base (▷) covered with a 50mm (2in) layer of sharp sand. To lay concrete bricks for a drive, increase the depth of hardcore to 100mm (4in).

Fully compact the hardcore and fill all voids so that sand from the bedding course is not lost to the sub-base.

Provide a cross-fall on patios and drives as for concrete (▷), and ensure the surface of the paving is at least 150mm (6in) below a damp-proof course to protect the building.

Retaining edges

Unless the brick path is laid against a wall or some similar structure, the edges of the paving must be contained by a permanent restraint. Timber, treated with a chemical preservative, is one solution, constructed like the formwork for concrete (▷). The edging boards should be flush with the surface of the path, but drive the stakes below ground so that they can be covered by soil or turf **(1)**.

As an alternative, set an edging of bricks in concrete **(2)**. Dig a trench deep and wide enough to accommodate a row of bricks on end plus a 100mm (4in) concrete 'foundation'. Lay the bricks while the concrete is still wet, holding them in place temporarily with a staked board while you pack more concrete behind the edging. When the concrete has set, remove the board and lay hardcore and sand in the excavation.

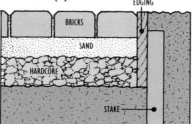

1 Wooden retaining edge

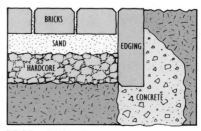

2 Brick retaining edge

SEE ALSO

Details for: ▷	
Brick bonding	216
Fall for patios and drives	226
Erecting formwork	228
Laying hardcore	229
Preservatives	47
Mixing concrete	225

Brick pavers
Clay brick pavers (top row) are made in a wide variety of colours and textures. *Concrete pavers* (bottom row) are less colourful but more shapes are available.

235

LAYING THE BRICKS

Having chosen your bricks, prepared the ground and set retaining edges (◁) you can start laying your paving. When bricks are first laid upon the sand they should project 10mm (⅜in) above the edging restraints to allow for bedding them in at a later stage (1). To level the sand for a path, cut a notched spreader to span the edging (2). If the paving is too wide for a spreader, lay levelling battens on the hardcore base and scrape the sand to the required depth using a straightedge (3). Remove the battens and fill the voids carefully with sand. Keep the sand bed dry at all times. If it rains before you can lay the bricks, either let the sand dry out thoroughly or replace it with dry sand.

Lay an area of bricks on the sand to your chosen pattern. Work from one end of the site, kneeling on a board placed across the bricks (4). Never stand on the bed of sand. Lay whole bricks only, leaving any gaps at the edges

to be filled with cut bricks after you have laid an area of about 1 to 2sq m (1 to 2sq yd). Concrete bricks have fixed spacers, so butt them together tightly.

Fill any remaining spaces with bricks cut with a bolster (◁). If you are paving a large area you can hire an hydraulic guillotine (see left).

When the area of paving is complete, tamp the bricks into the sand bed by striking a stout batten with a heavy club hammer. The batten must be large enough to cover several bricks to maintain the level (5). For a really professional finish, hire a powered plate vibrator. Pass the vibrator over the paved area two or three times until it has worked the bricks down into the sand and flush with the outer edging (6). The act of vibrating bricks works sand up between them, but complete the job by brushing more sand across the finished paving and vibrate the sand into the open joints.

SEE ALSO

◁ Details for:
Cutting bricks	218
Retaining edges	235
Brick pavers	235
Providing a base	235

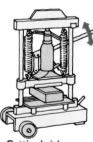

Cutting bricks
Hire an hydraulic brick-cutting guillotine to cut pavers.

1 Start by laying bricks 10mm above edging

2 Level the sand with a notched spreader

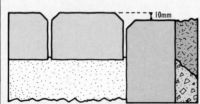

3 Or lay levelling battens on the hardcore

4 Lay the bricks to your chosen pattern

5 Tamp the bricks with a hammer and batten

6 A vibrator levels brick paving perfectly

Plain concrete-brick drive and parking space

Mottled-brick garden path

Interlocking concrete pavers

Bricks laid to a herringbone pattern

A

acoustic tiles 38
additives, paint 39
adhesives
  removing 38
  stainless steel 181
  tile 73, 76, 77, 78
aggregates 41, 224, 225, 231
air locks 171
alkali-resistant primers 23
aluminium, corrosion 37
aluminium spirit-based sealer 23
aluminium tape 106
aluminium wood primer 23
Anaglypta 60, 66
angle iron posts 210, 212
anti-siphon devices 207
arris rails 213
artificial respiration 129
asbestos cement 28, 102, 103
attics 115

B

banister brushes 42
base coat plasters 83, 85
basins 178, 193-6
bathrooms 19, 128, 153
baths
  bath enamel 197
  bath paints 57, 197
  bath/shower mixers 200
  installation 197-9
  panelling 199
  sealant 73
  taps 197
  types 197
batten holders 161
batteries, bell systems 158
bedrooms 17
bending, pipes 185, 189
bending springs 185
BESA boxes 162
bidets 203
binding, concrete 29
bituminous paint 57, 58
black lead 57, 58
blanket insulation 113, 114, 115
bleach 24, 32
blockages, clearing 178-180
blown fibre insulation 113
blowtorches 34, 36
bolts 97
bonding agents 85
booster pumps 200
border tiles 74, 76
bottle traps 178
branch pipes 178, 206
brass 37
  pipes 181
brick tiles 70
bricks and brickwork 24-8, 215-23, 235-6
  bonding 216, 221
  bricklayers' terms 215
  coping 216, 219, 220, 223
  cutting 218, 236
  laying 218-20, 235-6
  mortar 25, 215
  paving 235-6
  piers 216, 221-2, 223
  pointing 25, 220
  preparing to decorate 24-8
  preparing to plaster 84
  stretcher-bonded walls 219
brush seals 110, 111
bullnose tiles 73
burnishing 55
butt hinges 91

C

cables 140-3, 144, 149, 151
capillary joints 182
capping 210, 213
carlite plasters 83, 85
carpet tiles 70, 75, 77
cartridge fuses 133, 137, 138
casement locks 98
casement windows 50, 58, 98, 112
caulking compound 106
cavity walls 223
ceiling roses
  electrical connections 145, 160
  moulded, restoring 89
  painting behind 45
  papering around 68
  replacing 161
ceilings
  light fittings 161
  moulded 89
  painting 43-5
  papering 68
  repairing 31, 88, 89
  textured coatings 59
  tiles 38, 80
cellulose fillers 33
cement 224, 225
  asbestos 28, 102, 103
  paints 31, 40, 41, 43, 45
ceramic disc taps 194
ceramic tiles 38, 69, 72-4, 78
cesspools 180
chain link fences 212
chemical strippers 35, 36, 37
chimes 158
chimneys, stained 28
circuit breakers 127, 135, 137, 138, 166
cisterns
  maintenance 174-6
  see also cold water storage
    cisterns; WC cisterns
cleaning
  concrete 29
  concrete mixers 227
  masonry 24-5
  mouldings 31
  plasterwork 30
  tiles 38
closeboard fences 213
closed string stairs 101
cockspur handles 98
coiled flex 130
cold cure lacquers 46, 47, 48, 56
cold feed valves 169
cold water storage cisterns 168, 169
  draining 170
  installation 208
  insulating 114
  maintenance 174-6
cold water taps and pipes, draining 170
colour 8-9, 14
coloured preservers 46, 47, 48
compressed air guns 178
compression joints 182, 184, 187, 189
concave joints 220
concrete 29, 224-31
  block screen 223
  fence posts 210, 212, 214
  floors 29, 40, 41, 142
  formwork 228, 230
  ingredients 224
  laying 228-31
  mixing 225, 228
  pads 226-9
  paints 40, 41
  paths and drives 226, 230

paving 226, 232-4, 235
  preparing for plastering 84
  preparing and repairing 29
  quantities 227, 228
  ready-mixed 225
  surface finishes 231
condensation 105, 113, 115
connection units 152
connectors
  flex 132
  gunmetal 181
  pipes 182, 186, 189
consumer units 134, 136, 144, 151, 166
control joints 222, 226, 230
control units, cookers 155
cooker hoods 120, 154
cookers 125, 155-6
coping 216, 219, 220, 223
copper
  maintaining 37
  pipes 171, 181, 184, 185
  soldering 183
cork tiles 38, 71, 72, 75, 77
corners
  papering 64, 65
  repairing 31, 87
corrosion 36-7, 181
corrugated iron 37
corrugated sheet roofing 103
coverage
  finishes 40, 45, 48, 57
  plasters 85
  primers and sealers 23
cracks 26, 27, 29
crazy paving 234
Croydon pattern valves 175
cutting
  bricks 218, 236
  concrete slabs 233
  doors 90
  glass 92-3
  metal pipes 183
  slates 102
  soil pipes 191
  tiles 74, 76, 78, 79, 102
  wallcoverings 63
cutting-in brushes 50
cylinder rim locks 97
cylinders see hot water
  cylinders

D

damp 29, 105, 171
damp-proof course 216
decorating 20-80
  applying finishes 39-59
  means of access 20-2
  preparation and priming 23-38
  schemes 8-19
  tiling 69-80
  wallcoverings 60-8
diagonal tiling 75
dial meters 124
diaphragm valves 175, 176
digital meters 124
dimmer switches 163, 164
dining rooms 18
direct action WC cisterns 174
direct plumbing systems 168-9
dishwashers 125, 154, 206-7
distemper 31
doorbells 158
doors
  draughtproofing 108, 110
  fitting and hanging 90-1
  painting 48, 49
  papering around 65
  security fittings 97
  staining 53
  weatherproofing 91

weatherstripping edges 111
double glazing 108, 116-18
  demountable systems 117
  fitting extractor fans 122
  glazing positions 116
  hinged systems 118
  plastic materials 117
  renewable film 116
  sliding systems 118
downlighters 161, 162
downpipes 42, 58
drainage systems
  blockages 178-80
  cesspools and septic tanks 180
  maintenance 177
  rodding drains 180
  shower units 199
  types 168, 177, 192
draining the plumbing system 170-1
drainpipes, clearing 179
draught excluders 110
draughtproofing 108, 110-112
drilling, glass 93
drips 104
driveways 224-36
dry-lining 82
drying times
  finishes 40, 45, 48, 57
  primers and sealers 23
dual screws 98
dust particles 54

E

earth-leakage circuit breaker 135
earthing 126, 128, 135, 144
eaves 104
Economy 7 124, 157
efflorescence 24
eggshell paints 39
ELCBs 135
electric shock, first aid 129
electrical appliances 125, 152-9
  see also individual
    appliances eg cookers
electrical circuits
  basics 126
  bell systems 158
  checking 138
  cookers 155
  fuses 137-8
  immersion heaters 157
  lighting 139, 159-60, 165, 166
  power 146-51, 166
  radial 139, 151, 155
  ring 139, 149, 150, 151
  types 139
electrical fittings
  painting around 45, 59
  papering around 65, 68
  tiling around 74, 80
electricity 124-66
  assessing installation 144-5
  basics 126
  cables 140-3, 144, 149, 151
  circuit breakers 127, 135, 137, 138, 166
  colour-coding of wires 126
  conductors 126
  connection units 152
  consumer units 134, 136, 144, 151, 166
  earthing 126, 128, 135, 144
  economics 124-5, 157
  flex 130-2
  fuse boards 135, 144
  fuses 127, 133, 137-8, 145, 151
  lampholders 133, 161
  lighting 145, 159-65
  main switch equipment 134

measuring 127
meters 124, 134
off-peak 124, 157
plugs 133
regulations 126
safety 127-9, 132, 134
sockets 132, 144-5, 146-9, 150
switches 126, 144-5, 163-5
switchfuse units 156
terminals 131
Electricity Board 134, 135, 157
testing 127, 144, 156
electro-chemical action 181
electronic taps 194
emulsion paints 41, 43, 45, 57, 58
end-feed joints 183
English bond 216
epoxy putty 171
extenders
flex 132
paint 39
extension leads 132
exterior-grade emulsion paints
40, 41
extractor fans 121-2, 154
extractor hoods 120

F

fabric wallcoverings 61, 67
fans, extractor 121-2, 154
featherboards 213
felt roofing 104
fences and fence posts 210-14
fibre ceiling tiles 38
field tiles 69
filler boards 84
fillers
plaster 83, 85
repairing corners 31
wood 33
finish plasters 83, 85
finishes 39-59
see also individual finishes
eg paint
fireplaces 65, 87, 112, 119
first aid, electric shock 129
flaky paintwork 28, 34
flap valves 174
flashing tape 106
flashings 106
Flemish bond 216
flex 130-2
flex connectors 132
flex extenders 132
float arms 174, 176
float valves 169, 170, 175-6, 208
floats 174, 176
flock wallcoverings 61, 67
floor paints 40, 41
floors
concrete 29, 40, 41
draughtproofing 112
lifting floorboards 142
painting 40, 41
running cable 142, 143
staining 53
tiles 38, 75-9
varnishing 54
fluorescent lights 161, 163
flush doors 49
flush joints 25, 220
flux 183
foam strips 111
foamed polyethylene
wallcoverings 61, 67
foil wallcoverings 61, 67
footings 216, 217
formwork 228, 230
French polishing 47, 48, 55
French windows 50
fridges 125, 154

frozen pipes 171
fungicides 24
wallpaper pastes 63
fuse boards 135, 144
fuse carriers 137
fuse wire 137, 138
fused connection units 152
fuses 127, 151
cartridge 133, 137, 138
changing 138, 145
switchfuse units 156
types and ratings 137

G

galvanized metalwork 37
pipes 181, 184
gas torches 183
gate valves 170
gauge sticks 72
gel strippers 35
general-purpose primers 23
glands and seats 173
glass
buying 92
cutting and drilling 92-3
glazed roofs 106
in openable secondary glazing
systems 118
replacing in windows 94
see also double glazing
glass fibre wallcoverings 61, 67
glazing bars 50, 106
gloss emulsion paints 47, 48
gloss paints 39, 46
grain fillers 33
graining 51
grass cloth 61
gravel boards 213
grouting 72, 73, 78
growths, removing 24, 32
gullies 168, 169, 177, 179
gunmetal connectors 181
gutters 58
gypsum plasters 83

H

handles, cockspur 98
heat/light units 153
heated towel rails 125, 153
heaters 125, 153
water 125, 154, 156-7
hinge bolts 97
hinges 90-1
honeycomb bond 216
hot air strippers 35, 36
hot water cylinders 124, 156-7,
168, 169
draining 170
insulating 108, 109
hot water taps and pipes,
draining 170
hydrochloric acid 38

I

IEE Wiring Regulations 126,
128, 153
immersion heaters 125, 156-7
indirect plumbing systems 168-
9
industrial stripping 35
inspection chambers 177, 180,
231
instantaneous showers 200, 202
insulation 108-18
effect on ventilation 113,115, 119
floors 108
lofts 114

plumbing 108, 109, 114
priorities 108
roofs 108, 113, 115
specifications 108
types 113
walls 108
integral ring joints 183
interceptor traps 180
ironwork
black leading 58
corrugated iron 37
pipes 181
preparation 36

J

joinery see individual types eg
doors; wood and woodwork
joints
capillary 182
compression 182, 184, 187, 189
concave 220
control 222, 226, 230
dismantling 189
end-feed 183
flush 25, 220
integral ring 183
manipulative and
non-manipulative 184
metal pipes 182-4
mortar 25, 220
plastic pipes 186-9
push-fit 187, 188, 189, 191
raked 25, 220
soldered 183
solvent weld 187, 188
stair, repairing 99, 100
V joint 220
weatherstruck 25, 220
weeping 183, 184, 188
junction boxes 149, 150, 165
junction-box systems 139, 159-
60

K

keyholes 111
kitchen sinks 178, 204-5
kitchens 18, 120-2

L

lacquers and lacquering 46, 47,
48, 56, 58
ladders 20-2
lagging 108, 109
lampholders 133, 161
lath-and-plaster 31, 88, 146, 147
lead
corrosion 37
in paints 23
patching 106
pipes 181, 185
leaks 105, 106, 171
letterboxes 111
lichens 24
lighting 159-65
BESA boxes 162
circuits 139, 159-60, 165, 166
fittings 161-3
fluorescent lights 161, 163
pendant lampholders 133, 161
running costs 125
switches 163-5
tracks 161, 162
limewash 31
Lincrusta 60, 66
lining papers 60, 64
liquid sander 34
liquid strippers 35

living rooms 16
locks 97, 98
lofts 113, 114, 142, 143
loop-in systems 139, 159-60
loose-fill insulation 113, 114

M

main switch equipment 134
maintenance
cisterns 174-6
copper 37
drainage systems 177
general maintenance and repairs
82-106
roofs 102-6
valves 173
manipulative joints 184
masonry
chalky surface 28
cleaning 24-5
fixing sockets 146, 147
flaky paintwork 28
mortar 25, 215
paints and painting 40-3
preparing and repairing 24-9
see also bricks and brickwork;
concrete; walls
masonry facing tiles 70
mastic 53
matt paints 39
MCBs 137, 138
metal primers 23
metal tiles 71
metallic paint 57, 58
metals and metalwork
fence posts 210, 212
finishing 57-8
galvanized 37
pipes 37, 57, 58, 181-5, 189
preparation 36-7
mineral fibre tiles 71, 80
miniature circuit breakers 137,
138
miniature valves 170
mirror tiles 71
mitred tiles 73
mixer taps 173, 194
mortar 25, 215, 220
mortar boards 84
mortise locks 97
mosaic tiles 69, 78
mould, removing 24, 32
mouldings
metalwork 36
plasterwork 31, 89
woodwork 34

N

non-manipulative joints 184
non-slip paints 57, 58
nosings 99, 100
Novamura 61, 67

O

O rings 173
oil finish 46, 47, 48, 56
oil paints 39
metalwork 57, 58
walls and ceilings 43, 45
woodwork 46, 47, 48
one-way switches 164
open string stairs 101
organic growths 24, 32
overflow pipes 112, 169, 208
overflow safety valves 207
overflow units 198, 205

INDEX

P

pads
concrete 226-9
paint 44, 52, 53
paint reservoirs 45
paintbrushes 44, 45, 48
cutting-in 50
radiator brushes 57
staining wood 52, 53
varnishing 54
paints and painting 39-51, 57-8
additives 39
around electrical fittings 45, 59
blemishes 48
ceilings 43-5
common paint finishes 39
concrete floors 41
doors 48, 49
galvanized metalwork 37
interior walls 43-5
lead content 23
make-up of paint 39
masonry 28, 40-2
metalwork 36, 57-8
paint system 39
pipework 37, 57, 58
preparing paint 40
radiators 57
safety 40
skirting boards 51
staircases 51
wallcoverings 32
weatherboarding 51
windows 48, 50, 58
woodwork 39, 48
see also types of equipment eg
pads; types of paint eg emulsion
paints
panel doors 49
panel fences 214
panels
bath 199
staining 53
wall, fabric-covered 67
pans, WC 179, 190-2
papering 60-8
paste strippers 35
pastes, wallpaper 63
pasting brushes 63
paths 224-36
patios 224-36
pattern 13, 14, 232, 235
paving 224, 226, 232-6
pebbledash, patching 27
pendant lampholders 133
piers 216, 221-2, 223
pillar taps 172, 194
pipes and pipework 181-9
bending 185, 189
branch pipes 178, 206
concealing 193, 201
copper 171
corrosion 181
cutting 183
electro-chemical action 181
emergency repairs 171
fittings 182, 186
frozen 171
insulating 108, 109, 114
joints 182-4, 186-9
leaking 171
metal 37, 57, 58, 181-5, 189
overflow pipes 112, 169, 208
painting behind 42, 48
patching 171
plastic 186-9
service pipes 168, 169
sizes 181, 186
soil pipes 168, 169, 177, 179, 191,
196
supporting 189

tiling around 74, 76, 77, 78
types 181, 187
wastepipes 168, 169, 178, 187,
188, 196
pivot windows 98, 112
plaster of Paris 83
plaster and plasterwork 30-1,
82-9
applying plaster 86
buying and storing 82, 83
corners 87
cracks 30
crazing 86
making good 30
mixing plaster 85
mouldings 31, 89
patching holes 31
plastering techniques 82, 86
preparing to decorate 30-1
preparing to plaster 84, 86
repairing 31, 87-9
sealing fireplaces 87
types 83
plasterboard 30, 31, 82, 88, 147
plastic fence posts 210
plastic glazing 93, 117
plastic pipes 186-9
plastic sheet roofing 103
plinths, tiling 77
plugs 133
plumbing 168-208
air locks 171
baths 197-8
bidets 203
branch pipes 178, 206
cisterns 174-6, 190, 192, 208
dishwashers 206-7
draining and refilling the system
170-1
float valves 169, 170, 175-6, 208
overflow pipes 112, 169, 208
regulations 168
repairs 171-3
shower units 199-202
sinks 178, 204-5
taps 172-3, 194-5, 196, 204
traps 178, 180, 190, 196, 198, 207
types of system 168-9
washbasins 193-6
washing machines 206-7
waste disposal units 205
waste/overflow units 198, 205
water pressure 176, 199, 200
WCs 174-6, 190-2
see also drainage systems
plungers 178
PME 135
pointing 25, 220
polishes 46, 47, 48
polystyrene
double glazing 117
tiles 38, 71, 72, 80
wallcoverings 60, 67
polyurethane varnishes 46, 47,
58
Portsmouth pattern valves 175,
176
power circuits 146-51, 166
preparation
asbestos cement 28
concrete 29
for decorating 23-38
masonry 24-9
metalwork 36-7
paintwork 34
for plastering 84, 86
plasterwork 30-1
preparing cement paint 41
preparing lofts for insulation 113
preparing paint 40
tiled surfaces 38
wallcoverings 32, 60
woodwork 33-5

preservers, wood 33, 46, 47, 48,
53
priming
bricks and brickwork 26
cork tiles 38
metalwork 36, 37
plasterwork 30
types of primers 23
woodwork 33
printed wallpapers 60
protective multiple earth 135
protective wood stains 47, 48,
53
pumps, booster 200
push-fit joints 187, 188, 189, 191
putty 33, 53
epoxy 171
PVA bonding agent 23

Q

quadrant tiles 73
quarry tiles 69, 79

R

R-values 108
rack bolts 97, 98
radial circuits 139, 151, 155
radiator brushes 57
radiator enamels 57, 58
radiators 57, 65, 108, 109
raked joints 25, 220
RCCBs 135, 166
RE tiles 69, 74
ready-mixed concrete 225
recycling cooker hoods 120
refrigerators 125, 154
regulations
plumbing 168
wiring 126, 128, 153
reinforced emulsion paints 40,
41, 43, 45
relief wallcoverings 60, 66
render 27
renewable film double glazing
116
repairing
bath enamel 197
concrete 29
general repairs and maintenance
82-106
masonry 26
pipes 171
plasterwork 30-1
plumbing 171-3
render 27
taps 172-3
weeping joints 183, 184, 188
repointing
flashing 106
masonry 25
**residual-current circuit
breakers** 135, 166
reverse pressure taps 172, 194
rewiring *see* wiring and
rewiring
REX tiles 69
ridge tiles 103
ring circuits 139, 149-51
risers 99, 101
rising butt hinges 91
rising-spindle taps 194
rocker switches 163, 164
rodding drains 180
rollers 41, 42, 44, 45, 59
roofs
felt roofing 104
flat 104, 105, 113
glazed 106
inspecting 102

insulating 108, 113, 115
repairs and maintenance 102-6
sheet roofing 103
sloping 115
splits and blisters 105
tiles 102, 103
rounded joints 25
rounded-edge tiles 69
rubbed joints 25
rubber tiles 71, 75, 77
rubbers 52, 53, 55
rust 27, 36

S

safety
concrete mixers 225
electricity 127-9, 132, 134
lacquering 56
ladders 21
painting 40
slab cutting 233
sample boards 15
sand 224, 225
sanded plasters 83
sanding 33, 34
sash locks 98
sash stops 98
sash weight knot 95
sash windows 50, 95, 96, 98, 112
satin paints 39, 46
scaffolding towers 20, 22
scoring, wallcoverings 32
screens, concrete block 223
sealants 73, 111
sealing
concrete 29
draught sealers 112
types of sealers 23
sealing chambers 134
security fittings 97-8
security paints 57, 58
self-adhesive tiles 76
self-bore valves 206
self-levelling compound 29
septic tanks 180
service pipes 168, 169
shaver sockets 154
sheet insulation 113, 115
sheet roofing 103
shellac 55
shower units 125, 159, 199-202
shrouded heads 172
single stack waste systems 168,
177
single-coat plasters 83, 85
sinks 178, 204-5
siphonic pans 190, 191
Sirapite B 83, 85
skirting boards 51, 112, 142
slabs, paving 232-4
slate tiles 69
slates 102
small bore waste system 192
sockets
assessing condition 144, 145
extending ring circuits 149, 150
fitting and replacing 146-8
shaver 154
trailing 132
soil pipes 168, 169, 177
connecting 191, 196
unblocking 179
soldered joints 183
solvent weld joints 187, 188
solvent-base paints 39
space, manipulating 14-15
spalling 26, 29
spikes, fence post 211
spiral balances 96
spirit-thinned masonry paints
41

spray guns 42, 44
spur cables 149
stabilizing primer 23
stack bonding 216
staining 46, 47, 52-3
stainless steel pipes 181
stains, masonry 25
stairs 51, 99-101
stairwells 22, 66
stapled tiles 80
steam strippers 32
steelwork
  pipes 181, 184
  preparation 36
stepladders 20, 21
stepping stones 234
stone paving 234
stone tiles 69, 70
stopcocks 168, 169, 173
stoppers 33
storage cisterns see cold water
  storage cisterns
stretcher bond 216
strip footings 217
stripping
  cable 140
  chemical strippers 35
  flex 131
  metalwork 36
  mouldings 34
  wallcoverings 32
  woodwork 34-5
Supaglypta 60, 66
supplementary bonding 128
switched connection units 152
switches 126, 144, 145
  light switches 163-5
switchfuse units 156

T

tack rag 33
tank cutters 208
tapes 106
taps
  baths 197
  draining 170
  fitting and replacing 195, 196, 198
  kitchen sinks 204
  leaking 170-1
  mixer taps 173, 194
  pillar taps 172, 194
  reverse pressure 172, 194
  seats and glands 173
  types 194
  washbasins 194-5
  washers 172
terminals 131
texture 12
textured coatings 40, 41, 45, 59
thermostats 124
thinners
  masonry finishes 40
  metalwork finishes 57
  paint 39, 40, 45, 48
  woodwork finishes 48
thistle plasters 83, 85
thixotropic paints 39, 48
threshold draught excluders
  110
tile cutters 74
tile cutting jigs 74, 78
tile nibblers 74
tiles and tiling 38, 69-80
  bedding down 79
  ceilings 80
  cutting 74, 76, 78, 79, 102
  floors 75-9
  preparation 38, 84
  removing 38
  renovating 72
  ridge 103

roof 102, 103
setting out 72, 75, 78, 79
tile sections 69
types of tiles 69-71
walls 38, 72-4
see also individual types of tiles eg
  quarry tiles
timber see wood and
  woodwork
time switches 124
toilets see WCs
tone 10-11
track lighting 161, 162
trailing sockets 132
transformers 158
traps
  clearing 178, 180
  fitting 196, 198, 207
  types 190, 198
treads, replacing 100-1
trunking 120
tubular traps 178
two-pipe waste systems 168,
  177
two-way switches 164

U

U-values 108
undercoats 43, 45
universal tiles 69

V

V joints 220
valves
  adding to plumbing 170
  cold feed 169
  Croydon pattern 175
  diaphragm 175, 176
  flap 174
  float 169, 170, 175-6, 208
  gate 170
  maintenance 173
  miniature 170
  overflow safety 207
  Portsmouth pattern 175, 176
  self-bore 206
vapour barriers 113
varnishes and varnishing
  metalwork 57, 58
  woodwork 46, 47, 48, 54
ventilation 119-22
  effect of improved insulation 113,
    115, 119
  extractors 120-2
  fireplaces 119
  kitchens 120-2
  lofts 113
  windows 119, 122
ventilator grilles 119
vents, window 119
verdigris 37
verge drips 104
Vinaglypta 60
vinyl tiles 38, 70, 72, 75, 76
vinyl wallcoverings 32, 61, 66

W

wall brushes 63
wall panels 67
wallcoverings 32, 60-8
  cutting and trimming 63
  estimating quantities 62
  hanging 64-8
  painted 32
  pasting 63
  preparation 32, 60
  ready-pasted 63, 66

removing mould 32
types 60-1
washable 32, 61
wallpaper scorers 32
walls
  basic structure 216
  block screens 223
  bonding 216, 221
  brick 219-23
  cavity 223
  concrete 29, 223
  coping 216, 219, 220, 223
  damp-proof course 216
  external 24-9, 40-1
  fixing fences to 210
  fixing sockets 146, 147
  footings 216, 217
  hollow 141, 146
  insulating 108
  lath-and-plaster 31, 88, 146, 147
  light fittings 161
  mortar 25, 215
  painting 40-1, 43-5
  papering 64
  piers 216, 221-2, 223
  preparing and repairing 24-8, 30-
    1, 84
  running cable 141
  stretcher-bonded 219
  textured coatings 40, 41, 45, 59
  tiles 38, 72-4
washbasins 178, 193-6
washdown pans 190, 191
washers, replacing 172
washing machines 125, 154, 206-
  7
waste disposal units 154, 205
waste drainage systems 168,
  177
waste/overflow units 198, 205
wastepipes 168, 169
  clearing 178
  connecting 187, 188, 196
water heaters 125, 154, 156-7
water pressure 176, 199, 200
water repellent 23
water-based paints 39
waterproofing
  glazing bars 106
  masonry 26
wax polishing 46, 47, 48, 54, 56
WCs
  cisterns
  draining 170
  maintenance 174-6
  noisy 176
  types 190
  pans
    types 190-1
  unblocking 179
  replacing 190-2
weather bars 91
weatherboarding
  doors 91
  painting 51
  staining 53
weatherproofing, doors 91
weatherstripping 111
weatherstruck joints 25, 220
weeping joints 183, 184, 188
window vents 119
windows
  draughtproofing 108, 112
  fitting extractor fans 122
  painting 48, 50, 58
  papering around 65
  re-cording 95
  repairing 94-6
  security fittings 98
  spiral balances 96
  tiling around 72
  ventilating 119, 122
  working with glass 92-4

see also double glazing; individual
  types of windows eg sash
  windows
Wiring Regulations 126, 128,
  153
wiring and rewiring
  complete house 166
  electrical appliances 152-9
  electrical circuits 149-51
  lampholders 133
  light switches 164
  plugs 133
  running cable 141-3
  sockets 146-9
wood preservers 33, 46, 47, 48,
  53
wood primers 23
wood stains 46, 47, 48, 53
wood and woodwork 33-5, 46-56
  choice of finishes 46-7
  fences 210-14
  filling 33
  French polishing 47, 48, 55
  graining 51
  lacquering 46, 47, 48, 56
  oil finish 46, 47, 48 56
  painting 39, 48
  preparation 33-5
  priming 33
  staining 46, 47, 52-3
  treating new timber 33
  varnishing 46, 47, 48, 54
  wax polishing 46, 47, 48, 54, 56
woodchip paper 60
work platforms 22